McHenry
2009

Evelyn Waugh

Also by Selina Hastings

NANCY MITFORD: A BIOGRAPHY

Evelyn Waugh

A Biography

———

SELINA HASTINGS

HOUGHTON MIFFLIN COMPANY
BOSTON • NEW YORK

AUTHOR'S NOTE:
The sometimes eccentric spelling and
punctuation in the quoted material has been
transcribed from letters and journals.

———————————

For information about permission to reproduce
selections from this book, write to
Permissions, Houghton Mifflin Company,
215 Park Avenue South, New York,
New York 10003.

Library of Congress Cataloging-in-Publication Data
Hastings, Selina.
Evelyn Waugh : a biography / Selina Hastings.
p. cm.
Includes index.
ISBN 0-395-71821-X : $40.00
1. Waugh, Evelyn, 1903-1966 — Biography. 2. Authors,
English — 20th century — Biography.   I. Title
PR6045.A97Z689 1994
823'.912 — DC20   94-45396
[B]   CIP

First published in Great Britain in 1994
by Sinclair-Stevenson
an imprint of Reed Consumer Books Ltd
Michelin House, 81 Fulham Road, London SW3 6RB
and
Auckland, Melbourne, Singapore and Toronto

Printed in the United States of America

DOH 10 9 8 7 6 5 4 3 2 1

CONTENTS

For Tom

List of Illustrations

Acknowledgments

With every major writer there is room for at least three biographies: the memoir written by a personal friend; the academic biography; and thirdly a more general account, but drawing both on primary sources and on original research. Christopher Sykes, a close friend of Evelyn Waugh's since the 1930s, wrote the personal recollection. Martin Stannard's two volume life is the full-scale critical biography. This life of Waugh is of the third kind, a narrative account aiming to give as close an impression as possible of what it was like to know Evelyn Waugh, even something of what it was like to be Evelyn Waugh.

In the writing of this book I owe a large debt of gratitude to a large number of people, who gave me their time, their recollections and in many cases allowed me to see letters and papers which were invaluable to my research. Many whose generosity I depended upon are, unfortunately, no longer alive, but I would like to thank them nevertheless. Without the kindness of the following people this portrait of Evelyn Waugh would have been considerably less substantial.

First and foremost I would like to thank Auberon Waugh for his help during the writing of this book, and in particular for allowing me unrestricted use of Evelyn Waugh's papers and published works. Secondly, I would like to thank Alan Bell, Librarian of the London Library, for the time and scholarship that he put at my disposal, and for the attention with which he read the finished manuscript. I am also greatly indebted to Julie Kavanagh, who read the work in progress and made many valuable suggestions, and to Professors Roy Foster and Thomas F. Staley for their expert reading of the finished text. I would like to thank Duncan Fallowell for providing me with material on Alastair Graham; Antony Beevor for his help with the Crete campaign; and Nicholas Shakespeare for the loan of transcripts and family papers. I am also grateful to the Rev. Philip Caraman SJ, without whose patient teaching I would have been quite lost.

I would like to thank Mrs Drue Heinz for a stay of nearly six weeks at Hawthornden Castle, which was without doubt the most enjoyable, as well as the most rewarding, period of time spent at work on this book.

For access to collections of Evelyn Waugh's papers and related material I would like to thank the Bodleian Library, Oxford; the Rev. Francis Sweeney SJ and Boston College; Dr Howard B. Gotlieb and the Twentieth Century Archives, Boston University Libraries; the British Library; Cambridge University Library; Christ Church, Oxford; Columbia University, New York; Chatto & Windus; Georgetown University, Washington, DC; Hall Bros Ltd., Oxford; Dr Toby Barnard and Hertford College, Oxford; Sara S. Hodson and the Huntington Library, California; the National Library of Scotland; Oxford City Record Office; Michael Sissons and the Peters, Fraser & Dunlop Group Ltd.; Reading University; Professor T. F. Staley, Cathy Henderson, John Kirkpatrick, Pat Fox and the Humanities Research Center, University of Texas at Austin.

I would like to express my immense gratitude to the following for interviews, letters and advice: the Rev. the Hon. Charles Acton, Daphne, Lady Acton, Lord Acton, Lady Airey, Michael Alexander, Mark Amory, Lord Annan, Reginald Apthorpe, Lord Asquith, Clarissa, Countess of Avon, Don Bachardy, Sabina Bailey, Earl Baldwin of Bewdley, Countess Beauchamp, Olivia Bell, Georgiana Blakiston, Sarah Bradford, Sir Theodore Brinckman, John Brookes, Barbara Buck, Lucy Butler, Lady Campbell-Orde, C. L. Chamberlin, Edward Chaney, Winston Churchill, Lady Mary Clive, Philippa Codrington, Artemis Cooper, Jean Crowden, Teresa Cuthbertson, Teresa D'Arms, Michael Davie, Sir Robin Day, Sir William Deakin, the Duke and Duchess of Devonshire, Lord and Lady Donaldson, Harriet Dorment, Mary Dups, Lord Egremont, Peter Elwes, Michael Estorick, Richard Eurich, Peter Eyre, Daphne Fielding, Giles FitzHerbert, J. M. Flynn, Catherine Freeman, Jean Gabb, Dominic Gill, Elizabeth Gill, Sir Alexander Glen, Iris Goldsworthy, Celia Goodman, Bridget Grant, Harman Grisewood, Vera Grother, Graham Greene, Alice Gwynn, Luned Hamilton-Jenkins, Basil Handford, Sir Rupert Hart-Davis, Lord Hartwell, Ronald Harwood, Celia Haynes, Lady Dorothy Heber-Percy, Sir Richard Heygate, Peter Hiley, Lady Anne Hill, Bevis Hillier, Lavinia Hinton, Philip Hoare, the Rev. Geoffrey Holt SJ, Anthony Hobson, Major General R. D. Houghton, Laura Huxley, Richard Ingrams, John Jolliffe, John Keegan, Veronica Keeling, Sir Ludovic and Lady Kennedy, James Knox, Lady Pansy Lamb, Lady Lancaster, Deirdre Levi, Candida Lycett Green, James Lees-Milne, Petra Lewis, Herbert Lister, the Earl and Countess of Longford, Chloe MacCarthy, Sir Fitzroy and Lady Maclean, Hugh Massingberd, Michael Moberly, the Hon. Fionn Morgan, Lady Morrison, Charlotte Mosley, Diana, Lady Mosley, Major Patrick Ness, Viscount Norwich, Diana Oldridge, the Earl of Oxford and Asquith, Thomas Pakenham, Andrew Pares, Peter Parker, Burnet Pavitt, the Hon. Laura Ponsonby, Anthony and Lady Violet Powell, Janet Pennington, Sir Peter Quennell, Jenny Rambridge, Lord Ravensdale, A. L. Rowse, Lady Sibell Rowley, the Hon. Ianthe Ruthven, Professor Michael Shelden, Lord Shuttleworth, David Sox, the Rev. Dom Alberic Stacpoole OSB, Lady Stallard, Partrick Streeter, Sir Tatton Sykes Bt., Valerie Sykes, Tamara Talbot Rice, R. E. S. Tanner, Wilfred Thesiger, Renée Tickell, Jeremy Tomlinson, Sir Dermot de Trafford, David Twiston-Davies, Selina Turko, the Hon. Elizabeth Varley, Terence de Vere White, Hugo Vickers, Marjorie Watts, Capt. Andrew Waugh, James Waugh, Peter Waugh, Septimus Waugh, Virginia Waugh, J. S. Woodhouse, Mia Woodruff, Sir Peregrine Worsthorne, Sebastian Yorke.

Every effort has been made to trace holders of copyright. I much regret if any inadvertent omissions have been made, but these can be rectified in future editions.

Selina Hastings
London, 1994

The physical materials

The reputation of Evelyn Waugh rests on two premises: that he was one of the great prose stylists of the twentieth century, and that as a man he was a monster. To judge the first, one has only to read his books; to judge the second one must turn to the life.

According to James Lees-Milne, who barely knew him, Waugh was 'the nastiest tempered man in England, Catholic or Protestant'; according to Malcolm Muggeridge, who hardly knew him either, Waugh was 'a saint'. Certainly Waugh was capable of generosity and compassion; he was also romantic and affectionate. But in counterpoint to these agreeable qualities were other attributes; a deep seam of anger and resentment, notoriously exploding in demonstrations of cruelty and rage. Hilaire Belloc said on first meeting him that he was convinced the young man was diabolically possessed, and indeed Waugh had personal demons to contend with of a violence and tenacity unknown to most of us. As his alter ego, Gilbert Pinfold, asks despairingly, 'Why does everyone except me find it so easy to be nice?'

The demons were specifically his, but it is possible to see in Evelyn Waugh's forebears some of the trace elements of that difficult and complex character, 'the physical materials', as he phrased it in his autobiography, of which he was made. His parents were kind, gentle people; his paternal grandfather on the other hand was an irascible and sadistic character, known within the family as 'the Brute'. Once when sitting opposite his wife in the carriage, he saw a wasp settle on her forehead, and with cold deliberation leant forward and crushed it with the head of his cane, causing it to sting her.

*

Both Evelyn's parents came of Scottish stock. On his father's side his great-great-grandfather, the Revd Alexander Waugh (1754–1827), was descended from several generations of small tenant farmers in Berwickshire, while his great-great-grandfather on his mother's side was Henry, Lord Cockburn (1779–1854), the distinguished Scots judge, friend of Sir Walter Scott. Lord Cockburn was an eccentric and brilliant man, and his autobiography, *Memorials of His Time*, was widely acclaimed then and is still read today; his portrait by Raeburn at one time decorated the Scottish banknotes. One of Lord Cockburn's sons married the daughter of a lieutenant-colonel in the Bengal Army, and their daughter, Evelyn's maternal grandmother, forged a further link with the subcontinent by her marriage to Henry Raban, a magistrate in the Bengal Civil Service. (Evelyn never forgot at the age of seven watching his Uncle Bassett Raban, on the morning of the coronation of George V, walk down the Waughs' narrow garden path in Golders Green in the scarlet and gold dress uniform of an officer of the Bengal Lancers.) It was to India in the eighteenth century that several of the Rabans, originally a Staffordshire family by then settled in London, had gone to further their fortunes, the sons of Raban tradesmen and merchants – coal, saddlery, coach-building – making careers in the Army and the Indian Civil Service. By the early 1800s two of the brothers had returned with enough money for a sizeable house in Somerset and a coat of arms. When, at the end of the century, Evelyn's father, Arthur Waugh, met Catherine Raban, the Rabans could justifiably present themselves to the world as an established west country family. Soon after Catherine's birth, her father died, and her mother married again, a clergyman in the Indian Army and a cousin of her first husband's, also of the name of Raban. By him she had four more children, and after leaving India the family settled in 1885 in Somerset, in Paulton, the next village on the Bristol road to Midsomer Norton, the home of the Waughs.

Arthur Waugh's father, Alexander Waugh, was a prosperous general practitioner, whose prosperity was due not only to his success as a doctor but to a substantial income from a trust established by a childless great-uncle, and from a Welsh coal-bearing property deriving from his wife's family, the Morgans. Like Catherine's, Arthur's predecessors were from the professional middle classes, favouring careers in medicine and the church. It was the eighteenth-century Dr Alexander Waugh who first made good, spending most of his life in London as a distinguished and popular minister of the Scottish Secession Church in Wells Street. Among his ten children, two were notable in the line of descent: George, druggist to Queen Victoria, who had eight beautiful daughters, two of whom married in succession (and in defiance of the law against marriage to deceased wife's sister) the pre-Raphaelite painter Holman Hunt; and James Hay Waugh, Arthur's grandfather, a clergyman of the Church of England and rector of Corsley in Somerset. James Hay Waugh was a patriarchal figure, kind but authoritarian, who kept a good table and enjoyed a hand of cards. Like many churchmen an actor *manqué*, he was the first member of the family on record with a taste for private theatricals – a trait which was inherited by his son, grew to a passion with his grandson, Arthur, and became an intrinsic component of the character of his great-grandson, Evelyn.

Dr Alexander Waugh, 'the Brute', was tall and powerfully built, a gregarious extrovert, something of a roughneck, fond of shooting, fishing, cricket – and amateur dramatics. He had a large practice in and around Midsomer Norton near Bath, where he settled as a young man, and was doctor to both the monks and the school at Downside. He entertained heartily, and was well liked in the district. Only his family knew of another side to his character: fierce, unpredictable rages and an unrelenting autocracy in the home. There was, too, a streak of sadism in his nature which resulted in cruel behaviour towards his wife and children. He frequently reduced his three daughters to tears, would flog his younger son, Alick, with an energy that could only be described as demonic, and terrified the elder, Arthur, a pale, peaky boy, by forcing him to so-called tests of courage, at night ordering him into unlit rooms alone, and sending him downstairs to kiss his gun-case in the dark.

His wife Annie was the daughter of John Morgan, one of the first ophthalmic surgeons, and of Anne Gosse, of the family of Plymouth Brethren immortalised by Edmund Gosse in *Father and Son*. Perhaps taking after her grandfather, Thomas Gosse, a miniaturist and portrait painter, Annie was an artist of some talent, and in the drawing-room her pretty watercolours of local landscapes stood out for their originality from the usual display of birds' nests and cottage maidens. She was a timid, anxious woman who worried about everything. Her elder son, Arthur, was born on 24 August, and her chief torment during the latter weeks of her pregnancy was that her confinement should not interfere with her husband's first day of partridge shooting. It is not surprising that Arthur grew up subject to 'nerves', his vivid imagination feeding off his mother's insecurity and the frightening stories told him by his nursemaid, stories which imbued the long afternoons behind the staircase gate with a subtle spirit of fear. All his life Arthur conjured up for himself at the least opportunity visions of frightful catastrophe; and all his life he suffered from asthma, known to be a complaint exacerbated by emotional stress. As a boy he was prevented by it from playing football or swimming, although it was significant that his worst attacks always occurred not at school, but the moment he arrived back home after the end of term.

In the second half of the last century Midsomer Norton was a large, prosperous village. The exterior of the Waughs' house, concealed behind thick shrubbery, was plain and solid, as befitted the home of a well-to-do country doctor. But inside it was rambling and haphazard, full of strange souvenirs and curiosities, such as the charred walking-stick with which some relation had climbed Vesuvius, and in a glass phial a specimen of so-called 'white blood' which Dr Waugh had preserved from a patient dying of acute anaemia. There were five children: three sisters, Connie, Trissie and Elsie, and two boys, Arthur and a younger brother, Alick, a sailor, who died before he was thirty.

Arthur was sent first to a dame school in Bath, and then to Sherborne in Dorset, an old-established public school for which, in spite of the fact that his career there was not altogether happy (his asthma made athletic prowess impossible and he was jeered at for being a swot), he conceived a fervently romantic attachment which endured all his days. It was at Sherborne under the influence of a gifted English master that he developed his passion for poetry. At fourteen he was already a poet, and he wrote plays which were acted at home in the holidays. He edited one of the school magazines, and in his final term won the prize for English verse.

Arthur was a tender-hearted, sentimental child, deeply attached to his mother, frightened but admiring of his overbearing father, with whom he shared two of the three great passions of his life – cricket and the theatre. His love of cricket began at the age of twelve with the setting up in Norton of a village cricket club of which Dr Waugh was president, an appointment which ensured the attendance of his family at all the Saturday afternoon matches, and engendered in his son a lasting love of the game. Arthur's obsession with the theatre started even younger. In his engaging, discursive, nostalgic and slightly fatuous autobiography, *One Man's Road*, he admits that even as a child he was conscious of a strong desire to be centre-stage, and this, combined with Dr Waugh's vivid sense of the dramatic and a habit he had of declaiming scenes from Shakespeare and snatches of burlesque, encouraged in his elder son a strong enthusiasm for performing. During the holidays there were always amateur theatricals at home or at the houses of friends, and at Sherborne Arthur played his first rôle while still a new boy, at the end of his school career giving two memorable performances, one as Falstaff, the other as Katharina in *The Taming of the Shrew*. At Oxford, where he read Greats, he acted (but never joined OUDS because he was afraid the subscription was more than he could afford) and wrote a number of undergraduate plays and revues, lovingly and lengthily recalled in the pages of his autobiography and no doubt a contributory cause of his third-class degree. His sole academic distinction was to win the Newdigate Prize for Poetry on the subject of 'Gordon in Africa'.

On coming down from university in 1890, Arthur had to choose between making a career in the theatre and devoting himself to his third great love, literature, or, as he put it with typical flourish, making up his mind between 'the temptations of the greasepaint and the pen'. But the stage was out of the question for a sufferer from asthma, and although once settled in London, in comfortless lodgings off Gray's Inn Road, he formed the habit of going to the theatre at least once a week, it was 'the inky virus' that predominated. Arthur found writing both pleasurable and easy; he had the fatal facility of the second-rate, a facility inherited by his elder son Alec, and regarded with contempt by his younger son Evelyn, who referred dismissively to the 'deleterious speed' with which he composed both prose and verse. Arthur's first newspaper article, on 'The Decline of Comedy', appeared in

Lippincott's Magazine, and soon afterwards, through the influence of his cousin Edmund Gosse, he was taken on as reader by the newly established publisher, William Heinemann. Gosse also introduced him to a young American, Wolcott Balestier, who ran the London office of John W. Lovell, a New York firm specialising in popular fiction. It was Balestier who offered Arthur his first office job, which he enjoyed as the two men got on well, sharing a love of the business and a taste for the innovative and by no means universally popular work of writers such as Kipling, Ibsen, Yeats and Henry James. Unfortunately, Balestier, married by then to Kipling's sister, died suddenly of typhoid at the end of 1891, leaving Arthur in sole charge of what turned out to be a fast-failing operation. For a year Arthur did what he could to keep Lovell's London branch going, a year which through no fault of his was a commercial disaster, although it provided him with the professional experience on which to build his future career. During the same year he was commissioned by Heinemann to write his first book, a life of Tennyson which, rushed out only eight days after the laureate's death, was a runaway success and would have made a substantial difference to his financial standing had not the Lovell company soon afterwards been declared bankrupt, leaving Arthur under the self-imposed obligation of using every penny of his *Tennyson* royalties to pay the office salaries. This was a noble sacrifice, given that it meant the deferral of his longed-for and long-awaited marriage to the daughter of a neighbouring Somerset parson, Catherine Raban.

The Rabans had proved a great addition to local society. Mrs Raban's second husband, retired from his army chaplaincy in India, had had a restless career, taking duty at churches without regular incumbents and moving every few years from one west country parish to another. Arthur and Catherine (or Kate, as she was known) became acquainted when she and her half-brother and half-sister first called on the Waughs, dashing up in a smart dog-cart pulled by a high-stepping chestnut, Kate on the back seat, a tam-o'-shanter set becomingly on her long hair. The two young people quickly became friends, playing tennis, going for walks and waltzing together at parties. Arthur lent Kate books, pleased that she enjoyed the novels he recommended, if disappointed that poetry appeared to mean little to her. But the Rabans were not a literary family; Kate's brother, Bassett, when first shown

6

Arthur's bookshelves, famously exclaimed, 'All these books! and not one a feller could read!' and Arthur would later complain of the inability of the Rabans ever to sit down and write a letter. Kate enjoyed sketching, and after she became engaged there was a short-lived project for her to take lessons at an art school so that she would be able to supplement the marital income by teaching a few young ladies at home. Lovell's crash in February 1893, put an end to plans for a spring wedding, and it was not until the following autumn, eight years after they first met, and following an increasingly impassioned but scrupulously chaste courtship, that they were able to marry, on 5 October 1893, at Christchurch in Weston-super-Mare.

After a honeymoon in Malvern, Arthur brought Kate to London, to West Hampstead, that relatively countrified region still in reach of farms and fields. This district on the very outskirts of town had been chosen for its rural atmosphere, of importance to Kate who had never wanted to leave the country; for its reputation for clean air, beneficial for Arthur's asthma; and because it was the home of Sydney Pawling, a partner of William Heinemann and a great new friend of Arthur's. The Pawlings lived in Canfield Gardens, just behind Finchley Road station, and the Waughs found a small flat near the station above a dairy overlooking the Finchley Road itself. In the 1890s the lower end of the Finchley Road was a tree-lined thoroughfare of small shops and red-brick apartment buildings, while further up the hill at generous intervals stood secluded mansions surrounded by large gardens. To the north, from Fitzjohn's Pavement, the row of local shops, there was little building, mainly pasture and waste ground until the boundaries of Hampstead Heath were reached. To the south, behind the back windows of the first floor over the dairy, were trees and the pleasant green expanse of the Hampstead cricket ground. Like Arthur, Sydney Pawling was a keen cricketer, a noted fast bowler who had played for the county, known at the club in recognition of his status as 'the Skipper'. During the summer Arthur, often accompanied by Kate whose enthusiasm for the game almost equalled his own, went regularly to the nearby Lord's cricket ground to watch the county matches, which on occasion he extolled with effortless lyricism to the readers of the *Fortnightly Review*. 'With the dawn of May that merry monarch,

Willow the King, returns to his own again, and all his loyal subjects rise to pay him the salute of welcome . . .'

In most things Arthur and Kate (or K as he always called her) were well suited, her placid, unimaginative nature complementing her husband's highly strung temperament. She was small and neat and practical, rarely showing emotion, shy of any demonstration of affection. Although not 'literary', she enjoyed reading and being read to, and even kept a journal of sorts, three or four unrevealing lines written every day on the ruled pages of a Letts' Diary. Kate was her husband's most fervent and uncritical supporter, never failing to encourage and admire his writing, working hard to provide him with a secure and agreeable domestic environment in which to work. Having after her mother's remarriage been brought up in a rackety, populous household, largely indifferent to physical ease, she was determined to create in her own home surroundings of comfort and tranquillity. Her mother, accustomed to the idleness and lethargy of life under the Raj, had been a notoriously bad housekeeper, and it became a rule of Kate's that if she were not sure how something was done, she would think of what her mother would advise, and do the opposite. Kate had a gift for home-making, and spent hours of every day in housework. She loved nothing more than turning out a bedroom or dusting and rearranging Arthur's books; she did most of the shopping and cooking, and much of the sewing and upholstering: she made covers for the dining-room chairs, and would spend hours searching the Finchley Road for exactly the right pattern of fringe for a window blind; she washed, walked and clipped their beloved black poodle, Marquis, as well as looking after any other animal – a cat, a rabbit, some guinea-pigs – introduced at intervals into the household; and she made nearly all her own clothes ('Dressmaked' is a frequent entry in the diary). Although strictly speaking not a pretty woman, Kate was proud of her trim appearance, and took an interest both in her own clothes and those of her women friends. For a family wedding in July 1895, Kate records in words which would no doubt have made her son Evelyn wince, 'I had a lovely dress & looked tweetums. Everyone said I was the prettiest woman there, especially Hubbums.'

Although Arthur started married life in a financially precarious state, he also knew that he was now in demand, the success of his life of Tennyson having established his reputation in the eyes of the literary editors. He wrote for the *Literary World*, the *Academy*, the *Realm*, the *Daily Courier*, *Literature*, the *St James's Gazette*, the *Outlook* and the *Sun*; his became a regular by-line in the *Daily Chronicle*, and for two years he wrote a London Letter for the New York *Critic*. He also worked as a sub-editor on the *New Review*, for which he secured the serial rights of W. W. Jacobs's early stories. In 1894 he was asked to contribute an essay to the first number of the notorious *Yellow Book*, and had the good fortune to be singled out from almost universal condemnation of what was considered a scandalous publication for almost universal praise. Indeed it was this essay, on 'Reticence in Literature', that brought him to serious notice as a critic, and which made him realise that a career as a professional writer was within his grasp.

However, he now had a wife to provide for, and perhaps in time a family. And so when in January 1896 he was offered the job of literary adviser and assistant manager to the publishers, Kegan Paul, Trench, Trübner & Co., he accepted it, exchanging the uncertainty of a freelance career for the security of an office and a regular salary – a sensible choice for one of his temperament, easily made anxious and (as he dramatically phrased it) 'by nature and education a slave to discipline'. It was work to which he was well suited. Arthur knew and loved the publishing business, he enjoyed both the routine and the stimulation of office life, got on well with his colleagues and, as he could leave his office in the Charing Cross Road at four o'clock every afternoon, still had time for his reviewing and for the literary biographies (Browning, Meredith) which he was able to write start-to-finish in a matter of weeks. He included Kate in his professional life by occasionally allowing her to compile the index for a book. She was thrilled when her first opportunity came. 'Arthur brought me home an Index to do feel very proud!' she wrote; and two weeks later, 'When I returned home, my cheque from Kegan Paul was waiting for me £12.2.6. Such a proud K!!' Arthur stayed with Kegan Paul for nearly six years, until in 1901 he was offered the post of managing director of Chapman & Hall, distinguished as the publishers of Carlyle, Trollope, Thackeray and Dickens. Arthur was then thirty-five, and at Chapman & Hall he remained for the rest of his working life.

While Arthur was at the office, and when she had finished the day's shopping and housework, Kate spent most of her time paying and receiving calls from friends and neighbours, a small circle which included the Pawlings, her Cockburn cousins, the Circuitts, the Ledwards, the Gülicks and the Rhyses, Ernest Rhys a celebrity in the book world for his editorship of the Everyman Library. Sometimes she had an evening of whist or bridge while Arthur stayed in town to dine with a man friend or attend a meeting of the Sette of Odde Volumes, a bufferish dining club which his son was later to mock in *Brideshead Revisited*.[1] But most of their evenings they spent together, either at home playing chess or with Arthur reading Shakespeare aloud, or at the theatre; they went at least twice a week, locally in Kilburn or Golders Green, or in town where K would meet her husband for lunch (Lyons, the Gaiety) or dinner (the Comedy, Gatti's, the Italie in Old Compton Street) before the play. On 12 February 1895, Kate noted in her diary, 'Very happy day. Fetched Hubbie from Office, had lunch at "The Gaiety". Then went to "Santa Claus" which was very pretty – we both enjoyed it much.' On Saturday afternoons they went for long walks on the heath with Marquis, or sometimes skating at Wembley, or on an occasional visit to the zoo. On Sundays they went to church, usually to High Celebration at St Barnabas in Golders Green.

They entertained little – on Arthur's small income they could hardly afford to – and seldom went out on social occasions except to pay calls and to informal dinners at the houses of close friends – the Pawlings, or the Rhyses, or Richard Le Gallienne, whose brother-in-law, the actor James Welch, could sometimes be prevailed upon to perform his amusing sketch of a man making a speech while trying not to sneeze. On a grander scale than these modest entertainments were the dinner parties at Hans Place to which they were invited by Lady Lindsay, the separated wife of Sir Coutts Lindsay, founder of the Grosvenor Gallery, where they met such notable remnants of the Pre-Raphaelite Brotherhood

---

[1] 'It was a surprising association of men quite eminent in their professions who met once a month for an evening of ceremonious buffoonery; each had his soubriquet . . . and a specially designed jewel worn like an order of chivalry . . . they had club buttons for their waistcoats and an elaborate ritual for the introduction of guests; after dinner a paper was read and facetious speeches were made'.

as Lady Millais and the Burne-Joneses. But of greatest importance to Arthur was their regular attendance on Sundays at the literary salon of his cousin Edmund Gosse.

By the nineties Gosse was a distinguished man of letters with an influential circle of friends. Famously touchy but intrinsically kind, Gosse had welcomed the Waughs to his house in Maida Vale, where they drank their tea and ate their cake in the company of such famous figures as Thomas Hardy, Henry James, Austin Dobson, Coventry Patmore, Max Beerbohm and Andrew Lang. Gosse was an important influence on Arthur, in a sense his patron. It was Gosse to whom he had nervously gone for advice on coming down from Oxford ('We must remember', the great man had said teasingly to his earnest young cousin, 'that life is not all ices and lawn tennis'); through Gosse that he met Wolcott Balestier; after lunching with Gosse at the National Club the idea evolved of his contributing to the first number of the *Yellow Book*. The Gosses became good friends of Arthur and Kate, who enjoyed with them, and more particularly with their three children, known as the Goslings, a domestic relationship cosily underpinning the more glamorous world of the Sunday salon. There was a lot of coming and going between the two households, sometimes for small family suppers, at other times for more ambitious parties, such as the Gosses' Twelfth Night Party of 1899, which was noted appreciatively in Kate's diary. 'Very jolly with conjuror. Mr Sickert took me to supper.' Inevitably, with such a thin-skinned man as Gosse, there was the occasional falling-out, and Arthur soon saw through his mentor's self-importance: when Gosse was appointed to the librarianship of the House of Lords, Arthur wrote playfully, 'His manner is now pontifical to a degree, and I hide behind flower pots to avoid his domineering eye.' Nonetheless, it was a friendship that endured, one that was useful and gave pleasure to the Waughs.

At least once a year visits were paid to Kate's family at the vicarage in Bishops Hull and at Shirehampton, and to Arthur's at Midsomer Norton. The Rabans sent presents of game and fish to London, and at Christmas there was always a hamper from the Waughs. Kate loved Arthur's sisters, Connie, Trissie and Elsie, and welcomed their visits, although in private she made no secret of her loathing for her father-in-law, 'the Brute': his acts of domestic cruelty, the sudden irrational outbreaks of rage interspersed with patronising and theatrical displays of affection repelled her. Evelyn in his autobiography refers to his mother's account of a wet afternoon at Norton when Dr Waugh returned home unexpectedly to find the family playing snap with a pack of cards he kept specifically for whist. 'An appalling outburst of rage resulted,' Evelyn recalls his mother telling him – an incident referred to in her diary with characteristic reticence as, 'Scene about cards'. Later when Arthur and Kate had a house of their own and a spare bedroom, they saw even more of their relations. In 1898 Kate records that out of 365 days in the year, they had people staying for 230. Frequent guests were Kate's extended family, including her mother and step-father and, until he left for the Indian Army in 1900, her brother Bassett; there were also Arthur's sisters, though not his sailor brother who, having returned married from the Pacific in May 1899, died the following year at Norton after an attack of malaria.

In June 1895 Arthur and Kate were given notice by their landlord to leave the flat over the dairy. Arthur was now earning enough to be able to buy a house, and in October that year they moved into Number 11 Hillfield Road, just over a mile away, still in West Hampstead, still in easy reach of the Heath, of Lord's and of the Hampstead Cricket Club. Number 11 is one in a terrace of small, three-storey red-brick Victorian villas in a quiet cul-de-sac, each with its narrow strip of garden at the back, its little patch dividing it from what was then a public footpath at the front. It was far from being a fashionable address, but it was a quiet, pleasant part of outer London with plenty of trees and open spaces, mainly inhabited by middle-class families with incomes, like Arthur's, of around £600 a year, and in easy reach by railway and horse-drawn bus of the City and the West End. 'Very happy to be in our dear new Home!' wrote Kate in her diary.

Looking back years later Evelyn observed that his parents' life reminded him of *Diary of a Nobody*, with Arthur and Kate as Mr and Mrs Pooter, and himself as their rascally son, Lupin.[2] The second half of the comparison may not be strictly apt, but that

[2] In 1935 Alec Waugh described in his journal reading the novel to his wife. 'I read *Diary of a Nobody* aloud to Joan. We roared over Lupin's resemblance to my brother.'

12

there were Pooterish elements in the home life of the Waughs is undeniably true. Their modest domestic affairs ('Shopped in morning, and had my head champooed. Pruned three rows of raspberries while Bassett [Raban] weeded path. . . . Philip and Sylvia Gosse came to tea bringing the guinea pigs with them. Philip made lovely hutch . . .'); Arthur's swagger; Kate's unrelenting housework ('Very hard at work all day, Drawing-room finished & study nearly done, & carpet down in spare room'); her dressmaking, her cookery lessons ('Tried to make pastry. Very funny. Roasted pheasant. Very good'); their innocent amusements (ping-pong was a great passion, usually played after dinner, often with the Pawlings) and the entertaining of their acquaintance, cannot but bring the world of The Laurels, Brickfield Road, to mind. Arthur even had two friends, Mr Morgan and Mr Hamilton, who like Cummings and Gowing in the story irritated by their clumsiness, by the late hour at which they called after dinner and the inconsiderate amount of time they stayed. 'Mr Morgan called & wouldn't leave . . . Mr Morgan came after supper & missed last train . . . [Mr Hamilton] sat upon a hat when he came into church, & the gentleman whom it belonged to couldn't conceive how anyone could do such a thing.'

Arthur's favourite pastime, it hardly needs saying, was performing in amateur theatricals. He was president of the Merrie Andrews Dramatic Society, waggishly known to its members as the MADS, a company which had been started by Jocelyn Ledward, brother-in-law of Mrs Sydney Pawling, whose occasional productions were given for two nights at a time at the Bijou Theatre in Bayswater, a venue popular with amateur actors. There was also a Shakespearean society, known informally as the 'Shaker', which met regularly in the evenings for play-reading. Kate enjoyed taking part, but it was Arthur who was the star, as Puff in *The Critic*, Dr Roerlund in *The Pillars of Society*, Launce in *The Two Gentlemen of Verona*, with Kate as Silvia. He took the chair at meetings of the Dickens Fellowship, always an occasion of histrionic opportunity,[3] and at private parties could be relied upon to do a turn or give a recitation, to take centre-stage. Kate

[3] 'Arthur took the chair in his usual able manner. Mr Snowden Ward gave a magic lantern lecture & a member recited Pickwick on the ice. Miss Georgina Hogarth (a dear old lady) & Mrs Dickens were present & expressed themselves pleased with the entertainment.'

describes a party at the Pawlings at which scenes from *Alice's Adventures in Wonderland* were performed. 'Arthur twice times recited, he made the evening a great success, dancing & talking energetically. Delightful party, sorry when over.'

Apart from the increase in space and the fact that they were no longer living over the main road, for Kate the greatest pleasure in their new house lay in the garden. At once she began sowing beans and putting in bulbs, followed in the spring by geraniums, raspberry canes and strawberry plants. On his return from the office Arthur was set to putting up and painting a trellis, and made his wife a present of a lawn-mower. Together, and in common with, it sometimes seemed, the entire youth of the nation, they took up bicycling, a new sport which had quickly become a craze. After a few lessons, wobbling about on borrowed machines in the safety of Hillfield Road, the two of them, Arthur in plus-fours, Kate in a home-made costume of balloon sleeves and long skirt, would whirr off to Hatfield or Harrow, Barnet or St Albans, before returning pleased and tired to their evening meal. Traffic was sparse, and as their confidence grew they became more adventurous, travelling farther afield by train to spend a day riding in the country, stopping for a picnic lunch or for tea at a tavern or farm. The distances they covered were considerable: once they put their bicycles on the train to Richmond and from there rode to Chertsey, and another time Arthur and Mr Circuitt went as far as Hindhead, a distance of 58 miles, in one day. Arthur wrote a series of bicycling poems (one of which was called 'The Entraining Bicyclist'), which he later had bound and privately printed under the title *Legends of the Wheel*.

Such activity gives the impression of vigour and vitality, but in fact neither of the Waughs was robust, Arthur in particular suffering from a series of complaints mostly to do with his weak chest. 'Seedy' is a word that makes a frequent appearance in the diary. 'Shopped, rather seedy all day', 'Very seedy, stayed in bed to breakfast', 'Arthur came home to lunch feeling seedy'. Their doctor, Dr Andrews, was a regular visitor, treating Arthur's headaches and neuralgia and of course his chronic asthma, which during the winter often prevented him from going to work. In early summer he was a martyr to hay-fever, up all night with the

Himrod tray, his face swollen till it looked, in his words, 'like a linseed meal poultice'.

Although below average height, Arthur was a handsome young man, with a clear gaze and expressive features. His energy and enthusiasm, his remarkable memory for quotation and his ability to throw himself into any part made him a popular member of the relatively unsophisticated society in which he moved. In later life the dramatic utterances, the stagy performance became, at least to one member of his family, intensely irritating, making normal intercourse virtually impossible, but in his twenties and early thirties the habit had not yet hardened, he had not yet completely assumed the actor's mask. He was, too, very attractive to women. Of a warm and emotional nature, Arthur loved women, enjoyed being in female company, and although unquestionably faithful to his wife, from time to time pursued a number of harmless flirtations, not all of which left K entirely serene. There were a couple of girls who on visits to Norton had caught his eye, and during Kate's second pregnancy he formed an attachment to Katie Nicholas, a young woman who lived locally and with whom he took to going on long bicycle rides which were inclined to end in unexpected downpours, necessitating the taking of shelter and a very delayed return home. But his innocence and the purity of his motives are attested in a letter, revealing enough to be quoted at length, written some years later to a clergyman friend, Kenneth McMaster, after a course of treatment for rheumatism. The treatment, administered at home by a pretty young nurse, consisted of the application of infra-red heat and massage. The nurse,

a dark-eyed, curly-haired, smiling little fairy, of about 23 fair springs . . . assumed a shining white overall, attached the machine to the electric light, and whispered 'Will you please take off your trousers?' Trembling all over, I obeyed, & buried my face in the pillow. For twenty minutes she directed infra-red rays to my hinder parts, & put me to perpetual shame. Then I thought she had finished. Not at all. She waved her delicate fingers mystically, & began taking the most reprehensible liberties with my body. For another twenty minutes she persisted in her caresses; and, when at last she rested, I was ashamed to look my Wife in the face . . . It was the deepest enchantment I have ever undergone, but my conscience has tortured me ever

since. So I have come to my father-confessor for an epiphany
absolution. Say 'ite: missa est'. 'Bless me, even me also, O my
Father.' Thank you. I feel better now. With love & gratitude.
Ever your affectionate & innocent penitent, Arthur Waugh.

In November 1897, Arthur and Kate went to Brighton for a short
holiday. They stayed at the Royal Albion, walked on the pier,
visited the aquarium, and Arthur bought a new hat. It was very
jolly. Nine months later almost to the day, on 8 July 1898, Kate
gave birth to their first child, a son whom they called Alec.

As Arthur wrote later in his autobiography, Alec was the son of
his soul, the son through whom he could vicariously relive an
idealised version of his youth. From the very beginning the baby
was doted on by his father. When he was only a month old,
'Arthur sang & nursed & danced Aleck [sic] for more than half
an hour. He was so good & enjoyed it & looked with open eyes
all the time quite happy.' Arthur was entranced by him, and as
Alec grew older he spent more and more time with his little boy.
He drew for him, played soldiers with him and told him stories;
he made him a kite, and as soon as he was big enough would
sometimes come home from the office early to organise a baby
form of cricket in the nursery. Kate, helped by a nursemaid from
Somerset, Lucy Hodges, also adored her 'Baba', devotedly taking
him to Fortune Green to play bat and ball and wheeling him out
shopping in a little mail-cart she bought especially for the purpose. But it was his father whom Alec loved the most.

In December 1901, Arthur was offered the job of managing
director of Chapman & Hall, attending his first board meeting
on 31 January 1902. He took command quickly and efficiently
of the offices in Henrietta Street, of necessity moving fast to
prevent the disaster towards which the firm was effortlessly heading. For too long Chapman & Hall had coasted on the rich
revenue provided by the Dickens copyright, carelessly neglecting
most other aspects of the business. But the copyright would run
out in 1920, and Arthur saw it as a matter of urgency to restore
relations with living authors, establish contact with agents and
booksellers, revise existing arrangements with binders and printers, and make efforts to get to know his staff, which he did in
characteristic fashion by setting up a cricket club. 'I am much
too fat really to play,' he wrote to a cricketing friend in 1906,

'but the staff enjoy it more if I turn out with them.' In recognition
of his achievement and experience, he was appointed first chairman of the Publishers' Circle, formed for publishers to exchange
views and to promote and protect their mutual interests. He was
becoming a distinguished member of the world of the man of
letters, of the order of what he archly referred to as the 'Knights
of the Pen and Volume'.

At Hillfield Road, Alec, an outgoing little boy, was growing up.
For his son's fifth birthday Arthur gave him his first cricket bat,
for Alec had taken to the game with a passion that almost out-
stripped his parent's, learning by heart the names of the MCC
team, memorising the Test scores, and playing single-wicket
'matches' with his father in the narrow back garden. What he
lacked was a player nearer his age, one who did not disappear
every morning to the city.

On 28 October 1903, Kate, with no previous indication in her
diary that she was pregnant, notes that it was a wet morning, that
she had clipped Marquis, and that Arthur had come home early
with neuralgia. The day had passed without event – until the
evening. For in pencil is added, 'Evelyn born 10.30 in great haste
before Dr Andrews could arrive.'

Following the birth of her second son, Kate stayed in bed for
six weeks suffering from headache and depression; indeed, until
well into the new year she remained so fragile that Arthur grew
anxious enough to give up some of his acting commitments to
spend more evenings at home. On 7 January Evelyn was christened (Evelyn after 'a whim' of Kate's,[4] Arthur for his father, and
St John to please a godfather who insisted on the name of a
saint), and on the ninth he and his mother, accompanied by the
nursemaid Lucy, went down for a few days to Midsomer Norton.
On 9 February Evelyn was circumcised, as Alec had been, and at
the end of June Lucy went to Norton with the two children so
that Arthur could take Kate away for a recuperative holiday.
'Lucy & the boys left by the 10.45 at Paddington. I saw them
off, & then went on to Swan & Edgar's & bought a nice tussore
dress, then returned home & tidied up the nursery & sewed on

---

[4] 'I have never liked the name,' Evelyn recorded in his autobiography. 'In
America it is used only of girls and from time to time even in England it has
caused confusion as to my sex.'

Tweedledee's nose ... The house seems dreadful without the boys.'

They had chosen a Scandinavian cruise, the first time either of them had been away from England. However, once on board the *Cameo* they might almost have been at home in West Hampstead: on the first night out, the captain 'proposed a social evening. After dinner Arthur recited, & Mrs Nesbitt played, the captain did card tricks & sang. A very happy evening.'

In August Arthur went as usual to his parents, while Kate and Lucy took Evelyn to see her mother and step-father. 'Evelyn dreadfully frightened at the strange faces at Bishops Hull,' she wrote. 'I could not leave him a minute.'

A world of privacy and love

The first three years of Evelyn's life were spent in the little house in Hillfield Road. He and Alec shared a nursery on the first floor, the best room in the house, warm and sunny, its bow window looking south to the Crystal Palace and the Surrey hills. The small garden, where Evelyn, as soon as he was old enough for such things, was allowed to keep a rabbit in a hutch, was divided into lawn and kitchen garden; there was a willow and an apple tree, and at night owls could be heard hooting in the branches. The stairs and hall were lit by gas, the main rooms by oil-lamps, with candles on the chimney pieces. There was a maid in cap and apron, and Lucy Hodges to look after the children. It was a cosy house, but for six people decidedly cramped, especially with the demands made by Alec's cricketing activities. When it was too wet or cold to play outside, he spent entire afternoons obsessively bowling a tennis ball at the nursery wall, which not only dented the plaster of the wall but often landed on his brother's cot, only flimsily protected by a piece of netting. When the weather was fine, he turned his damaging attentions to the garden. 'Once more the borders of the garden are devastated by outs and switches to leg,' Arthur wrote proudly to Kenneth McMaster. 'There is no grass on the sward, and dust sails to the summit of the willow. Evelyn talks like a mob-orator, voluble and erratic: he runs up & down the path, roaring with laughter, & has red cheeks and sturdy legs.'

So it was decided to move. Arthur was doing well at Chapman & Hall, which now counted Bennett, Maugham and Wells among its authors, and in December 1906, Dr Waugh, 'the Brute', died, leaving Arthur a small legacy. With this Arthur was able to buy a modest plot of land in the village of North End, between Hampstead and the as yet undeveloped Golders Green. Here he built a comfortable, ugly suburban villa which he called Underhill, after a lane in Midsomer Norton, and here the family moved in September 1907, just over a month before Evelyn's fourth birthday.

Almost as soon as they had settled in, the district began rapidly to change. Underhill was just below the carriage entrance of North End Manor, one of the two local big houses, and North End Road was then a relatively quiet country thoroughfare bordered by a grassy footpath and low white railings. The village was a proper village with pub (the Bull & Bush), infant school, village hall, post office, shop (where telephone calls could be made, as Arthur refused to have an instrument in the house), and a dairy with china cows in the window run by the Misses Tooley, a couple of spinster sisters. In one direction, between the village and Golders Green, were farms, fields and market gardens; in the other the steep wooded hill leading to Hampstead and the heath. But in June that same year, 1907, underground railway stations were opened at both Hampstead and Golders Green, the new lines bringing with them a horde of builders and speculators, almost overnight turning Golders Green itself into a goldrush town, its surrounding country quickly disappearing in the mud and noise of the new development. From his window, Arthur could watch the rapid rise of the Garden Suburb, and soon North End had lost its rural character, grimily subsumed in the massive urban sprawl of Greater London.

Underhill, although far from beautiful, was a comfortable family house, and a great source of pride to Arthur. He loved its (to others) awkward shape, its dull suburban garden, the dark depressing oak of its interior. His love extended even to the house's fabric, and he took pleasure in referring, as though it were a ship, to its 'stout timbers'. On the ground floor instead of a family drawing-room there was a bookroom, complete with inglenook and a heavy stone fireplace from Norton; it was here that Arthur kept, on a shelf to themselves, the books he had reviewed, most of them with 'a kindly, grateful' letter from its author pasted to the flyleaf. On the first floor was a sitting-room for Kate, and overlooking the garden the boys' large, light daynursery with a wallpaper of figures in medieval costume. Arthur, who was at his office in Covent Garden every morning by nine o'clock, not returning home until after six, cared far less about the encroaching urbanisation than did his wife, who never became entirely reconciled to living in London. As far as was possible, she continued at Underhill to lead the life of a country-woman, spending hours every day in the garden, in her wash-leather gloves potting, planting, dead-heading, weeding, pruning fruit trees and digging vegetable beds. As she had at Hillfield Road, she took an active part in the running of the house, now with both a cook and housemaid to help her. Although she took trouble in training them, the cooks employed by the Waughs were not as accomplished as they might have been. Arthur, fond of his food and a big eater, made frequent querulous reference in his diaries to the disappointing quality of his lunch or dinner – although few instances were as frightful as the day Kate took Evelyn aged thirteen and Uncle George Raban to a matinée of *Where the Rainbow Ends*, coming back to Arthur and a dinner of steak-and-kidney pudding which was 'quite raw, absolutely uneatable. So Evelyn had to go down to the parade at 8 p.m. to see what he could buy, and found all shops closed except a busman's restn., where he bought two small pork pies.' Kate was always busy; if she was not gardening, then sewing, or in the kitchen making jam. With kind Miss Hoare, who lived with her widowed sister and a pack of West Highland terriers in North End House, she visited the poor – workmen's cottages down the hill and slum families in Shoreditch. She and Miss Hoare ran a clothing club for needy neighbours, and every year at the fairs on Hampstead Heath, as members of the St John Ambulance Brigade (Miss Hoare was the lady superintendent), they manned a first-aid station and a refuge for lost children.

His mother and his nurse, Lucy, were the calm, safe centre of Evelyn's world. He loved them both deeply. Lucy was kind and just; she was never cross or neglectful, but she was strict and laid great emphasis on the importance of telling the truth. She was a devout Christian, Chapel, not Church of England, and she read the Bible daily, systematically working her way from Genesis to Revelation every six months. She had a puritanical view of life, and silently disapproved both of Arthur Waugh drinking wine and of his wife playing bridge; she did not like it either when Evelyn began going to the theatre with his parents, remaining coldly unresponsive to his excited descriptions when he returned home. She was a strong influence in the nursery, although Evelyn, a cocky little boy, used often to answer her back. His fellow pupil, Stella Rhys, was shocked when after a scolding Evelyn said to her, 'Lucy has no business to speak to us like that.' 'Why?' asked Stella. 'Because we're of a much better class than she is.'

It was with Lucy that Evelyn first began to know the district, toiling up the hill to the heath, crossing the road at the Bull & Bush as Lucy did not care to walk near a pub, and on as far as the Whitestone Pond to watch people throwing sticks into the water for their dogs. Then they would either go down the hill one way to the shops in the Finchley Road, or, for more modest, local shopping, just as steeply downhill to Heath Street and Hampstead High Street, where there was the corn chandler with a decorative arrangement of grains in his window, the jeweller with his lion-head clock, and the chemist who had a gas burner to melt the wax with which he sealed the thick white paper wrapping his customers' parcels. When the great fairs took place on Hampstead Heath at Easter, Whitsun and August Bank Holiday, it was usually Lucy who took Evelyn to them, either in the morning or early afternoon, as in the evening the fair could turn rowdy. Once Evelyn went with his father, but this was not a success. When Arthur, after an entire morning indulging his son with the various amusements, turned for home, Evelyn in a rage rolled on the ground shouting at his parent, 'You brute, you beast, you hideous ass!', words which from that day became part of the family language.

When not with Lucy, Evelyn spent his time with his mother, with whom he often communicated in a secret language: 'Evoggles Goggles Moggles' stood for 'Evelyn Loves Mother'. The two of them had a great deal in common. Even as a small boy Evelyn took pleasure in good workmanship and in watching handiwork well done. He was particularly intrigued, for instance, by an ivory workbox from India which Kate kept in her sitting-room, its numerous trays and compartments made of sandalwood and full of tiny, exquisite sewing implements. And Kate was very good with her hands; it was she, not Arthur, who did the small carpentry jobs about the house, adept with hammer and screwdriver at hanging shelves or building a rabbit-hutch out of packing-cases. Although not a voracious reader (she got through one book a fortnight), it was she who taught Evelyn to read, and it was she who gave him his first lessons, shared with Stella Rhys, Ernest Rhys's little red-headed daughter. Under Kate's tutelage the children worked their way through *Reading without Tears* and *Little Arthur's History*, repeated their multiplication tables, and on walks on the heath learned by heart the names of wild flowers. As neither Kate nor Lucy (nor indeed Evelyn) was musical, nursery rhymes were taught as verse not songs.

Evelyn was an active, interested and cheerful little boy, but like his father he was of an emotional temperament, easily upset and made to cry. As with Lucy, so with his mother: with her dependable and reticent nature he felt safe. He knew she loved him. Whether allowing him to 'help' her in the garden, or at meals secretly holding his hand under the table, or at night hearing his prayers and tucking him up in a bed crowded with whatever possessions at that moment took his fancy, she inhabited with him 'a world of privacy and love'. By his mother he was exposed to none of the unpredictable and histrionic changes of mood to which his father was prone. Kate understood him, respected his modesty and sense of decorum, was firm when necessary, but never made the kind of invasive demands which were an integral part of Arthur's daily performance.

The irony was that while Arthur had always been determined that his children should never undergo the kind of upbringing he had endured, with its anxieties, its sadistic bullying and what he described as 'the terrible autocracy of the armchair'; had always intended to give his children everything he in childhood had been denied, to share their lives, be 'young with the young', in fact with his second son he remained, although much kinder, as distant and uninvolved as Alexander Waugh had been with him. It was indeed Alec who was the son of his father's soul, not Evelyn. And far from appearing young, Arthur in Evelyn's eyes never seemed anything but old and decrepit. Arthur spoke often and with solemnity of his imminent death, and the plot he had bought for himself and Kate in Hampstead churchyard was a favourite destination for walks. His bronchitis in winter and his chronic asthma brought on violent coughing and wheezing fits every morning, and in the evening the house reeked of the burning

23

powder of Himrod's Asthma Cure. He was also deaf in one ear as a result, when a subaltern in the Volunteers, of catching cold through sleeping on a damp pillow, and this, with the asthma, eventually made him reluctant to go out at night and gave him a dislike of parties. Evelyn resented his father. He resented the fact that Arthur's physical disability made impossible the kind of male pursuits at which fathers should be expert, such as football, boxing, and mending machinery. And he resented Arthur's interruption of the peaceful, happy life he enjoyed with his mother. Every evening during the week, Evelyn's pleasure in the day and in his mother's company was brought to an end by the sound of his father's key in the lock, and the invariable summons from the hall, 'Where is K? Where is my wife?' Arthur's subsequent visit to the nursery, although well-intentioned and meant to amuse, was brief and, to its occupant, unwelcome.

Evelyn was both fascinated and repelled by his father's theatrical behaviour. Arthur's feelings of insecurity and the pessimism and depressions inculcated by a difficult childhood were battened down under an exaggerated joviality. By this stage in his life, Arthur was never not on stage. ('Charming, entirely charming, and acting all the time' was the comment of one of the first adult friends Evelyn at the age of sixteen brought to the house.) His normal conversational tone was coloured by rhetoric and declamation. He was unbearably sentimental. Little was said without deliberate dramatic effect. He had an excellent memory for quotation, and loved making up ditties of his own which he sang to himself as he moved restlessly about the house in a cloud of pipe-tobacco smoke: 'Blast it! Darn it!/ Henrietta Elizabeth Barnett', or despondently and to a waltz tune: "Nobody loves me/ No, nobody loves me/ Nobody cares for me in the least/ Everyone thinks I'm a horrible beast'. Sometimes he parodied his grandfather delivering a sermon: ' . . . When this feeble voice is for ever silent and can no longer sound its note of warning . . .' Even when in the grip of an asthmatic attack and gasping for breath, he would cry to heaven for release in a wide variety of famous lines. With his large grey eyes, noble brow and head of thick hair, Arthur was a handsome man – small, like both his sons, but better looking – although for some reason he tried to avoid catching sight of his reflection, and if he saw himself in a glass, would start back crying, like the ghost in *Hamlet*, 'O, horrible! Most horrible!' Abnormally sensitive to criticism, he hated any form of confrontation, and when discussion arose within the family, however amicable, he put a stop to it with, 'Let the long contention cease!/ Geese are swans and swans are geese,/ Let them have it how they will!/ Thou art tired; best be still.' Of course all this was very entertaining, but it could also be frustrating, embarrassing, irritating, and to a child profoundly bewildering. Did his father mean what he said when he spoke like this, or did he not?

The difference between the two parents was exemplified by the treats which they separately provided. At Christmas there was the theatre: with Arthur, this meant seats in the stalls preceded by a large and exotic lunch in a Soho restaurant; with Kate, Evelyn had his lunch in a Lyons teashop after which they queued for seats in the gallery. With his mother he went by bus to Kew Gardens and the South Kensington museums; with his father it was the Tower of London, St Alban's Abbey and other sites of important historical interest, which Arthur would declaim over, liberally tipping the beefeaters and vergers and 'creating a little aura of importance about us'. Arthur was ill at ease with his younger son, and no amount of posturing could conceal the fact. A neighbour who was fond of Evelyn once tried to tackle the subject, a piece of impertinence that affronted Arthur. 'Mrs Fleming cordially told me that I had never been a good father to Evelyn, who was afraid of me, & at his worst in my presence!'

But the real and immovable obstacle to a close relationship with his father existed in the far closer relationship Arthur enjoyed with Alec. Arthur made no secret of the fact that Alec was his favourite,[1] expatiating in letters to his friends on the subject of Alec's achievements, his writing, his high marks, his athletic successes. Evelyn is rarely mentioned. On one awful occasion when Alec arrived home from school at the end of term, Arthur pasted a notice over the face of the grandfather clock in the hall, 'Welcome home to the heir of Underhill'. 'When Alec has Underhill,' asked Evelyn plaintively, 'what will be left for me?' The point was taken, and the notice never appeared again.

Through Alec, Arthur did his best to create for himself a

---

[1] In a letter to Alec's elder son on his christening in 1933, Arthur wrote revealingly, 'The three great things in my life have been my Mother, my Wife, & my son – your father. Nothing else has mattered much to me but their love.'

happier version of his own far from happy boyhood. To his friend, Kenneth McMaster, Arthur admitted, 'I know that I worry too much about Alec, and expect too much. But you see, I have built my earthly hopes on him – I do want to see him do some of the things I have had to give up hope of doing – not only on the cricket & football fields (where he romps to triumph weekly) but along the hard, beaten, stony path of life.' When Alec started at Sherborne in September 1911, it seemed the culmination of all Arthur's vicarious ambitions. 'I think your terms in IVA & VB were the happiest in my life,' he wrote to Alec in 1916, 'unless it was the weeks when you were getting into the XI.'

And Alec, a conformist at heart, revelled in school life; he loved the cups, the caps, the form promotions, the whole fiercely competitive drama of it. Even when he broke the rules and acted rebellious – for instance, going to a school match defiantly wearing his house rather than his school cap to show he was prouder of being a member of his house than of the First XI – it was always within the noble tradition of schoolboy scrape, acceptable behaviour for a spirited, sound-hearted boy. Arthur followed with passionate interest and paternal pride every stage of Alec's school career, several times a week writing to him at length and in unrestrainedly emotional terms. 'Dear Boy, I am sure there is some spiritual relation between you & me which transcends the merely material world . . . There is a rare sort of crucifix, found in one or two gothic cathedrals in France, in which behind the figure of the Son, as he hangs upon the Cross, is vaguely to be discerned the Figure of the God the Father also. The nails that pierce the Son's hands pierce the Father's also: the thorn-crowned head of the Dying Saviour is seen to be lying on the Father's bosom. And it is always so with you & me . . .' He discussed in admiring detail Alec's compositions in both prose and verse, guided his reading and lectured him solemnly about sex, in particular on the paramount importance of sexual continence and the appalling consequences of masturbation. 'The result of self-abuse, if carried on persistently, is first weakness both of body & mind, and finally paralysis & softening of the brain. This is absolutely true . . . Say it is Saturday night, and the idea attacks you. Put it from you at once. Think of cricket, of the day's game, of the probable team next week . . .' Arthur visited Sherborne regularly at weekends, was a keen spectator at the Saturday footer match, a generous host to Alec and his friends at the Digby Hotel in the evening, providing dinner and boyishly joining in the game of Coon-can which followed; he was a frequent and welcome guest of The Duffers, a literary society to which he was on several occasions invited to read a paper. 'I might almost be said to have lived at Sherborne in my imagination,' Arthur wrote in his autobiography, 'and I do not doubt now that, in reality as well, I lived there a great deal more than was wise.'

Far from resenting or feeling over-burdened by his parent's besotted attentions, Alec loved his father's company. As dark as in those days Evelyn was fair, Alec, although highly strung, was an extrovert, cheerful boy, pugnacious and competitive, fanatically interested in sport, in particular football and cricket. For Arthur and Alec cricket and Wisden were almost a form of religion, Lord's and the Oval the temples at which they worshipped.[2] At Sherborne Alec always bicycled keenly down to the post office to telegraph his cricket scores to Underhill; when awarded his first XI colours, his father wrote to him, 'the blue-and-gold of Sherborne has always been my Eldorado, and much as I would have given to see it on myself, I value it much more upon you.' During the school holidays Arthur on his return from Henrietta Street changed his office clothes for a grey suit, and he and Alec would walk arm in arm for an hour over Hampstead Heath. After dinner the two of them sat in the bookroom where Arthur in his armchair under the red-shaded lamp would read aloud from Kipling, Shakespeare and Tennyson.[3] 'My life centred round my father,' Alec later recorded. No wonder, then, that Evelyn felt excluded. And Alec himself did little to make matters easier.

In an unpublished fragment of autobiography, Alec wrote, 'For my first five and a quarter years I was an only child, and I remained an only child to all practical purposes right through my childhood, my brother Evelyn being in those early days no more than an encumbrance in a corner.' Unsurprisingly, Alec was

[2] 'Sunshine is wasted when it does not fall caressingly on white flannels and parasols and the sound of bat on ball,' Alec as a very young man wrote in a tone as besotted as his father's.
[3] Arthur firmly believed in the importance of the moral influence of great literature, 'in the possibility of each of us, in our own way, building up our character by the things we read, or, on the other hand, the certainty of our sapping and warping it by corrupt choice in reading'.

spoilt, possessed an exaggerated sense of his own importance, and was determined that nothing should threaten the position of privilege with his father. He did not grudge Evelyn their mother's company. ('Daddy loves Alec more than me, but you love me more than you love Alec,' Evelyn once said to his mother, to which Kate, with greater concern for fairness than accuracy, replied, 'No, I love you both the same.' 'Then I am lacking in love,' said Evelyn.) Just as Evelyn's emotional nature resembled his father's, Alec was more like his mother – even-tempered, reticent and apparently lacking in passion.[4] But Alec was never much interested in Kate. His father, on the other hand, he idolised, and by the time he was old enough to go away to school, the bond forged between them was unbreakable.

During term, Alec wrote regularly to his parents, occasionally appending to his letters a brief note for his brother. 'Dear It,' these missives usually began, often continuing with some accusation, such as that Evelyn was failing to send on his comics, 'Have you been hiding my *Chums*, and making my *Scout* a day late?' In the holidays the brothers slept in the same room, but Alec rarely came into the day-nursery, spending most of his time when he was not at football or cricket reading in his father's bookroom. The age gap was too great for the boys to have pursuits in common and, instead of allowing his little brother to worship him as hero, Alec effectively alienated him by his unkindness. Kate often had to lecture her elder son about his spiteful tongue, and when the situation got too bad and the taunting became unbearable, Evelyn would fling himself into the high-backed chair in which Kate sat at the dining-room table. 'Sanctuary, sanctuary!' he would cry, knowing that while he remained there it was understood he could not be touched, a ploy which no doubt maddened Alec.

After first attending a local day school, Alec had been sent to a prep school in Surrey, and he took pleasure in terrifying Evelyn with stories of life at Fernden, all thrashings, milk pudding and cold baths. When Alec attempted to teach his brother cricket it resulted only in inculcating in the younger boy a lifelong loathing

[4] In a letter to Alec dated 31 January 1917, Kate remarks on their similar temperaments: 'You are so like me in many ways. I can understand your joy of battle, your contrariness, your contempt of the approval of those you don't care for – we can really be in sympathy in the ways of life.'

of the game, typifying the rough-and-tumble male alliance so important to Alec and his father from which he was excluded. (Evelyn's boredom at the prospect of cricket is always forcibly expressed, even from the youngest age. 'I had a nice book to read naturaly wanted to read it: so far, so good; but all the rest were going to a cricet match and they got me to come by promesing that I could read my book,' Evelyn notes in his diary for 1914, 'which I did.') The process was not all one way. Evelyn, too, made sure that most of his activities were designed to keep out his brother. At one point a small billiard table was set up in the nursery for Alec, about which Evelyn was furiously resentful, regarding it as an intolerable invasion of his territory. And when on occasion Alec would ask friends in for tea and to play word games, Evelyn did his best to spoil the afternoon's fun with sarcastic repartee. 'We all disliked him heartily,' recalled one neighbour, then a little girl. 'We were thankful when he was at school and could not join in our cheerful social activities.' Most significantly, when playmates of Evelyn's were asked by their parents if their friend was an only child, they replied, 'Oh no, he has a brother at school whom he hates.'

Evelyn was a busy little boy. When not doing his lessons, or on walks with Lucy, or helping his mother, he was never at a loss for occupation. At the far end of the Underhill property behind the greenhouse was a fascinating area, acquired by Arthur when North End Manor was sold, where there had once been a kitchen garden, now overgrown with weeds; here there was a disused furnace house entered down a dark flight of stairs, and this secluded cellar Evelyn made his own. In the garden shed, equipped with test tubes and spirit lamp, he conducted 'chemical' experiments. Upstairs in his sunny first-floor nursery, he was very happy when nothing better offered making what he called 'different arrangements', moving the nursery furniture and rehanging the pictures. Perhaps as a legacy from his Gosse grandmother, and of his Uncle Alick, whose watercolour sketches and charts (still in use today) were much admired by his fellow officers in the Pacific, Evelyn was a skilled draughtsman, and painted and drew with enthusiasm, copying both pictures and lettering out of anything available, from Froissart's *Chronicles* to the pages of *Chums*. A keen reader, he was kept well supplied with books by his father, from whom when he was nine he received a history of the Roman Empire inscribed by Arthur with what looks now like uncanny prescience:

> All roads, they tell us lead to Rome;
> Yet, Evelyn, stay awhile at home!
> Or, if the Roman road invites
> To doughty deeds and fearful fights,
> Remember, England still is best –
> Her heart, her soul, her Faith, her Rest!

He collected coins, stamps, fossils, butterflies, beetles and wild flowers. He played with his lead soldiers, and for a time was possessed by a passion for conjuring, entertaining his audience with incompetent tricks performed to a facetious patter copied from the magicians he saw at children's parties. For a time he set up practice as a private detective ('Are you blackmailed? Send your cases to Messrs. Wuffles & Co.'). He had a microscope, a catapult and an air-gun. He was taught to ride a bicycle: 'It's very nice to ride a bike/ But I can't say I realy like/ The feal of falling off it.' He tried to construct a model town from instructions in the *Children's Encyclopaedia*, and at one time became so taken with the novels of Jules Verne that he started digging to the centre of the earth by way of the bootcupboard and thence down into the foundations of the house, a journey of exploration which when discovered resulted in a rare beating from his father.

But these were mostly solitary pursuits, and Evelyn was a sociable child, always ready to entertain, a keen participant of any party. To celebrate the New Year of 1914, the Waughs gave a fancy-dress dance for thirty, a jolly occasion enthusiastically described by Arthur as 'a whopping success – Both dining & book rooms were cleared, doors off their hinges, & musicians in the passage, who played right well. Supper up in the nursery – turkey, ham, pressed beef, tipsy cakes, meringues, creams, crackers, claret cup ad lib!! Alec took to supper the fair but pale Mistress Powell, who got no votes for her dress, but looked very sweet & seventeenth century – Mackintosh[5] bribed Evelyn to turn out the electric light between the dances because he wished to kiss Enid Archer on the stairs – an act of precocious gallantry which he had not, after all, the courage to attempt! We began at 6, & kept it up till 11, & even

[5] Hugh Mackintosh, a schoolfriend of Alec's.

then some of the guests protested that they did not want to leave. My poor Wife was nearly prostrated afterwards by the exertion.'

Unlike Alec, who knew almost nobody of his own age in the neighbourhood, Evelyn had made friends with a family of three children encountered one day when he and Lucy were out on a walk. Jean, Philippa and Maxwell Fleming lived in a house called Wyldesmead, less than quarter of a mile away in Morland Close at the back of Underhill. Evelyn quickly established himself as ring-leader, organising inventive games in the nursery, digging a dangerous tunnel, which he named 'Swylltinnon', in the sand near Wild's Farm, and leading skirmishing raids against local children, known contemptuously as 'the street cads'. In the eyes of his new friends he appeared fearless. When invited by them to a Christmas party, he turned up dressed all in white – white shoes, socks, shorts – and the other children, jeering, seized him by the legs and swung him round to polish the floor with his bottom. But Evelyn loved it, laughing helplessly as he was whirled round, growing filthier and filthier. It sometimes seemed that he preferred the Flemings to his own family. One day he turned up at Wyldesmead in a bowler hat. 'Eve! Fancy you in a bowler!' 'Yes,' said Evelyn. 'It belonged to father first, then descended to Alec, now to me. It has come down to me from generation to generation of them that hate me.'

Maxwell Fleming, a rather gentle boy, easily dominated, was his particular friend, and the two soon became inseparable; accompanied by the Flemings' Airedale, Warder, they roamed the heath in their thick jerseys, knee-length flannel trousers and stout shoes, looking for adventure. They found it once just outside Ivy Lodge, the house belonging to the ballerina Anna Pavlova. Pavlova kept swans, and one morning Evelyn and Maxwell, sauntering along towards the heath, saw that two of her big white birds had escaped on to the road. Ringing the door bell to report the fact, they were confronted by a strange man who, in reply to their story, poured out a torrent of incomprehensible verbiage. In a panic they flung at him the one foreign phrase they knew – 'Au revoir!' – and made a swift retreat. On another occasion, less well-intentioned, Evelyn led Maxwell through the fence and into the kitchen garden of North End Manor, where the boys, armed with sticks, ran up and down the rows of cabbages chanting, 'Here we come, the Cabbage Clopping Clan!' as they sliced the

31

cabbage-heads off their stalks, an act of vandalism not taken lightly by the old lady who lived in the manor, necessitating several peace-making visits on Kate's part before good relations were restored.

Evelyn, like his father and grandfather before him, loved to act. Now in imitation of the society to which Arthur belonged, the Merrie Andrews Dramatic Society (MADS), he formed the Wyldesmead Underhill Dramatic Society (WUDS). In the Easter holidays of 1914, his father gave him a professional make-up box, invaluable for the numerous productions which Evelyn produced, directing the Fleming children in the making of costumes and scenery and designing programmes with photographs of the chief performers. Most of the material he wrote himself, plays, sketches and revues, even a comic opera entitled *The Sheriff's Daughter*, with a chorus that effectively displayed the author's gift for personal invective. 'Shut your jaw you silly ass/ Can't you see the sheriff's lass . . ./ Silly ass shut your jaw/ You're just a silly ugly bore.' One of the most ambitious of the plays, written in collaboration with Jean Fleming, was called *The Man from Downing Street*, in which Evelyn, with cigarette and boater, took the part of the Man. When a new neighbour, a boy named David Malaher, joined their group and made particular friends with Maxwell, Evelyn was jealous and wrote *Come to the Coach House Door, Boys*, a drama showing the Malahers in a somewhat less than flattering light, the first act opening with this speech from David about his family: 'Fine is the clan of Malaher; of Scotch descent are we/ Whether in peace or war time, we are the first to flee/ We ran away at Bannockburn, we fled at Flodden field,/ In fact in every fight we are the very first to yield.' Evelyn, who played the part of David's father, made his first entrance with the memorable line, addressed to his wife (Jean Fleming), 'I'm sorry, dear, that I am late/ My son I've had to castigate.' The show was given at Christmas in the nursery in front of a full house, the play preceded by a short melodrama and a comic Cockney recitation spoken by Philla Fleming. 'The applause was tremendous,' Arthur recounted, '& at the close Philla was presented by Alec with a bouquet of mistletoe, & heartily kissed under it by myself!!'

Evelyn's talent for organisation found its greatest expression in the formation of the Flemings, David Malaher and himself into a small brigade known as the Pistol Troop. There was a very real fear at that time, the years just before the First World War, of German invasion, a fear fuelled by the German emperor's disquieting interest in naval expansion and intensified by the publication in 1903 of Erskine Childers's novel, *The Riddle of the Sands*. The reason for the Pistol Troop's existence was to repel the invading Hun ('Never be polite to Germans', ran one of the Troop rules. 'If you meet one, and feel capable of knocking him down, knock him down. If not, turn around and walk in the opposite direction.') Immediately after breakfast Evelyn would make his way to the bottom of the field opposite Wyldesmead and give the Pistol Troop call, 'Hoik! Oy-oik', his arm bent across his chest in the Troop salute. He and his 'men' would then prepare for the coming confrontation, forcing themselves to walk barefoot through nettles and concocting a poison soup to feed to the enemy. On a mound of clay in the middle of Morland Close, left there from the excavations of the many building works in the area, they constructed a sophisticated fortress, built ramparts, tunnelled through the interior, laid in stores in case of siege, and flew the Union Jack from a flagstaff – an abandoned scaffolding pole – on which they signed their initials in blood. In 1912 the Pistol Troop magazine was published, typed by Arthur's secretary, Miss Silk, and bound in red in full morocco by one of Chapman & Hall's best binders with a coat of arms designed by Evelyn stamped in gold. It had contributions from the Fleming children and various adult friends of the family, as well as a tale about racing by Alec and a six-page story by Evelyn called 'Multa Pecunia'.

'Multa Pecunia' was not Evelyn's first attempt at fiction. Indeed, almost as soon as he could hold a pencil, the volume of both his literary and graphic output was unusually large. He wrote poems and stories and stories told in pictures, most of them of a violent and bloodthirsty nature. At the age of six, he wrote 'The Curse of the Horse Race', a fast-paced tale of violence and murder in which bad Rupert, with 'a dark bushy mistarsh and flashing eyes', loses a bet with good Tom and tries to kill him. Tom dodges the blow, and it is the 'perlisman who had come to see what was the matter' who is killed. Justice is triumphant and Rupert is 'hung for killing the pulies man. I hope,' the narrator concludes with words in which the moral influence of Lucy is clearly detectable, 'I hope the story will be a leson to you never to bet.' The hero of 'Multa Pecunia', written three years later, is also called Tom, whose father, Sir Alfred James, was 'a great collector of books'. Underneath the house is hidden treasure, discovered simultaneously by Tom and by the butler, Smith. Now Smith 'was not usually a butler. He was really a proffessional thief', and it is his intention to make off with the treasure. However, after a couple of knock-out fights, Tom gets the better of him. Smith is sacked by Sir Alfred, arrested by Scotland Yard, 'and sent to Dartmoor convict prison'. In a third story, entitled 'Fidon's Confetion', written almost certainly in 1915, the year Alec left Sherborne, appears a miniature but unmistakable portrait of Alec. 'Sudenly the door opened and in came a young boy of nineteen he had just left his public school carrying away nearly every cup at the sports. He was certainly not clever clever for he had never got any higher than the upper fifth . . .'

As well as writing stories, Evelyn from the age of seven, perhaps at first in imitation of his mother, began keeping a diary, a practice he was to continue intermittently throughout his life. The first entry is for September, 1911: ' . . . We allways have sausages for breakfast on Sundays I have been waching Lucy fry them they do look funny before their kooked. Daddy is a Publisher he goes to Chapman and Hall office it looks a offely dull plase. I am just going to Church. Alec, my big brother has just gorn to Sherborne. The wind is blowing dreadfuly I am afraid that when I go up to Church I shall be blown away.' The following year Evelyn began 'My History', an early attempt at autobiography, 'ilastrated by the author'. 'My name is Evelyn, I live in a house called Underhill . . . It [was] futer to-day. I got 3 goles . . . I have had 1 shilling for being Vth in my form . . .'

Several times a year the routine of life at Underhill was interrupted by visits. There was one early and unsuccessful attempt at a family holiday in a small rented house in Ramsgate. Arthur detested it, and refused to repeat the experiment, ever after going abroad with Kate in June without the children. But Kate always took Evelyn on his own for a few days during the summer to some seaside resort, either Brighton or Broadstairs or Westcliff on Sea. They stayed at small family hotels, and spent their day on the pier and the beach, Evelyn sketching and swimming and playing 'Babmington'; in the evenings after dinner they took seats for a show. Evelyn was completely happy on these outings, and desired no other company than his mother's. Occasionally the Waughs took the boys with them to stay with Kate's mother and step-father at Bishops Hull. There were stables, and fruit ripening on the walls, and inside the house many interesting objects of Indian workmanship; the grown-ups were companionable and kind. Yet although Evelyn enjoyed himself, it never caught his imagination or rooted itself in his affections as did the house and the three maiden aunts at Midsomer Norton.

After Dr Waugh died in 1906, followed fifteen months later by his wife, Arthur visited Norton rarely, mainly because of an unpleasantness with his youngest sister, Elsie, over the will. After the death of their parents, Arthur said, Elsie 'developed a vindictive & bloodthirsty clutch upon all the family possessions.' She, Connie and Trissie, supported by an income mainly derived from a coal mine on the Morgan property in Wales, stayed on in the house where they had been born, looked after by Self, Dr Waugh's old coachman. Of the two elder sisters, Connie was pretty, Trissie plain; while Elsie, Evelyn's favourite, was selfish, capricious and sharp-tongued; early on in life she had decided to be an invalid, allowing herself to be waited on by the other two. For all three the parish church was the centre of their lives, and on Sundays each took a group of young men or girls for Bible classes in the house; they spent a great deal of time embroidering altar cloths and making doileys and table-mats for the church bazaar.

For a child like Evelyn, life at Norton was endlessly fascinating. The house was full of strange objects – fans, snuff-boxes, coins, medals, carved nuts; over the geyser in the bathroom was a frightening stuffed monkey with an evil grin, and downstairs an engraved facsimile of the death warrant of Charles I, which Evelyn ruined by upsetting a bottle of Indian ink while trying to copy the regicides' signatures. There were dogs, an old and ferocious cockatoo, and a pony to pull the trap. There were stables, a walled garden and a vine-covered verandah. There were frequent visits to church, which Evelyn much enjoyed; and there was always something being 'got up' at the church's instigation, a garden fête, a bazaar or sale of work, or amateur theatricals performed by the Girls' Friendly Society. In the summer there were frequent picnics. 'We set out at 12 o'clock & took our lunch with us Gorgeous lunch with hard boiled eggs cream slices & bananas. I got a lot of flowers ... [and] also found a pheasants nest and I bagged an egg which was too small to hatch.' Evelyn was never without company: he was an energetic, if not always effective helper to his mother and his aunts. 'Mother and Aunt Elsie were playing chess and they were cross yelling "Check" every few minutes and screeming and gigilling. I took out a golfe ball of Alec's and started bouncing it. Suddenly it bounced and I missed it, it bounced again and went up over Aunt Elsie and we thought it would drop on her but instead it went "pluck" into her cup.' He willingly joined in the varied and demanding social life of his contemporaries, two girl cousins from Chilcompton (Lucy's home village, where her brother had a milk-round on which he occasionally allowed Evelyn to accompany him), a boy of Evelyn's own age, and the children of Dr Bulleid, an archaeologist. With these colleagues, Evelyn several times a week had boisterous little parties, and on Sundays they used secretly to spy on the aunts' Bible classes, sniggering at Aunt Trissie's young miners arriving in their Sunday best, peeping through the conservatory door into the dining-room at Connie and her girls.

Evelyn was a friendly, happy and active little boy. Although not outstandingly robust, on the whole he enjoyed good health. He survived the usual childhood illnesses, such as croup, when he had to inhale over a kettle, head under a towel; and in May 1910 and June 1911 he went down in succession with measles and chickenpox, one preventing him from watching the funeral procession of Edward VII, the other the coronation procession of George V, for both of which Arthur had taken seats at his club, the Savile, then in Piccadilly.[6] But apart from circumcision as a baby, the only operation Evelyn underwent in childhood was for the removal of his appendix, which was performed on the kitchen table under chloroform during the summer of 1912 when he was

[6] In an article written in 1935, Evelyn recalled 'an obscure seat in the flag-draped bow windows of my father's club, to see a procession – though whether it was King Edward's funeral or King George's coronation I cannot remember – probably the latter, for the atmosphere seemed to be festive.' In *A Little Learning*, however, he says, 'My father belonged to the Savile Club – and he had seats for us there both for King Edward VII's funeral and King George's coronation. I missed both events, one for measles, one for chickenpox.' The probability is that Evelyn would have taken greater trouble to be accurate in his autobiography than in a magazine article, and it is possible in the former case that he was simply making use of a corporate family recollection.

eight. According to 'My History', he was kept in bed for a week 'with something wrong with my stomach', his distaste for his invalid state forcibly expressed in a little poem: 'I hate so much to stay in bed/ They seem to think I'm almost dead/ I want to sing, and dance, and leap/ And not to have to go to sleep/ O glory to the time when I/ May leap and shout mine own war cry...' Until the surgeon was actually in the house, Evelyn was kept in ignorance of what was to happen, and the period of convalescence which followed was almost as disagreeable as the operation. For ten days Evelyn, looked after by an unkind nurse whom he nicknamed the Scoundrel, was kept in bed and strapped down by the legs. His mother came and read aloud to him ('Mother read me a article ... called "How To Join the Navy" & I have made up my mind that I am going to be a "Merry Jack tar", if my eyes will pass Mother dous not think they will. If they do not I shall go board a "Merchantman" for I must go to sea.'). He was visited by his great chum, Maxwell Fleming, who came round to display his birthday presents ('He had a riping pair of pads & a pair of wickekeeping gloves & bat'), and by Miss Hoare, who brought some model soldiers in a little bag. But when at the end of ten days he tried to get out of bed, he was unable to walk.

A bizarre plan was devised for Evelyn to go on his own to recuperate at a girls' school situated at the mouth of the Thames near Southend. As it was the summer holidays, there were no pupils and, apart from the two mistresses in charge, his only companion was a little girl called Daffodil. Every day at low tide Evelyn paddled on the mud flats of the estuary to restore the strength in his legs; and three times a week a fat masseuse bicycled over to give him treatment with an electric battery. Nurse Talbot was a kind, motherly woman, and to her Evelyn confided his misery. She was concerned at his unhappiness and at her suggestion Evelyn left the school to spend the rest of his convalescence with her, her jolly, slightly drunken husband and daughter Muriel in their shabby little cottage on the marshes at Leigh. He and Muriel attended a local dame school together, and played in a tree house built for them by Muriel's father, where the two children showed each other their private parts. Evelyn, having been wretched, was so happy with Muriel and her parents that he forgot altogether about writing home, earning himself a letter

37

of emotional rebuke from his father that inspired not the remorse that was intended but a deep feeling of resentment.

When he finally returned home, he was still too weak to be sent back to school, and Kate asked if for a term he might join the Fleming children at Wyldesmead in the lessons given by their governess. Miss Brodie, or 'Broggie', as they called her, was a gentle little person, but to amuse the others Evelyn executed a series of drawings showing Broggie as torturer – Broggie turning the thumb-screw, Broggie operating the rack, and so on – drawings which he then posted down the cracks in the floorboards, where perhaps they lie to this day.

Unlike his brother, to whom religion meant little more than outward observance,[7] for Evelyn the spiritual life was always of paramount importance. Arthur, a practising Anglican, took his faith seriously but, although he suffered occasional doubts about the after-life, was not introspective and rarely questioned the tenets of the Church of England. It was the beauty of the language and the ceremony to which he responded, and the sense of tradition. He used to say revealingly, 'With a thorough knowledge of the Bible, Shakespeare and Wisden you cannot go far wrong.' At Underhill, in response to a specific request from his younger son, he read prayers to the household every morning, until just before the outbreak of war in 1914 when he stopped on the grounds that it was 'no longer any good'. On Sundays he and Kate attended choral celebration at St Jude's, a high Anglican church in the Garden Suburb, while Evelyn went with Lucy to the North End Rooms to hear Miss Hoare play the harmonium, a village congregation sing the hymns of Sankey and Moody, and lay preachers deliver sermons of a predominantly low-church nature. When Lucy left in 1910 to get married, Evelyn accompanied his parents to St Jude's, which was then in charge of the Revd Basil Bourchier. Bourchier, a cousin of the actor-manager, Arthur Bourchier, and satirised as the odious Cyril Boom Bagshaw in A. S. M. Hutchinson's bestseller, *If Winter Comes*, was an actor *manqué*, one of those flamboyant, theatrical priests who in every age are to be found showily performing from the pulpit. Arthur regarded the man as a rollicking joke, enjoying the novelty of each week's antics. Bourchier put a lot of thought into his dramatic effects: while his flock

[7] 'I accepted religion without belief,' Alec wrote in *The Early Years of Alec Waugh*.

were taking Communion, a large, red, electric cross was switched on over the altar; and the lesson was often acted out with impress-ive literalness. One Sunday Bourchier descended from the pulpit in cope and biretta, a large silver salt-cellar in his hands: 'My people,' he intoned, scattering salt before him, 'you are the salt of the earth.' Evelyn found Bourchier, with his love of the limelight and histrionic style of preaching, purely preposterous. However, as he later recorded, 'Despite all Mr Bourchier's extravagant display I had some glimpse of higher mysteries.'

Evelyn's spiritual nature was awake and responsive from an early age. Part of his happiness when staying with his aunts was associated with the churchy atmosphere that was such an integral part of the life there. Going to Evensong at Norton he found a positive pleasure, and he made friends with a pious young curate, a high-church ritualist, who to Evelyn's great satisfaction taught him to serve at the altar. He became 'intensely curious about church decorations and the degrees of anglicanism . . . which they represented'. Instead of drawing battles, he now drew saints and seraphim inspired by medieval illuminations, and was thrilled during one holiday when he was asked to paint some carved angels in Clandown church. Arthur remarked that his younger son seemed to be spending his entire summer 'serving at the altar, & going to picnics – a weird mixture of faith & frivolity', but it was a mixture that clearly suited him. Aunt Connie was able to report, 'We are all struck by the great improvement in Evelyn. He couldn't be nicer – so pleasant & so ready to do anything we want him to do, & pleased with any little joy we try to arrange. I don't think he is nearly so satirical as he used to be. We are all very happy together.' Back at Underhill he constructed beside his bed a shrine with brass candlesticks peopled with plaster statues of saints purchased from a religious emporium in Golders Green. Aged twelve, he wrote in his diary under the heading, 'My shrine', that the aunts 'promised to make me a frontal, Aunt Elsie is going to give me a crucifix when I'm confirmed[8] and Aunt Trissie has

[8] This took place at an evening service at St Jude's on 29 June 1916. In 'Charles Ryder's Schooldays', Ryder is confirmed 'incuriously, without expectation or disappointment. When, later in life, he read accounts of the emotional disturbances caused in other boys by the ceremony he found them unintelligible . . . The chaplain had "prepared" him and had confined his conferences to theology. There had been no probing of his sexual life; he had no sexual life to probe. Instead they had talked of prayer and the sacraments.'

given me two sweet brass bowls to fill with flowers.' For his father's
fiftieth birthday, he composed a holy poem, 'The World to Come',
in the metre of Hiawatha, describing the experiences of a soul
immediately after death.

Here the Devil laid his wager,
And on Job did cast derision.
Hence the cruelties of Nero,
Hence the anguish of the martyrs,
Hence the wailing of the slaughtered
And the shrieking of the murdered.
Here was hatched Our Lord's betrayal,
Here the thirty silver pieces,
Here Christ's Church was first divided
In this house of crime and torture.

As Arthur remarked, 'Not bad for twelve years old?'

On one level Christianity was an all-absorbing hobby, attending
church, learning ritual and spending pocket money on religious
insignia as another boy might collect birds' eggs or stamps. But
it went further than that. Evelyn began to talk of becoming a
parson, an ambition to which his mother, no doubt remembering
the comfortless clerical life of her childhood, was unsympathetic,
as she was unsympathetic to her son's obsession with high-church
practices and his self-conscious piety, refusing to hear his evening
prayers when he added to them lengthy recitations from
devotional texts. She was taken aback, having explained to him
the meaning of 'besetting sin', and pointed out that his was a
quick and unkind tongue, when he asked, after pondering the
criticism, 'You know, mother, what is your besetting sin?' 'No,
Evelyn, what is it?' 'A lack of faith in Catholic doctrine.'

One of Evelyn's favourite pastimes was bicycling about on
church hunts, a hobby shared by his Norton cousins. On holiday
with his mother at Westcliff in August 1916, he got her to
accompany him on his quest for 'spiky' churches, and during a
half-term holiday with her in Brighton the year before, he
recorded with a notable degree of self-satisfaction, 'In the evening
we went to church. We struck a horrible low one. I was the only
person who crossed myself and bowed to the altar.'

In September 1910, only a few weeks short of his seventh birthday,

Evelyn went for the first time to school. The plan was for him to follow Alec to his prep school, Fernden, in Haslemere, after a couple of terms at Heath Mount, a local establishment of good reputation, whose headmaster, Granville Grenfell, had been with Arthur at Sherborne. But in spite of its pleasant prospect among the Surrey woods and rhododendrons, and in spite of the very favourable terms which Arthur was offered (a discount of nearly 50 per cent for the first year) Fernden had not been a success for Alec; the discipline was harsh, the conditions spartan and the standard of teaching so poor that it was decided that Evelyn should stay at Heath Mount until old enough to go, like his father and brother, to Sherborne. Grenfell was delighted to have the boy, writing to Kate after Evelyn's first few weeks there, 'I am very pleased indeed with your young man. He is a smart boy, decidedly so, and promises extremely well. I do not know who has been teaching him, but he is better prepared than any boy of his age I have had for a very long time. You will I am sure, get an excellent report of his work and conduct generally at the end of the term.'

Founded in 1790, Heath Mount stood in that warren of twisting streets and high, narrow eighteenth-century houses off Heath Street, just below the Whitestone Pond. Every morning Arthur accompanied his son to school as it was on the way to Hampstead tube station, a twenty-minute walk from Underhill. It was during these early mornings that Evelyn first began to know his father. Arthur entertained him with stories, retailed with full dramatic effect, of the highwaymen, poets and painters who had lived in the locality, together with highly coloured accounts of fabulous creatures of his own imagining. For his first year, Evelyn, dressed in green tweed knickerbockers and green cap with yellow badge, attended school only in the mornings, where he had lessons with a governess and went home at 12.30 for lunch. In his second year he stayed for 'middle-day dinner' and was taught by masters, who at first overawed him with their not always playful threats and their loud masculine voices. The school day began with assembly in the gymnasium. At the call of '*Cave*', silence fell, and in bounded the headmaster, Mr Grenfell, a tiny, dapper figure with a goatee beard, dressed unvaryingly in tight-buttoned black coat, black trousers and a black silk stock with a pearl pin. 'Good morning, gentlemen', said Mr Grenfell. 'Good morning, sir',

41

chorused the boys. There were then prayers, followed by any necessary announcements before the boys dispersed to their classrooms. This routine was varied only on Saturdays when an alarming ceremony took place. On Saturdays Mr Grenfell appeared with a ledger from which he read first the names of boys who had done well that week, with appropriate commendation ('Geoghegan minor, plus three for Latin . . . Fine boy, Geoghegan minor'), followed by the names of boys who had not done well ('What is this I find? Fletcher. Fletcher has been idle. Stand out, Fletcher.'). Evelyn, quick to learn, was rarely reprimanded for bad work, although inevitably there were occasions when difficulties arose. One evening when he was sitting at the dining-room table at home after a high tea of eggs and fruit had been cleared away, the fire burning, curtains drawn, homework spread in front of him, miserably struggling without success to memorise some Latin verbs, he was rescued by his mother. Kate knew no Latin, but she devised a series of mnemonics: '*Molior*, to contrive. Remember the mole contrives to make a hole.'

Evelyn on the whole enjoyed Heath Mount, in spite of periods of exasperation. 'Fletcher got liked in Latin and I was made to sing, although Mr Grenfell said I need not. I have come to the conclusion that Heath Mount is the worst managed school in England.' But he was well up to his lessons, reasonably good at football and cricket, for which boys were taken by bus to playing fields in Bishop's Avenue, and he liked some, if not all, of the masters. The least popular were Mr Hynchcliffe who taught Classics and was eventually sacked for pinching little boys' bottoms, and Mr Stebbing who, when administering a beating, covered his ruler with chalk to be sure of always hitting the same spot. But one master whom he did like, who indeed became a friend of the family, was handsome Mr Ensor who taught English. Aubrey Ensor was stage-struck; he had written a play, for a time worked as stage manager at the Everyman Theatre, and owned a collection of 36,000 postcards of theatrical celebrities; he had the attractive habit, when in good spirits, of dancing round the classroom singing the popular songs of the day. It was he who introduced Evelyn to Saki, among other favourite authors, and it was probably as a result of Mr Ensor's influence that, with his friend Derek Hooper, Evelyn in his final year edited *The Cynic*, a subversive alternative to the official school journal, advertising itself as

'Cynical without being cheaply so. Piquant in moderation. Racy in excess.' 'By George when the term begins things will hum – Our first shell to smash the ramparts of convention is *The Cynic*, the most gorgeous paper out,' Evelyn wrote in his diary. Its purpose, clearly explained in the editorial of the first number, was 'to set out the views of the School rather than those of the masters as is the case with the *Heath Mount Magazine* which it is compulsory to buy, and therefore, much less appreciated.'

Among his contemporaries Evelyn's particular friend was Dudley Brown, a sophisticated boy from a well-to-do family, who kept an album of theatre programmes and knew in surprising detail about the private lives of actresses. It was he who told Evelyn his first obscene limerick (Evelyn was prudish and disliked it), and who first awoke his curiosity about the processes of reproduction, of far greater interest then than the sexual act, about which, in spite of Muriel's obliging lessons in female anatomy, Evelyn remained in complete ignorance. The two boys spent hours, the dictionary beside them, scanning the Bible for such thrillingly biological vocabulary as 'womb' and 'whore'.

Like many boys that age, Evelyn was pugnacious and enjoyed a good fight, gloatingly recording the action in his diary. 'Rostail entered [the cloakroom] and squatting temptingly on the edge of a basin proceeded to call me "Wuffles". I informed him that unless he refrain from using my name in a corupted form I would have to chastise him. He knowing that he was larger than me continued in the name whereupon I fulfiled my promise one hundredfold.' On another occasion, 'Hooper and I were going home when a kid about 10 yelled out "Silly old green caps"! We chased him about 300 yards when out came a biger brother who came at us with the usual "Ere d'you want a fight?" I answered yes and we set to with a mixture of wrestling and boxing ending in my victory.'

Taking after his grandfather, 'the Brute', Evelyn was already something of a bully. In a short story written over a decade later,[9] Evelyn describes a tormenting game he used to play with the cat at home,[10]

---

[9] 'The Balance' appeared in 1926 in an annual anthology, *Georgian Stories*, published by Chapman & Hall.
[10] As well as the inevitable poodle, the Waughs at this period also had a blue-grey Persian cat, described significantly by a friend of the family as 'a miserable grey animal'.

a game described with such startling veracity it is hard not to believe that it had its origins in fact.

> It was a game peculiar to himself and Ozymandias which Adam had evolved, and which was only played on the rare occasions of his being left alone. First, Ozymandias had to be sought from room to room, and when at last he was found, borne up to the nursery and shut in. He would watch him for some minutes . . . Then armed with a sword, gun, battledore, or an armful of bricks to throw, and uttering sadistic cries, Adam would pursue him round and round the room, driving him from refuge to refuge, until almost beside himself with rage and terror, he crouched jungle-like with ears flattened back and porpentine hair. Here Adam would rest, and after some slight pause the real business of the game began. Ozymandias had to be won back to complacency and affection. Adam would sit down on the floor some little way from him and begin calling to him softly and endearingly . . . mother-like he would comfort him, evoking some fictitious tormentor to be reproached, assuring him that he was powerless to hurt him any more; Adam would protect him; Adam would see that the horrible little boy did not come near him again. Slowly Ozymandias' ears would begin to come forward and his eyes begin to close, and the delectable exercise invariably ended with caresses of passionate reconciliation.

At school, where some of the pupils in self-defence had formed an Anti-Waugh Society, Evelyn's prime target was a beautiful boy with blond hair, thick eyelashes and an unforgivably girlish demeanour. His name was Cecil Beaton, and if ever there were a natural victim, little Beaton was it. Evelyn, backed by his gang of cronies, homed in on him at once, making a point of greeting him with 'Hullo, Cecil!' ('Awful score to a chap, you know, to find out his Christian name'), and in the playground looming over the younger boy with a menacing stare before bending back his arms to make him cry. Eventually the persecution was discovered by a member of staff, and Evelyn and his private army were soundly caned. But Beaton was marked for life. In middle age he wrote to a friend, 'Evelyn is a very sinister character, & I have been secretly frightened of him ever since my first morning at my first school when he came up in the "break" & started to bully me.'

In 1914, when in the normal course Evelyn would have started at Sherborne, the First World War began, and Arthur was informed by the *Daily Telegraph*, to which as a regular reviewer he looked for a sizeable part of his income,[11] that his services, except occasionally, would no longer be required.

I lost half my income the day the war was declared, by the stoppage of all literary work on the *Telegraph*, & it is only a question of *how long* we can go on paying full salaries at the office,' Arthur wrote gloomily to McMaster. 'We are making changes at once in our household arrangements – giving up our nice parlourmaid, Beatrice. We hope she may come back to us in better days. But the school bills loom ahead, and I want to pay them as long as any salary comes.

Chapman & Hall was not doing well, either, with authors away fighting for their country or too 'hypnotised by the war' to be able to write. Typically over-reacting, Arthur now decided that it was out of the question to afford a boarding-school for Evelyn, and he wrote to Mr Grenfell warning him that he might not much longer be in a position to pay the fees. Grenfell assured him that if necessary he would keep Evelyn at the school for nothing.

The war provided a welcome element of excitement both at school and at home. Kate was ready at once; as a member of the St John Ambulance Brigade she went daily as a VAD to a hospital first in North End Road then one in Hampstead Lane, work to which she was dedicated, in spite of the exhaustion it entailed. 'My Wife continues to nurse sick soldiers, regardless of the fact that she herself stands in urgent need of a month at a hydro,' Arthur complained, but later was persuaded to help out by conscripting the Fleming children to perform with him in one-act plays which they gave for the entertainment of Kate's convalescents. Soon signs of war were everywhere. Wounded soldiers in their bright blue suits and scarlet ties appeared in the streets, a Zeppelin came down over Potter's Bar, an anti-aircraft gun was set up by the Whitestone Pond, and at night there were frequent air-raids, after which the family would assemble in the bookroom for a midnight snack. Evelyn made a collection of war relics –

[11] £50–60 a month for a twice-weekly book review which he wrote for twenty-five years except for a brief period during the war.

bits of shrapnel, shell cases, a German helmet. At school two or three boys turned up for the new term with names suddenly anglicised: 'Kaiser' into 'Kingsley', for instance, and even Maxwell Fleming took the precaution of changing his name from 'Max' to 'Mac', which he remained ever after. A Dutch master was believed, of course, to be a spy. The boys subscribed to buy a watch for Mr Vernon who was leaving for the army ('I feel rather sorry now I used to rag him so'). Evelyn joined the Scouts and raised a school patrol, parading on Saturday afternoons and marching to the heath where, dividing into opposing forces, they engaged in a kind of fencing called 'ankle-tapping' before adjourning to a shop in the Vale of Health for tea and cakes. During the Easter holidays of 1915 Mr Fleming arranged for Evelyn and Maxwell to act as messengers at the War Office. The boys sat in a smoky cubby-hole in the company of an old soldier, waiting to be summoned to take files from one room to another. Evelyn passed Lord Kitchener's door, but to his regret was never called inside. In his drawing-books pictures of German cavalry galloping down among brave English infantry took the place of saints and angels. The Pistol Troop was dissolved, and its ex-members raised funds for the Red Cross by collecting and selling empty jam jars; they also cut up linoleum to sole slippers for wounded soldiers ('Some of our soles were dreadfully cut out specially Maxwell's'). But the initial excitement soon faded, and the dreariness of wartime made itself felt at Underhill. In August, Arthur reported that 'Kate is plunged in nursing again, & her sons complain that their holidays are the dullest on record. Evelyn goes out alone hunting butterflies, & Alec reads Marlowe & Beaumont & Fletcher in the loggia.'

In 1911 Alec had left Fernden for Sherborne. Evelyn, too, was much looking forward to going there, to the point of irritating Arthur by nagging him to be sure to earn enough money to pay his fees. But in June 1915, Alec, aged seventeen, was found out in a homosexual relationship of the kind entirely common among schoolboys. He managed to avoid expulsion, but Arthur, whose heart was '*really* nearly broken' by his adored son's disgrace, was asked to remove him at the end of term.

That September Alec enrolled in the Inns of Court OTC, passing out in January the following year to wait for his gazettement to come through. But the War Office had recently raised the age

limit for commissions in the army to eighteen and a half, and
Alec had time on his hands. He put it to good use by writing a
novel of school life, *The Loom of Youth*, which he completed in
seven and a half weeks. It was not published until July 1917,
shortly before its boy author, having passed through Sandhurst,
was within days of leaving for France. The book made a sensation,
in particular for its, in those days unheard-of, frankness on the
subject of schoolboy sexuality.[12] The ex-headmaster of Eton wrote
a ten-page attack on it in the *Contemporary Review*, both the *Spectator* and the *Nation* filled their correspondence columns for
weeks with letters from outraged teachers; and in many schools
the book was banned altogether and boys caned for reading it.
The headmaster of Sherborne, in a letter to Alec of frigid politeness, referred to the novel, which its besotted author saw as a
love-letter to his alma mater, as a monstrous libel, removing the
names of both Alec and Arthur[13] from the rolls of the O.S. Society.

But in 1916 *The Loom of Youth* was still in the future. After
Alec's departure from Sherborne in disgrace, Evelyn, who had
been due to go there in September, was obliged for reasons which
were never explained to him (Arthur had implored Alec to keep
the whole shameful business 'sacredly to yourself') to stay on at
Heath Mount while an alternative was found. Oundle, Gresham's,

---

[12] Frankness is a relative term. Most of the novel concerns itself with fierce inter-
house competition on the playing-field. The passage that caused such shock-
waves to run through the staff rooms of the public schools of England is: 'Thus
began a friendship entirely different from any Gordon had known before. He did
not know what his real sentiments were; he did not even attempt to analyse
them. He only knew that when he was with Morcombe he was indescribably
happy . . . Morcombe came up to Gordon's study nearly every evening, and
usually Foster left them alone together . . . During the long morning hours,
when Gordon was supposed to be reading history, more than once there came
over him a wish to plunge himself into the feverish waters of pleasure, and
forget for a while the doubts and disappointments that overhung everything in
his life. At times he would sit in the big window-seat, when the school was
changing class-rooms, and as he saw the sea of faces of those, some big, some
small, who had drifted with the stream, and had soon forgotten early resolutions
and principles in the conveniently broadminded atmosphere of a certain side of
Public School life, he realised how easily he could slip into that life and be
engulfed. No one would mind; his position would be the same; no one would
think worse of him. Unless, of course, he was caught. Then probably everyone
would turn round upon him; that was the one unforgivable sin – to be found
out . . .'
[13] In 1965 Alec was invited to return to Sherborne to present the school library
with the manuscript of *The Loom of Youth*.

Westminster and St Paul's were all considered and dismissed. Kate was in favour of a London day school, but this did not seem right to Arthur. Recognising the importance of religion to his younger son, he fixed upon Lancing in Sussex, a school about which he knew almost nothing apart from its reputation for high Anglicanism. This, he thought, would test the sincerity of Evelyn's faith.

Evelyn left Heath Mount, which at thirteen he was more than ready to do, and in May 1917, at the start of the summer term, went down by train with Arthur to begin his career at public school.

The flint-girt fortress

Lancing College had been founded in 1848 by Nathaniel Wood-ard, a high Anglican churchman, subscriber to the Oxford Movement, whose mission was to establish a network of schools providing a sound Church of England education for the professional classes, in particular for the sons of clergymen of modest means. In fact many of the Woodard schools were filled in the main by the offspring of tradesmen, and for this reason were socially looked down upon. Lancing College, however, was the first and best, the flagship of the Woodard fleet.[1] Built as an imposing affirmation of the Anglican faith, it stands, 'a flint-girt fortress,' high on the Sussex downs, the grey stone quadrangles and cloisters of the school dwarfed by a vast and magnificent chapel as big as a small cathedral,[2] a monolithic masterpiece of the Gothic revival, its apse rising like the prow of a ship over fields and hedgerows and the rolling, treeless downs. To the east could just be seen the outskirts of Brighton, to the west Worthing; south, beyond playing fields fringed with elms, was the coast road leading to Shoreham, and beyond that the estuary and the flat grey line of the sea. The tiny village of Lancing lay out of sight at the bottom of the hill leading up from the main road to the school.

It was to this isolated and monastic-looking settlement that

---

[1] In the portrait of Lancing which appears in Evelyn's short story fragment, 'Charles Ryder's Schooldays', the social status of the school is upgraded: boys talk of grouse moors and Scotland and of staying at Claridge's in the holidays.
[2] The chapel is exceeded in height only by Westminster Abbey, York Minster and Liverpool Cathedral.

Evelyn came on 9 May 1917, his sense of adventure at starting a new life strongly tempered by apprehension and a feeling that he was being sent into exile. Sherborne and the west country were well known to the Waughs; Sussex was uncharted territory. Compared with Alec and Alec's school career, he could not help but see himself as second best. Until his humiliating departure from Sherborne, Alec had been the ideal schoolboy, by his final term a prefect, house captain, a member of both the first XV and first XI, editor of the school magazine and winner of the English Verse prize. The talk at home had always been of Alec and Sherborne, Sherborne and Alec.

May the ninth was cold and damp. Arthur went with Evelyn on the train, changing at Brighton and arriving at Shoreham in the early afternoon. As their taxi crossed the timber bridge over the River Adur and began to climb uphill, Arthur, typically, began to quote, this time Belloc's words from 'The South Country' – 'Along the sky the line of the Downs/ So noble and so bare'.

Evelyn had been entered for Head's House which, with the headmaster, the Revd H. T. Bowlby, as housemaster, was the most prestigious in the school. Head's boys considered themselves a definite cut above the rest, although the only actual difference was £10 a year more in fees and the privilege of having the Bowlby children's old nanny act as matron. Mrs Bowlby gave the Waughs tea in her sitting-room, after which Arthur left to go back to London. Evelyn was introduced to his house tutor, Dick Harris, a friendly young man who took him into the empty House Room where he left him by himself with a book. Soon boys in boaters and black jackets began to trickle in, clustering round the notice-board, jostling each other, shouting out their news and ostentatiously ignoring the stranger. Eventually Evelyn was joined by the only other newcomer of that by-term, Fulford minor, a quiet, delicate little boy, son of a Suffolk clergyman, who was according to inflexible custom the only boy in the school with whom it was permissible to associate. Although they were later to become friends, neither at that stage would have chosen the other's company.

So began a period of loneliness and bewilderment, a 'bleak, untouchable epoch' with no one except Fulford as a friend, and a system of codes and regulations of labyrinthine complexity to be got by heart. The colour of your socks and tie, and where in the school grounds you might or might not walk were entirely governed by your status. Whether or not you could put your hands in your pockets was dependent on your position in the hierarchy (first years never; second years could, but with the jacket raised, not drawn back), as was the right to link arms with another boy (a two-year man might link arms with a one-year man, but not vice versa). One of the first ordeals, in the third week of term, was the New Men's Concert at which newcomers had to stand on a table and sing a song, to be pelted or applauded (usually the former) by the audience. Evelyn sang, 'My wife's gone to the country – hurray hurrah', words provided by Arthur. The school was lit by gas, but because of the war – on still days the guns could be heard from the other side of the Channel – there was a partial blackout, and the cloisters where boys were allowed to stroll in the evening were gloomy, shadowy places. 1917 was the year when the submarine blockade became properly effective, and food rationing was severe. Meals, inadequate and often uneatable, were served in tiny and repulsive portions: 4oz of meat per boy per day, milkless cocoa, jam not more than three times a week. At the tuck shop, known as the Grubber, choice was limited to fruit, when available, and oatcakes. Food parcels from home were forbidden for the duration.

The austerity, the isolation, the physical discomfort, the hunger and cold, the lack of feminine company or anything approaching a domestic atmosphere, and above all the lack of privacy, Evelyn found appalling. He was a fastidious, rather priggish child, and suffered from the fact that every moment of the school day was spent in the noisy, shoving company of mobs of boys. Most to be dreaded were the communal lavatories, known in school parlance as the Groves. These were a double row of tarred latrines in a white-washed yard, with no doors and built over a deep open pit. They were insufficient in number, smelt disgusting, and formed the centre of a boisterous social life, one of the few common meeting places for the four houses. Evelyn found himself unable to cope with the Groves: in spite of a statutory penalty of twenty-five lines, he preferred to absent himself from class to go to the lavatory in peace.

He was lonely, and in those early days frightened of being in any way conspicuous, to such an extent that when it was noticed that he received more letters from home than anyone else

('Another one for Waugh'), he asked his father to write less often, although Arthur's letters were a delight to him.

Arthur may have been a conscientious correspondent, but there was no question of frequent visits such as he had made to Alec at Sherborne. In *A Little Learning*, Evelyn gives the impression that his first three terms were a time of unalleviated misery and solitude. The war made travel difficult, but while other parents managed to get down to Lancing for sports days, and on 'Veniam days' to take their sons out, no one, he says, came for him, nor did he know anybody in the district whom he could visit. The culmination of this period of intense loneliness was reached on Ascension Day, the only whole holiday in the school year. Evelyn had not known what to expect when immediately after morning chapel the entire school dispersed on previously arranged outings. No dinner was served that day. It was raining. The House Room was locked. There was nothing for it but to wander off alone and shelter in some trees, where desolate and in tears he ate a 'ghastly galantine' provided at the last minute by the steward, and waited for the return of the holidaymakers. The memory remained bitter and deeply embedded. 'Ascension Day never passes without my thinking of the day now thirty years ago at Lancing which was the most miserable of my life,' he wrote in 1947.

No doubt it was. But although in his memoirs Evelyn mentions not one instance of his parents visiting him,[3] in fact they, and Kate in particular, spent several days with him each term. His first day at school was 9 May. The notorious Ascension Day holiday was on the seventeenth. Three days later, on a Sunday, both parents came down to take him out to lunch; the following day they took him to lunch and tea and on the Pier at Brighton, and the day after that collected him by car for lunch, tea and a long walk. In the summer term of 1918 (after holidays during which his mother complained Evelyn had been at his most bumptious and patronising), Kate spent over two weeks at Ditchling seeing Evelyn almost daily, providing picnics, taking him on the beach at Brighton, standing supper to his friends and accompanying him to church. The following year, when in March Evelyn went

[3] The nearest he allows them to come is when he records staying with them during a visit to friends in 1917 at the nearby village of Ditchling.

down with pneumonia and was confined to the sanatorium, she spent a week at Lancing with him before he was well enough to be taken home. Sometimes both parents came with Alec, and on at least one occasion they brought the Fleming children with them. And so it went on. But none of this was, apparently, remembered, or if remembered, not, in retrospect, recorded.

The end of that miserable first term brought with it a cruel disappointment. Evelyn kept a calendar marking off the days of his incarceration, each page decorated with a border of chains. As the holidays approached, his spirits rose. But just before the longed-for release, he and Fulford went down with mumps, and were confined in the sanatorium for two weeks. They were joined there by a member of another house, Christopher Chamberlin, who noticed this boy he didn't know curled up in the corner bed reading a book he refused to show around called *The Loom of Youth*.

The summer holidays of 1917, so eagerly looked forward to, proved a restless, uneasy time. Kate was out at the hospital most of the day at her VAD work, and Arthur was in a state of nervous anxiety about Alec, who was at the Front: the battle of Passchendaele was in progress, and long casualty lists were published daily in *The Times*. Evelyn was left very much to his own devices. However, when after his second term he came home for Christmas, he found an ally in a new member of the household, Barbara Jacobs, daughter of the writer W. W. Jacobs, who was an acquaintance of Arthur's.

Two years earlier Alec had fallen in love with Barbara, although she was then only fifteen. Alec had been conducting a tense and difficult courtship, under the censorious eye of W. W. himself, on his few intermittent days of leave from the Royal Military College in Camberley. His parents were pleased, as the Sherborne scandal was still very much on their minds, and they approved of Barbara who, like so many girls of her time, jumped at almost any chance of leaving home. She and Alec had become unofficially engaged immediately before Alec left for France. 'Not a word about Barbara,' he had written imploringly to his schoolfriend, Hugh Mackintosh. 'If my small brother knew, it would be all round Hampstead in a week.'

Nearly three years older than Evelyn, Barbara, dark-haired and pretty, was a congenial companion. Gentle and lively in manner, receptive and adventurous, she provided a very different feminine influence from the old-fashioned old ladies who up till then had constituted Evelyn's main experience of the opposite sex. Mrs Jacobs[4] had been a suffragette (had at one time spent a month in Holloway), and Barbara, following her mother's lead, was feminist, socialist and agnostic; she wore lumpy modern jewellery, bobbed her hair and was often seen in the street without a hat. She had not been well educated, but sharing Evelyn's interest in art listened admiringly as he instructed her on modern painting, on Vorticism, Cubism and the Post-Impressionists. She had wanted to enrol at the Slade, but her father, a die-hard reactionary, had forbidden it, and she was obliged to make do with a course of lectures at Bedford College in Regent's Park. As the Jacobs family lived in Hertfordshire, too far for a daily journey into town to be convenient, it was obviously sensible for Barbara to stay at Underhill. She was happy with the Waughs: Kate was endlessly kind, and Arthur, in spite of his sentimentality and the embarrassment of the over-theatrical readings-aloud in the bookroom after dinner, was much more sympathetic than her own father. But it was Evelyn she adored: years later she described Evelyn at fifteen as 'a darling, a perfectly darling boy. The nicest youngster you can imagine'. He called her 'Robert', as a variation of 'Bobbie', her more usual pet-name, and patronised her kindly: considerably younger than she, he was better read, far cleverer and much the stronger personality. Together they 'rushed' around visiting galleries and exhibitions, and frescoed with their own style of Cubist painting one of the walls of the old daynursery, now renamed 'the studio'. 'Barbara & Evelyn have been busy for two days defiling the studio with the most awful paint,' Arthur complained to Jean Fleming. 'They have painted the fireplace & walls all over cubes of colour, yellow, red, blue, in irregular splotches. You never saw anything so awful.' When they tired of this pastime, they went to the cinema and theatre and on shopping expeditions to Gamage's and Selfridge's. They explored London, 'careering about' for miles on the open top decks of buses, took a boat on the lake in Regent's Park, went for enor-

---

[4] It was Mrs Jacobs with whom Alec had first become infatuated, before transferring his attentions to her daughter.

mous walks, and sat and talked over disgusting wartime sundaes made mainly of egg-white at Stewart's in the Finchley Road. Evelyn had been taking dancing lessons, and he and Barbara gave some showy performances at *thés dansants* and local parties: 'The dance in the evening was excellent... Barbara and I did one wonderful one-step when we spun in and out only holding by one hand.' The only part of the holidays dreaded by both was the final day. Always miserable at having to return to Lancing, Evelyn stood white and trembling on the platform at Victoria while Barbara and his mother did their best not to show how agonised they were.

During the Easter holidays of 1918 came a report that Alec had been posted missing after the Ludendorff offensive. Both Arthur and Kate were thrown into a state of acute apprehension by the letter from Alec's captain: 'It is with the deepest regret that I inform you that your son, 2 Lt. Alec Waugh, is missing. In the days that followed Arthur in particular, already mentally in mourning, was shocked by the carefree attitude of Evelyn and Barbara, apparently unconcerned about the brave young soldier's fate as they happily desecrated the playroom walls with their hideous 'art'. 'Their loud laughter rings through the house. I sit alone & think of the other boy, lonely, cold, hungry, even if he is alive; and I wonder *what* their hearts are made of. Truly, it is a strange world.' Fortunately, news soon came through that Alec had been captured and was to be sent to a prisoner-of-war camp in Mainz,[5] reassuring news to his parents, who had naturally assumed the worst. Barbara, however, seemed unconcerned. Still rather childlike, she had almost forgotten Alec, and was far more interested in the company of his clever, funny schoolboy brother.

Alec, on the other hand, thought obsessively of her. Already he and Barbara had been apart for over a year, and before that had had little chance to get to know each other, had never been alone for more than a few minutes, and had kissed only once. But pent up in his prison camp, craving her presence, bored, depressed and wholly deprived of female company, in his fantasies he intensified and romanticised what had existed between them.

Through Barbara, Evelyn came to know the rest of the Jacobs

[5] Fulford remembered Evelyn fighting another boy on the downs for spreading the rumour that Alec had deliberately allowed himself to be taken prisoner by the Germans.

family: the fiercely fighting parents – he in Evelyn's uncharitable view tediously respectable, she a voluble booby – and the five children. The three boys Evelyn did not care for (Barbara's younger brother, Hugh, he referred to as 'the Hellswine'), and he disliked staying at Beechcroft, the large, ugly house in Berkhamsted where the Jacobses lived. But for a time he was mildly attracted to Barbara's younger sister, Luned, with whom he embarked on an inexperienced flirtation. 'Evelyn has become quite amorous, I regret to say,' Alec had reported before he left for France. '[He] loves Barbara's sister, a comely wench, and at odd periods of the day they are observed holding hands.' During the romping children's games that were played in the music-room at Beechcroft, Evelyn and Luned would find each other out and tangle silently together in a surge of unexpressed erotic feeling. They held hands in the cinema and exchanged clumsy kisses. Although Evelyn quickly tired of this and grew irritated by the emotional letters that followed him to Lancing, Luned for many years retained what she described as a 'foolish fondness' for him. He wrote callously about her in his diary – 'I think I shall have to snub her. She is really not worth it' and 'I find little attraction in Luned now. She has coarsened out a lot.' But he was never unkind to her, even when breaking off the friendship for good in January 1921: 'I have shut down, I think finally, the Luned affair. She wrote me a rather touching, but hysterical and, I fear, rather a self-conscious letter, asking me in almost as many words to go on kissing her. I wrote her a long letter back in which I explained my share in the whole thing and told her it was over.' He also went through adolescent infatuations, equally evanescent and immature, with a neighbour, Ursula Kendall, with pretty Betty Bulleid in Midsomer Norton, with Moira Mackintosh, sister of Alec's schoolfriend, Hugh, and with his childhood chum, Philla Fleming.

When the school reassembled in September 1917, although much of the strangeness had worn off, conditions were even harsher. The friendly housemaster, Dick Harris, had left to join the Army, together with most of the younger staff; food was in short supply; and the winter cold, when it came, was painful and unrelenting. Worst was getting up in the morning, climbing out of bed at 6.30 in an unheated stone dormitory to plunge straight into a cold bath – which had been standing filled since the night before, the same water for all the boys, the first in breaking the ice – in order to be ready in the classroom at seven o'clock for a lesson before breakfast. Here even the textbooks were war-issue shoddy, 'bound in a sort of greasy, limp oil cloth, "owing", a label half scratched off the back proclaimed, "to shortage of labour"; it was printed crookedly on a thin greyish paper with little brown splinters of wood in it . . .'

Evelyn was not a popular boy. 'Evelyn is a misfit, I'm afraid,' Alec commented to Hugh Mackintosh, adding smugly, '[He] hates Lancing. He shouldn't. A boy ought to like his school.' Although pleasant looking with his light-brown hair and fresh complexion, Evelyn was small for his age, wore spectacles and had a peculiar trudging walk – not, as the boys unkindly put about, the result of trench foot, but from having had his legs strapped down after his appendix operation. He was intellectually precocious and sharp-tongued ('Poor Evelyn has been getting in trouble at school again and all through that unwise tongue of his,' Kate wrote to Alec. 'Perhaps some day he will learn'), and his manner was eccentric; unlike his brother he was lamentably lacking in any sense of team spirit, his performance on the playing field rarely rising above the merely competent. Fulford was still his sole companion, and on walks across the downs, if Fulford were not there, he more often than not found himself walking alone.

His religiosity, too, set him apart. Although thin-skinned and on the surface anxious to conform, in this one area Evelyn took pride in carrying his devotional practices to ostentatious extremes. Lancing was a religious school with a strong high Anglican tradition. Attendance at chapel was compulsory both morning and evening during the week, with between three and five services on a Sunday. The school was administered as a diarchy by the headmaster, himself a clergyman, and the chaplain. Many of the boys were from clerical families.[6] There was, however, a commonsensical attitude towards religious practice which Evelyn deliberately flouted, making a point of kneeling during the Creed when everyone else remained standing, and at night in the dormitory taking noticeably longer than the others to say

[6] Out of the 97 boys in Head's House, 22 were the sons of clergymen.

his prayers ('dibs' in Lancing jargon) before getting into bed. 'That awful little tick Waugh' was a phrase that soon came to have a familiar ring to it.

It was not until the beginning of 1919 that there was any significant improvement in living conditions at school. With the war over, the Grubber was now plentifully stocked with whipped-cream walnuts, buns, chocolate and ices. 'Could you send me a few pennies, do you think?' Evelyn wrote to his parents. 'The cost of living is very high now that the Grubber has started having cream buns and éclairs . . .' Food could again be sent from home, and on Sundays for the seniors of the House Room there was the Settle[7] tea, provided by each member in turn. 'They began with crumpets, eight or more a head, dripping with butter. From there we swiftly passed to cake, pastry and, in season, strawberries and cream, until at six we tottered into chapel taut and stupefied with eating . . . [in their studies boys had] little pots of foie gras and caviar occasionally came from London and we were as nice in the brewing of tea as a circle of maiden ladies.' The inept and aging masters who had been brought in as a temporary measure were replaced by younger, energetic and in some cases remarkable men newly returned from the war. Among them were Adam Fox, later Warden of Radley and Professor of Poetry at Oxford; Evelyn's first housemaster, Dick Harris, who combined a keen athleticism with an inspiriting love of English literature; and that famously fascinating and charismatic teacher, J. F. Roxburgh, later to become the first headmaster of Stowe.

It was Roxburgh who exercised the greatest influence on that generation of Lancing boys. At thirty-one he had returned to teaching a hero, having been mentioned in dispatches and recommended for a Military Cross. He enthralled his pupils with his handsome, sardonic features, his flamboyance and panache. He was a dandy with an extensive wardrobe of no less than fourteen suits, some of them in most unusual colours, and his many silk ties, it was widely believed, were specially woven for him in Spitalfields. Striding into chapel a carefully planned few minutes late, the gorgeous gown of his Licenciat ès Lettres from the Sorbonne billowing behind him, he flowed down the aisle, as one of his

---

[7] The Settle comprised the top eight boys in the House Room who enjoyed certain privileges and authority.

admirers remarked, like the Prince of Glory passing on his way. Apparently indifferent to the service (his religious views remained a mystery on which he refused to be drawn), he would sit stooped in his seat looking like the prosecuting counsel in a cartoon by Daumier, reading not the Bible but, it had been discovered, the *Rubaiyat* of Omar Khayyam. Like many dedicated schoolmasters homosexual by nature, Roxburgh was a brilliant teacher, witty, unpredictable, flirtatious with his favourites (nearly always romantically in love with one of his pupils), and bitingly sarcastic with those slow to comprehend. He had about him the scent of the world, not, like most of the other masters with their pipes and leather elbows, of the tea-shop. Not for him the smudgily stencilled examination papers produced by the rest of the staff: Roxburgh had his elegantly printed, and his letters to parents written in his distinctive hand[8] were penned on heavy-weave writing paper personally embossed. He inculcated in his pupils an enthusiasm for subjects both on and off the syllabus; and in summer read aloud to his class in the garden, Greek and Latin poetry, English and French. 'Roxborough's [sic] French is really a joy,' Evelyn wrote in his diary. 'It is almost worth doing the wretched subject. He announced the work we were going to do in the "four delicious hours at our disposal".' He was fierce about precision in grammar and avoidance of slang and cliché. His performance was impeccable, and knowing exactly the sort of joke dear to the schoolboy heart, he made a point of using unusual words and phrases: poor reading was 'a concatenation of discordant vocables', a dreary essay 'a cacophonous collocation'; 'oo' in the margin of a piece of work stood for ''orrible oxymoron', 'ccc' meant 'cliché, cant or commonplace'. He never failed jocularly to refer to Leman's Thin Captains, the brand of biscuit served with cheese at dinner, as 'Emaciated Skippers'.

The headmaster, the Revd H. T. Bowlby, had been a housemaster at Eton, and had brought a certain Etonian aura with him to the College. He was a lean, distinguished-looking man, once vigorous but grown tired and frail with the stresses of war. 'Very exhausting, I find this teaching,' he once remarked to a surprised member of staff encountered in the corridor. A remote, rather

---

[8] Most of his pupils attempted an imitation of it; Evelyn's Greek 'e's, for example, were directly descended from those of his old schoolmaster.

Olympian figure to the boys, he was rarely seen even by members of his own house except for an occasional lesson in Divinity, at house prayers on Sunday evenings, and on infrequent dormitory inspections which he conducted with formality, like an officer inspecting his troops. Mrs Bowlby, on the other hand, was more approachable, a treasured figure in school lore for her silliness and a propensity for gaffes. For instance, during the war, as OLs (old boys) were killed and their photographs displayed in chapel, 'Oh, isn't that nice,' Mrs Bowlby one day exclaimed, 'to see a second row going up!' But she was kind to her boys and entertained them to tea in her sitting-room, so although they mocked her she was not disliked. The Bowlbys had four children, and during Evelyn's time there one of the sons got married, an occasion described with detectable irony in his diary: 'The Bowlby family were having a smart wedding, Cuthbert marrying money and J. F. and the Head radiant in morning dress and white spats.' One of the Bowlby daughters inherited her mother's genius for saying the wrong thing, most notoriously remarking, as the boys came back from a five-mile run soaking wet in thin cotton singlets and shorts, how odd it was that every one of them appeared to be carrying a penknife in his pocket.

The Christmas holidays of 1918, with Alec returned from the war, Evelyn described as 'the most joyous of my life'. In a fragment of a school novel written at about this time and set in March 1918, Evelyn's complex attitude towards his brother, half hero-worship, half resentment, is tellingly conveyed. The hero, Peter Audley, describes the homecoming from the war of his elder brother, Ralf.

> [Peter] was seventeen and a half; next year, if the war was still on, as it showed every sign of being, would see him fighting. He had learned much of what it was like over there from his brother, but Ralf saw everything so abstractedly with such imperturbable cynicism. Peter flattered himself that he was far more sensitive and temperamental. He was sure he would not be able to stand it.

A telegram arrives at school summoning Peter home to greet his brother.

> This was really the first time that Ralf had made any mark on

his life; he was five years older and had always kept himself
very much aloof. They had had many quarrels as brothers always
have. At times Ralf had been almost a prig, particularly when
he was head of the house at Selchurch.

As Peter descends from the train, he sees Ralf striding towards
him.

Peter had seen him in uniform before but then it had been with
the timid pride of a 1914 subaltern. Now after three years
fighting he looked wonderfully fit and handsome. A slanting ray
of sunlight lit up his fair hair . . .

The novel is dedicated by Evelyn to 'Evelyn Arthur St John
Waugh, to whose sympathy and appreciation alone it owes its
being'. In the following dedicatory letter, addressed to 'My dear
Evelyn', he makes his feelings of inferiority and resentment
towards both his father and Alec very clear. Not only did he suffer
from the usual younger brother's burden of getting and doing
everything second-hand, but he was well aware that he was considered a disappointment. Arthur never made any secret of the
fact that he had wanted his second child to be a daughter; if it
had to be a boy, then of course that boy should have been a
cricketer and as much like Alec as possible. Alec's honourable
war and his phenomenal success with his first novel made matters
worse.

Much has been written and spoken about the lot of the boy with
literary aspirations in a philistine family; little can adequately
convey his difficulties, when the surroundings, which he has
known from childhood, have been entirely literary . . .
    Many of your relatives and most of your father's friends are
more or less directly interested in paper and print. Ever since you
first left the nursery for meals with your parents downstairs, the
conversation; to which you were an insatiable listener, has been
of books, their writers and producers; ever since, as a sleepy but
triumphantly emancipated school boy, you were allowed to sit
up with your elders in the 'bookroom' after dinner, you have
heard little but discussion about books . . .
    . . . all this will be brought up against you. 'Another of these
precocious Waughs,' they will say, 'one more nursery novel.'
So be it. There is always a certain romance, to the author at
least, about a first novel which no reviewer can quite shatter . . .

Soon perhaps you will join the 'wordsmiths' jostling one another
for royalties and contracts, meanwhile you are still very young.
 Yourself,
 Evelyn

The fact that Evelyn's letter was written for his eyes only emphasises his sense of alienation: not only did he feel excluded by the
world of Alec and Arthur; he knew, too, that he was different
from them, that theirs was a world to which he had no wish to
belong.

When he went back to Lancing the following January, Evelyn set
about making an existence of his own instead of passively accepting his miserable lot. Having learned which way the current
flowed, he could now decide for himself when and how he would
swim against it. Never one to go with the crowd, Evelyn was not
entirely a rebel either. 'I did not admire the other boys. I did
not want to be like them. But, in contradiction, I wanted to be
one of them.' At heart conventional, he accepted tradition and
authority while at the same time making it clear that he accepted
them very much on his own terms. At school as at home he was
divided between his love of the world and his need for a refuge,
a retreat from it. The equivalent at Lancing of his private lair in
the cellar at Underhill was the school library, a large, light, vaulted
room with solidly built oak bookshelves on the tops of which
stood busts of the Roman emperors. Here, before he was sufficiently senior to be awarded 'library privileges', he was allowed
only for a rare and precious hour on Sunday evenings, when he
could read or draw or, which he loved, look through bound
copies of *Punch*. But although he needed solitude, he was also
intensely involved in school society, in some areas overtly dominating, in others subversive and undermining.

Among his contemporaries he fairly soon made his mark.
Evelyn was not widely liked but by the age of fifteen he had
begun to be noticed, to enjoy a certain repute, admired by some
for his spirit and eccentric humour, distrusted by others for a
streak of cruelty and an element of anarchy which lay disturbingly
close to the surface. One of his contemporaries, Max Mallowan,
remembered him as 'courageous and witty and clever but [he]
was also an exhibitionist with a cruel nature that cared nothing

about humiliating his companions as long as he could expose them to ridicule'. And Hugh Molson, who was a close friend at Lancing, chose not to resume the friendship in later life because he had so come to dislike the sadistic side of Evelyn's nature. Two boys in particular had their lives made wretched by Waugh: the head of the dormitory, a fat boy called O'Connor who was driven to extremes of misery by a loathing of his nickname, Dungy; and one Emlyn Bevan, known for clearly apparent reasons as Buttocks, whom Waugh and Fulford publicly humiliated at a New Men's Concert by singing a song about Bevan's behind. As Evelyn says in his autobiography, 'In Head's House we made life unbearable for anyone who incurred our displeasure . . . Towards our juniors we showed a kind of feudal benevolence. But we hunted as a pack to bring down our equals and immediate superiors.'

By this time, Evelyn had made friends other than the inevitable Fulford minor. There was Rupert Fremlin, full of gentle mockery; the sexually precocious, showily religious Tom Driberg; Hugh Molson, 'born middle-aged' in Roxburgh's opinion, and known as 'Preters' having replied 'preternaturally so' when asked if he were interested in politics; and the emotionally unstable Dudley Carew, always very much under Evelyn's influence. Dick Harris had moved to another house, but it was he who agreed to stand sponsor to a society devised by Molson to be known as the Dilettanti. This was a debating society divided into three categories – Political run by Molson, Literary under Fulford, and an Art group headed by Evelyn, whose proposal to include a dramatic club had been defeated by the others. The four of them sat in front of the fire in Dick's study planning the society's structure, and soon applications for membership started coming in. 'We want it to be perfectly democratic,' wrote Evelyn, '[but] I have great difficulty in warding off boys who obviously know nothing. One youth wished to join whose favourite painter was Landseer.' The initial meeting was on Sunday, 9 November 1919, and the following Tuesday Evelyn read his first paper, on 'Book Illustration and Decoration', a subject very dear to his heart.

Although a voracious and discriminating reader with a predilection for late Victorian and Georgian poetry, in particular that of Landor, Belloc, Dowson, Housman and Richard Le Gallienne, and although the author of a daily journal (resumed in 1919 after a three-year interval) of exceptional literary sophistication, Evelyn's ambitions at this time and for some years to come were as a draughtsman rather than as a writer. The precious hours in the library were now spent looking at books on art, especially of the Renaissance, the Pre-Raphaelites and a set of volumes reproducing paintings of every period illustrating the scriptures. He had won special permission to spend Third Evening, the half hour before bed at 9.30, in drawing. His father had obtained for him from Chapman & Hall some commissions to design book jackets, and these had been well received. 'This is really most encouraging,' Evelyn wrote in his diary, 'and is the sort of thing that cheers me up more than all the rags and jokes Lancing has to offer.' The image of himself as artist was an attractive one, and in the summer he took to wearing a red poppy in his buttonhole, considered 'jolly witty' in the idiom of the day. He spent much of his spare time on the downs sketching and painting, often in the company of the hero-worshipping Carew, the two black-jacketed boys with sketch-pads on their knees looking for all the world like a couple of maiden ladies. And at the end of the winter term of 1919 he won first prize in the Art Exhibition with an illuminated prayer. A perfectionist even at sixteen, he noted, 'If ever I paint anything really fine I shall make a huge collection of all my other work and have a jolly old bonfire. If I ever do anything better than that I shall destroy the first.'

Books and the making of books interested Evelyn intensely. There was an edition of Andrew Lang's *Leaves of Parnassus* in the library which he particularly coveted: 'It is printed very well on the most beautiful handmade paper and the feel of its crisp edges made me feel that I could buy no book on anything else again.' He read Lang on book-collecting, and anything he could find on lettering and binding. The expenditure of his small allowance was divided between food and books.

I have spent a lot of today pondering on the very important question of bindings. I think that if I live like a hermit this term I ought to be able to get one book bound, and with any luck I might get the wherewithal for another at Christmas. I have just thought what an excellent binding could be made of half black morocco, and half cloth of gold, but I have only enough of it to do a very small book and it would only be suitable for certain sorts, such as Oscar Wilde. It would be

rather a good idea to go through my little store next holidays
and mark each with what I think would suit them best, and
get them done, as best I can.

Dick Harris was succeeded as housemaster by E. B. Gordon,
'Gordo', nicknamed 'Pussy-foot' or 'Super-spy' because, although
full of goodwill, he was objectionably inquisitive, creeping along
the corridors in gym shoes so his approach would not be heard;
he also 'greased up' to the boys in a manner they judged sycophantic. Eventually, however, Gordo's nice qualities outweighed
the trying: he was always cheerful in spite of constant pain as the
result of a football injury; and, of even greater importance, he
allowed Evelyn the use of a small printing-press he owned, equipped with a jobbing printer's fascinating jumble of type and insignia – foxes' masks, hounds running, ornamented monograms
and ecclesiastical devices. And it was Gordo who was responsible
for bringing Evelyn to the notice of one of the two men
(Roxburgh being the other) who during his years at Lancing
exerted the greatest influence over him.

During his first summer term, Evelyn's parents, knowing of his
interest in calligraphy, took him to Ditchling, a small village at
the foot of the downs near Brighton which had been settled by
an arts and crafts community, predominantly Roman Catholic
and led by that eccentric genius Eric Gill. Arthur Waugh's host
was a London printer, and it was he who introduced Evelyn to
the great calligrapher, Edward Johnston. Johnston 'received me
with exquisite charm and demonstrated how to cut a turkey-quill
into a chisel-pointed pen and there and then wrote a few words
for me on the title-page of his book in what is now called his
'foundational' hand ... The sweep and precision of Johnston's
strokes were as virile as a bull-fighter's and left me breathless.'
The certainty of lettering appealed to Evelyn: as Eric Gill once
put it, 'Letters are things, not pictures of things. An A *is* an A,
not some vague approximation'; and he found satisfaction in the
tension between discipline and the free flight of the aesthetic
imagination. 'Once the barest respect has been paid to the deter-
mining structure of the letter, the pen is free to flourish and
elaborate as it will.' Although lacking the dedication to follow
the painstaking technique, Evelyn knew enough about what he
was looking at to recognise the superlative quality of Johnston's

artistry. Towards the end of his life, in 'Charles Ryder's School-days', Evelyn vividly conveys his fascination with illumination and manuscript:

> He worked happily, entirely absorbed, drawing in pencil, then tensely with breath held, inking the outline with a mapping-pen; then, when it was dry – how often, in his impatience, he had ruined his work by attempting this too soon – rubbing away the pencil lines. Finally he got out his water colours and his red sable brushes. At heart he knew he was going too fast – a monk would take a week over a single letter – but he worked with intensity and in less than two hours the initial with its pendant, convoluted border was finished.

One afternoon when Evelyn was changing after a boxing-match, Gordo summoned him to come and show his prize-winning work, the illuminated prayer, to an acquaintance of Gordo's, a plump, pink-and-white gentleman often seen in the side aisles at Sunday chapel, a figure of mild ridicule to the boys for his aesthete's garb of soft tweeds, cloak and strikingly coloured silk shirts and ties. His gait was mincing, his gestures feminine, his voice at moments of amusement shrill. His name was Francis Crease, an amateur scribe of small private means and an indeterminate background who lived in rooms in a farm at nearby Lychpole on the Tristrams' estate at Sompting Abbotts. Crease was dismissive of the script, but praised the illumination. Evelyn was intrigued, and so it was arranged that he should go over to Lychpole every Thursday afternoon for a lesson in calligraphy and sketching. On his first visit on 28 January 1920, Evelyn lost his way and was late, arriving to find Crease seated in front of the fire working on a piece of embroidery in a room furnished in old oak and decorated with some pretty china and reproductions of the Sistine frescoes. Evelyn did not altogether admire Crease's style of script, which was fanciful with a Celtic flavour deriving from the tradition of Beardsley and Walter Crane from whose influence Evelyn was then emerging, but he came to recognise that this precious, affected little person was an exceptional teacher. Exigent and sometimes peevish, Crease was on the whole encouraging, 'saying that I had real instinct for it and had the makings of a better scribe than he', although he didn't hesitate to make criticisms of the most personal nature: 'Threw up his eyes and hands and exclaimed "You come to me wearing socks of the most vulgar colours and you have just written the most beautiful E since the Book of Kells." '

The more he saw of Crease, the more Evelyn liked him, and soon Thursday afternoons became the most longed-for part of the week, Lychpole and Crease providing a tranquil refuge, his charming rooms and cultivated person a gentle, civilising contrast to the boisterous barbarity of school. Sitting in front of the fire they would have hot scones and tea drunk out of blue and white Crown Derby cups without handles; and Evelyn derived as much benefit from the conversation, an enticing mixture of gossip and aesthetics, as from the lesson itself. Sometimes Crease would accompany his pupil part of the way back, 'as far as the turn in the Roman Ditch round Steep Down where Lancing Ring suddenly comes into view, I eagerly questioning him about architecture or aesthetics or Limoges or Maiolica, he trying to turn me to the beauty of the evening and the downs'. And on days when they did not meet, Crease often wrote to his pupil, letters full of melancholy descriptive passages interspersed with sharp comments on Evelyn's moral failings. 'I wish you could have seen the flight of gulls in the fields on the left of the The Ring – against the softest greys & greens, blue & rose colours; hundreds of them suddenly took their way home to the sea in one long stream following each other & changing colour in the sunlight, & making sad music as a prelude to the coming symphony of colour,' one such missive dreamily meandered on, to be followed four days later by this: 'What is the matter is impatience nothing more or less – I can be as direct as you sometimes & you don't like it so much in others as in yourself – but it is good for you. You want a Friend who is a thorn in the flesh not an Echo! I shall disappoint you in many things. Alas! that it must be so – but in this I will not disappoint you.'

But towards the end of that spring term clouds started to gather over this entirely innocent friendship. J. F. Roxburgh, himself a man of undeniably homosexual tendencies with an eagle eye for similar leanings in others, thought he detected in the ladylike Crease a source of depravity. The two men had met over tea with Gordo, and the encounter had not been a success. 'The Sage of Lychpole, I presume,' drawled J. F. patronisingly, and Crease had retaliated by behaving in his most affected and hysterical manner.

Then Dick Harris began to have his suspicions and suddenly refused permission for Carew, whom Evelyn had allowed access to Lychpole, to go to tea there. Evelyn, to whom Crease appeared sexually neuter as a capon, was perplexed. 'I asked Carew about Dick's objection to Crease. Apparently he does not know anything against him but has heard scandal of him.' It was all very embarrassing, particularly as Evelyn had invited Crease to stay for a few days at Underhill during the Easter holidays. Unaware of the talk going on behind his back, and after a certain amount of neurotic, old-maidish panicking, Crease agreed to come. Fortunately the visit was a success; although Arthur was distrustful of his son's effeminate companion, Kate took to him, and Crease continued to visit Underhill, with and without Evelyn, for many years to come.

Soon after the beginning of the summer term, Crease went away. 'I am feeling very depressed and unhappy,' Evelyn recorded. 'Crease will be away a month and he is the only real friend I have here.' However, it was arranged that he should continue his weekly visits to Lychpole and practise at Crease's desk. Unfortunately, Evelyn used and damaged a favourite knife which Crease had forbidden him to touch. When Evelyn wrote to tell him what had happened, he was shocked to receive in reply an angry and deeply wounded letter: knife very old, quite irreplaceable, passionately fond of it, and so on. Evelyn sent the knife to be mended, and Crease followed up with a placatory postcard, but the damage was done; although lessons were resumed on Crease's return, the friendship was never the same.

Throughout his time at Lancing Evelyn remained divided between detachment and sociability, between a desire for solitude and a love of the world. It was Crease who represented the monastic, mystical side, Roxburgh the worldly. While Evelyn was having lessons every week at Lychpole, the influence of Crease was naturally dominant. 'I see the only way to get any pleasure out of life is to cut oneself off as much as possible . . . Crease's life is about the best after all . . . I owe anything at Lancing worth remembering to him.' But the estrangement over the broken knife was followed by Crease's absence for nearly nine months, an absence of which J. F. was ready to take full advantage. Recognising in Evelyn's obstreperous intelligence qualities of a potential prize pupil, he invited him to tea one Sunday in his study, or 'pit', where he fed his guest a large number of chocolate éclairs and put himself out to amuse and charm. That evening Evelyn went into chapel as usual and as usual saw Crease in his cape and soft cravat sitting in a side aisle. 'The spell is broken. His influence is quite gone. I just see a rather silly perhaps casually interesting little man,' he recorded. 'He seemed diminished. I did not exactly turn coat, but I knew that Mr Crease and J. F. were opposites and at about that time I transferred my allegiance to the more forceful and flamboyant person.'

Unlike his brother, Evelyn was no athlete, never an asset on the playing field and deplorably lacking in any desire to play up play up and play the game. But he was clever in so making a show of his indifference that it became an accepted part of his eccentricity. Slackness at 'Clubs', as games were called, was punishable by three strokes of the cane, but when Waugh was seen at a house football match positioned unmoving in one corner of the field, idly kicking the ball when it came his way, indifferent to its direction, then 'It was only Waugh'. Cricket, that obsession of his father and Alec, was of course even more boring than football, and the diary is dotted with yawning reference to school cricket matches. Of an away match at Brighton he wrote, 'We lunched modestly at one of the little tables by the ground off buns, bananas, chocolate, and ginger beer. We however made up for it at tea. Of the actual cricket I recall but vague memories . . . We won, I gather.'

But this was not the whole picture. Evelyn was intensely competitive, and although there were many aspects of school life, games in particular, which were not to his taste, he was nonetheless eager for success. He had no interest in furthering the reputation of the school: his ambitions were entirely personal, and during his first two or three years he worked hard, as inconspicuously as possible, to maintain a reasonable level of competence. As well as football and cricket, he swam, played rackets and fives, and being small ('I do wish I could get a little taller') did well in boxing, which he took seriously, going on long training runs and recording his matches in detail. As he moved up the school he grew more subversive, spreading, as J. F. complained, 'the contagion of disillusionment'. As always with Evelyn, there were two conflicting personalities: one side the conventional schoolboy, boisterous, sociable, anxious to excel; the other a world-weary cynic, crabby with contempt for the foolishness and frailty of men. Like the young Charles Ryder, he was aware of another voice in his inner counsels, 'a detached, critical Hyde who intruded his presence more and more often on the conventional, intolerant, subhuman, wholly respectable Dr Jekyll'. Evelyn worked on Fulford and Rupert Fremlin, and the three of them, joined by Driberg and Molson, became known for their rebellious attitude as the Bolshies.

After the end of the war there was among schools throughout the country a predictable reaction against militarism. It became very much the fashion to scoff at the patriotic and the soldierly, and to be deliberately slack at training sessions of the OTC. In tune with the times, and also because it ridiculed Alec and the established order, Evelyn made a point of despising parade-ground keenness. He and his contemporaries had been too young to fight and they were now determined to go to the other extreme and hold in derision what their older brothers had, some of them, died for. The army held no appeal for them at all; uniform was uncomfortable, the touch of cleaning materials 'revolting' (in chapel afterwards Evelyn 'could smell the cleaning stuff up his nails'), and arms drill was a misery, all that shouting and standing about 'with frozen fingers and rifles gnawingly cold'. Even worse were the tactical exercises which began with marching up the downs in a driving wind, struggling with ordnance maps that 'bulged with incorrect folding and flapped in the wind', before spending three hours on some elaborate pretend campaign until the whistles and bugles sounded the end of the afternoon's torture. 'They would then dismiss, hungry, bad tempered and with only twenty minutes in which to change for Chapel.'

Pretending to be inspired by high motives of pacifism, the Bolshies made as much trouble as they could, appearing on parade with puttees trailing, or with one boot polished, the other coated in mud; they dropped rifles, turned right instead of left, and on field days 'either hid from action or advanced immediately at the "enemy" so that we were "killed" at the first moment of battle'. This was all very annoying as far as it went, but then Evelyn had an inspiration, an idea for the ultimate rag; if Head's, famous throughout the school for its incompetence on parade, could win the Platoons' Shield, then the whole business would be sent up and made to look absurd. For a week before the competition 'the House was in a fever of military zeal. Manuals, hitherto ignored, were studied. Equipment was buffed. Prizes were awarded for individual smartness among the Lower boys.' Unfortunately the great effort came to nothing and Head's was placed third, to Evelyn's bitter disappointment. A day or two later he was summoned by Woodard, the house tutor, and given the choice of accepting a house captaincy, with all its privileges and constraints, or leaving the school – which was clever of Woodard, who had accurately assessed both Evelyn's qualities of leadership and his talent for disruption. Evelyn accepted the captaincy.

Lancing may have been more overtly religious than some public schools but that did not mean the level of morality among the boys was noticeably any higher. For most boys the years at public school were years of erotic and romantic passion, and many of Evelyn's contemporaries were engaged at one time or another in the pursuit of love, conducting amorous affairs with younger boys with and without physical expression. Dudley Carew's school diary is filled page after page with details of his courtship of a boy called John Onslow, a Restoration comedy of secret assignations, furtively passed notes and ecstatic descriptions of glances exchanged in chapel. Tom Driberg, admittedly an extreme example, wore powder and lipstick in the holidays, went on the downs with older men, and on Sunday evenings organised competitive masturbation sessions in his dormitory. Driberg was eventually asked to leave after propositioning a boy who, having turned him down, had then reported him to his housemaster. Evelyn, of course, was not immune to all this. There was a boy called Woodward who for a time attracted him, and in his last term he found himself drawn towards Carew's *inamorato*, the lovely Onslow. But unlike his brother, who had had at least two passionate affairs at Sherborne, he was prudish and anxious to maintain his self-respect; and so although in the changing rooms he enjoyed talking 'filth', as sex was called, and was fascinated by others' love affairs (boy lovers were referred to as 'tweatles'), he resolved to keep out of the emotional hot-house, aloof from the crude sexual bartering on the stock-exchange floor. 'I lead as pure a life as any Christian in the place, always excepting conversation of course', he wrote complacently. 'I do not approve of keennesses, myself, and have always tried, I think with some success, to suppress any such emotions.' As a result he was regarded as moral arbiter, a somewhat acerbic confidant in other men's affairs. Molson allowed himself to be argued out of a night's 'whoring' in the holidays ('All that day I wrestled with him in spirit') and another close friend, Hill, confided in him by letter his own 'filth experience . . . with Roberts[9] (I thought he could be corrupted no farther than he was already)' wrote Hill. 'If *you* have missed that experience, let me assure you've missed nothing – or at least not very much.' And Carew, of course, earnestly consulted him at every stage of the tortuous and tormenting Onslow affair.

This self-restraint on Evelyn's part required no great effort. Intellectually precocious, he was sexually and emotionally immature and not yet ready for these regions of experience. He was not happy at Lancing, never felt he belonged as part of the team; neither was he sufficiently at ease with himself or with others to allow on the one hand the freedom and intimacy, on the other the loss of power that such relationships involve. He preferred to remain detached, unconfiding, very conscious of playing a part. He had a number of friends; as well as Driberg, Fulford and the doggedly devoted Carew, there were Hale, Hill, and John Longe, a devout Christian for whom he had a particular regard. With these companions he huddled over the fire in the House Room, gorged on Settle teas, read the newspapers by the hot-water pipes in the study corridor, talked 'filth' by candlelight in the dormitory, picked blackberries on the Coombes road, lay and smoked on the banks of the Adur, in summer went into Shoreham for strawberries and cream, and ragged the fearful little oiks who came down from time to time to take parade. In June 1921 he wrote a poem to Hale and Longe ('Yet I know that just you two/ Mattered out of all I knew'), and Carew was jealous and had to be reassured. 'I mentioned the "just you two" of the poem,' Carew wrote in his diary. 'He was ripping about it & said that I counted in a rather different way to them; an intellectual friend-

---

[9] Roberts was a boy much in demand. Even the ascetic Crease had tried to persuade Evelyn to bring Roberts over to Lychpole: 'Apparently he wants to see him eat as he thinks he is like a kitten!'

ship cemented by personal affection & called me a silly ass but told me I really did count.'

Carew adored Evelyn and believed devoutly in his genius. He read what Evelyn read, adopted Evelyn's opinions, begged for his criticism, came to him for advice. In his diary he dotingly recorded his mentor's idiosyncrasies. 'I love the quaint mentality of his brain – his way of branching off and pointing out the beauty of a corner of a house or a shop-front. "Study street architecture Carey" ' – and his affectations – ' "There's a delightful squalor about Shoreham." ' He listened rapturously to Evelyn's emotional crises, crises brought on by the natural upheavals of adolescence and by frustration, by the restlessness and irritation common to those who are possessed of powerful creative feeling that is as yet undirected, as yet unexpressed. 'My divine fire's dying,' Evelyn told his friend. ' "I get depressed, Carey, the people I like never like me; besides its rotten when you think you've got a touch of genius and you don't know how things are going to turn out." ' Carew enormously admired Evelyn's writing, and Evelyn gave a great deal of time to criticising, often devastatingly and in great detail, Carew's imitative and inferior productions. 'A few days ago I wrote a poem which I thought had some slight merit, on the Chapel – & showed it to Evelyn. I got back a letter which stated in no qualified terms that it was thoroughly bad from beginning to end – "not a single phrase of any value".' The tougher Evelyn was, the more Carew loved it. He was toughest of all over the Onslow affair.

> Went for a tearing walk with Evelyn at 12.30 down in the valley & got thoroughly ticked off... 'How's Jo [John Onslow]? Been pouring your soul out on the hearth-rug again? My God nobody can see through your wretched little soul except me' . . . Evelyn keeping up a stream of invective & dashing up the slope at a terrific speed with [me] alternately trotting, walking, laughing & protesting at his side. All the same he does make me feel a bit of an ass & rather disturbs me . . . He more or less delivered an ultimatum – give up John or . . . He's got the most diabolical gift of caricature & while I laugh at him I wince. He by his ridicule has done far more to kill my belief in the fineness of our relations (John & I) than all the Dicks [Harris] and Gordons . . . in the world.

Three years after leaving Lancing, Carew published a novel, *The*

Next Corner,[10] in which the character of Dick Hirst is based on Evelyn, Hirst's friendship with the hero, John Blythe, clearly reflecting Carew's with Waugh. Hirst is described as fair-haired, 'a short, broad, strong-looking boy . . ., [who sings] completely flat and out of tune', refers to suicide as 'the triumph of reason over instinct', and parodies sentimental speeches on the Old School. Hirst is cleverer and more sceptical than Blythe: 'Hirst with his immature, yet strangely sincere, cynicism. Hirst with his contempt and his laughter for those things which at sixteen John was disposed to take with intense seriousness . . .'

Carew was perceptive in his judgment of Evelyn's talent as a writer. Evelyn's literary activity while at school was copious and wide-ranging. He was unusually well-read, and his output was prodigious. 'I must write prose or burst,' he recorded in his diary at the age of seventeen. He won the Poetry prize, the Scarlyn Literature prize, and edited and contributed to the *Lancing Magazine,* for which he wrote a number of articles; he composed poetry, started a novel, finished a number of short stories and a play, *Conversion,* which was performed to acclaim in front of the whole school. It was described as 'The Tragedy of Youth in three burlesques . . . Act I. School, as maiden aunts think it is. Act II. School, as modern authors say it is [a parody of *Loom*]. Act III. School, as we all know it is.' J. F. remarked of the epilogue that he thought it had a touch of genius, and J. C. Squire briefly showed interest in it for the *London Mercury.* And yet none of this compulsion, this exceptional industry, struck Evelyn or anyone else as unusual. He believed his artistic talent was as a draughtsman, and thought nothing at all of that extraordinary diary, that stream of consciousness flowing like a great subterranean river unregarded beneath the surface: a writer's diary, a novelist's record of introspection, characterisation, sharply recorded scene and dialogue, continuing day after day, which was to its author no more than part of the routine of his existence.

When school broke up for the summer holidays of 1920, Evelyn went for a week to OTC training camp at Tidworth, an exercise he found both dispiriting and dull. 'The chief result of the increased insight into people's characters led, I found, mainly to

[10] Published by Lane, 1924.

increased dislike ... The most instructive thing I saw was that
when the drum-major of the Gloucesters knocked his hat off with
his wand not a single man smiled.' When camp was struck he
returned thankfully to Underhill.

Alec Waugh and Barbara Jacobs had married in July 1919, and
because of the post-war housing shortage had been living at
Underhill for the past year. Now they had bought an ugly little
prefab in Ditchling, which Barbara was getting ready for them to
move into. Evelyn and Barbara were on the same easy terms as
before. He went down to Ditchling with her to look at the house,
Halfacre, and they bought a spaniel puppy from a farmer in the
village. Alec, however, Evelyn found inexplicably morose. Having
recently started work as a reader at Chapman & Hall, and just
back from a week's cricketing holiday, he should have been in
the best of tempers; instead he moped about the house sulking
and talking of suicide. Carew, who had come to stay for a few days,
remarked that 'Alec has an extraordinary chilling & repressing
influence. Directly he comes in Arthur stops making jokes, Evelyn
stops being clever, I stop talking & only Mrs is left undisturbed.
He has gimlety eyes [&] a baleful glare.' The cause of his
depression, it became known later, was an inability to consummate his marriage, a humiliating failure which not unnaturally
he had no wish to discuss with his little brother.

Evelyn went to Norton for a few days to see the aunts; then
back in London 'rushed' up to town almost daily with his mother
or Barbara for shopping and the theatre; he went six times to
the famous revival of *The Beggar's Opera* at the Lyric, Hammer-
smith, with sets and costumes by the much admired Claud Lovat
Fraser. On Sundays he went to Mass at St Jude's, where the usual
Bourchier performance was being staged. 'Basil, to enliven the
time when all his swell friends are out of town, has invented a
new festival "The Coronation of the blessed Mother of God"
which he observed with all pomp of copes and processions.' His
father gave him five guineas for passing his School Certificate ('I
am astoundingly elated'), and took him for the day to Oxford. 'I
have never seen anything so beautiful ... Father has put my name
down for New College and I am going to try for a scholarship at
the House. We saw the Sheldonian and the rostrum from which
Father recited the Newdigate; we saw the gate of Trinity which
James Waugh my great-uncle scaled at two o'clock in the morning;

and the Union where I hope to speak. We saw all over the good colleges... It was a splendid day; Father told me disreputable stories of his time.'

With the prospect of Oxford before him, Evelyn returned to Lancing full of enthusiasm for the new term. 'I have been put in the Upper Sixth. Roxburgh has given me a time table which suits me very well. I am doing no French, Greek, or Maths, a little English, a lot of History, some Latin and Divinity.' He had his own pit (study), in which he hung blue curtains and Medici prints, arranged blue cushions on the window-seat, and upholstered his desk also in blue: 'it looks very distinguished... with Father's brass candlesticks. Woodard has given us leave to have a bridge club. The term opens with great prospects. I am happier than I have ever been before at school. Being in the Sixth has greatly raised my social position in the House.' It was an improvement, too, having Alec and Barbara nearby at Ditchling, as sometimes on a Sunday they took him out to lunch in Brighton. 'We had an excellent lunch... discovered a new drink of ginger beer and burgundy... played with the slot machines on the pier – an everlasting joy – and saw an octopus fed at the aquarium.' And he started work on a novel, which he never finished, 'the study of a man with two characters, by his brother – but I never realized what an immense amount of labour it entails.'

The surging high spirits of the winter term did not last, however, and Evelyn's final year at school, 1921, was marked by depression, an increasing sense of alienation, and by an apparent loss of faith. His mother wrote to Alec that when Evelyn was at home during the holidays, 'he went about in a depressed manner and with contemptious [sic] looks'. Having been ambitious for high office – he was now house captain, editor of the school magazine and president of the Debating Society – he found his eminence lonely, felt cut off from many of his friends and 'in great danger of becoming self-important and even officious', as he noted with his customary unsparing insight in his diary. The writer of a letter in the *Lancing Magazine* made open reference to his unpopularity: 'I have never yet met a House Captain whose conduct the term before his promotion was such that his friends were only too glad to be able to drop him.' Evelyn was frequently in despair – 'I am bitterly unhappy. This evening, coming back to it all, I seriously began considering running away.' He was possessed by feelings of disappointment and self-loathing: 'I am burdened with failure this term, when I have been most successful really. Everything I have had has come to me shop-soiled and second-hand.' Like many boys his age, in a turmoil of ill-defined emotions and adolescent yearnings, sick in body and soul, every-thing vanity and vexation of spirit, he toyed with thoughts of suicide, even going so far as to draft noble letters of farewell to his friends. Desperate to get away from the claustrophobic atmosphere of the classroom, he took to going for long walks by the sea at night in the company of Hill and Longe. Unfortunately they were seen and reported and the matter came to his parents' ears. Clearly suspecting a repetition of Alec's Sherborne scandal, Arthur wrote a furious letter. 'Your mother and I had a sickening shock . . . years since we have heard anything that has so distressed us . . . you, a House captain . . . such a rotten and contemptible game . . . unworthy of the name of Waugh . . . appeal to you to send me by first post your honourable assurance that never again . . .'

This did little to improve relations between father and son. One of the last, indeed one of the few, occasions on which Evelyn had felt close to his father was on their visit to Oxford during the summer. Since then he had been increasingly irritated by Arthur's ineffectiveness and theatricality – 'Father has been inef-fably silly the whole holidays' – instinctively sensing not only the older man's weakness and emotional insecurity but also his second-rateness. It was not just that Arthur was old-fashioned, that his standards and tastes were out of date, that the men he admired had had their day, but also that few of them actually added up to very much. But if Evelyn read the angry letter with contempt, dismissing it as 'unconvincingly rhetorical' and 'absurd', he was privately relieved by his father's strong reaction, infinitely preferable to the usual evasive jocularity and clever, apt quotation. 'I am rather glad he has taken a strong line about something at last,' Evelyn wrote in his diary.

On his return to school in January Evelyn was appointed junior sacristan in chapel. The chapel with its fine, fragile Gothic arches, aqueous green windows and lofty, vast and vaulted roof was the central edifice, both figuratively and literally, of Lancing College, best appreciated, Evelyn always insisted, from out of doors lying on the grass staring up at the soaring stone and the sky. Its beauty and the beauty of the services, in particular the high standard of music under Alexander Brent Smith, could not but have a profound effect even on someone with little sense of religion. Evelyn was deeply religious. But over the last few months he had found an increasing sterility in the Christian message. In previous terms he had discussed religion exhaustively, in particular with Molson with whom he had visited the Carthusian monastery at Cowfold, with Longe and with Driberg, already noted for his high-church fervour and obsessive attention to ritualistic detail. But recently there had been some unsettling influences which, coinciding with his black view of himself and the world, drew him towards a drastic revision of everything he had until then unthinkingly accepted. A reading of Pope's *Essay on Man* had led to Leibnitz and to Arnold Lunn's *Loose Ends.* The dialectics of these very Christian writers shook him and led him to start thinking for himself, and to put to the test, as they had, the tenets of his own as yet untested creed. Then Roxburgh, as was his way, had posed without resolving some disconcerting questions about the nature of survival after death; and Mr Rawlinson, a dynamic young theologian from Oxford who taught Divinity, had been full of challenging agnostic argument. Evelyn wrote an essay arguing agnosticism for which he was congratulated by Rawlinson: 'No mean theologian, Waugh'. 'This learned and devout man inadvertently made me an atheist. He explained to his divinity class that none of the books of the Bible were by their supposed authors; he invited us to speculate, in the manner of the fourth century, on the nature of Christ.' All this worked together to obscure a belief in God. And it may be that even then Evelyn sensed in all the gorgeous ceremony of the Anglican church, in which he had been brought up and of which, with his clerical background, he believed himself an integral part, there was an essential element missing. Walking over the downs with Carew, he expatiated on his bleak new philosophy.

> Evelyn has come to the realisation of the minuteness of the world compared with the Universe & the minuteness of his life compared with the World. 'You must keep your nose down in the mud, Carey, once you look up, or even forward, you're

done. . . . Man is governed entirely by his own self-interest,
'Carey'. He has discovered he is an agnostic but is willing to
admit that God probably does exist as a force, like heat or
electricity. 'I am convinced there is no ultimate good or evil . . .
There's a kink in one man's brain which is attracted to what we
call good & in another to what we call evil.'

His fellow sacristan Tom Driberg was shocked when Evelyn in
this new mood, rebuked by holy Tom for leaving the altar cloth
hanging crooked, replied dismissively, 'If it's good enough for
me, it's good enough for God.' In his diary for 13 June Evelyn
wrote, 'In the last few weeks I have ceased to be a Christian
(sensation off!) I have realized that for the last two terms at least
I have been an atheist in all except the courage to admit it to
myself. I am sure it is only a phase and am not much worried.'
Worried enough, however, to make an appointment to discuss his
doubts with the chaplain. But when Evelyn arrived at Mr Fox's
room there was with him another master sitting smoking, and
this inhibited him and he came away feeling that his atheism had
been inadequately expressed and accepted with an unflattering
placidity.

During his last term, the Christmas term of 1921, Evelyn continued bored and restless. So bored that he founded a club, the
Corpse Club, 'for people who are bored stiff'. 'I am hating this
term,' he wrote, 'I am certainly making myself hateful.'

The Oxford scholarship examination was in December, and it
was on this that Evelyn set his hopes. Anything would be bearable
if only he could get to Oxford. The original intention had been
for him to try for his father's old college, New College, but as
the competition for scholarships there was exceptionally stiff, he
decided instead to aim for the less well known Hertford, whose
scholarship was worth more and where the advantage would be,
as his history master pointed out, 'that it is better to go up to
Oxford as a scholar in a smaller college . . . Apparently the dons
make more of you.' He and Molson went to Oxford together on
the fifth of December and sat their examinations on the sixth.
Evelyn wrote on the English Reformation and Pitt the Younger,
on Cavour, Kaunitz and the French Revolution. He was particularly proud of a phrase describing the nineteenth-century map
of the world as 'blushing scarlet with British Imperialism'. After

this he and Molson passed a couple of days 'bingeing' with OLs already at the university, including Hill and Mallowan, before returning to school. On the fifteenth, the last day of term, came the news that Evelyn had won the Hertford History Scholarship, worth £100 a year, together with a letter of congratulation from the dean of Hertford and senior history tutor, C. R. M. F. Cruttwell: 'Most of your work was extremely promising,' wrote Mr Cruttwell, 'and the quality of your English style about the best of any of the Candidates in the group.'

Evelyn was elated and spent the rest of the day saying his goodbyes, having a final interview with the headmaster and playing musical chairs in the dormitory. He felt wholly unsentimental about Lancing, and got on the train the following day without a backward glance. 'I am sure I have left at the right time – as early as possible and with success.'

An enclosed and enchanted garden

Oxford in the early 1920s was still a city of grey and gold, from its spiked and pinnacled medievalism to the plain ashlar beauty of the eighteenth century. The ancient colleges with their cloisters, lawns and quadrangles were networked with narrow streets and passages, beyond which lay woods and water meadows, a slow-moving river and the lush pastoral beauty of the Thames valley. Cattle were still driven through the streets to market, and at certain times of day nothing was heard except the sound of church bells. But this was the 1920s, and Oxford was also a city of sports cars and motor-bikes, jazz and gramophones, of the Black Bottom and Chili Bom Bom, of Jack Hulbert and Binnie Hale at the New, Mary Pickford, Harold Lloyd and Charlie Chaplin at the Super. Smart young men wore plus-fours and Charvet ties, while the aesthetes defied convention in polo-neck jumpers and Oxford bags. Christian socialists from Manchester and miners' sons from Cornwall could be found on the same staircase, breathing the same air as the young bloods of the Bullingdon[1] who hunted, played polo and got spectacularly drunk on incomes of £3000 a year.

Evelyn's college, Hertford, founded in the Middle Ages, was not one of the smarter colleges, having a reputation neither for social, nor academic, nor indeed architectural distinction. But if not prestigious, it was respectable, and its jumble of small, nondescript premises, figuratively if not literally overshadowed by the great medieval walls of New College, had a cosy charm. There

---

[1] The Bullingdon was an Oxford dining club for rich sportsmen.

were no wide lawns or ancient cloisters. Its advantages were an excellent kitchen, probably the best in Oxford, and an unusually relaxed attitude towards its Junior Common Room, for whose members there was neither early morning roll-call nor compulsory attendance at chapel. Partly as a result of this enlightened approach, Hertford was free of the schoolboy hooliganism so characteristic of many of the grander colleges.

As at Lancing, Evelyn came up in a by-term rather than at the beginning of the academic year, and so found that the best rooms were already occupied; the only set available was small and dark, overlooking New College Lane[2] and immediately next to the JCR buttery where teas were prepared. 'My chief memory of the staircase is of the rattle of dish-covers on foggy afternoons and the smell of anchovy toast and honey buns as the scouts filled their trays.' Although undergraduates were well looked after on a domestic level, conditions were primitive. Scouts brought up jugs of shaving water every morning and twice a day emptied the bedroom chamber-pot. There was a small number of privies concealed behind the chapel. To have a bath it was necessary to cross the Italianate 'Bridge of Sighs', as it was called (although modelled on the Rialto Bridge), which led over New College Lane into the New Building.

When Evelyn arrived in January 1922, he was still very much the schoolboy, and although excited by the prospects which he saw the university had to offer, during that first term was shy and sometimes lonely, his thoughts often turning nostalgically in the direction of the Sussex downs. Writing to Tom Driberg and Dudley Carew, both still at school, Evelyn, describing himself as 'an hungering OL', enquired keenly for news, anxious to know what people 'say of me now I have left'. 'If I came down to Lancing for a day,' he asked Driberg, 'do you think anyone would be glad to see me?' shrewdly adding, 'I imagine I am pretty well disliked now – as good God I deserved to be.' But soon the memory of school began to fade as the university in all its drama and magnificence took hold of his imagination.

Evelyn's rooms were on the ground floor, a vulnerable position

[2] Two New College men had rooms in the Warden's stables adjoining New College Lane, and their names, Best and Chetwynd, seen by Waugh every time he walked down the Lane, were amalgamated into Mrs Beste-Chetwynde in *Decline and Fall.*

as it was easy for people to drop in for a drink or cigarette, or, on their way somewhere else after a tutorial, simply to dump their books and gowns. And sometimes worse. One night when Evelyn was alone in his room a group of drunken Bullingdon hearties came roaring into the quad, made a quick circuit looking for trouble and then fortunately roared out again. All except one; a young man who walked shakily over to Evelyn's open window, leaned inside, and without saying a word was sick on his carpet – an incident later evoked by Charles Ryder's first encounter with Sebastian Flyte in *Brideshead Revisited*.[3] To many of the less raucously athletic undergraduates, the behaviour of the rich, hell-raising hearty was as fascinating as it was appalling. Not only is there the famous passage describing the barbaric behaviour of the Bollinger (Bullingdon) Club in *Decline and Fall* (characterised by 'the sound of the English county families baying for broken glass'), but there is also this description by Evelyn's friend and near-contemporary, Henry Yorke, of a typical bump supper evening at Magdalen:

> there was the difficulty of reaching my rooms unseen and then
> the wait far into the night with every now and then a rush of
> them through the cloisters, that awful screaming they affected
> when in motion imitating the cry when the fox is viewed, the
> sense curiously of remorse which comes over one who thinks he
> is to be hunted, the regret, despair and feeling sick the coward
> has.

In his first couple of terms, Evelyn followed the college routine: a huge cooked breakfast, lunch in his rooms of bread, cheese and ale, every evening dressed in subfusc dining in hall where the food was excellent and cheap and you paid for five dinners a week whether you ate them or not. Soon, however, a little group was formed, known as the 'Hertford underworld', which met in Evelyn's rooms in the middle of the day for sherry, followed by bread and cheese, steak-and-kidney pie or sausages, and quantities of beer. During this early period Evelyn was 'entirely happy in a subdued fashion'. He hung his Lovat Fraser prints on the wall

---

[3] 'There appeared at my window the face I knew to be Sebastian's, but not, as I had formerly seen it, alive and alight with gaiety; he looked at me for a moment with unfocused eyes and then, leaning forward well into the room, he was sick.'

and arranged his few fine bindings and collection of the None-such editions of English poets. Like any keen freshman he bought a cigarette box with the college arms, a panoramic view of the city for his study wall, took to smoking a pipe and learned how to ride a bicycle on which he explored the surrounding pubs and countryside, a way of life very much like that of Charles Ryder's in his first term, later described with such sophisticated contempt.

> On my first afternoon I proudly hung a reproduction of Van Gogh's *Sunflowers* over the fire and set up a screen, painted by Roger Fry with a Provençal landscape, which I had bought inexpensively when the Omega workshops were sold up. I displayed also a poster by McKnight Kauffer and Rhyme Sheets from the Poetry Bookshop, and, most painful to recall, a porcelain figure of Polly Peachum which stood between black tapers on the chimney-piece. My books were meagre and commonplace . . .

Evelyn kept company mostly with his old Lancing cronies, and briefly with Maxwell Fleming of the Pistol Troop, who had gone up to Wadham. He adopted the current Oxford idiolect which converted the Radcliffe into the 'Radder', St Giles into the 'Giler', the Martyrs' Memorial into the 'Maggers' Memogger', and the Bodleian into the 'Bodder'; he gave his maiden speech at the Union, 'not over well' he told Carew, noting that one of the tellers in the debate 'was an Earl of something'; and he briefly joined a hockey club, as there 'is a pleasant old world violence about the game which appeals to me strongly'. In fact, Evelyn was fast falling in love with the place, its beauty, its freedom, its apparently limitless opportunity. Like the heroine of one of his most loved books, Lewis Carroll's *Alice*, he had glimpsed that low door in the wall 'which opened on an enclosed and enchanted garden, which was somewhere, not overlooked by any window, in the heart of that grey city'. 'I can say little because I am too happy,' he told Carew. 'Life is good and Oxford is all that one dreams.'

But like the bad fairy at the christening, there was waiting in the wings one malevolent personage poised to break the enchantment.

When Evelyn won his History scholarship, instead of regarding it as the first step towards three years of industry and a first-class degree, he saw it as an achievement for which three years of idleness was the well-merited reward. Once he had passed History Previous at the end of his second term (to have failed this would have meant the loss of his scholarship), he settled down to a programme of almost no work at all. His interest in history was slight and his special subject, chosen in haste and almost by accident, was one which profoundly bored him. 'When asked by my tutor what I wished to read, I could remember the name of only one of these "special subjects": Representative Government. Nothing could have been drearier to me than the peculiarities of the various democratic constititutions of the world and no one was to blame except myself for directing me towards them.' A sympathetic teacher might have made all the difference, but unfortunately the dean of Hertford and senior history tutor, C. R. M. F. Cruttwell, was a man to whom Evelyn took an instant dislike, a dislike which quickly became mutual and irreversible. Cruttwell, a good-hearted though difficult man, had returned damaged from the war, in which he had fought gallantly. Although capable of great generosity and a devout Christian, 'Crutters' was also a bully and disciplinarian with a fierce temper, a lacerating tongue, and a tendency when dining out to get sottishly drunk. Women, referred to either as 'drabs' or 'breast-heavers', he regarded with fear and loathing, but even among his male colleagues he was notable for a brusque and often offensive manner, which only those who knew him well understood to conceal extreme shyness. As one of his colleagues put it, he had a fondness 'for the biting criticism and pungent phrase . . . [and was] full of odd quirks of behaviour that some people found very tiresome'. His appearance, too, was unprepossessing, a fact of which Evelyn makes the most in a cruelly memorable description.

> He was tall, almost loutish, with the face of a petulant baby. He smoked a pipe which was usually attached to his blubber-lips by a thread of slime. As he removed the stem, waving it to emphasise his indistinct speech, this glittering connection extended until finally it broke leaving a dribble on his chin. When he spoke to me I found myself so distracted by the speculation of how far this line could be attenuated that I was often inattentive to his words.

'It was', he added with palpable disgust, 'as though he had never cleaned himself of the muck of the trenches.'

Although under forty, Cruttwell was already arthritic and seemed an old man, his lack of sympathy with the frenetic frivolity of the younger generation typifying the unbridgeable divide between those who had fought in the war and those who had not. The fact that he was a distinguished military historian, an authority on the political history of the Rhineland, did little to endear him to a pupil who all too clearly neither knew nor cared where the Rhineland was.[4]

By the end of Evelyn's second term, Cruttwell had already targeted him for special treatment. At a meeting of the college Education Committee in June it was resolved that 'Mr Waugh should be fined £10 in the event of his failing to pass the History Preliminary Exam'. Fortunately the exam was passed, and Evelyn retained his scholarship. The crux came the following term at the beginning of the academic year after the customary 'freshers' blind. Evelyn, in common with at least one third of his colleagues, had been conspicuously drunk, and Cruttwell the next day warned him that he would do well to mend his ways as such behaviour was not the best way of ingratiating himself with the college. Evelyn insolently replied that college opinion meant nothing to him, and what the authorities chose to think was as far as he was concerned a matter of complete indifference. This was too much for Cruttwell, whose dislike of his pupil was by now profound; 'a silly little suburban sod with an inferiority complex and no palate', as he damningly described him. Cruttwell refused to give him any further tuition, and for a time (a 'blissful period') Evelyn had no teaching at all, until he was eventually handed over to a newly elected fellow, a courteous young man from whom he learnt almost nothing.

At any time during the next two years Cruttwell with complete justification could have sent Evelyn down on a number of charges from obstreperous conduct to neglecting his work. The fact that he forbore to do this did nothing to mitigate Evelyn's loathing. He neither forgot nor forgave Cruttwell's offences, and continued to persecute his tutor with vigour and ingenuity. He and another

---

[4] In his first tutorial Evelyn unfortunately let slip that he thought the Rhine flowed into the Black Sea.

Hertford man, Terence Greenidge, put it about that Cruttwell indulged in sexual intercourse with dogs. They invented a rhyme:

Cruttwell dog, Cruttwell dog, where have you been?
I've been to Hertford to lie with the Dean.
Cruttwell dog, Cruttwell dog, what did you there?
I bit off his penis and pubic hair.

They bought a stuffed dog from a junk shop in Walton Street and positioned it in the quad at what they considered an alluring angle, at night singing their ditty and barking suggestively under his windows. Soon in the minds of its two perpetrators the joke began to take on a crazy kind of reality: one rainy morning when Evelyn and his cousin Claud Cockburn were sitting in Evelyn's study drinking whisky, listening to the drone and thump of a vacuum cleaner in Cruttwell's rooms overhead, Cockburn was surprised by Evelyn saying gravely, 'Do you hear that? Now he's raping the poor brute. And at this hour in the morning, too.' In later years he continued the persecution, in his novels frequently giving the name Cruttwell to characters of particular repulsiveness,[5] unable to resist a passing swipe even in a travel book,[6] and would amuse himself when asked to list for some work of reference the books he had written by entering titles such as *The Mind and Face of Cruttwell, Cruttwell from Within,* and so on. When asked years later to name for a literary survey his personal favourite among his own works, Evelyn surprised his questioner by replying that his favourite had not yet been written, that it might be years before it was completed. 'It is the memorial biography of C. R. M. F. Cruttwell, sometime dean of Hertford College, Oxford, and

[5] Toby Cruttwell, the criminal friend of Philbrick in *Decline and Fall,* who also appears as a 'very silly' last-minute dinner guest of Lady Seal's in *Black Mischief;* the Conservative MP referred to by two snobbish ladies in the train in *Vile Bodies;* General Cruttwell, the shop-assistant with the fake tan in *Scoop;* Gladys Cruttwell, the unintelligent girl with fluffy hair with whom Tom Kent-Cumberland falls in love in *Winner Takes All;* the scoutmaster in *Work Suspended;* Mr Cruttwell, Brenda Last's bone-setter in *A Handful of Dust;* and the story about the lunatic Mr Loveday was originally titled, not 'Mr Loveday's Little Outing' but 'Mr Cruttwell's Little Outing'.
[6] The cathedral in Malaga, Waugh says, reminded him of the chapel at Hertford College, evoking memories of dons and undergraduates and, 'crouching in his stall, the venerable figure of my history tutor, ill at ease in his starched white surplice, biting his nails, and brooding'.

my old history tutor. It is a labour of love to one to whom, under God, I owe everything.'

Terence Greenidge, a second-year Greats man, was Evelyn's first close friend at Oxford. From the start Greenidge appealed to him enormously. He was a clown, an eccentric with an outrageous sense of humour, constantly in trouble with the university authorities. Terence made life hilarious with his practical jokes, his love of nicknames, his peculiar habit of declaiming Greek verse out of doors loudly and late at night. He was the founder of the university's Cinematograph Club, and during his first two years, before he became a convinced sceptic, was an enthusiastic follower of the Oxford Movement. His style of dress was bizarre, his favourite item a black sports coat edged in fur of which the pockets were usually bulging with the quantities of litter he felt compelled to pick up off the street. He had a habit, too, of quietly helping himself to any little thing – keys, nail-scissors, ink-pots – that caught his eye and his fancy in other men's rooms. Clever, childish and affectionate, Greenidge was precisely the right person to break Evelyn out of his self-imposed straitlacing, with his zany humour the ideal companion for the adolescent silliness which at Lancing he had largely denied himself.

In this return to childhood Evelyn was far from unique. For many of the middle and upper classes who were children of Victorian parents and too young to have fought in the war, frivolity was essential and games-playing a way of life. As Evelyn wrote in an article for *The Isis*,[7] 'We are all of us young at Oxford . . . and do not need a psychology text-book to cause us to yearn once more for the nursery floor.' Just as it was the fashion to pretend (for those for whom pretence was necessary) to be homosexual, so it was the done thing to behave like children. The universities, and Oxford in particular, were a kind of deregulated nursery where bread-and-milk was replaced by plovers' eggs and champagne, and nobody said anything about going to bed early or not answering back. The Bright Young People were encouraged to act like babies, in the words of a popular jingle, to 'Prattle and say "Ga!"/ [to] Suck a naughty cocktail at the Bad Boys'

[7] The two best-known undergraduate journals, *Isis* and *Cherwell*, in those days retained the definite article.

Nursery Bar.' In *Brideshead Revisited* Charles Ryder describes his
time at Oxford in just such terms: 'it seemed as though I was
being given a brief spell of what I had never known, a happy
childhood, and though its toys were silk shirts and liqueurs and
cigars and its naughtiness high in the catalogue of grave sins,
there was something of nursery freshness about us that fell little
short of the joy of innocence.' These mock and mocking adults
devoted themselves to foolery: instead of working for their
degrees or planning their careers, they spent their time inventing
pranks and amusing things to do: they played practical jokes, got
themselves up in fancy dress, devised nicknames for each other
and a sort of private language. Billy Clonmore gave a supper
party on the roof of a church. A group of Balliol men formed
the Hysteron-Proteron Club and lived a day in reverse, getting
up in evening dress and going to bed after breakfast last thing at
night. Tom Driberg and John Betjeman organised a concert
entitled 'Homage to Beethoven', at which bemused north Oxford
matrons were entertained to a symphony of typewriters and a
flushing lavatory. John Sutro founded the Railway Club, to which
Evelyn belonged, whose members dined on the Penzance–Aber-
deen express between Oxford and Leicester, returning from
Leicester to Oxford for speeches and liqueurs.

Evelyn and his cronies instigated a number of running gags,
most of them harmless, although annoying for the victim. In
Balliol, for instance, there was a man called Philbrick who had
unwisely confessed to having enjoyed beating smaller boys at
school. Evelyn, seizing on this, spread it about that Philbrick was
an unbridled flagellant, a notion keenly adopted by the frivolous
faction, so much so that when a film about African life was shown,
with a scene of a man being flogged, the entire cinema broke
into a rhythmic chant of 'Philbrick, Philbrick, Philbrick . . .' For
this achievement Evelyn was quietly but efficiently beaten up by
the flagellant himself, assisted by the thuggish Basil Murray,
with the result that Philbrick's name for a time joined that of
Cruttwell to be bestowed on the more disreputable figures in
Evelyn's fiction.[8] Equally successful in outcome, if less designedly
so, was an incident involving Edmund Gosse. It had become the

[8] For instance, the secretary at Maltby's School of Art in 'The Balance', and Dr
Fagan's criminal butler in *Decline and Fall.*

practice, particularly among the Hertford underworld, to use sexual terms in referring to ordinary, non-sexual intercourse: thus if Chris Hollis were seen in the Broad talking to Hugh Molson, Hollis would be described as having been 'lying with' Molson. Evelyn, idly referring to his distinguished cousin, said that he 'lay with' some lady with whom in fact Gosse enjoyed only the most casual acquaintance. Gosse came to hear of the slander, was incensed, and wrote angrily to Arthur Waugh that although he would be glad to continue the friendship with him, on no account would he see Evelyn again.

As Evelyn says in *A Little Learning*, 'At Oxford I was reborn in full youth.' And it was his Hertford friend, Terence Greenidge, who officiated at the birth, Terence who encouraged the childishness and pranks, and Terence who introduced Evelyn to the headquarters of that dissolute nursery world.

Because pubs were out of bounds to undergraduates, there had sprung up within the university precincts a large number of drinking clubs. One of the most notorious was the Hypocrites' Club (motto, in Greek, the opening line of Pindar's *Olympian Odes*, 'Water Is Best'), whose premises were a couple of rooms over a bicycle shop at 131 St Aldate's, just below Christ Church. The club, under its president Lord Elmley, a highly respected Magdalen man, had originally existed as a sombre meeting place for old Rugbeians and Wykehamists with a taste for folk-dancing, shove ha'penny and the Cowley Fathers. But by the time Evelyn was inducted there by Terence it was in the process of being taken over by a group of dissolute Etonians such as Brian Howard, 'Lulu' Waters Welch, Mark Ogilvie-Grant, Robert Byron, David Plunket Greene, Hugh Lygon and Billy Clonmore, who got wildly and noisily drunk, thumped out jazz on the upright piano, danced together (in spite of a notice on the wall which read, 'Gentlemen may prance but not dance'), kissed, cuddled and conducted themselves in a manner that the authorities, when they came to hear of it, regarded as shockingly improper. Although the membership was not entirely homosexual, there was little in the Hypocrites' behaviour to lead one to think otherwise. Tom Driberg dancing with a man friend one evening noted with interest the sight of Evelyn, very drunk, rolling with some unidentified boy on a sofa, 'with (as one of them said later) their tongues licking each others' tonsils'. Anthony Powell's first-ever sight of Evelyn was at the Hypocrites' sitting on Christopher Hollis's knee. Women were occasionally smuggled in, but more for the attraction of the dare than because members were much interested in the species. The quantity of alcohol consumed, mainly beer, was colossal, and total inebriation the nightly goal of most of the club's patrons, a goal which Evelyn had no difficulty in attaining. It became a familiar sight, Evelyn, 'very pink in the cheeks, small, witty and fierce', sitting in a high chair, his head lolling to one side, helplessly drunk. Occasionally his high spirits soared out of control, and he was temporarily suspended at one time for smashing up some of the furniture with his walking-stick. He was noisy when drunk, and would stagger out into the street shouting odd slogans. 'Shoo, shoo, go *away* little black cat. Shoo, shoo, go *'way*, little black cat.' One night when making an appalling racket outside Balliol, an acquaintance, Cyril Connolly, asked him, 'Why do you make so much noise?' 'I shout because I am poor,' came the disconcerting reply.

By the 1920s there had arisen a mystique about drinking beer, or 'ale', deriving mainly from the example and writings of Belloc and Chesterton – 'We are of the stout South Country stuff, / That never can have good ale enough'. To get drunk on beer was English and manly, part of the good old Anglo-Saxon tradition which Evelyn had adopted with enthusiasm. For him drink was a liberation, a release of 'the hot spring of anarchy', a freedom from self-consciousness, an invitation to sexual licence, and an intoxicating path to pure enjoyment. Drunk, he was no longer responsible for his actions. Drunk, Evelyn was inventive, uninhibited and wildly, wickedly funny, the purveyor of a non-stop series of inspired comedy turns. 'There was a drinking set and I was of it,' he says in *A Little Learning*. 'We enjoyed not only drink but drunkenness.' And so he got drunk, night after night, and frequently during the day. After a bibulous Offal lunch, as the underworld's midday gatherings came to be called, while the others would go out to the river or playing fields, Evelyn stayed behind. Back they would come at five for tea and anchovy toast, glowing with the effects of fresh air and exercise, and there would be Evelyn, still in his armchair in front of the fire, purple in the face, heat blotches on the backs of his hands, still drinking. During his first year he wrote to Driberg, 'Do let me most seriously advise you to take to drink. There is nothing like the aesthetic pleasure of being drunk and if you do it in the right way you can avoid being ill next day. That is the greatest thing Oxford has to teach.' In fact Evelyn was frequently sick but, fastidious as ever, would beg his companions to leave him as he could not bear the indignity of being seen to vomit.

It was during drinking sessions at the Hypocrites' Club, 'that noisy alcohol-soaked rat-warren by the river', as Claud Cockburn lovingly described it, where very strong beer cost only eight pence a pint, that Evelyn met many of the men who became his friends, and remained so long after university days had passed: Richard Pares, David and Richard Plunket Greene, that rakish Restoration figure Alfred Duggan, Hugh Lygon (Lord Elmley's sweet-faced younger brother), Anthony Powell, Tony Bushell, Christopher Hollis and the combative, difficult Robert Byron, famous for the passion with which he held to his prejudices and for his uncanny resemblance to the widowed Queen Victoria. There were also John Sutro, an ugly, baby-faced boy with a genius for mimicry, and David Talbot Rice, a studious young man engaged in the unusual pursuit of courting a female undergraduate, Tamara Abelson, a beautiful Russian girl at St Anne's, whom he was later to marry. In *A Little Learning*, Evelyn observes that there were three men among his acquaintance whom 'I did not greatly like but whom, in my innocence, I was proud to know'. These were Basil Murray, Peter Rodd and Brian Howard, all of whom were to make notable contributions to characters in Evelyn's fiction. Murray and Rodd, handsome, clever and delinquent, provided the inspiration for that bad buccaneer, Basil Seal; while the third, Brian Howard, a precocious and affected young man of striking beauty and an elegance that verged on the abnormal, acted as part-model for the fascinating and degenerate Anthony Blanche in *Brideshead*. Like many another effeminate exhibitionist of that era, Howard was physically tough, riding in university grinds and hunting, even going so far as to help smash windows after a Bullingdon dinner. From that time on, all three, Howard, Murray and Rodd, began 'to barge about in the corridors of Mr Waugh's early fancy', as V. S. Pritchett later described it.

Evelyn had introduced to the Hypocrites' Club another friend, met at a lecture given by G. K. Chesterton to a Catholic group at the Newman Society, a man who was one of the most charis-

matic figures of that Oxford era, Harold Acton. On the surface
no two people could have been less alike than Acton and Waugh:
Waugh, small and stocky, with his pugnacious insularity, his artsy-
craftsy liking for Lovat Fraser and Eric Gill, above all with his
beery exuberance; and the tall, elegant, widely-travelled, precocious and sophisticated Acton. Although educated at Eton,
Acton was far from typically English. His mother was American,
his father a wealthy art dealer with a great villa in Florence. As a
child Harold had moved regularly between Chicago and Italy; to
him baroque and rococo were familiar domestic styles; he knew
Geneva and St Moritz as well as he did London; spoke Italian as
seamlessly as he did English – although about his English, it was
thought, there was something indefinably foreign? perhaps a lack
of inflection, vowels too exquisitely enunciated? 'Oh my de-ar,'
he was heard to say as he passed a group of rowdy rowing men,
'we are so dec-a-dent, and they are so in-no-cent.' A man of
discernment, a true arbiter of taste, he was an enthusiast of the
modernist movement, a devotee of Eliot, the Sitwells, Gertrude
Stein and Ezra Pound. In reaction against the last frail exhalations
of art nouveau and the bluff rusticity of the Georgians, he had
innovated a craze for that then most unfashionable period, the
early Victorian. His rooms in Christ Church, painted lemon
yellow, were decorated with artificial flowers and wax fruit under
glass, and he himself, sporting long side-whiskers and rarely seen
without a rolled umbrella, had perfected a sartorial imitation of
the Victorian dandy, in grey bowler, silk stock, black velvet jacket
and voluminous check trousers. With his jade-smooth skin (he
was rumoured to use face cream at night) and seal-sleek black
hair, there was something oriental about his appearance, an effect
emphasised by a mandarin manner and the grey silk kimono
which he habitually wore as a dressing-gown.

Evelyn, always drawn to the dandy element, as at Lancing he
had been drawn to Roxburgh and Crease, was fascinated by this
affected and exotic person with his wit, his precocity, his knowledge of the world and his passion for modern poetry. Acton had
published a slim volume, *Aquarium*, in red-, black- and yellow-
striped cover, and it was he who introduced Evelyn to the novels
of Firbank and the poetry of Edith Sitwell. The two men shared
a love of literature, of frivolity, of the world's theatre of the
absurd. Harold Acton leaning out of his window in Christ Church

reciting 'The Waste Land' through a megaphone to a League of Nations garden party was the sort of performance that appealed to Evelyn. And Acton, one of those 'who did not fret for female society', for his part found Waugh disquietingly attractive with his charm, his dangerous energy, and those 'wide-apart eyes and curved sensual lips'. A faun, a little prancing faun, was how Acton whimsically portrayed Evelyn in his *Memoirs*, inscribing a copy of his poems to, '*Le faune d'un après-midi ou de plusieurs.*' ('I think much of it excellent,' Evelyn guardedly told Carew.) Acton was so taken with his new friend that, overcoming his distaste for rowdy male company, he would glide over to Hertford at lunch-time to sit fastidiously sipping a glass of water while Evelyn and the underworld cheerfully knocked back their beer and scoffed their bread and cheese.

The friendship with Harold Acton was important both aesthetically and socially, laying open regions of which Evelyn had had little experience. As both innovator and iconoclast, and a considerable wit, Harold had a great deal to offer. It was Harold, for instance, who brought to Evelyn's attention the work of T. S. Eliot and Gertrude Stein; it was Harold who introduced him to the Sitwells, taking him to the first public performance of *Façade* at the Aeolian Hall on 12 June 1923, and afterwards to a party at Osbert Sitwell's house in Carlyle Square, where among others Evelyn met Lytton Strachey, Clive Bell, Eugene Goossens and Ada Leverson. It was through Harold, too, that Evelyn came to know the eccentric John Fothergill, proprietor of the Spread Eagle, an old inn at Thame a few miles from Oxford with a reputation for good food and a relaxed attitude towards untrammelled behaviour. Fothergill had taken to inn-keeping in middle age, having failed to make a living as an art dealer and historian, and was now absorbed in the theatrical production of his new rôle, driving about in a dog-cart to deliver orders to the local tradesmen dressed in a costume of his own devising of knee-length white coat and buckled shoes. An associate of Oscar Wilde and Augustus John, the snobbish, irascible Fothergill was as sympathetic to the extravagances of Acton and his friends as he was contemptuous of most of his more conventional customers: he once added sixpence a head to a bill because he thought the party so ugly. Capable of appalling rudeness to guests he considered common or insufficiently appreciative, Fothergill was a good friend to those he considered worthy of his friendship; those he liked could get away with anything. For Lord Elmley's twenty-first birthday a dinner was given at Thame for fifty or sixty young men, including the entire membership of the Hypocrites' Club. Elmley, in a purple dress suit, himself provided the champagne, Harold made a learned speech about the beauties of the male body, Evelyn got silently drunk, Robert Byron festooned in lace passed out, and the night ended in wild dancing, persimmons thrown against the wall, and couples passionately embracing in the hearse Fothergill kept in the room next door.

Evelyn owed Acton a debt, acknowledged in the dedication of his first novel, *Decline and Fall*,[9] not only for extending his horizons but for recognising and encouraging his talent, steering him away from Lovat Fraser and Francis Crease, 'that nice old maid', and giving him the confidence to rely more on his own artistic judgment. Most important, it was Acton who encouraged him to write, commissioning a short story for his own publication, the *Oxford Broom*. But although the friendship endured, there was always at its centre a small residue of unease. For one thing, although Evelyn was dazzled and fascinated by this bird of paradise with his daring and display, he soon saw that it was the plumage that was brilliant, and that Acton's gifts as a writer were unremarkable. There was, too, the embarrassment of Evelyn's inability to reciprocate Acton's amorous interest, and Harold's consequent jealousy of some of Evelyn's relationships with other men.

> Please forgive me if I said what was in my mind about 'R. I. P.' last night. Truth will out, I suppose, in spite of the fact that I had tried hard not to hurt your feelings or to 'sneer' . . .
>
> At any rate, it was plain as daylight to me that you were beginning to think I was 'bloody awful' from the marvellous expression of complete boredom you managed to sustain on your face whenever you were with me, although, God knows, I have attempted to dispel it.
>
> You are, as I have said before, a faun, but I had never credited you with the fantastic whimsies of a faun, nor with the enigmas of one; now I do . . .

*

[9] 'To Harold Acton in Homage and Affection'.

R. I. P. was Richard Pares, a history scholar at Balliol, and the subject of Evelyn's first love affair. With fair hair and blue eyes, Pares, son of Sir Bernard Pares, the great authority on Russia, Professor of Russian at London University, was unusually good-looking in a girlish, Pre-Raphaelite way. Having repulsed the many offers that had been made him at Winchester, once at Oxford he had embarked like Evelyn on a period of sexual experiment. Oxford in the 1920s was a masculine world. The few women undergraduates were rarely glimpsed, and men who felt the need for female companionship usually went to London to find it – the last train back from Paddington was known as the 'Flying Fornicator'. Most of these young men, Pares and Waugh among them, were still emotionally immature. Accustomed to the all-male society of their public schools, they continued to find their friends and sometimes lovers within the confines of that same society, translated unchanging from school to university.

The affair almost certainly began in the summer term of 1922 when Evelyn was clearly happy, reporting to Tom Driberg that 'Life here is very beautiful. Mayonnaise and punts and cider cup all day long.' In June he wrote to Tom, 'By the way a friend of mine up here called Pares is sending a brother to Lancing next term . . . I wonder if you could make a note of his name &, when he turns up, be kind to him.' In a letter to Evelyn written probably at the beginning of that same summer term, Richard Pares tells him, 'I have been inwardly faithful to one boy for more than two years, and he is only dispossest this morning and by you, so I think I shall be constant to you for three years and then turn a Papist. How much I shall have to confess depends on you.'

While it lasted, the affair was intense ('My dear,' Acton said of Pares's role in the relationship, '*he lends his body*'). In reply to a letter of Evelyn's during the vacation Pares wrote

> In vain that you ate the bread of carefulness for – you have
> written me a love-letter . . . I am tired of pretending not to be
> in love with you – which I have done intermittently since the
> fourth week of last term . . .
> If only there were time to bring myself to the sticking-point I
> should stride up to Hampstead Heath and in through the
> French window of your drawing-room and – well, you know what
> happens when the hero (or heroine) strides in through the

French window of the drawing-room and finds the heroine (or is it hero?) sitting on the sofa . . .

For a time the two young men were always together. It was a familiar sight in town, the pair of them with heads close, arms linked, chattering away like a couple of clever monkeys. But while Evelyn remained resolutely immature, Pares, academically brilliant, was growing up; and underneath the adolescent high spirits was very serious indeed about his work; as an article in *The Isis* put it, 'his gift for absurdity and frivolity . . . never prevented the exercise of his sterner abilities.' He also found himself unable to keep up with Evelyn's heavy and habitual drunkenness. The two of them used to go to the Hypocrites' to dance and drink, but this kind of camp debauchery was not really to Pares's taste, who at heart was something of a puritan. He had, too, a weak head, suffered badly from hangovers and did not enjoy getting drunk. Evelyn, on the other hand, found it difficult to enjoy himself without getting drunk; he wanted to get drunk at every opportunity, and anyone who could not or would not drink with him was eventually and inevitably excluded from the inner circle. 'When I felt most intimate, he felt queasy,' Evelyn recalled, 'and this made an insurmountable barrier between us.'

The relationship was further undermined by another Balliol man, Cyril Connolly ('I was cuckolded by Connolly,' Evelyn is reported to have said), who in a letter to a crony dated 23 March 1923, wrote about Richard Pares, 'I have been rather gone on him ever since Wednesday night.' Connolly and Pares began spending time in each other's company, going up to London together, attending a service at Westminster Cathedral. And it was Connolly who encouraged Pares's adoption into the circle of that elusive but powerful figure, F. F. Urquhart, dean of Balliol, known as 'Sligger'. Sligger had the distinction of being the first Roman Catholic don in Oxford since the Reformation, and his Oxford salon and the select reading parties held during the vacations in his chalet on the foothills of Mont Blanc were a byword for their combination of scholarship and ephebic exclusivity. Unsurprisingly Evelyn took violently against Sligger: not only had he helped deprive him of Pares, but it was Urquhart who was the prime mover in the shutting down of the Hypocrites' Club. The morally austere Sligger had been gunning for the

Hypocrites' for some time, his opportunity coming in March 1924 with reports of a fancy-dress party so outrageous (nuns, Lord Byron, choirboys with vermilion lips) that he was able to have the club closed by the authorities for good – after which a funeral dinner was held for members, several of whom arrived by Fothergill's hearse, at the Spread Eagle at Thame. In a stroke of demonic revenge Evelyn took to walking across the Balliol quad late at night shouting at the top of his voice to the tune of 'Nuts in May', 'The dean of Balliol lies with men! The dean of Balliol lies with men!' But Sligger knew what he was doing. Pares was exceptional material – he went on to get a first class degree and a fellowship at All Souls – and it was high time he turned back to his books and away from the broad path of self-destruction down which Evelyn was travelling with such noise and speed.

At the end of the affair in the summer of 1923 Evelyn wrote to Carew, 'I have been having one of my periodic fits of melancholy – I am ... a worthless fellow.' For both Evelyn and Pares it had been a powerful experience: years later, Pares, then married and with a family, admitted to a close friend that never in his life had he known such passionate intensity; and, significantly, both men saw fit to destroy the diaries which they had kept during that period.[10]

Evelyn's admission of moral depravity would, had he known of it, have been seconded by Alec, who visited Oxford at least once a term, and was sometimes made uneasy by the blatantly homosexual atmosphere. As always, Evelyn's attitude towards his brother was ambivalent: fond, though mildly bored by him and unimpressed by his work. 'A thoroughly sincere artist ... Mr Waugh's opinions are those of the professional writer accustomed to the chatter of literary parties rather than of the aesthetician,' Evelyn in an unsigned review in *The Cherwell* had written of an early venture by Alec in autobiography. But on the whole the brothers got on well enough. Evelyn had given a party in his first Michaelmas term for Alec to meet his friends, since when Alec had taken an interested if peripheral part in university life, con-

[10] Pares's influence remained in Evelyn's choice of vocabulary: some of Pares's favourite words are often used by Evelyn, for instance, bogus, dim, and bonhomous.

tributing occasionally to *The Isis* and inviting Evelyn and some of his chums to parties in London.

Just before Christmas 1923, Alec, now divorced from Barbara, took Evelyn to dinner at the Cave of Harmony, a nightclub in Charlotte Street run by the actress Elsa Lanchester, his other guest Joyce Fagan, a girl he was at that time unsuccessfully pursuing. Joyce, lively and adventurous, was intrigued by Evelyn's Oxford stories, and said how she wished she could see that exclusive male society for herself, but from the inside, disguised as a man. To Evelyn such an idea was irresistible. As soon as term began, he threw a party in the rooms of a graduate friend in King Edward Street to which Alec, reluctantly, brought Joyce, in his eyes shockingly transformed by plus-fours, baggy jacket and a cycling cap under which her brown hair was slicked down with brilliantine. When at the end of the evening the proctors, attracted by the noise and scenting trouble, arrived to break up the party and take names, Joyce, lowering her voice, successfully passed herself off as 'Terence Greenidge, Hertford College'. For Evelyn the whole episode had been exciting and amusing; but Alec had found the ambience distastefully 'degenerate', and Joyce suddenly repellent in her boy's attire.

Tony Bushell, another Hertford man and friend of Evelyn's, said that he had never once seen Waugh open a book that had any relevance to the syllabus he was meant to be following. But although he may have left untouched the key texts of Representative Government, Evelyn was reading widely and involving himself energetically in several of the university's undergraduate 'professions'. Unlike his father, he showed no interest in joining any of the dramatic societies, preferring to confine his acting to private life, although he did enjoy taking part in debates at the Union, which in its way was as much high performance art as anything produced by the OUDS. He made his maiden speech in June 1922, and quickly established a reputation as an entertaining if lightweight speaker. Never in the same class as such outstanding orators as Douglas Woodruff, Christopher Hollis, Gerald Gardiner and Alec Douglas-Home, he nevertheless acquitted himself entertainingly, and his participation was reported humorously and with relish. Already skilful in playing to an audience, Evelyn turned up for a debate on King and Country wearing a Union

Jack waistcoat, which caused a sensation, and, as in later life, his expressed opinions were deliberately perverse. On the motion that 'the time has come when the enmities engendered by the war should give way to a friendly attitude towards all the peoples that fought under the Central Powers', Mr E. A. St J. Waugh (Hertford) 'said that this was purely a question of public sentiment, which could only be settled by the Man in the Street, an individual whom he claimed to represent, and indeed, boldly asserted that he was the only Man in the Street present'; 'that this House regrets that the population of England has come to exceed five millions', Mr E. A. St J. Waugh (Hertford) 'expressed his surprise at anyone being found to oppose the motion, and his conviction that the lives of the great majority of people in England were not worth living'; 'that the introduction of Prohibition would benefit this country', Mr E. A. St J. Waugh (Hertford) 'supported the motion because he was a Conservative and he thought Prohibition ought to be a Conservative principle'.

It was the performance, not the politics, which was the point for Evelyn, and the dignified setting, and the men in their white ties and tail-coats. He liked club life, too, and belonged impartially both to the Carlton (Conservative) in George Street and to the New Reform (Liberal) in the Cornmarket, as well as to the Chatham and to the White Rose, a dining club which existed to promote the Stuart cause. But he was never seriously interested in politics, and his political understanding was and remained simplistic and immature. Politics were rarely discussed at Underhill, regarded as 'at best a technical question in economics, at worst a mere accumulation of gossip about thoroughly boring individuals'. Largely through indifference Evelyn had adopted similar views to his father, a middle-of-the-road Tory who detested Lord Northcliffe on the one hand and Lloyd George on the other, was ignorant of social questions, and bored by economics and foreign affairs. As the prevailing climate at Oxford was then very much left of centre, it naturally suited Evelyn to assume the rôle of die-hard Conservative. 'I proclaimed myself a Tory but could not have defined Tory policy on any current topic,' he says in *A Little Learning*. 'I was as little concerned with the outcome of affairs of Westminster as with the Stuart restoration.'

Evelyn's other and much greater interest was in journalism. He reported Union debates for the *Oxford Fortnightly Review*, and contributed regularly to both *The Cherwell* and *The Isis*. He wrote articles, including an adulatory pen portrait of Acton and a rather less adulatory one of Cruttwell ('a badger-like figure, clad in ancient tail-coat and lop-sided white tie'); for a few weeks reviewed films under the heading 'Seen in the Dark', until he was obliged to desist because his notices were so vituperative that the managers of the local cinemas refused to allow him any more complimentary tickets; and adopting the pseudonym 'Scaramel' wrote light verse and short stories in which his fascination for madness, murder and the grotesque is consistently evident. In 'Conspiracy to Murder', for instance, there is a sinister don who knows nobody, speaks to nobody, spends hours sitting alone in the dark, and whose apparently homicidal intentions drive to insanity the young man living opposite him. The don, 'a strange shambling man of middle age ... ill-dressed and rather dirty', bears a not inconsiderable resemblance to a familiar badger-like figure.

But Cruttwell's most notable appearance is as Mr Curtis, the murdered history tutor in 'Edward of Unique Achievement'. Twice in his life, once at the beginning, once at the end,[11] Evelyn wrote a story that was an almost naked expression of personal wish-fulfilment. Here his loathing of and contempt for Cruttwell and a desire for his hideous end are given full rein. It is Edward who hates his tutor: 'Edward hated him with an absorbing and unmeasurable hatred, so that at last he became convinced that Mr Curtis' existence was not compatible with his own'; and Edward who kills him, although the blame is fixed on Lord Poxe, a stupid young nobleman; but he, on account of the authorities' respect for aristocratic status, gets off with a fine of thirteen shillings. 'Among tradesmen and dons he [Poxe] had always found his title of vast value.' Not content with Mr Curtis's dim nonentity, his horrid murder, a faked postmortem by a dissolute doctor who 'earned an irregular livelihood performing operations in North Oxford', and a funeral that was 'brief and ill-attended', Evelyn throws in as finale a brief bravura passage of sexual degradation, in which the Warden's wife, hearing the news, falls to her knees and pours out 'a tale of the most monstrous and unsuspected transactions between herself and Mr Curtis'.

[11] In *Basil Seal Rides Again* (1963), in which Basil prevents the marriage of his much-loved daughter to an objectionable young man.

It was to Harold Acton's short-lived *Oxford Broom,* for which he had designed covers for two out of its three numbers, that Evelyn contributed a morbid short story entitled 'Antony, Who Sought Things That Were Lost'.[12] Written in the mannered style of a Wildean pastiche, it tells the tale of two highly born lovers incarcerated in a squalid cell and watched over by a pox-marked turnkey. Gradually the Lady Elizabeth's love for Count Antony turns to hate as she becomes possessed by lust for her gaoler; 'and so the Lady Elizabeth, who had known the white arms of Antony, loved this turnkey who was ugly and low born'. For Antony, a noble soul who would die for his love's sake, the sight of his lady in the embrace of such a man is unbearable. Weak though he is and weighed down by his chains, he drags himself up from his bed of filthy straw: 'there was pain in him which raised him from his corner . . . between his hands was the heavy chain and he stretched it across her throat . . . the pain lent him strength and he prevailed; . . . thus the lady [sic] Elizabeth died . . .' The story's vocabulary emphasises the motif of disease, of sexual depravity and desolation. It was written in the early summer of 1923, at approximately the same time that Evelyn was writing to Dudley Carew about the end of his affair with Pares, 'I am depressed . . . [and] quite incredibly depraved morally . . . Believe me my dear Carey I have quite lost all self respect.'

Self-respect may have gone, but not a sense of humour. At about the same time and in very different mood, Evelyn began a column for *The Isis* entitled 'Children's Corner', in which, under the pseudonym 'Uncle Alfred',[13] he gives 'advice' to his readers in typically ironic vein: 'There is no harm in thoroughly enjoying our food – we must not "love it", of course, and we must always remember that there is no sauce like hunger sauce, and that a crust in the desert is nicer than a meringue in a teashop . . .' The column was not only comic, and with its mock-childishness very much in tune with the times, but it also gives a foretaste of the brilliant parodic dialogues of the early novels, the private jokes

---

[12] Harold Acton expressed himself pleased with the story at the time, but many years later admitted that his judgment had been at fault. 'Evelyn was particularly dear to me at the time he wrote "Antony" – I was under his elvish fascination – so it seemed rather better than it was in fact.'

[13] But in his last term continued in *The Cherwell* under the nom-de-plume 'Uncle Julius'.

and inventive infantilism used to such effect with some of Evelyn's future correspondents, in particular members of the Lygon family.

> Dear Uncle Julius, . . . We have a blak cat caled Sidny here and two cerneries called Kit and Spit . . . Sidny . . . was sik on the drawing-rum carpit . . . Charlie and i gave him som carster oil to mak him well, but he was sik *again*! . . . Uncle Gussie can play the Robba's Marsh on the piano, but Auntie dus not like it, cos it is vulgar and only plays Goono. Her favrit peace is Nasareth, she plays it on the hamoanyom in cherch.
>   Well I must stop now. Lots of love and kisses, From Gladys.

> Dear Uncle Julius, I feel I must write to thank you for your <u>delightful</u> gift of jujubes for my little girl . . . The parcel caused <u>immense</u> excitement, and we were all very much <u>amused</u> to find that the label was addressed to G. Hunter Blair,[14] Esq!!!!!! and as Gladys is only nine next month, we all <u>roared</u> till our sides quite <u>ached</u>! . . .
>   With many thanks, I beg to subscribe myself, Yours sincerely, Annie Hunter Blair.

Funny though this is, there was little at this stage to indicate that Evelyn's literary talents were anything remarkable. Yet with hindsight one has only to look at the early publications of some of his contemporaries to see how superior his were. Alec, Terence Greenidge and Christopher Hollis were feeble in comparison, and the three notable Oxford poets of the day – Harold Acton, Peter Quennell and Brian Howard – all as poets came to nothing.

Nevertheless, at Oxford Evelyn had a greater reputation as a graphic artist than as a writer, and as such was much in demand, designing covers for magazines, for OUDS programmes, book jackets for Chapman & Hall, and for the caricatures with which he had been so successful at Lancing, when he had bartered satirical sketches for cream slices and halfpenny stamps. During one vacation he took lessons in wood-engraving, after which he made bookplates for friends – Richard Pares's was a duck standing under a pear tree in front of a rising sun; Alec's a cricketer, a cupid and the Waugh family crest – and sold a number of prints to J. C. Squire for the *London Mercury* and to Clifford Bax for his

---

[14] In the previous issue a J. W. Hunter Blair had savagely attacked the quality of reviewing of *The Cherwell* music critic, Keith Douglas.

short-lived publication, the *Golden Hind.* Under Acton's influence
he developed a harsher, bolder technique. He went to classes in
nude life drawing at the Ruskin School of Art in Oxford, together
with a man from Balliol whom he had met with the Jacobses at
Berkhamsted, Peter Quennell. He exhibited to high praise twice
at the Oxford Arts Club, for *The Isis* did some queer illustrations
on the theme of drink (Beer, Brandy, Angostura and Soda), and
for *The Cherwell* made an extraordinary and disturbing series of
woodcuts, *The Seven Deadly Sins,* whose titles alone read like a
synopsis of an early Waugh novel: 'The Intolerable Wickedness
of Him who Drinks Alone', 'The Horrid Sacrilege of Those that
Ill-Treat Books', 'The Wanton Ways of Those that Corrupt the
Very Young', 'The Hideous Habit of Marrying Negroes', 'That
Dull, Old Sin Adultery', 'The Grave Discourtesy of Such a Man
as will Beat his Host's Servant', and 'That Grim Act Parricide'.

With life during term so full of interest and new experience it
was predictable that Evelyn should find the vacations at home
dreary and dispiriting. Golders Green was not enhanced by the
perspective of Oxford. To Evelyn's dismay, the postal address of
145 North End Road had recently been changed from
Hampstead to Golders Green; he now had to walk as far as the
Bull & Bush to post letters so that they would be franked with
the Hampstead postmark. After the stimulus and sophistication
of the university, Underhill was an embarrassment and a bore.
While Harold Acton was declaiming 'The Waste Land' from his
window, Arthur was dismissing Eliot's work as 'premature decrepitude', Pound's verse as 'wooden prose', and the poetry of the
entire modernist movement as 'unmetrical, incoherent banalit-
ies'. In a letter to Tom Driberg from Underhill during his first
vacation of Easter 1922, Evelyn talks of the 'melancholy mania'
with which he is afflicted in the company of his family. 'I hardly
know how I shall live through the next ten days until I go up.'
    Certainly the atmosphere was not easy. Alec and Barbara had
separated, and Alec was living at home. Now employed at Chapman & Hall, he was not getting on as well as usual with his
father. Their attraction had always been that of opposites, Arthur
passionate and impulsive, Alec, like his mother, careful and controlled. Attempting to work in tandem, the two men got on
each other's nerves. Alec found the work tedious and Arthur's

dictatorial methods maddening. The firm, too, was showing signs of instability. The lucrative Dickens copyright had expired two years earlier and profits were running steadily downhill, a decline for which Arthur felt he should stand responsible. The future worried him, and his mood was not improved by the presence of his younger son sulking about the house penniless and resentful, sighing heavily at his father's favourite anecdotes, and clearly counting the days until he could go back to Oxford. Like Charles Ryder's father in *Brideshead*, Arthur had assumed the attributes of a much older man, a pose that irritated Evelyn immensely.

> He was then in his late fifties, but it was his idiosyncrasy to seem much older than his years; to see him one might have put him at seventy, to hear him speak at nearly eighty. He came to me now, with the shuffling, mandarin-tread which he affected, and a shy smile of welcome. When he dined at home – and he seldom dined elsewhere – he wore a frogged velvet smoking suit of the kind which had been fashionable many years before and was to be so again, but, at that time, was a deliberate archaism.

The readings-aloud in the bookroom after dinner were, too, a source of acute suffering, as Arthur emoted his way through Pinero or gave jocular renderings from Gilbert and Sullivan. Evelyn saw something of his Lancing cronies, Carew and Molson, and a friend from Balliol, Christopher Hollis; but even that was not wholly a success. Carew, who liked and admired Arthur, was embarrassed by Evelyn's obvious irritation with him, and Molson was frankly appalled at his insolence. On one occasion in Molson's presence, Arthur made the mistake of enquiring in an injured tone how it was that Evelyn could be so charming to his friends and so unkind to his father. 'Because', came the bored reply, 'I can choose my friends, but I cannot choose my father.'

Christopher Hollis, a lifelong friend, was one of the many young men of that Oxford generation, so destabilised by the First World War, who became converts to Roman Catholicism, among them Graham Greene, Billy Clonmore, Giles Isham, Robert Speaight and Frank Pakenham. Hollis's father was an Anglican bishop, but his son having, like Evelyn, been through a period of calf piety in childhood, turned sceptic at Oxford. This was not unusual: the university chaplain, Monsignor Barnes, used to say that all young men give up religion at eighteen to return to it at

twenty-three. Just as at Lancing Evelyn had been fascinated by
the unswerving belief of his friend Longe, so was he now
by Hollis's determined quest for faith; although immediately
before Hollis in his early twenties was received into the Roman
Church, Evelyn was the only one of his acquaintance who tried
to dissuade him. Evelyn made a point of flaunting a particularly
aggressive brand of muscular agnosticism, always ready furiously
to debate and if possible shoot down the claims of Christianity.
'There is far too much religion in this University', he wrote to
Dudley Carew, and to Tom Driberg, '[I] never go to Chapel.' Yet
he remained very aware of religion, going to hear Chesterton
lecture to the Newman Society, Dean Inge preach at the university
church, and reading and rereading *The Pilgrim's Progress*. As always,
Evelyn was embroiled in the conflict between the asceticism and
detachment demanded by the religious life and the sensual self-
indulgence of the worldly, a conflict embodied in the person to
whom more than any other he now became deeply attached, a
young man named Alastair Graham.

Although Evelyn in his autobiography gives barely a page to
Graham, whom he calls Hamish Lennox, their relationship was
important, and his description of Alastair as 'the friend of my
heart' was no exaggeration. 'For two or three years', he says, 'we
were inseparable.'

Alastair Graham, nearly a year younger than Evelyn, was the
only surviving son of the younger brother of a Borders baronet,
an unashamed philistine who had no time for books or scholarship and spent his entire year, when not hunting and shooting,
salmon fishing in Scotland and Norway. Alastair's father had died
a year before he came up to Oxford, leaving Alastair and a much
older sister, Sibyl, in the care of their mother. Mrs Graham, born
Jessie Low, was the daughter of a cotton merchant from Savannah,
Georgia. Jolly, quick-tempered and energetic, she was fiercely
possessive of her son, who seemed designed to disappoint her in
almost every respect. In 1917 the Grahams had bought a house at
Barford in Warwickshire, a location chosen solely for its excellent
hunting. Alastair never hunted. Mrs Graham built on to the house
a large ballroom for Alastair's coming-of-age. The party never
took place. Under her management the house ran on oiled
wheels, and she worked hard at the garden, weeding and pruning
and rushing up ladders to cut down ivy from the clock tower. 'I

only keep this place going for Alastair,' she used to say. But he could rarely be persuaded to spend any time there and made no secret of his intention to get rid of Barford as soon as it became his. Alastair, who never cared for London and London society, loved the country, but he loved it as a place of refuge, uninterested in any of the traditional sporting or agricultural pursuits of the country gentleman. He loved lying in the garden, or wandering through the fields looking for edible fungi, or dreamily picnicking in a secluded wood, unproductive and time-wasting occupations which sent Mrs Graham into a frenzy of frustration. It was the same with his education. Alastair was bookish, and much had been expected of him. But he left Wellington ('ran away', according to family legend) before he was sixteen and was sent down from Oxford in only his second year.

Alastair was entirely unlike anyone Evelyn had met before. Small and good-looking, with a pale face and brown hair, he was both indolent and reclusive, indifferent to the material world, ascetic but at the same time profoundly sensual. He was, too, intriguingly elusive, and would silently disappear for days in pursuit of some genealogical project, an interest which he had inherited from an uncle, wandering round churchyards and copying coats of arms off ancient family tombs. This love of the past appealed strongly to the romantic in Evelyn, as did Alastair's languor, the impression he gave of *fin de race* etiolation, his air of decadence and melancholy. His sweet nature and a tone of flirtatious whimsy which he adopted when amorous made him all the more irresistible. In *A Little Learning* Evelyn says of him, 'I could not have fallen under an influence better designed to encourage my natural frivolity, dilettantism and dissipation or to expose as vulgar and futile any promptings I may have felt to worldly ambition.'

Graham arrived at Brasenose in the Michaelmas term of 1922. It is uncertain exactly when he and Evelyn met, although they knew each other well enough for Evelyn to bring Alastair to stay for the first time at Underhill in December 1923.[15] A number of Evelyn's friends later remarked that during Waugh's last year at the university they remembered seeing very little of him, that he

[15] In a diary entry for Christmas Day 1924, Evelyn notes that 'strangely enough my few romances have always culminated in Christmas week – Luned, Richard, Alastair'.

seemed to have withdrawn almost entirely from his old haunts and his old companions. In fact he had withdrawn with Alastair into a private world, each desiring only the company of the other. Unlike Richard Pares, Alastair 'had no repugnance to the bottle', as Evelyn put it, 'and we drank deep together', driving about the countryside from pub to pub in Alastair's little car, or else during long evenings in each other's rooms in college. In an undated letter from this period, enclosing a photograph of himself naked, Alastair wrote

> I have found the ideal way to drink Burgundy. You must take a peach and peel it, and put it in a finger bowl, and pour the Burgundy over it. The flavour is exquisite. And the peach seems to exaggerate that delightful happy Seraglio contendedness that old wine evokes . . .
>
> I don't know whether I ought to come to Oxford or not next week. It depends on money and other little complications. If I come, will you come and drink with me somewhere on Saturday? If it is a nice day we might carry some bottles into a wood or some bucolic place, and drink like Horace . . .
>
> I wish you felt merrier, and were not so serious.
>
> With love from Alastair, and his poor dead heart

In *Brideshead*, Sebastian Flyte says seductively to Charles Ryder, 'I've got a motor-car and a basket of strawberries and a bottle of Château Peyraguey – which isn't a wine you've ever tasted, so don't pretend. It's heaven with strawberries.'

This was a time for Evelyn of complete emotional and sensual fulfilment. He neither needed nor wanted anyone but Alastair. The two men were rarely apart and when they were remained in daily contact by letter. It is from this time that there was born in Evelyn the nostalgic and romantic image of Oxford to which he was to give such heady expression twenty years later in *Brideshead Revisited*.[16] It was the memory of this period that was to engender in his imagination the picture of a past Golden Age to which he always longed to return, to find again the little door in the wall leading to the paradise garden, a magical illusion for ever unattainable, which was powerfully to epitomise the sense of loss from which he suffered with such anguish in later life. For Alast-

[16] In the manuscript of *Brideshead Revisited*, Evelyn has more than once inadvertently written the name Alastair for Sebastian.

air, too, by nature a recluse, the hidden garden had an almost mythic significance, as he made clear in one of his letters to his lover. 'All the beautiful things that I have seen heard or thought of, grow like bright flowers and musky herbs in a garden where I can enjoy their presence, and where I can sit in peace and banish the unpleasant things of life. A kind of fortified retreat that no one can enter except myself.'

The Grahams' house at Barford also played its part in Evelyn's development. It was no Brideshead, not a noble pile in a land-scaped park, but an attractive, early nineteenth-century family house. Surrounded by a wall of weathered brick, it stands just off the main road into Barford village in the flat, agricultural country (so wonderful for hunting) between Warwick and Stratford-upon-Avon. The house, faced in white stucco, had a library, a conservatory, pilasters on either side of the front door, and a glass cupola on the roof. There were stables, and a garden with lawns, box hedges, a fish-pond and a stone gazebo. If it was not Brideshead, neither was it Underhill. Barford had claims to elegance and a kind of shabby, small-scale grandeur with which Evelyn was not familiar and which served to provide him with a form of trans-ition, an ideal introduction to the sort of upper-class, country-house life which he had yet to encounter but which was to exercise a potent and lifelong fascination.

When Evelyn met Alastair's mother, he took to her at once. Although bossy and quick-tempered, Jessie Graham was a good-natured woman, and Evelyn found her particular brand of eccentricity entertaining, using her later as a model for Lady Circumference in *Decline and Fall* and Mrs Kent-Cumberland in 'Winner Takes All'.[17] 'Mrs G' was perfectly easy to get on with, except when in the presence of her children: both Sibyl and 'Ali' took a delight in baiting her, and when either was at home there were constant, noisy rows. If there was one thing Mrs Graham could not abide it was idleness, especially in the young, and she made repeated and determined efforts to get Evelyn and Alastair out-side working in the garden. But they were adept at avoiding her.

[17] The Graham connection provided material for two other fictional characters: Jessie Graham's sister married Charles Guthrie of Craigie, and his sister was Lady Rennell of Rodd, mother of Peter Rodd, on whom Evelyn partially modelled Basil Seal; Lady Rennell was the main inspiration for the formidable Lady Montdore in Nancy Mitford's *Love in a Cold Climate*.

She tried, too, to enlist Evelyn's help in persuading her beloved boy to cut down on his drinking, which was beginning seriously to alarm her, but Evelyn was unresponsive to her pleas.

Naturally not all Evelyn's friends approved of the alliance. Harold Acton, as jealous of Graham as he had been of Pares, was wholeheartedly against it, describing Graham as a 'cock-tease', who disastrously encouraged Evelyn's already prodigious consumption of alcohol. And if Evelyn were inclined to idleness, Alastair did no work at all. Apart from playing in a couple of OUDS productions, he took little interest in the life of the university, and in his second year was sent down for failing his Preliminary examinations. Not to be beaten, Mrs Graham enrolled him in an architectural course in London which he abandoned without having attended a single class. She then sent him to the Shakespeare Head Press in Stratford to learn printing, but nothing much came of that either. Alastair preferred to drift; and Evelyn, as far as he was able, drifted with him.

Evelyn was due to sit his Finals in June 1924. In *A Little Learning* he says that at the beginning of this third year, realising that 'I was doing no good at my books, I wrote to my father asking to be taken away and sent to Paris,' a request which Arthur unhesitatingly turned down, insisting that Evelyn stay where he was, do some work and get a decent degree. In fact Evelyn, possibly alarmed by the direction in which his involvement with Alastair was taking him, had been in a state of much greater turmoil than his later recollection allows. 'My life here has been extremely precarious', he wrote to Carew.

> At present I am keeping my balance but I may crash any moment . . . I have been living very intensely the last three weeks. For the last fortnight I have been nearly insane. I am a little saner now . . . I may perhaps one day in a later time tell you some of the things that have happened . . .
>
> I want to go down for good but I cannot explain and my parents are obdurate.

Part of the trouble, if only part, was financial. Evelyn was by this time seriously in debt. His scholarship was worth £100 per annum, his allowance from his father £220, with a further £50 to be counted on from Christmas and birthday presents. This was not an unreasonable income on which to live. Evelyn did not run with the rich, and during his vacations stayed thriftily, if resentfully, at Underhill. The Oxford tradesmen were notoriously lax about credit: huge bills could be run up over long periods, but in the end they had to be paid. And Evelyn had cultivated some expensive tastes. He had developed a liking for a brand of Egyptian cigarettes called Vagiadis ('God made them in his own image', he told Driberg. 'Profound subtle and immeasurably satisfying . . . passing the love of boys.'). He spent generously on drink, ate often in restaurants – the most popular was the George, which with its band, punkahs and palm trees was the domain of the aesthete set led by Acton and Brian Howard and known as 'the Georgeoisie' – and four or five times a term gave a luncheon party in his rooms, elaborate meals ordered specially from the excellent Hertford chef. Although he was never able to afford the sartorial extravagances of the great dandies, with their Egyptian dressing-gowns, heliotrope silk shirts, their Carlsbad hats lined with hare's fur and their jade-coloured motor mufflers, Evelyn regularly overspent at Hall's, the university tailors in the High. At Hall's he bespoke well-tailored suits, soft tweeds and strikingly coloured waistcoats, his most expensive order being for a dress suit with silk facings costing £19; his hand-woven ties he bought from a shop in Dorchester, and at the end of his last term, following the fashion set by Harold Acton, he and Alastair both bought grey bowler hats, reduced to half price in Hall's sale. Books and beautiful bindings too were a matter of necessity to Evelyn. But so was finding the money to pay for them. In desperation at the beginning of 1924 he held an auction in his rooms and sold almost his entire library, at the same time moving into the cheapest and dingiest quarters the college bursar could provide. The bank having stopped his overdraft, Evelyn borrowed from his mother, from Alec, and £100 from Terence Greenidge whom he paid back at the rate of £5 a year. Even so he went down with debts of over £200, which took him another four years to clear.

Among undergraduates who had done insufficient work there was a consoling and popular tradition, based on the example of F. E. Smith, that three weeks' intensive study after three years of idleness was enough to obtain a first-class degree. Unfortunately the great Smith's methods worked only for Smith. An old Lancing acquaintance, Christopher Chamberlin, met Evelyn on top of a bus one morning in the week before Schools. Evelyn was far from sober and, apologising for this, explained that he was working like fury twenty-four hours a day and it was only by drinking that he could keep awake all night. In the event he came away with a third and a reproving letter from Mr Cruttwell informing him that the college would not be renewing his scholarship for the further term which would complete the nine terms necessary to qualify for a degree. 'I cannot say that your 3rd does you any thing but discredit,' wrote the old enemy. 'I hope that you will soon settle into some sphere where you will give your intellect a better chance than in the History School'; a letter which in the circumstances, although acid in flavour, cannot be considered entirely unreasonable. But to its recipient it was an act of blatant hostility: not only were Evelyn's hopes of a respectable grade disappointed, but so too were his plans for a final term of 'pure pleasure', for which he had already engaged to share rooms in Merton Street with Hugh Lygon.

On 29 July Evelyn returned to the Examination Schools for his Viva Voce dressed in the regulation white tie, dark jacket and scholar's black gown, and fortified by a large whisky. On the way he stopped at a jeweller's in the High Street and bought a ring for Alastair. The Viva, as he had known it would be, was the merest formality. Afterwards all that was left was for him to telegraph the news to Underhill and contemplate his miserable situation, a prospect of 'heart-breaking dreariness . . . with bills, over-fastidious tastes and a completely hopeless future'.

Teaching the mad boys

The first three months after leaving Oxford were heavily overcast by the imminence of Alastair's departure for Kenya. In the face of furious opposition from his mother, who hated the idea, Alastair had accepted an invitation to spend the winter with his sister Sibyl, now living there with her husband. For Evelyn the prospect was dismal: he was in despair at Alastair leaving and had no idea what to do with his future. In the time that was left the two men were rarely apart, moving aimlessly between London, Oxford and Barford. One entire Saturday they spent at Paddington Station, drinking, eating buns and watching the trains pull in and out. From London they went to the Empire Exhibition at Wembley, to Kew Gardens and Hampton Court. In Oxford there was an extended pub crawl with Richard Plunket Greene and David Talbot Rice, which ended in quarrels and broken glass. To escape Mrs Graham, they rented a squalid little caravan parked in the garden of the Abingdon Arms, a pub at Beckley, a village just outside Oxford, and here Evelyn spent what he described as one of the most wretched days of his life – rain leaking through the roof, Alastair in bed with a hangover, he himself reduced to reading Gibbon alone in a nearby church. The next day, after a drunken binge again with Richard Plunket Greene, Evelyn returned to the caravan to find Alastair snugly ensconced, and 'strangely enough Joyce Fagan, who had slept the night there'.

In August, and in direct defiance of Mrs Graham who wanted her son at home, Evelyn and Alastair left on a walking tour in Ireland. It was not an enjoyable excursion: neither had much money – they had passed the hat round at Barford before leaving and managed to raise £10 – the hotels were shabby and uncomfortable, the food poor and the beer 'ghastly'. Although Evelyn was still at this stage agnostic, Alastair had for some time been drawing near to Rome, and to satisfy his leanings in that direction they visited a large number of churches (seven in one day), and stayed a couple of nights in the monastery at Mount Melleray, which was achingly cold. It rained nearly all the time, and when the rain stopped clouds of flies materialised to torment them. On return to England, Evelyn left Alastair in Warwickshire with a very cross Mrs G while he went back to Underhill. Here his already fractious temper was made worse by the presence of one of his aunts, a half-sister of his mother's ('I cannot write or think or eat, I hate her so') and a loathsome new contraption of Arthur's, a wireless apparatus, 'a tiresome toy'. However, in spite of these vexations, he managed to make progress with a piece of work that had been in his mind for some time. In May he had written to Dudley Carew, 'Quite soon I am going to write a little book. It is going to be called "The Temple at Thatch" and will be all about magic and madness', the plot concerning a young man who moves into an eighteenth-century folly to practise black magic. But Evelyn's heart was not in it: 'a suspicion settles on me that it will never be finished', he correctly predicted. The day of Alastair's departure, 18 September 1924, was coming near, and in a conscious attempt to counteract despair and give himself some purpose, he enrolled in a course of study, beginning the very day that Alastair was due to leave, at an art school off the Tottenham Court Road.

Meanwhile he spent as much time as he could with his friend. On Saturday, 13 September, Alastair in Oxford was received into the Roman Catholic Church, an event about which Evelyn makes no comment, recording simply that he met him at Paddington afterwards and took him home to Golders Green, the next day, a Sunday, accompanying him to Mass in Hampstead. On Monday the two men were back in Oxford where Alastair had arranged to take Communion and have breakfast with his instructor, that industrious fisher of men's souls, Father 'Charlie' Martindale, SJ. To mark the event Alastair presented Evelyn with a Bible handsomely bound in green morocco. But that apart, it was a gloomy occasion; they had a disgusting dinner at the George, drank in a dismal and unfamiliar pub and passed an exceptionally uncomfortable night. 'Everything was inexpressibly sordid,' Evelyn observed. On Tuesday Alastair went to see his mother before coming up with her to London. Evelyn, forbidden to go with him to the docks, said his goodbyes at the station at midday, after which for some hours he wandered miserably about, 'feeling more than a little disconsolate'.[1] With Alastair gone, there was little pleasure to be had in anything, and 'my life of poverty, chastity and obedience commences'.

The start of the course at Heatherley's Art School did little to diminish his melancholy. The school, at 75 Newman Street, advertised itself as 'A Paris Studio in London', but in reality catered more for commercial draughtsmen than creative artists. Every morning Evelyn walked to Hampstead tube station, amusing himself by hiding pennies (once, when drunk, sixpences by mistake) along the route, collecting those which remained on his return in the evening. From ten until four, with a break in the middle of the day when he met Tony Bushell, now studying at RADA, for a pub lunch, he sat on a 'donkey' in an overheated studio, drawing from the nude in pencil and charcoal. The class was taught by the proprietor, an ineffectual old man with a red nose and trembling hands. As to the students, most of the girls were 'underbred houris', while the young men were bent only upon making careers for themselves 'by illustrating *Punch* or advertising things. It does not seem to me likely that I shall find any pals among them.' Two years later Evelyn incorporated a portrait of Heatherley's in his short story, 'The Balance', in which the second-rateness of the place, his own lack of real talent and his irritation with the teaching are made tellingly clear.

[The model] disclosed a dull pink body with rather short legs and red elbows; like most professional models her toes are covered with bunions and malformed. Young Mr Maltby sets her on the chair in an established Art School pose. The class settles to work.

Adam returns with some sheets of paper and proceeds to arrange them on his board. Then he stands for some time glaring at the model without drawing a line ... he works on for five or six minutes, during which time the heat of the stove

[1] Mrs Graham, having heard from Sibyl, reported that in Kenya 'Ali seemed completely *uninterested in everything*!!'

becomes increasingly uncomfortable. Old Mr Maltby, breathing smoke, comes up behind him.

'How have you placed it? What is your centre? Where is the foot going to come? Where is the top of the head coming?'

Adam has not placed it; he rubs it out angrily and starts again.

Evelyn found the experience both dispiriting and exhausting. 'Every evening I return wishing to do nothing except eat a pro-digious dinner and go early to bed after an evening of desultory conversation or, less profitably still, in "listening in" to Chap-man & Hall's[2] horrible wireless. The result is that I have read nothing or written nothing for a week.' He was quick to realise that although his drawings were far from being the worst in the class, they were not good enough, and that he lacked that 'obsession with solid form, the zeal for probing the structure of anatomy ... which alone could make the long hours before the models exciting'. Soon tedium set in and he began to cut classes to wander round museums and galleries or go to the cinema. By the end of October he had given up attending altogether. 'I learned', he wrote in his diary, 'that it is not possible to lead a gay life and to draw well.'

Much of this gay life he owed to Alec. Although Evelyn was as bored as ever by the obsessive interest in football and cricket,[3] and although he despised the literary lions such as Gosse and Jack Squire whom Alec, taking after his father, so looked up to, he nonetheless admired his brother's social gifts and was fasci-nated by the somewhat louche world in which he moved. Alec took Evelyn with him to nightclubs and parties, introduced him to his already large circle of friends, and put him up at his tiny flat in Earl's Terrace whenever Evelyn after a night on the town was too drunk to make the journey home. As Alec pertinently remarked, 'there is no stronger deterrent to one's enjoyment of an evening than the knowledge that one has at the end of it to get to Golders Green.' In his fragmentary second volume of autobiography, *A Little Hope*, Evelyn wrote

[2] 'Chapman & Hall' was the name by which Evelyn referred to his father when he was feeling most irritated by him: 'Chapman & Hall has a "quinsy",' he recorded in his diary for 5 January 1925, exasperated by the affectedly archaic word which Arthur typically used to describe his sore throat.

[3] A boredom vividly expressed in 'The National Game', a short story written by Evelyn and published in *The Cherwell* in September 1923.

Kate and Arthur Waugh with their beloved bicycles

Alec reading in the bookroom at Underhill

Evelyn as a child

Alec, Kate, Evelyn
and poodle
(Marquis's successor)
in 1912

The Pistol Troop: Evelyn, second from left, with the three Fleming children and David Malaher

Evelyn and David Malaher holding the Pistol Troop fort

Heath Mount: second row from top, Evelyn far left; his victim, Cecil Beaton, far right

Evelyn as a spectator
on the playing-field
at Lancing

J. F. Roxburgh at
Lancing

Barbara Jacobs
before her marriage
to Alec

Richard Pares as an
undergraduate at
Balliol

Alastair Graham at
eighteen shortly
before going up to
Oxford

C. R. M. F.
Cruttwell, the hated
Dean of Hertford

Henry Yorke, 'lean, dark and singular'

Harold Acton and Evelyn, young men about town

The Hon. Mrs
Evelyn Waugh (She-
Evelyn) in costume
for a fancy-dress
party

The two Evelyns at
a 'tropical' party during
their wretched last days together

Evelyn Gardner
after her divorce
from Evelyn Waugh

Arthur and Kate in
the garden at
Underhill

The Waugh brothers
playing with Alec's
elder son, Andrew

To me he [Alec] was someone who owned Havelock Ellis's *Studies in the Psychology of Sex* in which I lubriciously browsed, as a host who introduced me to the best restaurants of London, on whom I sponged, bringing my friends to his flat and, when short of money, sleeping on his floor until the tubes opened when I would at dawn sway home to Hampstead in crumpled evening-dress among the navvies setting out for their day's work ... [he] was already accumulating a large and heterogeneous collection of cronies, drawn from the stage, from journalism and literature ... [and] in the years of my poverty and obscurity I was constantly at his table.

'Baldhead' or 'Baldie', as his young brother ungratefully referred to him, was not only exceptionally gregarious but already at twenty-six well started on a lifelong career of womanising. The emotionally voracious demands made on him as a schoolboy by his father had sent him, metaphorically speaking, underground: in order to survive he had had to batten down his feelings, remain elusive, keep the escape route always open and accessible. But in spite of his failure with Barbara, a failure largely caused by unreal expectations on both sides, Alec, like Arthur, was highly sexed and loved the company of women. When he was neither at work nor on the playing field, Alec in his careful, self-contained way devoted himself to their pursuit, a pursuit in which, small stature and early baldness notwithstanding, his genuine admiration and sympathy and his quiet charm brought him considerable success. Despite what Evelyn described as a rigid orthodoxy (an orthodoxy that 'sends him to Jermyn Street for his shirts and Paris for his fornication'), Alec also had a taste for bohemian life and girls of easy reputation, both of which were to be found in the compulsive partying and numerous nightclubs so much a part of London life in the 1920s.

Among the artistic younger set, the most popular of the clubs was the Cave of Harmony in Charlotte Street. The Cave was run by Harold Scott and his partner, Elsa Lanchester, a fragile, red-haired beauty just starting on an acting career. In spite of the fact that it had no drink licence, the club was much patronised by young actors and journalists, for, as the premises were private and the audience members only, the rigorous laws of censorship did not apply, and well-known theatrical names took part in cabaret and one-act plays of a kind which would never have been licensed for public performance by the Lord Chamberlain. Alec went there nearly every Saturday, often taking Evelyn with him. They came to know Elsa quite well, even persuading her to take part in a cinema film which had been concocted by Evelyn and Terence Greenidge while still at Oxford.

The Scarlet Woman: an Ecclesiastical Melodrama was a typically exuberant undergraduate rag, with a comic plot written by Evelyn revolving round an imaginary attempt by the dean of Balliol to convert the king of England to Catholicism. It was financed by the two Greenidge brothers, John Sutro and Evelyn, each of whom put up £5.[4] During July of 1924 filming took place in Oxford, on Hampstead Heath and, watched lovingly by Arthur to whom it recalled the amateur theatricals of his youth, in the garden at Underhill. ('Evelyn & Terrance [sic] taking a cinema film in garden picked raspberries for dinner', was Kate's record of the occasion.) Elsa, in exchange for a free lunch on the days she spent on location, played the female lead, Beatrice de Carolle, a cabaret singer of Evangelical principles; Evelyn in a blonde wig took the part of Sligger, the dastardly dean, John Sutro was Cardinal Montefiasco, Alec the cardinal's old mother, Elmley the Lord Chamberlain and John Greenidge the Prince of Wales, who makes homosexual advances to the Pope. The first showing, at the Oxford University Dramatic Society with Lennox Berkeley in charge of the musical accompaniment, was followed by a request for a second by the Society of Jesus at Campion Hall; Father Martindale, the master, was so amused that John Greenidge took it upon himself to insert a subtitle, 'Nihil Obstat – projiciatur – C. C. Martindale SJ'. The film was clever, silly and high-spirited, and should have been fun, but Evelyn, although he clowned engagingly in front of the camera, did not really enjoy it, and badly in debt as usual grudged the expenditure. 'Looking back on it I think the money was ill spent', he sourly remarked.

Although naturally he resented having to rely so heavily on his brother's patronage – 'one wants a Bohemia of one's own independent of Alec!' – Evelyn assiduously accepted all invitations Alec procured. Most of the parties to which the Waugh boys were asked were distinctly raffish, parties often assembled at short

[4] Terence Greenidge was also involved in another film, *The Cities of the Plain*, with both Hugh Lygon and Evelyn in the cast. Evelyn, under the stage-name Wycliffe Hall, played a lecherous black clergyman.

notice, where most of the guests were actors, writers, painters, girls with short hair who smoked a lot and wore make-up, and young men recently down from university who had not yet decided what to do with their lives. There were parties at Gwen Otter's in Tedworth Square, at Mrs Torry's ('Black Torry', daughter of an Indian rajah) just off the Marylebone Road, and a particularly memorable one at 'Keith' (Mrs Cecil) Chesterton's flat in Fleet Street, at which 'pansies, prostitutes and journalists and struggling actors [were] all quite quite drunk and in patches lusty. Peter Pusey with whom Hugh Lygon sodomizes was there, and Elsa . . . Alec turned up late and a little drunk and, after his fashion, fixed upon the ugliest woman in the room, bore her off and lechered with her.' Alec gave a supper party at the flat of the novelist, Mary Butts, in Belsize Park. It was a hot evening in late September, and the large number of guests, Alec's football and cricket friends mixed with writers, actors and publishers, flowed out into the big untidy garden. For the first hour or two the atmosphere was decidedly sticky, until Evelyn had the inspired idea of lacing the claret-cup with brandy, after which the party went with such a swing that the butler hired for the occasion retired to the basement in disgust and the last guests did not leave until noon the following day. One of them, the novelist Douglas Goldring, recalled his last sight of Evelyn drunkenly playing football in the hall with the butler's top-hat.

After a party the evening would often continue with a couple of hours' hard drinking in a nightclub, if not the Cave of Harmony, then the 50–50, the Blue Lantern, Rector's, the 1917 or, when they were in funds or someone else was paying, Quaglino's, the Embassy and Mrs Meyrick's notorious 43 in Gerrard Street. Time after time Evelyn would come home at five or six in the morning, heavy-eyed with hang-over, and collapse into bed where he would stay until late in the afternoon. Not surprisingly, Evelyn's dissipation soon became a source of anxiety to his parents. Even the gentle Kate was provoked to anger after a particularly unrestrained occasion when her younger son gave a party at Underhill for some of his Oxford friends. 'There's a drunken beast *still* in the house!' she was heard to exclaim with uncharacteristic fury while surveying the damage the morning after. She was even crosser when Alec, who should have known better, took his brother to lunch with that eccentric, Rabelaisian figure, E. S. P.

Haynes. Haynes, a solicitor with literary tastes and an old friend
of Arthur's, was a generous host, and during the meal he and his
two young guests got through a bottle of burgundy each, two
different kinds of port and some 1870 brandy which they swigged
out of tumblers. That evening Evelyn, in a state of alcoholic near-
stupor, dined at Previtali with Tony Bushell, went on to drink
Chartreuse at the Café Royal, and when that closed, bought a
bottle of whisky and ended the evening at the Cave of Harmony,
where he made a heavy-handed pass at Joyce Fagan.

Joyce had been very taken with Evelyn ever since her appearance at his Oxford party dressed as a boy. The two of them
met fairly frequently, usually in the company of other people, in
particular, and to Evelyn's disgust, that of Joyce's lover, Douglas
Goldring, usually referred to as 'the toad Goldring'. Joyce was
the only guest invited to dine at Underhill on Evelyn's twenty-
first birthday, an occasion marked by a disappointingly decorous
celebration at home. The friendship remained playful, as Evelyn
was too unsure of himself and too depressed to attempt at this
stage to carry it further. On Christmas Day he wrote, 'Now with
Alastair a thousand miles away and my heart leaden and the
future drearily uncertain things are not as they were.'

With Alastair in fact rather more than a thousand miles away,
it was comfort of a sort to return to the places associated with
him. At the end of November, Evelyn had spent a weekend at
Barford alone with Mrs Graham, who loomed 'like some baffled
archangel beating in the void her voluminous wings in vain while
anger fills the room up of her absent son'. From there he went
to Oxford, a city still of magical allure, which Evelyn frequently
revisited in pursuit not only of his lost paradise but also to indulge
in bouts of oblivion-inducing drunkenness even deeper and more
prolonged than those he had become accustomed to in London.
On this occasion he attended a luncheon party (lobster, par-
tridges, plum pudding, sherry, mulled claret and liqueurs) of
John Sutro's, consisting, among other guests, of Harold Acton,
Hugh Lygon, Robert Byron and Richard Pares, who had just been
elected a fellow of All Souls. The afternoon was spent drinking
beer with Greenidge, Elmley and Byron, the evening downing
whisky with Claud Cockburn and Henry Yorke. 'After about this
stage of the evening my recollections become somewhat blurred.
I got a sword from somewhere and got into Balliol somehow and

was let out of a window at some time having mocked Arden [Hilliard] and Tony Powell and talked very seriously to Peter Quennell.' The following weekend he went again to Oxford for a party of Billy Clonmore's at Merton, where 'one man was sick and two or three in rut'. The next night there was another party, 'a grisly evening. Never have I seen so many men being sick together or being so infernally dangerous. They threw about chairs and soda water syphons and lavatory seats.' The tone of self-loathing and disgust increases as the Dionysian debauch continued, culminating in December with several days of massive, suicidal drunkenness. First there was a dinner party, at which 'I arrived quite blind after a great number of cocktails at the George with Claud. Eventually the dinner broke up and Claud, Roger Hollis and I went off for a pub-crawl which after sundry indecorous adventures ended up at the Hypocrites[5] where another blind was going on . . . Next day I drank all the morning from pub to pub . . . I ate no lunch but drank solidly . . . Alfred [Duggan] and I then drank double brandies until I could not walk. He carried me to Worcester where I fell out of a window and then relapsed into unconsciousness punctuated with severe but well-directed vomitings. I dined four times at various places and went to a drunk party at Worcester in someone's rooms I did not know.'

After this stupefying bender Evelyn returned to London finally convinced that such a self-destructive way of life must not continue. Much of his despair stemmed from the fact that he was still without direction, had not yet discovered his *métier.* The life of the man of letters was surely not for him, who despised the clubbable cosiness so relished by Arthur and his middle-brow cronies, with their ever-ready quotations and comfortable practice of mutual admiration. Evelyn had always sat resentfully silent at the literary At Homes which Arthur gave at Underhill for such as St John Ervine, G. B. Stern, Sylvia Gosse and the flamboyant Bourchier. The fact that Alec had joined the club made the prospect doubly off-putting: it was unthinkable to try to compete with a brother who by the age of twenty-six had published stories, poems, essays and reviews as well as four novels and two volumes

---

[5] The old Hypocrites' premises in St Aldate's, then occupied by Richard Plunket Greene.

of autobiography, and was regarded as one of the most promising younger members of the literary establishment.

So Evelyn turned to his early love of printing, first discovered at Lancing. He and Alastair had sometimes talked of setting up their own imprint, which in the days of small private presses like the Nonesuch, Shakespeare Head and Hogarth, was a trade both financially viable and socially acceptable. To this end Evelyn wrote to James Guthrie, owner of the Pear Tree Press at Flansham in Sussex, whose work, sweetly reminiscent of Lychpole and Crease, he had seen and admired, to ask if he might be taken on as apprentice. Guthrie on a visit to London met Evelyn and agreed to the proposal, Arthur was persuaded to pay the £25 indenture, and a week before Christmas Evelyn went down to the Guthries' ugly modern villa near Bognor Regis to start his training. Although he liked the family – the son, who met him at the station, was a pleasant young man; Mrs Guthrie, pink-cheeked and maternal, gave him an excellent lunch of pork and apple pie; and Guthrie himself, a follower of William Morris, was a skilled draughtsman and technician – it was clear at once that the project would not work. Pear Tree, it turned out, was dependent for most of its work on trade photography, which involved the use of zinc intaglios that were inked by hand and then pulled to reproduce drawings, a process which was of no interest to Evelyn. After a night in an uncomfortable bed he returned to London to face his father, still without a career and with a mountain of pressing debts which Arthur, displeased but resigned, agreed to pay off.

Evelyn had once written to Dudley Carew that 'no one in our class need ever starve because he can always go as a prep school master' (cheerfully adding, 'not a pleasant job but all roads lead to Sodom'). Although Evelyn may not have been starving, he was left with little alternative but to put this premise to the test. The next few days, having registered at the scholastic agency Truman & Knightley, he spent quietly at Underhill, 'writing out letters of praise of myself to obscure private schools and still attempting to rewrite "The Temple". A man from Arnold House, Denbighshire . . . seem[s] to show a little interest in me.' But such interest was small help in raising Evelyn's spirits. He was poor, his story was not working, and he could look forward only to the prospect of a job which held no attraction for him.

It was not all black, however. In his last year at Oxford Evelyn had come to know the two gentle and gigantic Plunket Greene brothers. David, nearly seven foot tall, was a languid dandy with beautiful manners; although most of his friends were homosexual, he himself appeared curiously neuter, his energies, it later became apparent, reserved for an addiction to heroin which was eventually to cause his death. Richard, Evelyn's friend, was almost as tall as his brother, dark-haired, good-looking in a piratical way, a heavy drinker, and intensely musical, in particular passionate about jazz. His love of music was inherited from both sides, his father, Harry Plunket Greene, being a well-known singer, while his mother was the daughter of the composer, Sir Hubert Parry, and a gifted amateur violinist. Their parents having separated, David and Richard lived with their mother and a sister, Olivia, in Hanover Terrace, and it was here on New Year's Day 1925 that Evelyn was brought to tea. 'I met Mrs Greene for the first time and loved her', he recorded in his diary.

Gwen Greene, with her mass of dark hair, heavy brows, and calm, beautiful face, was a most attractive personality, if unconventional as a parent. Tolerant and amusing, she lived with her children on terms of easy equality, allowing them to say what they liked and behave as they pleased, seeing no need to imbue in them any sense of practical responsibility for their extremely straitened circumstances. If the children wanted to spend extravagantly on drink or expensive magazines, she was not about to spoil their pleasure by telling them they could not afford it. This delightful, if improvident, unworldliness had its roots in a religious faith which was the centre of her existence. Under the influence of her uncle, the Catholic theologian, Baron Friedrich von Hügel,[6] Gwen at the time Evelyn met her was on the point

---

[6] Von Hügel was married to Gwen Greene's aunt, Mary Herbert. After his death Gwen published an edited selection of her uncle's correspondence, *Letters from Baron Friedrich von Hügel to a Niece* (Dent, 1928). Described by Dean Inge as 'Our greatest theologian and the ablest apologist for Christianity in our time', he was recognised as an outstanding intellectual and the international leader of the modernist Catholic movement; for this reason he was regarded with distrust by adherents of the rigid Ultramontanism so effectively established in England by Cardinal Manning.

of converting to Rome,[7] and her absorption in religious affairs, while remaining a matter of indifference to her two sons, had a profound effect on her daughter, Olivia; and, through Olivia, on Evelyn.

In *A Little Learning* Evelyn says of the Plunket Greenes that he fell in love with the entire family, but of necessity focused 'the sentiment upon the only appropriate member, an eighteen-year-old daughter'. Although in fact only seventeen when he met her, Olivia was already a formidable personality, a strange girl with an impressive intellect, utter contempt for social nicety, and a sexual magnetism that many men found overwhelming. She was not conventionally pretty, but with enormous eyes in a small white face, with dark hair and a slim figure, disturbingly attractive to those to whom her type appealed. Evelyn was drawn to her at once, fascinated by her outspokenness and lack of concern for general opinion, and by her physical allure. Olivia moved gracefully (she had studied ballet with Cecchetti) and was fastidiously dressed, usually in black. She was capable of spending an entire afternoon choosing a ribbon for a petticoat, always of the finest crêpe de chine, and took an unconscionable time preparing herself in the morning, never appearing until heavily made-up, her Elizabeth Arden 'face case' accompanying her everywhere.

The more Evelyn saw of Olivia, the more captivated he became. They started meeting for pub lunches, and spent hours talking in front of the fire at Underhill; in the evenings they went dancing and drinking at the Cave. For Olivia liked to drink almost as heavily as Evelyn. In this one direction it was she who was prepared to follow his lead. In a letter to her cousin, Matthew Ponsonby, she wrote, 'Evelyn was here yesterday afternoon quite drunk at 4 o'clock bringing 3 bottles of champagne under his arm. We drank them out of teacups & various pots & china & slop basins we found about, I have never drunk at that hour of the afternoon before & was in a very bad state to greet Anne & Dick Talbot who came to supper afterwards absolutely sober.' Evelyn was impressed by Olivia's originality and arrogance. She herself was without ambition of any kind, and equally indifferent both to the successes and the disappointments that concerned her friends. She was moody, subject to periods of untouchable

[7] She entered the Church the following year, 1926.

melancholy when she would withdraw into a depressed silence; at other times she seemed alight with a wild enthusiasm for something in which no one but she could see any point. Evelyn loved in her these reckless extremes.

A book, a play, a film, a ballet, a new, and usually deleterious friend, a public injustice, generally known and generally accepted, but suddenly discovered by Olivia, would totally engage her for a time; these crazes were mitigated by a peculiar fastidiousness, which did not prevent her from saying and doing outrageous things, but preserved her essential delicacy quite intact; also by shyness which made her unwilling to make any friends save those who were attracted by her and forced their way into her confidence. She nagged and bullied at times, she suffered from morbid self-consciousness, she was incapable of the ordinary arts and efforts of pleasing and was generally incapable of any kind of ostentation.

Even more than Evelyn, Olivia was fiercely judgmental, stringently rating her acquaintance on their sexual potential and ability to amuse. Her maternal grandmother was a Herbert, and she had inherited to the full the Herbert pride in the Herbert name, the belief that Herbert blood was of an invincibly superior quality to that which ran in the veins of other great English families. Disowning the Plunket Greene element in her genetic composition (the Plunkets, according to her, were 'bog Irish'), Olivia saw herself as pure Herbert, her character traits, she was convinced, deriving from the Woronzow connection that had been made at the beginning of the nineteenth century when a daughter of Count Woronzow had married the Earl of Pembroke, head of the Herbert family.

For both Gwen and Olivia, the most condemnatory terms were 'second rate' and 'middle class'. Unfortunately, by their empyrean standards, Evelyn was both.

Gratified though she was by the evidence of his growing infatuation, Olivia found Evelyn physically unappealing, his ideas and ambitions irredeemably mediocre. She loved nothing so much as intense intellectual argument; she became passionately absorbed in whatever she was reading – Browning, Plato, Dostoievsky – and then loved extensively to debate it, while Evelyn tended more to make a shrewd snap judgment and leave it at that. He was not always able to resist saying something purely for effect, while Olivia 'snapped like a lizard on any affectation'. However, far from antagonising him, this combination of intellectual aggressiveness and Herbert high breeding he found irresistible. 'I wonder whether I am falling in love with this woman', he wrote in his diary for 24 December 1924.

A few days after Christmas Alastair turned up unannounced at Underhill, back from Kenya, thin, dirty and unshaven. 'When he was washed,' said Evelyn, 'he began to be more beautiful.' But although the friendship between the two men was as strong as ever – as before, they went off to Barford where, as before, they spent most of their time quarrelling with Mrs Graham – for Evelyn the erotic element had faded. While Alastair remained committed to his own sex, Evelyn, although still aware of his power to attract men, had turned his attentions to women. Women in general, and Olivia in particular. But the more ardently he pursued her, the clearer it became that Olivia was unable to reciprocate. This resulted in some tortured meetings.

> I had promised to go to tea with Olivia and after wandering for miles in fog arrived at Hanover Terrace at about 5. We had a desolate tea alone in front of a gas fire quarrelling in a half-hearted sort of way. Most of the time she insisted monotonously, 'I don't think you love me any more' and then became aloof when I attempted to prove that I did. At about 8, deeply depressed, we set out to drink, and after some champagne cocktails at the Criterion we ate oysters and drank Chablis at the Café Royal . . . Olivia very drunk.

For another of Olivia's fascinations was her love of drinking and of getting drunk ('a ghost with a glass of gin in her hand', was how one contemporary described her). Like Evelyn, she found a kind of freedom in intoxication, a freedom which in her case allowed her a sexual licence that, sober, would have been unattainable. Olivia was both passionate and promiscuous. Highly charged sexually, she was intensely interested in every kind of amatory experience, which she sought avidly and with many partners, among them Tancred Borenius, Paul Robeson and the painter Stephen Toulmin. With these, unselfconsciously and wholly without prurience, she delighted in analysing refinements of technique, rather as a concert pianist might analyse his own and others' performance. Evelyn, however, she considered both too unattractive and in sexual matters too gauche to be admitted into this favoured freemasonry, an exclusion which, although only half understood, sent him into a frenzy of frustration.

A few days after the depressing evening ending at the Café Royal, Evelyn went to a dinner party of Alec's, 'almost wholly spoiled by the abominable manners of the Greene family who arrived fifty minutes late'. After dinner they went on to the theatre, then dancing at the Cave, where Olivia quickly got drunk on cherry brandy and started kissing the very handsome Tony Bushell. Evelyn was furious. 'I could not get drunk try as I might and was very rude to Olivia who was too drunk to mind.' The next day, 'with a glowing resentment against the Greene family', Evelyn sent word that they would not be seeing him for some time as he was going to the country. 'This high attitude was a little shaken later in the evening because I got quite, quite drunk with Tony [Bushell] and Bill Silk[8] and called at Hanover Terrace at about 12.30 . . . I refused to go until Olivia knelt down and apologized to me; she quite rightly did not do this. I also broke a gramophone record.'

However, before Evelyn did leave for 'the country', he and Olivia made it up. She came round to see him at Underhill and they sat and talked in the bookroom. She told him that he was a great artist and must on no account make a career as a schoolmaster. Too late. The next day, just as he had begun to feel that he might be winning her interest and approval, he was leaving to take up a post at some unheard-of establishment in North Wales. 'I went to bed feeling more desolate than I had felt since the embarkation of Alastair.'

Arnold House at Llanddulas on the bleak, beautiful Denbighshire coast, was a preparatory school catering mainly for the sons of professional families from Lancashire and Ireland. The school itself, plain, gabled and late-Victorian, was situated on top of a steep hill overlooking the windswept and featureless little town. Mr Banks, the headmaster, 'a tall old man with stupid eyes', had interviewed Evelyn in London, and offered him the job of teaching History, Latin and Greek for a salary of £160 a year. And so

[8] A hard-drinking actor-manager at that time in love with Tony Bushell.

it was that on 23 January 1925, the new usher with sinking heart arrived at Euston Station to take charge of a group of red-capped little boys on the train to Llanddulas. Once there, he climbed into the only taxi, immediately to be submerged in a pile of hand-luggage which the boys threw in after him. 'Oh sir, will you take my bag? Jolly decent of you, sir.' He was greeted reprovingly at the front door by the headmaster's wife. 'The boys know they must carry their own bags,' said Mrs Banks. 'You should not have let them do that to you, Mr Waugh.' This was the start of a mutual antipathy, Evelyn disliking Mrs Banks for her bossiness and snobbery, she despising him for his incompetence. The only time she softened towards him was when Mrs Graham and Alastair, manifestly her social superiors, came to the school to see him. 'Some *very* nice friends have called for you, Mr Waugh.'

Evelyn was put to live with two other masters in a house known as Sanatorium, but most of his day when not in class was spent in the staff common room, a cramped but cosy habitat with a linoleum-covered floor, dim gas lighting, some easy chairs, a fire and a gramophone. There were two other new masters, like Evelyn hastily hired to replace the three sacked for the usual reason the previous term: Watson, 'tall and grand and elderly', and Dean, 'squalid, with a blue chin, discoloured cheeks, cockney accent and severe cold'. Although in *A Little Learning* Evelyn admits that the school was well conducted and the boys 'healthy, happy, well-fed and well enough taught to pass into the public schools of their choice', the account written at the time lays emphasis on the school's more eccentric aspects.

> There are no timetables or syllabi or such offal. All that happens
> is that the Headmaster Banks wanders into the common-room
> in a blank kind of way and says, 'Oh, I say, there are some
> boys in that end classroom. I don't know who they are . . . Anyway
> they've got their Latin books and they shouldn't have those so
> I think it would be best if someone took them in English.'
> Then the least lazy gets up and does that . . . Poor Mr Watson
> groans for a timetable but I find the arrangement quite agreeable.
> I sat out all the morning today.

This leisurely régime was not to last, however.

> Things get steadily more busy and as they become more busy
> more tedious . . . On Sunday I started on an awful thing called

week's duty. It means that I have no time at all from dawn to
dusk so much to read a postcard or visit a water-closet . . . my
nerves are distraught.

In spite of his insistence that he found teaching boring and the
boys of no interest and small ability, Evelyn was one of the more
popular masters. He had made an immediate and favourable
impression with his distinctive sartorial style. Instead of the neat
dark suits universally favoured by the rest of the staff, Mr Waugh
sported a striking tweed coat with leather buttons, very full plus-
fours and a high-necked jumper[9] over which protruded half an
inch of check shirt. On Saturdays he wore a flamboyant pair of
Oxford bags. In the classroom his wit and originality were much
appreciated, as was his enlightened policy of laisser faire, leaving
to their own devices those who did not want to work while taking
trouble with those who did. He allowed the top form, in what
were supposed to be history lessons, to read French novels not
included on the curriculum, and during evening preparation,
instead of patrolling the room, sat at his desk absorbed in his
own work. 'A history of the Eskimos', he unvaryingly replied when
asked what it was he was writing. A similar method of teaching
was adopted at Llanabba Castle by Paul Pennyfeather in *Decline
and Fall.*

> He was a distinct success with his form; after the first day an
> understanding had been established between them. It was
> tacitly agreed that when Paul wished to read or to write letters
> he was allowed to do so undisturbed while he left them to
> employ the time as they thought best; when Paul took it upon
> him to talk to them about their lessons they remained silent,
> and when he set them work to do some of it was done.

Unsurprisingly, 'Mr Banks frequently expresses himself dissatisfied with the work I am doing – perhaps not without cause.' The
one area in which it was generally accepted that he was no good
at all was games, and it was soon arranged that he should be

[9] This was a style of jumper he had first noticed being worn at Oxford at the
party he attended in Merton at the end of the previous year. 'Everyone was
wearing a new sort of jumper with a high collar rather becoming and most
convenient for lechery because it dispenses with all unromantic gadgets like
studs and ties. It also hides the boils with which most of the young men seem
to have encrusted their necks.' He had later bought one for himself, in which,
disappointingly, '[I] look exactly ten years old.'

restricted when on the playing fields to umpiring the ten-year-olds.

In letters and in the diary Evelyn makes much of his incompetence ('A short time ago I poured the milk into the teapot instead of the hot water and said "damn". The two little boys next to me looked inexpressibly shocked and then gave a ghastly snigger') and of his distaste for the job. 'It is a sorry waste of time and energy,' he wrote to Harold Acton. 'I do not think that I am good at teaching – at any rate I have not succeeded so far in getting any idea into anyone's head.' However, there is no doubt that Arnold House took strong hold of his imagination. Always very much alive to the grotesque in any situation, Evelyn made the most of what was turning out to be a copious opportunity, dwelling lovingly on all the more ludicrous aspects of school life, the diary entries growing longer and more detailed as he allows the comedy to develop.

[On St Patrick's Day] I got up late for chapel and arrived in breakfast to find it looking very much like my idea of a Masonic banquet; all the boys had been up for hours decorating themselves like maypoles with red, white, blue, green, and orange rosettes and streamers. Mr Dean had draped a red curtain round his shoulders and looked so strange. Some of the older and more opulent boys wore green shirts and stockings. It was a horrid carnival.

Ever the perfectionist, he was attentive to the details of his own rôle: he wore spectacles, grew a moustache and took up smoking a pipe.

Temporary escape from the irritations of school and the confines of the staff-room was essential, the most effective route being through drink, consumed either on the premises or in various pubs and hostelries in town. One evening Waugh and some of the other masters got drunk in Watson's room on whisky and sherry: 'the result was that I was sick'. Occasionally he went into Rhyl, 'the Naples of the North', and dined at the Grand Hotel. There was also the bar of the Queen's Hotel in Colwyn Bay, and the local pub, the Fairview, in Llanddulas. Here 'an aged eunuch has tried to teach us Welsh. I have learned very little, however, except *Iechyd da i bob un* and *Ilyrddiant ir archos*, which are toasts, because he gets too drunk to say anything else.' Evelyn also subscribed for a course of riding lessons at the local livery stables, his initial experience ending in humiliation when he was seen by the entire school returning home on a leading rein. Nonetheless he enjoyed it. 'On Wednesday Gordon and I and the attendant rode miles over the hills . . . It is not an easy sport or a cheap one but most agreeable.'

In spite of the considerable amusement value, Evelyn was well aware that he was wasting his time in an occupation that bored him. 'There was no happiness,' he was to write in recollection, 'merely hilarity.' Although he got on with them well enough and was glad of their company in the pub in the evenings, there was not one among his colleagues with whom he found any true fellow-feeling. 'We all do nothing but talk bawdy and lay absurd wagers – 6d in the pool for the man who can keep the ash on his cigar longest, etc.' He was depressed, too, by the hopelessness of his love for Olivia, for whom he was designing a bookplate, described as an 'Impietà', of a naked Salome dancing to a horn gramophone while holding aloft the head of John the Baptist. Like Alec in his prison camp at Mainz yearning for Barbara, Evelyn in his prison camp in Wales yearned for Olivia and ideal-ised her. 'All the term I have been allowing her to become a focus for all the decencies of life, which is foolish of me and not very fair to her.' He wrote to her regularly, letters 'full of sorrow and devotion', but her replies were brief, infrequent and dis-appointingly impersonal. In counterpoint to his melancholy situ-ation was that of Olivia's brother, Richard, also working as a schoolmaster, also unhappy because he could not marry the woman with whom he was in love. 'It makes me sad for them', Evelyn noted, 'because any sort of happiness or permanence seems so infinitely remote from any one of us.' However, the Easter holiday was approaching ('I should dearly like to spend it at the feet of Olivia but can hardly afford it'), and there was a chance of a tutoring job which would bring in some money; there was also a plan to go with the Plunket Greenes to Lundy Island where they had rented a house; and he had an idea for a book, he told Harold Acton, 'about Silenus – very English & sentimental – a Falstaff forever babbling o' green fields'. On one of the last nights of term, 'Gordon and Dean and I gave dinner to Watson at the Queen's Hotel and we drank a lot and sang all the way home.'

*

The first few days in London were spent in all the occupations Evelyn liked most: he ordered new clothes, went twice to the theatre, to the music hall, an exhibition, dined at Previtali with Tony Bushell, and got very drunk in the company of Olivia and his old acquaintance Audrey Lucas. But in the middle of one night Evelyn woke in his bedroom at Underhill and 'considered gravely how very little I have really enjoyed the last three days'.

Worse was to follow. Evelyn and Olivia had planned a party to which they asked, among many old friends, Olivia's cousin, Matthew Ponsonby.[10] Matthew, having driven up from his home in Sussex, arrived at Hanover Terrace at 6.30, and was immediately sent out again, with Evelyn, to collect a case of drink, after which Evelyn asked to be driven home so that he could change. They stopped more than once for beer on the way, drank more beer at Underhill, stopped again for beer en route to the Greenes, and were finally waved down by the police while Matthew was attempting to drive the wrong way around a traffic island in the middle of the Strand. According to newspaper reports, '[with Ponsonby] was another man in the car who was incapably drunk. A quantity of liquor found in the car was afterwards claimed by this man.' The two men were taken to Bow Street police station and put in separate cells. Matthew's father, Arthur Ponsonby, until recently Secretary of State for Foreign Affairs, used his influence to bail out his son, but did nothing ('rather ill-naturedly, I thought') for Evelyn, who was obliged to spend four hours in a cell before being summonsed to appear at Bow Street the following day and fined £2. Matthew, who was in very real danger of a prison sentence, in the event got off with a year's disqualification and a fine of £21 9s, of which Evelyn offered to pay half. 'After all I was rather more than half to blame & I got off so lightly myself.' Of far greater concern was that the world in general, and the Ponsonbys in particular, seemed to be laying the blame not only on Evelyn ('I do not the least mind how virulently I am abused by people who do not know me') but on the decadent influence of Richard Greene and Olivia. 'I am rather overcome with shame for us both,' he

[10] Matthew Ponsonby's father, Arthur Ponsonby, had married Gwen Greene's sister, Dorothea.

wrote to Matthew, 'when I see poor Mrs Greene so much troubled about something for which neither she or her children are remotely responsible. Do you think you made Olivia's part in it all quite clear to your family?'

But after this very low point the situation improved. Alec had come up with the possibility of a job for his brother in Tuscany as secretary to Charles Scott-Moncrieff, the great translator of Proust, which would be infinitely preferable to schoolmastering. And the expedition to Lundy, 'in spite of the insistent sorrows of unrequited love', turned out to be enjoyable. The party included all the Greenes, Elizabeth Russell, to whom Richard had now defiantly announced his engagement, Terence Greenidge and the difficult, talented Julia Strachey. They went for walks, out in a boat, listened to Gwen ('Lady Plunket', as Evelyn called her) reading aloud, played silly paper games and in the evenings got drunk, the conversation and behaviour often degenerating into a bawdiness which Evelyn now found distasteful and depressing. Julia Strachey slept most of the day, while Richard and Elizabeth wandered around blissfully happy in a world of their own. When everyone else had gone to bed Evelyn and Olivia sat up talking. 'Olivia and I sat in the dark until nearly 4 and I became very sentimental and no doubt tedious, but she bore it with much kindness.' It was becoming increasingly clear that he was getting nowhere with her: 'The sad thing – the only sad thing about this party – is that I cannot cure myself of being in love with Olivia. It is so trying for us both. While I was in Denbighshire I had hoped that I only loved her as a personification of all the jolly things I had left behind.'

Evelyn in love with Olivia, Olivia it appeared in love with Tony Bushell, and, to complete the random dispositions of Fate, Audrey Lucas, daughter of Arthur's old friend, that prototypical man of letters, E. V. Lucas, had fallen in love with Evelyn, who was unable to regard her with anything other than fraternal fondness. Now Audrey had written to tell him of her engagement to Elsa Lanchester's partner at the Cave of Harmony, Harold Scott, an engagement that he suspected was a gesture of despair on Audrey's part. It was the final irony in the unhappy situation: 'I am still sad and uneasy and awkward whenever I am with Olivia, and she of course is more than half in love with Tony which makes things less possible and now here is Audrey linking herself up for life, with a person whom I am sure she does not much like. Amen. So be it.'[11]

Thus high spirits gave way to melancholy – until the last morning when Evelyn's mood lightened at the prospect of temporarily exchanging the emotional rack of Olivia's company for a few days' hard drinking with Alastair. On their way through Oxford they collected a group of friends – Tony Bushell, Claud Cockburn, David Greene, Robert Byron, John Sutro and Harold Acton – and with them went on to Barford for 'a lovely drunk tea party', followed by a peaceful evening alone together drinking port in the library. Mrs Graham was away taking the cure at Harrogate, which should have made for perfection; however, 'it seems unkind but I much prefer Barford when it is being run by Mrs G. Things are very vague now and there are not enough fires.'

Before returning to Wales, Evelyn spent a gloomy twenty-four hours in London. Arthur was having one of his depressions, and there was a last, 'rather dismal' evening at the theatre with the Greene family, Peter Quennell and Alastair.

But nothing so dismal as the return to Arnold House. 'In school I find a certain perverse pleasure in making all I teach as dreary to the boys as it is to myself . . . I set them in sullen rows all day long to learn grammatical definitions – "a syllable is a single sound made by one simple effort of the voice," etc. – ad nauseam.' But bleak though it was, the term did have its better moments. Evelyn had had an idea for a novel, with which he was very much engaged. 'I am making the first chapter a cinema film and have been writing furiously ever since. I honestly think that it is going to be rather good'; and there were two new additions to the local cast list, both of whom immeasurably brightened the scene.

The first, Professor R. M. Dawkins, Evelyn had known slightly at Oxford when he had for a time provided an aegis for the Hypocrites' Club. 'A fidgety, learned, humorous bachelor' with a walrus moustache, Dawkins, it turned out, owned a house near the school; he appeared as 'a rescuer sent to me in the desert from that green world', his house an oasis from the discomforts of school. The second newcomer was a young man in his early

[11] In fact, Audrey Lucas married Harold Scott because she found she was pregnant by him.

thirties very different from the colourless characters who up till now had inhabited the common room. W. R. B. (Dick) Young was a true eccentric, a larger-than-life figure whose unrestrained recountings in the local pub of his disgraceful past appealed immediately to Evelyn's imagination: expelled from Wellington, sent down from Oxford, forced to resign his commission in the army; 'has left four schools precipitately, three in the middle of the term through his being taken in sodomy and one through his being drunk six nights in succession. And yet he goes on getting better and better jobs,' Evelyn delightedly recorded. After a school picnic on Snowdon in honour of Mrs Banks's birthday, always for the masters a gruesome and much dreaded occasion, Young surprised his exhausted colleagues by boasting that he had enjoyed the day enormously. *Enjoyed?* 'What did you find to enjoy?' 'Knox minor,' he said with radiant simplicity. ' . . . I took Knox minor away behind some rocks. I removed his boot and stocking, opened my trousers, put his dear little foot there and experienced a most satisfying emission.'

But for the rest, it was a period of unrelieved misery: silence from Olivia; a coldness with the Plunket Greenes over his and Matthew Ponsonby's drunken arrest, which had so scandalised the Ponsonby parents; and as always a frightening number of creditors pressing for payment, which had driven Evelyn to go yet again to his father who had agreed yet again to pay up, but this time on condition that his profligate son now surrender his allowance. Added to this was a letter of disparaging criticism from Harold Acton, to whom Evelyn had sent his novella, 'The Temple at Thatch'. The great arbiter was woundingly dismissive. 'Too English for my exotic taste. Too much nid-nodding over port. It should be printed in a few elegant copies for the friends who love you . . .'[12] Evelyn consigned the manuscript to the furnace in the school boiler-room, and sank even deeper into depression. 'I debate the paradoxes of suicide and achievement . . . and negotiate with the man Young to buy a revolver from him.' Then came the news that the job in Italy with Scott-Moncrieff was not after all going to materialise. This was serious, as not only had Evelyn been basking in visions of a future 'drinking Chianti under olive

---

[12] Years later Acton wrote of it, 'it was an airy Firbankian trifle, totally unworthy of Evelyn, and I brutally told him so. It was a misfired jeu d'esprit.'

trees and listening to discussions of all the most iniquitous out-
casts of Europe', but so sure had he been of the post that he had
given his notice to Mr Banks, who had accepted it with alacrity.
No going back there. 'The phrase "the end of the tether" besets
me with unshakable persistence,' Evelyn wrote. 'I have a heart of
lead and nerves of fire and can see no hope of anything ever
happening.'

According to his autobiography, but not recorded in the diary
nor mentioned in any existing letter, Evelyn one night did go so
far as to attempt suicide. He went down to the beach in the
moonlight, took off his clothes and, having left with them an apt
quotation from Euripides, started to swim out to sea. But then,
as so often in his novels, the grand gesture thwarted by some
ridiculous and extraneous incident, he was stung on the shoulder
by a jellyfish, stung again, and so decided to return to life on
shore. Whether or not this incident really took place is almost
irrelevant; what matters is that Evelyn was miserable enough to
have thought that he wanted to die, even if not quite miserable
enough to pursue the ambition to its end.

'After some few valedictory discourtesies', Mr Banks allowed
Evelyn to leave a few days before the end of term, and he returned
to Underhill to set about finding himself another job. His situation compared to that of most of his friends, impoverished
though some of them were, was markedly more precarious.
Dudley Carew had published a novel and was assistant editor on
a weekly newspaper; Robert Byron, having done a stint as cub
reporter on the *Daily Mail*, had a commission to write two books;
Richard Pares was ensconced in All Souls; Anthony Powell at
Duckworth's, the publisher; Tony Bushell was enjoying a success
on the stage and had played opposite Gladys Cooper; even Alastair, that dedicated drifter, had the promise of a posting as honorary attaché at the British legation in Athens.

There was a suggestion from Evelyn's old headmaster, Granville
Grenfell, that he should teach at Heath Mount, but nothing came
of it. In an attempt to get away from schoolmastering, Evelyn
wrote a number of letters of application to galleries – including
the National Gallery – and to the editors of art magazines. But
nothing came of that either. Finally he heard from Richard
Greene, who was teaching at a school in Buckinghamshire, that
there was a vacancy there that might suit him. Just over a week

later, after a visit to the school, the news came that he had been accepted for the post, to teach English, History and Art at the same salary as before, £160 a year. Richard and Olivia Greene, Elizabeth Russell and Alastair were coming to dinner that night, and the occasion should have been celebratory, but 'I was tired and ill at ease, as I usually am with Olivia, and my father's jollity seemed more than usually distressing . . . After the others had left Alastair and I sat up until 4 talking and drinking beer and smoking.'

The remaining weeks of August and September Evelyn divided between Alastair and the Greenes, going first to Barford, where there was a stupendous row when Mrs Graham found out that her son had been guaranteeing Evelyn's overdraft. Luckily she was on the point of leaving to stay with her sister, and after her departure the two young men were able to enjoy a peaceful time together, Alastair working at his printing on a press bought second-hand from Leonard Woolf, Evelyn at a short story 'odd, but, I think, quite good'. In the evenings 'we dined in high-necked jumpers and did much that could not have been done if Mrs Graham had been here.' From Warwickshire Evelyn went to Happisburgh in Norfolk to join the Plunket Greenes, taking with him a kitten as a present for Olivia.

He was followed by a pleading letter from Alastair. 'My dearest Evelyn, I feel very lonely now. But you have made me so happy. Please come back again soon. Write to me a lot . . . My love to you, Evelyn; I want you back again so much . . . Please come back again. I can pay your fare . . .' A few days later Alastair wrote again, this time clearly resigned to the inevitable.

Thank you for your letter.[13] Evelyn, it was very serious for a poor careless, happy person like me. Of course I want you to treat me as your nature wishes to. I don't understand how one could treat anyone otherwise without being insincere. Tonvail [unidentified] is a charming spiced memory that I am most pleased to think of in my quiet moments. It is those memories that I live on . . .

In the third week of September Elizabeth Russell drove Richard and Evelyn to Aston Clinton, near Aylesbury. The school, a Greek revival house set in an immense park, was huge and ugly, with

[13] Evelyn's letters to Alastair appear not to have survived.

echoing, ill-lit passages and a 'frightful' common room. With a complement of about thirty pupils, it specialised in coaching backward boys for university entrance. In imitation of Eton, the boys wore top hats. The headmaster was Dr Crawford, and apart from Waugh and Plunket Greene there were only two other teachers, one 'dull, but tolerable. The other is dull, dour, & objectionable.' But after a glum start ('I took languid, lengthy, and incredibly ignorant boys in English'), Evelyn began to cheer up. He was near both London and Oxford, and friends were close at hand, Richard actually on the premises, his cousin Claud Cockburn only a few miles away at Tring, and there were frequent visits from Alastair, Terence and John Greenidge, and of course Liza Russell coming to see her fiancé. Evenings were spent at the local pub, The Bell, or at the cinema in Aylesbury, or dining with the Cockburns. During the day, 'taught the poor mad boys and played football with them'.

In short the new school was in every way preferable to Arnold House – in every way except one. Arnold House had been unlike anything Evelyn had experienced before. With its eccentric head-master and collection of misfits in the staff-room, it had a quality both grotesque and absurd; above all it was isolated, hundreds of miles from London, deep in the mountainous heart of North Wales, and surrounded by a small, dark people speaking an incomprehensible tongue. Because during term there was no possibility of escape and Evelyn was forced to become an inhabi-tant of this strange kingdom, it took root in his imagination in a way that Aston Clinton, with its home-counties normality and easy access to the outside world, did not. In Buckinghamshire Evelyn did his best with the material at his disposal, referring to the boys as 'mad', meaning stupid, or 'mad and diseased', meaning stupid and with acne. One of the other masters, Captain Hyde-Upward, at first appeared promising, with a habit of cleaning out his pipe while standing at his bedroom window naked, but even he turned out to be disappointingly ordinary. The comic ingredients were just not there, as they had been so abundantly among the Welsh, and Evelyn's heart was not in it. He was, however, a conscientious teacher, making his classes as interesting as he could, and dutifully umpiring on the football field. He directed one lot of boys in a scene from *The Tempest* ('they act contemptibly'), took over the literary society, and worked on the school magazine for which he

designed a cover. He even became quite fond of several of his
pupils, and described to like-minded friends the pleasure he
took in caning them. But most of his energies, intellectual and
emotional, were directed elsewhere.

In the holidays, as though attempting to recapture his lost
youth, to evoke a longed-for golden age, Evelyn returned again
and again to Oxford. On one occasion with Harold Acton,
Richard and Elizabeth, he 'dined at the George and became
enormously drunk. It was quite like the old Hypocrite days: trying
on the hats of strange men, riding strange bicycles and reciting
Edith Sitwell to the chimneys of Oriel Street. Eventually, I found
my way to a party at the House . . . where I think we were not
well received, but I was too drunk by then to mind.' Another
time he went to a party, also in Christ Church, given by Bryan
Guinness and Acton's younger brother, William, where enormous
quantities of champagne were consumed and a dangerous mixture concocted by William of champagne, gin and absinthe. The
evening ended 'raging drunk' with a fight, vomiting and a nightmare drive back to the school in Richard's car. A couple of weeks
later there was a party of Tom Driberg's, again at the House, at
which Evelyn arrived drunk and with a broken ankle, having leapt
out of the window of the Clarendon Hotel to avoid Liza Russell,
with whom he was engaged to dine. 'I was behaving very oddly,
I think.'

The result of this particular episode was several days' enforced
rest at Underhill, which Evelyn spent lying on the sofa in the
bookroom reading about the Pre-Raphaelites, in whom he had
recently become interested. 'I want to write a book about them,'
he wrote in his diary. From Underhill he returned to Aston
Clinton, where, still immobilised by his ankle, he continued his
researches into the Brotherhood, with whom he began to develop
an almost hallucinatory empathy.

I can say without affectation that during this last week I have
lived with them night and day. Early in the morning with
Holman Hunt – the only Pre-Raphaelite – untiring, fearless,
conscientious. Later in the day with Millais – never with *him*
but with my biography of him – a modish Lytton Strachey
biography. Later, when firelight and rum and loneliness have
done their worst, with Rossetti, soaked in chloral.

Firelight and rum and loneliness, or their equivalents, now became a constant refrain. Like Rossetti, Evelyn began seriously to suffer from insomnia, for which in later life, like Rossetti, he became so deleteriously dependent on chloral.[14] In his diary he makes frequent record of sleeplessness and depression. 'Very tired and sad . . . I am writing in the middle of the night because I am tired of trying to sleep. I never can nowadays for hours and hours after I go to bed.' The treats, so eagerly anticipated, turn out 'dismal', 'disappointing' or 'dreary', ennui enveloping him like a noxious fog. Gwen Greene wrote sympathetically, 'Dear Evelyn I love you very much & I hope life *somehow* will so interest you that you'll be happy.' But there was not a great deal to be happy about. His short story, 'The Balance', had been rejected by three publishers, including Leonard Woolf. And misery over his relationship with Olivia was made more acute by the constant presence of Richard Greene and Elizabeth, 'remote from me behind an impenetrable wall of happiness': not only had Richard at last landed a good job, as music master at Lancing, but his engagement was now officially recognised. He and Elizabeth were married in London on 21 December 1925, with Evelyn as best man. The reception was in Halkin Street at the house of the bride's aunt, Lady Mary Morrison. That evening, after a dinner party given by Liza's mother, Evelyn, Olivia and a group of friends went to the Berkeley, where they sat about drinking beer, discussing the likelihood of the bride's still being a virgin, and watching Olivia perform what Evelyn described as 'that disgusting dance of hers'.

The disgusting dance, for which not only Olivia but the youth of the entire country had, it appeared, gone mad, was the Charleston. Bishops condemned it, newspapers described it as vicious, but among the Bright Young People, 'literally Charleston crazy', it had become as addictive as a drug. At parties and nightclubs Olivia in her dead-white mortuary make-up wandered restlessly about until she found some corner of the floor where she could dance alone and with abandon. Evelyn found this exhibitionism both distasteful and disturbing. Olivia's conduct – her drinking, her manic dancing, her increasingly promiscuous behaviour –

[14] Chloral, pungent and oily, is a solution of chlorine and alcohol, much used as an anaesthetic and hypnotic.

was driving him into a state of fury.[15] Her deportment was deliberately and overtly sexual: when in company and under the liberat-
ing influence of alcohol, she indulged in a form of erotic display
which was aimed at every man in the room, it sometimes seemed,
except Evelyn. Everything about her, from her clothes and
painted face to the way she moved and the subjects of her conversation (the topic of Elizabeth Russell's virginity was a typical
choice), was inflammatory and provocative. At parties she gave
herself freely to the embraces of almost any interested male,
rolling about uninhibitedly in full view of the other guests. 'Olivia
as usual behaved like a whore and was embraced on a bed by
various people.' She was particularly interested in 'Negroes', who
at that time were regarded as something of a fashionable novelty,
thanks to the success of such celebrated entertainers as Paul
Robeson, the Blackbirds and the jazz pianist 'Hutch'. 'Olivia
could talk of nothing except black men', Evelyn disapprovingly
remarked after lunching with her one day.

But Olivia's feverish sexuality was not the sole aspect that compelled Evelyn's fascination. Like Alastair, only far more extreme
in degree, she embodied the two opposing sides of his own
temperament, the sensual and dissolute with the reclusive and
ascetic. The antithesis of Olivia's licentiousness was a loathing of
the world coupled with an appetite for lacerating self-discipline,
which was to find expression in a religious mania which now
invaded her like an ague.

For several years Gwen Plunket Greene had been corresponding on religious matters with Friedrich von Hügel and, although
he was firmly opposed to proselytising, Gwen under his teaching
had become convinced of the rightness of the Roman faith,
tactfully waiting until after his death to be received into the
Church. Like her uncle, Gwen was uninterested in making converts. She was very happy to talk to Evelyn about religion, to
lend him von Hügel's *Letters,* but she scrupulously refrained from
leading him in any particular direction. To her daughter, Olivia,
however, Roman Catholicism, which had struck with all the terrifying force of divine revelation, became not only the burning centre
of her life but a vital message which she felt it her mission to
bring to lost souls, of whom Evelyn was conspicuously one.

---

[15] Years later Evelyn was to describe Olivia as '⅓ drunk ⅓ insane ⅓ genius'.

Although dismissive of his mental ability and what she saw of his ambitions, Olivia felt compassion for Evelyn's sense of disillusion, understood the despair always threatening to engulf him. She was acutely aware of the abyss, of the dark night of the soul, and exceptionally sensitive to those writers, painters and musicians who in her view were able to explore and transcend the spiritual agonies of human existence. Among this number she included Schubert, El Greco, Browning, Dostoievsky, St John of the Cross, and some of the greatest Victorian writers for children, in particular George Macdonald and Edward Lear. Evelyn was as excited by Olivia's mind as he was by her person; but although when it came to intellectual discussion her generosity was limitless, she continued to deny him even the most tentative physical embrace. And this was painful.

The antidote was a return to the old undergraduate way of life, with inebriated late-night parties in the company of Alastair and other men of similar inclinations who had been Evelyn's colleagues long before the tormenting existence of women such as Olivia had even been imagined. 'Alastair and I both got very drunk indeed' appears frequently in the diary. To many of his friends, none of them abstemious, Evelyn's drinking appeared almost suicidal. The reverberations of his drunken arrest in the Strand had done little to improve an already dissolute reputation. And Dudley Carew had been badly shaken by an incident in a pub near the British Museum: arriving to meet Evelyn for lunch, he found him already semiconscious and swaying like a punch-drunk boxer, the landlord repeating again and again that he'd never seen anything like it, never seen anyone drink so much so quickly and with such devastating effect. Carew noted that Evelyn 'went at the bottle as though he was engaged in a desperate, murderous struggle with one who was at the same time deadly enemy and devoted comrade ... Evelyn's drinking at that time was not, then, the sort of part-time vice in which most of us indulged; it was a serious, not to say deadly business.'

At the end of December 1925, Evelyn went abroad for the first time, to Paris with Bill Silk, the 'toping actor-manager' so smitten with Tony Bushell. It poured with rain, and because of the Christmas holiday many of the galleries and museums were shut. They stayed in a cheap hotel near the Louvre, ate at Prunier, Voisin, the Crillon and the Tour d'Argent, and drank massive quantities of wine while Silk talked obsessively about the beautiful Bushell. On their second evening they went to a male brothel discovered by Bill in the rue des Ourses. According to Evelyn, 'I arranged a tableau by which my boy should be enjoyed by a large negro who was there but at the last minute, after we had ascended to a squalid divan at the top of the house and he was lying waiting for the negro's advances, the price proved prohibitive and, losing patience with Bill's protracted argument with the patron, I took a taxi home and to bed in chastity. I think I do not regret it.' He was in Paris again nine months later, with Alastair. They ran into Hugh Lygon and Elmley, and the four of them made an expedition to Luna Park to see the big wheel by which Otto Silenus illustrates his philosophy of life in *Decline and Fall.* But the trip was not a great success, mainly because Alastair was 'so ignorant about Paris and French. This surprised me,' Evelyn wrote, adding, 'I think I have seen too much of Alastair lately.'

The return to Aston Clinton for the spring term was made marginally more bearable by the present of a Douglas motor-bicycle from Richard Greene, possession of which immensely raised Evelyn's status in the eyes of his pupils.[16] The bike was both a source of pleasure – providing mobility, a means of instant escape to London or Oxford – and of extreme vexation, constantly breaking down and having to be expensively repaired. On its first trip to Barford, during which it rained nearly all the way, the bike broke down three times, after which Evelyn bought a Francis-Barnett, a smaller but more reliable machine.

Another bonus was the acquisition of a sitting-room, a room over the stables which with the help of his two favourite pupils, Edmund and Charles, he managed to make reasonably comfortable. Although most evenings were still spent drinking at The Bell ('My account there must be getting very large'), he was now able to entertain his friends away from the fug and monotonous masculine drone of the common room. Charles and Edmund were asked to tea, and so on one occasion were the Waugh parents. Evelyn's only comment was that 'it rained all the time',

[16] Eleven years later Evelyn wrote of his time at Aston Clinton, 'At first the boys despised me, but I bought a motor-bicycle and from that moment was the idol of the school. I bribed them to behave well by letting them take down the engine.'

but Kate in her diary was fractionally more expansive. 'Arthur &
[I] went to Aston Clinton lunched at the Bell. Tea in Evelyn's
room. Tea beautiful, prepared by Edmund. Water boiled in
biscuit tin. [Nick] Kelly to tea. Claud C[ockburn] came in
after.'

Another guest that term was Dick Young from Llanddulas, who
'was rather a bore – drunk all the time. He seduced a garage boy
in the hedge.'

Evelyn's sitting-room was a valuable retreat; here in his spare
time he was able to read and write in peace. He had been reading
widely, Sir Joshua Reynolds's *Discourses*, Plato's *Republic*, 'The
Waste Land', and under Olivia's influence, Bergson, Bertrand
Russell and Dostoievsky. His most recent work, originally planned
as a novel, was 'The Balance', a short story subtitled 'A Yarn of
the Good Old Days of Broad Trousers and High Necked Jumpers',
described by himself in a letter of application to Chatto & Windus
as 'rather odd in shape & scheme, I am afraid'. It tells the story
of Adam Doure, a young art student who is unhappily in love
with a society beauty, the strikingly named Imogen Quest. She
casually ends the affair, he unsuccessfully attempts to drown himself. After the attempt he discusses with his reflection in the river
what it is that governs the will to die and the will to live, 'the
balance of life and death', concluding cynically that the destiny
of the individual is unimportant and apparently random and in
the end all depends on circumstance.

> Reflection: 'That is the balance then – and in the end
>   circumstance decides.'
> Adam: 'Yes, in the end circumstance.'

There is a great deal of Evelyn's own experience in this story:
Adam at Oxford and art school; Adam's sense of detachment and
attempted suicide; Imogen's indifference to his love; and in
several aspects it foreshadows the devices and preoccupations of
the early novels. There is, for example, the cinematic technique,[17] the highly developed sense of comic irony, and a faultless

---

[17] This is comparable to the cinematic effect used in *A Handful of Dust*: 'Adam
[in Oxford] is lying on his face across the bed, fully clothed. He turns over
and sits up. Again the vision of the native village; the savage has dragged himself
very near to the edge of the jungle. His back glistens in the evening sun with
his last exertion . . . Adam steadies himself at the foot of the bed and walks to
the dressing table . . .'

ear for dialogue, used brilliantly in the opening scene to characterise the absent hero. A group of bright young people are playing a game of Analogies. ' "Poor Adam, I never thought of him as Dublin, of course it's perfect." "Why Cactus?" "So phallic, my dear, and prickly". "And such vulgar flowers" . . .' Also introduced are some soon-to-be-familiar themes: blind fate; a passive and blameless hero; a sophisticated society that is cruel, frivolous, funny and amoral; and a beautiful and selfish heroine, who in this case probably owes more than a little to Olivia Plunket Greene. ' "Imogen, you never really cared, did you?" . . . "Adam dear, why will you always ask such tiresome questions. Don't you see how impossible it all is? We've only about five minutes before we reach Euston." '

'The Balance' eventually appeared in 1926 in *Georgian Stories*, an annual publication of Chapman & Hall, under the editorship that year of Alec. Evelyn was paid £2 5s 6d, and found himself in the company of William Gerhardie, Aldous Huxley, Liam O'Flaherty, Gertrude Stein and Somerset Maugham. 'The Balance' received little notice apart from a loyal piece in *The Cherwell* calling to its readers' attention the impressive accuracy of the description of drunken vomiting after a 'blind'; there was also 'a very silly review' in the *Manchester Guardian* commending Evelyn's contribution, 'but in his opinion 'for all the most futile reasons'.

The summer term of 1926, for the first week of which only five boys turned up, the rest detained by the once-in-a-lifetime opportunities of the General Strike, was characterised by boredom and melancholy. A barber had 'made savage inroads on the rather scant beauty of the school' and, except for Edmund and Charles, Evelyn had little interest in any of it. He was glad to get away as often as he could, spending most evenings either in London or Oxford, riding back in the dawn on his motor-bike and sleep-walking his way through the day's duties. With Alastair again abroad, he went for one hot, lazy weekend to Barford to stay with Mrs Graham. Returning to Aston, 'I found Edmund out of bounds and beat him with mixed feelings and an ash plant. He was very sweet and brave about it all. I have given him a Sulka tie as recompense.' With his two favourites he sat talking in his room over the stables, eating strawberries, and reading aloud from *The Wind in the Willows.*[18]

When Alastair came back, he and Evelyn, with Claud Cockburn and the young married Greenes, went to a pub 'and got very drunk and Alastair swam the canal with a glass of beer in each hand and drank them'. It was during this weekend that Alastair suggested Evelyn write something for him to print, as he now had a press of his own. 'All this week accordingly I have been writing the essay which I made notes for when my ankle was sprained last year, on the PRB. I think it is quite good. I got it done in four and a half days, in between correcting exam papers.'

The Pre-Raphaelite Brotherhood was an attractive subject, with its extreme romanticism and a style founded in the Walter Crane–William Morris tradition. The Pre-Raphaelite was, too, a very literary genre (every picture tells a story), with the added recommendation of being despised by Bloomsbury and wholly out of fashion with the modernist movement. There was also Evelyn's personal, proprietary interest deriving from Holman Hunt's having married in succession two of his Waugh great-aunts. *PRB* is a short, lucid account of the group and its work, interspersed with some fictional scenes (it begins with an imaginary dialogue between Millais – 'now nearly sixteen; a precocious child of agreeable but prosaic appearance' – and Hunt) and some forcible expressions of personal opinion: *The Awakening Conscience*, for instance, is categorised as 'the noblest painting by any Englishman'.

Returning in September for the start of the school year, Evelyn was determined to make yet another attempt to lead 'a life of sobriety, chastity and obedience'. His mother had given him £150 with which to pay his debts, and he was working on a contribution to a light-hearted essay series published by Kegan Paul entitled *Today and Tomorrow*, of which the most notable to date had been Robert Graves's 'Lars Porsena, or the Future of Swearing'. Evelyn's idea was that he should write on 'Noah, or the Future of Intoxication'.

[18] Kenneth Grahame's novel was a great favourite of Evelyn's. In his first book, a life of the painter Rossetti, he describes the fall from fashion of Benjamin Haydon in the following words: 'Poor Mr Toad, deserted by Rat, Badger, and even Mole, with the stoats and the weazels permanently established in his inheritance!'

As usual the term quickly deteriorated into featureless weeks of boredom and depression. The food was bad, the boys 'increasingly given to sordid malefactions', it rarely stopped raining, and there were only evenings drinking at The Bell to look forward to. 'I find myself shouting at the children and neglecting to make my corrections and losing my mark book and reading Edgar Wallace and being quite unable to understand the essays of Herbert Read – and there are five more weeks of this term nearly... All day I have been rude to the boys and am ashamed of it,' he wrote, entering two days later only the word, 'Bored'; the week after that, 'Tired and bored'. The days dragged on 'cold and beastly... yesterday I caned a boy for blasphemy'. Term ended on the tenth of December, and Evelyn with difficulty got a promise from the headmaster of a rise in salary of £10 per annum. 'I think next term will be my last.'

To escape from the tedium of a holiday at home, on Christmas Eve 1926 Evelyn left London for Marseilles en route to join Alastair, who was in Athens about to take up his post as honorary attaché to the British legation under Sir Percy Loraine. The ship, *Patris II*, was smart and clean, but the passengers were uninteresting – Evelyn shared a cabin with a Greek currant merchant who for five days never left his bed – and the weather rough, so most of the voyage was spent reading William James's *The Varieties of Religious Experience* and making drawings for a book Evelyn had briefly in mind to be called 'The Annals of Constitutional Monarchy'. Alastair was a generous host, his apartment 'very modern indeed with baths and lavatories and electric lights'. But Evelyn, his tastes now tending in other directions, was no longer wholly sympathetic to the unrestrained paederasty indulged in by his friend (at last free of his mother and the laws of Great Britain), complaining that 'the flat is usually full of dreadful Dago youths called by heroic names such as Miltiades and Agamemnon with blue chins and greasy clothes who sleep with the English colony for 25 drachmas a night.' He and Alastair patronised the British Club and spent a lot of time sitting in cafés. 'All the drinks taste either of camphor or medicine and everything smells of drains.'

As a present on parting Alastair gave him an old icon, and renewed his supplies of brandy, razor blades and lavatory paper.

Thus equipped Evelyn, after a week, went on his own to Olympia, where he saw in a shed the Hermes of Praxiteles, 'embedded in concrete before a grey plush curtain. It is quite marvellous and well worth all the trouble I have taken to see it.' He then took the boat at Patras for Brindisi, stopping on the way at Corfu. Of this first brief experience of the island, Evelyn wrote later, 'It seemed to me then one of the most beautiful places I had ever seen. So much was I impressed, that when, later, I found myself writing a novel about someone very rich,[19] I gave her a villa in Corfu, as I thought that, when I was rich, that was one of the first things I would buy.' He arrived in Rome on 11 January 1927, where he spent three days sight-seeing and in a futile search for night life. He enjoyed it only so far: Rome at that stage was just Rome. He reached home on 22 January, very dirty, very hungry, and unimpressed by 'abroad'. 'I am afraid I have inherited over-much of my father's homely sentiments. The truth is that I do not really like being abroad much . . . from February [I want to] shut myself up for the rest of my life in the British Isles.'

At Underhill there was a letter from Kegan Paul turning 'Noah' down – 'rather a blow as I was counting on the money for it but perhaps it is a good thing. I was not pleased with it' – a disappointment counterbalanced by an offer of ten guineas for a short story for Hugh Chesterman's anthology, the *New Decameron*.

By the end of January 1927 Evelyn was back at Aston Clinton, but not for long. His prophecy that this would be his last term was correct. During the holiday Dr Crawford had engaged two new members of staff, a poor-spirited usher named Attwell ('almost a teetotaller when he came but I have so far corrupted him that last night he was sick'), and an 'admirable' matron who had previously worked at Lancing and seemed friendly and fun. But she was not as accommodating as at first appeared. 'While Attwell and I were sitting over the fire laughing about our drunkenness of the night before, Crawford suddenly arrived and sacked us both, on the spot . . . Apparently that matron had been making trouble.' Attwell, in recognition of his minor rôle as accessory, was allowed to stay till the end of term, but Evelyn had to go at

[19] Mrs Beste-Chetwynde in *Decline and Fall.*

once. 'I packed hurriedly leaving my books to come on by goods and slipped away feeling rather like a housemaid who has been caught stealing gloves. I rang up my parents first to apprise them of my coming, and dined in a very sorrowful household.'[20]

The version of events prepared for consumption at Underhill was that he had been dismissed for drunkenness, but other, less fragile audiences were told that Evelyn had been sacked for attempting to seduce the matron. The truth was a combination of both: Dr Crawford had finally lost patience with the nightly noisy inebriation of Attwell and Waugh, and so when matron complained that Evelyn, coming back one night drunk as usual, had made a semi-facetious pass at her as she came out of the bathroom in her dressing-gown, he took the opportunity to get rid of them both. At least two of Evelyn's pupils regretted his departure. 'Dear Evelyn, I cannot tell you how sorry I am that you have left,' wrote Edmund. 'I do not know what Pig & I will do now without your room to go up & tidy or wash up . . . I went up there yesterday to see what you had done with all your things & it looked so bare without your books & candle sticks and the Ikon (I cannot spell it.)'

Arrived home, Evelyn wrote portentously in his diary, 'the time has arrived to set about being a man of letters.' First, however, he had to find a job. The very day of his dismissal he had had an appointment to see a Father Underhill to discuss the possibility of becoming a clergyman. It had not been an encouraging interview. '[Father Underhill] spoke respectfully of the Duke of Westminster and disrespectfully of my vocation to the Church.' Religion having failed him, there was nothing for it but to try again at schoolmastering. He applied and was accepted for a post at a down-at-heel academy in Notting Hill at £5 a week. 'This relieves me of immediate anxiety but it looks like being a dreary job.'

The school, described by Evelyn in terms of Dickensian horror, was far, far worse than either of his previous establishments. 'All

---

[20] In an article in *Passing Show* two years later, Evelyn wrote of schoolmastering, 'The early hours, the close association with men equally degraded and lost to hope as yourself, the derision and spite of indefatigable little boys, the gross effrontery of matrons and headmasters' wives, all these and many minor discomforts too numerous to mention are the price you must pay for bare subsistence.'

the masters drop their aitches and spit in the fire and scratch their genitals. The boys have close-cropped heads and steel-rimmed spectacles wound about with worsted. They pick their noses and scream at each other in a cockney accent.'

This was the nadir of his experiences as a schoolmaster. Fortunately, it was not to last. With the end of that term came a complete change of fortune, a change opening up opportunities which only a few weeks previously had been unthought of. Now his career as a man of letters, until then considered only as a subsidiary means of generating income, suddenly took on new importance. And in further sloughing off the old life, he managed finally to extricate himself from his unhappy love affair with Olivia.

This relationship had been growing increasingly torturous. Several of Evelyn's friends were convinced that the influence of the Plunket Greenes was an unhealthy one. Harold Acton, as sour in his disapproval of Olivia as he had been at Oxford of Richard Pares, condemned the whole family as 'esurient narcotics', while in the opinion of another acquaintance, Robert Speaight, the actor and Catholic convert, Olivia's combined rôle of saint and prima donna was completely bogus: it was, he said, 'simply unintelligent to confine one's reading to *Vogue* and St John of the Cross'. By such critics her company was found depressing, her appearance morbid; she had 'a face like a fungus', said one of the Russell uncles. Evelyn was disturbed by what he saw as Olivia's sordid and unstoppable decline. There had been a particularly depressing occasion when he had visited her one Sunday from Aston Clinton, and 'found her packing bottles in a bedroom littered with stockings and newspaper. Fatter and larger generally, unable to talk of much except herself and that in an impersonal and incoherent way. I sat on her bed for some time trying to talk to her with my heart sinking and sinking.'

But he was still in love with her, still passionately attracted. The more he yearned, the more distant she became, until during an agonising confrontation Olivia finally made it plain that she could never love him, would never allow him to sleep with her. Evelyn, who was smoking, took hold of her wrist and held the burning tip of his cigarette against her bare skin.

This act of spontaneous sadism, far from shocking Olivia, moved her deeply. For the first time Evelyn had shown himself worthy of respect; and the mortification of the flesh was something to which Olivia, recently committed to a form of religious servitude in which pain and suffering were requisite, greedily submitted. Although she had not yet been received into the Catholic Church, she had taken to her new faith with a fanaticism that to many seemed dangerously unbalanced. The prospect of marriage had never interested her, 'those dreadful relationships', but now she went further along her chosen path of self-denial. Taking to the limits of interpretation the teaching of von Hügel, who had always emphasised the importance of joy through renunciation, 'the Cross *and* the Crown',[21] Olivia believed that the road to spiritual purity lay only through extreme anguish; she had thus decided to renounce what she knew she could least do without, and as a result, she believed, of divine direction had taken a vow of chastity. Evelyn knew nothing of this, but at last he had to accept that although he could continue to regard her as mentor and friend, as a lover Olivia was for ever out of reach.

Yet this period was far from being one of unmitigated despair. The change in his relationship with Olivia, although harrowing, was also something of a relief; and for once there were several promising prospects in view, the first being a job on the *Daily Express*. This was offered as part of a probationary scheme by which graduates were given the chance of working in Fleet Street, while conveniently providing the paper with some extremely cheap labour. The idea was that at the end of three months the probationer would either be taken on at full union rates (very rare) or (more usual) have his contract terminated. On the same day as Evelyn's successful interview with the editor, word came that his short story, 'The Tutor's Tale', a mildly black comedy involving two favourite themes, madness and the aristocracy, had been accepted for the *New Decameron*. To celebrate, Evelyn had dinner at Kettner's with Harold Acton, now living in 'rather a charming flat in John Street, Adelphi, with a Chinese servant and many paintings of himself'.

The celebration was both timely and appropriate: the end of the hated schoolmastering, a promising new job, publication of his second story. Not only that: through the good offices of

[21] 'Holy suffering is the very crown of holy action,' he had written to Gwen on 7 October 1921.

his old Oxford acquaintance, Anthony Powell, Evelyn had won a commission from the publisher, Duckworth, to write a full-length biography of Rossetti for the centenary of the painter's birth the following year.

And, he recorded in his diary for 7 April 1927, 'I have met such a nice girl called Evelyn Gardner.'

My mock marriage

Exactly how Evelyn Waugh met his first wife is open to dispute. Dudley Carew was under the impression that it was he who first introduced Waugh to Evelyn Gardner, at a party at his flat in Red Lion Square. Carew was surprised that the two seemed to get on as well as they did. '[Evelyn Gardner] was a girl it was impossible to dislike,' he recalled, 'or, rather, I could imagine only one person who might dislike her, and that was Evelyn Waugh.' The other, more probable, version credits Alec with the introduction. He had gone to talk to Evelyn Gardner and her flat-mate, Pansy Pakenham, for an article he was writing about the Modern Girl, and had been enchanted by them both. 'Utterly delightful,' he told Anthony Powell, whom he met while crossing Sloane Square on his way back from the interview. 'Very modern, but not at all *brassy*.' Soon afterwards the two girls invited him to a party, and it was to this that Alec, as so often before, took his brother.

That spring, the spring of 1927, Evelyn Gardner and Pansy Pakenham were sharing furnished lodgings at 107 Ebury Street, two rooms with breakfast for 35s a week, £1 extra for use of sitting-room if notified in advance. In those days it was unusual, to say the least, for young ladies of good family to be living together unchaperoned, entertaining whom they pleased, one (Pansy) even going out to work. But their mothers, both widows, were old friends, and both believed (mistakenly as it turned out) that the other's daughter would have a stabilising influence on her own. Pansy's mother, the Dowager Countess of Longford, had always liked Evelyn Gardner and admired her spirit, while Evelyn's mother, the Dowager Lady Burghclere, had been impressed by an incident in the recent past when Pansy had succeeded in persuading her feckless daughter out of an unsuitable engagement. The friendship between the two girls was on the face of it an unlikely one: Pansy earnest and idealistic, Evelyn essentially frivolous; but they had in common an antipathy to conventional upper-class life and a longing to escape from home.

Until then, home for Evelyn Gardner had been a succession of rented houses in Mayfair. Her father, Herbert Gardner, 1st Lord Burghclere, was a distinguished politician, a Liberal Member of Parliament who had served under both Gladstone and Rosebery. He was a charming, clever and affectionate man, devoted to his children and, like Arthur Waugh, passionately fond of amateur theatricals.[1] Unfortunately he had died in 1921 when Evelyn was little more than a child, leaving her, much the youngest of four children, all girls, in the sole care of her mother. Lady Burghclere was something of a bluestocking, author of a couple of historical biographies. Like Olivia Plunket Greene, she was a Herbert, and thus a member of the chosen race, her father the 4th Earl of Carnarvon, her brother, the 5th Earl, famous for his discovery of the tomb of Tutankhamen. Dark and prim, with a caressing manner that did little to temper the iron will beneath, she was determined to make something of her youngest daughter. The Burghcleres had never been rich, but the three elder girls had married well, two of them to very wealthy men, Alathea to Geoffrey Fry (Fry's cocoa), Mary to George Hope-Morley (Morley underwear), and it was made crystal clear to Evelyn that it was her duty to do the same. Not unnaturally Evelyn thought otherwise. Although like all Herberts she had a strong sense of family, she could hardly wait to exchange the stuffy, respectable world into which she had been born for the anonymity and freedom of the more liberal society into which she now found her way.

In adolescence Evelyn Gardner had been rather plump, but she soon fined down and, although never a beauty like her sisters, was extremely pretty, with a round face, little upturned nose, huge eyes and a flawless porcelain complexion. She looked, said Harold Acton, like a china doll; 'like a china doll with a head

---

[1] Lord Burghclere's mother, Julia Fortescue, was a professional actress who had lived openly with her lover, the 3rd Lord Gardner, for fifteen years and borne him five children before belatedly he married her.

full of sawdust', added Diana Guinness, less entranced than some by Evelyn's modish inanities. The androgynous styles of the period, so unbecoming to more voluptuous women, could have been designed for Evelyn. Proud of her resemblance to Edna Best, star of that popular play, *The Constant Nymph*, she was the personification of the flapper. With her shingled brown hair, her long legs and boyish figure – divine in the narrow tube dresses then in fashion – she looked like a ravishing page-boy as she mixed a cocktail or deftly practised her Charleston on the hearth-rug in front of the fire. She loved clothes, particularly in shades of apricot and orange, and was extravagant with her modest allowance of £400 a year. She had a cloche hat decorated with painted hearts pierced by arrows, and a handbag shaped like a Pekinese whimsically referred to as 'Androcles'. Her speech was slangy and up-to-date, full of 'sick-makings' and 'too-too-shame-makings'. Far from unintelligent, she read Proust, but under-mined this sign of intellectual discernment by referring to him always as 'Prousty-wousty'. She gushed with enthusiasm, was lavish with dearests and darlings, addressing all her friends indiscrimi-nately as 'angel-face' and 'sweetie-pie'. She loved company, hated spending any length of time on her own. Lively, light-hearted and a tremendous flirt, she was a great success with men. When Pansy reported home that Evelyn as a child had claimed she was descended from a fairy bear, the Pakenham governess snorted, 'More like a bare fairy!'

Of the two girls, beautiful, blonde Pansy was the more serious and mature. Having done a course at the Central School of Arts and Crafts, she had got a job working for the archi-tect George Kennedy, while Evelyn, apart from a little light journalism and an amateurish attempt at writing a play, concen-trated on parties and dances and entertaining her growing number of friends to tea. Young for her age, living only for the moment, determined to take nothing too seriously, Evelyn wanted fun, fun as far away as possible from the basilisk eye of Lady Burghclere. Later, Evelyn was to accuse her mother of inducing a crushing sense of inferiority by her sarcasm and constant snubs; she felt that Lady Burghclere's rigid prudishness had kept her 'innocent' far beyond the age when innocence was natural. The result of such an overdisciplined upbringing was that 'some of us suffered'. Evelyn's naïvety and a puppyish eagerness to embrace everything and everyone that came her way were undoubtedly engaging, but her childishness sometimes took her friends aback. Over breakfast one morning she startled Pansy by announcing in a little-girl voice, '*I* think it's time something *nice* happened!'

The party to which Alec had been invited that April evening was typically Ebury Street bohemian, with guests from the literary and theatrical worlds mixed with Pansy's sisters and those of Evelyn Gardner's old débutante friends, like Nancy Mitford, who were also in rebellion against strict and conventional families. Noël Coward had been invited but was unable to come, so Alec Waugh, well-known young novelist, was the lion of the evening. The first guest to arrive at 9.30 was Lady Brooke, wife of Sir Charles Vyner Brooke, white rajah of Sarawak, who turned up accompanied by her husband's ADC, the dark and handsome Barry Gifford. With a choice of gin, beer or marsala, the party soon got under way, the guests amiably crowded into the tiny sitting-room and overflowing into Evelyn's adjacent bedroom. With all the noise and the heat and the crush of people, it is little wonder that Evelyn, busy with her duties as hostess, took small interest in Alec Waugh's younger brother, a short, brown-haired young man with sticking-out ears and an intense stare. In any event the focus of Evelyn's attention that evening was Lady Brooke's ADC, to whom, in spite of the fact that he was quite a few years older and not yet divorced, she had until recently been engaged.

Evelyn got engaged as easily as other girls bought hats. (Rumour had it that she was engaged nine times before she finally married.) With her high spirits and flirtatious manner, she was attractive to men but quickly bored by serious suitors and surprised when they acted hurt when she tired of them and turned them away. Among her several fiancés was Ulick Verney, a young guardsman of impeccable background but in Lady Burghclere's eyes inadequate income. In order to put an end to this particular bit of nonsense, her mother had packed her off to Australia in the company of one of her sisters – from where she returned engaged to the ship's purser. It was this attachment that Pansy successfully urged her to break, whereupon she instantly took up with the equally unacceptable Gifford. Eventually convinced of the impossibility of marrying a middle-aged divorcé, Evelyn Gardner was once more on the loose. And it was at this point that she met Evelyn Waugh, himself only just emerging from a long period of unhappiness.

After the torment of the relationship with Olivia, Evelyn Gardner, pretty, playful and uncomplicated, presented an alluring prospect for Evelyn Waugh. But attracted though he was to this new playmate, Waugh was still very much enmeshed with Olivia, continuing to see her, talking to her almost daily on the telephone, and doing what he could to help her through increasingly frequent periods of depression, with which he could sympathise only too well. But he was not depressed: life for once was full of promise. 'Mr Toad on top!' as he used to say when expressing satisfaction with his fortunes.

First there was the job with the *Daily Express*. Osbert Sitwell had provided Evelyn with an introduction to the editor and, although he stayed for less than two months, the terrain was new and interesting. It had recently become quite the thing for Oxford graduates to go into Fleet Street. Evelyn's cousin Claud Cockburn was working for *The Times*; Patrick Balfour, another Oxford contemporary, joined the *Weekly Dispatch* before going to the *Daily Sketch* as Mr Gossip; and Tom Driberg was given a job on the *Express* only months after Evelyn had left it. Before Lord Beaverbrook built his great black glass palace, the premises, like all the other newspaper offices in Fleet Street, were old and grimy; there was a small entrance for staff in Shoe Lane, opposite the sausage shop much frequented for cheap meals. For £5 a week Evelyn as a probationer was expected to cover minor news stories (fire, theft, accident) none of which, in his case, ever appeared in the paper. This may account for the flippant tone in which a couple of years later he gave advice to the aspiring journalist. When sent out on a story, 'the correct procedure is to jump to your feet, seize your hat and umbrella and dart out of the office with every appearance of haste to the nearest cinema . . . [there to sit] for an hour or so and smoke a pipe'. Evelyn was directly answerable to the news editor, J. B. Wilson, but he was given little to do, and most of the day was spent lounging about the hot, noisy office chatting to his fellow probationers, making particular friends with one, Inez Holden, who later won a small reputation as a novelist and writer of short stories.

Evelyn started work on the *Express* in April. He was sacked in May, leaving him free for his next undertaking, the life of Rossetti, for which Tom Balston at Duckworth's had paid him an advance of £20, 'which I spent in a week'. Arthur, who would never have paid an advance to an untried author without seeing at least part of a manuscript first, disapproved of Balston's irresponsible extravagance. 'Balston will never see that book,' he discouragingly predicted. 'I suppose I'll have to make it good.'

Before getting down to work, Evelyn joined Alec and his parents for a holiday in the South of France. They stayed first at Nîmes, then went on to Les Baux, visiting Arles, Avignon and Aigues-Mortes, before ending up at Marseilles where they were to see Alec off on a voyage to Tahiti and the Far East. After six and a half years, Alec had left his uncongenial job at Chapman & Hall to embark on the first stage of a lifetime's nomadic voyaging round the world in search of copy. The two brothers, without their parents, spent the last evening together, 'beginning decorously at Basso's with caviare and Meursault and ending less creditably in the slums', in particular the red-light district in and around the notorious rue Ventomargy, a street 'said to be the toughest in Europe', a schedule followed almost to the letter a year later by Paul Pennyfeather in *Decline and Fall.*

By the end of July *Rossetti*, under the temporary title, *The Last Born of Eve*, was well advanced. In August, after a night of drunken debauch with Alastair 'that sickened me of London for the time', Evelyn went on his own to the Abingdon Arms at Beckley, going into Oxford most days to work quietly in the Union library. He called several times on Francis Crease, who was now living in the nearby village of Marston, and for whom Evelyn had written a graceful introduction to his book (small edition, privately printed), *Thirty-Four Decorative Designs*. Crease was pleased. 'Could you have seen my enjoyment whilst reading your essay – I won't say you would have been rewarded, but certain of my appreciation in a way that a letter can't convey.'

Evelyn also went to Barford for a weekend with Mrs Graham, 'that unquiet lady' of whom he was nevertheless fond, Alastair having gone up to Scotland to stay with his Forbes relations. When she and Evelyn were alone together, they got on well: the house was comfortable and there was an attic, furnished with a table, chair and a dressmaker's headless dummy, where Evelyn could work undisturbed. It was Mrs Graham who took him to tea at Kelmscott where William Morris had lived, and where Miss Morris, 'a ·singularly forbidding woman', showed them 'two exquisite Rossetti crayons of her and her sister as children – innumerable sketches of Jane Morris and a large painting and the studies for the predella of Dante's Dream'. Back in London, Evelyn went to see Sir Hall Caine, the novelist and critic who had befriended Rossetti in the last years of his life, and in whose arms the great man had died: 'He received me in bed . . . wore a white woollen dressing-gown and looked like a Carthusian abbot. Enormously vain and theatrical but more genial and humorous than I had expected. He told me a lot of really profitable things about Rossetti and Fanny Cornforth and Lizzie's suicide.'

Rossetti: His Life and Works is a vigorous and opinionated account written in a manner combining the chattily informal (Elizabeth Siddal's brother was 'slightly dotty', Millais's father and mother were 'sweet to him') with the grandiose. The most grandiose sentence of all – 'Turner was seventy-one years old, sinking like one of his own tremendous sunsets in clouds of obscured glory' – was lovingly transposed almost word for word from *PRB*. As a subject, the rich romanticism of Rossetti's work and his anguished personality were immensely attractive, as was the fact that the Pre-Raphaelites were then, largely thanks to Roger Fry and the Bloomsbury group, wholly out of fashion. In character and circumstance there was much in Rossetti with which Evelyn could identify. Both men believed in the importance of meticulous craftsmanship, both had a loathing of music: 'in later life [Rossetti] was inclined to regard it as an invention of his enemies devised expressly for his own discomfort'. There were further, prophetic affinities in the drinking and insomnia, and in the delirious paranoia, fuelled by an addiction to chloral, which so tormented the artist at the end of his life.[2] More importantly, both men felt out of joint in place and time. Evelyn empathetically describes Rossetti as

[2] The painter's drug-induced hallucinations described by Hall Caine in his *Recollections of Rossetti* are strikingly similar to those experienced by Waugh and described in his autobiographical novel, *The Ordeal of Gilbert Pinfold.*

the baffled and very tragic figure of an artist born into an age
devoid of artistic standards; a man of the South, sensual,
indolent, and richly versatile, exiled in the narrow, scrambling,
specialised life of a Northern city; a mystic without a creed; a
Catholic without the discipline or consolation of the Church;
a life between the rocks and the high road, like the scrub of a
Southern hillside, sombre, aromatic, and impenetrable.

Ultimately however, Evelyn condemns Rossetti as a second-rate
artist who was able only occasionally to overcome his spiritual
inadequacy and create a great work. He was lacking 'the *moral*
stability of a great artist . . . All his brooding about magic and
suicide are symptomatic not so much of genius as of mediocrity.'
This inadequacy was shamefully exemplified by Rossetti's decision
to disinter manuscript poems from his wife's grave.

There is no reason why one should look upon the grave as more
sacred than the dung-heap. The point is that Rossetti did so look
upon it, and it is his reluctance to comply, coupled with his
compliance, that clearly indicates a real degradation in his
character. In burying the poems, he was, according to his lights,
performing a sacramental act, and in digging them up he
violated that sacrament, and one can discern no motive for this
violation other than frank, disagreeable vanity.

Rossetti was the first full-length book Evelyn had written, and still
he thought of himself as a painter and craftsman first, a writer
second. When he came to the last sentence, he inscribed, 'The
End. Thank God'.

The book was not due to be published until the following spring,
and for the present, the autumn and winter of 1927, there was
as always the problem of money. Through Arthur's influence
Evelyn had started writing occasional reviews for the *The Bookman*,
which brought in a few pounds, and he had a tiny salary from
part-time teaching at a school in Golders Green, a job of which
he was so ashamed he would never afterwards speak of it. He
had also promised to take part in a symposium planned by Robert
Byron and Brian Howard entitled 'Value', his contribution to be
a drawing of God consisting entirely of abstract form, 'yet in
some measure coherent and having perhaps some slight relation
to the revelation of St John the divine'. 'I deal with God as best

I can,' he wrote to Robert. 'I suppose a treatise on the relationship between painting & photography wouldn't fit into your scheme anywhere? I am at work on one now.' But the project was never realised. In desperation Evelyn appealed to his father, who agreed to give him an allowance of £4 a week to tide him over while he looked for proper employment. Living at Underhill, of course, cost nothing, except the energy expended in resenting it.

> How I detest this house and how ill I feel in it. The whole place
> volleys and thunders with traffic. I can't sleep well or work . . .
> Mother is away at Midsomer Norton where Aunt Trissie is dying.
> The telephone bell is continually ringing, my father
> scampering up and down stairs, Gaspard barking, the gardener
> rolling the gravel under the window and all the time the traffic.
> Another week of this will drive me mad.

But in spite of these unserene surroundings, Evelyn recorded on 3 September, '[I] have begun on a comic novel.' And the following day there is this entry in the diary: 'I sat up last night unable to sleep, reading my Lancing diaries. Wrote to Balston about my comic novel which I think is amusing.'

Meanwhile there was the more urgent matter of earning a living. Perhaps inspired by his Pre-Raphaelite researches and his visit to William Morris's house, Evelyn enrolled in October for a carpentry course at the Central School of Arts and Crafts in Southampton Row,[3] preparatory to making a career as a cabinet-maker.[4] Here he came across Tony Powell, who had been sent by Duckworth's to learn about printing. Powell, surprised to run into Evelyn of all people, asked what he was doing there. 'Oh, Tolstoy, and that sort of thing', Evelyn blandly replied. But unlike his wastrel experience at Heatherley's, Evelyn took his lessons seriously and enjoyed them, 'all except the carving in the evenings'. Some years later he recalled that brief period with pleasure.

> Those were delightful days, under the tuition of a brilliant and
> completely speechless little cabinet-maker who could explain

[3] Founded in 1896, deriving from the Art Workers' Guild and drawing its inspiration from Ruskin, Philip Webb and Morris himself.
[4] Kate Waugh more than once expressed the opinion that Evelyn would have done better as a cabinet-maker than as a writer. 'Furniture is so useful; besides he would have been happier designing furniture.'

nothing and demonstrate everything. To see him cutting
concealed dovetails gave me the thrill which, I suppose, others
get from seeing their favourite batsman at the wicket or bull
fighter in the ring . . . I never got as far as veneering curved
surfaces, but I made an indestructible mahogany bed-table,
which I gave to my father.

But none of this was bringing in money, and although board and
lodging were free, Evelyn's preferred way of life was expensive,
particularly now that he was beginning seriously to pay court to
Evelyn Gardner. They went to the theatre together, and he took
her to lunch at the new Green Park Hotel, and to dinner at the
Gargoyle Club in Dean Street, that raffish meeting place of
the louche and fashionable to which he had recently taken out
membership. On one occasion described by Evelyn Gardner the
two Evelyns and Alec went to a dinner party at the Ritz and then
on with a group of friends to the Gargoyle. 'An awful old woman
in the party insisted on leaning her head on Evelyn's shoulder &
holding his hand. Poor Evelyn simply didn't know what to do
about it. Afterwards we came back here, and woke up Pansy &
drank coffee and sherry!' Over the last few months Evelyn Waugh
had become a regular guest at the tea parties given by Evelyn
Gardner and Pansy, the flapper and the 'beau-monde blonde', at
their new flat, a maisonette over a tobacconist at 54 Sloane
Square, on the corner of Cliveden Place. Evelyn Gardner had
jokily inscribed 'Blondes' under their names on the doorbell.

She was clearly intrigued by her latest suitor. Still being pursued
by Barry Gifford and having just turned down a proposal from
yet another 'shady bore', she seemed to be enjoying this innocent
and playful courtship, in which the ardour, as Pansy noted, was
all on Waugh's side, an ardour which most of the time he had the
sense to keep under control, his good behaviour only occasionally
undermined by the effects of alcohol. At a drunken party given
by one of Evelyn Gardner's ex-boyfriends, 'Evelyn [Waugh] got a
little tight too, and was furious because I wouldn't let him take
me home. When I got back about 1.30 the telephone rang, & a
small precise voice said, "Is that Miss Gardner?" "Yes." "What I
want to say is, Hell to you!" Clang went the receiver. I did laugh
so much. Evelyn apologised profusely the next day, he is so sweet.'
A friend of Evelyn Gardner's described her as having 'immense

charm & a very generous nature, but she was essentially light, not sexy except in a superficial way', a view borne out by her description of her relationship with Evelyn Waugh. 'Lately we have become such terribly good friends, and it's such a good plan, because I know he would never make love to me, & everyone else does, & it's such a bore.' From time to time she took fright and backed away, but Pansy, who liked Waugh and thought him far more interesting and worthwhile than the bounders with whom her friend had previously been entangled, vigorously argued his case. Pansy was conducting a love affair with the painter, Henry Lamb, a man not only more than twenty years older than she, and bohemian, but as yet undivorced from his first wife. As Anthony Powell put it, the household at Cliveden Place 'at that moment had some of the air of a play: the two charming girls; the two detrimental but gifted suitors; the very situation come into being most dreaded by the two dowager mammas.'

It was Henry Lamb who offered to take Waugh down to Bourne-mouth to see the cabinet-maker, Romney Green, with a view to being taken on as apprentice. However, two days before the planned interview, Waugh, alarmed by sudden talk of a trip to Canada, took Evelyn Gardner to dinner at the Ritz and proposed marriage. It was not a graceful proposal, no declaration of undying love, more along the lines of, 'Why don't we try it and see how it goes?', an unfortunately off-hand phrase which Evelyn Gardner did not care for. Her reply was 'inconclusive'. After dinner, Waugh 'rang up Pansy who advised in favour of marriage. Went to Sloane Square and discussed it. Went to Bourdon Street and told Olivia. Home late and unable to sleep.' Next morning Evelyn Gardner telephoned to say that she had thought it over and had decided to accept. Waugh was overjoyed. 'Went to Southampton Row but was unable to work. Went to pub with Dudley and told him of engagement. Tea Evelyn.' A day or two later Tony Powell met Waugh, obviously in the highest spirits, on the Underground. 'I'm going to be married,' he announced, beaming.

Foolhardy although it may have been, marriage for both Evelyns appeared as a life-saving solution. They were both adrift and the proposal at the Ritz had been well-timed. It is true that at twenty-four they were not only very young, but very young for their age;

neither of them had any money, and little in common except high spirits and a taste for frivolity. Nonetheless, each saw in the other not only an ally but a deliverer.

Since leaving Oxford, Evelyn Waugh had been without direction, with little sense of purpose or identity. He had been profoundly unhappy, more than once on the brink of the abyss, dangerously driven by an instinct of self-destruction. As a married man he would immediately assume an identity, would have a road to follow. And although his parents exasperated him, the safety and stability of their marriage must have set an encouraging example. Underhill was dull, yet it never failed to provide a safe haven; and once in a home of his own, with a wife, such a haven could surely be his. The fact, too, that his fiancée was so obviously attractive to men was of importance to Evelyn, prone to self-loathing and sexually unsure, his confidence badly damaged by Olivia's rejection. Previously he had been existing in a kind of no-man's-land, poor, drinking too much, wasting time in hopeless jobs which bored him. But by marrying Evelyn Gardner, his status as a displaced person would change: he would immediately belong, not only as husband and provider, but as a member of that secure and desirable world inhabited by the English upper class.

For Evelyn Gardner the situation was slightly different. She liked Evelyn Waugh, was fascinated by his cleverness and originality, but for her marriage was first and foremost a means of escape from home. With Pansy in love with Lamb and hoping to marry, the prospect of a return to her mother and Green Street loomed dangerously near.

Once engaged, the two Evelyns, He-Evelyn and She-Evelyn as they were cutely called, had to face some formidable opposition. Lady Burghclere was not about to see her youngest daughter marry an unemployed carpenter with £4 a week, an irredeemably middle-class background and a father virtually in trade. ('It never occurred to me to think I wasn't a gentleman until Lady Burghclere pointed it out,' Waugh wrote later.) Nor, once she had made up her mind, was there much chance of persuading her to a more lenient view. 'She is an impossible person to discuss anything with,' her daughter complained, 'because unless you agree with her every word she is furious.' Lady Burghclere had seen off a number of undesirable suitors in the past, and her tactics were ruthless and efficient. The first step was to conduct some private researches into the young man's character. There were plenty of useful rumours about Waugh's behaviour at university,[5] but hard evidence was what was needed, and for this Lady Burghclere paid 'a scavenging visit' to Oxford. On her return she insisted that her daughter move into Green Street for at least a fortnight, and there she confronted her with the results of her interview with

> a Mr Crutwell [sic] (palpitating with perverse vices) & the Dean of Hertford. They said he used to live off vodka and absinthe (presumably mixed) & went about with disreputable people (then followed a string of French remarks about 'ces vices' something or other, all beautifully pronounced but unintelligible).

Lady Burghclere had further discovered that Waugh lived off his parents, ill-treated his father, lacked moral fibre, and was sure to drag his young wife 'down into the abysmal depths of Sodom & Gomorrah'. The upshot was that there was to be no engagement for at least two years.

Evelyn himself was then summoned, to be submitted to an extremely unpleasant interview, during which his future mother-in-law criticised his drinking habits ('The late Lord Burghclere always said that "a young man might drink champagne but not spirits" '), his general character, and his unsuitable friends ('The late Lord Burghclere always said "a man is known by his friends" '). Waugh, completely unafraid, counter-attacked by threatening to marry within the week, which so took Lady Burghclere aback that she reluctantly agreed to a wedding in September on condition that Waugh find a job first. 'Victory for the Evelyns!' her daughter triumphantly proclaimed.

Pansy, in love with a thoroughly unsuitable man and having to deal with similar opposition from the Longford camp, was the Evelyns' most sympathetic supporter. She was delighted by the engagement, she told a friend of hers, John Maxse,

> but then my opinion of Evelyn Waugh, always high, has greatly increased in the last few months & I had been hoping that he would propose & she would accept. After all these toughs &

[5] 'Evelyn Waugh did much worse than drink! and anyone seen with him lost his reputation at Oxford at once!!!' a friend of Matthew Ponsonby's delightedly reported.

cavemen that make up her & Mary H[ope] M[orley]'s usual clientèle, E. Waugh seems like claret after whisky ... to me the chief question is has Evelyn G. the guts & nerve necessary to marry on very little without much family blessing. E. Waugh was anxious to take the plunge at once & I was *greatly* in favour of this as I thought E. Gardner had lost her nerve about marriage & that if she didn't do it at once she would let it peter out out of sheer funk. And then what sort of man would be her next choice? I tremble to think ... This also means a complete break with the hair-raising Barry [Gifford] who Evelyn Waugh so detests that he has practically forbidden Evelyn G. to have anything to do with him. ...

 Of course immediate prospects are not very bright & neither of them are really suited to extreme poverty ... there are certainly a most depressing number of snags between them & what is called a happy marriage.

Fortunately, both Arthur and Kate found their son's fiancée charming. They had first met when Evelyn brought her to dine at Underhill in November 1927 with Terence Greenidge and Dudley Carew. The evening had been a success. 'Old Mr Waugh is a complete Pinkle-Wonk', declared She-Evelyn approvingly. 'He wears a blue velvet coat at dinner, just like Papa did, and talks about the actresses who were the toasts of his young days. I like that kind of thing.' After the two Evelyns became engaged, Arthur went to see Lady Burghclere. In spite of no doubt vociferous arguments on her part, he refused to stand in his son's way. During December, Evelyn Gardner came to lunch or dinner every few days, and was introduced to the Fleming girls from Wyldes-mead. 'Very pretty' said Jean afterwards; 'a tight-lipped, snobby little thing', said Philippa. Over Christmas she stayed at Underhill for a week, accompanying Alec, Evelyn and their mother to the theatre, and treating Kate and Aunt Elsie to the circus at Olympia. The two brothers were constantly bickering, and Evelyn Gardner made it her business to smooth relations between them. After-wards she wrote to Kate thanking her for the happiest Christmas of her life: she had loved staying at Underhill, she said, and was grateful for the cherishing manner with which she had been made welcome. 'Somehow I thought that you wouldn't be pleased [about the engagement], because Evelyn is such an exceptional person and I know how proud you are of him. I hope that I shall

be able to make him happy. I think that when one loves someone as much as I love Evelyn, one is terrified of disappointing
them.'

As soon as the Christmas holiday was over, He-Evelyn went to
The Bell at Aston Clinton to work on his book, the comic novel
which had begun to take shape in his mind while rereading his
old Lancing diaries. '[It] does not get on,' he told Harold Acton,
adding, 'I should so much value your opinion on whether I am
to finish it.' But finding time to concentrate was not easy. He was
back in London after only a few days, in time to take Evelyn
to Barford for the weekend, and then set about finding some
employment that would satisfy Lady Burghclere, who, although
she was still putting difficulties in the way, seemed at last prepared
to accept the match as a distant, if distasteful, possibility. The
Evelyns were hoping to marry in April, but as She-Evelyn predicted, 'I do not see much hope of it before June', adding gloomily, 'Evelyn detests Mama'. Waugh had been made to promise
that he would not do anything 'rash' without first informing 'the
Baroness', as he called her, and if the engagement were to be
considered official, then it would have to be lengthy, the devious
dowager no doubt believing that given time her daughter would
yet again throw over her young man: what, after all, made this
one any different from the rest? Inevitably, as Pansy was quick to
observe, 'the first fine careless rapture has died down under
pecuniary difficulties & the marriage is not likely to take place
until May at the earliest. He is trying to get a job in the BBC –
though he really hopes to earn his living by writing. Evelyn G. is
beginning to get rather depressed by the delays. Unfortunately,
[she] is really afraid of poverty & so is anxious for a certain solid
support from relations.'

Evelyn Waugh, 'kind & bracing' though he was with his fragile
fiancée, was also depressed. His interview at the BBC had gone
well, and it had been a sharp disappointment to learn that he
was not after all to be offered the job. What he did not know was
Lady Burghclere's Scarpia-like rôle in his rejection. Evelyn had
been seen at Savoy Hill by Lance Sieveking, a member of the
Corporation staff and a friend of Geoffrey Fry. Sieveking had
been impressed by Waugh, who had arrived in his office armed
with a note of recommendation from Fry, and would certainly
have offered him employment had he not already received a

second note, also from Fry, asking that he go through only the motions of an interview, and then be sure to turn the young man down. Waugh was hoping to marry Alathea' s sister, Fry explained, but was very much disapproved of by the family. Soon after this, Waugh wrote despairingly to Patrick Balfour, 'As soon as I see any hope from my window in the Slough of Despond I will let you know. As a matter of fact I think there will probably be an elopement quite soon.'

But instead of eloping, he moved back to the country to work on his novel. Both Pansy and Evelyn Gardner had decided that they too wanted to write novels, that they too wanted to move to the country. To this end they had taken rooms in a boarding house at Wimborne in Dorset, conveniently near Henry Lamb who was then living at Poole, and here Evelyn Waugh joined them, staying at the Barley Mow, a pub in Colehill, a village just outside Wimborne. '[Waugh's] engagement still prospers,' Pansy reported. 'Evelyn G. is really much better than I have known her for a long time . . . I don't think she is wildly in love with E. W. but I doubt if she is capable of sustained passion, but she is very fond of him & looks up to his brains & respects his strength of character.' Although Lady Burghclere was for the moment out of the way ('Mama has gone off to Egypt, to flirt with Howard Carter and Tutankhamen at Luxor. She fondly believes that no-one knows of our engagement'), her implacable opposition was still the main obstacle. However, if Evelyn's 'book on Rossetti is a success there is some chance of the marriage taking place in June.'

Rossetti: His Life and Works was published in April 1928, and dedicated to Evelyn Gardner, a dedication removed in later editions. Harold Acton sent a letter of ambiguous congratulation: 'Peter Quennell . . . said it might have been made so infinitely more amusing, but I myself am glad you did not fall a victim to that vulgar temptation . . . You have written in your own genuine and agreeable style, and dealt quietly and eloquently with your subject'. Evelyn replied: 'I am not proud of the book. I think it has some eloquent phrases but there are few pages I can read without a shiver at some place or other.' On the whole, however, the critics took a more benign view. J. C. Squire in the *Observer* praised the book for its elegance and wit, while Roy Campbell in the *Nation & Athenaeum* congratulated Waugh on his sense of balance. 'He is fully alive to the comic aspects of his subject, but does not make this a pretext for adopting a superior tone . . .' Less appreciative was a dismissive notice in the *New Statesman* by Quennell,[6] and a long and disparaging piece in the *Times Literary Supplement* in which the anonymous reviewer[7] wrote, 'Miss Waugh approaches the "squalid" Rossetti like some dainty miss of the 60s bringing the Italian organ-grinder a penny . . .' This drew from Evelyn a letter of complaint which is a small masterpiece of comic offensiveness.

> . . . Your reviewer refers to me throughout as 'Miss Waugh'. My
> Christian name, I know, is occasionally regarded by people of
> limited social experience as belonging exclusively to one or
> other sex; but it is unnecessary to go further into my book
> than the paragraph charitably placed inside the wrapper for the
> guidance of unleisured critics, to find my name with its correct
> prefix of 'Mr'. Surely some such investigation might in merest
> courtesy have been taken before your reviewer tumbled into
> print with such phrases as 'a Miss of the Sixties'.

This, when it was published, resulted in a gratifying letter from Rebecca West, already becoming known as a novelist and free-thinker. 'Dear Mr Waugh, May I tell you how much I liked *Rossetti?* – to say nothing of the incidental entertainment of your letter to the *Times Lit. Sup.*, which was a model of how one might behave to that swollen-headed Parish Magazine.'

While *Rossetti* made its appearance before the public, Evelyn finished his first novel. 'Do you like "Untoward Incidents" as a title?' he had written to Tony Powell. 'The phrase, you remember, was used by the Duke of Wellington in commenting on the destruction of the Turkish Fleet in time of peace at Navarino. It seems to set the right tone of mildly censorious detachment.' But in May the title was changed to *Facing Facts: a Study in Discouragement*, with the alternative of *Picaresque, or the Making of an Englishman*. At the end of the month, having changed the title yet again,

---

[6] For which Quennell later made a patronising apology: ' . . . Certainly I didn't mean my reference to be unkindly: it still doesn't read unkindly to me . . . Meanwhile let us avoid anything so silly as a definite quarrel, and content ourselves with being, perhaps, a little frigid and surprised at the mention of each other's name. Though even that, I very much hope, won't last for ever . . .'
[7] T. Sturge Moore.

this time to the Gibbonian *Decline and Fall*, Evelyn wrote to Harold Acton from Poole, where he was staying with Henry Lamb, who was painting his portrait,[8] 'I have finished the novel. I think it is quite amusing. I am at work doing illustrations for it. May I dedicate it to you?'[9]

Soon word began to get round among Evelyn's friends that this novel of his was something out of the ordinary. After dinner one evening at Underhill when his parents had gone to bed, Evelyn took Dudley Carew into the bookroom and sitting in Arthur's chair, read him the first fifty pages. '[Evelyn] roared with laughter at his own comic invention and both of us at times were in hysterics.' He also read part of it to Tony Powell, who was enormously impressed, although worried that it was almost too clever and funny to have a popular success. Alec found it 'hilariously funny', and Evelyn Gardner wrote to John Maxse, 'it is really screamingly funny, & I think there is a good chance of its being a success if not a bestseller,' adding confidently, 'I don't think our mothers will approve of it, certainly mine won't!' Harold Acton, pleased by the dedication as a graceful acknowledgement not only of a formative friendship but of the significance of his literary taste and influence, wrote at once, having read the first half of the book, to convey 'my sincere great admiration and appreciation of *Decline & Fall'*.

Duckworth, however, to whom Evelyn had submitted the manuscript, were not so impressed. While recognising the book's skill and originality, they were worried by the indelicate nature of some of its scenes. The head of the firm, Gerald Duckworth, had a brother who was married to Evelyn Gardner's aunt; he was well acquainted with Lady Burghclere's opinion of her prospective son-in-law and what she shudderingly described as 'ses moeurs atroces'. Tom Balston, one of the directors, wrote to Evelyn listing the words and passages of dialogue considered unacceptable, requesting him to substitute less offensive alternatives. The main objections concerned references to lavatories, incest, knocking-shops and the alleged Welsh practice of mating with sheep; the

---

[8] The portrait was to be paid for by Bryan Guinness, and in recognition of this generous patronage, Evelyn agreed to sit for it holding in one hand a glass of Guinness.

[9] The previous year Acton had dedicated a book of poems, *Five Saints and an Appendix*, jointly to Waugh and Desmond Harmsworth.

scene in which the hero is debagged also had to go, said Balston, as must the schoolmaster Grimes's explicitly homosexual interest in one of his pupils.

At first Waugh agreed to do what he could, but changed his mind when Gerald Duckworth himself, no doubt with Lady Burghclere breathing down his neck, began interfering in an intolerably high-handed manner. This was too much, and Evelyn removed his manuscript, taking it three doors down Henrietta Street to his father's company, Chapman & Hall. Although it was not the kind of novel he personally found appealing, Arthur recognised its quality, but felt uneasy about the morality of accepting a work by a member of his family. Fortunately the dilemma was avoided by his leaving at the crucial moment for the annual holiday in France with Kate, during which the board met and decided – by one vote – to publish.[10]

The story of Paul Pennyfeather, and the vicissitudes of his progress, passive and unquestioning, through an anarchic world, is an accurate reflection of its creator's mind. Waugh's highly developed sense of comedy, his taste for inspired lunacy, his love of the macabre and the grotesque, inform and infiltrate every sequence. With schoolboy high spirits and an unscrupulous adolescent cruelty under the restraint of a suave and urbane prose, Evelyn fiendishly satirises the entire English establishment: education, the church, politics, the legal system and the aristocracy. But as in his own character, beneath the extreme funniness, effervescence and frivolity, there is a serious moral dimension, a stern judgmental eye coldly observing the surreal and savage circus. And, as in his own life, it is clear that he loves the world he castigates. Mrs Beste-Chetwynde, vicious, heartless and wholly without conscience, is rendered with a degree of admiration that almost overcomes the loathing.

The book owes a visible debt to Dickens, to Lewis Carroll, Kenneth Grahame (young Beste-Chetwynde's favourite reading, apart from Havelock Ellis, is *The Wind in the Willows*) and

---

[10] In a preface to a new edition of *Decline and Fall* issued in 1962, Evelyn wrote that Chapman & Hall had asked for a few emendations; they had considered it, for instance, 'more chaste that the Llanabba Station Master should seek employment for his sister-in-law, rather than for his sister'.

to Ronald Firbank. In an essay on Firbank written the following year, Waugh acknowledges this debt with an analysis of
Firbank's technique that might almost be a description of his
own.

> [Firbank's] later novels are almost wholly devoid of any
> attributions of cause to effect; there is the barest minimum of
> direct description; his compositions are built up, intricately and
> with a balanced alternation of the wildest extravagance and the
> most austere economy, with conversational nuances. They may
> be compared to cinema films in which the relation of caption
> and photograph is directly reversed ... From the fashionable
> chatter of his period, vapid and interminable, he has plucked,
> like tiny brilliant feathers from the breast of a bird, the particles
> of his design ...

A reference to another favourite work, *Pilgrim's Progress*,
was removed when Evelyn deleted the title of the first part,
which was originally to be 'Doubting Castle: the City of Destruction'.

In spite of a disclaimer at the front of the first edition ('I hope
that somewhere a school like Llanabba may exist, and a staff like
Dr Fagan's, but it has never been my good fortune to come across
them'), Llanabba Castle in North Wales derives directly from
Arnold House, Denbighshire, just as Scone College, Oxford
(where Paul as an undergraduate comes straight from 'a creditable career at a small public school of ecclesiastical temper on
the South Downs') derives from Hertford. Like most novelists,
Evelyn was irritated by his readers' insistence on 'identifying'
characters in his novels with real people; in an article published
the following year, he wrote, 'A novelist's trade ... is the only
one in which his acquaintances insist on coming right into the
workshop and playing with the tools. One of the most mischievous
forms which this interference takes is the attribution to him of
living models for his characters.' But as with all such defensive
arguments, there is a large element of the *faux-naïf* and in *Decline
and Fall* there are two characters at least whose similarities to
living models are undeniable.

First, that determined survivor, Captain Grimes, the outrageous,
hard-drinking, paederastic schoolmaster, is immediately recognisable as Dick Young, the homosexual renegade who so delighted

Evelyn when he turned up at Arnold House.[11] And secondly, Lady Circumference bears a distinct resemblance to Alastair's mother, Jessie Graham. Increasingly in his diary, Evelyn had been working Mrs Graham up as a Red Queen character, and in his most recent descriptions of staying at Barford had risen to new heights of comic embellishment.

> Went to a quarry with four dogs where Mrs G bought mountains of mustard-coloured stone from a deaf man with second sight who rode a tricycle . . . This morning there was great trouble with a large truculent under-gardener who is under notice to go and will not allow his successor to use his cottage. Mrs G: 'Here am I left without a *man* in the house' – looking hard at me – 'if Hugh were alive he'd have *kicked* him out.'

The distance is not far from this (and memories of Mrs Graham bossing Evelyn and Alastair about in the garden) to Lady Circumference, 'a stout elderly woman dressed in a tweed coat and skirt and jaunty Tyrolean hat', laying down the law to Dr Fagan.

> 'Nonsense!' said Lady Circumference. 'The boy's a dunderhead. If he wasn't he wouldn't be here. He wants beatin' and hittin' and knockin' about generally, and then he'll be no good. That grass is shockin' bad on the terrace, Doctor; you ought to sand it down and re-sow it . . . What d'you pay your head man?'

As well as these two portraits, there are several sharply pointed references to old enemies and favourite targets. Cruttwell is commemorated in the figure of a brutal burglar who castrates a Harley Street abortionist; Philbrick, the Balliol flagellant, gives his name to Philbrick the protean criminal who so mysteriously dogs Paul's footsteps. The much despised J. C. Squire puts in an appearance as Jack Spire. Cecil Beaton comes on stage as David Lennox, the society photographer, who 'emerged with little shrieks from an Edwardian electric brougham and made straight for the nearest looking-glass'; he photographs Margot Beste-

---

[11] Dick Young, under the pseudonym Richard MacNaughton, himself wrote a novel set in a school in Wales very like Arnold House. In *Preparatory School Murder* (Fenland Press, 1934) the chief suspect is one of the masters. Mr Erard was not entirely satisfactory. 'His rooms began to smell of drink, and more than once I surprised him emerging from the public-house in the village . . . he seemed to have got out of tune with the normal conditions of life – to be unable to adapt himself, if you see what I mean, to the social outlook of his fellows.'

Chetwynde before her wedding, taking 'two eloquent photographs of the back of her head and one of the reflection of her hands in a bowl of ink'. Evelyn was obliged to alter the names of a couple of other flamboyantly homosexual characters: Martin Gaythorn-Brodie (an amalgamation of Eddie Gathorne-Hardy[12] and Paddy Brodie, one of Brian Howard's more notorious friends) to Miles Malpractice, and Kevin Saunderson, based on Gavin Henderson,[13] to Lord Parakeet. There were other changes of name in the final version: Avonforth was altered to Metroland, Lord Water became Lord Tangent, and the title of the Earl of Codrington (after the Codrington Library in All Souls) was changed first to Christendom, then finally to Circumference.

Just occasionally Evelyn himself can be glimpsed almost without disguise, as in the scene in which Paul practises his somewhat unorthodox teaching methods.

'If there's another word from anyone I shall keep you all in this afternoon.' 'You can't keep me in,' said Clutterbuck; 'I'm going for a walk with Captain Grimes.' 'Then I shall very nearly kill you with this stick. Meanwhile you will all write an essay on "Self-indulgence". There will be a prize of half a crown for the longest essay, irrespective of any possible merit.' From then onwards all was silence until break.

Finally there is this, an evocative recollection of Alastair at Oxford, disconcertingly different in its emotional overtone from the rest of the novel, and closely anticipating the portrait of Sebastian Flyte in *Brideshead*. At the very end of the novel, Paul is sitting late one evening in his study at Scone.

Peter Pastmaster came into the room. He was dressed in the bottle-green and white evening coat of the Bollinger club. His face was flushed and his dark hair slightly disordered.
   'May I come in?'
   'Yes, do.'
   'Have you got a drink?'
   'You seem to have had a good many already.'
   'I've had the Boller in my rooms. Noisy lot. Oh, hell! I must have a drink.'

[12] A younger son of the 3rd Earl of Cranbrook, and part of the Acton–Howard set at Eton and Oxford.
[13] Gavin Henderson, later 2nd Baron Faringdon, was another member of the aesthete circle surrounding Acton and Robert Byron at Oxford.

'There's some whisky in the cupboard. You're drinking rather a lot these days, aren't you, Peter?'

Peter said nothing, but helped himself to some whisky and soda.

'Feeling a bit ill,' he said. Then, after a pause, 'Paul, why have you been cutting me all this time?'

'I don't know. I didn't think there was much to be gained by our knowing each other.'

'Not angry about anything?'

'No, why should I be?'

'Oh, I don't know.' Peter turned his glass in his hand, staring at it intently. 'I've been rather angry with you, you know.'

From the moment that Evelyn Gardner and Pansy came back to London from Wimborne events began to move fast. Instead of returning to Ebury Street, they moved into lodgings in Montagu Place, north of Hyde Park, to be nearer their future husbands, Evelyn Waugh in Hampstead, Henry Lamb in Maida Vale. On 12 June Pansy had given it as her opinion that '[Evelyn Gardner's] marriage still seems remote & it is hard to imagine exactly how much she cares for the other Evelyn. Not enough to follow him barefoot through the world, certainly, but on the other hand she is happier with him & since this engagement than she has been for a long time.'

Just over a fortnight after this was written, the two Evelyns were man and wife. They had appeared one day in the big, sunny drawing-room in Montagu Place and told Pansy they could no longer bear the prospect of a long engagement, that they were going to get married as soon as they could. To this end, Evelyn Waugh had taken a room in nearby Portman Square, where Robert Byron had a flat. The two Evelyns spent much of their time with him, 'as their own rooms', said Robert, 'are so disgusting'. On 22 June, Waugh wrote in his diary, with assumed insouciance, that 'Evelyn and I began to go to Dulwich to see the pictures there but got bored waiting for the right bus so went instead to the vicar-general's office and bought a marriage licence.'

The church they had chosen was St Paul's, Portman Square, an unbeautiful, unfashionable, 'horribly low' church, with ARE YOU SAVED? placards posted outside it. Here, telling almost no one, at midday, on 27 June 1928, the two Evelyns were married. The night before, Evelyn Gardner had had an attack of nerves and told Pansy she could not possibly go through with it ('this elusive, timid creature trapped at last'), but when Robert Byron, who was to give her away, arrived to collect her, she was ready and composed, soignée in a yellow and black crêpe de chine jumper suit with pleated skirt, her cropped hair hidden under a black cloche hat. The groom, small and slender, was immaculately dressed, as was the best man, Harold Acton, tall, balding and heavily side-whiskered. The two witnesses were Pansy and Alec. A table covered in a black velvet pall served as an altar, and, as his services cost two guineas less than those of the vicar, the ceremony was conducted by a curate, whose moustache, heavy black boots and cockney accent made the bride giggle. She giggled again when her husband-to-be promised to endow her with all his worldly goods; her voice was barely audible as she whispered, 'I do'. When it was over there were champagne cocktails at the 500 Club before a celebratory luncheon hosted by Acton at Boulestin in Covent Garden. In the afternoon the newly married pair left for their honeymoon, going by train to Oxford, then by taxi to Beckley, the village in which Evelyn and Alastair had had their caravan, where they were greeted by village women with bouquets of flowers.

It was only then that Evelyn wrote to his parents. As always in June, the Waughs were on holiday in France, and although the news may have taken them by surprise, they remained unruffled. 'Good walks morning & afternoon,' Kate wrote in her diary. 'Arthur well again. Evelyns married.' They had no objection to the match, and Arthur 'forked out handsomely'.

Lady Burghclere, on the other hand, who was not informed of the catastrophe until three weeks after it happened, was very angry indeed, not only with the disobedient young couple, but with Pansy, whom she had trusted. Describing herself as 'quite inexpressibly pained', she insisted on immediately putting a notice in *The Times*, 'to avoid scandal & misconstruction', and then issued a command that the delinquent pair should call on her in Green Street to be interviewed separately, a 'hideous' occasion for which they eccentrically chose to dress in formal attire, He-Evelyn in tails and a top hat.

On their return to London at the beginning of July, the young Waughs stayed at Underhill while they looked for somewhere to live. The solution to the problem was provided by an old friend,

Joyce Fagan. Joyce, who had kept up her friendship with Evelyn and his parents, had recently married Donald Gill, an American businessman with whom she was now living in Knightsbridge; however, she had not yet disposed of her bachelor flat in Islington, a handsome if unfashionable part of London which, largely thanks to such as Joyce and her friends, was beginning to be popular among indigent young writers and painters. It was arranged that for £1 a week the two Evelyns should take it over, and at the end of August, during an oppressive heatwave, they moved in.

17A Canonbury Square was on the first floor of a terrace house in a broad, beautiful Georgian square near Highbury Corner, with a pretty communal garden down its centre. 'Half a house in a slum', Waugh in a letter to Henry Yorke described it, exaggerating as usual. 'Delapidated Regency.' Comprising five rooms, with the use of a laundry in the basement of which She-Evelyn to the day she left remained unaware, the flat was let unfurnished, but they had been given a bed, a sofa and a dining-room table, and the junk shops in Essex Road and Upper Street were a good hunting ground for cheap furniture, which Waugh enjoyed repairing and ornamenting. He pasted magazine covers on an old black chest, converted a clock case into a cocktail cabinet, and decorated a coal scuttle with used postage stamps bought in packets at the local stationer. Harold Acton called one day to 'find him squatted on the floor, deeply preoccupied, surrounded by confetti-like pools of these bright little stamps which he would stick in elaborate patterns on an ugly old coal-scuttle, his hair all tousled and his fingers dabbled in glue. Later he would give the object a coating of varnish.' It was a dinky little flat, bright and fashionable, with the air, according to Acton, 'of a sparkling nursery', an effect emphasised by some voguish wedding presents from the General Trading Company, such as wineglasses with coloured animals in the stem, and a couple of mugs inscribed 'Evelyn' and 'Evelyn' positioned at either end of the mantelpiece.

Against such a backdrop their friends saw them as a couple of anthropomorphic characters out of a fairy story or a tale by Beatrix Potter. Daphne Weymouth[14] noted how well matched they

---

[14] The writer Daphne Fielding, daughter of the 4th Baron Vivian, in 1926 married Viscount Weymouth, heir to the Marquess of Bath.

were physically, both the same diminutive height, and watching them dancing likened them to 'a pair of squirrels – round-eyed and reddish nutkin colouring'; Harold Acton, inevitably, described She-Evelyn as 'a fauness with a little snub nose . . . one hoped to see cradles full of little Evelyns in the near future, baby fauns blowing through reeds, falling off rocking-horses, pulling each others's pointed ears and piddling on the rug'; while Peter Quennell compared them to a couple of prize pigeons, glossy and sleek. They themselves, playfully taking advantage of the topical joke that, with the current fashions, it was impossible to tell boys from girls were photographed by Olivia Wyndham looking as much like each other as possible.

At the end of November the two Evelyns gave a cocktail party, to which invitation cards were sent backed with a map showing the route to Canonbury from Buckingham Palace. Among the guests were He-Evelyn's parents, Arthur and Kate, She-Evelyn's sister, Alathea, and her husband, Geoffrey Fry, Diana Mitford, and Pansy's younger sister, Mary Pakenham. There were also a number of Evelyn Gardner's débutante friends, who had arrived agog to see what had happened to their rebellious chum. 'How *could* she leave all that delicious *food?*' shrieked one, remembering the unusually high standard of Lady Burghclere's cuisine. Everybody seemed to be in high spirits, the room packed, the chatter deafening. But at the end of the evening, as Geoffrey Fry got into his car, he was heard to murmur, 'And when they buried her the little town had never seen a merrier funeral.'[15]

Neither Evelyn Waugh nor Evelyn Gardner had any realistic conception of what married life entailed. They were playing at marriage, and their flat and its cheerful accoutrements were their toys. But two aspects of the game did have to be taken seriously. The first was lack of money. Although both were well used to having very little, both were inclined towards extravagance. Waugh had started on a life of Wesley for Duckworth, '[which] will be rather amusing, what with the family ghost & the women in the congregation who fell in love with him', his wife cheerfully predicted, and he was also experimenting with a detective story, but neither was likely to earn much. 'The happy pair will not be

[15] A play on lines from Tennyson's *Enoch Arden*: 'And when they buried him the little port/Had seldom seen a costlier funeral.'

poorer than they were before,' wrote Pansy, 'as long as they don't start a family. To prevent this they have invoked all the magic of Marie Stopes & the shops in the Charing Cross Road.' The second serious consideration was She-Evelyn's health. From childhood she had been delicate and vulnerable to infection, but now it seemed as if her whole system were in rebellion against a situation which, at some profound level unrecognised on the surface, was proving unbearable. In the weeks immediately following the move to Canonbury she had appeared cheerful. She had enjoyed arranging the flat, spending hours sitting in the kitchen talking to the daily charwoman, Mrs Stammers; and she had enjoyed receiving the first visitors, among them Acton, Tony Powell ('full of scandal about the Sitwells'), and Joyce and Donald Gill. In the first week of October the Waughs had given a dinner party, with Tom Balston of Duckworth's, Alec, and the Charles Drages.[16] Everyone was in good form, and 'the dinner was admirable, eggs and sweet corn, poussin, passion fruit and savoury.' But four days later Waugh came home from having tea with Olivia to find his wife with a temperature. 'I imagine a touch of influenza', he noted casually.

The next morning, however, she was worse, and Waugh so alarmed that he summoned his mother from Underhill. Taking one look at her daughter-in-law's mottled face, Kate sent for the doctor, who found his patient slightly delirious and with a temperature of 104. During the next fortnight Kate, assisted by Evelyn Gardner's old nanny, remained at Canonbury Square to nurse the invalid while Evelyn Waugh stayed at Underhill with his father. On the day that the correct diagnosis, of German measles, was at last made, Lady Burghclere decided to swallow her anger and pay her first visit, bringing grapes and a chicken, and managing to make some 'more or less kindly comments on the flat'. Aunt Margaret Duckworth sent a generous £20 to help with medical expenses, and Alathea Fry a parcel of turtle jelly, ham mousse and other delicacies from Fortnum & Mason.

On 21 October Waugh returned to the marital home, before taking his wife to Oare at the Frys' invitation for a fortnight's convalescence, 'thus relieving us of what had become a considerable anxiety about [the cost of] an hotel'. Here She-Evelyn tink-

---

[16] Friends of Evelyn Gardner's.

ered with her novel and some articles on decoration for the
Evening News, while Waugh made notes on Wesley. But no sooner
were they back in London than Evelyn Gardner fell ill with a bad
sore throat, and in January went into a clinic in Wimpole Street
for an operation.

It was during this anxious autumn that *Decline and Fall* was published. This was the book on which so much depended, the
critics' reaction crucial to the direction of Waugh's future career.
Fortunately, praise was almost unanimous. That most influential
of reviewers, Arnold Bennett, wrote in the *Evening Standard* that
'*Decline and Fall* is an uncompromising and brilliantly malicious
satire, which in my opinion comes near to being quite first-rate';
according to the *Observer*, '[Mr Waugh] is an important addition
to the ranks of those dear and necessary creatures – the writers
who can make us laugh'; and Cyril Connolly, never one to be
over-generous with his praise, informed the readers of the *New
Statesman* that in *Decline and Fall*

> there is a love of life, and consequently a real understanding of
> it. . . . The humour throughout is of that subtle metallic kind
> which, more than anything else, seems a product of this
> generation. A delicious cynicism runs through the book . . .
> though not a great book, it is a funny book, and the only one
> that, professionally, he [this reviewer] has ever read twice.

Anxious to be on good terms with influential reviewers, Evelyn
invited Connolly to lunch. 'I remember that lunch very well
because it lasted all day,' Connolly later recalled.

> It was a very small spick and span little bandbox of a house, and
> his wife was like a very, very pretty little china doll, and the
> two of them were this fantastic thing of the happily married
> young couple whom success has just touched with its wand.
> They started to talk about Arnold Bennett who had also
> recognised *Decline and Fall* and whom they had had to dinner
> the night before.

The only let to Evelyn's enjoyment of his good notices was an
embarrassment concerning Harold Acton. Harold was still in
Evelyn's eyes the arbiter; it was still assumed by those, like Evelyn,
who had fallen under his exotic influence at Oxford that it would
be Acton who would achieve real fame as a writer. As bad luck

would have it, Harold's first novel, *Humdrum*, came out at exactly the same time as *Decline and Fall*, with the inevitable result that the two books, by two contemporaneous 'Oxford' authors, were reviewed in tandem. And whereas Evelyn's novel received universal praise, Harold's was the target for universal condemnation, many of the reviewers using the excellence of Waugh to point up the inadequacies of Acton. 'As a satire, *Decline and Fall* seems to possess every virtue which it [*Humdrum*] lacks ... *Humdrum* reads like a painstaking attempt to satirise modern life by a Chinaman who has been reading Punch' (Cyril Connolly). '[Waugh's] book is dedicated "In homage" to Mr Harold Acton, author of *Humdrum*. Mr Waugh owes no homage to Mr Acton as a novelist, for the latter's story is a poor thing, showing us nothing but a vast social superiority to every body and everything' (J. B. Priestley). Not unnaturally, Harold was dismayed by such hostile reaction, and replied thankfully to Evelyn's suggestion that Waugh should try to redress the balance by reviewing the novel in the *Observer*: although privately Evelyn held no very high opinion of the book, he had found it 'amusing in places' and could, therefore, be appreciative in print without perjuring himself. Grateful as Harold was for this act of solidarity, it nonetheless altered the friendship between the two men. Acton grew increasingly jealous of the success of his one-time protégé in an area in which he himself, contrary to early expectation, was never to make much mark. As Evelyn complained to Christopher Hollis, 'I don't know what to say to Harold. If I tell him I'm going to lunch at the Ritz, he says, "Of course you're a famous author, but you can't expect a nonentity like me to join you there." And if I suggest we go to a pub, he says, "My de–ar, what affec*ta*tion – a popular novelist going to a pub." '

Decline and Fall came out in September, and by December was into its third impression, with a print-run of nearly 3000 copies. It had also been bought by Doubleday & Doran in America for $500. '*Decline & Fall* seems to be going well,' Evelyn told Balston. 'I am threatened with four civil actions & a horse whipping but so far James Doyles [?] & the public prosecutor have been silent.' She-Evelyn, who had been following the sales figures with interest, reported that, 'Our finances have vastly improved, at times we are absolutely rolling in money, and at others we have to live on haddock and potatoes, but it is all very amusing.' As the author of a bestseller, her husband was 'now quite a lion and we were asked to meet Max Beerbohm, Hilaire Belloc and Maurice Baring the other night'. More important, Waugh's by-line was suddenly much in demand by newspapers and magazines. Knowing very well that he needed to make the most of this opportunity, Alec introduced his brother to A. D. Peters, his literary agent, who was to become a crucial figure in Evelyn's professional career.

On coming down from Cambridge, Augustus Detlof Peters had a job for a brief, bored spell as theatre critic on the *Daily Chronicle*, before setting up his agency in 1924 in premises in Buckingham Street, listing among his early authors J. B. Priestley, Rebecca West, C. S. Forester, Cecil Day Lewis, Hugh Walpole and V. S. Pritchett. Pale, thick-set, with reddish-blond hair, Peters was terse and unforthcoming in manner, but impervious to bullying and displays of temperament; he knew his business and knew very well how to handle his clients. Alec, of course, never gave any trouble, but his brother was made of different material. At this early stage, however, Evelyn, anxious to consolidate his position and earn some money, was only too eager to please, grateful to accept anything that came his way. In a letter thanking Peters for obtaining a commission from *Vogue*, he wrote, 'Please fix up anything that will earn me anything – even cricket criticism or mothers welfare notes . . . Yes I should be pleased to write "Wyndham Lewis stuff" or any other kind of "stuff" that anyone will buy.' Indeed, so eager was he to supply what the market required that when the *Evening Standard* misread as 'The Mothers of the Younger Generation' a proposal of his for an article on 'The Manners of the Younger Generation', Evelyn barely hesitated ('[The misunderstanding] is unfortunate but not disastrous'), before sitting down to write about mothers instead of manners. He was full of ideas; for instance,

> a humorous serial called *Young Man* dealing with the arrival in London of a young, handsome and incredibly wealthy marquess hitherto brought up in seclusion and the attempts made by various social, religious, political bodies and ambitious mothers to get hold of him.
>
> I would also write a detective serial about the murder of an author rather like Alec Waugh.
>
> I have both these stories fairly clear in my mind.

And to Peters's assistant, W. N. Roughead, he wrote, 'Could you get the *Express* to take an article on the Youngest Generation's view of Religion?' – to which the answer was, No: 'The *Daily Express* say that they have had enough of religion lately.' They were, however, prepared to consider other suggestions, and it was for the *Express* that Evelyn composed his first feature article, on censorship, for which he was paid four times his original weekly salary by the editor who fifteen months previously had given him the sack. This was followed by articles for the *Manchester Guardian* (4 guineas) and the *Evening Standard* (10 guineas), for *Passing Show* and the *Observer.*

With the exception of book reviews for the latter 'quality' paper, the tone was on the whole facetious, the subjects light-hearted. Evelyn understood his market: he was versatile and resourceful, good at self-promotion and at turning in the kind of performance he knew would go down best. Thus, although he often found the writing arduous ('I find humorous articles an awful strain', he admitted to Roughead), always the craftsman, he was more than ready to satisfy demand, ready to be interviewed, perform 'stunts' (climb a tower at a house party, present an unknown woman in a restaurant with his tie), and express opinions on any subject under the sun. In all this he was following exactly the advice he propounded in an article on 'The Way to Fame', in which the aspiring writer is instructed first to write a biography, '[choosing] as a subject someone very famous who has had plenty of books written about him quite recently'; then a novel, 'preferably a mildly shocking one . . . The reviews matter very little in the case of a novel. The important thing is to make people talk about it. You can do this by forcing your way into the newspapers in some other way.'

One of his most shrewdly selected rôles was as the Modern Young Man ('It seems to me that it would be nice if we could persuade them that I personify the English youth movement'), in which guise he wrote a piece entitled 'Too Young at 40: Youth Calls to the Peter Pans of Middle-Age Who Block the Way', affecting to complain of the manner in which those who had fought in the war were obstructing the younger generation.

In business, in the professions, in art, in the public services the way is blocked by the phalanx of the Indestructible Forties. A fine, healthy lot, these ex-captains and majors work by day, dance by night, golf on Sundays, nothing is too much for them, and nothing is going to move them for another thirty years. How they laugh and slap their thighs and hoot the horns of their little two-seater cars. I don't suppose that I shall be heard at all when I diffidently whisper that *there is a younger generation.*

After a Christmas spent at Coombe Bissett in Wiltshire with Pansy and Henry Lamb, who had married in August, Evelyn wrote to Peters with a new proposal: he was planning, he said, a voyage on a cargo boat around the Black Sea. 'Would anyone like travel articles about that? . . . I shall be quite pleased to adapt my plans to editorial tastes. Would they for instance like me to go to Salonika? I shall be drawing hard. Would *Vogue* like something on the "Night Life of the Near East". I feel they might, with drawings of Turkish night clubs etc.' Peters, perhaps aware that roughing it on a cargo boat was not in the best interests of She-Evelyn's precarious state of health, instead negotiated free passages on a luxurious Norwegian vessel for a cruise in the Mediterranean, the voyage paid for by a series of articles to be published as a book. The Waughs were delighted: the timing was ideal, as there had been neither money nor opportunity for a proper honeymoon, and She-Evelyn was badly in need of sun and a period of recuperation. They left on 10 February 1929, Kate seeing them off at Victoria, a departure loyally reported by Patrick Balfour in the *Daily Sketch*. '[Mr and Mrs Waugh] were about to spend the proceeds of *Decline and Fall* in a tour of Southeastern Europe and the Levant,' his readers were told. Mr Waugh made it clear that he still thought of his future as a draughtsman rather than a writer: 'I hope I can bring back enough sketches to hold an exhibition in June, and, if it is successful, abandon writing for painting.'

Changing trains in Paris, they went on to Monte Carlo, where they were to join their ship. It was an arctic winter; in London people shrank, as Evelyn put it, even 'from the icy contact of a cocktail glass', and the weather grew no warmer as they travelled south. The windows of the train frosted over, and She-Evelyn sat huddled and shivering in her fur coat. She had a high temperature, and the crême de menthe her husband persuaded her to drink made her feel so much worse that, in spite of the expense,

Evelyn hired a couchette so that his wife could have some privacy and lie down. When they arrived in Monte Carlo the next morning, it had been snowing, and they had to walk from hotel to hotel before they found one that would take in such an obviously ill woman. Two days later they boarded the *Stella Polaris*, 6000 tons of gleaming white elegance, for the start of a voyage which was quickly to assume the elements of nightmare.

As the *Stella* moved down the beautiful Italian coast towards Naples and the Straits of Messina, the cheerful chatter of her passengers provided a grotesque counterpoint to the frightening condition of She-Evelyn who, growing noticeably worse with every day that passed, had begun to cough up blood. Waugh, who was inexperienced with women, and had never had to look after anyone, now found himself alone with, and wholly responsible for, a woman who to all appearances had not long to live. He sent Pansy a postcard saying that by the time she received it, She-Evelyn would probably be dead. In this state of anguish, Waugh still had to work, had to justify his passage and produce the light-hearted prose on pleasure cruising which his contract demanded. With the other holiday-makers he disembarked at Naples, Messina and Catania, conscientiously touring the sights. 'I did not really enjoy those two days in Naples very much', he wrote in a veiled account of his visit to the city. 'I was ill at ease all the time, and impelled by a restless sense of obligation to see a great deal more than I intelligently could.' When the ship reached Haifa, where he went ashore and picked a bunch of wild flowers, a nurse was brought on board for his wife, 'a squat young woman of indeterminable nationality', who with her rough incompetence made her patient if anything feel worse. Finally at Port Said She-Evelyn's condition was so bad that she was taken off the ship on a stretcher, looking, said her husband, 'distressingly like a corpse'. At the British hospital double pneumonia and pleurisy were diagnosed, and her state considered so perilous that for two days she was left on her stretcher as it was thought dangerous to move her.

The *Stella* sailed on, and the Waughs remained in Port Said for a month. Every day Waugh visited his wife's bedside, reading aloud from P. G. Wodehouse, which in her feverish, semi-conscious state she found completely unintelligible. The rest of the time he kicked his heels and explored with increasing boredom the ugly, squalid little port. 'In spite of all reports this is an intolerably dull town,' he told Harold Acton. 'Two expensive & very dirty hotels, one brothel, a cinema & this awful club where the shipping-office clerks try to create an Ethel M. Dell garrison life by drinking endless "gin & tonic" & talking about "the old country" & "pukka sahibs".' To his father he wrote, 'There are three good bookshops but none of them sell *Decline & Fall.* There is a cinema and a dance every Saturday. I went last Saturday with the consul's harlot wife. She opened her mouth and invited me to throw sugar into it.' Gradually She-Evelyn began to recover. 'Today she is sitting up in bed knitting & reading & falling deeply in love with her doctor,' Waugh wrote to Tom Balston, and soon she was strong enough to be taken for short drives. A plan was made to go to Cyprus for a few weeks' convalescence, but then it was found that there was no hotel of suitable standard on the island. 'We have had to give up the idea of Cyprus . . . [we] are going South instead to Helwan or Heliopolis or Luxor,' Waugh reported to Arthur; 'wherever in fact I can persuade an hotel to give me advantageous terms in return for commendation in my book.'

As worry over his wife's health receded, so Waugh's anxiety about money grew. With all the stress and business of the illness – talking to doctors, cabling relations – he had been unable to make much progress with his work, although 'I hope now things are easier to start on a new novel,' he wrote to Acton; and to Tom Balston, 'I am struggling to write you a book inspite of every obstacle.' Substantial medical expenses and the cost not only of a month in Port Said but of a further month's convalescence outside Cairo had somehow to be met. 'We are frightfully broke', he told Balston. 'However I think this is an occasion when a nice man overdraws recklessly.' Lady Burghclere sent money ('Evelyn's mama has come out rather well about her illness really'), and so did Alathea Fry. Several anxious letters were despatched to Peters in London, and Alastair Graham, alarmed by what he described as 'a pathetic SOS from the Evelyns', came over from Athens for a couple of days, and gave his old friend enough money to 'struggle along for another week or two'.

On the first of April the two Evelyns left Port Said, and moved to the Mena House Hotel in the shadow of the pyramids: 'enormous and hideously expensive but sunny & I think a good place for Evelyn's recuperation'. Waugh wrote to Harold Acton: 'There is a huge garden full of garish flowers & improbable insects – all rather like the final scene of a Paris review. The people range from exquisitely amusing Australian trippers with sun helmets & fly whisks to Cairo demi-mondaines in picture frocks – one with a pet monkey in silver harness which sits & fleas its rump on the terrace.'

Waugh was in better spirits here than he had been since their departure from England, not only because his wife was now fit but because at last he was able to write. 'The travel book is going to be *very* good', he told Balston, adding that he wanted to change its title from *The Quest of a Moustache* ('I am growing a moustache', Evelyn had written to Peters just before leaving) to *Labels*, with the cover 'all made of labels'.

From Egypt they went to Malta, where they rejoined the *Stella* and continued their interrupted free cruise back to England. 'We are getting a little fed-up, and shall be glad to get home,' wrote She-Evelyn. But now at least they were able to have some fun and behave like normal holiday-makers, He-Evelyn joining the ship's Sports Committee while She-Evelyn organised the fancy-dress ball. At Constantinople, they were invited to a 'rather uneasy' luncheon party at the British embassy, where their fellow guests were Osbert, Sacheverell and Georgia Sitwell, the Sitwell brothers 'combining a gay enthusiasm for the subtleties of Turkish rococo with unfathomable erudition about Byzantine archaeology and the scandals of Ottoman diplomacy'. Georgia Sitwell recorded of the 'little Evelyns Waugh . . . [that] he is dapper and baby-faced like a drawing by Mabel Lucie Attwell . . . she has rather popping eyes but is pretty. Neither of them appear to have anything very amusing to say but they were painfully shy.' In Athens in an atmosphere of high camp the Waughs spent their time with Alastair and his like-minded compatriot, Mark Ogilvie-Grant. 'Their new hobby is to talk Greek with a cockney accent so it is all very much like home from home. Mark very sweet & skittish feeling relieved of the burden of keeping up appearances and having terrific affairs in an atmosphere of garlic & Charlie Chaplin moustaches.' The voyage home took them to Ragusa, Venice and Monte Carlo, then via Barcelona, Algiers and Gibraltar to Lisbon and Harwich, arriving back in London at the end of May.

During the three months he had been away, and in spite of the constant and enervating demands made on him, Evelyn had continued to work whenever he could and at a furious rate, sending articles to Peters in London on any topic for which his agent had been able to secure a commission. From Mena House he had written cheerfully, 'I will send you about twenty articles in about twenty four hours . . . [and] I shall bring you two books at the end of May to serialise. A travel book and a fairly funny novel.'

The travel book, *Labels*, giving little hint of the unhappy circumstances under which the journey was made, takes the form of an apparently personal narrative, describing the narrator's adventures, his pleasure in the ship, his curiosity about his fellow passengers, and in particular his interest both in the people and the architecture of the countries he visits. The two days in Naples are described in terms of comic frustration, with the tourist, in the grip of 'that obsession by panic and persecution mania which threatens all inexperienced travellers', trying in vain to see the sights unencumbered by the relentless attentions of the touts. Predictably, Evelyn is most intrigued by two mummified corpses in the church of San Sansevero: 'They were quite naked and dark brown in colour.' As in his letters, he tellingly conveys the seediness and dim colonial atmosphere of Port Said. In Cairo he admires the treasures, discovered by She-Evelyn's uncle, Lord Carnarvon, from the tomb of Tutankhamen. In Constantinople he expresses contempt for all things Turkish. 'They seem to have been unable to touch any existing work or to imitate any existing movement without degrading it.' The greatest enthusiasm is reserved for his discovery in Barcelona of the work of Gaudí, in particular the great unfinished cathedral of the Sagrada Familia.

Gaudí bears to these anonymous contractors and job-builders
[of the debased English architecture of the period]
something of the same relation as do the masters of Italian
baroque to the rococo decorators of the Pompadour's boudoir,
or Ronald Firbank to the author of *Frolic Wind.* What in them is
frivolous, superficial, and chic is in him structural and essential;
in his work is apotheosized all the writhing, bubbling,
convoluting, convulsing soul of the Art Nouveau . . . a great
example, it seems to me, of what art-for-art's-sake can become

when it is wholly untempered by considerations of tradition or good taste.

But underneath this vigorous and witty traveller's tale, like the faint tracings of a palimpsest, can be seen the story of himself and Evelyn. In the book, the narrator, travelling alone,[17] befriends a young married couple whom he calls Geoffrey and Juliet,[18] first encountered on the train to Paris.[19]

> The young man was small and pleasantly dressed and wore a slight, curly moustache . . . His wife was huddled in a fur coat in the corner, clearly far from well . . . Every quarter of an hour or so they said to each other 'Are you quite sure you're all right, darling?' And replied, 'Perfectly, really I am. Are you, my precious?' But Juliet was far from being all right.

Several times Geoffrey has to cable from the ship to Juliet's sisters for money to pay the doctor, and then to pay for the nurse taken on board at Haifa, where 'the hills were covered with asphodel and anemones and cyclamen . . . I got out to pick a bunch for Juliet'. Juliet develops pneumonia, and at Port Said has to be lifted off the ship on a stretcher, 'looking distressingly like a corpse', and driven to the British hospital. The 'I' of the story stays with Geoffrey for the month in Port Said to try to cheer him up; but 'Geoffrey was not to be consoled so easily'. The narrator then accompanies the couple to Cairo, where they part, Geoffrey and Juliet bound for Cyprus, the narrator to complete the rest of the journey on his own.

As the *Stella* at last sails into home waters, she runs into a sea-mist and has to sound her fog-horn. The penultimate paragraph (written later that summer during a period of intense unhappiness), like the ship's horn warning of danger, strikes a chilling note. 'I woke up several times in the night to hear the horn again sounding through the wet night air. It was a very dismal sound, premonitory, perhaps, of coming trouble, for Fortune is the least capricious of deities, and arranges things on the

---

[17] In America, the book was published under the title, *A Bachelor Abroad.*
[18] Both names in Evelyn Gardner's family: Juliet was her elder sister, Geoffrey Fry one of her brothers-in-law.
[19] In *Hot Countries*, a travel book published in the same year as *Labels*, Alec uses the same device, attributing to fictional characters a love affair of his own.

just and rigid system that no one shall be very happy for very long.'

Then, with characteristic toughness, Evelyn ends the book thus. 'We came into harbour at Harwich early next morning; a special train was waiting for us; I lunched in London.'[20] When the book came out the following year, an unsigned review in the *Observer* perceptively remarked that,

> It would be difficult to imagine a more devastating exposure of the fatuity of modern travel than Mr Evelyn Waugh's Mediterranean journal. Merely turning over his pages we suffer all the fatigue, ennui, and disgust of being transported from one disappointment to another by contrivances whose luxury seems as vain as the pleasures to which they profess to carry us.

Waugh's original intention on returning to England had been to take 'a minute house & [settle] somewhere in the country for the summer', so that he could work on his 'fairly funny novel', while at the same time producing as much highly paid journalism as was physically possible. 'We found bills of over £200 waiting for us and each overdrawn at our banks so I must write a lot quickly', he explained to Henry Yorke. But this was not a plan which appealed to his wife. A married woman now, free from restrictions, the last thing She-Evelyn wanted was to bury herself in the country. For the past year she had been dogged by ill health; most of the previous three months had been spent in hospital or as a convalescent, much of the time with only her husband for company. As urgently as Waugh now wanted to be alone, his wife, pretty and only just twenty-five, wanted to have fun. It was June, and after a slow start occasioned by a general election at the end of May, a particularly gay season was in full swing. She-Evelyn was longing to dress up, go out, see and be seen. There was nothing she hated more than being left alone in the flat, in a part of London with which she was unfamiliar. (The previous year she had written tellingly to John Maxse, that to be left entirely alone evening after evening was enough to make her feel quite desperate.) Thus it was decided that after a

---

[20] Peters's associate in New York, Carl Brandt, was, like Peters himself, less than enthusiastic about the book, complaining, when he received the manuscript, that 'I don't think it is complete. It ends on p. 134, rather abruptly.'

week spent with Arthur and Kate, she would move back to Canonbury Square while her husband went to Beckley during the week
to write, returning to London only at weekends. So that she
should not be lonely, a chum, Nancy Mitford, was to move into
the guest-room. And various trustworthy men friends from Oxford
days, such as Bobby Roberts, Tony Bushell and Harold Acton,
and a new friend, John Heygate, were deputed to keep an eye
on the two women and act as dancing partners at parties.

There were a lot of parties that summer. 'We hardly ever saw
the light of day, except at dawn,' Nancy Mitford recalled. 'There
was a costume ball every night: the White Party, the Circus Party,
the Boat Party, etc . . . Soon the door of my tiny room would no
longer shut because of the huge pile of costumes that I had not
the courage to pick up.' One of the most popular venues was on
board the *Friendship*, a boat permanently moored at Charing
Cross, where the Bright Young People, dressed as pirates or cow-
boys or gods and goddesses, danced on deck until dawn. There
was the Catalan Party in Lowndes Square, the Baby Party in
Rutland Gate, the Bath and Bottle Party at the St George's Swimming Baths, the Heroines of History Ball at Claridge's, and Olga
Lynn's Literary Party, where guests had to come as the title of a
book. John Heygate threw a Party Without End, during which
people could come and go as they pleased, fortified by an
inexhaustible supply of exotic sandwiches. And on 25 June Bryan
and Diana Guinness gave an 1860s Party at their house in Buckingham Gate. 'I danced blissfully with Evelyn at Bryan's last night',
Harold Acton reported reassuringly to Beckley. But there was
another fancy-dress dance given that evening, a Watteau party
held on board the *Friendship*. After leaving the Guinnesses, a
number of guests went on to it, among them John Heygate and,
noted the *Bystander*, 'the Hon. Nancy Mitford and the Hon. Mrs
Evelyn Waugh whose husband has isolated himself in the country
in an attempt to excel his first novel'.

John Heygate and Evelyn Waugh had met relatively recently
through an old Oxford acquaintance, Bobby Roberts, and had
taken to each other at once. Although in no way remarkable,
Heygate, with his affable manner, jokey conversation and slightly
raffish good looks, was agreeable company. Heir to an Irish baron-
etcy, he was the son of an Eton housemaster so priggishly conven-.
tional that 'doing a Heygate' became the accepted phrase for

doing the most priggishly conventional thing. His mother, who adored him, was descended from the diarist, John Evelyn, and her son only just escaped being christened Evelyn in commemoration – which, given the subsequent course of events, would have turned an already complicated situation into one bordering on farce. In 1929 Heygate was working as a news editor for the BBC, having failed, after coming down from Balliol, for the diplomatic service. Like Waugh, he was a hard drinker; he was also attractive to women, and had the gift of being completely at ease in any society. A generous host on his own territory – a small flat in South Kensington – in others' houses he was looked on as the ideal 'spare man'. After the Waughs married and moved to Canonbury, Heygate became one of their most frequent visitors, a happy member of 'such a happy trio', as he himself described it. When She-Evelyn went into hospital in the month before the cruise, it was Heygate who took Waugh out to dinner, together with Harold Acton and Eleanor Watts, an undergraduate with whom Heygate fancied himself in love. And Heygate was one of the few friends from whom Evelyn received a condoling letter while coping with his wife's illness abroad.

It was only natural that on the Waughs' return the friendship should resume. Which, for a time, it did. The three of them lunched together in London, and while Evelyn was at Beckley, Heygate and Eleanor drove She-Evelyn down to see him. Heygate was present at the Watteau party, one of the last to leave, which no doubt is why he fell asleep at the table the following evening at a dinner of Tom Balston's for the young Waughs and Rose Macaulay. Later that same week, the last week of June, Heygate and the Waughs were guests at a cocktail party given by Anthony Powell and Constant Lambert at Powell's basement flat in Tavistock Square. The Waughs arrived separately, seemed not to enjoy themselves, and left early, She-Evelyn having had some kind of disagreement, it was observed, with Heygate. That weekend both Waughs and Tony Powell stayed with Heygate at his parents' house at Milford-on-Sea, opposite the Isle of Wight. On the Saturday evening they went to the New Forest Hunt ball, and on Sunday were taken to tea with Lady Montagu at Beaulieu, her step-daughter, Elizabeth, being an old friend of Heygate's. The tea party was not a success, Elizabeth Montagu later recalled, with

Evelyn Waugh for some reason in heavy sulks, his wife irritatingly vivacious, and Heygate trying far too hard to be funny.

Waugh returned to Beckley, where in the silence of the Oxfordshire countryside he had already finished the first 10,000 words of his novel, 'a welter of sex and snobbery', which he had entitled *Vile Bodies*. As each section was completed he posted it to his wife who was responsible for having it typed before sending it on to A. D. Peters. Waugh found the atmosphere at Beckley tranquil, the company restfully undemanding. 'In the evenings I sit with the farmers in the kitchen drinking beer. I like so much the way they don't mind not talking.'

During his stay, he was visited by a new acquaintance, Randolph Churchill, who drove over with Basil Murray. Randolph recalled that '[Evelyn] was dressed in a rough shirt and a pair of corduroy trousers and shod, I seem to remember, in sandals. It was a lovely day and we sat outside the pub drinking rum and water from large pewter tankards and eating bread and cheese.'

On 20 July Evelyn wrote to Henry Yorke, 'I have written 25,000 words of a novel in ten days. It is rather like P. G. Wodehouse all about bright young people. I hope it will be finished by the end of the month.' But well before the end of the month he received a letter from his wife confessing that she and John Heygate had fallen in love.[21]

Stunned by this wholly unexpected news, Evelyn went at once to London where he was confronted by a semi-hysterical, rather frightened young woman, who told him that not only were she and Heygate in love, but that they had become lovers. It then transpired that the affair had begun at a party to which Heygate had taken Eleanor Watts. Eleanor, having just turned down his proposal of marriage, left early, while Heygate stayed on with the

---

[21] Later that year Bryan Guinness began work on a novel, *Singing Out of Tune* (Putnam, 1933), which was partly based on Evelyn's oral account of the breakdown of his marriage. In it the hero receives a letter from his wife, breaking the news of an adulterous relationship. ' "Darling Arthur," it began, "something has happened between me and Peter Blekinsopp which has made me decide to leave you. I have fallen in love with him, and he with me. The thought of your reproachful face is more than I can endure, so I am going away and leaving this letter to tell you..."

'... [it was] the phrase "something has happened between me and Peter", that had a sinister ring. He pictured her rolling entwined in the greedy arms of the little hunchback. He saw them tugging at each other's clothes, at each other's bodies.'

express intention of getting drunk. At the end of the evening She-Evelyn had accompanied the rejected suitor to his flat in Cornwall Gardens and stayed the night.

Waugh at first was unable to believe that what he took to be mere physical passion could be that important. He thought that the situation was not beyond saving. He told Evelyn he would be prepared to continue as though nothing had happened on condition that she give her word she would never see Heygate again. Evelyn promised, but it was not a promise she was able to keep.

Although the news had come as an appalling shock to her husband, others had already detected signs of trouble. Balston, on the morning after his dinner party, had reported a strained atmosphere between the Evelyns; and Anthony Powell, who had spent a day in Brighton with She-Evelyn and Heygate, had been uncomfortably aware of the extramarital electricity.

For the next fortnight Evelyn Waugh stayed in London in a miserable attempt to repair his marriage. The couple went together to Henry Yorke's wedding, where Henry's aunt, Margaret Wyndham, was amused to see She-Evelyn behaving in an uncharacteristically genteel manner, 'butter not melting in her mouth'. Grimly, Evelyn accompanied his wife to the parties she so loved, including a 'tropical' party given by Oscar Wilde's son, Vyvyan Holland, where the *Bystander* flashlighted them looking startled and ill at ease in their safari kit. 'The Hon. Mrs Evelyn Waugh and her husband . . . on board the *Friendship*. The author of *Decline and Fall* looks somewhat scared, although there were no fierce Zulus on board.' It was a ghastly two weeks. The weather was unusually hot, and the tension between the two Evelyns at breaking point, Waugh at one moment even accusing his wife of trying to murder him. 'It's terrible,' she told Alec, whom she had arranged to meet at the Gargoyle. 'Evelyn's drinking much too much, which makes him feel ill. And he thinks I'm trying to poison him.'

Semi-paralysed by misery and to escape the noxious atmosphere for a few days, Waugh went to Cheshire to stay with Eleanor Watts at her parents' house, Haslington Hall, near Crewe. A sympathetic relationship had evolved between them based on mutual unhappiness, as Eleanor was painfully regretting having turned down Heygate, with whom she was more than a little in love. They sat around the house all day drinking Black Velvet and endlessly analysing the events of the past weeks, while Evelyn with his paintbox made desultory sketches for the dust-cover of *Vile Bodies*. In a letter almost incoherent with wretchedness, he wrote to Balston,

> I am afraid my book is not written. When I gave the end of July
> as a date I had every expectation of delivering the ms. then,
> but the last weeks have been a nightmare of very terrible
> suffering which, if I could explain, you would understand. You
> shall have the book, unless I go off my head, as soon as I can
> begin to rearrange my thoughts. At present I can do *nothing*
> of any kind.

With the heightened awareness of her emotional state, Eleanor sensed that Evelyn was not, probably never had been, deeply in love with his wife, but that it had been a powerful infatuation and that the possession of such an attractive woman had meant a great deal to him in restoring his masculine confidence. Now all this rebuilding had been demolished. 'You must put it out of your mind,' she told him. 'I *can't*, I *can't*,' came the unvarying reply. On the first of August they returned to London, Eleanor at the wheel of her little Morris Oxford, Evelyn urging her all the way to go faster.

She-Evelyn, meanwhile, had succeeded in bringing matters to a crisis in her husband's absence by being photographed at a party in the company of Heygate. 'What shall I do?' she asked her flatmate, Nancy Mitford. To Nancy, the problem was not serious: it was the sort of mischance that at a party could happen to anyone. 'Tell Evelyn it wasn't your fault', she said, 'and that you love him.' 'But I don't love him', She-Evelyn replied, going on to confess that she had never loved her husband, had married only to get away from home.

Clearly any reconciliation was out of the question. 'Evelyn so obviously was determined to make it impossible for Waugh to take her back,' wrote Pansy, 'that while promising to return to him if he wished, she took care that he shouldn't ... Her excuses for infidelity were that Waugh was too difficult to live up to[22] & that he secretly hated her when she was ill!' But although Waugh may

[22] Evelyn Gardner 'has to work hard for him [Waugh] which is the best thing for her', Pansy had written soon after the two Evelyns had got engaged.

have resented his wife's illness, resented the expense and the time it took away from his work, there was no doubt that he had been genuinely concerned and had done what he could to take care of her. It is far more likely that She-Evelyn had hated *him*, hated his masculine inhibition and lack of demonstrativeness, sitting by her bedside smoking his pipe and doggedly reading P. G. Wodehouse when what she craved were caresses and endearment. Later she confided that she had felt very lonely and had painfully missed feminine company, specifically the company of her sisters. As her second husband later said of her, she suffered 'constriction from He-Evelyn's brain, knowledge and occasionally sharp tongue . . . she wanted to [be allowed to] develop in her own rather childlike self.' Sexually the marriage had been far from satisfactory: hers was a warm temperament; her husband's, she said, was not. The probability is that before his marriage Waugh had had little or no experience with women, an assumption borne out by his wife's subsequent complaint to a girl-friend that Evelyn had been 'bad in bed', and also by a veiled reference in the most autobiographical of Evelyn's novels, *The Ordeal of Gilbert Pinfold*: '[on honeymoon] many a young couple spend a wretched fortnight together through not knowing how to set about what has to be done.' She-Evelyn suspected, too, that her husband's real preference was for men; his sexual technique she found unpleasurable, a technique which had, after all, been learnt in affairs with men, and she had been perturbed during the few days staying with Alastair and Mark Ogilvie-Grant in Athens by how congenial Waugh had found their conspicuously effeminate behaviour.

For his part Evelyn Waugh had believed in the permanence of his marriage, and had no inkling of the measure of his wife's dissatisfaction. And yet in retrospect, there are indications that he must have known that all was not entirely well. After lunching at the Ritz the following year with Nancy Mitford, who was unsuccessfully trying to persuade an extremely reluctant young man into marriage, he wrote, 'I explained to her a lot about sexual shyness in men.'; and in an article on marriage for *John Bull*, which appeared in August 1930, Evelyn argued that

[People say] 'You cannot lead a happy life unless your sex life is happy.' That seems to me just about as sensible as saying,

'You cannot lead a happy life unless your golf life is happy.' ...
It means that the moment a wife begins to detect imperfections
in her husband she thinks her whole life is ruined. ... Sex
instinct in most cases is a perfectly mild and controllable
appetite which would never cause most of us any serious trouble
at all if it was not being continually agitated by every sort of
hint and suppression. ... By the present system of education the
one thing that is hidden is the actual facts about sex; as a
natural result they [ie young people] regard this as the most
important thing of all. When they find that after some time of
marriage sexual relations are not so absorbingly interesting as
they had been led to suppose, they think it is because they
have made a mistake in their choice of a mate. Then they get
into the divorce courts ...

Now all that remained was to go through with what Waugh
described as 'my smutty lawsuit'.

Heygate had left for a motoring holiday in Germany with Tony
Powell. Having spent a few untroubled days in Berlin, they
reached Munich, where Powell found a telegram waiting for him:
'Instruct Heygate return immediately Waugh'. Evelyn asked Alec
to break the news to their parents. 'It's going to be a great
blow to them,' said Alec, at which his brother laughed wryly.
Arthur's priorities were expressed with an equal lack of tact. 'Your
poor mother', he said. 'Your poor, poor mother.' Arthur was in
no doubt as to where the blame lay, and refused to see his
daughter-in-law again, whereas Kate, although disapproving of
She-Evelyn's adultery, believed that the fault was partly her son's
for having left his wife too much alone. Eventually Evelyn brought
himself to write to his parents in person.

'I asked Alec to tell you the sad & to me radically shocking
news that Evelyn has gone to live with a man called Heygate. I
am accordingly filing a petition for divorce ... Evelyn's defection
was preceded by no kind of quarrel or estrangement. So far as I
knew we were both serenely happy. It must be some hereditary
tic,' he added, a reference to the fact that Evelyn was the third
of Lady Burghclere's daughters to divorce. In reply to a somewhat
insensitive enquiry from Harold Acton as to the cause of the split
('Are you so very male in your sense of possession ... is it the fact
of its being Heygate? Or is it due to quarrels and boredom? ... As
you know, I have a low opinion of all women'), he replied,

'Certainly the fact that she should have chosen a ramshackle oaf like Heygate adds a little to my distress but my reasons for divorce are simply that I cannot live with anyone who is avowedly in love with someone else', commenting in a letter to Henry Yorke, 'It is extraordinary how homosexual people however kind & intelligent simply don't understand at all what one feels in this kind of case.'

Arthur and Kate went to see Lady Burghclere and Geoffrey Fry (who, as one-time private secretary to Stanley Baldwin, had experience in treaty negotiation), after which Evelyn was persuaded to delay matters while She-Evelyn stayed in Venice with an aunt to think things over. But while there she heard from Heygate that he was waiting for her, and so, burning her boats once and for all, she returned to London and moved into his flat.

On 3 September Evelyn Waugh, through Arthur's old friend, the well-known divorce lawyer, E. S. P. Haynes, filed a petition against his wife, she having honourably insisted that she be legally recognised as the guilty party. Pansy, who had always done what she could to promote what Waugh later referred to as 'my mock marriage', now felt miserable at its collapse. 'I fear [She-] Evelyn's affairs are now past praying for,' she wrote. 'The only hope is that she will not marry John Heygate who is null, unpleasant & penniless. It will be rather difficult as she has lived with him for a week & is incapable of living by herself... She is so eminently unsuited for marriage... the terrible thing is she really seems to enjoy the publicity her conduct entails.'

Far from enjoying it, sunk in a state of black despair, Waugh turned for refuge to Richard and Elizabeth Plunket Greene. Richard was away, and Elizabeth, who had been planning to join her husband, seeing the state Waugh was in, gave up her plan, and took him to stay with her brother and his wife at Shere, near Guildford. 'He was miserable, talking of suicide, and quite beside himself but determined to divorce.'

Almost simultaneously She-Evelyn was encountered by Margaret Wyndham,[23] who was staying with Henry and Pansy Lamb at Coombe Bissett. '[She was] looking quite unmoved.... I never saw Pansy alone so could ask nothing, but Shevelyn [sic] seems

---

[23] Margaret Wyndham's elder sister was the mother of Pansy's friend John Maxse; her other sister was the mother of Henry Yorke.

to have behaved rottenly.' It was during this weekend that the solicitor's letter arrived explaining that her husband was suing for divorce. 'Well,' said Evelyn in her little-girl voice. 'Well, you can't call life dull!'

Waugh, meanwhile, was writing to Harold Acton, 'I did not know it was possible to be so miserable & live but I am told that this is a common experience.'

The island of sanity

Although it is useless to speculate what Evelyn Waugh's life would have been had he remained with Evelyn Gardner, there is no doubt that he was much better off without her. They had so little in common. Once the enchantment had worn thin of her prettiness and playful ways, he would have had small sympathy with her passion for parties and her lack of spiritual dimension, while she would have felt miserably neglected by a husband who when working needed to spend long periods on his own.

Now Evelyn Waugh was free, but the cost of his freedom had nearly crippled him. He was conscious only of shock and humiliation: shock that an alliance he had assumed would last a lifetime could be so easily destroyed; humiliation that a pretty woman had publicly rejected him for a man whose powers of attraction were obviously superior to his own. In Waugh's eyes Evelyn Gardner had slammed the door shut on the safe nursery world he had hoped to recreate. By leaving him, she had confirmed his inadequacies, and now, like Tony Last, he heard and saw little except 'the all-encompassing chaos that shrieked about his ears'.

Although he behaved with dignity and restraint, Evelyn's unhappiness was profound and like a virus attacking the weakest part of the system, it erupted in an outbreak of paranoia and self-loathing. When John Sutro, hoping to cheer him up, took him to dinner at the Savoy, Evelyn was made wretched by a conviction that the other diners were laughing at him. Desolate and displaced, he was overwhelmed by the pain inflicted by his wife's desertion and by an intense hatred of her lover. 'I wish I was handing Evelyn over to someone less radically contemptible than Heygate,' he wrote to Tom Balston, 'but clearly that is a matter in which I cannot exercise any choice.' And to Henry Yorke he admitted, 'My horror and detestation of the basement boy[1] are unqualified. There is practically no part of one that is not injured when a thing like this happens but naturally vanity is one of the things one is most generally conscious of – or so I find.' Hard to bear, too, were the copious expressions of sympathy which poured in unwelcome from every quarter. Even when he managed to escape for a couple of weeks to Ireland, 'wires arrive in green envelopes every two hours', and 'everyone is talking so much nonsense on all sides of me about my affairs, that my wits reel. Evelyn's family & mine join in asking me to "forgive" her whatever that may mean.' For the moment he was rudderless, had nothing in mind except a strong desire to get away from people he had known with his wife. 'I confess to being shy of meeting anyone just at present,' he wrote to Balston, and to Henry Yorke, 'Can you suggest anything for me to do after Christmas for six months or so – preferably remunerative but that is not important – but essentially remote & unliterary?'

Unable to endure the well-meant commiseration of his parents, Evelyn preferred the company of his friends, particularly his married friends, who had more of an insight into his predicament than such as Harold Acton and Alastair Graham, or even than his bachelor cousin, Claud Cockburn who, writing from New York to sympathise, insensitively enquired, 'Have you tried quickly sleeping with someone else practically as pretty?' But Richard and Elizabeth Plunket Greene understood very well what he was going through, as did Henry and Pansy Lamb, with whom he stayed in their little Georgian house at Coombe Bissett while Henry painted his portrait. They both had been distressed by the breakdown of the marriage, Pansy especially, as she felt responsible for having promoted it so enthusiastically in the first place. Some of the strongest support came from that 'strange mixture of dash and melancholy', the sardonic Henry Yorke, a comparatively new acquaintance. While still an undergraduate at Magdalen, Yorke, under the pen-name Henry Green, had published a first novel, *Blindness*. Evelyn read it, admired it and had written to express

[1] Evelyn described Heygate as 'the basement boy' because he met him in Anthony Powell's basement flat.

his admiration, after which the two men quickly became friends, identifying with each other's jaundiced view of the world and anarchic sense of humour. Both Evelyns had been present at Henry's wedding in July 1929, when he married Adelaide ('Dig') Biddulph; and now Henry sided passionately with Waugh over what he saw as a monstrous betrayal. 'I do hope that you are in a towering rage about it. Divorce is the only possible attitude to take up. I am absolutely furious with her ... It is the sort of meanness which is beyond any toleration & an underhand attack on one's emotions which only a woman can produce. In the circumstances one of the dirtiest tricks I've ever heard of.'

The nomadic existence on which Evelyn now embarked was to continue for seven years. In August, he went to Ireland, first to Belfast for the motor races, probably with David Plunket Greene who was a keen amateur racing driver ('I am escaping to Ireland for a weeks motor racing in the hope of finding an honourable grave', he told Harold Acton), before moving south to stay with Bryan and Diana Guinness at Knockmaroon, just outside Dublin. It was here that he had the unenjoyable task of composing an article for the *Daily Mail* entitled 'Let the Marriage Ceremony Mean Something', in which he argues that 'The real value of marriage to any two people is not so much the opportunity for each other's society which it provides as the illusion of permanence.' If the *Mail* did not use the piece promptly, Evelyn wrote wrily to Peters, 'they will be printing my austere views on the sanctity of marriage in the same issue as the report of my divorce.' He returned from Ireland at the beginning of September, and the following month went to Paris to stay again with the Guinnesses, who had the use of the luxurious family apartment in the rue de Poitiers.

Diana Guinness was already expecting her first child, and it was during her pregnancy, when for weeks at a time she was confined to bed and able to spend hours in talk, that Evelyn fell romantically in love with her. On his return from Ireland he had written to Henry Yorke, 'Do you & Dig share my admiration for Diana? She seems to me the one encouraging figure in this generation – particularly now she is pregnant – a great germinating vat of potentiality like the vats I saw at their [the Guinness] brewery.' A flawless classical beauty – '*Voici la Grèce!*' the painter

Helleu used to exclaim as the fifteen-year-old Diana came into the room – she was tall and slender, with blonde hair and enormous blank blue eyes. If not as acerbic as her elder sister, Nancy, she shared her love of frivolity and her insatiable sense of humour. Although only eighteen when she married, desperate, like Nancy, to escape from home, Diana's tastes were surprisingly mature and far removed from the likes and dislikes of the conventional débutante. She read widely, passionately admired the new young novelists such as Evelyn and Henry Green, and adored the clever, camp young men she had come to know through Nancy, such as Harold Acton, Mark Ogilvie-Grant and Robert Byron. Bryan Guinness, whom Evelyn had known slightly at Oxford, was a gentle, literary young man, a poet and connoisseur of the arts. With him Diana met the Sitwells and Augustus John, as well as members of the Bloomsbury group: Lytton Strachey, whose penetrating intelligence and malicious wit particularly appealed to her; Dora Carrington and Boris Anrep, from both of whom she commissioned work. Like all Mitfords, Diana saw it as a courteous obligation to perceive life as endlessly amusing; she adored gossip and chat, and was ready to scream with laughter at the slightest provocation ('shrieking' was a favourite Mitford word). This beautiful and high-spirited young woman provided the perfect antidote to Evelyn's melancholy, an appreciative audience for his jokes, an unfailing admirer of his unordinary intelligence. 'He was the best company imaginable,' she wrote of this time. 'Never was there a more agreeable man. He had a very deep laugh, about an octave lower than his voice, and we laughed all the time.' Had he still been married, they would never have grown so close. 'One couldn't have had him constantly in the house if he'd been saddled with the other Evelyn, who though very pretty, wasn't much else.'

With Diana's youth and high spirits and her love of being entertained, it is hardly surprising Evelyn made light of his unhappiness. Diana saw not the slightest indication of any depression, and from that assumed that the wound had not gone deep, that his feeling about his divorce was predominantly one of relief. Nancy, too, was staying in the rue de Poitiers, and as she, Bryan and Evelyn had books in progress, the morning was devoted to work, the afternoons to dress-shows and sight-seeing. Evelyn, with his taste for the macabre, conceived a passion for the waxworks in the Musée Grevin, going again and again to look at a bloodthirsty tableau of Christians and lions and the model of an old mad woman in a cell in the Bastille.

When Evelyn left the glamorous Guinnesses it was to go to David and Tamara Talbot Rice, both of whom he had known at Oxford and who now had a tiny flat in the rue Blomet. It was immediately apparent to Tamara that in spite of a courageous front Evelyn was profoundly unhappy, and that 'he minded intensely about his marriage break-up'. But then the Rices were old friends: David, now a Byzantine archaeologist, had been a member of the Hypocrites', Tamara a home student at St Anne's. Living out of college she been able to keep a dog, an Alsatian called Ghost, and several afternoons a week Evelyn had called round to walk with Tamara and Ghost in Christ Church Meadow. The Rices, recently returned from a dig in Constantinople, were poor, and David was having to work hard on his thesis, while Evelyn spent hours talking to Tamara, mainly about religion. When she was unavailable, he went by himself to the Bal Nègre, a rackety, ramshackle club where he was fascinated by the loose-limbed dancers from Guadeloupe and Martinique. 'The chief instrument in the band is a cocktail shaker full of gravel which is called a Cha Cha. The girls put their arms round the men's necks, the men round the girls' waists, if expert each keep one hand on their own hip – jauntily, they stay mostly in the same place, frigging.' Evelyn had met and was being energetically pursued by Marcella Gump, a one-time girlfriend of Alec's and daughter of a Chicago paint millionaire. Every evening she telephoned to ask him out, and with the Rices as chaperones, all three would go 'Gumping', they called it, drinking and dancing with the heiress at Le Boeuf sur le Toit.

Evelyn returned to England at the end of October invigorated and with his spirits greatly improved. 'I am going to stop hiding away from everyone,' he wrote to Henry Yorke. 'I was getting into a sort of Charlie Chaplinish Pagliacci attitude to myself as the man with a tragedy in his life and a tender smile for children. So all that must stop and one conclusion I am coming to is that I do not like Evelyn & that really Heygate is about her cup of tea.' Now the important thing was to concentrate on work.

The first draft of his novel, *Vile Bodies*,[2] had been finished before he went away in October. He had written then to Henry Yorke, 'It has been infinitely difficult ... It all seems to shrivel up & rot internally and I am relying on a sort of cumulative futility for any effect it may have.'

And indeed, although presented as high comedy, the novel paints a bleak and chilling picture both of human nature and of the period, 'one of the meanest and most fraudulent decades staining the annals of history'.[3] In an interview given over thirty years later, Evelyn said that it was in the middle of his writing *Vile Bodies* that his first wife had left him; and indeed there is a distinct change of mood which takes place at the beginning of Chapter VII – from indications in the manuscript precisely the point at which Waugh broke off, and then restarted. On only the third page of this new section, there is a sour reference to 'cocktail parties given in basement flats by spotty announcers from the BBC', and the novel's heroine, Nina, soon turns to callous infidelity.

The members of this savage society are rootless and amoral, most of them possessed by an almost hysterical sense of futility. Adam Fenwick-Symes, although not as passive in character as Paul Pennyfeather, is as helpless a victim of fate. Adam is a young and unsuccessful writer, and the furniture of his world, a combination of the bookish and social, is very similar to those of his creator. He has no money, but is a friend of Lady Metroland (harder and more sinister than in *Decline and Fall*), and is invited to parties at Pastmaster House. The theme of Adam's on-off engagement to Nina Blount, a shallow young woman, is threaded through the novel as a bitter running gag, in which can be heard poignant echoes of Evelyn's relationship with his wife. ' "I don't know if it sounds absurd," said Adam, "but I do feel that a marriage ought to go on – for quite a long time, I mean. Do you feel that too, at all?" ' After they first go to bed together, Nina says, ' "My dear, I never hated anything so much in my life ... still, as long as you enjoyed it that's something," ' only later climbing down suf-

[2] The title is taken from Philippians 3:21, 'the Lord Jesus Christ who shall change our vile body, that it may be fashioned like unto his glorious body, according to the working whereby he is able even to subdue all things unto himself'.
[3] Richard Aldington in his review of *Vile Bodies* for the *Sunday Referee*.

ficiently 'to admit that perhaps love was a thing one could grow to be fond of after a time, like smoking a pipe. Still she maintained that it made one feel very ill at first, and she doubted if it was worth it.' In a sentence that was deleted from later editions, the narrator revealingly remarks, 'The truth is that like so many people of their age and class, Adam and Nina were suffering from being sophisticated about sex before they were at all widely experienced.' When Nina eventually decides not to marry Adam, her new fiancé, Ginger, innocently observes, ' "After all, damn it, what does being in love mean if you can't trust a person?" ("What, indeed?" thought Adam).' As the story moves towards its terrifying climax, the author's perspective becomes increasingly disillusioned and more stark. Nina in an aeroplane looks down on a country that typifies Evelyn's disgust with the modern world:

> a horizon of straggling red suburb; arterial roads dotted with little cars; factories, some of them working, others empty and decaying; a disused canal; some distant hills sown with bungalows; wireless masts and overhead power cables; men and women were indiscernible except as tiny spots ... The scene lurched and tilted again as the aeroplane struck a current of air. 'I think I'm going to be sick,' said Nina.

The final chapter, entitled 'Happy Ending', is even grimmer. Adam is sitting on 'a splintered tree stump in the biggest battlefield in the history of the world ... The scene all round him was one of unrelieved desolation; a great expanse of mud in which every visible object was burnt or broken. Sounds of firing thundered from beyond the horizon – '

The Bright Young People, funny, frenzied and frivolous, caper their way from party to party ('Oh, Nina, what a lot of parties') like a troupe of Dionysiac dancers, dotty with drink, heavily painted, and chattering on heedlessly in their bright young fashionable idiom. ' "Well," they said, "Well! how too, too shaming, Agatha, darling," they said. "How devastating, how unpoliceman-like, how goat-like, how sick-making, how too, too awful." '
Evelyn's observation of the various strata of London society, ruled over by 'those two poles of savagery Lady Circumference and Lady Metroland', are made with a scientific exactness; he delineates precisely the difference between the younger, livelier, but rather raffish set to be found at Margot Metroland's and the grand, dull,

deeply respectable society invited to Anchorage House, where
'the Presence of Royalty was heavy as thunder in the drawing-
room'. Miss Runcible and her friends would never be guests
of Lady Anchorage, although they provide a consuming topic of
conversation at her receptions. ' "What I always wonder, Kitty
dear, is what they actually do at these parties of theirs. I mean,
do they – ?" "My dear, from all I hear, I think they do." ' Just
such a naughty party is Archie Schwert's, again retailed with
perfect pitch: 'There was a famous actor making jokes (but it was
not so much what he said as the way he said it that made the
people laugh who did laugh). "I've come to the party as a wild
widower," he said. They were that kind of joke – but, of course,
he made a droll face when he said it.'

Also at the party are two aristocratic gossip columnists, Lords
Vanbrugh and Balcairn, whose existence owes not a little to the
real-life columnists Lords Castlerosse and Donegall, as well as to
Evelyn's two friends, both engaged in the society racket, Tom
Driberg (Dragoman of the *Express*) and Patrick Balfour (Mr
Gossip of the *Daily Sketch*). Balcairn, unable to obtain an
invitation to Lady Metroland's dance, kills himself, and Adam
takes over his job as Mr Chatterbox of the *Daily Excess*, whose
owner, Lord Monomark, bears a close resemblance to Lord
Beaverbrook. Adam enlivens his column by reporting invented
stories about invented people, and by testifying to fictitious fads
and trends, for instance, the buffet at Sloane Square underground
station as the most popular haunt of the artistic coterie, and
green bowler hats as the latest word in chic (this piece of nonsense curiously echoed by a report in Driberg's column one
morning that, 'The new drink is green beer [only to be found
at] the enterprising Bury-street restaurant where Londoners were
first introduced to champagne rosé, champagne nature and
camel soup.').

One of the book's great comic characters is Lottie Crump,
proprietor of Shepheard's Hotel in Dover Street, a bare-faced
portrait of the famous Rosa Lewis, proprietor of the Cavendish
Hotel in Jermyn Street. Rosa Lewis was one of the glories of
the Edwardian age: 'One can go to Shepheard's parched with
modernity any day, if Lottie likes one's face, and still draw up,
cool and uncontaminated, great, healing draughts from the well
of Edwardian certainty.' She had worked for the Comte de Paris,

Lady Randolph Churchill and for the Prince of Wales himself, before eventually opening her own hotel, an establishment at once respectable and shady, patronised both by dowagers up from the shires and dissolute young Guards officers dining and spending the night with young women no better than they should be. Evelyn was never an habitué (Rosa, like Lottie, 'true to the sound old snobbery of pound sterling and strawberry leaves', did not care for writers), although he went there occasionally, having been introduced by Alastair Graham, by whose uncle, Willie Low, Rosa had once been employed. Rosa was seen by Evelyn as an incomparable clown, and there was an irresistible *Through the Looking-Glass* quality to the Cavendish, with Rosa as both Red and White Queen, with her inconsequential remarks and confusion over names, her 'off-with-his-head' manner and unconventional method of dealing with clients.

> 'What about a little drink? Here, you over there, your honour Judge What's-your-name, how about a drink for the gentlemen? Bottle of wine,' said Lottie, 'with Judge Thingummy there.' (Unless specified in detail, all drinks are champagne in Lottie's parlour . . . but Lottie has an equitable soul and she generally sees to it, in making up the bills, that the richest people pay for everything.)

The last occasion on which Evelyn went to the Cavendish was after dinner the night before Henry Yorke's wedding – 'Rosa was having some trouble at the time over a cheque with a man called Lulu Waters-Welch . . . She fixed me with fierce eyes and said: "Lulu Waters-Waugh take your arse off my chair" ' – but after the publication of *Vile Bodies* he was never allowed back. 'There are two bastards I'm not going to have in this house,' Rosa was heard to say. 'One is that rotten little Donegall[4] and the other is that swine Evelyn Waugh.' She sent a letter to Chapman & Hall threatening litigation, after which Evelyn wrote a disingenuous paragraph in an article for the *Daily Mail*, entitled 'People Who Want to Sue Me':

> Not long ago I published a novel in which a few pages were devoted to the description of an hotel. In order to avoid trouble I made it the most fantastic hotel I could devise. I filled

[4] The Marquess of Donegall was a columnist on the *Sunday News* against whom Rosa Lewis was threatening to bring a libel suit.

it with an impossible clientèle, I invented an impossible proprietress. I gave it a fictitious address, I described its management as so eccentric and incompetent that no hotel could be run on their lines for a week without coming into the police or the bankruptcy court . . . Imagine my surprise, therefore . . .

Scattered through *Vile Bodies* are a number of private jokes and references. Cruttwell gets off lightly, his name given to a Conservative MP, Captain Cruttwell, whom Adam overhears mentioned approvingly by two snobbish Tory ladies in a train. And the way of life of Alastair Graham and Mark Ogilvie-Grant, both so happy to quit England for their diplomatic postings abroad, is recalled in the subterranean existence of Miles Malpractice, an existence punctuated 'by ambiguous telephone calls and the visits of menacing young men who wanted new suits or tickets to America, or a fiver to go on with'. Most bizarre of all this secret semiclogy is the adjective 'sheepish' to describe Archie Schwert's house in Hertford Street. Evelyn had originally written 'divine' ('a perfectly divine house in Hertford Street'), but at the request of Diana Guinness's little sister, Jessica, who had a much-loved pet sheep, he substituted this unusual term of approbation.

Although Evelyn was to outgrow his taste for Firbank ('I think there would be something wrong with an elderly man who could enjoy Firbank', he said in an interview in 1962), in *Vile Bodies* the influence is still strong, apparent not only in the novel's baroque artifice but in the use of dialogue on its own to convey character and further plot. Lewis Carroll's imprint is again clearly visible; there are two quotations from *Alice Through the Looking-Glass* as a frontispiece, and Nina's father, Colonel Blount, is plainly a direct descendant of the White Knight.

[Adam] went up the steps to the front door. He rang the bell and waited. Nothing happened. Presently he rang again. At this moment the door opened.

'Don't ring twice,' said a very angry old man. 'What do you want?'

'Is Mr Blount in?'

'There's no Mr Blount here. This is Colonel Blount's house.'

'I'm sorry. . . . I think the Colonel is expecting me to luncheon.'

'Nonsense. I'm Colonel Blount,' and he shut the door.

Towards the end of the book, Colonel Blount becomes involved in making a film about the life of the Methodist peeress, Selina, Countess of Huntingdon, and the two rivals for her love, Wesley and Whitefield (in one episode, Wesley in America is 'rescued from Red Indians by Lady Huntingdon disguised as a cowboy'[5]). This joke at the expense of the Protestant church is generously balanced by a sending up of the Church of Rome by means of the Machiavellian figure of Father Rothschild SJ, who conforms in every detail to the caricature image of the slippery Jesuit. Father Rothschild, first met carrying a borrowed suitcase in imitation crocodile containing a false beard and 'six important new books in six languages', had the 'happy knack' of remembering 'everything that could possibly be learned about everyone who could possibly be of any importance'. He is, of course, among the guests at Anchorage House; as the party comes to an end, 'Father Rothschild pulled on a pair of overall trousers in the forecourt and, mounting his motor-cycle, disappeared into the night, for he had many people to see and much business to transact before he went to bed.' It is to this joke Jesuit that Evelyn, abandoning the joke, gives a strangely dissonant speech of disillusion and foreboding, using the priest as his own mouthpiece in the only undisguisedly serious part of the book.

> 'I know very few young people, but it seems to me that they are all possessed with an almost fatal hunger for permanence. I think all these divorces show that ... We long for peace, and fill our newspapers with conferences about disarmament and arbitration, but there is a radical instability in our whole world-order, and soon we shall all be walking into the jaws of destruction again, protesting our pacific intentions.'

Vile Bodies, with Evelyn's own cover design, was published by Chapman & Hall on 14 January 1930. To celebrate, Evelyn gave 'a very upper-world' lunch party at the Ritz.

Letters of congratulation came pouring in, one of the most perceptive from Henry Yorke, who enthusiastically described the

---

[5] Evelyn had gone to some trouble to find out about Lady Huntingdon, borrowing material about her from her direct descendant, Viscount Hastings, heir to the then Earl of Huntingdon, who was a close friend of Alec's. It is clear from the novel, however, that the use he made of this authentic material was slight.

novel as 'a most frightfully depressing book in the best possible way . . . Everyone acts in it true to himself & there is dust & ashes everywhere just as there is in real life.' The critics on the whole were favourable, although a few had reservations. Arnold Bennett wrote in the *Evening Standard* that although among the younger humorists, 'the chief in my view is Evelyn Waugh . . . *Vile Bodies* is less successful [than *Decline and Fall*]. It has a few satirical sallies of the first order of merit, but the lack of a well-laid plot has resulted in a large number of pages which demand a certain obstinate and sustained effort of will for their perusal.' Rebecca West, however, praised it, remarking on 'an extremity of desperation which makes his work as touching as it is amusing. *Vile Bodies* has, indeed, apart from its success in being really funny, a very considerable value as a further stage in the contemporary literature of disillusionment.'

Whatever the critics' reaction, the novel quickly became a bestseller. Arthur, retired from Chapman & Hall, now kept a daily journal in which, among much else, he recorded the progress of his sons' books. Alec's travelogue, *The Coloured Countries*, published the same month to reviews that were 'friendly, but unenthusiastic', was subscribed for 350, *Vile Bodies* for 1800. Sales were soon amounting to nearly 2000 copies a week, and by the end of the year it had been reprinted eleven times. 'Those *Vile Bodies* seem to be selling like hot cakes,' Evelyn reported with satisfaction to Peters.

The immediate consequence of Evelyn's success was his revaluation as a literary property. At this stage Evelyn was dealing directly with his two English publishers, Duckworth and Chapman & Hall, so that Peters was involved only with his client's journalism and with his affairs abroad, predominantly in America. There was now a sudden flurry of activity in New York. Alfred Knopf were expressing interest, and Carl Brandt, Alec's American agent, was anxious to establish that he was to continue handling Alec's younger brother ('you know how deep our interest in his work is'). At the same time, Peters's American partner, the Ann Watkins Agency, in spite of the fact they had found *Vile Bodies* 'excessively smart-aleck', admitted they were anxious to get their hands on him. The next project, they had heard, was to be a life of Dean Swift, and they were keen to let Peters know that thanks to clever promotion on their part, the firm of Little, Brown were 'crazy to get Waugh' and would 'crash through with a swell offer for the Swift biography'. Evelyn's travel book, *Labels*, scheduled for publication in the autumn, had still to find an American buyer. 'Did I tell you I saw a man called Lathom who is an American something to do with publishing,' Evelyn wrote to Peters. 'Well what I thought would be nice would be a whacking great advance from Lathom on signature of contract for *Labels* & perhaps Swift too if he can afford such a high up author as me.'

Meanwhile, in London, newspapers and magazines were competing to secure Evelyn's services. Joyce Reynolds of *Harper's Bazaar*, who had rejected the serialisation of *Vile Bodies*, asked if she could commission a short story ('He is so tremendously amusing'); while the *Daily Express* were obliged to consent to some exigent terms in order to secure his by-line: '£15.15 a thousand,' Evelyn instructed Peters, '[and] I will only do feature articles – not side columns like Heygate – with photograph of me and general air of importance.' A deal was arranged with the *Graphic* for a weekly page of book reviews at ten guineas,[6] while the *Daily Mail* agreed to a staggering 30 guineas for regular light features. As well, there was freelance work from the *Week-End Review*, *John Bull*, the American *Bookman* and the *Architectural Review*. In May Evelyn noted in his diary that all this had brought his regular income 'temporarily up to £2500 a year. I feel rather elated about it.'

Labels was finally published in the last week of August, four extracts having already appeared in the *Fortnightly Review*. It was in general well received, with appreciative notices in the *Observer*, the *Bystander* and the *New Statesman*, and an enthusiastic recommendation from Harold Nicolson in the *Express*. The book was also reviewed by the author himself in a nicely calculated piece of self-promotion in the *Graphic*: 'The book that interests me most this week is a new travel book issued by Duckworth's . . . [which includes] an accurate and full description of the night life in Port Said.' As always, Evelyn had given careful thought to the marketing of his product, writing to Tom Balston from Ireland,

> Thinking things over I feel very strongly that *Labels* ought to come out *at the beginning* of October at the latest as otherwise it

[6] In 1930 Evelyn reviewed 84 books in 18 weeks for the *Graphic*.

has such a short run before Xmas. You say it should wait until
rich people are back in London but I want poor people to buy
it too. When are review copies going out? I should like to inscribe
personal copies to Harold Nicolson & the other more
influential critics. Are you entering it for the Book of the Month.
I feel Priestley might be helpful there. Can any steps be taken to
push it with booksellers in Cairo, Athens etc [illeg] on the tourist
route. Might it not be worth while sending them a letter saying
it is all about tourism and their tours . . .

The original intention, at Evelyn Gardner's suggestion, had been
to dedicate the *Labeliad,* as Evelyn called it, to Alec and Alastair,
but this would have revived too many unpleasant memories, and
in the event, as with *Vile Bodies,* the dedication was made to
Bryan and Diana Guinness, 'without whose encouragement and
hospitality this book would not have been finished'.

With his name so frequently before the public, Evelyn was pursued by fashionable hostesses, assiduously tracked by those two
great lion-hunting ladies, Sibyl Colefax and Emerald Cunard. He
entertained lavishly, often at the Ritz, and his week was filled with
luncheon parties, cocktail parties, dinner parties and dances.
Astute enough to know the ephemeral value of such attentions,
he was not yet astute enough 'to avoid the manners of the new
rich' when it came to name-dropping and showing off, although
as always he was more than ready to mock. 'No-one has a keener
appreciation than myself of the high spiritual and moral qualities
of the very rich,' he wrote in the *Mail.* 'I delight in their society
whenever I get the chance.' His fellow-traveller in these realms
of gold was Frank Pakenham, Pansy's brother, who, not long
down from Oxford, was as fascinated as Evelyn by such a world,
such a dazzling amalgam of high society and upper-class intelligentsia. Like Evelyn, Frank had lived in Golders Green and, as a
younger son with no money, had little in the way of prospects.
They were glad of each other as they 'climbed the slopes of
London society together', Frank pleased to have the friendship
of the fashionable young novelist of the moment, Evelyn anxious
to learn from the socially adept Frank how to comport himself

in patrician circles.[7] Lacking the necessary finesse, Evelyn was aware that he did not always come up to scratch. At a party of Emerald Cunard's, among whose guests were Oswald Mosley, Princess Bibesco, George Moore, Nancy Cunard, Harold Nicolson, Lady Lavery and Lord Ivor Churchill, Evelyn noted, 'Lady C. very restless throughout the evening, obviously dissatisfied with me as a lion.' A number of people who now met Evelyn for the first time remembered how nervously irritable, how ill at ease he often seemed, sitting in silence hour after hour smoking and drinking while others danced and chattered around him. But the time was not wasted: he was listening and watching, learning the language and becoming familiar with native customs.

He had tea with Edith Sitwell ('Stale buns and no chairs'), tea with Lady Oxford and the Prime Minister on the terrace of the House of Commons ('They talked of spiritualism'), and lunch with Noël Coward at the Ritz ('He has a simple, friendly nature. No brains'). At the end of June, at the height of the London season, he dined with the Duke and Duchess of Marlborough.

> There were two ambassadors and about forty hard-faced middle-aged peers and peeresses. The Duchess very battered with fine diamonds. The Duke wearing the Garter: also a vast silk turban over a bandaged eye from which his little hook nose protruded. When I left, the Duchess said, 'Ah, you are like Marlborough. He has such a mundane mind. He will go to any party for which he is sent a printed invitation.'

After leaving a dinner party, he would often end the evening at Quaglino's, the Eiffel Tower, the Blue Lantern ('very squalid') or the Gargoyle, not returning home till the early hours of the morning. 'Evelyn, having revelled till 3.0 am, lay abed' is a typical entry in Arthur's diary of this time. During the summer, Evelyn made a number of country visits. He was a guest of the Guinnesses at Pool Place in Sussex, went with John Betjeman and Frank Pakenham for 'a delightful weekend' at Sezincote, and with Robert Byron for ten days to Renishaw in Derbyshire to stay with the Sitwells.

[7] In Frank Pakenham's autobiography, *Born to Believe* (Cape, 1953) he writes of that time, 'After I left Oxford I had quite a little vogue in London society as a coming young man. Not that my status approached that of even the dimmest eldest son, but I had what might be called a respectable niche in the second line at dances.'

Sachie likes talking about sex. Osbert very shy. Edith wholly
ignorant . . . The household was very full of plots. Almost
everything was a secret . . . The recreations of the household
were bathing, visiting houses, and Osbert's Walk . . . [which]
consisted of driving in the car quarter of a mile to Eckington
Woods, walking through them, about half an hour (with
bracken), the car meeting him on the other side and taking
him home. He did this every day. There was a golf club where
we had morning drinks. This too was a secret.

Immediately after Christmas, Frank Pakenham invited Evelyn to
Ireland, to Pakenham Hall in Westmeath, home of his elder
brother, Edward, who had succeeded to the earldom of Longford
after the death of their father at Gallipoli. He and his wife,
Christine, loved entertaining Frank's friends, especially writers
(Edward was a poet and playwright, Christine a novelist), and
Edward in particular, sweet-natured and enormously fat, had a
boisterous sense of humour and a very ungrown-up appetite for
rags and romping. 'I have seen at Pakenham what I have seen
nowhere else,' Evelyn wrote later, 'an entirely sober host literally
rolling about the carpet with merriment.'

Pakenham, a moated and battlemented Gothic mansion of
towers and turrets, was surrounded by a garden full of ivy-strang-
led yews beyond which was a wooded park, the trees encircling a
lake. Its slightly sinister, fairytale atmosphere appealed enormously to Evelyn, as did the gloomy grandeur of the house inside.
Never interested in grandeur for its own sake. – the stultifying
way of life of many of the great houses would have bored him to
distraction – what he found irresistible was ancient lineage, with
all its romantic, historical associations, accompanied by intelligence, charm and that unshakeable self-confidence which, as
Evelyn saw it, was the enviable birthright of the upper classes.
Bookish, clever, eccentric and kind, the Longfords very much
represented the world to which he now aspired, but in which he
still felt himself at a disadvantage. On his second visit at the
end of August, he persuaded Alastair, who was used to such
surroundings, to go with him. It was assumed by the other guests
that they were lovers. Although Alastair was darker and a little
taller, they were similar physically, Alastair was known to be uninterested in girls, and Evelyn when with him used to put on a

high, whiny voice which gave a convincing impression of effemi-
nacy. Edward and Christine were amused by the little pair, 'like
a couple of twins', they said, 'perfectly sweet'.

Evelyn, in spite of the lively and often contentious discussions
at every meal, spoke less than usual, preferring to test the ground
before taking possession of the territory, encouraging others to
perform rather than taking centre-stage himself. No such inhi-
bitions affected John Betjeman, who had also been invited. He,
as ambitious as Evelyn and in much the same direction, worked
hard at being the focus of attention, clowning energetically
during tennis matches, and making a great hit with his hosts by
singing revivalist hymns at the piano, organising charades, giving
mock-Shakespearean recitations and inventing elaborate jokes
about an obscure Irish peer, one of the Pakenham neighbours,
which almost everyone found terribly funny. 'John B.', Evelyn
recorded, unamused, 'became a bore.'

Frank had fallen in love with the beautiful Elizabeth Harman,
whom he had met at Oxford, and was now in a state of agonising
indecision whether or not to commit himself to a proposal of
marriage. She, too, as the daughter of a professional man, a
Harley Street eye surgeon, was an outsider, and perhaps sensing
a natural ally, Evelyn put himself out to be agreeable, encouraging
her to inject some vim into Frank's dithering suit. On the last
night, as everybody was going upstairs to bed, Evelyn hissed in
her ear, 'Go after Frank. Follow him. Go on.' So Elizabeth followed Frank into his bedroom, where the two of them had a long
and decisive talk about their future. Evelyn in his diary wrote,
'Frank and Harman slept together on Frank's last evening but
did not fuck.'

Back in London, Evelyn continued to see his old Oxford acquaintance – John Sutro, Patrick Balfour, Cyril Connolly, Billy Clonmore, and of course Harold Acton. But just as success had
brought him closer to his fellow novelist, Henry Yorke, so it
had begun to put a strain on the friendship with Acton. With
Henry, 'lean, dark and singular', Evelyn was now on terms of
some intimacy; they exchanged long, gossipy letters, and Evelyn
had been to stay at Henry's parents' house, Forthampton, in
Gloucestershire. Evelyn was as much intrigued by Henry's uncon-

ventional way of life as by his radically experimental literary technique. Mrs Yorke was a Wyndham, brought up at Petworth;
Henry's father, a master of foxhounds, was the proprietor of an
engineering works in Birmingham. On coming down from
Oxford, Henry had gone to work on the factory floor, where
Evelyn had visited him and, ever the craftsman, been impressed
by 'the manual dexterity of the workers. Nothing in the least like
mass labour or mechanization – pure arts and crafts. The brass
casting peculiarly beautiful: green molten metal from a red caul-
dron.' When Henry's second novel, *Living*, set in a factory, came
out in 1929, Evelyn gave it a perceptive and favourable review in
the *Graphic* describing it as 'a work of genius', a judgment for
which its author was grateful. '[Your review] was quite excellent
in every way & said I had accomplished all the things I most
wanted to do in *Living* & had told no-one of.' When Evelyn was
working on *Vile Bodies* in June of the same year, Henry wrote, 'I
am longing to read it, I am really, as I think you & I are the only
people who can write at all.'

Unfortunately, the same could not be said by Harold Acton,
whose reputation withered as Evelyn's continued to flourish.
When Harold sent Evelyn the manuscript of part of his book on
The Last Medici, Evelyn noted, 'Most unsatisfactory and I am afraid
will do him no more good than his novel – full of pompous
little clichés and involved, illiterate passages. Now and then a
characteristic gay flash but deadly dull for the most part.' Inevitably, a certain sourness was engendered on Harold's part,
expressed in sulks and the picking of petty quarrels. 'Vain, jealous
and too rich', was Robert Byron's brisk diagnosis of the trouble.
At Oxford, Harold had been the mentor, Evelyn the disciple; now
the rôles were reversed, with Evelyn trying to persuade a not very
receptive Harold to appreciate new talent such as Henry Green
and Ivy Compton-Burnett. 'I have just read *Brothers & Sisters*
through twice & think it magnificently humorous and well
managed. Do try it again.'

But far more distressing was the rupture which now took place
with Diana Guinness. From September 1929, Evelyn had been
constantly in the company of both the Guinnesses. The day after
he returned from Paris, they gave a birthday luncheon for him
at the Ritz; he stayed with them in Sussex and Ireland, and spent
Christmas Day with them at Buckingham Street. They in turn

lunched at Underhill, and on several occasions Evelyn brought Diana to tea with his parents, travelling up with her from Victoria in her enormous chauffeur-driven Daimler as part of the 'carriage exercise' prescribed by the doctor during her pregnancy. It was the fact of Diana's pregnancy that made such a close friendship possible: she was still only nineteen, had not long been married, and in normal circumstances there would have been no question, with her husband out all day studying for the Bar, of spending time alone with an unattached man. But in her condition Diana was grateful for the attentions of this charming and hilarious companion, who was ready to spend hours entertaining her as she rested in the afternoons, happy to eat his dinner on a little table at the end of her bed and, when she felt like it, to accompany her on expeditions to the zoo. It passed the time very pleasantly. To Evelyn, however, the friendship meant much more: Diana had become his private and exclusive property, and when, after the birth of her baby in the middle of March, she returned gladly to crowds of friends, to dancing and fancy-dress parties, he felt bitterly betrayed, rejected yet again by a beautiful woman who yet again had failed to love him as he required.

The breach did not happen immediately. Evelyn went to the baby's christening, and he took part in a spoof art exhibition staged by Bryan and Diana, for which he wrote the preface to a catalogue of paintings by 'Bruno Hat', a mysterious German émigré; in fact, the paintings were done by Brian Howard, while Tom Mitford, a fluent German speaker, dressed up as 'Hat'. But by June the cracks had started to show. For her birthday, Evelyn gave Diana 'an umbrella from Brigg which' he recorded in his diary, 'she broke next day.' In fact Diana kept the umbrella for many years, and treasured it. He refused an invitation to Knockmaroon, but in July went to Pool Place, where he made himself consistently disagreeable. 'Diana and I quarrelled at luncheon. We bathed. Diana and I quarrelled at dinner and after dinner. Next day I decided to leave. Quarrelled with Diana again and left.'

Two days later at a party of Cecil Beaton's, he made a point of cutting her, and after a party at the Sutros', at which Diana had been 'friendly and reproachful-looking', he sent her a note, 'trying to explain that it was my fault that I did not like her, not hers. I don't suppose that she will understand.' What he wrote to her was, 'I must have seemed unfriendly lately and I am sorry. Please believe it is only because I am puzzled and ill at ease with myself. Much later everything will be all right.' Much later indeed. Not until a few weeks before his death in 1966 did Evelyn and Diana become properly reconciled.

> You ask why our friendship petered out. The explanation is very discreditable to me. Pure jealousy. You (and Bryan) were immensely kind to me at a time when I greatly needed kindness, after my desertion by my first wife. I was infatuated with you. Not of course that I aspired to your bed but I wanted you to myself as especial confidante and comrade. After Jonathan's birth you began to enlarge your circle. I felt lower in your affections than Harold Acton and Robert Byron and I couldn't compete or take a humbler place. That is the sad and sordid truth.[8]

Since leaving Canonbury Square, where Evelyn Gardner and Heygate were now living, Evelyn had been without a base. He would spend a night or two with the Richard Plunket Greenes in Holland Park or at the Savile, Arthur's old club, of which he and Frank Pakenham had recently become members. But more often than not, as it cost him nothing, he slept at Underhill. He dined there regularly, was not above an afternoon of charades with his father and the neighbours, and often treated his mother to lunch and a matinée in the West End, leaving Arthur, 'abandoned' and slightly querulous, to his crossword puzzle in front of the fire. Although Evelyn flinched from any discussion of his personal problems, his relations with his mother were easy and affectionate; with his father they were habitually constrained.

This was a difficult time for Arthur. Recently retired as managing director of Chapman & Hall, he was very much missing the structure and society of his office day, with all the attendant business of visitors, telephone calls and correspondence. Although he retained his chairmanship of the board of directors, he felt lonely and uncomfortable with so little to do, and as a

[8] Years later, after Evelyn's death, Diana wrote of this episode to her sister Nancy, 'When Evelyn got fed up with me he wrote to Jonathan then aged 2 or 3 months complaining about me . . . I thought he just stopped coming when I began to recover from pregnancy and he was no longer the only (practically) pebble on the beach. I remember he was so horrid when he did come that one didn't miss him at all.'

result was pushing himself unnecessarily hard over the writing of his autobiography, spending hours a day in his study on the first floor, which had been newly converted from the boys' old nursery. He had grown corpulent, and his asthma was frequently so bad that after meals he sometimes had to hold on to the mantelpiece gasping for breath. He was worried, too, by the gentle but steady decline in the firm's finances, for which he felt he was held largely to blame. His timidity and anxiety, together with his old man's fussiness, at times irritated Evelyn beyond bearing. On one occasion when Arthur was entertaining friends at home, 'Evelyn glared at them all the time & refused to speak', while at an important luncheon for the aviator, Amy Johnson, at Henrietta Street, 'Evelyn never turned up for it, nor let anyone know where he was' – perhaps not surprisingly as the lunch was held the day before the wedding of Heygate and Evelyn Gardner. The references in Arthur's diary to his younger son are tinged with disapproval and self-pity. 'Evelyn left, without bidding me goodbye . . . At 4 o'clock Evelyn returned, demanded aspirin, and took his mother to the pictures . . . Evelyn came back to dinner, & sat with K in the bookroom, while I spent the evening alone upstairs.' There was no open quarrel, however, and from time to time Evelyn made conscious efforts to be attentive, bringing his father expensive delicacies when Arthur was confined to bed feeling 'seedy', and inviting him to a sumptuous lunch at the Savile. 'It cost him £11. I sat between Priestley[9] & Frank Pakenham, & enjoyed myself much.'

The decree nisi had come through on 17 January 1930, and in the months that followed Evelyn indulged in a kind of sexual free-wheeling that he had not known even at Oxford. In April he and Alec spent a few days together in the South of France, Alec on the point of leaving for his first visit to America, Evelyn en route to a rendezvous in Monte Carlo. As his brother, who had been doing such things for years, explained, 'He was able for the first time in his life to say to an attractive female: "What ghastly weather we are having. Don't you think three weeks in Monte Carlo would be a good idea?"' (Alec, a dedicated womaniser, used to put rings round the many dates in his appointment diary

[9] J. B. Priestley was, as Evelyn reminded Balston, in an influential position as regards the choice of Book of the Month.

on which, as he put it, 'fate accorded me the delights of dalliance'.) In Villefranche they stayed at the Welcome, a small, pretty hotel on the waterfront much patronised by artists and writers. They both enjoyed their few days together, but it was the last time there was any real intimacy between them. Alec was about to begin his long love affair with the United States – 'that absorption in and ultimate identification with the American scene that was eventually to make New York my operative base instead of London' – a country which to his brother came to symbolise everything contemptible about the modern age. And Evelyn was on the verge of a spiritual journey, the nature of which was incomprehensible to Alec. 'You cannot appraise a stained-glass window if you look at it from the outside,' Alec wrote in retrospect, '[and] I cannot enter imaginatively into the mind of a person for whom religion is the dominant force in his life.'

On the day of departure they went to the station together. On opposite platforms the two brothers sat by their suitcases in the sun, facing each other with the tracks between them, waiting for their trains to take them on their disparate roads.

When Evelyn returned to England, there was little outward sign of the upheaval that was taking place within as he approached nearer to a resolution of his spiritual problems.

He revived his old friendship with Audrey Lucas, now married to Harold Scott of the Cave of Harmony. Audrey, unhappy in her marriage, had always been attracted to Evelyn and was more than ready to drift into an affair. Evelyn took her to Pool Place, but 'Audrey felt ill all the week and we left on Monday.' Then she told him she was pregnant, but if she hoped this would provoke any demonstration of commitment, she must have found his response disappointing. 'Audrey says she thinks she is going to have a baby. I don't much care either way really...' Later, '[Audrey] says she is not going to have a baby so all that is bogus.'

During the summer Evelyn also had at least one encounter with Dorothy Varda, ex-wife of the art-historian, Gerald Reitlinger, and always known, after a short career as one of C. B. Cochran's Young Ladies, as 'the beautiful Varda'. 'Went back and slept with Varda,' he records after dining with Richard and Elizabeth

Plunket Greene. 'Both of us too drunk to enjoy ourselves.' As Alec later remarked, 'such passades . . . were brief and shallow.'

Much more significant was his meeting a young woman with whom he was now to fall seriously in love. Like Evelyn Gardner, Teresa ('Baby') Jungman typified the flapper. Frivolous and fashionable, intelligent and full of verve, she was extremely pretty in a fair, watercolourish way, and very attractive to men. Michael Duff, 'Bloggs' Baldwin (son of the former prime minister), Lord Ebury's son, Robert Egerton, Charles Brocklehurst, 'Boofy' Gore (later Lord Arran), and handsome Tom Mitford, Nancy's and Diana's brother, were among the many who admired her. Unlike Evelyn Gardner, Baby was rich. She and her sister Zita were the daughters of the wealthy Mrs Richard Guinness by her first marriage to Nico Jungman, a painter of Dutch extraction. The Jungman girls adored parties and were much in demand. They were invited to stay at those two pinnacles of grandeur, Hatfield (the Salisburys) and Taplow (the Desboroughs), and were frequently photographed in *Tatler* wearing fancy-dress or taking part in private theatricals. It was they, with Eleanor Smith and Elizabeth Ponsonby, who several years before had started the fashion for the treasure-hunts and masquerades that became such a craze in the 1920s. The sisters lived with their mother at 19 Great Cumberland Place, where they entertained lavishly, society mingling with artists such as Nöel Coward, Gertrude Lawrence, William Walton and the Sitwells. But there was another side to Baby: she was a devout Roman Catholic and, like Alastair, had an elusive, mysterious quality about her, an underlying seriousness that made her simultaneously more substantial and more tantalisingly seductive.

As Evelyn either did not write or later destroyed his diary for the eighteen months after the disintegration of his marriage, the first reference to Baby Jungman does not appear till 26 May 1930, in an account of a supper party at the Savoy given by Frank Pakenham. However, there is evidence that Evelyn met her first at the beginning of that year: found in his prayerbook at his death was a dried corsage of an orchid and a frond of maidenhair fern labelled in his own hand, '19 January 1930'. At Frank's party Baby is described as 'anxious to be friendly and very sweet'.

Friendly she may have been towards this clever, successful and amusing young man but, like Olivia, Baby was incapable of finding

Evelyn attractive. Physically, 'she couldn't stick him', a fact which unfortunately did nothing to diminish his feelings for her. As they had many friends in common, he saw her frequently, but these sightings were not always productive. At a luncheon given by the Acton brothers in Lancaster Gate, '[Baby] left early and sat at the other end of the table so I couldn't speak to her'; and at a party of John Sutro's, '[I] saw Baby in the distance, v. thick with Tom Mitford.' In June Evelyn himself gave a luncheon party at the Ritz, to which Baby agreed to come, but 'chucked . . . on Friday with peculiar insolence', so much annoying her host that he devoted that week's article for the *Mail*[10] to the rudeness common among the spoiled daughters of the rich. Entitled 'Such Appalling Manners!' he argues, 'The trouble comes entirely from young women . . . I have been to very few luncheon or dinner parties during the last month where someone has not "chucked" usually within an hour of the meal . . .'

During the period of his most acute misery after his wife had left him, Evelyn had found Richard and Elizabeth Plunket Greene among his kindest comforters; he had stayed with them several times, on one occasion taking their flat in Holland Park while they were away. Evelyn was grateful for their tact and sympathy, but there was little anyone could do to alleviate his profound despair. He felt lost, isolated, and wholly without purpose. More and more he found himself drawn towards a contemplation of the Christian faith he had superficially abandoned while at Oxford. But now his inspiration was not the Anglican Church in which he had been brought up, but the Church of Rome.

In this direction he was encouraged by his old friend, Gwen Greene, and by Olivia, who had recently followed her mother into the Catholic Church. Gwen, after instruction by the distinguished Dominican, Bede Jarrett, had 'gone over' four years earlier, but had been scrupulously careful not to influence her daughter. 'I must tell you', she assured her sister, Dolly Ponsonby, 'that I have never even thought of converting Olivia. Far from it. I have opposed her on it.' But to one of Olivia's temperament, 'the great, tremendous and dazzling lure of the Catholic Church' was irresistible. '[She] is marvellously happy about it,' her mother

[10] 'Wrote my *Mail* and *Graphic* articles. The *Mail* one all against Baby Jungman . . .'

reported. 'So changed I can't get over it.' Throughout May and June Evelyn had long discussions with them both. Olivia's faith was intensely emotional, finding its most profound inspiration in the writings of the great sixteenth-century Spanish mystics, St Teresa of Avila and St John of the Cross. For Gwen, on the other hand, a disciple of the austere and practical von Hügel, 'the call came unadorned by any joy or emotion, only a hard and naked will to follow God.' And although it was Olivia to whom Evelyn turned when he wanted to find a priest, his approach to his religion was closer to Gwen's. He experienced none of Olivia's feelings of near-ecstasy (he said that reading St John of the Cross was like reading 'about the habits of some strange tribe'). Instead Evelyn saw his new faith unclouded by emotion, his conversion in terms of a 'grim reality . . . a mariage de convenance'.

Olivia had received instruction from a Jesuit, the mystical and charismatic Father Roy Steuart, and presumably on his advice she sent Evelyn to the Reverend Martin D'Arcy. Father D'Arcy was at Farm Street only temporarily, at the age of thirty-six about to return to Oxford to teach Moral Philosophy at the University's Jesuit foundation, Campion Hall, of which he was soon to become master. As a priest he was well known in more elevated Catholic circles for his strong logical mind, his eloquence and his success in bringing into the Church numbers of prominent converts.[11] An unashamed tuft-hunter, he faithfully followed the Jesuit tradition established in England of concentrating on the upper echelons of society, on the well-tried principle of the bigger the stone, the bigger the ripple. Father D'Arcy, with his black hair, dark eyes, pale face and air of subtle sophistication, had an almost Mephistophelean look about him; he was worldly and amusing, an apostle of the drawing-room, very much at home with the old recusant families, intensely proud of his distinguished Norman ancestry. He had a talent for friendship and intimacy while yet remaining aloof, always maintaining what one colleague described as a 'noli me tangere atmosphere'. He, like Evelyn, regarded the modern age with distaste, looking back with nostalgia to a romantic and dignified past as represented by the great houses and ancient lineage of the old Catholic nobility.

[11] In her novel *The Girls of Slender Means*, Muriel Spark, herself a Catholic convert, says of one of her characters that, 'he could never make up his mind between suicide and an equally drastic course of action known as Father D'Arcy.'

On 8 July Evelyn went for his first appointment to the Jesuit clergy-house, 114 Mount Street, in the heart of Mayfair. 'Went to Father D'Arcy at 11. Blue chin and fine, slippery mind . . . We talked about verbal inspiration and Noah's Ark.' Over the next two weeks Evelyn returned several times to Mount Street, before going down to Coombe Bissett, where he was staying while the Lambs were away, and where the doctrinal dialectic continued with his visitors. First came Douglas Woodruff and Christopher Hollis ('They are very settled in their minds on all debatable topics'), followed by Olivia. 'Olivia and I drove into Salisbury and bought some very good port . . . That evening we got a little drunk and talked about religion.' At the end of August before leaving for Pakenham (where he gave no hint during his stay of what was uppermost in his mind), Evelyn wrote to Father D'Arcy:

> I wonder whether it will be possible for me to continue my instructions when I get back from Ireland. Shall you be in Oxford? I could easily come to live there or near there for a time. As I said when we first met, I realize that the Roman Catholic church is the only genuine form of Christianity. Also that Christianity is the essential and formative constituent of western culture. In our conversations and in what I have read or heard since, I have been able to understand a great deal of the dogma and discipline which seemed odd to me before. But the trouble is that I don't feel Christian in the absolute sense. The question seems to be must I wait until I do feel this – which I suppose is a gift from God which no amount of instruction can give one, or can I become a Catholic when I am in such an incomplete state – and so get the benefit of the sacraments and receive faith afterwards?

His instructor's response was obviously reassuring. Twenty years later Evelyn wrote, 'With me, [D'Arcy] saw it was no good hoping for much & the thing to do was just to get the seed in anyhow & hope some of it would come up.'

Soon after his return from Ireland, Evelyn broke the news of his intention to his parents. 'K very, very sad over news of Evelyn's secession to Rome,' Arthur recorded in his diary, while Kate, unrevealing as ever, wrote, '[Evelyn] told me he was being received into Roman Church next week. Shopped with Janet.' On 29 September 1930, Evelyn was received by Father D'Arcy at the Church of the Immaculate Conception in Farm Street, his only godparent the charwoman then on duty, his only witness Tom Driberg, with whom ten years before he had served at the altar in the chapel at Lancing, and to whom he had confided his adolescent loss of faith. Tom, a devout high Anglican, was puzzled by the invitation, and could only think that as at the time he was writing the 'Talk of the Town' column on the *Express*, this was Evelyn's method of most efficiently spreading the news.[12] That evening Evelyn and Tom dined at the Café de Paris where they listened to a new black singer from America; and next morning readers of 'Dragoman' learned that among other members of the smart set come to hear her – Lady Ravensdale, Tallulah Bankhead, the Marquis of Casa Maury – 'watching critically from the balcony [was] Mr Evelyn Waugh, who had earlier in the evening been received into the Roman Catholic church'.

Although the Church of Rome has traditionally appealed to the artistic temperament, partly for its mystery, partly for the beauty of its music and language, Evelyn always insisted that he was wholly uninfluenced by any aesthetic consideration. (Music he had never cared for, loathed Gregorian chant and regarded Palestrina as a penance.) In an essay entitled 'Come Inside', he wrote,

a first interest in the Catholic Church is often kindled in the convert's imagination by the splendours of her worship in contrast with the bleakness and meanness of the Protestant sects. In England the pull is all the other way. The mediaeval cathedrals and churches, the rich ceremonies that surround the monarchy, the historic titles of Canterbury and York, the social organization of the country parishes, the traditional culture of Oxford and Cambridge, the liturgy composed in the heyday of English prose style – all these are the property of the Church of England, while Catholics meet in modern buldings, often of deplorable design, and are usually served by simple Irish missionaries.

---

[12] That this supposition of Driberg's was probably correct is indicated in a remark made by Evelyn to the Revd Philip Caraman SJ at the time of Edith Sitwell's entry into the Church in 1955: 'What I fear is that the popular papers may take her up as a kind of Garbo-Queen-Christina. I was incomparably less notorious when I was received and I know that I suffered from the publicity which I foolishly allowed then.'

Evelyn's conversion sprang from the recognition that in looking at the Catholic faith, he was looking at truth, the absolute, unarguable and historical truth of the universal Christian Church as established in Rome and founded by Christ in the person of St Peter: 'Tu es Petrus, et super hanc petram aedificabo ecclesiam meam' [Matthew 16.18].[13] To the Holy, Roman and Apostolic Church all roads must lead. This was the Christian revelation, 'a proposition [which] seemed so plain to me that it admitted of no discussion . . . and so on firm intellectual conviction but with little emotion I was admitted into the Church'. Martin D'Arcy's account reiterates this.

> I have never myself met a convert who so strongly based his assents on truth [he recalled]. He was a man of very strong convictions and a clear mind. He had convinced himself very unsentimentally – with only an intellectual passion, of the truth of the Catholic faith, and that in it he must save his soul. Hence in his instructions or talks he always wanted to know exactly the meaning and content of the Catholic faith, and he would stop me, raise difficulties – then immediately he was satisfied, he would ask me to go on.

For cumulative historical reasons, the time at which Evelyn entered the Church was one of the most active periods of Catholic conversion in England. There had been the restoration of the hierarchy in 1850, the veering towards Rome among both lay and clergy instigated by the Oxford Movement, the pervasive influence of Cardinal Newman, the continuing mass immigrations from Ireland, the traumatising effects of the First World War; and with a fast growing Catholic population, an enormous increase in 'mixed' marriages, requiring the instruction of the 'outsider' and a commitment that the children of such marriages be brought up within the Roman Church. In the years between the wars, unprecedented numbers of men and women 'embraced the Scarlet Woman', as the process was facetiously called; by the 1930s there were some 12,000 converts a year in England alone. Several of Evelyn's closest friends had gone over, or were in the process of going over to Rome: Christopher Hollis, Alastair

[13] In 1962, Evelyn said in an interview with the *Paris Review*, 'I reverence the Catholic Church because it is true, not because it is established or an institution.'

Graham, Billy Clonmore, Olivia Plunket Greene; Baby Jungman
was Catholic, so was Douglas Woodruff; Harold Acton, born Catholic, brought up Protestant, had made an early return to the
Church in which he had been baptised.

Evelyn had a religious temperament – he was, after all,
descended from a long line of clergymen; and even when going
through his most atheistic period at Oxford had attended church
occasionally and remained intensely interested in questions of
religion. In an important sense his conversion to Rome was a
measure of urgent necessity. He had reached the stage when life
had become 'unintelligible and unendurable without God', and
in the words of his fellow-convert, Graham Greene, 'he needed
to cling to something solid and strong and unchanging.' Always
prone to depression and despair, Evelyn suffered acutely from a
sense of worthlessness, of accidie, of a terror of being subsumed
in chaos. In an article explaining his conversion, Evelyn wrote,
'the essential issue is no longer between Catholicism, on one side,
and Protestantism, on the other, but between Christianity and
Chaos.'

The Catholic Church, in whose teaching despair was regarded
as a mortal sin, offered a safe and solid structure, a discipline,
an ordered way of life, which once adopted held out a clear
prospect of salvation. To this foundation, and to this alone, Evelyn
was prepared to offer absolute submission. For Evelyn the Church
of England, with its comfortable complacency and flexible accom-
modations, could not compete with the rigour and unrelenting
orthodoxy of Rome. In rejecting the Church of England, he was
rejecting his father's faith, Basil Bourchier's posturing performances, and Golders Green. He was rejecting the parochial and
familiar for the Pope and the Latin Mass and transubstantiation,
for the confessional, for penance and indulgences, for holy relics
and images of saints and a flickering red flame signifying the
perpetual presence of the Host. By changing sides, he was joining
that small but dangerous band which, in the view of Anglicans
such as his parents, had for centuries attempted to undermine
the fabric of the established Church. That this attempt had been
visited with notable success in the last half century, with the rise
of the Oxford Movement and the shocking defection of John
Henry Newman, gave rise in some quarters to passionate anti-
Catholic feeling:

God give our wavering clergy back those honest hearts and true
Which once were theirs ere Popish snares their toils around them
   threw;
Nor let them barter wife and child, pure hearth and happy home
For the drunken bliss of the strumpet kiss of the Jezebel of Rome.

But Evelyn was never one to swim with the tide, and the fact that
Catholics in England were a minority, a small élite, which,
although fast growing in strength and no longer persecuted, was
still frowned upon by the majority and distrusted, enormously
appealed to what Father D'Arcy recognised as his 'spirit of revolt'.
In addition, for a man with such a profound antipathy towards
the barbarous modern world, a universal Church that had stood
essentially unchanged for nearly two thousand years offered a far
stronger bastion against barbarity than one that had been in
existence as an inadequate compromise only since the Reformation.

In such a view all that was still sound of the ancient fabric of
England was exemplified by the old Catholic nobility, with their
encumbered estates, their history of continental exile and persecuted ancestors. The words Evelyn later wrote about the churchman and novelist, Hugh Benson, another convert to Catholicism,
could as well be applied to himself.

> Superficially he was an aesthete, but the Catholic church made
> little aesthetic appeal to him ... What he sought and found in
> the church was authority and catholicity. A national church,
> however wide the empire (and in his life time the empire
> seemed boundless and indestructible), could never speak with
> universal authority and, because it was provincial, it was
> necessarily narrow, finding room for scandalous doctrinal
> aberrations but forever incapable of enclosing the vast variety of
> humanity. Transplanted the Church of England became merely
> the church of the golf club and the garrison ...

Evelyn was a perfectionist, and his desire for perfection penetrated every aspect of his life, its lack often causing him acute
distress. The Catholic Church was the nearest to perfection this
earth could offer. And as an artist, he was attracted to its logic,
by the way in which, once the basic premise was accepted, every
piece fitted. He appreciated the workmanlike attitude of its
officers, the priest as craftsman, who with his apprentice 'stumped

up to the altar with their tools and set to work without a glance to those behind them'.

This essential combination of the mundane with the magnificent which meant so much to Evelyn is nowhere better described than by his distinguished predecessor in the ranks of the converted, Cardinal Newman:

> . . . a Catholic Cathedral is a sort of world, every one going about his own business, but that business a religious one; groups of worshippers, and solitary ones – kneeling, standing – some at shrines, some at altars – hearing Mass and communicating – currents of worshippers intercepting and passing by each other – altar after altar lit up for worship, like stars in the firmament – or the bell giving notice of what is going on in parts you do not see – and all the while the canons in the choir going through their hours matins and lauds or Vespers, and at the end of it the incense rolling up from the high altar, and all this in one of the most wonderful buildings in the world and every day – lastly, all of this without any show or effort, but what every one is used to – everyone at his own work, and leaving every one else to his.

Once 'inside', Evelyn admitted later, 'it took me years to begin to glimpse what the church was like.' Immediately after his reception, however, he was aware of one crucial difference, aware that now he had access, as he described it, to a little island of sanity in a raving world.

VIII

Remote people

The plan for an expedition to Abyssinia originated in a frivolous conversation in the library at Pakenham during Evelyn's visit there in August 1930. His desire to distance himself was as strong as ever, and during the past few months he had contemplated trips to Canada, the Antarctic, China and Japan. But then Alastair Graham started talking about the forthcoming coronation of the Emperor Haile Selassie in Addis Ababa and the idea took hold. Alastair knew enough about his subject to make the picture attractively grotesque. He and Mark Ogilvie-Grant, known in diplomatic circles as 'the Embassy girls', had been transferred to Cairo when Sir Percy Loraine left Athens to become high commissioner to Egypt and the Sudan. It had fallen to them to arrange a luncheon for two visiting Abyssinian princes, who arrived wearing silk capes and bowler hats which they insisted on retaining throughout the meal. As they spoke no known tongue, it had been a tricky occasion, which Alastair had soon worked up into an extremely funny story, now embellished with further enticing details, such as the fact that the Abyssinian church had canonised Pontius Pilate, that it consecrated its bishops by spitting on their heads, that the people lived on raw meat and mead, and that the rightful heir to the throne had for years been 'hidden in the mountains, fettered with chains of solid gold'.

For Evelyn, this was more than enough, and he lost no time in dispatching a postcard to Peters. 'I want very much to go to Abyssinia for the coronation of the Emperor. Could you get a paper to send me as special correspondent? ... P. S. this is a serious suggestion.' Peters, having tried and failed to sell the idea to the *Mail,* the *News* and the *Telegraph,* eventually managed to persuade the *Graphic,* for which Evelyn was doing regular book reviews, to take three articles reporting the occasion, although they refused to pay more than the usual ten guineas a piece. Through the good offices respectively of Douglas Woodruff and Tom Driberg, Evelyn also managed to get himself accredited to *The Times* and the *Daily Express.*

Alastair, having suggested the project, was indirectly responsible for the ending of Evelyn's friendship with Mrs Graham. While staying at Barford shortly before leaving for Abyssinia, Evelyn, anxious to acquaint himself with his destination, tore out of the big *Times Atlas,* always kept on a long stool in the ballroom, the full-page map of Africa. Mrs Graham discovered what he had done, ordered him out of the house, and never saw him again.

It was mid-October when Evelyn embarked at Marseilles. *Azay le Rideau* was a shabby little vessel, her passengers mainly French colonials, with 'inconceivably ill-disciplined children', and members of the various delegations – Polish, Dutch, French, Egyptian – on their way to the coronation. The voyage took ten days, ten days of cards, deck-games, noisy sweepstakes and on the last night a fancy-dress ball; when the ship docked at Djibouti at dawn, one grey-faced couple was still dancing.[1] Immediately there was confusion, the start of a 'preposterous *Alice in Wonderland* fortnight', during which a large cast of pantomime characters in exotic costume behaved in a manner which, seen through Evelyn's eyes, had little connection with civilised normality. As in *Alice,* he found in Abyssinia that 'peculiar flavour of galvanized and translated reality, where animals carry watches in their waistcoat pockets, royalty paces the croquet lawn beside the chief executioner, and litigation ends in a flutter of playing-cards'.

Contrary to expectation, there was no seat for Evelyn on the only train, which had been reserved for official delegates, including the British party headed by the Duke of Gloucester. Eventually, however, a place was found, and the train which left Djibouti after dinner on Friday arrived at Addis Ababa on Sunday morning, where the assorted grandees, by now changed into ceremonial uniform, were welcomed by a guard of honour drawn

---

[1] *Remote People,* the book Waugh wrote about this expedition, was published in America under the title, *They Were Still Dancing.*

up on the platform: 'but for the bare feet below their puttees, they might have been the prize platoon of some Public School O.T.C.', Evelyn noted with relish. The nieces of the British minister, Sir Sidney Barton, were there to meet him, charmless girls who discomfited him by shrieking with derisive laughter when they discovered he had not had the foresight to engage a room. The town was full: he would *never* find one now! Hating to be laughed at, particularly by women, Evelyn from that moment took against the Bartons.

The impression of an upside-down, Wonderland world was further reinforced by 'the tin and tarmac squalor' of Addis, a primitive and dilapidated town, with bazaars, *tedj* houses,[2] thatched native huts looking like hollow haystacks at one end, and at the other a featureless European quarter. Wide dusty streets planted with straggly eucalyptus ordered from Australia in bulk by the Emperor Menelik were lined with half-built houses and with little shops roofed in corrugated iron owned by Armenians, Greeks and Indians, and selling everything from bicycles to Seidlitz powders. There were several rather primitive hotels, three nightclubs with cinemas attached, and a *quartier réservé* of doorless cabins where native girls nightly earned their living amid raucous music and loud drunken quarrelling. The legations were outside town in their own spacious compounds, many of them, most remarkably the British, surrounded by lavish and elaborate gardens. Over recent weeks the population had doubled several times over, now a picturesque mixture of savagely armed tribesmen meekly followed by their veiled women, of a crumpled and bewildered press corps, and of the gold-braided, feather-helmeted representatives of western royalty. Large, gleaming motor-cars driven by uniformed chauffeurs blasted their way through packs of slow-moving mules, horses, donkeys, camels, and white-robed pedestrians into whom frantic policemen armed with whips were trying to instil a basic road sense.

For the visitors the days passed in a crazy jumble of ill-organised luncheon, garden and dinner parties, in sight-seeing and shopping, and in sitting through interminable and incomprehensible ceremonies of barbaric splendour, occasions frequently missed by the press because of the impossibility of obtaining a reliable

[2] Tedj is a strong liquor made from fermented honey.

timetable. Nothing was trustworthy, nobody seemed capable of telling the truth. 'Evelyn Waugh after various interviews returned sulky and saying everyone told "lies lies lies",' as one member of the English delegation observed. Evelyn made comic copy not only from the bizarre displays surrounding the coronation itself, but from the cut-throat competitiveness among the journalists, most of whom realised early on that it was easier to invent than to go through the hoops necessary to obtain an eye-witness account. 'It was highly interesting to me, when the papers began to arrive from Europe and America, to compare my own experiences with those of the different correspondents. I had the fortune to be working for a paper which values the accuracy of its news before everything else.' Not so, apparently, the others. Among a number of highly imaginative versions, one had the emperor leaving his palace for the cathedral in a magnificent procession at sundown, although 'it was late at night before he arrived, and then with the minimum of display'. Another 'stated that the emperor's banqueting-hall was decorated with inlaid marble, ivory, and malachite . . . In actual fact there were photographs of Mr Ramsay MacDonald and M. Poincaré, and a large, very lifelike oil-painting of a lion, by an Australian artist.'

Evelyn's amateurish insistence on actually being present at the events he described resulted in victory for the competition. As a telegram from the *Daily Express* curtly informed him, 'Coronation cable hopelessly late beaten every paper London'.

In the diary and also in *Remote People*, the book which came out of Evelyn's Abyssinian adventure, there are several characters whose comic potential is skilfully exploited. One of the coronation guests was Irene Ravensdale, eldest daughter of the great Lord Curzon. Although Lady Ravensdale had been well-disposed towards Evelyn, and they had spent a certain amount of time together, he privately found her pretensions ridiculous, recording in his diary some of her choicest pronouncements. 'After all Evelyn, you may think it's nothing but I *am* Daddy's daughter. I *am* Baroness Ravensdale.' (She for her part recorded in her diary that she thought Waugh a 'silly little creature', and his newspaper articles 'very poor and trite'.) More hostile treatment was reserved for the British minister and envoy extraordinary, Sir Sidney Barton, his family and members of his legation. 'I have rarely

seen anything so hysterical as the British legation all this last week
– or so incompetent to cope with their duties. A half-baked consul
called Barton is minister,' Henry Yorke was told by Evelyn, still
smarting from the fact that he had been left off the legation's
invitation list for one of the most important of the official entertainments. In Evelyn's novel, *Black Mischief*, Barton is reincarnated
in the dotty and inconsequential figure of Sir Samson Courtenay,
who with his family and staff are made to enact scenes of sublime
ludicrousness; at the end of the book, Sir Samson's daughter is
cooked and eaten by cannibals.

Nothing quite so awful befalls Professor Thomas Whittemore,
given a leading part in the first section of *Remote People*. A distinguished Boston academic, friend of Henry James and one of the
leading authorities on Byzantine art, Professor Whittemore
caught Evelyn's fascinated attention when he sat next to him at
the long coronation service in the cathedral, during which this
'expert of high transatlantic reputation on Coptic ritual' kept up
a running commentary remarkable only for its inaccuracy. ' "They
are beginning the Mass now," "That was the offertory," "No, I
was wrong; it was the consecration," "No, I was wrong; I think it
is the secret Gospel," "No, I think it must be the Epistle," "How
very curious; I don't believe it was a mass at all," "*Now* they
are beginning the Mass ..." and so on.' It was with Professor
Whittemore that Evelyn visited the famous focus of spiritual life
in Abyssinia, the great monastery at Debra Lebanos, celebrated
for its ancient library in which among a priceless collection of
manuscripts and incunabula there had recently been discovered
an early version of Ecclesiastes. Needless to say, the reality was
something of a disappointment. The monastery turned out to be
a squalid commune inhabited by a few eccentric old men served
by a mob of scrofulous boys '[who,] we learned later, were the
deacons', and the contents of the ancient library 'of which
the world stood in awe ... two coloured lithographs, apparently
cut from a religious almanac printed in Germany some time
towards the end of the last century ... Professor Whittemore
kissed them eagerly ...'

On their return to Addis, Evelyn made enquiries about the
possibility of a journey into the interior, to the dry desert country
inhabited by the notorious Danakil. Disappointingly, this was
judged impracticable. 'It would take many weeks and more money

than I could conveniently afford; even so, I would have attempted it if I had been able to find a companion, but no one seemed ready to come.' In fact, Evelyn might well have gone, for an expedition was about to set off, headed by a young Englishman who had succeeded, with Sir Sidney Barton's help, in obtaining official permission for just such a venture. Wilfred Thesiger, whose father was British minister at the legation before the war, had been born in Addis Ababa, loved what he described as 'the age-old splendour of Abyssinia', knew the people well, and would have been the ideal guide. However, when asked if he would take Waugh with him, he unhesitatingly refused, having felt an instant aversion to the 'little pip-squeak' with his grey suede shoes, floppy bow tie and ridiculously wide trousers. The two men had met at an embassy reception, during which Thesiger watched with distaste the spectacle of Waugh 'holding court' and making fun of the noble Abyssinians. 'He struck me as flaccid and petulant and I disliked him on sight.' It had been one of Thesiger's boyhood dreams to go up-country, and having Waugh tagging along would have ruined it. Not only that: if he had come, 'I'd have been tempted to knock him off.'

That diversion having been denied him, Evelyn was glad to accept an invitation to stay with the British consul at Harar, a town situated due east of Addis. Harar could hardly have presented a greater contrast to the capital. Instead of the brown, barren country of the Amharic region, this area was green and fertile, with lakes bordered by flocks of flamingoes and hillsides terraced with well-tended coffee plantations. Harar, an ancient and attractive Moorish town, was the scene of three encounters crucial to Evelyn. One was a chance meeting with a French bank clerk, who put forward the 'deplorable' but compelling suggestion that Evelyn should go home not by the most direct route, as he had planned, but via Dar es Salaam, the Congo and the African west coast. Secondly, there was a long talk with the Bishop of Harar, Monsignor Jerome, who was the last man alive to have known Arthur Rimbaud. '[Rimbaud] used to live with a native woman in a little house, now demolished, in the square . . . a very, very serious young man, the bishop repeated. He seemed to find this epithet the most satisfactory – very serious and sad.' And thirdly, there was Mr Bergebedgian, the inspiration for that irresistible rogue, Mr Youkoumian, the Armenian fixer in *Black Mischief*.

Proprietor of the Lion d'Or, one of the town's only two inns, Mr Bergebedgian

> spoke a queer kind of French with remarkable volubility, and I found great delight in all his opinions; I do not think I have ever met a more tolerant man. Unfortunately his hotel was less admirable. Most of his business was done in the bar, where he sold great quantities of colourless and highly inflammatory spirit distilled by a fellow countryman of his and labelled, capriciously, 'Very Olde Scotts Whiskey', 'Fine Champayne', or 'Hollands Gin' as the taste of his clients dictated.

It was Mr Bergebedgian who took Evelyn out on the town, first to a dire musical party at Government House, then to an indigestible dinner washed down with 'a disturbing liqueur labelled "Koniak"', and finally to a wedding, for which, disconcertingly, Evelyn's host armed himself and his servants with an automatic pistol, a bandolier of cartridges and four or five wooden clubs – 'all very much like Rat's preparation for the attack on Toad Hall'.

The next two ports of call, Aden and Zanzibar, Evelyn had expected to dislike, but in spite of the ferocious heat he found both surprisingly sympathetic. It is in his description of Aden that Evelyn achieves two of the great comic *tours de force* in *Remote People*. The first is a scene in which a Somali boy scout is being tested in scout law.

> He knew it all by heart perfectly. 'First scoot law a scoot's honour iss to be trust second scoot law . . .' et cetera, in one breath.
> 'Very good, Abdul. Now tell me what does "thrifty" mean?'
> 'Trifty min?'
> 'Yes, what do you mean, when you say a scout is thrifty?'
> 'I mean scoot hass no money.'
> 'Well, that's more or less right. What does "clean" mean?'
> 'Clin min?'
> 'You said just now a scout is clean in thought, word, and deed.'
> 'Yis, scoot iss clin.'
> 'Well, what do you mean by that?'
> 'I min tought, worden deed.'
> 'Yes, well, what do you *mean* by clean?'
> Both parties in this dialogue seemed to be losing confidence in the other's intelligence.

'I mean the tenth scoot law.'

A pause during which the boy stood first on one black leg, then on the other, gazing patiently into the sun.

'All right, Abdul. That'll do.'

'Pass, sahib?'

'Yes, yes.'

An enormous smile broke across his small face, and away he went capering across the parade ground, kicking up dust over the fire-makers and laughing with pleasure.

The second episode recounts Evelyn's experience with that eccentric Frenchman, the powerful, charming and impossibly elegant M. Besse ('Leblanc' in *Remote People*). Antonin Besse, self-made millionaire, dealer in coffee and hides, Aden's representative for Shell Oil, later in his life founder of St Antony's College, Oxford, was the only European magnate in the Settlement. He entertained Evelyn at his luxurious penthouse in the Aidrus Road in Crater, and, a physical fitness fanatic, invited him on a walk. Evelyn readily agreed. 'After the torpid atmosphere of Aden it would be delightful to take some gentle exercise in the cool air.' The experience was terrifying. What for M. Besse, who daily climbed the crumbling volcanic cliffs round Crater and swam fearlessly in shark-infested waters, was an easy and customary form of exercise ('Besse gave a lithe skip and swarmed straight up a perpendicular cliff') half kills his guest. By the end of the afternoon, 'my shoes were completely worn through, and there was a large tear in my shorts where I had slipped among the cinders and slid some yards. Mr Leblanc had laid out for him in the car a clean white suit, a shirt of green crêpe-de-chine, a bow tie, silk socks, buckskin shoes, ivory hairbrushes, scent spray, and hair lotion. We ate banana sandwiches and drank very rich China tea.'[3]

To Evelyn one of the recommendations of Aden was the predominance of bachelors; it was this that made the English community there 'so unusually agreeable ... there is never anything essentially ludicrous about English officials abroad; it is the wives they marry that are so difficult.' This sour misogynistic streak is much in evidence throughout the trip, the one exception Evelyn's

[3] According to Besse's biographer, David Footman, this description is not entirely accurate. '[Besse] never wore crêpe de chine shirts – only airtex [*sic*] cotton. And he would not wear, or allow his staff to wear, socks with shorts. His mercerised cotton stockings were specially made for him in India.'

infatuation with the lovely, witty, cocaine-addicted American, Kiki Preston, who had been a fellow-passenger on the ship between Aden and Mombasa. It was while staying with Kiki and her husband on the edge of Lake Naivasha in Kenya that Evelyn met a 'delightful' and obviously like-minded English general. 'One day after dinner we talked about marriage and found ourselves in agreement on the subject.'

In its every aspect Kenya enchanted Evelyn. He saw in this beautiful country with its young, hedonistic and glamorous society a last, precious vestige of a golden age, an age long vanished from Europe. Here there was a quality

> which I have found nowhere else but in Ireland, of warm
> loveliness and breadth and generosity ... The Kenyan settlers are
> not cranks of the kind who colonized New England, nor
> criminals and ne'er-do-wells of the kind who went to Australia,
> but perfectly normal, respectable Englishmen, out of sympathy
> with their own age, and for this reason linked to the artist in an
> unusual but very real way.

This having been idealistically stated, Evelyn is then immediately captivated by one of the most unartistic, near-criminal ne'er-do-wells in the country. Raymond de Trafford, tall, charming and diabolically handsome, was a gambler, a heavy drinker and an indefatigable womaniser. He was from an old Catholic family in Lancashire, and before settling in Kenya had been obliged to leave both Downside and the Coldstream Guards as well as having done a spell in borstal for manslaughter. At the time Evelyn met him, he was involved in a typically ramshackle piece of profiteering, setting up a scheme for capturing gorillas, 'prompted by the information that they fetched two thousand pounds a head at the Berlin Zoo'. Evelyn was entranced by him. 'Raymond de T. is something of a handful v. nice but so BAD and he fights & fucks and gambles and gets D.D. [disgustingly drunk] all the time.' In Nairobi Evelyn accompanied him to the races ('[Raymond] told me what horses to back. None of them won'), dined with him at the Muthaiga Club, and then stayed for a fortnight at his house in Njoro. 'A delightful if rather irregular visit ... Sometimes I had no breakfast; sometimes I found Raymond, if he was at home, sitting up in bed with a tin of grouse paste and a bottle of soda water, and forced him to share these things with me.' One evening, '[Raymond] got very drunk and brought a sluttish girl back to the house. He woke me up later in the night to tell me he had just rogered her and her mama too.'

After leaving his Kenyan idyll, Evelyn went west to Lake Victoria and over the border into Uganda, where he spent five days in Kampala with a Dutch Catholic priest, Father Janssen. He then travelled due south, crossing Lake Tanganyika to reach the Belgian Congo, where at Elizabethville he had hoped to find an air service to the coast. But there was no aeroplane, and nothing for it but to undertake an arduous journey by rail through Rhodesia to the Cape, where with only £40 in his pocket he managed to secure a third-class berth on a ship sailing that day. On 10 March 1931, five months after taking leave of his mother at Waterloo, he docked at Southampton.

On the publication of *Remote People* at the end of 1931, Evelyn was criticised by reviewers for his emphasis on how bored he had been. Even Rebecca West, one of his most enthusiastic admirers, complained that 'Mr Waugh has failed to observe that it is an iron law of literature that the minute one begins to describe how one has been bored one becomes a bore.' But for Evelyn boredom had always been a menacing, almost tangible presence, and during this trip, on a number of vividly recalled occasions, the old enemy had been victorious. In his book Evelyn categorises three sections of his journey as 'Nightmares', the last nightmare being the evening of his arrival back in London, the first taking place during the four days between leaving Harar and arriving at Djibouti.

This brief period in hell begins with missing the train for the coast on Saturday evening, necessitating a wait till the following Tuesday for the next. 'Never', wrote Evelyn, 'have I been so desperately and degradingly bored as I was during the next four days; they were as black and timeless as Damnation.' He stayed at a scruffy little hotel where the only place to sit was on a hard rocking-chair in a small white-washed parlour. It was unbearably hot. He had nothing to read except a pocket edition of Pope's juvenile poems and a tiny French dictionary. After a couple of hours he gave up on those and wrote letters 'to everyone in England whose address I could remember'. In the evening he was joined by an English couple who lent him some old copies of *John o' London's*, three issues of which he read right through before going to sleep under his mosquito net. The following morning he read the fourth, then visited the bank where he 'dragged out the cashing of a small cheque to the utmost limits of politeness'. The train journey was passed in considerable discomfort: hammering heat, very slow progress through flat, featureless country, and only the irritating conversation of one of the Misses Barton to distract him. Arrived at Djibouti, there was a further wait of two days for the ship to Aden, a period of monotony that turned out to be 'the most deadly of all'. Two and a half months later on a four-day voyage across Lake Tanganyika he endured the second period of nightmare when a paralysing ennui again threatened to overwhelm the traveller; this time, however, he was more prepared. 'I fought boredom, and to some extent overcame it, by the desperate expedient of writing – it was there, in fact, that I ground out the first two chapters of this book.'

Boredom is frequently the concomitant of despair, and throughout his five months abroad, Evelyn determinedly sought out the supportive structure of the Catholic Church. On his arrival in Addis, he attended Mass at seven in the morning, noting in his diary that the church was 'island sanity in raving town'. In Mombasa he called on the apostolic legate, who helped him arrange his journey to the Congo; at Tabora in Tanganyika he had tea with the the bishop; in Kampala most of his time was spent with Father Janssen, who took him to see a local convent.

At the convent they manage a small farm and hospital, and in recreation time do skilled needlework. It does not sound very remarkable to a reader in Europe; it is astounding in Central Africa – this little island of order and sweetness in an ocean of rank barbarity; all round it for hundreds of miles lies gross jungle, bush, and forest, haunted by devils and the fear of darkness, where human life merges into the cruel, automatic life of the animals; here they were singing the offices just as they had been sung in Europe when the missions were little radiant points of learning and decency in a pagan wilderness.[4]

[4] In 'Out of Depth', a story published in *Harper's Bazaar* (9 December 1933), Rip, a complacent, middle-aged American, a lapsed Catholic, is magically transported five hundred years into the future, where he finds a primitive and savage society grubbing a living on the mud-flats and grass-grown wreckage of what had once been London. Suddenly he comes across 'the word "Mission" painted on a board; a black man dressed as a Dominican friar . . . Rip knew

Just as this passage reveals Evelyn's perception of the Church as an island of order in the midst of chaos, so was his experience at Debra Lebanos an illustration of the vast distance between the highly evolved Church in Europe and the superstitious mumbo-jumbo of its eastern equivalent. While staying at Debra Lebanos, Evelyn and Professor Whittemore after a night of appalling squalor and discomfort attended early morning Mass. To their dismay, the liturgy was incomprehensible, the rite barbaric and obscure.

> For anyone accustomed to the Western rite it was difficult to think of this as a Christian service, for it bore that secret and confused character which I had hitherto associated with the non-Christian sects of the East... At Debra Lebanos I suddenly saw the classic basilica and open altar as a great positive achievement, a triumph of light over darkness consciously accomplished... And I began to see how these obscure sanctuaries had grown, with the clarity of Western reason, into the great open altars of Catholic Europe, where Mass is said in a flood of light, high in the sight of all.[5]

On returning to England, Evelyn went almost at once for a Holy Week retreat to Stonyhurst, the old-established Jesuit school in Lancashire where Christopher Hollis, recently married, was now a master. His plan then was to go to a small hotel in the Thames valley in order to write, but no sooner had he arrived at the Beetle & Wedge in Moulsford than he felt so unwell that he turned round and came back to Underhill to be looked after by his mother. His symptoms were unpleasant: a high temperature, very sore throat and the inside of his mouth covered in ulcers. Kate called in Dr Andrews, who diagnosed not some tropical disease, but poisoning from watercress. She also brought in an agency nurse, who was obliged to spend most of her time on a

---

that out of strangeness, there had come into being something familiar; a shape in chaos. Something was being done. Something was being done that Rip knew; something that twenty-five centuries had not altered... The priest turned towards them his bland, black face. "Ite, missa est." '

[5] That Evelyn's view of the centre of Abyssinian spiritual life was not unduly exaggerated is upheld by a passage in Dean Stanley's study of *The Eastern Church*. '[The Church of Abyssinia] furnishes the one example of a nation savage yet Christian; showing us, on the one hand, the force of the Christian faith in maintaining its superiority at all against such immense disadvantages, and, on the other hand, the utmost amount of superstition with which a Christian Church can be overlaid without perishing altogether.'

chair reading outside Evelyn's bedroom as he found her presence too annoying to bear. Not to be outdone, Arthur in an aggrieved bid for his wife's attention now took to his bed complaining of feeling ill, in spite of the fact that the doctor could find nothing wrong with him. As Evelyn so disliked his nurse, Kate was obliged to take over many of her duties, but the more time she spent with her son, the more demanding her husband became. As Evelyn began to recover, he saw the comedy of the situation, which he referred to as 'les malades jalouses', and to make it up to his father bought him a dozen quarter bottles of champagne and presented him with £5 towards a week's convalescent holiday with Kate in Sussex.

In June Evelyn, Alec and their parents went for a month to the Welcome Hotel in Villefranche. Arthur loved France, his unchanging choice for the annual holiday. 'France all round me, happy, happy, happy', he would say as the train pulled out of Calais or Boulogne. While he and Kate pottered gently about, occasionally venturing on little excursions (Evelyn took his mother into Monte Carlo: 'Lovely time. Had a champagne cocktail'), the 'boys' enjoyed a rather more active holiday. Also staying at the Welcome were Patrick Balfour, the only close friend Evelyn and Alec had in common, and Keith Winter, a good-looking young man, novelist and later playwright, who had caught the roving eye of Somerset Maugham. Maugham, anxious to pursue the acquaintance, invited the four young men first to dine, then two days later to lunch at the Villa Mauresque at Cap Ferrat. Another day, while Alec went into Nice with a girl he had picked up in the bar, Evelyn and Patrick dined with Nina Seafield, young, very rich, and a peeress in her own right, who, like Nancy Mitford, had become an honorary member of that aesthete homosexual set led by Hamish Erskine and Nina's cousin, Mark Ogilvie-Grant. Evelyn also went to Sanary to visit Cyril Connolly and his wife, who introduced him to the Aldous Huxleys and took him on a tour of the red-light section of Toulon. 'The district is full of chums, Connolly, Aldous H, Willy Maugham, Nina, Eddie S-West, Alex Waugh, etc,' Evelyn wrote to Henry Yorke. 'Also Godfrey Wynne [Winn] also Tennyson Jesse . . . I meant to do work but it is all very gay and we bathe a lot and get sleepy.'

But despite the appearance of conviviality, Evelyn was not happy, and took little trouble to conceal his discontent. Nina

Seafield was soon pronounced a menace, her house-party composed of 'all the biggest bores on the Riviera'. He also took
against Keith Winter, refusing to speak to him except through
the intermediary of Patrick Balfour; made an appalling upset over
a pair of grey flannel trousers he insisted on having sent out
to him from London, and was ingeniously rude to Maugham,
pretending not to know who he was when they were introduced.
'How I hate the south of France and everyone here,' he wrote
with less than Christian charity on a postcard to Father D'Arcy.
He longed to move on, but money he was expecting from
England failed to arrive, immobilising him in Villefranche. When
Alec went into his brother's room one morning, he found him
lying on his bed, one leg swinging loose over the side, his hands
under his head, staring at the ceiling. He ignored Alec, who came
back an hour later to find his position unchanged, still lying on
his bed, still staring at the ceiling. In the end, Evelyn's bad mood
had such a lowering effect on the rest of the family that Arthur
agreed to advance him the 1500 francs he needed to go to a
monastery he had heard of near Grasse in the little mountain
village of Cabris.

Here at least he was on his own and could get down to work
on his travel book, although the accommodation was far from
luxurious. 'I am living in a pension kept by a priest,' he informed
Balfour. 'The lavatory smells so that whenever I go to shit, I vomit
instead. The food is bad. The bed is lumpy & bugridden. The
other pensionnaires are crazy ... I am writing very quickly and
boringly & shall have finished that book in eleven days.' He was
back in England on the last day of June to deliver the speedily
written *Remote People* to be typed. The transcribing of the manuscript was not an easy job. 'I regret slight delay in returning these
Chapters owing to extreme difficulty in reading the handwriting,'
the typist, a Mr Alex McLachlan from Deal, complained to Peters.
'Every care has been taken, but despite magnifying glass, encyclopaedia and two visits to Dover Reference Library, I have been
unable to decipher many of the words.'

Evelyn did not remain long at home, and three weeks later was
again in France, this time with the Yorkes at the Grand Hotel at
Le Canadel in the Var, where he found 'Henry amazingly cheerful. Doing little turns imitating people like Olivia and drinking
heavily.' Henry and Dig, however, had privately been disconcerted

when Evelyn arrived not alone but accompanied by a young married woman, Mrs Reginald Marix, with whom he then proceeded exhaustively to quarrel. Pixi Marix, whom Evelyn had met through Patrick Balfour, was a flighty character, very pretty, whose speciality was what she called 'brinking', allowing men to take her to bed while stopping short of actual consummation. This was what was giving rise to the quarrels. 'That girl has made a fool of me & taken all my money,' Evelyn wrote furiously to Balfour. 'It is all very distressing & humiliating. Apart from anything else she is so boring and so American at heart. I could drown her with pleasure.' Eventually he made it clear to Pixi that either she give in, or she would have to find her way home at her own expense. Hard up and not wishing to cut short her holiday, Pixi decided to change tactics. Having insisted on separate rooms, she now barely left Evelyn alone, appearing ready and eager the moment he went upstairs for a siesta, keeping him with her most of the night, coming into his room again before breakfast. Mollified, Evelyn wrote to Patrick, 'I said some hard things about your Mrs Marix. Well subsequent events have not justified my first estimate of her character . . . [she] is a nice girl really.'

The Pixi episode had been expensive, and Evelyn returned to England at the beginning of August with no money and extremely anxious to see his book published before the end of the year. He had dedicated it to the subject of another of his transient affairs, the wife of the painter, Sir John Lavery. Evelyn had first met Hazel Lavery the previous year, shortly before leaving for Abyssinia. She was sixteen years older than he, American, lapsed Catholic, and very beautiful with her ivory skin and huge hare's eyes. Her husband had painted her many times – *Hazel in Rose and Gold, Hazel in Black and Gold, Portrait of Hazel in a Mirror* – and had depicted her as the Irish colleen with shawl and harp that appeared on the Irish Free State bank notes. Hazel's style was dramatic: her face, heavily made up, was dead white and slashed with scarlet lipstick, her hair dyed vivid red, and she favoured picture hats, paste jewellery, ostrich-feather fans and theatrical costumes in black and purple. *Tatler* spotted her one evening at the theatre in a cloak of rose velvet with an enormous Harrisi lily in her Titian hair. A sufferer from nephritis, she was easily exhausted, but this did little to dampen a restless search for novelty and excitement. She was a dedicated *salonière*, her guests mainly artists and politicians. 'If there was only the cat in the room,' Sir John wearily remarked, 'Hazel would feel that she had to entertain it.' She also had a reputation for what some described as nympho-mania, others less censoriously as obsessive romantic attachments, and for a time she pursued Evelyn with ardour. He, although slightly embarrassed by her flamboyant attentions, was nonethe-less flattered, and quite ready to enjoy a brief liaison. He took her to tea with his parents, and allowed her to drive him about when he had errands to do. But he soon grew bored by the hysterical demands, rebuffing her unkindly, behaviour which, when Hazel died in 1935, caused him to suffer remorse. He had a Mass said for her which he attended very early in the morning as a penance.

He had written his book in haste, and had not enjoyed the writing, finding the result 'very dull', a judgment with which his agent in New York, Carl Brandt, wholeheartedly agreed. 'The difficulty', as Brandt complained to Peters, 'is that it simply isn't amusing.' *Remote People* was published on 3 November to reviews that were polite rather than enthusiastic. 'Africa eludes him,' wrote the anonymous critic in the *Times Literary Supplement*, going on to complain that the author fails to make his subject attractive. 'It would be odd if he did; for the state of mind that he records most frequently is lack of interest.' Rebecca West was forced to admit in the *Telegraph* that his new book was 'well beneath his proper form . . .', an opinion with which Peter Fleming in the *Spectator* was one of the few to disagree. '[Waugh] is not ashamed to admit to boredom, and describes it exquisitely.' *Remote People* managed to climb into the bestseller category for a week, before dropping off Duckworth's list and out of sight.

Glad to be done with it, Evelyn now turned his attention to the novel he had in mind, also based on his African experiences. As soon as he returned from holiday in France with the Yorkes, he had gone down to Beckley to start work, telling Henry Yorke that he was 'writing what I take to be a good novel about the Emperor of Ethiopia . . . My word it is good.' First, however, there were problems to be sorted out with his American publisher, Harrison Smith, at the New York branch of Jonathan Cape. Because *Labels* had not sold well in the States, Hal Smith had tried to persuade

Evelyn to cut by $600 his agreed advance for *Remote People*, a
suggestion to which Evelyn reacted with scorn. And as Peters
wrote to the Brandt office which was handling the deal, Waugh's
attitude was not unreasonable. 'Authors, especially young authors,
often make bad bargains with publishers, and they have to stick
to them. It is not surprising that they expect publishers to do the
same.' Now that 'a real dyed in the wool best selling novel' was
in progress, Evelyn's reluctance to give it to Cape – 'I don't feel
disposed to give it to anyone who fusses so much. Damn the
United States' – was matched only by Cape's reluctance to take
it. As Carl Brandt explained in a wire to Peters, 'Cape agreed
fulfill contractual commitments Waugh but his lack of enthusiasm
for author made change of publishers advisable.' Fortunately,
Peters had no difficulty in making the transfer. John Farrar of
Farrar & Rinehart was delighted to add the young novelist to his
list, although he begged to suggest that if between novels Waugh
intended to continue writing non-fiction that he concentrate on
biographies or essays. 'One very important literateur [sic] said to
me the other day, "I think you have the most important of the
young English writers in Evelyn Waugh, but my God, will you
stop him writing travel books!" '

Once these matters had been satisfactorily settled, Evelyn
turned with relief to *Accession*, the working title of his novel.
Unable to concentrate at home, he went to Barford to stay with
Alastair, but that was scarcely more productive. 'We just sit about
sipping sloe gin all day,' he complained to Patrick Balfour. 'I am
reading all the case histories in Havelock Ellis and frigging too
much.' Patrick, who had just left his job on the *Sketch* to write a
book himself, was sympathetic, and it was he who suggested that
Evelyn go down to Devon, to the Easton Court Hotel near Chagford, where he would find exactly the quiet and comfortable
environment he needed. In *Enemies of Promise*, Cyril Connolly
gives it as his opinion that the writer's 'rightful place of composition [is] the small single unluxurious "retreat" of the twentieth
century, the hotel bedroom'. In the past Evelyn had stayed at
various inns and hotels in search of solitude, none of them
entirely satisfactory. There had been the Bell at Aston Clinton,
the Barley Mow at Wimborne, the George at Appledore, the
Abingdon Arms at Beckley and the Spread Eagle at Thame, where
John Fothergill sometimes let him have cheap rates during the

week, but all had their drawbacks. Chagford, however, was ideal. Not only was it an inconvenient distance from those two cities of the plain, London and Oxford, it was run specifically to suit the needs of writers (its advertisement in the PEN Club journal described it as 'understanding writers' ways'). An old thatched farmhouse with low ceilings and tiny windows, the Easton Court had been turned into an attractive hotel by its proprietors, an American divorcée, Carolyn Postlethwaite Cobb, and her partner, Norman Webb, inevitably known as 'the Cobbwebbs'. Mrs Cobb's transatlantic background meant that in style and standards of comfort her hotel was luxuriously unEnglish: no chintz, no draughts, no linoleum; other exotic touches included central heating, well-sprung mattresses and by every bedside a reading lamp that worked. There was a pretty and peaceful walled garden. The food was excellent, and although there was no drink licence, regular guests were encouraged to keep stocks of their own in the cellar, favoured clients being asked in to a preprandial cocktail in Mrs Cobb's own room, where she spent most of her day in the company of a smelly old dog called Nannie. (The hotel's telegraphic address was 'Nannie, Chagford'.) Evelyn in facetious mood described the hotel on his first visit as

> very odd. Kept by a deserter from the Foreign Legion[6] and an American lady named Mrs Postlethwaite Cobb who mixes menthol with her cigarettes. And we drink rye whisky in her bed room and there are heaps of New York magazines & rather good, sophisticated food. I think it is a distributing centre for white slaves or cocaine or something like that. They never give one a bill. Mr. B[alfour] hasn't had one since he came six weeks ago.

This letter was written to three sisters, Lady Sibell, Lady Mary and Lady Dorothy Lygon, whom Evelyn had only recently met, although he had been at Oxford with two of their brothers, the 'monumental' Elmley and the handsome, hard-drinking and feckless Hugh. Earlier in the year, their father had been the subject of a notorious scandal. The 7th Earl Beauchamp, immensely rich and immensely grand (KG, PC, KCMG, Chancellor of London University, Lord Lieutenant of the County, Lord Steward of the Royal Household, Lord President of the Council,

---

[6] Norman Webb had been living in Morocco working for an animal charity when Mrs Cobb first met him.

Lord Warden of the Cinque Ports), was married to the sister of that bad bully, Bendor, Duke of Westminster. In spite of the fact that Lord Beauchamp had fathered seven children, the duke claimed to be outraged by what he had heard of his brother-in-law's homosexual predilections. (According to the gossip of the time, Lord Beauchamp's little weakness came unavoidably to notice through the heavy clunk of the footmen's bracelets as they changed the plates at dinner.) In fact, it was as much a matter of jealousy as of moral outrage: Westminster had always resented the fact that unlike Lord Beauchamp, he had no son and had never held distinguished office. Slightly crazy as well as powerful, he forced his 'bugger-in-law', as he now offensively referred to him, on pain of public prosecution permanently to leave the country. The laws of the land being what they were, Lord Beauchamp was given no alternative but to resign all his appointments and decamp to the Continent, there to begin his exile. His disgrace split the family in two: Lady Beauchamp in a state of nervous collapse and refusing ever to see her husband again, moved with her youngest son, Richard, into a house provided by her brother's Grosvenor estate, while Elmley, Hugh and the three unmarried girls, all of whom sided passionately with their father, were left in possession of generous incomes – and Madresfield.

Madresfield Court, an immense moated manor house, stands surrounded by garden and half hidden in trees in the middle of a park on the wide Worcestershire plain beneath the Malvern hills. It is a remote, almost secret part of the country, and Malvern itself quaintly old-fashioned, still retaining the refined atmosphere of the last century when it was much patronised by the dyspeptic well-to-do who came to take the waters at the spa. Lygons had lived at Madresfield since Jacobean times, but in the last century the house had been extensively rebuilt by the younger Philip Hardwick, architect of the Great Western Hotel at Paddington and a specialist in Gothic and Elizabethan 'restorations'. Except for the entrance across the moat, Hardwick had left untouched little of the original building, replacing wattle and daub with bright red brick, adding a 'Jacobean' wing, and putting in an extraordinary inner courtyard, a riot of half-timbering and fretted gables, like an Arts & Crafts set for *The Merrie Wives of Windsor*. Indoors the original fifteenth-century minstrels' gallery was left in place, but to the great hall which it overlooked was added a second great hall in black and gold, connected, by a staircase with a crystal balustrade, to a second gallery. In 1865 a chapel was constructed out of what had been two bedrooms on the ground floor, and this Lady Beauchamp had had decorated as a wedding present to her husband in 1902, in a style of exuberant art nouveau pastoral memorably recalled in *Brideshead Revisited*. 'Angels in printed cotton smocks, rambler-roses, flower-spangled meadows, frisking lambs, texts in Celtic script, saints in armour, covered the walls in an intricate pattern of clear, bright colours . . . the altar steps had a carpet of grass-green strewn with white and gold daisies.' On either side of the altar were life-size portraits of Lord and Lady Beauchamp, fully robed and kneeling in prayer, while flitting round them were winged cherubs with the faces of their children.[7]

Evelyn saw Madresfield for the first time after meeting Mary (Maimie) Lygon at a luncheon party in London given by Baby Jungman's mother, 'Gloomy Beatrice'. Maimie, much taken with this amusing Oxford friend of her brothers ('my brothers were rather reticent about their Oxford life,' she complained), and discovering in the course of conversation that he was planning to travel down to Malvern that very day to begin a course at the local riding academy, insisted that he go with her to Worcester-shire in the family's big chauffeur-driven Packard. By the time they arrived it was dark, and Maimie's younger sister, Dorothy, running out in the starlight to greet the arrivals, stopped in surprise when she saw this unknown and unexpected young man climbing out of the car.

The household to which Evelyn was now introduced was as engaging as it was unconventional. The permanent residents were the three girls (the eldest, Lettice, having left home the year before to marry), Sibell, Maimie, and Dorothy the youngest, at nineteen not long out of the schoolroom. Sibell and Maimie were beauties, while Dorothy had a large, plain face and wore spec-tacles. Elmley, recently elected Member of Parliament for East

---

[7] In the novel, Lord Brideshead asks the painter, Charles Ryder, his opinion of the chapel. ' "Is it Good Art?" "Well, I don't quite know what you mean," I said warily. "I think it's a remarkable example of its period. Probably in eighty years it will be greatly admired." "But surely it can't be good twenty years ago and good in eighty years, and not good now?" "Well, it may be *good* now. All I mean is that I don't happen to like it much." '

Norfolk, was much of the time busy in London and his constitu-
ency, while Hughie, who had been working with a racehorse
trainer near Salisbury, was farming and settled in a house in the
village. In their father's day, an elaborate formality had been *de
rigueur* at Madresfield. Lord Beauchamp, known in the family as
'Boom', was a courteous if condescending host, whose sense of
his own dignity permeated every department of his domestic life.
Whenever opportunity allowed, he wore his blue Garter ribbon
at dinner and always referred to his children by their titles, Lord
Elmley, the Lady Lettice, the Lady Sibell. There was a swimming
pool in the garden, and even here protocol was meticulously
observed: the ladies were expected to leave the water first, whereupon Lord Beauchamp would turn to the gentlemen and say,
'The ladies have left us: you may lower your costumes,' meaning
that the men could roll their bathing-suits down to the waist.
Now all this had gone, replaced by an easy-going and high-spirited
atmosphere, a rare situation in which great luxury was untrammelled by adult restraint or responsibility. Officially the girls were
chaperoned by their old governess, Miss Brown, but in fact they
were free to do very much as they chose. Although their father's
disgrace and the bitter division it caused within the family must
painfully have affected his daughters, they gave little sign of it,
revelling in their freedom and filling the house week after week
with fun-loving friends, most regular among them Hubert
Duggan, Robert Byron (who had been visiting Madresfield since
his time at Eton with Hughie), Bloggs Baldwin, Teresa Jungman
and David Plunket Greene.

Evelyn was entranced by Madresfield, by its beauty and freedom, by the nursery innocence of this private, self-contained little
world. The girls adored him, and he was enrolled at once as an
honorary member of the family, of whose jokes and games he
quickly became the prime mover. Like children forming a secret
society, nicknames were invented, and a cast of comic characters
to people the stage. Evelyn, currently fascinated by masonic rituals
and insignia, frequently embellishing his letters with pentangles,
swastikas and encircled triangles, assigned to himself the masonic
name of 'Boaz', often shortened to 'Bo'; Maimie became 'Blondy',
and Dorothy 'Pollen' or 'Poll', Grainger, Maimie's one-eyed Pekinese, became P. H. (Pretty Hound) Grainger, and a member of
the Lord's Day Observance Society. Neighbours and friends, too,

were allotted their rôles, such as Tommy McDougal, a dashing master of foxhounds, who Evelyn affected to believe was retarded and illiterate, making McDougal insistently interrupt Bo's letters to Blondy and Poll with his childlike questions.

> When we meet again it will be gay and terribly exciting and not at all like a biscuit box.
> WY LIKE A BISKIT BOCKS PLESE?
> Wait till you are a little older Tommy and you will understand.
> Well I am living with the bright young Yorkes.
> Last night I saw a terribly drunk man with a prostitute.
> WOTS A POSTATUTE PLESE?
> Ask your little playfellow Dorothea, she will show you, Tommy.

Others had their names incorporated in the Lygon language. A 'jagger', a kind, selfless but unsycophantic friend, was derived from Miss Jagger, a devoted and generous-hearted spinster who lived permanently at Madresfield; 'to lacock', after Robert Laycock, meant to chuck a social engagement at the last moment ('Very very sorry for lacocking tea', Evelyn apologised to Maimie); and 'Dutch' was applied to anything awkward or difficult, in honour of Teresa Jungman, who was part-Dutch and where Evelyn was concerned always awkward and always difficult. (When a Dutch edition of *Black Mischief* was in preparation, Evelyn wrote, 'What a difficult book it will be – bound upside down with the pages in wrong order & bits left out...'[8]) 'Mad Carew' from the poem, 'The Green Eye of the Little Yellow God', meant 'jealous' ('So sorry I was mad Carew') and 'lascivious beast', adopted from a now-forgotten limerick, was the recognised term for 'priest'. (After returning from an Easter retreat, Evelyn wrote, 'I went to Stonyhurst and saw the lascivious beasts. God they were lascivious', and in 1935 when he was working on his life of the Catholic martyr, Edmund Campion, he told Maimie, 'I am going to spend a very studious autumn writing the life of a dead beast.')

The jokes, the fantasy, the secret-garden aspect of life at Madresfield made of it a sunlit refuge to which Evelyn in his imagination was repeatedly to return. In an enclosed part of the garden a little way from the house was a luxuriant herbaceous border where stood a sundial inscribed with the words, 'That day is wasted on which we have not laughed.' Walking in the garden

[8] The Dutch edition was dedicated to Teresa Jungman.

one day with Maimie, Evelyn remarked, 'We haven't wasted many days, have we?'

While Evelyn was at Madresfield a routine was established whereby he disappeared after breakfast to work on his book, sitting at a table in the old nursery where in theory he would be left entirely alone until lunch. But the three sisters, led by his playfulness to believe that he, like them, preferred to take nothing seriously, failed to understand that his writing was in a different category altogether; and when he made an amusing act of reluctantly hauling himself upstairs, groaning and complaining of the horror of work, they took this to mean that any interruption would be welcome. 'We hindered more than we helped,' Dorothy merrily recalled, 'and had no conscience about disturbing him and dragging him away to join in whatever was going on, or even just to chat while we stitched away at an enormous (and never finished) patchwork quilt.' As a result, when he was asked to return to Madresfield at a time when he was under pressure to finish his novel, Evelyn was obliged to refuse. 'The trouble about poor Bo is that he's a lazy bugger,' he explained, 'and if he was in a house with you lovely girls he would just sit about and chatter and get d.d. and ride a horse and have a heavenly time but would he write his book? No, and must he? By God he must.'

That having been said, it was of course the sitting about and chattering and getting disgustingly drunk that he enjoyed. There was a very childlike side to Evelyn's character, part of the source from which his comic genius derived, and both in his novels and in life he enjoyed translating the adult world into nursery terms: he had done it at Oxford, again in the little Canonbury Square flat with Evelyn Gardner, and now with the Lygons at Madresfield. Evelyn made everything amusing, and Sibell, Blondy and Poll were an appreciative audience. When he was designing the cover for *Black Mischief,* he made the girls pose for him (Maimie's foot appears in a picture of Prudence sitting on the end of the bath). They laughed helplessly at the elaborate jokes delivered with a dead-pan expression, and loved to take part in whatever running gag was chosen as the theme of each visit. While *Private Lives* was playing in the West End, the four of them, orchestrated by Evelyn, endlessly imitated Nöel Coward and Gertrude Lawrence: 'What fools we were to ruin it all, utter utter fools . . .' (Shortly afterwards Maimie and Evelyn ran into Coward in the Ritz, collapsed in giggles and had to rush away.) On one occasion Evelyn found Dorothy's diary, a naïve and schoolgirlish little record, to which Evelyn added purple passages describing incestuous orgies and every kind of outlandish debauch. On her innocuous drawing of a carthorse, he inked in a gigantic penis. 'It was', she said, 'like having Puck as a member of the household.'

When he was away from them, the Lygon girls were kept generously supplied with letters, in which, returning to the 'Children's Corner' style pioneered by Uncle Julius in *The Isis* and *The Cherwell*, Evelyn continued to weave his fantastic embroidery around the activities of himself and his friends. Part of the joke was the lewd tone in which the most innocent undertakings were described, as though he and they were naughty boys talking smut in the boiler-room at school. 'Darling Maimie,' Evelyn wrote from the Savile Club. 'Thank you 100 times for the lovely handkerchiefs. I have tied one to each ball and one to my cock and it looks very becoming.' Even the beloved Baby Jungman was subjected, behind her back, to this treatment. 'Look after that dear Dutch girl,' he wrote facetiously while staying at Chagford, 'and don't let her roger anyone with clap.'

One of the most fruitful areas of fabrication was the fashionable riding academy in Malvern run by an ex-cavalry man, Captain J. H. Hance. Hance and his daughter, Jackie, taught serious horsemen and women from all over the country – steeplechasers, competition show-jumpers – as well as those of the hunting fraternity who wanted to improve their skills. Evelyn, who had no great interest in horses or riding, had decided to take up hunting mainly as a means of social advancement. At many of the houses in which he now stayed, hunting was very much the thing; the Lygons in particular were passionate about it, in the winter going out several times a week. Although he had no natural gift – Dorothy thought he rode worse than anyone she knew – Evelyn was courageous and determined, and Captain Hance was famous for transforming even the most unpromising material. 'I may say that the Captain is dead nuts on me,' Evelyn reported to Blondy and Pollen at the start of his course.

He talks to me all the time not only about riding but politics & art & everything. He smokes my cigars. Mrs Captain & Jacky

came & had cocktails with me this morning & Mrs Captain told
me that Jacky's teeth were false – did you know that? – having
been rolled out by a horse when she was 14. She also gave me
a bright red ointment which cures stiffness so I am well in with
that family.

A few weeks later, in a letter headed by a masonic pentangle,
Evelyn wrote,

As for poor Boaz his stock has fallen pretty seriously at the
Academy. First, on Saturday, a little horse called Tom Tit threw
me on my head over a fence. All the sluts laughed except Miss
Jagger who was sympathetic. Then this morning on
Gingerbread I muddled up all the school & was in deep disgrace.
So I tried to have a come back by tippling with the Captain.
That went fairly well for a bit but he said Do you know So-&-So
and I said no so he said He must have been at Eton about
your time and I said I wasn't at Eton and the Captain was
shocked and finished his glass and strode straight out of the
bar and now he doesn't even like me as a chap. I have also
strained my back in a place between my shoulders where I
can't reach it with Ma's red ointment and it hurts like nothing
on earth and I do wish you were here to rub it for me. So what
with one thing & another I feel pretty low.

Back in London, Evelyn wrote to the sisters,

Well this is the last time I shall write for days. I'll tell you why,
you see I find suddenly there is no more money in my bank and
about six tradesmen have written to say look here this bill is
going too far what about it. So I went to my agent & said give
me some money and he said well if it comes to that you owe *me*
quite a bit one way and another. So I am broke. Well what I
am going to do is to go to a boarding house called Easton Court
Hotel, Chagford, Devon (where you must write to me) because
Patrick Balfour lives there & I argue that if he can so can I
because he is worse broke even than me. Well at Chagford
I pretend to my London chums that I am going to hunt stags
but to you who are intimates & confidantes I dont mind saying
that I shall sit all day in my bedroom writing books, articles,
short stories, reviews, plays, cinema scenarios, etc. etc. until I
have got a lot more money.

As with many writers, Evelyn's working life was characterised by bursts of intense industry interspersed with stretches of profound idleness, the latter often to the despair of his agent. 'It is always difficult to pin Evelyn Waugh down to work,' Peters wrote resignedly to Brandt during one of these periods of creative lethargy.

But now books, articles, short stories, reviews were being hammered out under high pressure for regular employers, such as *John Bull, Woman's Journal* and *Harper's Bazaar.* For Joyce Reynolds at *Harper's Bazaar* Evelyn wrote two short stories, 'Bella Fleace Gave a Party', which was set among the kind of derelict Irish society he had observed at Pakenham, and 'Cruise', composed in the form of a series of letters written from a cruise ship by a silly (and familiar-sounding) young woman who makes a set at the purser and becomes thoughtlessly engaged one after the other to all the young men on board.

At the beginning of the same year 1932, Evelyn was asked to write the treatment of a film for Basil Dean, chairman of Ealing Studios. The story was based on a novel by Sapper, the salary an irresistible £50 a week, and while he was at work on it, Evelyn was to stay in a set of chambers in Albany in Piccadilly, not only one of the most prestigious and historic addresses in town but one located dangerously near the Ritz. 'Well, I am living like a swell, in Albany, as it might be Lord Byron, Lord Macaulay, Lord Lytton, or any real slap up writer!' Evelyn wrote cheerfully to Bloggs Baldwin. Most of the day was spent getting dressed for lunch at the Ritz, having lunch at the Ritz, getting dressed for cocktails at the Ritz, making personal telephone calls, drinking cups of tea, and entertaining his collaborator, John Paddy Carstairs, with slapstick versions of the preposterously melodramatic scenes with which he intended to enliven a script that in the end was hastily cobbled together by the two men just in time to meet their deadline.

Evelyn rewarded himself with a week's holiday alone in Spain, looking at Gothic cathedrals. 'I wish we could see Gothic as the Gothic revivalists did. I mean living in Northern Europe so much, one's palate gets debauched by so much imitation and reproduction Gothic, that it is an effort to understand it when one meets the real thing,' he told Baldwin.

On his return he found another dramatic project under way, an adaptation for the stage of *Vile Bodies* by a young man called Dennis Bradley, whose first version had been refused a licence

by the Lord Chamberlain, with the result that it had only a brief
run at the Arts Theatre Club in October 1931. The following
year, Bradley having rewritten the offending passages, the play
was passed for public showing and put on at the Vaudeville for
six weeks from the fifteenth of April. Evelyn had no high opinion
of the play or its author – 'The new version of *V. B.* is stinking',
he wrote to Peters – but he made the most of the attendant
publicity, on the opening night taking a large party consisting of
Maimie Lygon, Hubert Duggan, Irene Ravensdale, Eleanor Smith,
Billy Clonmore, Frank and Elizabeth Pakenham, Henry Yorke,
Gerry Wellesley, Raymond de Trafford and Hazel Lavery. The
results were gratifying. 'So Boaz is momentarily a social lion,' he
reported to Baldwin, 'and Lady Cunard (whom God preserve)
calls him Evelyn and makes him sit on her right hand at luncheon & dinner every day of the week.'

The one name conspicuously absent from this glamorous first-
night gathering was that of Baby Jungman. 'Did little Miss Jungman send me a line of good wishes from Ireland?' he continued
to Bloggs. 'Not on your life. And did I look through a sheaf of
telegrams with trembling hands looking for one loved name and
was I surprised at its absence? I can't say I was.' As neither Evelyn
nor Baldwin, who with his white face, ginger hair and heavy
spectacles was not easily accepted as a romantic prospect, was
making any progress in their pursuit of Baby, they had formed a
friendly alliance based on a mutual need for commiseration. In
January Evelyn had written, 'The more we stick together the
happier the New Year will be!' But in that aspect at least the New
Year was far from happy. Teresa remained as resolutely uninterested as Evelyn remained resolutely in love. Not only was she
unable to respond to him physically,[9] but as a Catholic it was out
of the question for her to consider any kind of amatory relationship with a man who, in the eyes of the Church, was married to
another woman. Naturally enough, and in spite of the seriousness
of his own faith, her intransigence provoked some explosive reactions. In the three letters from Teresa which survive (kept in an
envelope, together with letters from Harold Acton and Alastair

[9] 'Although I loved him very much, I was not *in* love with him and that made
everything difficult.'

Graham, marked 'Sentimental Friendships') she begs him to accept the situation.

> I was so sad to see you again last night and find that you were treating me as if we had had a quarrel – It is hard to believe that you can't see me without wanting to have an affair with me – but if that is so I do *implore* you not to feel bitter about it . . . If only you would be less obstinate about having evil intentions we could perfectly well go on seeing each other . . . I am afraid that it is my fault that you are cross with me. Perhaps you feel that I made too much use of you during those weeks when I was sad. Forgive me if I did. It was only because I felt you were sympathetic and trusted you completely *not* only because you were a Catholic because after all there are a good many others who might have been able to produce kisses and advice for me.

In another she writes,

> Darling Evelyn – Don't be cross with me and keep ringing off all the time – you *know* how fond I am of you . . . If you weren't married you see it would be different because I might or I might not want to marry you but I wouldn't be sure – As things are, I *can't* be so unfair as to go on when I am quite determined about what I mean to do.

For Evelyn the outlook was doubly depressing: not only was there the intractability of Teresa, but by the implacable laws of his newly adopted faith he had to face the strong probability that he would never be able to remarry. This meant either a lifetime of emotional and sexual restraint or a series of temporary liaisons, which while indulged would place his soul in a state of mortal sin. Outwardly, Evelyn expressed little of his anguish;[10] but for a man who never much enjoyed himself abroad, his compulsive desire to travel – Moscow, Peking, Jerusalem were now being considered as destinations – is hardly indicative of inner content. He wrote to Maimie Lygon, 'I wish I were dead you said that before yes but I wish it all the time.'

Evelyn's professional priority was to finish the novel based on his Abyssinian experience, whose title at the request of the Americans

---

[10] Except probably in his letters to Teresa Jungman, but these are said to have been destroyed.

had been changed. '*Accession* as such means practically nothing in America,' John Farrar had complained to Peters. Farrar was also making anxious enquiries as to when he could expect delivery of the manuscript. In the second week of May, Evelyn wrote briskly to Roughead, 'You can tell these troublesome yanks that the novel will be called *Black Mischief* and will be ready for them in about 3 weeks. It is extremely good.'

Black Mischief is a transitional work, halfway between the semi-surrealism of *Decline and Fall* and *Vile Bodies* and the next novel, the more mature, more realistic *A Handful of Dust*. Its theme is again the triumph of barbarity over progress, its action divided between those two moral jungles, London and Azania, with the link between them a rascally adventurer called Basil Seal. A comic colossus, Basil Seal is both irresistibly funny and a savage embodiment of anarchy. Evelyn's sense of despair and impending chaos and his loathing of the modern age provide the novel's dark foundations; but just as Evelyn's accidie was offset by an ability for intense enjoyment and an inspired comic vision, so in *Black Mischief* the underlying pessimism is almost obscured by the high hilarity that soars above it. It is Basil Seal who is responsible for much of the novel's humour, but it is also Seal who expresses a *tedium vitae*, a disgust with metropolitan life very similar to that experienced by his creator, with a similar longing for escape. 'Isn't London hell?' is Basil's refrain; 'Don't you hate London?'

The structure of the plot rests on the attempts of Seth, the new ruler of Azania, to impose a façade of modernity on his backward, fractious country, in which doomed ambition he is helped by his old Oxford acquaintance, Basil Seal. Instructions are issued daily to the hastily founded Ministry for Modernization for a national museum, for a birth-control pageant, boots for the barefoot army (the hungry soldiers gratefully cook and eat them), and for a national bank.

'Seth, what's the Imperial Bank of Azania?'
The Emperor looked embarrassed.
'I thought you might ask . . . Well, actually it is not quite a bank at all. It is a little thing I did myself. I will show you.'
He led Basil to a high cupboard which occupied half the wall on one side of the library, and opening it showed him a dozen or so shelves stacked with what might have been packets of writing paper.

'What is that?'

'Just under three million pounds,' said the Emperor proudly. 'A little surprise. I had them done in Europe.'

The corruption and depravity endemic in Azania, where cannibalism and murder are concurrent with the emperor's 'progressive' innovations, are more subtly if no less accurately reflected in the moral turpitude of society in London. When Basil invites himself to dinner with Alastair and Sonia Trumpington in their flat in Montagu Square, he arrives to find them in bed playing backgammon.

> Each had a separate telephone, on the tables at the side, and by the telephone a goblet of 'black velvet'. A bull terrier and chow flirted on their feet. There were other people in the room: one playing the gramophone, one reading, one trying Sonia's face things at the dressing-table. Sonia said, 'It's such a waste not going out after dark. We have to stay in all day because of duns.'
>
> Alastair said, 'We can't have dinner with these infernal dogs all over the place.'
>
> Sonia: 'You're a cheerful chap to be in bed with, aren't you?' and to the dog, 'Was oo called infernal woggie by owid man? Oh God, he's made a mess again.'

Although some of his rakish glamour is owed to Raymond de Trafford, Basil Seal derives mainly from two men Evelyn had known at Oxford, both of them, like Seal, handsome, arrogant, attractive to women, very brave, very clever, often drunk, and persistent in the kind of behaviour best described as delinquent. Both Basil Murray and Peter Rodd were the sons of distinguished fathers. Basil Murray (who at Oxford had helped beat up Evelyn after the Philbrick affair) was the son of Gilbert Murray, Regius Professor of Greek; Peter Rodd's father was that exquisite flower of diplomacy, one-time ambassador in Rome, Sir Rennell Rodd. Both men were drifters, wayward, constantly having to be bailed out of trouble of one sort or another. Both had great charm. Murray, described by Evelyn in his autobiography as 'satanic', had been a scholar at New College, where he earned a reputation for irascibility, heavy drinking and sexual profligacy; he was not overpunctilious, either, when it came to matters of money and personal hygiene. Peter Rodd, or Prod, as he was universally known, was a rebel and buccaneer, sent down from Balliol for having a woman in his rooms, always getting into scrapes, drawn like a magnet to wars and revolutions, preferably in remote and dangerous corners of the world. He was handsome, sexy, argumentative and often aggressively rude; he was also exceptionally well informed about almost everything, and loved nothing better than to instruct his audience, completely insensitive to that audience's desire to be instructed, a trait notoriously shared by Basil. ' "No, the truth about Basil is just that he's a *bore*. No one minds him being rude, but he's so *teaching*. I had him next to me at dinner once and he would talk all the time about Indian dialects . . ." '

Several familiar characters appear again. Lady Metroland is briefly glimpsed, brought on stage mainly to point the comic contrast to Basil's mother, Lady Seal, who, like Lady Anchorage in *Vile Bodies*, inhabits a far more respectable milieu than Margot's. The description of Lady Seal, stupid, innocent and dull, preparing for a dinner party is a miniature masterpiece. Basil, coming in late having failed to turn up for it, asks his mother, ' "Was the party a success?" "Yes, I think so, so far as can be expected. I had to ask poor Toby Cruttwell. Who else *was* there I *could* ask at the last moment?" '

In Azania, a thinly veiled caricature of Abyssinia, many of the landmarks and *dramatis personae* are recognisable, either from *Remote People* or from recent Abyssinian history. Two English ladies in knitted suits Evelyn saw searching Addis for evidence of 'vice' are translated into Dame Mildred Porch and Miss Sarah Tin of the League of Dumb Chums. Amurath is the Emperor Menelik II; Achon his successor and grandson, Lej Yasu; Seth the westernised Ras Tafari. The native Azanians are presented as funny savages in a manner that would have had Wilfred Thesiger reaching for his revolver. Here are the emperor's crack troops, irreverently reminiscent of the dancers at the Bal Nègre: 'hard, bare feet rhythmically kicking up the dust, threadbare uniforms, puttees wound up anyhow, caps at all angles, Lee-Enfield rifles with fixed bayonets slung on their shoulders; fuzzy heads, jolly nigger-minstrel faces, black chests shining through buttonless tunics, pockets bulging with loot.' Mr Bergebedgian, proprietor of the Lion d'Or in Harar, is gloriously reincarnated as the Armenian fixer, Krikor Youkoumian, while the sublimely ridiculous British minister, Sir

Samson Courtenay, with his family and staff at the legation take the place of the Bartons, with Sir Samson's daughter, Prudence, coming to an undignified end in a cannibal pot. The words in which Prudence expresses her disappointment with her sexually lethargic boy-friend, the honorary attaché at the legation, bring to mind She-Evelyn's exasperation with her first husband: ' "I think you're effeminate and under-sexed," she said, "and I hate you" ', a resemblance that may go some way to explaining the frightfulness of Prudence's fate.

One of the highlights of the Azanian episodes, as it had been of Evelyn's Abyssinian expedition, is the description of the monastery at Debra Lebanos, making an appearance here as the monastery of St Mark the Evangelist, and delineated with a satiric ebullience that was to bring Evelyn a great deal of trouble. The cluster of mud huts that formed the monastery stood beside a stream which, according to tradition, was

> the brook Kedron conveyed there subterraneously; its waters were in continual requisition for the relief of skin diseases and stubborn boils. Here too were preserved, among other relics of less certain authenticity, David's stone prised out of the forehead of Goliath (a boulder of astonishing dimensions), a leaf from the Barren Fig Tree, the rib from which Eve had been created and a wooden cross which had fallen from heaven quite unexpectedly during Good Friday luncheon some years back.

Black Mischief, dedicated 'With love to Mary and Dorothy Lygon', was published in October 1932, to reviews that were somewhat ambivalent. Although Eric Linklater in the *Listener* described the novel as 'an all-round growth of strength', and L. A. G. Strong in the *Spectator* thought it 'amazingly well-written', the *Express*, in the person of James Agate, found the satire 'heavy-handed', the *Telegraph* thought that '[Mr Waugh] grows a trifle weary of the cap and bells', while the *Bookman* frankly regretted the Book Society's choice of the novel for Book of the Month.[11] 'With all respect to Mr Evelyn Waugh, the Society might have looked further and found better.'

---

[11] So, too, did the Book Society, which returned to Chapman & Hall 760 copies less than a month after publication. However, in November, Arthur noted after a board meeting that the firm's October sales were 'over £9000, chiefly owing to Evelyn'.

Evelyn had a small special edition printed on rag paper, bound in best morocco, numbered and signed, to give to friends. In return, he received the usual appreciative letters, although even here there was the occasional note of equivocation. Henry Yorke, congratulating his friend on 'a very great achievement', and on the admirable conciseness of his style (a quality which above all Yorke studied to attain in his own work), admitted to some reservations. 'Of course you know how I deplore travel and how little I sympathize with the black races. How admirable if Seth had been white – a rich man who did not know what to do with his money or in other words a Bryan Guinness.' This judgment was tactfully presented more as personal prejudice than objective criticism, but Henry Yorke had hit the nail on the head: the sections of the novel set in Azania, outside Evelyn's familiar territory, are very much less effective than the scenes set in London among his own kind. In an article written the following year for the *Daily Mail*, Evelyn, like Joseph Conrad before him, gave it as his opinion that it was important for novelists to travel because 'one cannot neglect the study of human nature in unfamiliar surroundings; the aspects of character that are visible in civilized life give one material for only a superficial survey.' *Black Mischief* is the perfect illustration of how ill-conceived in his case this notion was.

One recipient of the special edition, whose good opinion was of particular importance, was a new acquaintance, Lady Diana Cooper, daughter of the Duke of Rutland,[12] wife of the clever, irascible Tory Member of Parliament, Duff Cooper, and considered one of the great beauties of the day. She and Evelyn had met during the early summer at a dinner party of Hazel Lavery's, at which Evelyn had had great success with an imitation of Emerald Cunard, which, said a fellow-guest, 'made us laugh till it hurt and we wanted him to stop'. The dinner had been preceded by a motorised treasure hunt, which ended at the Café de Paris at Bray on the Thames. Evelyn, sharing a car with Lady Diana, had quickly fallen under her spell, while he in his turn captivated her

---

[12] In fact, the illegitimate daughter of the Duchess of Rutland and the handsome Harry Cust, Member of Parliament, poet and one-time editor of the *Pall Mall Gazette*. Diana was, however, accepted by the duke, and brought up as one of his own five children at Belvoir Castle.

with a well-polished version of the Captain Hance saga, with scenes featuring all the supporting cast, their characters, their habits, their diets, their tempers. By the end of the recitation, she could hardly wait to have the story continued at the next meeting.

Although nearly forty, Diana Cooper was still lovely, with her pale skin, fair hair and huge 'love-in-a-mist' blue eyes. She possessed in abundance all the qualities Evelyn most admired: arrogance, breeding, intelligence, an astonishing self-assurance, as well as a spirit of adventure and a highly developed sense of fun. Enormous personal charm more than made up for a devouring vanity, richly nourished by a permanent and doting chorus of sycophantic admirers. At that time Diana, who liked to dabble in the drama and had already acted in a couple of films, was appearing at the Lyric Theatre in a revival of *The Miracle*, a mock-medieval mime play, German in origin and produced by Max Reinhardt, in which she took the part of a statue of the Madonna. Her rôle required her to stand exquisite and immobile for long periods while Tilly Losch as the fallen Nun and Leonide Massine as the satanic Spielmann capered about the stage. In April Evelyn had been taken by Baby Jungman to see the play. 'I went to a disgusting thing called *The Miracle*,' he told Dorothy Lygon, describing himself as having been 'sickeningly bored... I sat next to the Duke of Norfolk. He didn't know me but I knew him & I thought here is the man I respect as the natural leader of English Catholics and why is he at this blasphemous play because it is full of blasphemy as an egg is full of meat.' Meeting the Madonna herself, however, tempered Evelyn's dislike of the play, for when it went on tour in the autumn, he went with it, joining Diana in Manchester, and then, with Diana's mother, the Duchess of Rutland, in Glasgow and Edinburgh. 'My passion for shows is still a great trouble to all about me,' he wrote to Christine Longford from the Midland Hotel, Manchester. 'They have had to make all the *Miracle* chorus dance in bare feet as the only way of keeping me off the stage.' At night Evelyn sat contentedly in Diana's dressing-room, during her rest periods reading aloud from that seminal text, *The Wind in the Willows*, and waiting till after the performance when he could take her to dinner. By day the two of them visited some of the great houses, Chatsworth, Hardwick, Belvoir (the Duke of Rutland's seat), and Lord Brownlow's house, Belton, where Evelyn later stayed on several occasions. 'A house of staggering beauty', he described it. 'Built by Christopher Wren. Grinling Gibbons throughout. Marble Wren fire places, tapestry early 18th cent. with pseudo-Indian scenes. Inconceivably lovely.'

The more he saw of Diana, the more infatuated he became, but as with his earlier Diana, Diana Guinness, another bold, beautiful woman, his feelings were intensely romantic. She was his *princesse lointaine*; he wanted to win her heart but without seriously aspiring to her bed – fortunately for the future of the friendship, as Diana Cooper was physically cold, voracious for admiration, indifferent to sexual love. There had been one or two ill-fated passages of arms. Evelyn reported a 'strained hour in Diana's dressing-room' in Edinburgh, while she remembered dismissing with contempt 'his dribbling, dwarfish little amorous singeries'. But to the relief of both such half-hearted gestures to convention were quickly dropped. The strength of Evelyn's emotional attachment shows itself in his attempt to cure her frequent bouts of depression, initiating a dialogue on a specific theme that was to continue, sometimes irritably and always ineffectively, until his death. 'Wish I could persuade you to be Catholic,' he wrote in November 1932. 'You see you have the real mens catholica (Latin for Catholic mind) and all that isn't happy in your nature would be made straight. But I won't go on – at least I will, but not in writing but when I see you.'

In August, before *The Miracle* tour, Evelyn had been in Venice at the same time as the Coopers, having gone there with Hugh Lygon and Raymond de Trafford. 'My word,' Evelyn had written to Dorothy, 'I am glad Hugh is coming to Italy because between you and me and the w.c. Raymond de T. is something of a handful.' Evelyn, together with Duff and Diana and Chips Channon, stayed at the Palazzo Brandolini as guests of that indefatigable social climber, Laura Corrigan, whose mission in Venice was to provide extravagant entertainment for the grand English, among them Randolph Churchill, Cecil Beaton, Emerald Cunard, Oliver Messel, Juliet Duff, the Guinnesses, Abdys and Castlerosses. Nearly every night there were dinner parties for seventy or eighty, the beautiful salons of the palazzo lit by candles, the tables loaded with tuberoses; by day Mrs Corrigan's motor-launches ferried her guests to and from the Lido, where liveried footmen set up backgammon boards on the beach, poured drinks and served a large and elaborate luncheon. Evelyn, 'a confirmed heliophobe', much preferred to spend the hottest part of the day wandering through the cool, dark depths of the many churches, saving his social energies for the evening, when everybody converged at Florian's or Harry's Bar to discuss the latest party before going off to dress for the next. One evening there was a picnic on Torcello. Evelyn amused himself by conversing in Latin with one of the friars. '*Mulieres stridentes et vestitae immodestissime*', the holy man complained. Another night he went to sea with the Chioggia fishing fleet, trawling for scampi. 'We cooked them on a charcoal brazier and ate them in their shells at dawn – with cups of hideous coffee compounded, it seemed, of chicory, garlic and earth.' To celebrate Diana Cooper's fortieth birthday on 29 August, a party was held on Murano, starting in demure pastoral mode with glassblowers and gondoliers picturesquely dancing with the guests, but ending in a disgraceful brawl as four men – Richard Sykes,[13] Randolph Churchill, Oliver Messel and Cecil Beaton – came to blows and fought each other 'like bears'.

When Evelyn returned to England he was greeted by the news that Alec was engaged, his fiancée, Joan Chirnside, a pretty girl from a wealthy Australian family whom he had met with his old friends, Jack and Cristina Hastings. They were married on 25 October, but his brother's good fortune, with the prospect of domestic happiness renewed, served only to underline the bleakness of Evelyn's situation, the probability that he himself should never be able to marry, making it all the more pressing that he put as much distance as possible between himself and home. His chosen destination this time was British Guiana and Brazil, where, he told Peters, he planned to spend his time 'among the wildest possible forest people'. To finance the trip, he asked his agent to guarantee an overdraft of £100 on the strength of the sale of some short stories, the American royalties on *Black Mischief*, and fees to be earned from travel articles for which, it was hoped, commissions would be quickly forthcoming: 'far flung stuff impenetrable Guiana forests, toughs in Diamond mines, Devils

---

[13] This incident gave rise to a new term in the Waugh private vocabulary, 'to sykes', meaning to strike or demolish.

Island, Venezuela'. Peters agreed to the overdraft, but found selling the 'far flung stuff' more difficult. One of his regular customers, Alison Settle at *Vogue*, explained that 'we don't deal with scenery or life in the raw, as you know and whether the *Vogue* woman reaches British Guiana, Florida, Cannes or New Zealand she merely reflects on the outward differences of social customs, comforts that she meets and whether or not there is anybody who can give a good party.'

Although Evelyn cared very little where he went as long as it was far away, South America had caught his fancy because of the stories in the press over the past few years about the mysterious disappearance of Colonel Fawcett. In 1925, Colonel P. H. Fawcett had led a small expedition into the Matto Grosso in Brazil in confident expectation of finding a fabled lost city, the ruins of which had last been reported by a party of Portuguese in the eighteenth century. Fawcett had set off into the jungle, never to be seen again, but although he had certainly died, the story had not, kept alive by a series of tantalising reports from returning travellers of a white man worshipped as a god, of a white man being kept captive by the Indians, and so on. Peter Fleming had recently returned from the latest of the 'finding Fawcett' expeditions, reporting on it for *The Times*, before publishing a successful book, *Brazilian Adventure*. He was one of the people Evelyn consulted about equipment, the other being Ivan Davson, a businessman with commercial interests in British Guiana, who over lunch at the Ritz gave Evelyn an introduction to his agent in Georgetown.

Baby Jungman was the third member of the party on this occasion. 'She sat quiet while he [Davson] and I spread a map on the table and talked of Guiana,' Evelyn noted in his diary. Their relationship was no easier. They had continued to meet, Evelyn remaining very much in love, Teresa friendly but detached. 'Usual Ritz usual Dutch girl', Evelyn wrote in October reporting his week to Diana Cooper, mysteriously adding 'I went to communion with dutch girl to ratify treaty (morbid).' In November he told Diana, '[I] had a very pious few days going to church with that Dutch girl.' Whether deliberately engineered by Teresa or not, Evelyn found it difficult during his last days in England to see her alone. At the beginning of December, three days before he was due to leave, she went to Northamptonshire for a dance, while Evelyn was left to dine by himself with the Yorkes. He dined with her and the Simon Elweses the following evening at the Savoy, and only on the night before his departure finally took her to dinner by herself at Quaglino's.

The next morning, 4 December, they went to early Mass at St James's, Spanish Place, breakfasting afterwards at a nightclub, the Slip-In, where Teresa presented him with a medallion. '[The Dutch girl] gave me a St Christopher on a chain to put round my neck – gold, Cartier, very expensive saved out of her pocket money. Deeply moved.' Teresa drove with him to the docks in her mother's car. 'Deadly lonely, cold, and slightly sick at parting . . . Teresa drove off to lunch with Lady Astor in London. We sailed at about 2.30. Down the river in heavy rain and twilight. Heart of lead.'

Heavy Catholic trouble

'What a snare this travelling business is to the young writer,' wrote P. G. Wodehouse referring to the South American sequences in *A Handful of Dust*. 'He goes to some blasted jungle or other and imagines that everybody will be interested in it.' That Evelyn was aware of this widely held attitude, and himself not remotely interested in the 'blasted jungle', is apparent from the defensive tone of most of his travel articles about it. Although admitting to a genuine fascination for 'distant and barbarous places, and particularly in the borderlands of conflicting cultures and states of development', and while relishing some of the grotesque characters encountered in these borderlands, as a novelist he was always most engaged, always at his most true, subtle and profound when depicting members of his own society: Mr Todd in *A Handful of Dust* is a caricature, as are Mr Youkoumian in *Black Mischief* and the Jacksons in *Scoop*. There can have been few travel writers, too, who show less curiosity about their surroundings. Although prepared to note the architecture, go to Mass, and drink with members of the expatriate population, Evelyn rarely displays more than a superficial inquisitiveness about the country or its indigenous inhabitants. In Guiana and Brazil, the spectacular jungle and lush riverside scenery are considered 'unendurably monotonous', while the Indians are cursorily dismissed as 'unattractive, squat and dingy, with none of the grace one expects in savages'. In the description of his South American journey, *Ninety-Two Days*, there is barely a glimmer of excitement or enjoyment, none of the intellectual avidity of Robert Byron, nor the exuberance of Peter Fleming. Instead it was as though the whole expedition had been undertaken as a form of penance, with even the book's title sounding as if the sufferer had been counting off the hours and minutes as well as the days.

As if to underline this penitential aspect, Evelyn included a detailed debunking of the myth that 'the greatest physical and mental well-being can be attained only in the wild parts of the world . . . For instance, *that one felt free.* On the contrary, there seemed no limit to the number of restrictions with which the "open life" hampered one . . . *That one was untrammelled by convention.* The toilet of the tropics, with all its hygienic precautions, is every bit as elaborate as dressing for dinner . . . *That one eats with a gay appetite and sleeps with the imperturbable ease of infancy.* Nonsense . . . However hungry I was I found it difficult to swallow and impossible to digest the *farine* and *tasso* of the ranches . . . As for sleep, I scarcely had a single good night in the open.'

But this interpretation omits the single overwhelming advantage of enduring such discomforts: when struggling to survive in conditions of extreme hardship in hostile surroundings among members of a disintegrating society, there is little energy for the contemplation of personal despair. In this sense the hostility and chaos of the external world provide a welcome distraction from the hostility and chaos of the world within.

The voyage out on a battered old cargo ship, SS *Ingoma,* 'was as depressing a time as I have known in adult life'. The ship was cold, and there were bed-bugs in the cabins. Part of the second-class quarters had been converted for the accommodation of two prize bulls, a racehorse, a couple of fox hounds and some hens, with inevitably squalid results. 'The sailors will not clear up their shit on account of being Indians and it would be unclean.' The weather was bad, and most of the passengers seasick. 'Very little sleep at nights. Tempers becoming uncertain. Nothing to do all day except read. As usual I brought all the wrong books.' Once past the Azores, the wind dropped and it grew warmer, but by this time Evelyn had developed a heavy cold and felt incapable of doing anything except sitting in a corner with a pile of detective stories. However, after the first week he noted in his diary, 'I feel less tied to London than when I started and have thrown off all the hesitations about the jungle which I felt driving down with Teresa.' When they reached Antigua, Evelyn went ashore to see the sights, bathe, drink rum swizzles and visit the cathedral; he did the same at the next ports of call, Barbados and Trinidad, both of which were perfectly pleasant without in any way engendering much enthusiasm. 'General impression of Trinidad that I don't want to see it again.' In *Ninety-Two Days*, Evelyn makes only the briefest reference to these Caribbean islands because of a bargain struck with Alec. 'Like me, poor fish, he lives by writing books, so on one of our rare but agreeable meetings we made a compact each to keep off the other's territory; with a papal gesture he made me a present of the whole of Africa and a good slice of Asia in exchange for the Polynesian Islands, North America and the West Indies.'

The coast of British Guiana was first glimpsed as a misty fringe of palm trees only just visible in pouring rain. As the ship swung into the mouth of the Demerara, there came into view a dismal perspective of windswept wharves, factory chimneys and corrugated-iron roofs; there was a strong smell of brown sugar and clouds of bees around the customs sheds. 'I have never seen a less attractive harbour; hope dried up in one at the sight of it; only the heavy reek of sugar occupied the senses.' The capital, Georgetown, with its broad, untidy streets and two-storey wooden buildings, was 'not at all a nice town', and 'I don't mind how soon I leave it.' Evelyn was obliged to stay for a fortnight, however, in order to assemble provisions and lay his plans for going up-country, a fortnight that was made more agreeable than it might have been by the kindness of the governor and his wife. Sir Edward and Lady Denham invited him to dinner at Government House on Christmas Day, and at New Year took him on a three-day trip up the Essequibo River to see the settlement at Mazaruni, a former convict station. Guiana, a country of vast tracts of jungle and wide savannah, is remarkable for the beauty and abundance of its flora and fauna, some species of which are found in no other parts of the world. This was Evelyn's first experience of the magnificent rain-forest and its exotic specimens. 'Saw countless ants,' he recorded in his diary, 'some flowers, fine butterflies and tortoise.'

It was during this trip that Evelyn was persuaded by Edward Denham to think again about a plan that had briefly attracted him of exploring the head waters of the Essequibo where, it was said, 'unsophisticated' Indians were still to be found. The suggestion had come from Dr W. E. Roth, curator of the George-town museum and a distinguished biologist whose knowledge of Indian culture was profound. Evelyn had found him 'an opinion-ated and rather disagreeable old man', and was at first taken aback to be told that the trip would last three months and cost £300, 'but later grew more enthusiastic and saw the possibility of a good book in it'. However, Denham's description of Roth's notorious irresponsibility towards time, money and physical danger, together with Evelyn's personal antipathy towards the man, decided him not to pursue the idea. But the episode was typical of a curious lack of motivation on Evelyn's part: he seemed not to care where he went, completely indifferent to his direction, swayed by the most recent suggestion, as though anything would do. He arrives in Georgetown with no plans, decides to go with Roth, decides not to go with Roth; soon afterwards he meets a Mr Haynes, commissioner for the Rupununi district, who happens to have a boat going up-river, so with a shrug Evelyn settles for going with Haynes; later on, having heard talk of the celebrated city of Manaos, he decides on the spur of the moment to go to Manaos, but then, discovering that the boat service is unreliable, abandons that project in favour of a visit to a settlement whose sole attraction is that Evelyn had met a man he liked who lived there.

Mr Haynes, with Evelyn, left Georgetown on 3 January 1933. They went first by train down the coast to New Amsterdam, and from there by boat up the Berbice River to Takama, which was where the arduous part of the journey began. The next desti-nation was Kurupukari, a three-day ride across a vast stretch of parched savannah, whose monotony was broken every half mile or so by the remains of dead cattle, some still being picked clean by crows, others no more than skeletons with grass growing between their ribs. Their mounts were thin, dispirited little ponies, 'too lethargic even to switch away the horse flies that clustered on their quarters; mine had been attacked by a vampire bat during the night and bore a slaver of blood on his withers'. Every evening Evelyn and Haynes stopped in what were officially described as rest-houses, in fact only primitive, open-sided shelters under which to sling a hammock. 'A hammock is one of the most agreeable things for an hour's rest, but it needs practice to adapt it for a night, particularly when it is tied to the same framework as three others, whose occupants with every movement set it vibrating.' Ten or eleven hours in every twenty-four were spent in their hammocks, as darkness fell as soon as they had eaten dinner, after which there was nothing to do except lie back and suffer the pains of indigestion consequent upon the unvarying and almost uneatable meal of farine, a kind of sawdust-like flour produced from cassava root, and tasso, a blackened, tough and fibrous form of dried beef.

At this stage the physical discomforts were not overwhelming; harder to bear was the company of Mr Haynes. Haynes, referred to as 'Bain' in *Ninety-Two Days*, was a middle-aged Creole, ·emaciated by frequent attacks of fever and a sufferer from constant and appalling bouts of asthma which kept him and everyone else awake for most of the night. Throughout the week's ride, there was not one moment of silence, for when Mr Haynes was not coughing, retching and wheezing, he was talking.

> Many of his stories I found to strain the normal limits of credulity
> – such as that he had a horse which swam under water and a
> guide who employed a parrot to bring him information; the
> bird would fly on ahead, said Mr Bain, and coming back to its
> perch on the Indian's shoulder whisper in his ear what he had
> seen, who was on the road and where they could find water . . . I
> soon fell into what now seems to me an ungenerous and
> exasperating habit of cross-examination, which usually
> disinterred some closely concealed nucleus of verbal truth.

Most of Mr Haynes's anecdotes concerned his own exceptional honesty, courage and knowledge of local lore.

> There was one insect which buzzed in a particular manner.
> 'Listen,' said Mr Bain one day, 'that is most interesting. It is
> what we call the "six o'clock beetle", because he always makes
> that noise at exactly six o'clock.'
> 'But it is now quarter past four.'
> 'Yes, that is what is so interesting.'

After a week, Evelyn, unable to endure his companion any longer, struck out on his own, accompanied by two boys and Haynes's foreman, 'a large middle-aged black of unusual ugliness'. In his book, Evelyn writes that, 'I was sorry that this stage of the journey was over,' but in a letter to Diana Cooper he admitted he had grown 'sick with boredom' of Mr Haynes and was delighted to see the last of him. From then on, however, conditions swiftly deteriorated. Except in the early morning, the heat of the savannah was intense, glaring up off the earth so that even under a broad-brimmed hat the skin of Evelyn's face and neck was burned raw. Thirst was overwhelming and unassuagable. 'All through the blazing afternoon I found that I thought of nothing except drinking. I told myself very simple stories which consisted of my walking to the bar of my club and ordering one after another frosted glasses of orange juice; I imagined myself at a plage, sipping ice-cold lemon squashes under a striped umbrella, beside translucent blue water.'

Most tormenting of all were the insects, mosquitoes, fleas, ticks, which had to be burned off with a cigarette end, jiggers, whose eggs had to be dug out of the soles of the feet with a pin, and *bêtes rouges*, 'a minute red creature which brushes off the leaves of the bush on to one's clothes and finds its way below one's skin where it causes unendurable itching'. Worst of all were the clouds of tiny *cabouri* fly whose bite left a savage irritation, and which unfailingly found their way to any exposed flesh, making necessary the wearing of cotton gloves and towels to cover the face. 'It is quite accurate to say that in the weeks from leaving Kurupukari until some time after my final return to Georgetown, there was not a two-inch square on my body that was not itching at some time of the day or night.'

At intervals on the trail there were ranches at which the traveller could stay as a welcome relief from the comfortless rest-houses. The first of these, belonging to a man called Christie, Evelyn reached after a particularly bad day, when the miseries of climate and terrain had been greatly aggravated by the behaviour of his mount. 'One-eyed horse played up on being bridled and threw himself over backwards. Five miles out stopped; repeated performance twice more, finally reared and fell over. Lost trail once but found it. Intolerably hot ride.' At four o'clock Evelyn arrived at the ranch, both he and his horse staggering with fatigue, to be met by the sight of the owner, an old black man with white hair and moustache, reclining in a hammock while sipping water from the spout of an enamelled teapot. This was Mr Christie, 'the fantastic figure of Mr Christie', who was to play a leading rôle in Evelyn's treasury of eccentrics.

Hobbling across to shake hands with his exhausted visitor,

Christie greeted him and at once began to ply him with large quantities of rum. All evening they drank, and Mr Christie talked. He talked mainly about mystic numbers, about religion ('Lately he had been privileged to see the total assembly of the elect in heaven. "Were there many of them?" "It was hard to count because you see they had no bodies but my impression is that there were very few" '); about his translation of the Scriptures into Macushi, and about the visions he personally had experienced. ' "I always know the character of any visitors by the visions I have of them. Sometimes I see a pig or a jackal; often a ravaging tiger." I could not resist asking, "And how did you see me?" "As a sweetly toned harmonium," said Mr Christie politely.' The effect on Evelyn was strange and dreamlike. 'The sweet and splendid spirit, the exhaustion of the day, its heat, thirst, hunger and the effects of the fall, the fantastic conversations of Mr Christie translated that evening and raised it a finger's breadth above reality.'

The following day, having left Christie behind him in fact if not in imagination, Evelyn came to the next ranch, whose Portuguese manager gave him an excellent breakfast, 'a dish of fried eggs minced tasso fried with herbs, bananas and delicious Brazilian coffee'. At the third ranch, belonging to an American, a Mr Hart, Evelyn was received in the owner's absence by his wife, who allowed him to examine her husband's collection of books, 'a curious library, much ravaged by ants, filled, like the boxes outside secondhand booksellers, with works on every conceivable subject, hygiene, carpentry, religion, philosophy, and among them a number of fairly recent best-sellers left presumably from time to time by passing travellers'. Evelyn's next destination was the Jesuit mission of St Ignatius outside Bon Success, where, having accepted Mrs Hart's offer of a lift into town in her motor van, he arrived 'in a third of the time it would have taken by horse', completing the last two miles to St Ignatius by bullock cart.

The mission, a draughty, two-storey building of wattle, thatch and corrugated iron, with a small church and primitive school-house nearby, was run by Father Mather, a gentle, self-effacing man whom Evelyn came to admire without reservation. When he arrived in the early afternoon, he found the priest at work in the carpentry shop. Father Mather had himself made much of the mission furniture, 'firm, finely jointed and fitted, delicately finished, a marked contrast to the botched, makeshift stuff that prevailed even in Georgetown'. He was also a dedicated entomologist, of necessity confining his studies, as he rarely left his post, to the insects that collected round his reading-lamp in the evenings. Most of the year he lived entirely alone, running the ranch attached to the mission and acting both as priest and doctor to the Indians. 'He had once been desperately ill from fever and had frequent slighter recurrences; he had constant toothache for he was two hundred miles from the nearest dentist.' The mission itself was 'as lonely an outpost of religion as you could find anywhere', and yet Father Mather was 'one of the happiest men I met in the country'.

Evelyn had to wait over a week for the return of the head *vaquero* who was to guide him on the next stage of his journey to Boa Vista. But this period of enforced immobility was for once passed in the greatest tranquillity and contentment, reading, writing and talking to Father Mather, who cut his hair, made him a walking-stick, and touched his guest by ingeniously constructing as a leaving present a camera-case out of calfskin, deerskin and an old duster.

After the miseries of the journey so far, Boa Vista had taken on the qualities of a mirage, assuming in Evelyn's mind the features of a sophisticated European capital, with hotels and cafés, shady boulevards, and fast motor-launches plying constantly to and from the great port of Manaos. In fact the town turned out to be no more than 'a squalid camp of ramshackle cut-throats', with half a dozen seedy shops and two cafés, one little more than a shed, selling farine, bananas, warm beer and fish. There were no boulevards, no comfortable hotels, no one knew anything about a launch to Manaos. The people looked ill and discontented, '[they] are naturally homicidal by inclination, and every man, however poor, carries arms; only the universal apathy keeps them from frequent bloodshed.' Fortunately, Evelyn had a letter of introduction from Father Mather to Father Alcuin, a gloomy German-Swiss who ran the Benedictine priory in Boa Vista, and here he was able to stay until the arrival of the Boundary Commission boat on which he hoped to secure a passage to the coast. The time passed slowly. Father Alcuin, in the grip of chronic fever and melancholia, was not an enlivening companion. 'I do not think he ever liked me much or understood what I was doing in his house, but he accepted my presence without complaint as he accepted all the other hardships of Boa Vista.' For four days Evelyn suffered what he described in his diary as 'degrading boredom', when, with nothing to distract him, he was overwhelmed by loneliness and depression. However, having been attacked for describing his ennui so feelingly in *Remote People*, in *Ninety-Two Days* he was to be careful to make light of the subject.

> I will not say I was bored in Boa Vista but merely remark that I found very little to occupy my time . . . I could walk to the wireless office and learn that no news had been heard of the Boundary Commissioner's boat; I could visit the English-speaking blacksmith and watch him tinkering with antiquated automatic pistols . . . I could give bananas to the captive monkey and I could study the bottled worms in the laboratory; I could watch the carpenter, in his rare moments of industry, sawing up lengths of plank. There was really quite a number of things for me to do, but, in spite of them all, the days seemed to pass slowly.

In a letter to Diana Cooper he allowed himself a greater frankness.

> Goodness the boredom of Boa Vista . . . I am already nearly crazy . . . There are no books except an ant eaten edition of Bossuet's sermons and some back numbers of a German pious periodical for children. One cannot get drunk as the only liquor in the village is some very mild, very warm beer, which I can drink at a table in the store in a cloud of flies stared at by Brazilians in pyjama suits and boaters. There are of course no cars or boats for hire and nowhere to go in them if there were . . . No amount of fun compensates for this sort of misery and I shan't ever again undertake a journey of this kind alone. I am getting homesick and shall return direct as soon as I get to Manaos. I don't think there will be a book in my experiences up to date. However I have been able to brood a bit in solitude and discern solutions to some of my immediate problems.

Evelyn never did get to Manaos. After six days the boat arrived, but the commissioner flatly refused to take on a passenger. 'It was in a despondent and rather desperate mood that I heard his boat chugging away out of sight down the Rio Branco.'

By now in a state of desperation, Evelyn was forced to turn to writing to combat his ennui, sending Peters what he described as 'a grade A short story', which had been in his mind since the night at Mr Christie's ranch, and '3 grade B articles', one of which, on the Rupununi district, he was later dismayed to see headlined in the *Daily Mail*, 'My Escape from Mayfair'.

It has been assumed that the 'grade A short story' was 'The Man Who Liked Dickens',[1] later used as the final section of *A Handful of Dust*. The story tells of an ideal English gentleman, Tony Last, who in despair after the breakdown of his marriage, joins an eccentric explorer in search of a ruined city in Brazil; lost in the jungle, with the explorer dead, Last is eventually taken prisoner by a madman, clearly modelled on Mr Christie, who forces him to read Dickens aloud every day for the rest of his life. In his diary for 12 February while at Boa Vista, Evelyn wrote, 'thought of plot for short story'; and on 14 February, 'finished short story'; his letter to Peters is dated 15 February. Further evidence seems to support the assumption that his reference is to 'The Man Who Liked Dickens', as on the typescript of the final section of *A Handful of Dust* Evelyn wrote in pencil, 'This was originally written at Boa Vista, Brazil, as a short story. Original ms. lost. EW.' There are problems with this, however. First, it is unlikely that a story of such length and complexity could have been completed within two days, even if the plot had been evolving in Evelyn's mind since he left Christie's ranch. Second, and more conclusively, there are important episodes in the story closely based on Evelyn's experiences in South America, which at the time of his sojourn in Boa Vista had not yet occurred. For example, the explorer, Dr Messinger, takes with him a selection of what he calls 'trade goods' for barter with the natives, among them some mechanical mice. 'They were of German manufacture; the size of large rats, but conspicuously painted in spots of green and white; they had large glass eyes, stiff whiskers and green-and-white-ringed tails; they ran on hidden wheels, and inside them were little bells that jingled as they moved.' Towards the end of Evelyn's trip, over a month after leaving Boa Vista, he spends some days with a diamond prospector called Winter, who ran a makeshift store for the benefit of his Indian workforce. 'Whenever

[1] 'The Man Who Liked Dickens' first appeared in *Hearst's International & Cosmopolitan* in September 1933.

he went to Georgetown he came back with some new supply of novelties . . . He had a great success shortly after Christmas with some mechanical mice, emerald green drawers and a gramophone.' In the story, Tony Last is deliberately made drunk by his captor, Mr McMaster (his name changed in the novel to the more sinister-sounding 'Mr Todd'), who presses on him large quantities of an intoxicating liquor, brewed by the Indians and known as *pivari*, after which Last passes out for two days. Again several weeks after leaving Boa Vista, Evelyn is given a strange native drink known as *cassiri*, very similar, he notes, to another native drink named *piwari*.

> It is made from sweet cassava roots, chewed up by the elder members of the community and spat into a bowl . . . after the fermentation has been under way for some time, they [the villagers] all assemble and drink the entire quantity. It usually takes some days, beginning sombrely like all Indian functions, warming up to dancing and courtship and ending with the whole village insensibly drunk.

The likelihood is that with the writing of 'The Man Who Liked Dickens', Evelyn's memory was at fault, and although he may have begun the story at Boa Vista, he probably finished it at a later date, and that what he sent Peters was something else altogether.

Evelyn's experiences staying with Christie, at St Ignatius and at the Hart ranch – Christie's surreal mingling of erudition and madness, the ant-eaten library at Hart's, the volumes of Dickens lent him by Father Mather – are all woven into the story of Tony Last.

> 'I have all Dickens's books here [says Mr Todd] except those that the ants devoured. It takes a long time to read them all – more than two years.'
> 'Well,' said Tony lightly, 'they will well last out my visit.'
> 'Oh, I hope not. It is delightful to start again. Each time I think I find more to enjoy and admire.'
> They took down the first volume of *Bleak House* and that afternoon Tony had his first reading.

Eventually, unlike Tony Last, Evelyn got away. Deciding to return to Guiana, he headed for Dadanawa, three days' ride away on the other side of the river. As before, Evelyn had no particular reason for going there, 'except the desire to visit the manager whom I had greatly liked in Georgetown'. After a long and frustrating series of delays, he at last set off with a guide and three broken-down horses, two for riding, one for pack. The most practical route was due east across the Takutu River, and then north back to Bon Success and the St Ignatius Mission. On the second day Evelyn, convinced that he knew the way, set out alone, well ahead of his guide. Within hours he realised that he was not only hopelessly lost, but in serious danger of physical collapse. 'It was', he says, 'one of the low spots of the journey. I had been given a medal of St Christopher before I left London. I felt that now, if ever, was the moment to invoke supernatural assistance. And it came.' (Evelyn later calculated that the odds against rescue were one in 54.75 million.) Suddenly there was a river, a hut, food, and a well-disposed Indian who, most unusually, spoke English and was himself on the point of setting out for Bon Success. From there it was only a short ride to St Ignatius. 'I had just returned to the carpenter's shop, when Mr W. rode up on his weary horse,' recalled Father Mather, with whom Evelyn, exhausted and painfully sunburnt, thankfully spent several days resting, continuing to read Dickens, writing letters to England, and trying to make up his mind where to go next. A village called Kurikabaru was selected, its sole distinction that it stood at the farthest point of the mission itinerary, where even now Father Mather's colleague, Father Keary, was heading on his pastoral rounds.

At a place called Tipuru Evelyn caught up with Father Keary, a tall, dour, raw-boned Irishman. In practical terms the priest's presence made the going easier, although he was a depressing companion, trudging along hour after hour silently telling his beads. It was acerbically noted in the diary that, 'whenever Father Keary gives up the idea of saying Mass with special intention for our journey we have a better day.' Conditions were atrocious. It was the rainy season and to protect themselves against *cabouri* fly the two men had to walk in rubber-soled canvas boots, their hands in cotton gloves, their necks and faces swathed in handkerchiefs. Supplies were beginning to run short. An unusually heavy downpour kept them awake all of one night, while on another sleep was impossible because of the inflammation caused by jiggers in the soles of their feet. The next morning Evelyn had to have more than a dozen dug out with a pin, and the pain of this, aggravated by a poisoned toe, made him helplessly lame. Luckily they managed to hire a fat little stallion on which he could ride bareback through the forest, although as the trail had been cut head-high for men on foot, the discomfort of this was nearly as hard to bear as the discomfort of walking. 'While I was riding – face down, blind on the horse's neck and nervously anticipating more jostling than ever came to the swollen foot – I longed avidly to walk; and while I walked – hobbling one pace to every two up and down the sides of the valleys – I longed to ride.'

The next main staging post marked the beginning of the last leg of the journey. This was a riverside camp belonging to the Mr Winter whom Evelyn had met during a convivial evening in Georgetown, and who ran the primitive local store among whose novelties were the mechanical mice. When they reached Mr Winter's camp, Father Keary took his leave ('Father Keary went off at 9. Glad to see last of him'), while Evelyn lay in a hammock for ten days, reading *Martin Chuzzlewit* and waiting for his foot to heal. At the end of the first week in April, he was back in Georgetown. Here there was some time to wait before the arrival of the ship home, and Evelyn sent the Lygon girls a merry letter, giving the impression of high spirits. 'The delight of these simple people at my return is very touching. A public holiday has been declared and all the men & women prostrate themselves in the dust & bring me their children to bless; great banners & bonfires decorate all the streets & several elderly niggers have already died of excitement.' But on reaching England he confided to Henry Yorke that he was just returned 'after a journey of the greatest misery.... Am getting rid of some of the horrors of life in the forest'.

Evelyn arrived at North End Road on 1 May 1933, 'cheery, red-cheeked, with a car-full of luggage, and 5 stuffed crocodiles', which he had brought with him as presents. It was the last time he was to stay at Underhill, for his parents, anxious to economise, were on the point of moving to a small flat in Highgate. To avoid the consequent upheaval, Evelyn went down to Bath to stay at the Grand Pump Room Hotel, where in comfort and quiet and surrounded by the restorative effects of classical Georgian architecture he could deal with his correspondence, categorised as 'mostly Christmas cards and press cuttings', and what was ominously referred to as 'heavy Catholic trouble'.

The trouble concerned *Black Mischief*, and had blown up in January while Evelyn was away. Before leaving, he had written about the book to Diana Cooper, 'I think people may enjoy it without any grave sacrifices of intelligence or taste,' a judgment which had obviously been over-optimistic. Somewhat belatedly the novel had come to the notice of Ernest Oldmeadow, editor of the respected Catholic weekly, the *Tablet*. Oldmeadow had been outraged by what he regarded as an obscene, immoral and sacrilegious work, and in a frenzy of inquisitorial vigour had flown to the attack. 'Whether Mr Waugh still considers himself a Catholic, *The Tablet* does not know; but, in case he is so regarded by booksellers, librarians, and novel-readers in general, we hereby state that his latest novel would be a disgrace to anybody professing the Catholic name.' The diatribe continued at length, its tone growing increasingly hysterical and abusive, so abusive that a number of distinguished readers were shocked into action.

Oldmeadow, a personal appointment of the paper's proprietor, Cardinal Bourne, cardinal archbishop of Westminster, whose stringent views as to the censoring of 'unsuitable' Catholic literature he was relied upon faithfully to echo, was known for his litigious temperament. A Nonconformist minister before his conversion, he still retained a number of Nonconformist characteristics, among them a zest for theological controversy and a decidedly puritanical zeal in hunting down anything that could remotely be described as morally dubious. He was constantly engaging in pointless polemics with the editor of the *Church Times*, and filling the columns of the *Tablet* with furiously controversial articles written by himself under a variety of by-lines on subjects of very little interest to the majority of his subscribers. Circulation had badly fallen off, with Oldmeadow considered something of an embarrassment, yet so far nothing had been said. But now he had gone too far: instigated by the publisher, Tom Burns, twelve well-known Catholics, including three distinguished Jesuits (Fathers D'Arcy, Martindale and Steuart), the prior of Blackfriars (Bede Jarrett OP) and two celebrated artists (Wyndham Lewis and Eric Gill), signed a letter of protest. 'We think these sentences exceed the bounds of legitimate criticism and are in fact an imputation of bad faith. In writing, we wish only to express our great regret at their being published and our regard for Mr Waugh.' Unbowed, the editor returned to the battle and the row raged over several weeks, Oldmeadow, who refused to refer to the disgusting publication by name, delivering his anathemas under the heading 'A Recent Novel'. Among much else that was objected to was the passage in which Prudence goes alone into Basil's bedroom, the incident near the end when Basil unwittingly consumes part of Prudence, cooked, at a cannibal feast, and the reference to the Nestorian monastery, whose venerated cross 'had fallen from heaven quite unexpectedly during Good Friday luncheon, some years back'. If, thundered Oldmeadow,

> the twelve signatories of the above protest find nothing wrong with 'during Good Friday luncheon' we cannot help them . . . [Mr Waugh's book] abounds in coarse and sometimes disgusting passsages, and its climax is nauseating. Nowhere in its three hundred pages is the reader's mind lifted to anything noble. Of the very many characters, hardly one is other than contemptible or ridiculous. Religion and altruism are extensively mentioned; but invariably in a spirit of cynicism and, in some places, offensively. There may be books in which sordidness of detail does not overwhelm the spirituality of the pervading idea; but Mr Waugh's is not one of them. On his dunghill no lily blooms.

Shocked though he was by the violence of the attack, Evelyn was equally shocked by its injustice. Oldmeadow's condemnation was a gross insult to Waugh both as artist and Catholic, and he had little choice but to defend himself. Nonetheless, it was necessary to tread with care. Although privately he had no very high opinion of Bourne, the cardinal was Catholic primate of Great Britain; Oldmeadow was his employee, the *Tablet* his personal property. Evelyn's redress took the form of an open letter to the cardinal in which point by point he countered the charges of blasphemy, obscenity and irreverence. Written with an elaborate formality refined by barely restrained rage, Evelyn deals with Oldmeadow's accusations coldly, scathingly and in great detail, allowing himself to descend to personal insult only in the grand oratorical finale.

> Had the Editor of *The Tablet* found, as I hope he may shortly find, employment more suited to his temper, and had his attack on me appeared in an organ where its tone would have been

less inappropriate, I should have known how to treat it and should not now find myself dragged into this distasteful quarrel. Your Eminence's patronage alone renders this base man considerable, and it is with the earnest petition, as much for the good name of the Faith as for the comfort of all intelligent English Catholics, that a scandalous misuse of your patronage may be corrected, that I ascribe myself, Your Eminence's very humble and obedient servant, Evelyn Waugh.

In the event the pamphlet was never published, although Evelyn had a number of copies printed privately. As Tom Driberg succinctly paraphrased it in his column in the *Express*, 'Influential priests induced him to withdraw it, on grounds that (a) more authoritative representations re. *Tablet* were being made to the Cardinal, (b) the Cardinal was seriously ill.' But in a sense Evelyn had his revenge: within a few months of Oldmeadow's latest attack, Bourne was dead, Oldmeadow dismissed, and the *Tablet* sold to three laymen – A. H. Pollen, Douglas Woodruff and Tom Burns – the first occasion in sixty-eight years that the journal had passed outside clerical control.

The affair, nonetheless, had shaken Evelyn badly. As a recent convert, he was particularly sensitive about his standing in the eyes of fellow Catholics, and although it was easy enough to dismiss Oldmeadow as a hysterical fool, for Evelyn, like a new boy reluctantly brought to the attention of the headmaster, any brush with the upper echelons of the hierarchy could only be regarded as damaging. Father D'Arcy, who continued to keep a kindly eye on his protégé, realised what Evelyn was going through, and that this was the moment for some stabilising, suitable and supportive Catholic influence. To this end he suggested Evelyn should join him and a group of companions on one of Arnold Lunn's Hellenic cruises, the ostensible reason given that Waugh should act as minder to his old Oxford acquaintance, Alfred Duggan. Duggan had given up his Catholic faith and taken to the bottle, and it was hoped that Evelyn could help him return to the former and abandon the latter.

The company could hardly have been better chosen, and the members of the two families Father D'Arcy had particularly in mind as friends for Evelyn, the Herberts and the Asquiths, took to him at once. Gabriel Herbert was twenty-two, a handsome, amusing, athletic girl, daughter of that dashing adventurer,

Aubrey Herbert. Katharine Asquith, at forty-eight one of the older
members of the party, widow of the brilliant Raymond Asquith,
was travelling with two of her children, Julian (known as 'Trim'),[2]
soon to go up to Oxford, and his older sister, Helen. Gabriel
Herbert's father had died in 1923, after which her mother had
converted to Rome, taking her four children with her; Katharine
Asquith had done the same after the death of her husband during
the Great War. Indeed the Catholic presence on the ship was
formidable – Peter Acton, Laura Lovat and her daughter Magdalen Fraser, Chris and Maidie Hollis, the Infanta Beatrice of Spain.
The number of black-suited priests, the intense discussions of
Roman affairs, and Mass held twice every morning, were looked
at rather askance by the other passengers.

The SS *Kraljica Marija* left Venice at the beginning of September 1933. Evelyn wrote to the Lygon girls,

> So I am in the sea of Marmora and it is very calm & warm and
> there are lots of new & old chums on board and I have seen
> numbers of new & old places and am enjoying myself top-
> hole . . . The ship is full of people of high rank including two
> princesses of ROYAL BLOOD. There is not much rogering so
> far as I have seen and the food is appalling . . .
>
> There are several beasts of various religions & they are jealous
> of each other and there is a Protestant Canon with a beard
> who talked to one of the princesses with his fly buttons undone
> and she was disgusted . . . Perhaps that handsome Dutch girl is
> staying with you. She was expelled from Capri by Mussolini for
> Lesbianism you know.[3] Give her my love & a kiss on the arse.

As on all such ventures, little groups began to form. Evelyn's
group, known as the Catholic Underworld and comprising the
Asquiths, Hollises, Alfred Duggan and Peter Acton, liked to collect after dinner in the bar to listen to Father D'Arcy, frail and
white-faced, expounding on doctrine. 'There was the usual rather
unusual conversation,' Mrs Asquith noted in her diary after one
such evening's entertainment. 'Father D'Arcy explaining religious
principles to Evelyn and Mr Duggan. Mr Duggan rather drunk,

---

[2] Raymond Asquith saw his son, born in 1916, only once, when the baby was
sucking greedily at his mother's breast; this inspired his father to call him
Trimalchio, after the famously greedy *parvenu* in Petronius's *Satyricon*.
[3] Translated, the joke refers to the fact that Teresa had once visited Capri with
her mother.

but very attentive, Helen and Mr Hollis arguing about something else all the time.' Evelyn, she was quick to note, was the one who 'spreads scandal and nicknames them all . . . Helen and Trim and I have got rather friendly with him. He is exceedingly amusing and a great collector of ship's gossip.' Evelyn for his part was greatly taken with the Asquiths. Mrs Asquith was judged 'decent', a high term of praise, while the boy Trim was found to be 'big on good sense and good manners. Studious, holy and respectful'. Gabriel Herbert also won Evelyn's approval, but others were not so fortunate. 'The lovely Magdalen Fraser is ugly as hell and dull as mud,' while her mother, Lady Lovat, well-known for her charm, prettiness and chic, was described as a neurotic giantess who 'gets into such odd postures at mass that no one can look anywhere else'. The antipathy was returned, eventually reaching such a pitch that Katharine Asquith decided to defuse the situation by arranging a dinner party at which, she hoped, Evelyn and Laura Lovat could make up their differences. It was not a success, and the well-meaning hostess regretfully recorded that the evening had failed 'to bring about a greater mutual appreciation'.

When at the end of the cruise the ship returned to Venice, Evelyn found himself at a loose end. He and Alfred Duggan had been invited by Gabriel Herbert to her family's house at Portofino, but not for another week. Diana Cooper had half promised to meet him, but had failed to turn up. Alfred, who had started out well at the beginning of the cruise, drinking only beer, had with disastrous results latterly switched to brandy, and had disappeared on some ploy of his own. Fortunately Evelyn managed to prevail on Katharine Asquith and Trim to go with him to Ravenna and Bologna for a few days. The two men made a game of missing nothing in their sight-seeing, ransacking an old 1913 Baedeker for obscure churches, the three of them collapsing exhausted every evening either in the cinema or over a drink in a piazza café. On their last morning in Bologna, 'there was a fine procession of Blackshirts who marched past the hotel at ten o'clock, singing cheerfully and followed by the whole population of the town'.

The Villa Carnarvon, or Altachiara,[4] as it was informally known,

---

[4] A direct translation of Highclere, Lord Carnarvon's seat in Berkshire. 'Highclere' had become a term of the highest approbation in the Waugh-Lygon private language when Sibell had come home after staying at the castle full of praise for its luxury and comfort.

the Herberts' house at Portofino, had been built by the 4th Earl of Carnarvon, Aubrey Herbert's father, who had purchased a large expanse of that beautiful peninsula, choosing a site at the top of the steep promontory which overlooked the harbour on one side, and on the other the Mediterranean, three hundred feet below. Here he built a large, comfortable suburban villa, more appropriate to Berkshire than to the Ligurian coast, surrounded by acres of steeply terraced vines and olive trees. Constructed of a pinkish-white stone, its most attractive features were an outside dining-room and drawing-room on a spacious terrace shaded by two enormous ilex trees. When Evelyn and Alfred arrived, they found a large and rather noisy house party in progress. Their hostess was Mary Herbert, Gabriel's mother, tall, gaunt and fearlessly outspoken, with the face of a handsome hawk. All four children were with her: as well as Gabriel, there was a beautiful middle sister, Bridget, a shy 'white mouse named Laura', and the youngest, their eleven-year-old brother, Auberon, an 'astute urchin with neurotic tendencies'. As well as several friends of the family hitherto unknown to Evelyn – David Peel, a boy-friend of Bridget's, Johnny Churchill, Francis Howard – there were also Peter Acton and the dreaded Magdalen Fraser.

Diana Cooper was told that it was 'a very dangerous house where all the young people are covered in festering sores... There is a little boy [Auberon] who throws stones at his elders... Music all the time and philosophic discussion with a nit-wit mural decorator [John Spencer-Churchill]. Mr Acton is staying here too I believe but he hasn't woken up since his arrival. There is a decent hostess who makes barking noises when the orchestra is not playing.' The Asquiths received a more decorous account. 'It is most enjoyable here... Delicious simple food and the wine not at all as you described it.' The weather was perfect, there was a boatman to take them swimming, and all meals were eaten out of doors under a canopy. In spite of the potential embarrassment of Mrs Herbert's relationship by marriage to Evelyn Gardner (her late husband was Lady Burghclere's half-brother) everything went smoothly, except for an incident at lunch one day when Evelyn and Peter Acton began making facetious reference to Ireland and the Irish. Mary Herbert, daughter of Viscount de Vesci, brought up in Ireland, had the possessive, passionate devotion to that country common to Ascendancy families, and quickly lost her temper. Grabbing some hard bread rolls from a basket on the table, she threw them at the two men, before ordering them out of the house, leaving Bridget to drive them around the countryside until she reckoned her mother had cooled down sufficiently for them to return.

The summer of 1933, between Evelyn's return from Guiana and his leaving on the Hellenic cruise, was of necessity devoted to earning as much money as quickly as possible, for as always after a long absence abroad he was desperately short of funds. From Bath, where he was working on a series of articles for *Passing Show*, he asked Peters if there were any chance of securing a weekly literary page, which would at least bring in a regular income. Peters's reply was not encouraging – 'A weekly literary page is going to be hard to fix, but I'll try' – and his attempts predictably unsuccessful. A rising star he may have been, but at this juncture Evelyn's work did not always find favour with nor did his manner endear him to his employers, and Peters had to put a great deal of effort into persuading dissatisfied editors to give his talented, difficult and sometimes lazy young client a second chance. Part of the trouble was that Evelyn demanded very high fees which were not always justified by the quality of his work. Richard Sharman of *Vanity Fair* had complained to Carl Brandt about an article on 'Boredom'.[5] 'I am very sorry about this piece by Evelyn Waugh, but it has been read by every member of the editorial staff, and we all agree that it is – to be frank – rather a hastily put-together job; it reads as if it were a manufactured paper on a topic about which the author really cared very little.' Even more outspoken was a letter from Mark Goulden of the *Sunday Referee*, who angrily regretted having agreed to pay thirty guineas for what he described as 'one of the most uninteresting and uninspired contributions it has ever been my misfortune to publish'. The *Bystander* returned a short story which they considered sub-standard, and the *Daily Mail* sent back two articles on Brazil, while another, 'Debunking the Bush', remained unsold. Peters did what he could, telling Brandt that he knew 'Evelyn has not been doing his best lately. I have had a serious

[5] 'Here is the boring article on Boredom,' Evelyn had written only too accurately to Peters.

talk with him about it, and he agrees that it is time that he pulled up his socks.'

Although loyal to his client and supportive when necessary, Peters was never afraid to confront Evelyn with the truth. 'I wasn't greatly surprised, I fear, when the *Bystander* boys rang up today saying that they couldn't possibly use your story, that it wasn't a story at all and that they proposed to send it back. I protested, but must admit to you that I didn't think very much of it.' 'You can't tell me a thing I don't know about the low quality of my journalism,' came the submissive reply, while to another piece of acerbic criticism forwarded on from a disappointed editor, he wrote to Peters, 'Hard words. Hard words. I do not think you would send these messages on if you realised how much they wound the artist in me.' But if docile with his agent, Evelyn took a rebarbative stance towards editors, never willing to accept a reduction in price, however poor the standard of his product. To the *Referee*'s demand that he take a 50 per cent cut for the piece, 'Did We Overdo It?' ('The heading of the article seems strangely prophetic,' Mark Goulden bitterly remarked), Evelyn, unrepentant, replied, 'Mr Goulden must be off his rocker. Any article I write is worth exactly what I have been offered for it,' adding offensively, 'Tell him I'll make it pounds if he will give ten shillings to the Society for the Conversion of the Jews.' Even less was he prepared to take any nonsense from the Americans. Brandt had enraged him by failing to obtain payment for the *Vanity Fair* piece, which had after all been commissioned. 'Please transfer my American business to someone else,' Evelyn brusquely instructed, at the same time sending a gratuitously insulting letter to Brandt himself, which very much annoyed Peters.

But the poor quality of Evelyn's work was due more to depression than idleness. During the late summer and autumn, he stayed for weeks at a time at Aldwick, near Bognor Regis in Sussex, where the Coopers had put at his disposal West House, a small Regency villa divided only by a walled garden from the beach. Here, looked after by the caretaker and his wife, Evelyn was able to concentrate undisturbed on his articles and on the travel book about his South American journey, which he wrote from beginning to end in a month. 'The book has begun,' he told Diana unexcitedly, '500 words the first day, 1,500 yesterday and a little over 2,000 today. Time was I could write 3,000 a day and think nothing of it. Still it is getting longer and if I go on even like this it will be done some time. What is more I am getting a little interested in it. Not much, but when I am not writing I think of it sometimes instead of never.' Although to Diana he was polite about the house – 'I am much under compliment about this decent house' – to Dorothy Lygon he wrote, 'It is a very sad life I lead, very lonely, very uncomfortable, in a filthy cottage in the ugliest place in England with only mice for company like a prisoner in the tower.'

He was deeply unhappy, too, about Teresa. 'Trouble is I think of dutch girl all day and not sweet voluptuous dream, no sir, just fretful and it sykeses the work,' he told his hostess, while to Maimie he was even more explicit. 'The pope G. B. H. won't let me use her (nor will she). God how s[ad]. . . . Can't help loving that girl.' On 28 October, he wrote again to Maimie, 'I was thirty on Saturday & feel sixty. I celebrated the day by walking into Bognor and going to the Cinema in the best 1/6 seats. I saw a love film about two people who were in love; they were very loving and made me cry. Then I had a synthetic welsh rarebit to my dinner and went to bed at 10 with 3 dial pills. I bought myself Sitwell's new book & find it as heavy as my heart . . . It is very hard to be 30 I can tell you . . . oh dear oh dear I wish I was dead.'

On 18 October, ten days before this unhappy birthday, Evelyn came up to London for the first stage in what was to prove a painfully protracted business, the annulment of his marriage to Evelyn Gardner.

It was Christopher Hollis who had encouraged him to bring the case. While they were on the Adriatic cruise together, Hollis had been aware of Evelyn's intense misery over his situation. Some time afterwards Evelyn had been staying with the Hollises at Stonyhurst when at dinner one evening an American Jesuit, Father Vincent Watson, an authority on Roman ecclesiastical law, had discoursed knowledgeably on the notorious Marlborough nullity case of 1926, in which the marriage of the Duke and Duchess of Marlborough had been annulled by Rome in spite of the fact that they had had two children. Naturally there had been a furore in the Protestant press, which had excelled itself with a rich seam of inventive anti-Catholic propaganda, including the accusation that the case had been won by the duchess personally bribing the pope with her Vanderbilt millions. The facts were rather different: the seventeen-year-old Consuelo Vanderbilt had been forced by her mother into a marriage to which she was passionately opposed; as canon law stipulated that one of the impediments to marriage was 'lack of real consent', and as Mrs Vanderbilt herself testified that she had compelled her daughter with 'duress and fear', the Sacred Roman Rota, supreme tribunal for the Holy See, had little hesitation in granting an annulment. It was 'the lack of real consent' that struck both Evelyn and Hollis, the latter persuasively arguing that in his view and on those same grounds Evelyn would almost certainly be awarded a declaration of nullity.

The next step was for the case to be submitted to the ecclesiastical tribunal in the Diocese of Westminster, under the aegis of the archbishop, Cardinal Bourne, where it was scheduled to be heard in five sittings during October and November. The tribunal's report would then be sent to the Rota in Rome, which would make the final judgment, a process normally taking between six and nine months.

By church law the burden of proof falls on the petitioner, who must establish to the court's satisfaction the existence of one of the recognised impediments to holy matrimony, for instance, that one or both parties were under marriageable age, that there was a prohibited relationship, or, as Evelyn was to argue, a lack of real consent. Evelyn brought in to testify for him his brother, Alec, his ex-sister- and brother-in-law, Alathea and Geoffrey Fry, and Pansy Lamb. Waugh and She-Evelyn met for the first and only time since their civil divorce to discuss matters over lunch at a nearby restaurant immediately before the hearing. 'I shall be in London on Wed to take my poor wife to be wracked by the Inquisition,' Evelyn had written to Dorothy Lygon.

The court room, in a building adjoining Westminster Cathedral, was hung with scarlet, the black-robed members of the tribunal sitting on either side of a long table, with at its head the officialis, or principal judge, Monsignor William Heard. The crux of the argument for nullity rested on two specific grounds, first, that the couple entered marriage on the understanding that the union could be dissolved at the wish of either party, and second, that children were to be entirely excluded for an indefinite period ('*ad tempus indeterminatum*'). Regarding this second clause, Waugh stated that he and his wife had agreed not to have children to begin with, 'but that when financial considerations made it possible, the matter would be reopened and examined anew', evidence in essence repeated by Mrs Heygate, who told the court that, 'We agreed to exclude children until we judged that we were rich enough,' adding that she had been prepared to continue using contraception for as long as her husband wished it. But although accepted by the tribunal, this particular impediment was to be rejected by the Rota as it was not considered to meet the required standard of proof.

Next to be examined was the nature of the compact existing between the couple with regard to divorce; whether permanence had been specifically excluded from the marriage by 'a positive act of will'. Both Evelyns had described themselves as at the time nominal Anglicans, to whom the church wedding was no more than a conventional formality. Alec, himself a divorced man, said that in the milieu in which the couple lived marriage was regarded as a contract that could be dissolved in accordance with civil law. Pansy and Alathea had both assumed that the marriage was unlikely to last, given Evelyn Waugh's dissolute reputation and financial irresponsibility and Evelyn Gardner's previous record of broken engagements. 'When they were still engaged I had long discussions with my sister about what they would do if the marriage was not happy,' Alathea told the court. 'Such discussions provided the occasion for the couple to make explicit their intention to divorce should the marriage turn out badly, and to do so before witnesses ... My sister said explicitly that if her marriage was not happy, divorce would be the solution, and she would make use of it if the occasion arose.' Pansy said much the same. 'They came to an agreement in my presence that if the marriage was not happy, they would not be bound by it, and Miss Evelyn said to me that she had no intention of remaining married if the marriage did not turn out well.' This was important evidence with which both Evelyns separately concurred.

In spite of this clearly witnessed intention, the Westminster tribunal expressed serious reservations, reservations which were, however, dismissed by the Rota, whose Curia had no hesitation in awarding a declaration of nullity, concluding that 'It is established beyond doubt on the evidence that the parties excluded the indissolubility of the bond of marriage by a specific act of the will.'[6]

This was a welcome judgment, but a long time was to pass before it was delivered. Father D'Arcy was instrumental in preparing the petition for Rome, fully expecting to hear the result by the following Easter. But for nearly two years the papers lay forgotten and gathering dust in the archiepiscopal office in London, while Waugh grew ever more anxious and uneasy. Eventually he made contact with Bishop Myers, one of Cardinal Bourne's two auxiliary bishops, and over an expensive luncheon at the Ritz asked him if the papers had indeed been sent to Rome. Myers assured him that they had. More time passed, and still nothing was heard. Finally Evelyn requested a meeting with the notary of the diocesan tribunal, and asked him to confirm that the tribunal's report was with the Rota. The notary was shocked, for he knew very well that it was not, and found himself obliged to explain that Myers's information had been less than accurate. 'Bishop Myers had a very distinctive speech impediment,' the priest charitably observed, 'and it may well be that Waugh misunderstood him.' By this time, January 1935, old Cardinal Bourne had died and a new man, Archbishop Hinsley, appointed in his place. The notary made it his business to inform Hinsley of the dilatoriness of his predecessor's office. '*Post hoc* and possibly *propter hoc*, one of his [Hinsley's] first acts on arrival in Westminster was to accept Bishop Myers's resignation from the office of diocesan judge.' The papers were immediately sent off, the Rota duly condemning Westminster's 'reprehensible delays', but even so it was not until 4 July 1936, nearly three years after the original hearing, that the long-awaited annulment was finally granted.

Father D'Arcy, worried that such a disillusioning experience might have damaged Evelyn's faith, was relieved to receive a letter in which Waugh reassured him that 'no matter how "discreditable" the ecclesiastical authorities turned out to be, his faith was completely intact.'[7]

---

[6] For much of this material I am indebted to Donat Gallagher's masterly summarising of the hearing in his article 'Evelyn Waugh and Vatican Divorce' in *Evelyn Waugh: New Directions* edited by Alain Blayac (Macmillan, 1992).

[7] There exists an undated note to Maimie Lygon, almost certainly written when Evelyn was in Rome in December 1935, in which he appears to be making reference to a personal appearance before the Curia. 'So I am in the eternal city god it is cold & I have to wait to be cross examined by beasts re my wife . . .'

But in the autumn of 1933 the possibility of such a delay had not occurred. Indeed, so confident was Evelyn at the prospect of being freed at last from his miserable marriage that, he told Maimie, he took Teresa out to dinner and proposed to her. 'Just heard yesterday that my divorce comes on today so was elated and popped question to Dutch girl and got raspberry. So that is that, eh. Stiff upper lip and dropped cock. Now I must go. How sad, how sad.'

On the face of it, proposing to Teresa was an unlikely risk to take for someone as vulnerable to rejection as Evelyn. He must surely have understood that there was no chance of her accepting him. And yet there had always been something ambiguous in her behaviour, perhaps enough to give grounds for hope: she had after all allowed him to continue seeing her, often alone, and not long before had written to him of his being in love with her, 'I enjoy that situation too much not to encourage it as much as I can in a subconscious way,' and even more encouragingly, 'If you weren't married you see it would be different because I might or I might not want to marry you . . .'

In this difficult and depressing period, Evelyn derived much comfort from his friendship with Katharine Asquith. This austere, handsome and high-minded woman lived her life permanently in the shadow of her husband's death, her sadness profound and palpable. During her widowhood she had found consolation in Catholicism, turning to Rome largely through the influence of her old friend, Hilaire Belloc, and in the face of vigorous opposition from her family. This opposition came predominantly from her father-in-law, the ex-prime minister, H. H. Asquith (of whom it was said that his two lifelong aversions were to eating rabbit and the Roman Catholic Church), and from her mother, old Lady Horner, who, witty, vivacious, clever and sharp-tongued, had in her day been a leading member of the Souls. Since the sixteenth century the Horners had lived at Mells in Somerset, having bought the estate, originally part of the demesne of Glastonbury Abbey, at the time of the dissolution of the monasteries.

The Manor House at Mells is a grey-stone Elizabethan house of outstanding beauty, surrounded by an ancient and abundant garden within high ivy-clad walls; next to it stands the old church, a yew avenue leading through the graveyard into open fields. Mells is a tranquil, timeless place, the country round it lush and wooded, full of secret lanes, small farms and hidden waterways. In spite of the fact that Lady Horner had lost her only son in the Great War, and her husband, Sir John, a few years later, she nonetheless continued at Mells the tradition of large and lively house parties which since her girlhood had been the pattern of her life. As a member of the Souls and for twenty years the *inamorata* of the painter, Edward Burne-Jones, Frances Horner had accumulated a large circle of writers and artists, as well as a more political element attracted by the Asquiths, among her weekend regulars, Sir James Barrie, Maurice Baring, Lord Haldane, T. E. Lawrence, the Duff Coopers and Desmond MacCarthy. At Christmas and during the summer holidays, her daughter and grandchildren, then living in London, would come to stay, with the understanding that Katharine could invite only those friends whom her mother found amusing. These most emphatically did not include the Catholic contingent, not even such luminaries as Hilaire Belloc and Ronald Knox, although an exception was made in time for the witty and socially seductive Father D'Arcy.

It was little wonder that Katharine was apprehensive about introducing Evelyn into the household, although she wanted him to come, knowing how depressed he was. J. M. Barrie was staying that weekend, and Katharine, anxious that her mother should accept her difficult new friend, made Barrie promise to promote Evelyn to Lady Horner, at the same time instructing Evelyn to be especially nice to Barrie. Both men behaved impeccably, with Evelyn listening attentively to the famous writer's every word, treating his opinions with civility and respect. Katharine was pleased. 'Did you like him?' she asked Evelyn afterwards. 'Bored my pants off,' he replied. But the ruse had worked, and from then on Evelyn became a frequent visitor to Mells.

Katharine Asquith was someone before whom Evelyn always tried to appear at his best, slightly in awe of her aristocratic bearing, piety and air of religious melancholy. After staying at Mells, he sent her his last two books, writing rather nervously,

Remoters and *Blackers*. Well I don't know what the effect will be. I don't think there's much to bring a blush in *Remoters* & yet I don't know – is it justified teleologically? As for *Blackers* there are bits in that to make your hair stand on end worse than Garnett or Maugham. But what was I to do? There the books were and any minute you might come across them & the fat would be in the fire, cat out of bag etc. So it seemed best to take a risk & send them on and perhaps the result will be no more lovely week ends like the last.

But however hard he tried, Evelyn was never able, or indeed willing, to meet Katharine's high spiritual standards. He had shocked her during the cruise by his vindictive attitude to his wife, making a point of buying an English newspaper at every port of call, 'Just to see if Mrs Heygate is dead or any other good news.' And he shocked her further at Mells by announcing it was almost impossible for a bachelor to live chastely, and that he was not prepared to try; he asked her if she would mind if Trim slept with women, a question she found in the worst possible taste. However, Mrs Asquith, if judgmental, was a kind and perceptive woman, and understood very well the depths of unhappiness that lay behind this objectionable behaviour.

By the middle of November, Evelyn's travel book, *Ninety-Two Days*, was finished, and Chapman & Hall agreed to give him an advance of £100 so that he could go abroad to work on a novel. On 28 December 1933, after lunching with his parents at Highgate, he left for Morocco, probably at the suggestion of Norman Webb, co-proprietor of the Easton Court Hotel, who had lived and worked in that country.

Disembarked at Tangier, Evelyn went by train to the ancient walled city of Fez. To Katharine Asquith, he wrote an appropriately decorous description of

a city of astonishing beauty with running streams & fountains everywhere and enormous covered gateways in very narrow streets – no wheeled traffic, miles of bazaar, elaborate medieval fortifications, hills all round dotted with forts, olive trees, sand cliffs & spring grass, waterfalls. Dense crowds of moors and a few French soldiers – mostly Senegalese or Foreign Legion – practically no touting for tourists.

I haven't done anything about taking a house yet as its too cold. I live in a French pension just outside the walls where the officers come in to play a kind of billiards. Good cooking & tolerable local wine . . .

Some French Franciscans have made a chapel a kilometre away so I haven't got away from that . . .

Reading the life of Charles de Foucauld[8] – so thats edifying.

The Lygons were treated to a less expurgated version.

> It was very gay [in the red-light district] and there were little
> Arab girls of fifteen & sixteen for ten francs each & a cup of
> mint tea. So I bought one but I didn't enjoy her very much
> because she had a skin like sandpaper and a huge stomach
> which didn't show until she took off her clothes & then it was
> too late . . . There is also a brothel full of white ladies very
> cleverly named Maison Blanche but they cost 30 francs each so
> I haven't bought any of them.

And to the broad-minded Diana Cooper Evelyn wrote,

> I have formed an atttachment for a young lady named Fatima.
> She has a round brown face entirely covered by a network of
> blue tattooing – very becoming. She is very unlike the Dutch
> girl in all particulars. I see her a lot but as we neither speak a
> word of the other's language our association is rather limited. I
> am thinking of taking her out of the quartier réservé and setting
> her up for my exclusive use but the legalities are formidable . . .
> She is about 15 years old . . . Don't tell Mrs Asquith about
> Fatima.

As so often when abroad, Evelyn was listless and lonely. As he
spoke little French, his social life was limited to the occasional
meal with the British consul and silent evenings with Fatima, a
routine very much as that later described by the novelist, John
Plant, in *Work Suspended*, published in 1942.

> I used to work on the verandah of my room, overlooking a
> ravine where Senegalese infantrymen were constantly washing
> their linen. My recreations were few and simple. Once a week
> after dinner I took the bus to the Moulay Abdullah [the
> brothel]; once a week I dined at the Consulate. The consul
> allowed me to come to him for a bath. I used to walk up,
> under the walls, swinging my sponge-bag through the dusk. He,
> his wife and their governess were the only English people I
> met; the only people indeed, with whom I did more than
> exchange bare civilities. Sometimes I visited the native cinema

---

[8] Charles de Foucauld (1858–1916), 'the Hermit of the Sahara', was a French
soldier and explorer who became a Trappist monk.

where old, silent films were shown in a babel of catcalls. On other evenings I took a dose of dial and was asleep by half-past nine. In these circumstances the book progressed well.

After a month of this uneventful way of life, Evelyn took a week off work to visit Rabat, Marrakesh and Casablanca ('WOT¿ KARSA BLANKER¿ It is a large town on the Atlantic coast of Morocco, Tommy, WAS IT DESINT No Tommy it was bloody'). He was, however, pleased with his progress on the novel, telling Diana Cooper that, 'What I have done is <u>excellent</u>, I don't think it could be better. Very gruesome. Rather like Webster in modern idiom.'

As soon as Evelyn arrived back in England at the end of February, he went down to Chagford to finish the book. Anxious that it should generate as much income as possible, he had instructed Peters to try to sell the pre-publication serialisation rights. The American *Harper's Bazaar* agreed to take it, although the author did not yet know how the story would end. 'It may be much the same ending as that short story ['The Man Who Liked Dickens'] in *Nashs-Cosmopolitan* in which case they wouldn't want it presumably.' The presumption was correct, but the problem not insuperable. Having decided to use as the novel's final section the short story in which the hero is held prisoner in the jungle by the terrifying Mr Todd, Evelyn quickly wrote an alternative, and artistically much more complementary, ending for the magazine version.[9]

The book's original title, 'A Handful of Ashes', was changed first to 'Fourth Decade', which was rejected by the Americans, and finally to *A Handful of Dust*. All this involved Peters in a great deal of transatlantic correspondence on Evelyn's behalf. Relations between Waugh and Carl Brandt had now deteriorated beyond

[9] This version, in which Tony and Brenda are reconciled, appeared on its own as 'By Special Request' in the short story collection, *Mr Loveday's Little Outing* published by Chapman & Hall in 1936. It was John Farrar who suggested that the magazine serial should be called 'A Flat in London', which gave Evelyn the idea for the alternative ending to the novel. He wrote to thank Farrar, an unexpected politeness which led the publisher misguidedly to believe that this would inspire in his author some sense of obligation, a belief that Peters was obliged to dispel. 'I am aware that John Farrar suggested the title,' he wrote to Carol Hill. 'But he little understands this young man's mentality if he imagines that it will make any difference to his attitude towards him when it comes to the question of a new contract.'

saving – 'God how I hate Americans,' Evelyn exploded to Peters after Brandt had the temerity to press for delivery of the new ending. Brandt had readily agreed to release Waugh so that he could be taken on by Carol Hill, Peters's opposite number in New York, who, though delighted to add him to her list, was not unaware of the difficulties involved. Now they had to find a publisher. 'Evelyn is more interested in money than in publishers,' Peters warned Hill. '[It is] only fair to let Farrar & Rinehart bid when the time comes, but I do not want them to get him because I think it is a mistake to have Evelyn on the same list as Alec. I know that both Evelyn and Alec feel the same.' The agents' first choice was the firm of Alfred Knopf Inc., but the response from that direction was far from encouraging. 'No one here, on the strength of past work and sales, can get up the proper enthusiasm today for Evelyn Waugh,' came the reply from Blanche Knopf, Alfred Knopf's wife and partner. 'Interest has waned, he is yours to sell.' Soon Carol Hill was writing anxiously to London,

[Waugh's] sales record, which is shockingly bad for anyone so well known,[10] plus the rather uneven production he has given, has made a great many people say they weren't interested in him; that is not [un]interested simply in terms of making contracts and a proposition, but just not interested in him at all.

Of course I personally would rather see him with Little, Brown than anyone in the world. If you think you want to hold off and anticipate a better offer I will cope accordingly. Personally I don't feel it would be wise.

The reaction of Alfred McIntyre of Little, Brown was, if hardly ecstatic, the best that had been met with so far. Having read *A Handful of Dust*, he pronounced it 'quite good', and offered an advance of $1500, 'rather more than Evelyn Waugh has any right to expect as things are at present', Peters crisply remarked. By this time both John Farrar and Stanley Rinehart had also read the novel and were back-pedalling fast. Carol Hill wrote to Peters,

---

[10] By September 1934 Evelyn's American sales were as follows: *Decline and Fall* (Doubleday, Doran & Co.) 1473; *Vile Bodies* (Jonathan Cape & Harrison Smith) 9766; *Bachelor Abroad* (Jonathan Cape & Harrison Smith) 2399; *Black Mischief* (Farrar & Rinehart) 2753; *Remote People* (Farrar & Rinehart) 1171.

> [They] are not interested in continuing with Evelyn Waugh on
> any basis other than the terms of the existing contract . . .
> Stanley thinks this new Waugh book quite bad . . . though I did
> make them admit that they thought it was considerably better
> than *Black Mischief* . . . [this] confirms the reasons for my trying
> to get a good contract for Evelyn Waugh before he has another
> flop.

Alfred McIntyre, about to leave for Europe, civilly expressed the
hope of meeting the promising young writer while he was in
London, a prospect which gave rise to new anxieties for Peters
and Hill. 'Whether you think it is advisable for him [McIntyre]
to meet Evelyn Waugh in London is something you are in a better
position to judge than I', wrote Hill.

> I do know that Blanche Knopf was strongly influenced in terms
> of the personal element when she decided not to publish
> [him] . . . I know that Evelyn Waugh successfully offended both
> Stanley Rinehart and John Farrar and I do beyond that know that
> Alfred McIntyre is not the most flexible personality nor the most
> tolerant, so that unless you have Evelyn in his best bib and tucker
> with his company manners on perhaps it would gain nothing.

In the event Waugh and McIntyre did not meet, and Farrar &
Rinehart published *A Handful of Dust*, their lack of faith in its
author reflected in the lack of effort they put into the book's
promotion. 'Farrar and Rinehart are keeping the publication of
A Handful of Dust a secret from the general public. There is no
publicity or advertising,' Carol Hill told Peters.

Meanwhile, *Ninety-Two Days* had come out, to reviews that were
more respectful than enthusiastic. 'Though the book is far from
being dull – the digressions especially are often brilliant – it is as
nearly dull as anything Mr Waugh can write,' was the opinion of
Peter Fleming in the *Spectator*, one of the most appreciative of the
book's critics.[11] Evelyn already had his next project in mind, a
life of the sixth-century pope, Gregory the Great, responsible
through his missionary, St Augustine, for the Christian conversion
of England. In April he wrote to Maimie Lygon from Chagford,

[11] The previous year Evelyn had reviewed Fleming's book, *Brazilian Adventure*,
also in the *Spectator* (11 August 1933). After praising it highly and predicting
its wide success, he criticises Fleming for a facetious self-consciousness which,
he says, almost spoils the genuine excitement of his story.

I have finished the G[ood] T[aste] book god it is G. T. . . . I am
going to live in Oxford all the summer and write a life of
Gregory the Great.
WHO WAS GREGRY THE GRATE?
He was a famous Pope, Tommy.
POPE GOES THE WEEZIL?
No, be quiet and rub your cock like a good boy.

After an account of a day's hunting ('a very good run & did not
fall off'), he ends his letter with the news that, 'I am going to
stay with G. Herbert & P. Lamb on the way to London.'

With the Lambs at Coombe Bissett he had often stayed before,
but this was the first visit to the Herberts' house, Pixton, in
Somerset. In a letter to Maimie, he says only that he went stag-
hunting, that his horse ran away with him, and that Gabriel
Herbert was planning to go to Captain Hance for a course of
instruction. Of the composition of the party that weekend, however, Maimie learned little, only that all three 'tender Miss Herberts' were there, and that 'there are so many dogs in this house &
they all sit in chairs so that I have to stand all the time & that is
tiring.' Of the youngest Miss Herbert, Laura, the 'white mouse'
of Portofino, nothing was said.

Instead of Oxford, most of the next couple of months was spent
in London. At the beginning of July there was a heatwave. On
the fifth, having attended a tea party given by Gerald Berners,
where he saw Bridget Herbert and both Dianas (Cooper and
Guinness), Evelyn wandered over to the Lygons' town house,
Halkin House, off Belgrave Square, to see if any of the girls were
at home. To his surprise he found only Hughie, alone in the
library drinking gin. In two days' time, said Hugh, he was leaving
for Spitzbergen with a young man, Alexander ('Sandy') Glen,
who although still in his early twenties had twice been to the
Arctic while an undergraduate at Oxford. He knew the Lygons
and had stayed at Madresfield. On the spur of the moment,
Evelyn decided to join them.

He went back to the Savile to change for the evening. 'While
I was in my bath Sandy Glen rang up and came to see me. We
had some champagne while I dressed. He said it was all right my
going to Spitzbergen with him. I gave him £25 for fares and he
gave me a list of things I should need.' The subsequent evening's

entertainment exemplified exactly what it was that made Evelyn jump at such an opportunity for escape. There was a dull dinner party in town, after which everyone went on to a party of David Tennant's in the country. 'The drive took an hour. Someone had removed the signposts David had put up to show the way. It was a very bad party. I met Colin Davidson who said it was a bad party so we left together. I got to bed soon after 3.' This was typical of the aimless social life into which Evelyn so easily drifted when bored and depressed, his conduct much the same as during the miserable, drink-sodden, post-Oxford period when he was living at Underhill. Now as then, he drank to drown his dejection (he was seen at this period 'disgracefully gibberingly drunk' at a dance at Wilton), and now as then his late hours and dissipated behaviour were an unfailing source of annoyance to his father. '[Evelyn] did not come back till we were abed, left all doors open, & lights on ... Woken at 1.45 by Evelyn's return ... Woke at 2.30, to find Evelyn not back. Lay awake till 5. He did not return till 6.30 ... Evelyn stayed in bed till noon ... Just before 4 Evelyn arrived in cheerless mood ... A very edgy afternoon.'

But now there was the journey to the Arctic and only twenty-four hours in which to prepare. The next day he and Hugh bought skis, ice axes and balaclava helmets at Lillywhite's, wind-proof clothes and sleeping bags at a shop in Holborn. Evelyn spent the night with a tart called Winnie employed at Mrs Meyrick's club, the 43, half speakeasy, half brothel (and the model of the Old Hundreth in *A Handful of Dust*). The diary entry for the day of departure, 7 July, begins, 'To Farm Street to confess Winnie. A few more purchases including a birthday cake for Teresa.'

The three men went by train to Newcastle, where they embarked, arriving in Bergen the following day. Here they boarded another ship, on which for three days they steamed slowly north,

> threading between islands and up fjords and stopping three and
> four times a day at little, wood-built villages ... The scenery
> becomes more Arthurian as we get further north ... We read
> Edgar Wallace, look at maps and play cards ... Our chief
> interest is in the growth of our beards, Hughie's is golden and
> even. Mine appears to be black and patchy, with the making of
> fine Dundreary whiskers, but too little on the chin. Sandy shaves.

On Friday the thirteenth they reached Tromsö, a small sealing and whaling port on an island off the northern coast of Norway. It was a bleak little place with few diversions, so Evelyn and Hughie bought a bottle of spirits and sat in Hughie's bedroom playing piquet in their shirtsleeves, while Sandy Glen tracked down his various contacts. In the early afternoon of 14 July, they set sail on the last part of their journey. 'The leader had warned us that this was to be the most disagreeable part of the expedition, but like most of his predictions – notably that Tromsö was a cosmopolitan resort full of bars and hotels – this proved wholly inaccurate.' It is clear from the tone of Evelyn's diary that he had already taken against Glen, 'the leader' as he pointedly refers to him. The trouble almost certainly stemmed from the fact that Evelyn did not care for taking orders from a man nearly ten years younger than himself, whom he quickly saw to be less efficient and experienced than he had believed, and who persisted in remaining cheerful and optimistic in the face of every danger and setback; it is probable too that, intensely possessive over his friendship with Hugh Lygon, Evelyn was jealous of Hughie's easy amiability with Glen. To underline Glen's alien status, Evelyn made a point when the three of them were together of talking to Hugh of people and places of which Glen could know nothing. But the fact that the young man thoroughly enjoyed such conversations, roaring with laughter at jokes only half understood, in the end undermined Evelyn's resistance.

The voyage from Tromsö to Spitzbergen took three days. At first it was hot, sunlight streaming into the cabin almost all night, making sleep impossible; but the next day it turned cold, there was a heavy swell and everyone was seasick. Evelyn took a treble dose of Dial and slept for thirteen hours. At about seven in the evening of the following day they came in sight of the south cape of Spitzbergen. 'Black mountains with glaciers flowing down to the sea between them – occasionally a magnificent burst of light on a narrow silver strip between iron grey sky and iron grey sea, the glaciers brilliantly white, the clouds cutting off the peaks of the mountains.' Arriving in Advent Bay early in the morning, they could see no sign of life on shore, only a crooked little street with low timber buildings. Eventually a small whaling boat came to take them within reach of their camp, four derelict huts at the foot of a glacier, stocked with some meagre stores left behind by last year's Oxford University Expedition. Having unloaded their gear, they returned to the whaler to say their goodbyes, Glen presenting the crew with one of their few precious bottles of rum, a gift which both Hughie and Evelyn passionately resented.

The whaler chugged off, leaving the three men alone on the desolate shore, the shingle covered partly by moss, partly by snow. They had a tent, a boat, a sledge and provisions for about six weeks. The plan was to make a way up the glacier and sledge across the inland ice to some unexplored territory in the northeast. In preparation for this, a day and a half was spent repacking stores and waxing skis. Late the second evening they rowed across the bay into another, smaller bay where there was another derelict hut. The glacier they intended to climb was three miles distant, across a mosquito-infested valley of mud and sharp stones, and all stores had to be carried on their backs. 'We made two journeys a day, taking between thirty and forty pounds in a load. It was beastly work.' Both Sandy and Hugh, who had trained as a heavy-weight boxer, were reasonably fit and took this in their stride, but Evelyn was overweight and in poor shape physically and, although he did not complain, suffered badly from exhaustion and strain. Once on the ice, it should have been easier, but owing to an exceptional thaw, pulling the sledge over soft, wet snow was extremely arduous.

For a week they plodded monotonously on, walking ten hours at a time and covering on average five miles a day. Their clothes were soon soaked in sweat and snow, and could not be dried; much of the time they were shrouded in a thick white mist. Fortunately, their provisions were plentiful, and they had two primus stoves on which to heat their food, twice a day cooking up nasty but nourishing messes of oatmeal and pemmican, which were made slightly more palatable by the brandy, whisky and cigars which Evelyn and Hughie had insisted on including. To provide variety in their menu, Sandy Glen shot a seal, which they roasted over a wood fire. Excited by his success, Glen prepared to shoot another but was stopped by Evelyn, who lectured him at length on the sacredness of life, animal as well as human.

In spite of the physical privations, conditions could have been worse: it was never very cold, and when the sun came out the country was spectacularly beautiful, covered in saxifrage and wild poppies, with nests of duck, tern and geese every few feet; at night there was the huge, light Arctic sky and never a breath of wind.

The glacier when they got to it proved to be too heavily crevassed to ascend, so Glen suggested they make for a trapper's cabin remembered from a previous expedition. The going, through thick fog, was hard, and they were forced to abandon the sledge, carrying everything again on their backs. Once the cabin had been reached, Hugh and Glen set off almost at once to retrieve the sledge, leaving Evelyn to put the filthy cabin in order. Here he was woken from a deep sleep by Glen in a state of great agitation: one of the little streams easily forded on their way had in the space of a few hours turned into a torrent. Hugh being tall had succeeded in wading across, but Glen had not. Now he had come back to fetch Evelyn as Hugh, who had gone on to find the sledge, would need help to bring it back.

For at least half an hour before they reached the stream, Evelyn and Glen could hear the roar of the flood. 'The flow was terrific ... running at a dizzy speed, full of boulders and blocks of ice whirling down in it.' Evelyn and Glen roped themselves together with a length of tarred twine, and managed to get near where Hugh was standing laden with the pack off the sledge. Throwing him the string on a ski-stick, they started to drag him across, but no sooner had Glen reached the bank in safety when the twine snapped, and Hugh and Evelyn were swept down into the powerful current. 'I had time to form the clear impression that we were both done for,' Evelyn recalled. Fortunately, soon afterwards, 'I found myself rolling in shallow water and was able to crawl ashore. Hugh was stuck on a small iceberg in midstream. There did not seem to be any way of helping him. We shouted to him throw away his pack. But he got to his feet and came across, fully loaded.' Although it ended safely, it had been a frightening experience. Evelyn had panicked and for a few seconds genuinely believed he was going to die, which accounted for the fact that he was 'remarkably angry' with 'the leader' afterwards, accusing him of irresponsibility and gross ineptitude.

Somehow they got back to the cabin, where with no rations remaining, they were faced with a difficult decision: they could again attempt the river; they could wait for the trapper to whom the cabin belonged, due in about a month; or by taking a much longer route, climbing up into the mountains and above the river, they could try to get back to the original base where they had left stores and their boat. Glen was in favour of waiting, Hugh, detached and fatalistic, was indifferent, while Evelyn, desperate to get away, was for the overland route. It was Evelyn who prevailed, although the undertaking, a trek of some seventy miles without map, tent, climbing rope, ice axes or crampons, and with only half a bowl of pemmican each a day, was, as he later put it, 'the first time I despaired of my life'.

In fact, they did the journey in three days, although it was not without incident. At one moment on top of a col with a storm threatening, they were obliged to take shelter, huddling uncomfortably under an overhanging rock. Hughie had somehow nestled peacefully into a little niche, leaving Sandy Glen and Evelyn to stand pressed together and bolt upright on a narrow ledge. Evelyn, still in a rage with Glen, and even angrier at their present predicament, spat at him, 'This is typical of your folly. If I hadn't joined the Church of Rome, I could never have survived your appalling incompetence!'

Evelyn and Hughie returned home disgruntled with the entire experience, agreed that Glen had proved 'a dull dog', and the adventure not worth the immense effort involved. To Blondie and Poll they claimed they had had mountains named after them, although none such ever appeared on any map. Evelyn told Tom Driberg that Spitzbergen had been 'hell – a fiasco very narrowly retrieved from disaster'; and except for a short essay entitled 'Fiasco in the Arctic',[12] he made no literary use of his polar experience, even abandoning his diary halfway through as though in disgust. However, there was little time to brood, for on the third of September was published Evelyn's new novel, *A Handful of Dust*.

[12] Published by Chapman & Hall in 1935 in an anthology edited by Theodora Benson, *The First Time I* . . .

X

I have to wait wait wait
god it is sad

It was during his two months in Morocco at the beginning of 1934 that Evelyn wrote the major part of *A Handful of Dust*. From the start he realised that this was different from anything he had attempted before, more serious and more mature than the semi-surreal black comedies that had preceded it. 'I peg away at the novel which seems to me faultless of its kind,' he told Katharine Asquith, significantly adding, 'Very difficult to write because for the first time I am trying to deal with normal people instead of eccentrics.' 'The Man Who Liked Dickens', the short story about the captive in the jungle, had remained fermenting in his mind. 'I wanted to discover how the prisoner got there, and eventually the thing grew into a study of other sorts of savage at home and the civilized man's helpless plight among them.' The civilised man is Tony Last; chief among the savages are his wife, Brenda, and her cold, caddish lover, John Beaver,[1] who between them drive Tony to destruction. As so often, the relationship between anger and the precision of high comedy is a close one. The fury underlying the narrative is rooted in Waugh's rage at the annihilation of his own happiness by Evelyn Gardner. Brenda Last's heartless betrayal of her husband is on the surface light

---

[1] In the course of a conversation during the 1950s, Waugh said that technically his most difficult achievement was to turn a woman into a man, in other words to create a male character based on a female original, as he had done with John Beaver. (Richard Acton in the *Spectator*, 19 September 1992.) Anthony Powell, on the other hand, remembers Waugh telling him that Beaver shared a number of characteristics with both Hamish Erskine and Murrough O'Brien, a friend of the Lygons often referred to in Evelyn's letters as 'Sponger'.

years away from the facts of Waugh's own experience, and yet it is all there, the chilling nature of the tale clearly signalled in the title, taken from 'The Waste Land': 'And I will show you something different from either/Your shadow at morning striding behind you/Or your shadow at evening rising to meet you;/I will show you fear in a handful of dust.'

At first sight, Brenda, unfaithful wife and feckless mother, is wholly to blame, while her husband, devoted, tolerant and kind, is the innocent victim. In Tony's eyes, his existence is perfect. He is in love with his wife, by whom he has a son; although not rich, he is completely content with his peaceful life as a country squire; and he is passionately attached to his family home, Hetton. 'Not a worry in the world.' Tony is the last to find out about Brenda's affair, and even when confronted with the truth is for a long while unable to break 'the habit of loving and trusting Brenda'. Brenda acts with utter ruthlessness. She wants Beaver, and in spite of the fact that she knows he is a sponger, morally degenerate, incapable of love, a bore, a snob and has no feeling for her at all, she is determined to have him, and gives not a thought to the hurt and humiliation she causes in the process. Yet although it is Brenda's behaviour that is damnable, it is her blameless husband who is punished: she makes a contented second marriage, while Tony ends his days in the jungle as a prisoner of the diabolic Mr Todd. Such was Evelyn's pessimistic perception of the workings of Fate.

However, although Brenda is the chief target, Tony is not wholly undeserving of his punishment. A true gentleman, chivalrous and good, he is nonetheless naïve, incurious and immature, another in that line of passive heroes, like Paul Pennyfeather and Adam Fenwick-Symes, to whom Fate is always so cruel. The reader is forewarned at the beginning by the words of Jock Grant-Menzies, Tony's friend, 'I often think Tony Last's one of the happiest men I know. He's got just enough money, loves the place, one son he's crazy about, devoted wife, not a worry in the world,' words uneasily reminiscent of the ending of *Labels*: 'Fortune is the least capricious of deities, and arranges things on the just and rigid system that no one shall be very happy for very long.' The clues to Tony's personal fallibility lie in the shallowness of his nature, in his lack of religion (a serious flaw in Waugh's judgment, if not necessarily in that of the reader), and in the fantasy nature of his domestic environment. Tony, apart and protected from the real world, has grown complacent. He attends church every Sunday, but more as a matter of convention than of faith, and when, after his son is killed in a hunting accident, the vicar calls, Tony is embarrassed by his proffered consolation. 'After all the last thing one wants to talk about at a time like this is religion.' This sentiment is addressed to the mysterious Mrs Rattery, herself a manifestation of Fortune, arriving literally out of the skies, a *dea ex machina* in her little aeroplane, come to impose temporary order on Tony's 'all-encompassing chaos'.

The fantasy environment is Hetton Abbey. Hetton is essentially a fake; like Madresfield, it was redesigned as part of the mid-Victorian Gothic revival. The execution of its 'medieval' theme is ugly, dark and cumbersome, the great hall swathed in ecclesiastical gloom, 'half-lit by day through lancet windows of armorial stained glass, at night by a vast gasolier of brass and wrought iron, wired now and fitted with twenty electric bulbs'; the cold, uncomfortable bedrooms are named after characters in the *Morte d'Arthur.* Tony's bedroom is Galahad, Brenda's Guinevere. To Tony the abbey is a haven he never wishes to leave, a fairyland of primal innocence and beauty. When he realises that to meet the terms demanded by Brenda in the divorce, he will have to sell Hetton, Tony is stunned. 'He hung up the receiver and went back to the smoking-room . . . A whole Gothic world had come to grief . . . there was now no armour glittering through the forest glades, no embroidered feet on the green sward; the cream and dappled unicorns had fled.'

Brenda, on the other hand, hates Hetton and is bored by the life there. 'Me? I *detest* it . . . at least I don't mean that really, but I do wish sometimes that it wasn't all, every bit of it, so appallingly ugly.' One of her first acts of barbarism is to commission that fashionable fixer, Mrs Beaver, to 'do over' the morning-room. 'My poor Brenda, it's an appalling room,' says Mrs Beaver, looking with revulsion at the plasterwork and the dado and the pink granite chimneypiece. 'Supposing we covered the walls with white chromium plating and had natural sheepskin carpet . . .' For three guineas a week she provides Brenda with a snappy little bachelor flat in town, designed and decorated precisely for the kind of adulterous affair which Brenda is conducting with John Beaver. When at the end of the book Tony sets off with Dr

Messinger to find a fabled lost city in the Brazilian jungle, the vision of it he conjures up in his mind is of 'a transfigured Hetton ... all vanes and pinnacles, gargoyles, battlements, groining and tracery, pavilions and terraces ... pennons and banners floating on the sweet breeze, everything luminous and translucent'. But when, as a prisoner for life in the hands of Mr Todd, Tony in his delirium sees the destruction of his earthly paradise, he sees it in terms of the destruction wrought by the Beaver-barbarians. 'I will tell you what I have learned in the forest, where time is different. There is no City. Mrs Beaver has covered it with chromium plating and converted it into flats. Three guineas a week, each with a separate bathroom. Very suitable for base love.'

Interestingly, in the alternative, and far more congruent, ending to *A Handful of Dust* commissioned by the American *Harper's Bazaar*, the balance is completely reversed. Tony leaves England not for the jungle but on a luxury cruise, returning wiser, tougher and more cynical, to find Brenda humbly hoping to be taken back. It is Tony who discreetly retains the bachelor flat.

'You know,' said Tony, 'I've been thinking. It's rather a useful thing to have – a flat of that kind.'

'It is *necessary*,' said Mrs Beaver.

'Exactly. Well I think I shall keep it on. The only trouble is that my wife is inclined to fret a little about the rent. My idea is to use it when I come to London instead of my club. It will be cheaper and a great deal more convenient. But my wife may not see it in that light ... in fact ...'

'I *quite* understand.'

'I think it would be better if my name didn't appear on that board downstairs.'

'Naturally. A number of my tenants are taking the same precaution.'

'So that's all right.'

'That's quite satisfactory. I daresay you will want some little piece of extra furniture – a writing-table, for instance.'

'Yes, I suppose I had better.'

'I'll send one round. I think I know just what will suit you.'

The table was delivered a week later. It cost eighteen pounds; on the same day there was a new name painted on the board below.

In this version Waugh in a sense parts company with himself. The Tony Last of *A Handful of Dust* is a man with whom Waugh identifies, recognising that men such as he and Last, when betrayed by their wives, are doomed to end up dying among savages. The Tony Last of the short story is the personification of the man Waugh would like to be, the betrayed husband who can shrug off his betrayal, remain invulnerable to his wife, and take a flat in Mayfair in which to conduct his affairs.

There are other parallels between the Tony Last of the novel and his author. Tony's yearning for his lost golden age echoes Evelyn's for his, just as Tony's despair at Brenda's shocking infidelity evokes Evelyn's despair, when he too was sunk in an 'all-encompassing chaos that shrieked about his ears', when he, like Tony, went through that agonising period, 'rehearsing over and over in his mind all that had happened ... searching for clues he had missed at the time; wondering where something he had said or done might have changed the course of events'. 'The scenes of domestic playfulness [that] had been more or less continuous in Tony and Brenda's life for seven years' at Hetton recall the nursery element in the domestic life at Canonbury Square; and there are a number of personal characteristics that Brenda shares with She-Evelyn. Brenda had the same 'very fair, under-water look', the same pretty ways: 'She leant forward to him (a nereid emerging from fathomless depths of clear water). She turned her lips away and rubbed against his cheek like a cat. It was a way she had.' Like She-Evelyn in hospital in Port Said, Brenda hated her husband's reading aloud. '[Tony] had always rather enjoyed reading aloud and in the first year of marriage had shared several books in this way with Brenda, until one day, in a moment of frankness, she remarked that it was torture to her.'

Brenda is allowed no saving grace.[2] The most chilling moment of revelation is in the famous scene when she is told her son has been killed out riding, and her split second of relief when she

[2] In 'The Man Who Liked Dickens', Evelyn originally made Brenda much more sexually promiscuous, as the following passage shows, the words in italics deleted from the finished version: '[Tony] lay in the hammock staring up at the thatched roof and thinking about Brenda, *rehearsing over and over again different incidents in their life together, most often the affair with the tennis professional and the latest scenes about the soldier* ...'

realises that it is John Andrew who is dead, not, as for an instant she had believed, her lover, John Beaver.

'What is it, Jock? Tell me quickly, I'm scared. It's nothing awful, is it?'

'I'm afraid it is. There's been a very serious accident.'

'John?'

'Yes.'

'Dead?'

He nodded.

She sat down on a hard little Empire chair against the wall, perfectly still with her hands folded in her lap, like a small well-brought-up child introduced into a room full of grown-ups. She said, 'Tell me what happened. Why do you know about it first?'

'I've been down at Hetton since the week-end.'

'Hetton?'

'Don't you remember? John was going hunting to-day.'

She frowned, not at once taking in what he was saying. 'John . . . John Andrew . . . I . . . oh, thank God . . .' Then she burst into tears.

For a man who always made such a point of disliking children, Evelyn's portrait of John Andrew is exceptional not only for its veracity but for the affection with which it is drawn. The little boy is given one of the funniest scenes in the book.

'Where's mummy gone?'

'London.'

'Why?'

'Someone called Lady Cockpurse is giving a party.'

'Is she nice?'

'Mummy thinks so. I don't.'

'Why?'

'Because she looks like a monkey.'

'I should love to see her. Does she live in a cage? Has she got a tail? . . .'

They were having tea together on the afternoon of Brenda's departure. 'Daddy, what does Lady Cockpurse eat?'

'Oh, nuts and things.'

'Nuts and what things?'

'Different kinds of nuts.'

For days to come the image of this hairy, mischievous Countess occupied John Andrew's mind. She became one of the inhabitants of his world, like Peppermint, the mule who died of rum. When kindly people spoke to him in the village he would tell them about her and how she swung head down from a tree throwing nutshells at passers-by.

'You mustn't say things like that about real people,' said nanny. 'Whatever would Lady Cockpurse do if she heard about it?'

'She'd gibber and chatter and lash round with her tail, and then I expect she'd catch some nice, big, juicy fleas and forget all about it.'

Evelyn knew that *A Handful of Dust*, if not the masterpiece it is now judged to be, was on a level of achievement very much higher than any he had previously attained. However, although the book was an immediate success with the public – a Book Society choice for Book of the Month, running into five impressions before the end of the fourth week – its reception by the critics was no more than mildly appreciative. Several declared themselves exasperated by Tony Last's passivity ('Tony is so incapable of helping himself that he is not worth helping,' was the opinion of an irritated reviewer in the *TLS*), while the consensus was that Waugh's latest work was admirable in its way, certainly showed a new maturity, but was not as funny as his previous efforts. William Plomer in the *Spectator* epitomised this tepid reaction when he wrote, 'There is no waste, no whimsy and no padding; the book holds the attention throughout and is of exactly the right length.'

Among the many letters of praise from friends and admirers, including Rebecca West, Lord Beaverbrook, Diana Cooper, David Cecil, Desmond MacCarthy, Maurice Baring, Hilaire Belloc and John Sparrow, there were one or two querulous voices. J. B. Priestley in his bluff Yorkshire way informed Waugh that 'All the people in the book are altogether too light weight. It did not matter to me what happened to Tony and Brenda and Mrs Beaver,' while Katharine Asquith, applying a doctrinaire Catholic gloss to her reading of the text, wrote, 'O Evelyn the book! – it's brilliant in its way but it made me so miserable – you know how I admire the way you write – though I quarrel dreadfully with your subject matter. Oremus pro invicem.' The most incisive criticism came as usual from Henry Yorke, who instantly identified the one great flaw.

The book was entirely spoilt for me by the end – the end is so
fantastic that it throws the rest out of proportion. Aren't you
mixing two things together? The first part of the book is
convincing, a real picture of people one has met and may at
any moment meet again. Then comes the perfectly feasible, very
moving, & beautifully written death of that horrible little boy
after which the family breaks up. Then the father goes abroad
with that very well drawn horror Messinger. That too is
splendid & I've no complaints. But then to let Tony be detained
by some madman introduces an entirely fresh note & we are in
phantasy with a ph at once. I was terrified towards the end by
thinking you would let him die of fever which to my mind
would have been false but what you did do to him was far far
worse. It seemed manufactured & not real.

Evelyn replied calmly.

Very many thanks for your letter of criticism. You must
remember that to me the savages come into the category of
'people one has met and may at any moment meet again'. I
think they appear fake to you largely because you don't really
believe they exist ... I think I agree that the Todd episode is
fantastic. It is a 'conceit' in the Webster manner – wishing to
bring Tony to a sad end I made it an elaborate & improbable
one ... The scheme was a Gothic man in the hands of savages –
first Mrs Beaver etc. then the real ones, finally the silver foxes
at Hetton. All that quest for a city seems to me justifiable
symbolism.

The elegaic theme of the lost city which so haunted Tony Last
remained to haunt Evelyn, reaching its most poignant material-
isation in the Epilogue to *Brideshead Revisited*, when Charles Ryder,
looking back at the desecrated house, sadly recalls the opening
words of *Lamentations*, 'Quomodo sedet solas civitas ...' ('How
doth the city sit solitary ...')

On the whole Evelyn was pleased with the novel's reception. The
good-taste book was a success: 'wherever I go the people shout
Long Live Bo & throw garlands of flowers in my path,' he told
Maimie, adding, 'I am going to spend a very studious autumn
writing the life of a dead beast,' a reference to a projected biography of Edmund Campion, the sixteenth-century Jesuit martyr.
Evelyn felt it important that he should now make his presence

felt as a reputable member of the Catholic community, and along the route to respectability Campion was an ideal means of transport. The book was commissioned by the Catholic publisher, Sheed & Ward, in association with Longmans, royalties to be made over in perpetuity to Campion Hall in Oxford: the lease of the premises in St Giles' was about to run out, and a fund had been set up under the aegis of the master, Father D'Arcy, to raise money for a new Hall to be built in St Aldate's. 'I am doing a little book with Sheed & Ward,' Evelyn wrote to Roughead. 'The proceeds of both author & publisher are going to a Catholic charity so don't think I am making bootleg or black leg contracts behind your back.'

Evelyn went several times to stay with the Brownlows at Belton, the Abdys at Newton Ferrers, and to Chagford in order to work on Campion and also to finish a couple of stories. 'Mr Cruttwell's Little Outing'[3] and 'On Guard' were described to Dorothy Lygon as 'a funny short story about a looney bin and a very dull one about a dog who bit a lady's nose'. The first, about a murderous psychopath, was originally intended for Joyce Reynolds at *Harper's Bazaar*; of the second he wrote to Peters, 'It is not very good & the question whether it goes to the *Strand* or *Nash's* seems to resolve itself into the one: does the editor of the *Strand* know a bad story when he reads it. I should say not to judge by what he prints.' But then Miss Reynolds decided that 'Cruttwell' had too sinister a theme – 'I personally like it,' she wrote to Peters, 'but I don't know about my ridiculous readers' – and turned it down. For once Evelyn was prepared to be tolerant: 'If it was anyone else I'd tell her to go to hell, but she is an old customer and has proved herself a girl of honour on more than one occasion,' so she was allowed to have the despised dog story, while 'Cruttwell' went to *Nash's*. At the same time as these negotiations were in progress, Evelyn was asked by the BBC to write a short dramatic dialogue, an assignment he was prepared to accept, he told his agent, for a minimum fee of £30. The Corporation's final offer of fifteen guineas was curtly rejected in a postcard to Roughead, 'B.B.C. L.S.D. N.B.G'.

As well, Evelyn continued regularly to review books, the tedious

---

[3] When this story was published by Chapman & Hall in a collection in 1936, it was retitled, 'Mr Loveday's Little Outing'.

but necessary hack-work of many a writer's career. Cyril Connolly once remarked that Evelyn was well-read without being literary, and Evelyn confessed that he early lost his taste for reading purely for pleasure. Unlike Connolly and his friends, he did not care for literary discussion, and approached most of his reading in a spirit of professional enquiry. He was interested in the work of his contemporaries in the sense that a craftsman is interested in the work of others in his field, and much of it he admired, especially the novels of Henry Green, Graham Greene, Ivy Compton-Burnett and Anthony Powell. He admitted to having been technically influenced by Forster and Firbank, and also by Hemingway, in particular Hemingway's experimental use of language in *The Sun Also Rises*, and 'the way he made drunk people talk'. Above all he paid homage to P. G. Wodehouse, whom he read throughout his life with unfailing enjoyment. 'One has to regard a man as a Master who can produce on average three uniquely brilliant and entirely original similes to every page.' Evelyn despised Aldous Huxley and D. H. Lawrence, was on the whole unimpressed by Virginia Woolf, and believed that James Joyce, although initially interesting, had gone 'dotty' halfway through *Ulysses*.

This studiedly workmanlike attitude evolved partly in reaction to Arthur's exaggerated reverence for English literature. Although Evelyn shared some of his father's tastes, for instance a failure to appreciate most modern poetry ('I simply don't understand anything later than Tennyson'), he rejected many of Arthur's favourite authors. He was bored by Galsworthy, highly critical of Hardy, and came to loathe Dickens, supreme in the pantheon for Arthur, who had edited the Nonesuch Edition and often read extracts from the novels in the after-dinner one-man show performed in the bookroom at Underhill. Only for one brief period did Evelyn rediscover his love of Dickens, and this was during his two recuperative sojourns with Father Mather in Brazil. 'I had not for ten years read a book for the mere pleasure of the process,' he recalls. 'At Father Mather's I began to read with this motive, and by good chance the books he had were just those which were meant to be read in that way, and when I left him I took away a copy of *Nicholas Nickleby* and read it with avid relish during the ensuing journey, bit by bit while the light lasted, grudging the night every hour of her splendour and the day its toil, which kept me from this new and exciting hobby.' But once back home, this liking for Dickens never returned, and *Dombey and Son*, one of the titles devoured so avidly at the mission, was later dismissed as 'the worst book in the world'.

In order to start serious work on *Campion* in the new year of 1935, Evelyn took rooms in a cottage belonging to the estate at Mells, an ideal arrangement in that he could join in the social life of the manor without actually being part of the household. Mells he loved as much as ever, in spite of one or two objectionable local characters, chief among them Conrad Russell, a neighbour loved by the Asquiths and Horners and, even worse, adored by Diana Cooper. Russell was a gentleman farmer on a modest scale, a soft-spoken man, charming, kind, widely read and immensely entertaining. Tall and handsome with a fresh complexion and thick white hair, he specialised in romantic attachments to beautiful women, among them Diana Cooper and Daphne Weymouth, attachments of a sentimental, flirtatious but entirely platonic nature.

Evelyn was jealous of Russell's privileged position, and found unbearably affected his self-consciously rustic rôle, retired from the world, happy among his cows, peaceably cultivating his garden. Russell for his part did not care very much for Waugh – 'I'm afraid not quite a gentleman, not quite, not quite,' he was heard damningly to say behind his back – and was far from pleased to find him so often in residence. Adopting Diana's babyish nickname for Evelyn, he complained to her that every time he went to the manor now, there was Mr Wu, 'always always Mr Wu... I know the moment is approaching when Katharine will ask me if I am now fonder of Mr Wu – and to be honest I don't think I am.' Russell took the trouble to pass on to Diana some uncomplimentary remarks Evelyn had made about the discomforts of staying at Bognor, and gloatingly revealed, having finally opened *Decline and Fall*, that '[it] doesn't amuse me much and after reading 100 pages with difficulty I've laid it aside ... now I know why poor Mr Wu himself appears to enjoy such very low spirits. It must be a sad task to write like that.'

It was at the end of December 1934, immediately before going to Mells, that Evelyn went to stay for a second time with the Herberts at Pixton. Beautifully placed in its park on a wooded hillside above the village of Dulverton in Somerset, Pixton is a handsome Georgian house, spacious and comfortable, solidly built rather than architecturally distinguished. The high-ceilinged rooms are well proportioned, the furniture was good, but the Herberts were unaware of appearances and indifferent to physical comfort. Like an Anglo-Irish house, Pixton was hospitable and chaotic. Generations of dogs and the comings and goings of energetic young people had produced a homely shabbiness. There were cigarette burns on the veneer, and broken springs and stuffing could be seen protruding out of chairs and sofas, which much of the day were occupied by the resident canine pack, for whose benefit, whatever the weather, the tall windows were left open at the bottom so that they could jump in and out as they chose, barking furiously at every disturbance. Everyone smoked a lot, drank a lot, and talked incessantly. There was always a lot of business to be arranged over the care and transporting of horses.[4] As is not unusual among converts, there was an intense interest in Catholic affairs; an old laundry a little way from the house had been turned into a private chapel, and there was nearly always a priest in residence, often Father D'Arcy or Father Ronald Knox; Hilaire Belloc, who at one time had acted as unofficial tutor to Aubrey Herbert, was a frequent visitor. As head of the household, Mary Herbert, looking like the Monarch of the Glen, ruled her domain with absolute authority. In the evenings before dinner she stood in front of the fire with her glass of gin and her cigarette, pushing back her tangled hair and demanding, 'What? What?' when, as often, she could not quite hear what was being said. (She was nicknamed 'Mrs What-What' by her children's friends.)

When Evelyn arrived, he found a large, young and rumbustious

---

[4] An example of which is faithfully reproduced in *Scoop*. 'For over an hour the details of Priscilla's hunt occupied the dining-room. Could she send her horse overnight to a farm near the meet; could she leave the Caldicotes at dawn, pick up her horse at Boot Magna, and ride on; could she borrow Major Watkins's trailer and take her horse to the Caldicotes for the night, then as far as Major Watkins's in the morning and ride on from there; if she got the family car from Aunt Agnes and Major Watkins's trailer, would Lady Caldicote lend her a car to take it to Major Watkins's; would Aunt Anne allow the car to stay the night; would she discover it was taken without her permission?'

house party in progress, with hockey and hunting during the day, noisy games of charades in the evening. Everyone seemed tireless, he complained, and made him feel very middle-aged. Previously his particular friend in the family had been Gabriel, but now his attention was caught by her younger sister, Laura. 'I have taken a *great* fancy to a young lady named Laura,' he told Maimie.

> What is she like? Well fair, very pretty, plays peggoty beautifully. We met on a house party in Somerset.[5] She has rather a long thin nose and skin as thin as bromo as she is very thin and might be dying of consumption to look at her and she has her hair in a little bun at the back of her neck but it is not very tidy and she is only 18 years old, virgin, Catholic, quiet & astute. So it is difficult. I have not made much progress yet except to pinch her twice in a charade and lean against her thigh in pretending to help her at peggoty.

Although Laura was only eighteen, Evelyn was quick to recognise in her the qualities he most desired in a wife. She was kind, quiet, stable, innocent and true. She was also pretty, well-born and devout, with a subtle sense of humour and an admirable dislike of London and sophisticated society. Although in manner still rather childlike, Laura had a stronger character than might at first appear. Youngest of the three sisters, she was very different from both Gabriel and Bridget. They were tall, energetic young women, outgoing and impatient, talking loudly, shouting with laughter, striding about the house calling to their dogs and throwing themselves on to the broken-springed sofas. Superb horsewomen, they went out several times a week during the hunting season, fearlessly galloping up and down the steep valleys and jumping the terrifying stone walls of Exmoor. Laura, on the other hand, was physically far from robust, a bout of rheumatic fever in childhood having left her delicate. Although she hated riding, she loved animals, like all the Herberts, but while her sisters went in for big, muddy labradors and setters, Laura's dog was a whippet called Imp. 'Imp-Imp-Imp', she would be heard calling, clacking over the uncarpeted floors in her impractical high heels. She was not a beauty like Bridget – her long nose had been broken by an accident with a cricket bat when she was small – but her fragile

---

[5] Laura's presence during Evelyn's stay at Portofino the previous summer had obviously made little impression.

features, pale skin and huge dark eyes gave her an ethereal, fairytale look.

Thin and frail though she was, and seemingly overshadowed by the forcefulness of her mother and sisters, Laura was no cipher. When in company she contributed little, being extremely shy as well as socially lazy, but nonetheless she had a mind of her own and firm opinions about the people she met. She could be surprisingly judgmental, and to some observers there was a quiet arrogance about her, often a slight curl to her lip. As one of her schoolfriends observed, '[Laura had] a very definite personality with a quirky way of criticising people'; another remarked that she was 'pretty unforthcoming, but a very strong character'. In her own eyes her worst fault was a violent temper, so violent that when in its grip she would take to her bed for the day as the attempt to control it made her physically ill. As a result of this drastic form of self-discipline, Laura became adept at suppressing her emotions. As one of her daughters was later to say, 'Mummy had a very strong character, but very suppressed. Everything was very suppressed with mummy.' But she also possessed a great appetite for enjoyment, and loved being made to laugh; safe within the family circle she could be very funny, with a talent for mimicry. 'Behind the veil of good manners, she mocked everybody and everything.' She had, too, all the Herbert self-confidence and family pride, indeed felt little need to make friends or pursue interests outside the family pale. There was, said Gabriel of her at this time, 'a quality of self-containedness and irony . . . [as one who] steered a determined course of non-involvement'.

Laura's father had died when she was only seven. An intrepid and romantic adventurer (the model for Sandy Arbuthnot in John Buchan's *Greenmantle*), Aubrey Herbert, second son of the 4th Earl of Carnarvon, had spent much of his life abroad. He had an heroic war, acting as go-between with the Turks at Gallipoli, and as a member of the Arab Bureau conspiring with T. E. Lawrence in the Near East. He had a ready command of French, Italian, German, Turkish, Arabic and Greek, had travelled widely throughout the bandit-infested Ottoman Empire, and was twice offered the throne of Albania. At home he pursued a career in Parliament, first as the Conservative member for South Somerset, later representing Yeovil as an Independent. Devoted to his wife, he was not otherwise much interested in human relationships, preferring causes to people. Of the children, Gabriel was his favourite. For her part, Mary Herbert never made any secret of the fact that her husband came first, her son and daughters very much second. The beautiful only child of Lord and Lady de Vesci, Mary Vesey had been worshipped by her mother, who had been widowed young, and adored and flattered by her mother's friends, a form of homage which she received with indifference, being wholly without personal vanity and too secure in her self-assessment to need reassurance from outside. Widowed in her early thirties, Mary Herbert took on the running of an estate once extending over 5000 acres but now much depleted by a disastrous combination in Aubrey of impassioned commitment to impractical causes and a complete lack of business sense.

Soon after her husband's death, Mary Herbert converted to Rome, in the face of furious opposition from her mother-in-law, whose contempt for the Catholic Church was bottomless. Old Lady Carnarvon used to refer to 'the bloody robe of Mary', and her hostility affected Laura, who for several years resisted all persuasion, refusing to follow her mother's example until she was well into her teens.

The daily lives of the Herbert children, like those of the servants, were briskly and efficiently administered by their mother. In accordance with the custom of their class and generation, the three sisters were initially brought up by nannies and governesses, their relations with their parents affectionate but formal. Although Laura's governess was generally disliked, the children loved their nanny, who when she retired continued living at Pixton, playing patience in her little room upstairs, like Nanny Hawkins in *Brideshead*. Later the girls were sent to school in London, while their brother, Auberon, attended a small Catholic prep school in the Black Country run by a son-in-law of Mr Belloc's, and then Ampleforth. Holidays were spent at Pixton or in the summer at Portofino, interspersed with occasional visits to London when the family stayed at Lady de Vesci's old town house at 28 Bruton Street.

In 1927 Gabriel, the eldest, was taken away from school to keep her widowed mother company at home, and Laura sent in her place to join Bridget as a weekly boarder at Albemarle House on the edge of Wimbledon Common. This was a welcome change as Laura was never entirely happy at Pixton. The only unmusical member of a musical family, the only one who cared nothing for hunting, she often felt left out by the others. She longed for the friendship of her older sister, Bridget, but Bridget's close alliance was with Gabriel, leaving Laura to the inadequate companionship of her little brother, to whom as a result she was consistently unpleasant.

Albemarle was a small establishment with rarely more than twenty pupils, run by Miss Margaret Parratt, daughter of Sir Walter Parratt, organist of St George's Chapel, Windsor. As a result of the headmistress's background, there was a strong emphasis on music; Bridget was taught cello, Gabriel had violin and singing lessons. There was also a strong drama department in both French and English: the teacher of French drama was head of the French department at the Royal Academy of Dramatic Art (RADA), Ellen Terry attended end-of-term performances, and Mrs Patrick Campbell directed a production of Aristophanes' *The Frogs*, in which Laura distinguished herself in the rôle of Euripides. For such a reserved personality Laura was surprisingly forthcoming on stage. Amateur dramatics had been very much a part of her childhood, both at Pixton and with the Asquith children at Mells, she and Trim having given memorable performances in Maurice Baring's *Diminutive Dramas* with Trim as Henry VIII, Laura as Catherine Parr. At Albemarle Laura's closest friends were Chloe Buxton[6] and Mary Herbert's niece, Bridget Vesey. At weekends Laura and Bridget Vesey went to Englefield Green, near Windsor, to stay with Laura's grandmother. On Sunday mornings the two girls were escorted to Mass by Lady de Vesci's parlourmaid.

In 1932, Laura left Albemarle for the Convent of the Holy Child at Neuilly to be 'finished', an experience she at first enjoyed, especially as her sister Bridget was also in Paris continuing with her cello lessons. 'I am not sure yet about all the girls,' she wrote to Chloe Buxton in a childishly misspelt letter soon after her arrival, 'but all the nuns are charming, especially the reverent [sic] Mother.' There were visits to the Louvre and the Comédie Française, lessons in German ('very difficult') and cookery ('not so amusing as I had hoped'), and occasionally

---

[6] A member of the well-known Norfolk family, Chloe Buxton was to marry Michael, son of Desmond MacCarthy, whose daughter, Rachel (later married to David Cecil), was also at Albemarle with Chloe and Laura.

the girls were allowed to attend dances ('I have put on too much lipstick & I know the reverent mother will be shocked'). By Easter the following year, Laura was more than ready to leave. She had not yet made her début, and looked forward to her first season with apprehension. 'You must be nice to me when I come out,' she wrote to Chloe in January 1933, 'and introduce [me] to lots of people ... I really do wish I could come out this year as everyone I know is coming out this year and next year there will be a very frightening and beautiful lot coming out, namely Liz Paget and Isabel Manners and several others.'

Meanwhile some occupation had to be found. Laura dreaded returning to Pixton, and begged to be allowed to live in London. Her mother refused to countenance her taking a job, but for some reason was perfectly agreeable to her training as an actress, an ambition of Laura's more to do with staying away from home than with a serious love of the stage. She was enrolled in a course at RADA, where, as her end-of-term reports made clear, her talent was unremarkable. 'Holds herself badly and is inclined to force her voice ... A keen student – but without any subtlety of characterisation. She also lacks grace. Lacks control & makes difficulties for herself through being over-anxious.'

It was at this stage in Laura's life, when she was eighteen, he thirty-one, that Evelyn fell in love with her. He began to pay court, writing to her and seeing her whenever he could in London, where he returned between stints working on his book at various country houses. From Belton he wrote, 'Darling Laura, Its discouraging that we never meet. I begin to despair of ever seeing you again ... I'm pegging away at Campion. Hope to arrest him this afternoon and rack him before I leave. Then I will hang, draw & quarter him at Mells.'

It was not an easy courtship. Laura was shy, and fiercely guarded by her dominating mother, who was far from pleased that this, in her view, vulgar, slightly common person, who had been such a nuisance to her husband's half-sister, Lady Burghclere, should now be in pursuit of one of her daughters. 'I thought we had heard the last of that young man,' remarked Laura's aunt, Lady Victoria Herbert, who as aunt also to Evelyn Gardner had been through this before. Evelyn knew he had to tread carefully. 'I am sad and bored and need your company,' he wrote to Laura. 'If you have a spare evening between now and when you leave London, please come out with me. Any time will suit me as I have no engagements that I cannot gladly break.

'Ask your mother first and tell her I wanted you to ask... Please come. I will behave respectfully, I promise.'

Laura, for her part, was at first uneasy at being the focus of such passionate attention from a man considerably older than herself and quite unlike anyone she had met before. Until now the young men who had found her attractive were of her world – Trim Asquith, Terence O'Neill, Henry Howard and William Douglas-Home. It was not until Mary Herbert put her foot down and forbad her daughter to continue the unsuitable friendship with Evelyn Waugh that Laura's interest was properly aroused. She enjoyed conducting a forbidden correspondence and the meetings in secret, and by the time her mother began to relent she found herself falling in love.

By early summer 1935 Evelyn had finished *Edmund Campion*, which was published in September. The story of the gentle, brave and scholarly priest martyred for his faith is told with a romanticism far removed from Evelyn's customary stance of ironic detachment. It is a passionately partisan book, in which the Catholic Church is the source of all good, Protestantism the source of all evil.[7] In his preface to the second edition, Waugh states that the book is not a work of scholarship, but the work of a novelist attempting to present a complex sequence of events as a single unified narrative. More than this, the book is a polemic for the Church, in a sense Evelyn's personal affirmation of his new-found faith. The arguments that he found most moving at the time of his conversion are all present in his story of Campion. The Roman Church in England at the time of the Reformation he describes as 'something historically and continuously English, seeking to recover only what had been taken from it by theft', while Cam-

---

[7] In a letter to Canon F. E. Hutchinson written in 1936 after the book's publication, Waugh gives a characteristic explanation for the reasons for his severe judgment of the Church of England. 'I daresay I am at fault in giving too grim a picture of the Anglicans. There must have been sincere men among them. Obviously in Mary's reign and later, under Laud, there were hundreds. But I do think that at Campion's particular epoch the English church, at the top, was run almost exclusively by arrivists. That's the impression I formed though it's hard to substantiate in detail ... Campion didn't seem to come across the good Anglicans – I believe because they were left out of influential positions.'

pion's mission is stated as the desire to disseminate the simple truth 'which lies at the root of all Catholic apologetics, that the Faith is absolutely satisfactory to the mind, enlisting all knowledge and all reason in its cause; that it is completely compelling to any who give it an "indifferent and quiet audience".' The image which is repeated again and again throughout Evelyn's writing about religion is repeated here, that of the Catholic Church as the triumph of clarity and light over obscurity, as a lone beacon illuminating a benighted world, '[a] pure light shining in darkness, uncomprehended'.

Predictably, the most favourable reviews came from the Catholic press – and from the *Spectator*, whose critic was Graham Greene. Elsewhere, although there was a certain amount of objection, some of it vehement, to the author's anti-Protestant bias, reception was generally favourable, with the influential Desmond MacCarthy praising it in a broadcast talk, and Peter Quennell in the *New Statesman* describing the author's prose style as 'dry, witty, well-modulated [and] exceedingly effective'.

A few weeks before *Campion*'s publication, Evelyn spent a couple of days at Pixton, during which his happiness was soured by the absence of any news from Rome about his annulment. After he left, Laura wrote to him, 'You can't know how happy I was & how much I loved having you here this weekend – I don't think I've ever loved anything so much.' She then retailed a couple of unremarkable events – visiting Nanny, buying a meatsafe – before concluding, 'All my love to you darling I do love you so very much more than I can say – I do hope Abyssinia's fun & not dangerous.'

This last was a reference to a proposition of Evelyn's to return to Abyssinia, this time as a war correspondent reporting on the imminent invasion of that country by Mussolini. As a result of the international situation, anyone with even the most meagre knowledge of the region was in demand by a press desperate for informed opinion. Men like Evelyn, who had not only been to the place but could also write, were at a premium, and he was not slow to take advantage of his position, seeing in it both an opportunity to make money and an excuse to escape from the problems of his private life, to which there could be no resolution until he heard one way or the other from the Curia.

Although Evelyn was never seriously interested in politics, there were aspects of the current crisis which specifically appealed to him. To begin with, there was the satisfaction of holding a minority view. The pose of right-wing Conservative assumed with such deliberate provocation at Oxford was no longer a pose. While most of the British nation sided passionately with the Abyssinians, believed sincerely in the League of Nations, and were appalled by Mussolini and his fascist régime, Evelyn perceived the situation differently: he saw the Abyssinians as cruel and lawless savages; by conquering them Italy would provide this wretched people with a hope of salvation and the world with a supreme example of the triumph of order over barbarity. He had nothing but contempt for the League and its dithering efforts to impose sanctions on Rome, and no time at all for the popular view of Haile Selassie as the pathetic but noble victim of a bullying aggressor. In an article in the *Evening Standard*, Evelyn argued the case. Abyssinia was a primitive country, Italy highly civilised.

> It is in the nature of civilization that it must be in constant conflict
> with barbarism . . . Now Abyssinia is still a barbarous country . . .
> [By this] I mean that it is capriciously and violently governed and
> that its own governmental machinery is not sufficient to cope
> with its own lawless elements. It is entertaining to find a country
> where the noblemen feast on raw beef, but less amusing when
> they enslave and castrate the villagers of neighbouring countries.

To 'sentimentalists' who ask 'what right have Europeans to interfere?' the answer was straightforward:

> throughout the greater part of the country the Abyssinians are
> just as much foreigners as the Italians . . . The Emperor
> Menelik succeeded to a small hill kingdom and made himself
> master of a vast population differing absolutely from himself
> and his own people in race, religion and history. It was taken
> bloodily and is held, so far as it is held at all, by force of arms.
> In the matter of abstract justice, the Italians have as much right
> to govern; in the matter of practical politics, it is certain that
> their government would be for the benefit of the Ethiopian
> Empire and for the rest of Africa.

An added attraction, although not mentioned in the article, was the alluring prospect of a new Roman empire. Like Hilaire Belloc, Evelyn tended to the belief that no country could be called civilised that had not been conquered by Rome. For Catholics in particular, Mussolini was the great bulwark against Hitler, the only effective barrier to the threatened Nazi annexation of Catholic Austria. To oppose the duce's imperialist plans for Abyssinia would not only involve a backward and impoverished country in an unwinnable war, but would almost certainly drive the Italian leader into an alliance with Berlin.

Evelyn did not expect to encounter much difficulty in finding employment, but he was particularly fortunate in the terms that Peters managed to secure, by luck offering his client's services to the *Daily Mail* at precisely the moment when that newspaper had lost its most prestigious foreign correspondent, Sir Percival Phillips, who after a quarrel with the proprietor, Lord Rother-mere, had resigned and gone over to the *Telegraph*. The *Mail* needed someone immediately available and with a well-known by-line; someone, moreover, who could be relied upon to support their pro-Mussolini stance.[8] Peters made an approach to the paper, the ubiquitous Diana Cooper had a word with Lord Rother-mere (just as Mrs Stitch, her alter ego in *Scoop*, had a word with Lord Copper on behalf of John Boot), and the thing was done. Towards the beginning of August Evelyn told Diana, 'So it is all OK about Abyssinia and unless those mischiefous [sic] peace makers bugger it up I sail on 12th. God it is decent. The *D. Mail* is the one so it is all your doing.' Not only was Evelyn to receive a handsome salary with generous expense account, but he also signed a contract with Longman's for the enormous sum of £950, as Tom Burns, alert to the sudden craze for all things Abyssinian, was anxious for an important book about the war which would be sure to give the Catholic perspective.

Evelyn was looking forward to the adventure, if not to leaving Laura. By now he was deeply committed, and yet his situation was a wretched one. Still there was no word of an annulment, and no question of being able to possess Laura without one. As Evelyn wrote drunkenly to Maimie after missing a train one day, 'so I have to wait wait wait god it is sad'. Laura herself was very young and very much under the control of her mother. Mary Herbert did not like Evelyn, and he knew it. But now he found himself in the unusual position of having to make himself accept-

---

[8] The only two other newspapers who were pro-Italian were the *Observer* and the *Morning Post*.

able to an enemy whom in other circumstances he would have taken pleasure in antagonising. His letters to Laura often end with a self-conscious attempt to ingratiate himself with her mother. 'It is odd I don't say more about love to your mother and Gabriel etc that is to be taken for granted. It is very sincere love so please tell them.' He was shrewdly aware, too, that his involvement in the war and his Catholic viewpoint could only work to his advantage, perhaps reminding the Herberts of the kind of crusading in a foreign field that had been such a speciality of Aubrey's. Evelyn wrote with satisfaction to Diana Cooper that it was all 'Sir Garnet' with Laura's family 'on account of this lucky war', adding that he was sure to get a successful book out of it which would result in 'great prestige', with the successful author ending up the 'hero of Pixton'. Just before departure, he wrote to Laura, 'Darling darling Laura please dont find that you are just as happy without me. I am not nearly as happy without you bless you my darling love child.'

Evelyn set off for Abyssinia on the fifth of August. 'At 9.30 Evelyn left on his adventure, having been very kind to us to the last,' Arthur wrote in his journal. 'Felt sad & apprehensive, to see him go.' Evelyn had called at the flat in Highgate accompanied, his father noted, by a girl who did not come in but remained outside waiting in the car.

It is possible that the girl was Joyce Gill. As Joyce Fagan, she had known Evelyn when he was an undergraduate (it was Joyce whom Alec had smuggled into an Oxford party dressed as a boy), and since then the two of them had maintained a casual but flirtatious friendship. When Joyce married, to an American businessman called Donald Gill, it was her flat in Canonbury Square into which the two Evelyns had moved. Joyce was lively, attractive, intelligent and fun. Half Irish and a couple of years older, she could hardly have been more different from Evelyn in taste and temperament: very musical, a committed socialist, an agnostic briskly dismissive of religion, she was unconventional even by the standards of the bohemian world in which she moved. Where he was self-conscious and controlled, Joyce was impulsive and given to histrionics. Although she always had the greatest admiration for his work, there was a side of Evelyn that in her view was ridiculously strait-laced and conventional. When before her marriage he used to visit her in Canonbury, she would tease him for his dapper appearance – 'a natty young man', she called him – and after his Catholic conversion made no secret of her contempt for what she saw as sentimental self-indulgence.

Joyce's father had been vicar of Newlyn in Cornwall, an irascible and eccentric character who ran off to New Zealand with one of his parishioners, leaving his wife to bring up four children on her own. The family moved to Birmingham where Joyce won a place at the university, leaving after a year to join a music-hall troupe known as 'Dancin' Time'. For eighteen months she toured the provinces, before giving up her stage career to come to London, where she got a job as secretary to the playwright Clifford Bax. Joyce's friends were nearly all writers and artists; the novelist Douglas Goldring was one of her lovers ('that toad Goldring'), and through her friendship with Goldring and another writer, Lewis Wilkinson,[9] she was introduced to Bloomsbury, the Powyses, to Edmund Gosse and Arthur Waugh. Through Arthur she met Alec, and through Alec, Evelyn.

Whatever happened between Evelyn and Joyce must have come to a head during the summer of 1935, for shortly before his departure for Abyssinia Evelyn asked Joyce to leave her husband and go with him. The probability is that although deeply in love with Laura, Evelyn was overwhelmed by the depressing likelihood that he would never be able to marry her. On the point of going abroad for an indefinite period, in a state of heightened emotional and physical responsiveness, the temptation of an affair with Joyce was irresistible. He knew her well and was fond of her, she was an experienced, emancipated woman and, unlike Baby Jungman and Olivia Plunket Greene, Joyce possessed the added recommendation of finding him physically attractive. It was, she later told one of her daughters-in-law, the most painful decision of her life: the affair was a passionate one, the prospect of adventure extremely tempting; but she loved her husband, by whom she now had two little boys, and so decided against running off with Waugh.

Although for Evelyn the proposition was inspired less by love than loneliness, for Joyce it was a more serious matter. Two and a half years later, at the end of February 1938, when Evelyn was

[9] Lewis Wilkinson wrote under the pseudonym, Lewis Barlow.

married to Laura, and shortly expecting their first child, Joyce wrote him a letter which casts a revealing light on what had passed between them.

It is too difficult not to write to you now, Evelyn, because things have not been going well, because – it's nearly March 13th which was the day you jokingly suggested that we might meet – each year until I am 70. And so I suppose that day will be for me a kind of lovely agony for ever and ever . . . I have arranged my life now, as I think best, to give the least trouble to you or to Don [Gill]. When you were married I found that to drive the children back to their Prep-school I had to pass very near to you. So, to be out of temptation, I arranged to have them living at home. It is better so, anyway . . . In compensation, I do what you suggested & what – in my foolishness, I thought almost a crime. I think of you all the time when I am making love, until the word and Evelyn are almost synonomous! And in the darkness each night & in the greyness of each morning when I wake I remember your face – & your voice and your body and everything about you so earnestly and intensely that you become almost tangibly beside me. And after that I can forget you for the day (except when I am alone). It is a kind of exercise, which, together with being tied hand & foot by the family, keeps me from behaving like the pitiable sort of fool I was 2 years ago. At least I hope it will keep me from it. It is only for the next few years. After I am 40 I won't want to see you . . . Then even the impossible possibility of having your child will be gone. And I suppose that is at the roof of this – this – I can't call it infatuation – because I know that that is an unworthy word for it; because I know, darling, that love is a juster description. And every night I tell myself that your wife now has your child in her body and I think of it and of you always, so that when I do hear or read about it I shall not be unprepared. I tried to do the same thing about your marriage, but darling, it was the dearest kindest thing of you to write about it, and it is because you are like that – because you are Evelyn, that I shall try most terribly hard to conform to the normal convention of 'decency' (Christ! what a phrase), and not bombard you with love letters. And if I do ever write, darling, it is not a 'begging letter', only because I remember that once you said 'write to me if it helps'. I know that was before you were married again . . . Almost I could be contented if every night I could write & say 'Evelyn, I love you,' & every morning I could say

'Evelyn. God bless you – ' But what nonsense! of course I could not be content. I have only to remember your eyes – your mouth and my heart aches as if it were a stone cut by a diamond . . .

Clearly the affair with Joyce Gill was intense. But she was not the only woman Evelyn pursued during that unhappy period when he was left in limbo by the archbishop's office in Westminster. Unlike Alec, Evelyn was never a womaniser, probably less highly sexed than either his brother or father. But during the 1930s, with a broken marriage behind him, still a young man, fond of female company and susceptible, he embarked, or attempted to embark on a number of casual entanglements. There was an affair with a married woman, Clare Mackenzie, whom he took to Chagford, and according to a heartbroken letter from Mrs Mackenzie, there walked out on her.

Was it absolutely necessary to leave me when I needed you so desperately badly? . . . One kind word last night would, I believe, have saved me cracking so badly . . . My hand is so shaky this morning I can hardly hold the pencil steady. But the doctor's given me some soothing medicine which may help. And God do I need it after your note this morning. I shan't stay here long now; what's the use, I should only be miserable without you . . . Please ignore a telegram in very bad taste if it reaches you – I hope it doesn't. I'm afraid I felt so ill I lost all sense of proportion & broke the rules.

Meticulously applying a somewhat convoluted Catholic perspective, Evelyn was scrupulous in selecting for his attentions women who would not be damaged by them, women outside the pale of the Roman Church, women who were morally unencumbered and sexually experienced. According to Alec, Evelyn during this period drew back from an affair with a young actress who was much taken with him because he was afraid of endangering her soul. The danger to his own immortal soul of deliberately indulging in such occasions of sin he was apparently prepared to risk.

Eileen Agar, the surrealist painter, was one of the emancipated women considered fair game. She had caught his eye at Alec's wedding to Joan Chirnside, although Evelyn already knew her and her Hungarian lover (later husband) Joseph Bard, had visited them in the South of France and at their little flat in Half Moon Street. At Alec's wedding, no doubt well fortified by champagne,

Evelyn behaved, said Eileen, 'like a malignant demon with a red hot poker', announcing in a loud voice to all and sundry that the beautiful Miss Agar was to be his next target. Later, staying with Alec and Joan at Oswalds, their house in Kent, Evelyn made a determined attempt to seduce Eileen, teasing her, charming her, pleading with her, eventually trying to push her into some bushes while out on a walk. The more resolutely she refused, the more insistent he became, finally after everyone had retired for the night loudly arguing with her through her bedroom door. Next morning at breakfast, resentful at his rejection, he made himself unpleasant in a manner ingeniously designed to be felt by an artist of the surreal. '[Evelyn] asked me if I had made my mark yet as a painter. With those kidney-shaped eyes you should have, he said, stabbing a kidney in two . . . For Evelyn, it seemed to be all or nothing, and he refused to be friends though we did bump into each other from time to time.'

He was no more successful with another strong-minded and unconventional young woman, Penelope Chetwode, although in her case his failed attempts at seduction did nothing to detract from a friendship that was to last a lifetime. Like Joyce Gill and Eileen Agar, Penelope Chetwode was intelligent, outspoken and eccentric. She was also a devout Anglican. Evelyn had met her for the first time at Pakenham, where she had been taken by her fiancé, John Betjeman. Penelope was horse-mad, and Evelyn, fresh from the hands of Captain Hance, had gone riding with her. To Evelyn her naïvety, her athletic good looks and forthright demeanour were immensely attractive, and in spite of vigorous discouragement on her part, he continued to lay siege to her both before and after she married. Although in middle age he claimed that he had enjoyed 'carnal relations' with Penelope Betjeman, this was probably a tease. 'I remember being very shocked as he was a practising Roman Catholic,' Penelope later recalled. 'He never attracted me in the very least.' And one of her closest confidantes, Lady Mary Pakenham, said of Penelope's attitude to sex that,

> [it] was rather like that of a child who has just heard how babies are born and thinks it screamingly funny. She egged people on to tell her about kinky sex and roared with laughter over sex habits of natives, erotic Indian sculptures & so on. When Evelyn

made a pass at her she was very surprised, rather flattered,
shocked and amused, made a funny story out of it & rushed
to tell me. She was not attracted to him and never talked about
him at all self-consciously . . . I can't prove it but I am fairly
certain she did not sleep with him whatever he said.

As in his letters to the Lygon sisters, Evelyn when writing to
Penelope indulged in a kind of sexy schoolboy smut, usually with
him an indication of a non-physical relationship. But Penelope
was both more prudish and less sophisticated than Blondy and
Poll, and she did not care for it.

Evelyn left England on the now familiar journey by Golden Arrow
via Paris to Marseilles, where he joined his ship. He wrote to
Laura,

> The *Daily Mail* have given me a type writer and told me I mwust
> learn to use it so I thought it bestbt to practuce on you. It is
> really quite easy if tou go slow and know how to spell . . .
>   This is a very decent ship but the people very dull all French
> colonials except for another journalist going to Abyssinia,
> called Emeny you will think I have spelled that wrong but no it
> is his name. He is a married man and does not want much to
> be killed and has a gas mask and a helmet and a medicine chest
> twice the size of all my luggage and I have told him so often
> that he is going to certain death that I have begun to believe it
> myself . . .'[10]

At Port Said, another Englishman came aboard, Francis Rickett,
who aroused the suspicions of both Waugh and Emeny by receiving long, coded telegrams, apparently from his huntsman at home
(' "He says the prospects for cubbin' are excellent" '). His
unlikely explanation for his mission to Abyssinia was that he was
carrying funds for the Red Cross donated by the Coptic Church.
Scenting scandal, Evelyn wrote to Penelope Betjeman, who lived
near Rickett in Berkshire, asking her to find out all she could
about their mysterious fellow passenger: 'I want particularly to
know how he earns his living, whether he is in the British secret
service and whether he is connected with Vickers or Imperial

[10] Stuart Emeny was employed by the *News Chronicle*, like most of the British
press a paper fervently opposed to Italian intervention.

Chemicals. Don't on any account mention my name in your enquiry. Be a good girl about this and I will reward you with a fine fuck when I get back.'

Evelyn was right to believe that the man was not what he seemed, and the eventual uncovering of Rickett's secretly obtaining from Haile Selassie massive and exclusive concessions for an American oil company was to turn into one of the biggest scoops of the war. Unfortunately, Evelyn's amateurish methods of investigation proved unproductive, and the story was carried in triumph on 30 August by Emeny in the *Chronicle*, by Associated Press, and worst of all as far as the *Mail* was concerned, by Sir Percival Phillips in the *Daily Telegraph*. 'Badly left oil concession suggest you return Addis immediately,' was the angry telegram which reached Evelyn, contentedly engaged at the time on a leisurely expedition up-country.

As the ship steamed on through the stifling heat of the Red Sea towards Djibouti, Evelyn's arrival in Addis Ababa was awaited with a certain apprehension by at least one of his compatriots. Patrick Balfour, representing the *Evening Standard*, was pleased at having the company of a friend who at least, as he put it, spoke the same language, although anxious at the nature of that friend's reception. 'Evelyn comes next week,' Patrick informed his mother, Lady Kinross. 'I rather dread his arrival as his name is mud here since *Black Mischief* & half the European population is out for his blood. This will make it unpleasant for him & awkward for me.' As indeed it proved. On arrival in Addis, Evelyn wrote to Laura, 'I am universally regarded as an Italian spy. In fact my name is mud all round – with the Legation because of a novel I wrote which they think was about them (it wasn't), with the Ethiopians because of the *Mail*'s policy, with the other journalists because I'm not really a journalist and it is black leg labour.' The allegation of being an Italian spy had its foundation in Evelyn's quarrel with the British legation. Sir Sidney Barton and his family had been deeply offended by what they took to be a cruel caricature of themselves as the Courtenays in *Black Mischief*. Esme Barton, believing herself to have been used as the model for the promiscuous Prudence, had been particularly outraged, so much so that when she ran into Evelyn one night at the Perroquet, one of the town's three nightclubs, she threw her glass of champagne in his face. The novelist was declared *persona non grata* at the legation, thus cutting him off from one of the main official sources of information, and encouraging him towards a friendly acquaintance with the charming Italian minister, Count Vinci, who was delighted to extend hospitality and feed stories to a British journalist with such an unusually sympathetic understanding of his country's position.

Evelyn joined Patrick Balfour in a comfortable pension, the Deutsches Haus, run by the Hefts, a pleasant German couple well known in Addis for their good food and efficient service. On either side of the Deutsches Haus was a row of native brothels, in front a pretty fenced garden full of lilies and sweet-peas, fiercely guarded by a couple of bad-tempered geese which attacked painfully and without prejudice the ankles of anyone coming up the path. Since Evelyn's first visit five years before Addis had changed very little. There were the same well-stocked general stores, the same French hairdresser, the cinema clubs, the stationer's where you could buy the European papers once a week, the pastrycook's at which the expatriate community congregated for cakes and coffee in the mornings. On one of the three hills stood the cathedral, on another the emperor's old palace, on the third his new palace, a grey concrete office block with an interior designed by Waring & Gillow.

But whereas in 1930 the town had been full of foreigners come for the coronation, now it was full of foreigners waiting for the start of the war; instead of diplomats and minor royalty the hotels were crammed with journalists, photographers, newsreel cameramen, munitions dealers, concession hunters and freelance adventurers of every type and nationality. Before, the climate had been temperate; now, it was the middle of the rainy season: the town was enveloped in a thick Scotch mist, and for three or four hours a day heavy rain drummed down on the corrugated-iron roofs and filled the gutters with a viscous yellow mud. For the first forty-eight hours Evelyn took to his bed with an attack of dysentery and depression, but the daily cables from London insistently demanding copy soon forced him into action.

The members of the press corps and their ingenious methods of supplying their various newspapers with stories soon attracted Evelyn's inquisitive attention. Among the English-speaking cadre there was a clearly established hierarchy; at the top were such as Sir Percival Phillips of the *Telegraph* and the two American stars of Hearst International, Carl von Weigand and H. R. Knicker-bocker; at the bottom were the representatives of the popular press, 'men with strong cockney tastes, an interest in curios and not much knowledge of the world'. Evelyn was almost unique among them in having been to the country before, and he lost no opportunity in mocking the others' inexperience, their terrors (particularly of tropical disease) and their ludicrously elaborate luggage. (The young man from the *Morning Post*, William Deedes, had arrived equipped with camp-bed, sleeping-bag, two uniform cases, a box of emergency supplies lined with zinc to keep out ants, a medicine chest and a trunk, as well as a large suitcase containing among much else riding boots, winter and summer riding breeches, and three tropical outfits specially made at Austin Reed. These Deedes never wore as Addis, 8000 feet above sea level, was cold and damp, and he was obliged to spend his entire time in the tweed suit in which he had left London.) With cables costing 2s 6d a word, Fleet Street understandably discouraged impressionistic pieces about local landscape and native customs. ('Colour', Corker explains to William Boot in *Scoop*, 'is just a lot of bull's-eyes about nothing. It's easy to write and easy to read, but it costs too much in cabling, so we have to go slow on that. See?') Hard news, however, was scarce. Until war was declared, there was little to report, what news there was having to be garnered from official statements sporadically issued by the Abyssinian press bureau, and from the evening radio bulletins from London and Rome.

The general atmosphere among the journalists was one of profound distrust. Every few days there was an acrimonious meeting of the Foreign Press Association in the Hotel Splendide, in theory to protest against the lack of co-operation from the authorities, in fact for the different nationalities to air grievances against each other. The French were perpetually 'insultés' by the English and Americans, the Germans resented the fact that no one spoke German, the Americans complained that the English treated everything as a joke, and the English that the Americans took it all too seriously. The wireless station employed only two operators, so on the rare occasions that a story broke, there was a rush for the station usually followed by a long wait before an operator was free. Competition for an 'exclusive' was made even fiercer by the transmitters' practice of selling to the highest bidder their highly confidential material. It was not unusual for fights to break out, and rivals frequently cribbed, stole, denied and destroyed each others' stories.

In between these brief bouts of excitement there were days of idleness, when numbers of highly paid journalists were left with little to do but drink, play cards and bicker among themselves. (The cameramen, most of them on lower pay and living six to a room, were reduced to facetiously photographing each other lying in bed, developing their negatives at the washstand afterwards.) Boredom, unrestricted supplies of alcohol and the rarefied atmosphere made people bad-tempered, and there were several violent quarrels. After a game of poker one evening Evelyn had a punch-up with Knickerbocker because the American had had the temerity to class Waugh with the despised Aldous Huxley as the two leading novelists of their generation.

It was not long before Evelyn came to loathe the position in which he found himself, far less adept than his colleagues in coping with the unsatisfactory conditions. 'I do my work very badly all the others beat me on all news. That makes me depressed,' he wrote to Diana Cooper. Instead of resigning himself to the situation, he fretted at the waste of time and was not nearly as skilful as the rest at manufacturing important-sounding items out of air. He resented the obligatory call every morning at the press bureau, when after a wait of an hour or two a polite secretary would make a note of any questions and apologise for the absence of the press director – who would of course be there on the morrow; and he grew increasingly impatient at the government's refusal to let any journalist leave Addis.

Not that there was anything to report. Although Italian troops could clearly be seen massing on the Eritrean border, as yet there was no war; with no war, no story, a detail which the *Daily Mail* in particular failed to take into account, making the life of its special correspondent miserable with a constant demand for hard news. 'Evelyn gets hell from the *Daily Mail* by telegram all the time,' Balfour remarked, while to Laura Evelyn complained, 'There is no news and no possibility of getting any, and my idiot editor keeps cabling me to know exactly what arrangements I am making for cabling news in the event of the destruction of all means of communication.' The more miserable his situation, the more bad-tempered he became, ostentatiously lighting his breakfast cigar with that morning's telegram, and offending almost everyone with his bellicose behaviour. Patrick Balfour noted pityingly that, '[Evelyn] is getting pretty depressed: a bad mixer: dislikes people a lot, & suffers from persecution mania on account of repeated angry telegrams from the *Daily Mail* & reputed hostility of Addis inhabitants because of his books.'

Evelyn's lack of experience put him at a serious disadvantage; he was often late with his copy, his material judged disappointing and consistently bettered by his rivals. He took refuge from his inadequacies in emphasising his contempt for the work – 'I am a very bad journalist, well only a shit could be good on this particular job' – and loudly despising his more professional colleagues. 'The journalists are lousy competitive hysterical lying,' he wrote to Katharine Asquith.

> It makes me unhappy to be one of them but that will soon be
> O.K. as the *Daily Mail* don't like the messages I send them and I
> don't like what they send me but I don't want to chuck them
> on account of honour because they have given me this holiday at
> great expense and would be left in soup if I stopped sending
> even my unsatisfactory messages; they don't want to sack me
> for identical reason. So it is deadlock and we telegraph abuse at
> 4 and something a word.

Although he made much of his scorn for the press and its workings, Evelyn was by nature competitive and by his own lights did his best to do a good job. In this he was not as incompetent as he liked to make out, the *Mail* running over sixty of his cables between 24 August and 20 November. Desperate for copy, he and Patrick hired a couple of professional informants to keep them supplied with stories, but industrious as their two spies were, neither Waugh nor Balfour quite dared relay to London a report that twenty-four Japanese officers had landed secretly and were proceeding towards the Ogaden, or that a mutiny among the boy scouts had been put down single-handedly by the eleven-year-old Duke of Harar armed with a machine-gun. (As Balfour cynically observed in his account of the war, 'If you were conscientious you searched for some confirmation of such fantasies before telegraphing them to London. If you were not you telegraphed them to New York as they were.')

Then at last came the chance of a genuine scoop. As nothing was happening in Addis, Evelyn and Balfour decided to go south, where it was generally accepted the main campaign would be fought. On 26 August they finally obtained permits, and accompanied by an English friend, Charles Milnes Gaskell, who had turned up at his own expense as an observer, managed to get as far as Harar, and from there by lorry to Jijiga, where they learned the astonishing news that the French consul had been thrown into prison and was about to be shot as a spy. Convinced that for once they were on to a good thing, the two men hurried to dispatch the story to London, but when they returned to Harar, expecting to find cables of congratulation from their respective newspapers, they found instead furious messages of rebuke. While they had been pursuing the French consul, the far more important story had broken in Addis of Rickett and the American oil concession. It was at this point that, as William Deedes delicately phrased it, 'a certain disenchantment fell between the *Daily Mail* and Evelyn Waugh.'

During the rest of his time in Abyssinia, Evelyn succeeded once more in getting hold of an important story, but this time it was the paper's fault, not his, that it was never used. Count Vinci, as a reward for the *Mail*'s support, gave exclusively to Waugh advance warning that he was intending to withdraw his staff and leave the country. This was crucially significant information, infallibly indicating that Italy was at last preparing to invade. Knowing that the wireless operators would have no compunction in making his scoop available to any hack prepared to pay, Evelyn hit on the cunning expedient of transmitting his copy in Latin. Unfortunately the sub-editor in London who received it, assuming it was some kind of incomprehensible joke, spiked the story.

This was the final straw. For weeks Evelyn had endured physical discomfort, appalling weather, corrosive boredom and the company of men nearly all of whom he disliked, in particular the 'swaggering' Americans, 'armed to teeth & talking like E Hemingway'. To pass the time he taught Deedes and Emeny to play bridge and to ride, barking at them in a very fair imitation of Captain Hance; and for amusement bought a baboon as a pet, 'but he seemed incapable of affection and he kept me awake in the afternoons so I threw him away'. There were not even any attractive women. 'It is a chaste life perhaps the altitude too & the great ugliness and illness of all women here it would not do to die in mortallers or yet to come back alive and marry miss herbert & give her a dose.' He hated Addis, hated the work and longed to be out of it. Finally on 13 September he wrote to Diana Cooper, 'well I have chucked the *Mail* it was no good they sent me offensive cables twice a day & i took umbrage & they wanted me to stay in Addis & I took despair . . . 74 journalists mostly american all lying like hell & my job to sit here contradicting the lies they write. then it is the altitude too which makes umbrage come easy so I shall be a free man in 2 weeks.'

But it was not as easy as that. The *Mail*, having accepted Waugh's resignation, sent out a replacement, W. F. Hartin. Hartin got as far as Djibouti, but there he remained, the Abyssinians refusing to issue a visa until the other *Mail* representative had left the country, which Evelyn, contrary as ever, was now reluctant to do. War was imminent, and having waited so long, he was determined to see it through. 'On account of my great honour I cant chuck the mail,' he wrote to Diana with his version of the story. 'I have got to hate the ethiopians more each day goodness they are lousy & i hope the organmen gas them to buggery.' On 3 October the Italians bombed Adowa, and on the seventh the army under General de Bono crossed the border from Eritrea. 'They began their war last week,' Laura was told. 'For a day or two things here were quite gay with air raid scares and the Americans losing nerve,' but soon it became depressingly clear that, war or no war, little had changed. 'No one is allowed to leave Addis so all those adventures I came for will not happen. Sad.' The only encouraging feature was that hostilities were unlikely to last long. As that old Ethiopia hand, Wilfred Thesiger, put it, while the Italians had a highly efficient modern army, 'the Abyssinians lacked everything but courage,' and by the end of the month it was clear that the fighting would soon be over. 'I think I shall be home soon – anyway by Christmas,' Evelyn told Laura. 'There is no possibility of getting to the front. Charles Milnes Gaskell has been expelled as a spy, Patrick Balfour has gone to Aden. I am lonely and bored and have all the material for a jolly good novel about journalists which I want to do before it gets

Olivia Plunket Greene
on Lundy Island

Teresa (Baby) Jungman with
her sister Zita James
taking part in a review
at the London Pavilion

Brian Howard and David Plunket Greene making-up from Olivia's 'face-case'

The four Lygon
sisters at Madresfield
with their brother
Hugh

Diana Guinness and
her sister Nancy
Mitford

Evelyn at Pool Place with
Bryan and Diana Guinness and Pansy Lamb

Evelyn with friends at a Circus Party given by John Sutro

Christopher and
Camilla Sykes on
their wedding day

Evelyn in pyjamas
staying with
Raymond de
Trafford in Kenya

Arthur
congratulating
Evelyn after the
presentation of the
Hawthornden Prize

Joyce Fagan before
her marriage

Laura Herbert as a
child

Mary Herbert, the
'Monarch of the
Glen'

Laura in a school
play at Albemarle
House

The opening of the new Campion Hall in 1936. Back row: unknown, Evelyn, Lady Horner, Katharine Asquith, Mary Herbert; front row: Edwin Lutyens, Martin D'Arcy, the Duke of Berwick and Alba, A. D. Lindsay (Master of Balliol), Ronald Knox

Mells, 1936: Osbert Sitwell, David Cecil and Evelyn

Mells, 1938: Jeremy Hutchinson, Katharine Asquith, Lady Horner, Julian Oxford, L. P. Hartley, Evelyn

Evelyn and Laura leaving church after their wedding

Evelyn in front of Piers Court

stale to me. I want to see you again. In fact for every reason I want to get back.'

Finally, at the beginning of December and enormously to his relief, Evelyn was officially recalled. He wrote to Diana Cooper in an access of good humour,

> I didnt realise how much I hated this job until I got the cable. Now I am deliriously happy. I suppose it is priggish to despise ones job but there it is. I felt ashamed all the time.
>
> Now I am going to Bethlehem for Xmas and soon shall be on the steps of Gower Street. I have made a great number of resolutions first among them to be deeply loving to you and all my friends and not ungrateful any more. Then I am going to give up the snobbish attempt I have made for some years to be low brow and to be just as fastidious as my nature allows, to read books again and so on as I used before my 1928 debacle. Then to get a fixed abode. Then to be sober often and always two days before doing anything with you. Remind me of these if you find me falling.

From the Holy Land he went to Baghdad, then to Damascus and Rome, where, on condition that he would not write about it, he obtained through the British embassy an interview with Mussolini. The duce received him courteously in his office in the Palazzo Venezia, where he was given by his English visitor a pessimistic account of the difficulties facing the army in Abyssinia. Evelyn was impressed with Mussolini, seeing in him little of the ridiculous, bombastic personality portrayed with such hostile relish in the British press.

Evelyn arrived in London at the beginning of January 1936, and almost at once began work on his book, only to realise that events were moving so fast that he would have to return to Abyssinia to gather material for his concluding chapters. At the end of July he travelled to Rome, where he spent several days obtaining a visa, making his travel arrangements and persuading the Italian authorities to underwrite his expenses. While waiting for all this to be done, he visited Assisi, writing to Katharine Asquith, 'Off to Africa full of the gloomiest forebodings I am sick of Abyssinia and my book about it. It was fun being pro-Italian when it was an unpopular and (I thought) losing cause. I have little sympathy with these exultant fascists now.' On 7 August he sailed from Naples, reaching Djibouti on the 18th. ('Evelyn is

341

back in Abyssinia, fortified with the blessings of Mussolini and the Pope', Arthur wrote to Kenneth McMaster. 'He is welcome to any comfort he can derive from such benedictions. I prithee have me excused.')

Here, contrary to his predictions, Evelyn found not the foundations of a well-ordered colony but a country in a state of complete chaos: there were stories of starvation in the cities, imminent famine, derailed trains, summary executions, telegraph lines severed, planes immobilised, bridges blown up, and incessant harassing of the occupying forces by the Abyssinian resistance movement. 'Truth appears to be Wops in jam', Evelyn noted in his diary. In Addis he called on the Hefts, whose Deutsches Haus had been renamed the Pensione Germanica, and on Marshal Graziani, the Italian commander-in-chief, whom he found charming and civilised and ready to oblige his visitor in any way he could. Evelyn met Strohm, the German *chargé d'affaires*, also discovered to be delightful and a great admirer of *Black Mischief.* The days that followed were arduous in the extreme, travelling in great heat by tiny aeroplane and ancient motor-car to Asmara, a 'profoundly depressing town'. His host in Asmara was the head of the press bureau, a Captain de Franchi. This delightful man,

> like many others before him, was deluded by my Christian name and for two days flitted between airport and railway station, meeting every possible conveyance, in a high state of amorous excitement. His friends declared that he had, with great difficulty, procured a bouquet of crimson roses. The trousered and unshaven figure which finally greeted him must have been a hideous blow, but with true Roman courtesy he betrayed nothing except cordial welcome, and it was only some days later, when we had become more intimate, that he admitted his broken hopes.

Evelyn was allowed to go wherever he wished, his published observations (not always in accord with the notes made privately in his diary) confirming his expressed conviction that the Italian conquest of Abyssinia was 'attended by the spread of order and decency, education and medicine, in a disgraceful place'. Franchi took him to Aksum to see the antiquities. It was a long day, but what impressed Evelyn were not the famous ruins ('very ugly'), but the magnificent trunk road still in the process of being built, which, starting in the north, was to drive through the country from Massawa on the Red Sea through the still unconquered territories of the south to the Somali coast and Mogadishu. The Italian road-building programme in Abyssinia had already been much admired; the *New York Times* had described it as a 'marvel', adding, however, that the project could be compared to the building of the pyramids not only for its magnificent scale but also for 'the terrible conditions' in which the work was carried out. In his diary, Evelyn records what he saw with the appreciative eye of the craftsman, taking note of 'tarmac, concrete parapets, cuttings, graded, cambered, cuttings faced with stone, little beds of patterned pebbles'. By the time he came to write of it in his book, however, the road has become a triumphant symbol of the great new Roman empire.

> [Soon] new roads will be radiating to all points of the compass, and along the roads will pass the eagles of ancient Rome, as they came to our savage ancestors in France and Britain and Germany, bringing some rubbish and some mischief; a good deal of vulgar talk and some sharp misfortunes for individual opponents; but above and beyond and entirely predominating, the inestimable gifts of fine workmanship and clear judgment – the two determining qualities of the human spirit, by which alone, under God, man grows and flourishes.

The journey home was by way of Cairo, Tripoli and Rome. In Rome '[I] had intended to bathe, change, fuck, and eat a luxurious dinner. Instead spent the evening driving to pay my debt to the English College in smuggled lire.'

On arrival in London, Evelyn was met by the shocking news that Hugh Lygon had mysteriously died while on a motoring holiday in Germany.

After Oxford Hughie had abandoned the prodigious and habitual drinking bouts in which, like Evelyn, he had indulged, but his health had always been frail. On 19 August after a hot day spent driving in an open car, Hugh stopped to ask directions, got out of the car and fell to the ground, fracturing his skull. He never regained consciousness and died the same night. This was the second tragedy suffered by the family within the space of a few weeks. In July Lady Beauchamp had died, but her husband, thanks to the untiring efforts of the Duke of Westminster, had been prevented from attending her funeral: at the time living in Venice, Lord Beauchamp had got as far as Dover on the cross-channel steamer, but while still on board he was warned that if he set foot on land he risked immediate arrest, and so he was persuaded to turn round and go back to the Continent. This time, however, the home secretary, informed that Beauchamp would be present at his son's burial whatever the consequences, out of pity relented. The warrant for his arrest was suspended and later annulled, and the following year Lord Beauchamp returned to live permanently at Madresfield. All this had happened while Evelyn was abroad, but the story made a deep impression on him, later contributing an important strand to the plot of *Brideshead Revisited*. 'It is the saddest news I ever heard. I shall miss him bitterly,' he wrote to Maimie. 'Do write & tell me what happened.'

Much of *Waugh in Abyssinia* was composed while staying at Mells and in a cottage on the Ellesmere estate in Shropshire lent him by the Brownlows, to whom it is dedicated. Evelyn wrote about it to a new friend, Daphne Acton, Mia Woodruff's sister-in-law whom he had met at Ellesmere: 'If the book bores its readers nearly as much as it is boring me to write it will create a record in low sales for poor Mr Burns.'

The book falls into three sections, the first a historical resumé of the situation, the second and longest part comprising the writer's own experience, the third a triumphal eulogy to the conquerors' achievement.[11] Although he makes good comic business out of the incongruous collection of journalists, the maddening caprices of the Abyssinian press bureau, the ghastly weather and conditions, and his own incompetence, the result is disappointing,[12] Evelyn reserving his best material for the novel he was to write on the subject the following year. In *Waugh in Abyssinia*, the wittiest and most novelistic passages are those concerning Emperor Haile Selassie and the Italian minister, Count Vinci,

[11] In the selection of his travel writing published in 1946, *When the Going Was Good* (Duckworth), very little of the first section and none of the last are retained.

[12] Evelyn had wanted to call the book *A Disappointing War*, but Tom Burns, foreseeing disappointing sales, insisted on the punning alternative, which Evelyn disliked.

both of whom are represented as highly skilled players in a Jacobean comedy of greed, ruthlessness and guile. The emperor, far from being the 'noble savage' portrayed in the British press, is seen as an extremely shrewd operator who was doing his considerable best for his beleaguered country by craftily playing off the various foreign interests fighting over it, while Count Vinci is portrayed as a modern Machiavelli, devious and cynical, expertly manipulating a dangerous situation with a mixture of charm, sang-froid and comic dexterity that won Waugh's whole-hearted admiration.

Except in the Catholic press, *Waugh in Abyssinia* did not have a notably favourable reception. By the end of 1936 when it was published, interest in Abyssinia had faded, pushed out of the headlines by the civil war in Spain, and the author's contempt for the Abyssinians (the Abyssinian, according to Evelyn, was remarkable chiefly for 'his venality, treachery, lack of patriotic consciousness, his bluster in victory and collapse in reverse') and his adulation for their Italian aggressors was not a popular stance in Britain. The consensus, mildly expressed in the *Times Literary Supplement*, was that '[Mr Waugh] should perhaps temper his judgment with a little generosity.'

But if the Abyssinian war aroused small interest in England, in America there was none at all, and in spite of strenuous efforts by Carol Hill, the book failed to find a publisher in the United States. To Evelyn, affronted by the lack of enthusiasm shown by 'the American swine', this was a bad set-back, as yet again he was in serious financial difficulties. But this time he had good reason not to be downhearted. In May he heard that he had won the prestigious Hawthornden Prize for *Edmund Campion*, and in July came the long-awaited telegram about his annulment, signed by Monsignor Godfrey, rector of the English College in Rome: DECISION FAVOURABLE.

Lovely house, lovely wife, great happiness

With the arrival of the long-awaited cable from Rome, Evelyn was free to make a new start, his disastrous first marriage annulled, cancelled, wiped from the slate.[1] For the past eighteen months, since the crucial visit to Pixton at the end of December 1934, he had known what he wanted: marriage to Laura. Indeed so eager was he for this that even before hearing from the Curia, and some weeks before his third visit to Abyssinia in August 1936, he had written to her from the Brownlow estate at Ellesmere with a proposal.

> Tell you what you might do while you are alone at Pixton. You
> might think about me a bit & whether, if those wop priests
> ever come to a decent decision, you could bear the idea of
> marrying me. Of course you haven't got to decide, but think
> about it. I can't advise you in my favour because I think it would
> be beastly for you, but think how nice it would be for me. I
> am restless & moody & misanthropic & lazy & have no money
> except what I earn and if I got ill you would starve. In fact its
> a lousy proposition. On the other hand I think I could do a
> Grant[2] and reform & become quite strict about not getting
> drunk and I am pretty sure I should be faithful. Also there is
> always a fair chance that there will be another bigger economic

---

[1] Evelyn had even forgiven John Heygate. Heygate, now living with She-Evelyn in a cottage in Sussex, had been told by his local bishop that in order to attend Communion he must obtain the forgiveness of the man he had wronged. To this end Heygate wrote to Evelyn, and received in reply a postcard: 'O.K. E. W.'

[2] Eddie Grant, married to Laura's sister, Bridget.

crash in which case if you had married a nobleman with a great house you might find yourself starving, while I am very clever and could probably earn a living of some sort somewhere. Also though you would be taking on an elderly buffer, I am one without fixed habits. You wouldn't find yourself confined to any particular place or group. Also I have practically no living relatives except one brother whom I scarcely know. You would not find yourself involved in a large family & all their rows & you would not be patronized & interfered with by older sisters in law & aunts as often happens. All these are very small advantages compared with the awfulness of my character. I have always tried to be nice to you and you may have got it into your head that I am nice really, but that is all rot. It is only to you & for you. I am jealous & impatient – but there is no point in going into a whole list of my vices. You are a critical girl and I've no doubt that you know them all and a great many I don't know myself. But the point I wanted to make is that if you marry most people, you are marrying a great number of objects & other people as well, well if you marry me there is nothing else involved, and that is an advantage as well as a disadvantage. My only tie of any kind is my work. That means that for several months each year we shall have to separate or you would have to share some very lonely place with me. But apart from that we could do what we liked & go where we liked – and if you married a soldier or stockbroker or member of parliament or master of hounds you would be more tied. When I tell my friends that I am in love with a girl of 19 they look shocked and say 'wretched child' but I dont look on you as very young even in your beauty and I dont think there is any sense in the line that you cannot possibly commit yourself to a decision that affects your whole life for years yet. But anyway there is no point in your deciding or even answering. I may never get free of your cousin Evelyn. Above all things, darling, dont fret at all. But just turn the matter over in your dear head . . .

Eight days from now I shall be with you again, darling heart. I don't think of much else. All my love Evelyn.

In this revealing testament Evelyn lays himself open as if for the confessional, his weaknesses unflinchingly described, his few perceived virtues clearly marked, scrupulously giving weight to the constancy and cleverness as well as to the restlessness, misanthropy and sloth. It was typical of Evelyn to present a matter of supreme importance in such an apparently casual manner; typical to present his failings unrelieved by qualification; typical, too, to be so dismissive of his family, referring only to a brother and making no mention at all of his parents. Most significant is the reference to his work: not many men deeply in love and suing for marriage would have the strength of mind to state without compromise that his future wife, unless she chose to share his solitude, must expect to live alone for 'several months each year'. But for Evelyn, writing was the motivating force, and it was essential that this be understood. As the basis of a contract, his argument is a model of integrity, and if Laura read it carefully, as she must have done, and took it seriously, then there can have been few surprises in the years ahead.

Laura's reply must have been encouraging for the tone of Evelyn's subsequent letters to her are trusting and happy, and the references to his situation in letters to his friends are cheerful. After dropping her off at RADA in Gower Street one day, he wrote to her, 'Lovely child, you have been sweet to me all this last week and I have loved it all and I look forward tenderly to Monday . . . I shall think of you for about 17 hours in the 24 and dream of you for the other five. Darling Laura. I love you. Thank you for loving me.' Diana Cooper was informed, 'It has been a very happy summer so far living in seclusion at Perry's office in Ellesmere and going away for occasional jaunts to see L. Herbert and loving her a lot and she being exquisitely unDutch. Goodness she is a decent girl.' While to Maimie he wrote in nursery French and high spirits, 'La jeune fille paresseuse, Mlle Herbert, a écrit beaucoup de lettres plein d'amour . . . On m'a donné un prix, qui s'appelle le "Hawthornden", à cause de la bon gout de mon livre *Edmund Campion*, . . . je suis bien content de cette affaire parce qu'il me fera beaucoup de bon avec Mde Herbert la mère de la jeune fille paresseuse au nez énorme.'

For the moment, what existed between Evelyn and Laura was no more than a private understanding; Laura was a minor, her mother's permission a legal requirement for her marriage. Evelyn was well aware that in Mrs Herbert's eyes he was far from the ideal son-in-law; he urgently needed to make as good an impression as possible, and for this the prestigious Hawthornden Prize was important. The Hawthornden, worth £100, was given annually for an outstanding work of literature by a British author under the age of forty-one. As A. D. Peters explained to Carol Hill, it was 'the most important literary award made in England', and although ostensibly won by Evelyn for *Campion*, '[it was] really, of course, for his work in general.' Pleasing though this was, what mattered in the circumstances, as Evelyn told Henry Yorke, was that it had registered with the very consciously Catholic Herberts 'that a prize of that kind should go to a specifically Catholic book'. The ceremony was on 24 June at the Aeolian Hall. Arthur was in the audience, Charles Morgan and the despised Jack Squire among those who spoke in commendation. Evelyn, looking shy, responded briefly.

The only notable absentee was Peters. The agent had been obliged to spend the afternoon at the police court in order to save his award-winning client from imprisonment for debt, a sentence only narrowly avoided by the immediate cabling to America for royalties due from Alexander Woollcott, followed two days later by Evelyn's signing of a five-novel contract with Chapman & Hall for an advance of £1000.

With marriage in view, Evelyn desperately needed money. *Campion*, thanks to his generous gesture to the Catholic cause, had brought in nothing at all, *Waugh in Abyssinia* very little. In July Chapman & Hall published a collection of his magazine stories, *Mr Loveday's Little Outing*, but although favourably reviewed (Maurice Bowra in the *Spectator* referred to 'the confident touch of an accomplished master'), the income from it was small, even smaller in America where it had been reluctantly issued by Little, Brown in a limited edition of 750. (Alfred McIntyre, Carol Hill told Peters, had had 'no wish whatever to publish [Waugh's] short stories either before or after his [next] novel.')

The protagonist of the title story, a psychopathic murderer who is released from a lunatic asylum after many years of exemplary behaviour, only to murder again, was originally named not Loveday, but the don. However, this was changed before publication, perhaps because Cruttwell (who, ironically, was to die insane) had recently been in the news and might be in litigious mood. While Evelyn was in Abyssinia the previous year, Joan and Alec Waugh had telegraphed the gratifying information that the don, standing as Conservative candidate for Oxford University, had been defeated in the by-election by A. P. Herbert. 'It was delightful of you and Alec to cable me the news of Cruttwell's ignominy.

It has made my week,' Evelyn wrote to his sister-in-law. 'Really Cruttwell's failure is supremely comforting.'

Included with 'Mr Cruttwell/Loveday' are 'By Special Request', the alternative ending to *A Handful of Dust*, 'Bella Fleace Gave a Party', and 'Incident in Azania', which sheds an intriguing light on English expatriate life as Evelyn observed it in Addis Ababa. Biographically the most significant is 'Winner Takes All', the story of two brothers, Gervase and Tom. Gervase, the elder and his widowed mother's favourite, is given all the advantages: he goes to Eton and Christ Church, his coming of age is lavishly celebrated, the family estate strained to indulge his every extravagant whim. Tom, meanwhile, is sent to a very minor public school after which a poorly paid job is found for him in the motor trade in Wolverhampton. When he falls in love with Gladys Cruttwell, a common young woman employed as a clerk in the same office, he is packed off to a sheep farm in Australia to forget her, returning two years later engaged to the only child of a self-made millionaire. Convinced that such a prize would be wasted on her younger son, Mrs Kent-Cumberland breaks up the relationship, sending Tom back to Gladys, while Gervase marries the heiress. Although its tone is light, the story conveys much of Evelyn's resentment against Alec, 'the heir of Underhill'. In Evelyn's view, Alec, their father's darling, had always been given the best, while to him everything came 'shop-soiled and second-hand'. Alec, like Gervase in the story, had even ended up with a rich Australian wife.

Evelyn's finances improved the following year, 1937, when Chapman & Hall issued an edition of his *Collected Works*, and Penguin brought out *Decline and Fall* in a sixpenny paperback. But as in the past the bulk of his income still had to be earned from journalism, most of it produced under pressure and in disciplined loneliness at Chagford and Mells. He now had a weekly column in the *Spectator*, whose literary editor, Derek Verschoyle, was an old pupil from Arnold House, and he was writing regularly for the *London Mercury* and the *Morning Post*. For what he described as 'joke wages' he contributed to the *Tablet*, now edited by his friend, Douglas Woodruff, and for no wages at all to Hilaire Belloc's magazine, *G. K.'s Weekly* ('In evening wrote free stuff for Belloc,' he recorded in his diary. 'Hope I get to heaven that way.') By far the most lucrative commission, appreciatively referred to as a 'jam job', was from *Nash's Magazine*, for which he was to write twelve articles, '30 guineas a month for less than 2,000 words on anything I like'. Unfortunately, the magazine folded before Evelyn had completed more than half his contract, as at the end of the same year did the sophisticated *Night & Day*, edited by Graham Greene, for which Evelyn, after some tough haggling, had agreed to write a weekly book page.

Always workmanlike in his approach, Evelyn knew precisely the value of his hire. He wrote for money, not enjoyment, so much money for so many words, and with his book-trade background was well acquainted with the few perquisites of his trade, chief among them the sale of review copies for half their marked price, a source of income accepted by the Inland Revenue as non-accountable. To this end he brazenly suggested to Greene that all review copies should be sent straight from the publishers to him, without going through the *Night & Day* office first.

> Yes, the pay is rather disappointing but I am getting spliced & want as many regular jobs as I can get. Six guineas a week would be worth it (a) if this was on the understanding that it would be raised to ten if the paper became a success (b) I could have, either to keep or sell, all the review books. That is to say you'd circularize the publishers saying you were a new weekly etc. that I was doing the book page & that books are to be sent direct to me. This would save trouble in selection, add to my library and supplement the wages very considerably.

Greene having rejected this plan, Evelyn was forced to climb down ('I had no conception that the output of new books was so big . . . I quite see that the literary editor must decide what books are given chief notice') and was not, therefore, disposed to be amenable when a few months later Greene found himself in trouble, with the magazine running out of money and an expensive libel action threatened. Desperately trying to stave off collapse, Greene cabled his contributors, asking them as an emergency measure to accept a temporary cut in fees. Waugh replied, 'I received your telegram this morning after the enclosed article had been written. As it had been definitely commissioned . . . I am afraid I must hold you to your offer, whether you print it or not.'

Less congenial but financially far more rewarding was an offer from the ebullient Hungarian film producer, Alexander Korda. In November 1936, Evelyn had been briefed at Korda's studio in Denham on a 'vulgar film about cabaret girls', originally entitled *Lovelies from America*, for which he was to write the script. This was hack work of the lowest level, but Evelyn made an acceptable job of it: the final version was completed in April, for which he was paid £750. The fact that nothing came of it and the film was never made, was a matter of indifference to its writer who, thankful to be done with it, could now return to the novel, for which ever since his return from Addis he had been 'itching & full of ideas'.

It was shortly before his final journey to Abyssinia that news of his annulment had come through. Evelyn had been in Donegal on a pilgrimage to Lough Derg. 'The grimmest pilgrimage in Christendom,' as he later described it, 'Patrick's Purgatory' involves spending two nights in prayer on a small island in the middle of the lake, walking barefoot over sharp rocks, keeping at least one all-night vigil, with no sustenance but oatcakes and sugarless tea. '[It] very rarely fails and is *horrible.*' On 7 July Evelyn arrived back from Ireland to find that his prayers had indeed been answered. His train from Holyhead reached Euston at 5.30 a. m.; he had gone straight to his club, the St James', and there he found the telegram waiting. 'Bath, shaved; lay down but did not sleep. At 8 rang up Bruton Street and was told that Laura had gone out to church. Dressed and went to Farm Street. Laura and Mary there. Knelt behind them and told Laura news in porch. Walked back to Bruton Street to breakfast.'

For the rest of the month Evelyn spent nearly every day with Laura. They lunched, dined and supped together, went to the cinema, the theatre, to Mass at Farm Street; they visited Kew, and called on Nancy Mitford who lived nearby. 'They had both been caught in a storm in Kew Gardens and were soaking wet,' Nancy recalled. 'Laura looked like an exquisite piece of Dresden china, so fragile that one felt she must snap in two'. Evelyn went to see Laura in an end of term production of *Macbeth*, before spending a weekend with her at Pixton. The previous week he had had an interview with Mary Herbert at Bruton Street, during which Mrs Herbert had made it plain that they must wait until October before announcing their engagement, and at least until Christmas for the wedding, later extending the period of the 'unofficial' engagement to the middle of December. Until then, their intentions were to be kept strictly private, with only one or two close friends, although not yet Evelyn's family, let into the secret. Maimie, the Lygon sister to whom Evelyn was closest, was one.

> You will be greatly be surprised to hear I have got engaged to
> be married to Miss L. Herbert. I don't think I have ever told
> you about her. She is lazy with a long nose but otherwise jolly
> decent. When I say engaged Miss H. and the Pope and I and
> Gabriel have made up our minds but it is not to be announced
> until after Xmas . . . So I shant be married for a long time.
> That is sad. Also Gabriel thinks it is wrong to fuck in Lent. So
> you must not tell people I am engaged or Driberg will put it
> in the papers. And dont tell pauper[3] as he will spread foul lies
> about Miss H. in his unchivalrous way. And don't tell Capt.
> Hance or he will take Miss H. away from me on account of his
> superior sex appeal.

In spite of the thirteen years between them, and although in some ways young for her age, Laura was old enough to know her mind. Like Evelyn Gardner, she was anxious to leave home, but unlike her predecessor she was by now genuinely in love. And Evelyn Waugh, difficult though he could be, was a man of formidable attraction to those who found him attractive, as is attested by the devotion shown throughout his life by a large circle of friends. He was very affectionate, had enormous charm, was still in his early thirties good looking, and he could be funnier than any man alive. For a young girl like Laura to have concentrated upon her the full force of his emotional and intellectual energies must have been intoxicating. And no doubt she sensed his vulnerability, and responded to his need for her.

In spite of the difficulties caused by Mary Herbert's lack of enthusiasm for the match, this was one of the few periods when Evelyn came near to being completely happy. The actualities of married life were still to be realised; meanwhile in contemplating his future with Laura he could look forward not only to the longed-for safe haven, but to emotional fulfilment with a woman to whom the spiritual dimension, as in himself, was highly

---

[3] Patrick Balfour.

developed. From Assisi in August, he wrote to her in a tone that combined lyrical romanticism with religious passion.

> My darling, It is a night of inconceivable beauty – cool after a stifling day. They have put on the lights in the garden for the first time since I've been here and are proud of them. 'The garden' is a little terrace roofed in leaves with a monkey in a cage and two doves in another. There is an absurd little fountain . . . From the terrace one can see the lights of Perugia and all the Umbrian plain . . . I feel transported with the beauty of the night & wish you were here to share it. Assisi seems to be full of the Grace of God. Darling Laura I do so wish you were here . . . I need you all the time – when I'm vexed and uncertain & tired – but more than ever on a night like this when everything is unearthly & lovely.
>
> You see, darling child, so often when people fall in love & want to be married, it is because they foresee a particular kind of life to which the other is necessary. But I dont feel that. . . . what I do know is that I cant picture any sort of life without you. I have left half of myself behind in England and I am only dragging about a bit of myself now.
>
> And I don't at all regret the haphazard, unhappy life I've led up till now because I don't think that without it I could love you so much. Goodnight my blessed child. I love you more than I can find words to tell you.

On his return from abroad in September, Evelyn was immediately confronted with more delaying tactics on the part of Mary Herbert. 'My darling,' Laura wrote in a welcome-home letter, 'I'm afraid I've got one hard blow for you . . . Mother & I have talked over plans about when we could be married – And as mother is still adamant about our not being publicly engaged until Christmas it really will be impossible for us to be married till directly after Easter . . .' Evelyn, expecting to marry in the new year, was furious, but there was little he could do: unlike Evelyn Gardner, Laura was not prepared to defy her mama. 'Decided nothing,' he remarked tight-lipped after spending the day at Bruton Street, 'except to be civil'; four days later, 'Worked myself into rage with Mary at night and had to take dope'; and the next morning, 'Rage justified by letter from Laura saying would I decide if I wanted to share London house with Mary. Mind boggled.' Soon afterwards, however, Mary Herbert declared herself finally 'reconciled' to the marriage, although still insisting it should not take place until the spring.

Now at least the Waugh family could be told. Alec wrote to congratulate his brother, his wife, Joan, generously offering to pay for the honeymoon. Unfortunately, it was Alec, not Evelyn, who was the one to break the news at Highgate. 'He [Evelyn] has not written to us!' Arthur, piqued, noted in his journal, and it was not until a week later that the expected letter arrived.

> My dear Father, I hope that you did not think it unfilial to delay telling you of my engagement . . . [Laura] is very young, very thin, rather poor, dead silent, long nosed, laudably devoid of literary, artistic or social ambition, lazy, affectionate, timid, ignorant . . . She is the youngest daughter of Aubrey Herbert of whom you probably know more than I do. I gather he was a popular & prominent figure in his day. Her mother is a sporting Irishwoman with an interest in foreign politics. I can't hope that you will find much in common with her.

Soon after this, Evelyn brought Laura to dinner. 'Seemed to go quite smoothly', was the laconic entry in the diary. For both Arthur and Kate, however, the occasion was exciting. 'Great preparations for Evelyn & Laura. The evening was delightful. She behaved charmingly; he was at his best; and the dinner was good . . . [the next day] K & I had a pleasant talk over dinner, about our happy evening . . . By last post a dear little note came to K from Laura, thanking us for being "so sweet" to her, wh: sent us to bed happier still.'

The only jarring note as Evelyn introduced Laura to his acquaintance was sounded by Diana Cooper. Diana was a friend of Mary Herbert's, and was extremely put out that Evelyn, her faithful admirer, should not only prefer another woman to herself, but choose the daughter of one of her oldest friends. Instinctively she recognised, too, that the clear-sighted Laura was unlikely to become a worshipper at the Madonna's shrine. When the two women met, Diana was brusque to the point of bad manners. 'Afternoon with Diana who was at first in tearing form imitating the King and Mrs Simpson, then, when Laura came to fetch me, suddenly became foully rude. Very shocked.' Diana's hostility, which continued unabated for several years, wounded Laura, and later helped fortify her dislike of Evelyn's smart social life in London, in which she could rarely be persuaded to take part.

On 13 January the engagement was finally announced in *The Times*, pre-empted, to Laura's dismay, by an item the day before in Tom Driberg's column in the *Express*. Unsuspected by her, this had been supplied by the bridegroom himself. 'I don't imagine the story will be of great news value but if you care to publish it you can have it a day ahead of *The Times*,' Evelyn had written to his old school friend. 'In return could you oblige me in one particular? I think that by now most people have forgotten or have never known that I was married before. That marriage has been annulled by the papal courts and it would be very painful both to me & my young lady to have it referred to . . . Apart from that you can have all the details you need.'

During these early weeks of their engagement, while Laura concentrated on her trousseau, Evelyn devoted himself to house-hunting. Both were agreed that they did not want to live in London. During his first period as war correspondent in Abyssinia (and learning how to type), Evelyn had described to Laura exactly what he had in mind for himself. 'When i get home i shall buy a cottage. Please find me one. Dorset or Somerset near water sea or river long way main road but near main line station. I wouldnt mind the Berners Betjeman country. On no account the Juliet Beaton Pembroke country. No pine trees. Sanitation light etc no consideration. Find me a house like that theres a poppet preferably thatch but not beams. Think of Mr Beverley Nichols famous cottage and get the opposite.' The region they both preferred was the west country, in particular the area round Mells, a part of Somerset which had the advantage for Laura of being within easy reach of Pixton, and which was familiar to Evelyn from his childhood: Midsomer Norton was in Somerset, as was the rectory at Corsley and the vicarage at Bishops Hull. By now his plans were more ambitious: a thatched cottage would do very well for a bachelor, but for a married man it must be something grander, preferably Georgian, preferably set in its own acres.

Domestic architecture had always been a consuming interest. In common with many of his Oxford generation, and encouraged by the eccentric enthusiasms of John Betjeman, Evelyn had made a study of the subject, and had already collected a small library of standard works. John Plant, the protagonist of *Work Suspended*, the unfinished novel written during 1939, is typical of this breed of informed amateur. He and his friends, says Plant, 'professed a specialized enthusiasm for domestic architecture. It was one of the peculiarities of my generation . . . When the poetic mood was on us, we turned to buildings, and gave them the place which our fathers accorded to Nature – to almost any buildings, but particularly those in the classical tradition, and, more particularly, in its decay. It was kind of nostalgia for the style of living which we emphatically rejected in practical affairs.' In an essay published in *Country Life*, Evelyn described his Georgian ideal, 'the solid, spacious houses of the bourgeoisie, with their regular rows of well-placed windows, their low stone steps spread out to the pavement, fanlight and pediment above the panelled doors, and behind them half an acre of walled garden, an old mulberry tree staining the grass . . . A lovely house where an aged colonel plays wireless music to an obese retriever.'

While at Mells, Evelyn came across just such a perfect property in the village of Nunney. 'Very small, next to the castle and farm buildings. Exquisite eighteenth-century façade . . . Inside and out it is very dilapidated but of the highest beauty. Panelled rooms, very fine oak and walnut staircase, Norman cellars. For a considerable sum it could be made one of the loveliest small houses in England.' Laura was taken to see it (she 'seemed to like [it]'), and Evelyn began negotiations with the elusive owner, a Major Shore, who after much havering, reluctantly agreed to let, though not to sell. Evelyn proposed terms, but the weeks went by and Shore never replied to his letters.

Eventually losing patience, Evelyn abandoned his hopes of Nunney and reluctantly resumed the hunt. The weekend before Christmas he and Laura spent at Faringdon with Gerald Berners; on the Monday they were collected by Mary Herbert, who was to drive them to Pixton for the holiday. On the way they stopped for a pub lunch at Stinchcombe, near Dursley in Gloucestershire, and to look at a house called Piers Court. 'Absolutely first-rate, delighted', Evelyn recorded in his diary. To Diana Cooper he wrote, 'Laura and I have found a house of startling beauty between Bath and Stroud, so that is where we shall live. All love and Xmas greetings. Bo.'

In the period leading up to his wedding, when Evelyn was seeing Laura almost daily, showered by presents and congratulations, absorbed in plans for Piers Court, it might have seemed as though he had everything he wanted, that at last his demons could be laid to rest. Of course they could not; but for the time his chief tormentors were lying dormant. In answer to a letter of congratulation from Georgia Sitwell, he wrote, 'It is, as you say, a great step but goodness how I am looking forward to it . . . I needn't tell you much about her – except that I discover new, lovely things daily.' Now at last he was loved, secure, with a partner who asked nothing more than to play the part of devoted and protective wife, just as in his parents' marriage Kate had always done for Arthur. Laura was docile and undemanding: like Kate she was modest, quiet and emotionally undemonstrative; she did not make scenes, nor wish for expensive clothes, nor visits to London, nor holidays abroad, nor even, apart from seeing her family, any social life of her own, remaining more than content for Evelyn to sustain his sophisticated friendships without her involvement. Again like Kate, although strong-minded she was uncompetitive, her calm temperament a soothing influence on his violent and volatile moods. Laura had no great gift for domestic life – was haphazard in her arrangements and not much interested in either food or physical comfort – but her love of the country and of farming, the very ordinariness and routine of such a way of life, was to provide Evelyn with exactly the tranquillity he needed, just as her firm Catholic faith, unswerving and unquestioning, acted as an anchor for his own often agonised relationship with his Church.

But even with all this in mind, the engagement was not without its tensions, many of them generated by an endemic lack of sympathy between Evelyn and the Herberts. Although later on Evelyn and his mother-in-law developed a mutual respect, before his marriage the relationship between them could be described at best as one of wary truce. The Herberts, accustomed to the company of writers and artists, conceded his literary talent but, with the traditional snobbery of privilege for actual achievement, looked down on his professional background, and found distressingly vulgar his exaggerated admiration for the upper classes. For his part Evelyn found many of the Herbert relations downright dull, and he positively disliked Laura's brother, Auberon, a dislike that was returned with interest.

Laura, too, was clearly under strain. She was very young, had led a sheltered existence, and never in her life had had to stand up to her mother or go against family opinion. In counterpoint to the frequent record in the diary of Evelyn's insomnia and depression ('Low spirited. Sleeping badly') are equally frequent references to Laura's tears and melancholy, and at one point to her physical collapse, apparently from undernourishment. 'Lunched with Laura at Simpson's. She cried. Cinema alone . . . Dined Berkeley buttery, returned Mulberry Walk[4] where Laura again cried.' 'Went to drink sherry with Grants who were frightfully dull. Laura very tired and gloomy. Foul dinner at Bruton Street. Heavily drugged sleep.' An even lower point was reached at Christmas, spent at Pixton with the Herberts, Grants and Alick Dru, Gabriel's future husband. 'Family fun. No sleep', Evelyn noted grimly. On Christmas Eve, 'Father D'Arcy came, very dotty . . . Felt very low. Midnight Mass in main room.' On Christmas Day, 'Church again. Felt very ill. Family fun'. In the new year, 'Terrible suffering Pixton', and the following day, 'Hideous sufferings'. 'Xmas was great hell on account of family & feudal feeling,' he later told Maimie. But the one great advantage of staying at Pixton was its propinquity to Piers Court. Lady de Vesci as a wedding present had given the couple £4000 with which to buy a house, and on 22 January Evelyn's offer of £3500 was accepted.

Piers Court, on the very western edge of the Cotswolds, was splendidly situated, just above the village and with a sweeping view across the Berkeley Vale to the Severn estuary and the distant Forest of Dean. Within only a few miles of Bristol, Gloucester and Bath, Stinchcombe was then still in the depths of the country – rich, agricultural country – the house surrounded by over forty acres of garden and farmland. Built of the lovely grey-gold Cotswold stone, Piers Court, although not large, is a beauty. At the front it presents the fine façade of a Georgian manor house, with raised parapet and a crowning pediment over the porch, while at the back unravelling into a jumble of small but extensive domestic offices dating from the sixteenth century. During the

[4] Laura was staying with Bridget and Eddie Grant at Mulberry Walk in Chelsea.

Civil War it was said to have been used as a refuge for the Royalists, owned from 1640 until the end of the eighteenth century by the same family, the Pynffolds. Although of architectural merit, Piers Court was in a poor state of repair and almost completely unmodernised. 'The main objection to the house is the lack of water, light and gas and all the chief rooms face due North,' Evelyn told Diana Cooper. 'Also the snow gets in through holes in the roof.'

Laura had to oversee the work as at the beginning of February Evelyn retired to 'a large warm sitting room' at Chagford, where he remained until Easter writing his film script, book reviews and his Abyssinian novel. He was passionately interested in the house, however, and Laura received detailed instructions almost daily.

> Re. Hancock. What he must do first is to see the present wiring, examine the existing plant & see where you want the new light points. I can't be any help over this and grudge the time. Will you deal with him . . . about the kitchen quarters. You better see him about that. I said we shall want a new range but couldn't give details. I shall have a use for the paving stones in the kitchen so don't spray them with liquid insulation. Take them out & put in properly ventilated deal floors . . . Sorry to put all this on you, but I really am very busy . . . & as it is correspondence takes $1/2$ my morning.

Evelyn's personal contribution was the buying of furniture and fittings. On a visit to London, '[I] bought a chimney-piece and mirror, both Adam, and two very fine carved pedestals which I am having converted at enormous expense into bookcase ends'; and while at Chagford, '[I] ran amok at village shop and bought a great deal of old furniture, fenders etc'.

Evelyn had grand ideas for Piers Court, particularly for the garden and library. He had long learned to appreciate country-house living, first experienced while staying with Alastair Graham at Barford, and since then had visited some of the finest houses in the country. With his love of architecture, his artist's eye and craftsman's instinct, his taste was both educated and well defined. More than that, his moving into Piers Court, the big house of the neighbourhood, presented him with an opportunity of assuming a part that much appealed to him, that of landed country gentleman. Now he was marrying into the aristocracy, into that stratum of upper-class intelligentsia to which by temperament and inclination he most wished to belong. His own background he regarded as not only irredeemably middle class but mediocre. Recently, in a fit of irritation, he had wounded Arthur by saying he felt ashamed of being the son of Balestier's office boy. When reminded that some of his antecedents were aristocratic, that the distinguished Scottish judge, Lord Cockburn, was his great-great-grandfather, he replied dismissively that that did not count, that 'Lord Cockburn was ennobled for practical reasons. I would like to have been descended from a useless Lord.'

In a brief but revealing note found among his papers after his death, undated but almost certainly referring to Piers Court, Evelyn had written, 'It is the kind of house which takes a lot of living up to. Everybody who comes in says "What a lovely house you've got." But I haven't got it: it has got me. How am I to impress my personality (if I have one) on a house whose atmosphere is not mine? And how long will it be before the place begins to impress its personality on me?' One way was by laying emphasis on his own line of descent. Now that he was, as he put it, 'marrying procreating & purchasing property', it was time to establish his credentials. Shortly before his wedding, Evelyn wrote to Alec about

> a thing which excites my curiosity . . . the validity of our coat of arms & crest . . . I have always had some doubts about whether we are entitled to it. We have certainly used it since the end of the 18th century but stationers at that time had a way of inventing arms without reference to the College of Heralds. Do you think it worth asking them, and, if it proves spurious, having a grant made? It would be made to our father so that we should both be entitled to it and I would share the expense – about £80 I believe . . .
>
> There is a further point. Since Robert Raban has become an American the Raban family will be extinct in the male line in England. In the circumstances I think that – mother being the only married daughter – we are entitled to quarter her arms, which are certainly genuine[,] with ours. That is more ornamental and I think well worth doing. The College of Heralds would register this for us at the same time.

Alec having given his consent, this was duly done, and the Waugh coat of arms, carved in stone, was prominently placed in the pediment of Piers Court.

Meanwhile, there was the question of wedding presents. Again it was Laura, minutely instructed by her fiancé, who had to make most of the effort involved in extracting what they wanted out of their friends and relations. Soon after she returned from a trousseau-buying trip to Paris, Evelyn dictated tactics regarding an offer of linen from his sister-in-law, Joan. 'You should write to her, say Evelyn has told of her kind offer etc. and make out a big list of what we need – two double beds, three single (at least) & towels for five guests. You might hint at table cloths, table napkins etc.' The results were deemed disappointing. 'Joan Waugh is mean as hell. Well I suppose I must pay for having neglected her these last 2 years.' His parents did rather better.

> My mama is giving us a little mahogany bureau which is of great
> sentimental value to her, the apple of her eye as it belonged
> to an Aunt she was brought up with & revered, so you must say
> nice things about it when she shows it to you. It is a very decent
> piece actually. My papa says will we come & choose a bit of silver
> from what he has left of his grandfathers, wrapped up in
> flannel under his bed. Also he will give us £25 to buy 'something
> definite & lasting – to remind you of me' I think thats decent
> considering his reduced circumstances & the fact that he forked
> out handsomely for my mock marriage some years back. So
> what would you like? I thought perhaps a candle thing for the
> dining room table. £25 wouldn't go far in silver, I think, but we
> might get one of those branch candlesticks in Dresden china or,
> if we decide on a period 1850 room, in Victorian bronze. Or
> books? He'd enjoy choosing them & it could be the nucleus of
> a library. Or cutlery? Or a picture? Or a chimney piece in the
> library built of local stone to my design. Or a clock? or mirrors?
> Well you choose.

Otherwise the haul was disappointing. 'Presents have come in, mostly of poor quality, except from the Asquiths who have given us superb candelabra, sconces, and table.' The Coopers sent a glass chandelier which arrived in smithereens, as Evelyn recounted in unsparing detail to Diana. A box full of broken glass, it looked like at first, but 'we were able to put together enough of the chandelier to see how beautiful it must have been and how clever and generous of you and Duff to find it and give it to us.'

The wedding was set for 17 April. Evelyn wrote to Maimie, 'Capt Hance G.B.H. has said yes to his invitation but all my other chums are abroad. Do please all of you come without fail to the wedding & to the party the day before because I shall be very lonely among all Laura's high born & [illeg] aunts. Mr Herbert [Auberon] sent the invitations out with $\frac{1}{2}$d stamps so all my friends thought they were bills & tore them up. G how s.'

On the first of April Evelyn took his mother to see Piers Court. 'Loveliest expedition to Stinchcombe', she wrote in her diary. 'Very happy time with Evelyn & Laura.' He then retired to Chagford for a few days before going to Pixton for some obligatory pre-nuptial entertaining. 'Cocktail party that afternoon for Laura's neighbours – not much pleasure to me,' and on the following day, 'Ball beastly at newly rebuilt, badly redecorated house of Lord Fortescue . . . Alick [Dru] full of fun.' On the twelfth he went to London, staying with his parents at Highgate, and on the thirteenth met Laura for the wedding rehearsal, at which Father D'Arcy showed himself 'sensationally ignorant of simplest professional duties'. The following day he moved out of his parents' flat to put up at his club. On the Friday was the Herberts' cocktail party. 'Highly enjoyable. Rather tipsy', was Evelyn's comment, while Arthur in Pooterish vein recorded that 'The party was v. nice. Evelyn & the Herberts very gracious, presents splendid, refreshments first-rate. Had a talk with Lord Bath about my father.'

On Saturday, 17 April 1937, a wet, chilly day, Evelyn, Laura, the Herberts and Woodruffs went to early Mass at Farm Street conducted by Father D'Arcy, after which Evelyn returned to the St James' for breakfast and champagne with Douglas Woodruff, Francis Howard[5] and Henry Yorke. 'Changed and pick-me-up at Parkin's[6] and to church where got married to Laura.'

The church was the Church of the Assumption in Warwick Street, the Nuptial Mass was celebrated by the curate, Father Roderick More O'Ferrall, assisted by Father Alfred Gilbey and Father D'Arcy. Laura, white-faced in a long veil and narrow dress

[5] Lord Howard of Penrith.
[6] The chemist in Piccadilly.

of ivory crêpe embroidered with silver lamé, arrived accompanied by the sixteen-year-old Auberon, who had spent the short drive from the house almost in tears, imploring his sister to change her mind. In marked contrast to Evelyn's first wedding, the church was full, the atmosphere solemn – so solemn that little Andrew Waugh, Alec's son, acting as a page, took fright and refused to join the bridal procession up the aisle. Auberon Herbert gave the bride away, Henry Yorke was best man; the witnesses were Sydney Herbert MP, Maurice Baring, Hilaire Belloc and Lord Howard. Among Evelyn's family and friends were his parents, Alec and Joan, Katharine Asquith and Trim, the Woodruffs, Alfred Duggan, Pansy Lamb, Coote and Maimie Lygon, John Sutro, the Brownlows, the Betjemans, Billy Clonmore, Nancy Mitford, and Mrs Cobb and Norman Webb from Chagford.

Afterwards the newly married pair drove to Englefield Green to thank Lady de Vesci for her magnificent present before catching the Paris plane at Croydon, where Mary Herbert and the dreaded Auberon arrived at the last moment to wave them goodbye. A cable was sent to Highgate: 'Just off. Very happy. Best love.' Arrived in Paris, Evelyn and Laura dined off pressed duck and fraises de bois at the Tour d'Argent before boarding the night express to Rome.

The first part of the honeymoon was spent at Portofino. 'Lovely day, lovely house, lovely wife, great happiness,' Evelyn wrote in his diary. They spent the week bathing, shopping and going to church. Laura gave her husband a medal of St George, patron saint of England, soldiers and boy scouts. From Portofino they went to Rome, where they attended a public audience with the pope, did some sightseeing, lunched and dined with English friends, and had the first real quarrel of their married life. 'Laura very bad temper. Also I.' From Rome they moved on to Assisi where, tormented by mosquitoes, Evelyn got drunk, and Laura spent most of one day in tears; from there they went to Florence. 'Laura very drunk at dinner in cellar bought cat (clockwork).' After this they returned to Portofino till the end of May, Evelyn resuming work on his novel, *Scoop*. He wrote contentedly to Dorothy Lygon, 'So it is very decent to be married, very decent indeed,' and to Peters, 'Honeymoon is being all that honeymoon should be. First class.'

At Portofino Evelyn had enjoyed in almost unlimited supply

the two components most necessary to his peace of mind, the company of Laura and undisturbed tranquillity in which to write. Back in England he found nothing but distraction. As Piers Court was not yet habitable, the Waughs were lent the Grants' house in Mulberry Walk, but in such temporary accommodation and surrounded by all the lures of London, Evelyn found it hard to concentrate. He was anxious to have the novel finished in time for publication by Christmas, and as usual was trying to milk the product for all it was worth by negotiating preliminary serialisation rights. Having failed in this, Evelyn then reworked the first chapter to stand on its own as a short story, but that found no buyer either. Eventually the situation was saved by an offer of $250 for serial rights from the American magazine, *Town & Country.*

At the end of August Evelyn and Laura moved into Piers Court, but if in London work had been difficult, in the new house in all its disarray it was next to impossible. And within days of moving in, Laura found that she was pregnant.

Apart from attending board meetings at Chapman & Hall, of which he was now a director, Evelyn stayed away from town, immersing himself in his new life in the country. In those early days he was prepared to play the part expected of a newcomer in the district, receiving calls from neighbours ('The Misses Leigh and the parish priest from Nympsfield came to tea. I fetched them and drove them back. Sticky party.'), accepting invitations to cocktail and garden parties, and benignly assuming the rôle of local squire, even to the extent of presenting prizes at the Dursley secondary school and inspecting the local orphanage. His heart was not in it, however; county society, once experienced, was perceived to be boring and to be avoided at all costs. 'Dined with Lady Featherstone Godley', ran a typically depressed entry in the diary. 'Bad dinner, bad wine, middle-aged military men boasting about their ancestry.' Much more to Evelyn's taste was working on the garden, work undertaken with energy and enthusiasm. One Sunday, 'As the men were away I had the run of my own tools and spent a happy day in the garden, where the new trees are in . . . I moved two castor-oil plants and a holly and some berberis to the corner of the field-gate under the laburnum trees. The clearing of the slopes above the gates is having the best possible effect.' A few days later, 'Pegged out circular lawn in front of house . . . Cut down big Portuguese laurel on line of front door. Gates being rehung in field. Planted hollies by laburnums at field-gate.' He and Laura were learning to drive, but 'yesterday we took our driving tests in Gloucester and both failed which is very inconvenient as we have to hire a man to sit with us on the box whenever we go shopping in Dursley.'

Even with so much in the house unfinished, the Waughs immediately had guests to stay, among the first, Mary Herbert, Gabriel, the Woodruffs and Father D'Arcy. The running of the house, staffed by two couples, the Ellwoods and the Müllers, was Laura's responsibility, Evelyn's territory his library, the cellar and the garden. Just before Christmas 1937, Patrick Balfour, who had been abroad and so unable to attend the wedding, arrived for a weekend. 'Lovely house: quite big, almost a "place",' he told his mother. 'Evelyn v. happy & exaggeratedly domestic: they hardly ever see anybody. All right in the meantime, but I should think she would begin to want something more sooner or later. She is v. young & very much under Evelyn's thumb, & the question is how long she'll be content to stay under it. Wives must have *some* life of their own!'

But there was never to be much chance of that. On 9 March 1938, Laura gave birth to her first child, a daughter. She went to London for the birth, while her husband, establishing an almost unchanging pattern, joined her only after the baby was born. His pleasure in the event, although ironical in tone, is clearly expressed in his letters. 'Laura's baby was born yesterday morning,' he told Peters. 'The daughter huge & loud. No one has had the insolence to suggest it is like me,' while to Tom Balston he wrote cheerfully, 'I foresee that she will be a problem – too noisy for a nun, too plain for a wife. Well standards of beauty may change in the next 18 years.' Maria Teresa was christened on 16 March, before being taken back to Gloucestershire, where shortly afterwards her Waugh grandparents were invited to stay, both of them predictably entranced by the little girl. Much effort was put into entertaining the older Waughs: the aunts from Midsomer Norton were asked over for lunch, and Evelyn showed Arthur and Kate the local sights; Kate, more energetic than her husband, went for long walks and worked in the garden, while Arthur sat at home with Laura, doing the crossword and enjoying 'the first intimate talk that I have ever had with her. She was very gentle & kind.' They stayed for five days, but it is plain that in spite of all the good intentions, before the end of the visit Evelyn's habitual irritation with his father had begun to surface. 'Evelyn & Laura both very tired. Too much entertaining! After dinner K & Laura played chess. Evelyn read, & I kept quiet,' Arthur wrote in his diary.

At the beginning of 1938, *Scoop* was finally finished. Never before had Evelyn taken so long to complete a book. The idea had first come to him as early as October 1935, when he had written to Laura from Abyssinia that at least all his sufferings and frustrations in that benighted country would 'make a funny novel'. But it was another year before he began, recording in his diary for 15 October 1936, that he had 'made a very good start with the first page'. He worked on it intermittently while staying at Mells, and then at Chagford right up to the week of his wedding; he returned to it on honeymoon in Italy, while living at Mulberry Walk, and after the move to Gloucestershire while coping with guests and renovations at Piers Court. 'Work on *Scoop* going slowly, with infinite interruptions and distractions,' he wrote at the beginning of January 1938.

> Several visitors during the last month. Father D'Arcy who had difficulty with his motor car and finally drove off without his luggage. Alick Dru arrived with a very serious hangover . . . Julian Oxford and Christopher Hollis. Helen Asquith. Carolyn Cobb . . . Work in the house: stripping, not with perfect success, of the library chimneypiece; building of cupboards in the night nursery. I have engaged Evans, one of Mr Jotchman's carpenters, at £3 5s 0d a week . . . Negotiations with the West Gloucestershire Power Company go on slowly; I have agreed to pay £120 if they will connect me by the end of March. Mrs Awdry threatens to build a cottage in the further of the two arable fields which originally went with Piers Court . . .

Scoop was published on 7 May. Abandoning the sombre realism of *A Handful of Dust*, Evelyn here returns to the realm of comic fantasy, in which, as in *Decline and Fall* and *Vile Bodies*, an innocent and passive hero is catapulted into chaos. Although the book is uneven in quality, reflecting the numerous interruptions that befell its writing, it radiates high spirits. This time Evelyn's comic genius is riding a wave of cheerfulness and good humour, with none of the previous undercurrents of bitterness and resentment. His mellow mood shows itself at every level. The hero, William Boot, unlike his predecessors, is allowed not only to survive but to succeed, and the corrupt world into which helpless he is dispatched, the world of the professional journalist which Waugh so loathed, is treated with an exuberance that almost suggests affection.

The three main comic themes in *Scoop* are the mores of Fleet Street as represented by the *Daily Beast* and its proprietor, Lord Copper; William Boot and his misadventures as a newspaper reporter in the war zone of Ishmaelia; and the savagery and cynicism of the foreign correspondents in the field.[7] As always, Evelyn achieves some of his best effects not by invention but by highlighting and exaggerating the ludicrous but true, particularly by revealing the childish side of the apparently adult. This is especially relevant in his depiction of Lord Copper, the megalomaniac press baron. Like Lord Beaverbrook, who inspired the portrait, Lord Copper was rich, ruthless and omnipotent, and again like Beaverbrook, ran an absolute dictatorship while maintaining the pretence that he never interfered with his staff.[8] The Megalopolitan Building in Fleet Street, very similar to the black glass palace housing the *Daily Express*, was a monument to power, money and bad taste. William Boot is dazzled by its grandeur, by its Byzantine vestibule dominated by a vast chryselephantine statue of Lord Copper himself. The proprietor's office is many floors above, sealed off by 'massive double doors, encased in New Zealand rose-wood which by their weight, polish, and depravity of design, proclaimed unmistakably, "Nothing but Us stands

---

[7] Evelyn's own assessment of the novel is summed up in a memorandum he wrote in 1957 when a film version was under consideration. 'This is a light satire of modern journalism, not a schoolboy's story of plot, counterplot, capture and escape. Such incidents as provoke this misconception are extraneous to the main theme which is to expose the pretensions of foreign correspondents, popularised in countless novels, plays, autobiographies and films, to be heroes, statesmen and diplomats.'

[8] '[Beaverbrook] used his papers without inhibition to pursue his enemies and to cement relations with friends and allies ... He adopted early on the pretence, used as required, that he had no power or influence over his papers, which gave him an alibi when criticised ... The notion that Beaverbrook, as he constantly claimed, left his staff to carry on their duties in their own way was always fanciful.'

between you and Lord Copper." Mr Salter [the Foreign Editor] paused, and pressed a little bell of synthetic ivory. "It lights a lamp on Lord Copper's own desk," he said reverently. "I expect we shall have a long time to wait." ' Eventually we are allowed a glimpse of the great potentate alone in his sanctum.

> [Lord Copper's] massive head, empty of thought, rested in sculptural fashion upon his left fist. He began to draw a little cow on his writing pad. Four legs with cloven feet, a ropy tail, swelling udder and modestly diminished teats, a chest and head like an Elgin marble – all this was straightforward stuff. Then came the problem – which was the higher, horns or ears? He tried it one way, he tried it the other; both looked equally unconvincing; he tried different types of ear – tiny, feline triangles, asinine tufts of hair and gristle, even, in desperation, drooping flaps remembered from a guinea-pig in the backyard of his earliest home . . . None looked right. He brooded over them and found no satisfaction.

William Boot, although hopelessly naïve, is nonetheless a far more positive character than Paul Pennyfeather, Adam Symes or Tony Last. Living in the depths of the country at Boot Magna Hall, William is entirely innocent of sophisticated city life, his only contact with the capital his fortnightly article for the *Beast*, a half-column of nature notes entitled 'Lush Places', 'ignominiously sandwiched between Pip and Pop, the Bedtime Pets, and the recipe for a dish called "Waffle Scramble".' His job with the paper, at a guinea a time, is of great importance to William, and he is horrified one week to discover that in a carefully researched piece about the habits of the badger, his sister, finding his manuscript, had for 'badger' playfully substituted 'crested grebe'.[9] ('His mail had been prodigious . . . A major in Wales challenged him categorically to produce a single authenticated case of a great crested grebe attacking young rabbits.') Summoned to Fleet Street convinced he is about to be sacked, William is seen by

[9] Waugh had chosen the great crested grebe after spending a weekend with John and Daphne Acton at Aldenham in Shropshire. John Acton insisted that Waugh walk as far as the lake to see the grebe which was nesting there. Waugh, who had drunk a great deal at luncheon, refused; Acton insisted; Waugh with bad grace gave in. They walked to the lake and looked at the grebe. 'Waugh was furious at its inadequacies and gave vent to his feelings: "It's a pathetic bird, a miserable bird, a wretched bird". A few months later Waugh began *Scoop* . . .'

Mr Salter, who to his astonishment offers him the prestigious post of war correspondent in Ishmaelia. But William is not without backbone.

' "And you'd go on paying me my wages?" he asks. "Certainly."

' "*And* my fare there *and* back, *and* my expenses?"

' "Yes."

'William thought the matter over carefully. At length he said: "No." '

He does go, of course, beneficiary of a case of mistaken identity, providing an endless source of jokes arising from the interaction between his own unworldliness and the wily, ruthless and unscrupulous hacks among whom he is flung. Evelyn's miserable experience as a newspaperman in Abyssinia is here transmuted by a form of comic alchemy into a sublime ludicrousness combined with absolutely accurate observation. Jacksonburg/Addis itself, the boredom, the frightful weather, the disgusting food, the bad-tempered journalists, the corruption and capriciousness of the Ishmaeli/Abyssinian authorities are all vividly reproduced; even the Deutsches Haus with its little garden and bizarre menagerie makes an appearance as the Pension Dressler. William's associates – his particular friend, Corker, and Corker's colleagues, Shumble, Whelper and Pigge – are almost endearing in their awfulness. 'Shumble, Whelper, and Pigge knew Corker; they had loitered together of old on many a doorstep and forced an entry into many a stricken home.' The professionals are up to all the tricks, spoiling each other's stories, stealing each other's cables, and in spite of a dearth of news, keeping their offices in London well supplied with impressive-sounding developments. William's methods, on the other hand, are deplorably amateurish and he misses all the important leads, for which he is severely reprimanded by his paper: NEWS EXYOU UNRECEIVED STOP DAILY HARD NEWS ESSENTIALEST STOP REMEMBER RATES SERVICE CABLES ONE ETSIX PER WORD BEAST. Politely William cables back, NO NEWS AT PRESENT THANKS WARNING ABOUT CABLING PRICES BUT IVE PLENTY MONEY LEFT AND ANYWAY WHEN I OFFERED TO PAY WIRELESS MAN SAID IT WAS ALL RIGHT PAID OTHER END RAINING HARD HOPE ALL WELL ENGLAND WILL CABLE AGAIN IF ANY NEWS. But in the end, thanks to the intervention of the mysterious Mr Baldwin (a figure who owes not a little to the mysterious Monsieur Besse, who made such an impression on Evelyn in Aden), it is

William who gets the big scoop, and returns to England a hero. Back at Boot Magna he happily resumes the writing of 'Lush Places', as innocent of the savage reality of the countryside as he was of the savage realities of his life in Ishmaelia.

Here the situation at the beginning of the novel is reversed, with Mr Salter leaving Fleet Street to enter the unfamiliar rural world of Boot Magna, just as William had left home for the strange urban territory of London and Lord Copper. William is as wholly ignorant of the workings of a newspaper as is Mr Salter of life in the country. ' "Tell me," ' William asks Mr Salter who is showing him round the *Beast* offices, ' " – I've often wondered – do you keep a machine of your own or send out to the printers?"

' "We have machines of our own."

' "Do you? They must work jolly fast."

' "Yes." '

To Mr Salter, obliged to walk six miles across fields and ditches in his city clothes in order to find William, the country appears both hostile and bewildering. Boot Magna Hall and its inhabitants exist in a time-warp, in a secret, sheltered world of their own, the house dilapidated, its inmates eccentric to the point of lunacy. The Boots owe not a little to the Herberts and the way of life at Pixton, with their shabby house and furniture, their intense interest in horses and dogs, and the relaxed informality of their retainers. 'Ten servants waited upon the household and upon one another, but in a desultory fashion, for they could spare very little time from the five meat meals which tradition daily allowed them.' (When at the start of William's adventure, Mr Salter tries to tempt him with the lavish expenses to be provided by the *Beast*, describing the extravagant meals he will be able to have in expensive restaurants, William naïvely replies, 'But you see I don't like restaurants and no one pays for dinner at home, anyway. The servants just bring it in.') At Boot Magna, the ultimate haven, there is no pressure to do anything, and one day, one year, is exactly like the last. '[William's] mother, Priscilla, and his three uncles sat round the table. They had finished eating and were sitting there, as they often sat for an hour or so, doing nothing at all. Priscilla alone was occupied, killing wasps in the honey on her plate.'

Among a number of familiar features is the figure of Fate or Fortune, here under two guises in the persons of Mrs Stitch and

Mr Baldwin. It is Mrs Stitch, ubiquitous and full of guile, who at Lady Metroland's luncheon party obtains from Lord Copper the job of foreign correspondent for her protégé, the fashionable young writer, John Boot, with whom later William is so disastrously confused; and it is Mr Baldwin who, in Ishmaelia, comes at the crucial moment to the rescue of William, very like Mrs Rattery descending out of the sky from her aeroplane at Hetton. In this case, however, the dispositions of Fate are benign, and for once the author allows his hero to triumph.

Two years earlier Evelyn had recorded in his diary, 'Made a very good start with the first page of a novel describing Diana's early morning', and it is Diana Cooper who in almost every detail is the template for Mrs Stitch. Evelyn adored Diana, and she was flattered by her fictional alter ego, and yet underlying Mrs Stitch's goddess-like qualities there is something curiously repellent, almost sinister, as though Evelyn in his heart was ambivalent about his feelings for her, as though subliminally his admiration for her beauty, her arrogance and ingenuity was tempered by an instinctive unease. The description of Mrs Stitch's levée, as she lies in bed simultaneously dictating to a secretary, signing cheques, talking on the telephone, hearing her daughter's homework, completing the crossword and giving instructions to the young man painting a mural on the ceiling is clever and funny. It is also the preliminary strokes of a portrait of a woman cold, spoiled, selfish and vain. '[Mrs Stitch's] normally mobile face encased in clay was rigid and menacing as an Aztec mask.'[10]

Desmond Shawe-Taylor in a perceptive review for the *New Statesman*, remarked 'I like Mr Waugh best when he remains within his own territory, which I take to be the circles radiating outwards – not too far – from the lunch-table of Lady Metroland,' and indeed the scenes set in England, and those dealing with the English journalists abroad, are much the most successful. The satirical description of the *Beast* office is a comic masterpiece, as is that of Boot Magna, but when the spotlight moves to Ishmaelian/ Abyssinian affairs, the standard drops. Evelyn had already written about Abyssinia three times (*Black Mischief*, *Remote People* and *Waugh in Abyssinia*), and the subject had little left to offer. His

[10] On 7 July 1936 Evelyn had written in his diary, 'Message to call on Diana; found her with face expressionless in mud mask.'

treatment of the Ishmaeli revolution engineered by the Jackson family with their comic left-wing names – Huxley Jackson, General Gollancz Jackson, Earl Russell Jackson – although efficiently produced as a kind of silent-film farce, is comparatively poor stuff, as tedious in its way as the treatment of the civil war in *Black Mischief.*

Also disappointing is the character of Kätchen, the fey German girl marooned in Jacksonburg with whom William falls in love. Another of those pale, under-water girls in the Evelyn Gardner/ Baby Jungman mould, she never for a moment comes alive, and her tiresome involvement with William is not only boring but technically inappropriate (William as a comic character should not fall seriously in love), impeding an otherwise fast-moving plot.

For the benefit of those in the know, the personal references and private jokes were laid like little land mines below the surface. Cruttwell appears as General Cruttwell, a superannuated explorer now reduced to working as a salesman (assisted by a Miss Barton) in the emporium at which William is sold his ridiculously elaborate tropical kit. 'The shop paid him [the General] six hundred a year and commission, out of which, by contract, he had to find his annual subscription to the R.G.S.[11] and the electric treatment which maintained the leathery tan of his complexion.'

Tilting at another enemy, Ernest Oldmeadow, Evelyn attributes to the Ishmaelites some religious practices as certain to enrage the ex-editor of the *Tablet* as the incident of the cross which fell from heaven during Good Friday luncheon at the Nestorian monastery in *Black Mischief.* 'Various courageous Europeans, in the seventies of the last century, came to Ishmaelia... None returned. They were eaten, every one of them; some raw, others stewed and seasoned – according to local usage and the calendar (for the better sort of Ishmaelites have been Christian for many centuries and will not publicly eat human flesh, uncooked, in Lent, without special and costly dispensation from their bishop).'

Evelyn's personal debt to 'the Master', P. G. Wodehouse, in this most Wodehousian of all his novels, is acknowledged in the last chapter, when Uncle Theodore Boot, a supremely Wodehousian character, present at the ghastly banquet given by Lord Copper to honour William's journalistic achievement, discovers to his joy

[11] Royal Geographical Society.

that he and his neighbour 'had both, in another age, known a man named Bertie Wodehouse-Bonner'.

Scoop was received on the whole with enthusiasm by the critics, although there were reservations. Among the best notices were those from the *Times Literary Supplement*, whose reviewer described the book as 'ingenious, satirical, extremely funny', and Evelyn's old pupil, Derek Verschoyle, in the *Spectator*. Verschoyle had not, he said, found *Scoop* 'as good as some of Mr Waugh's other books', and, like Desmond Shawe-Taylor, was of the opinion that 'Europe [is] a more effective background to his characters than the other continents,' but he described the novel as intelligent, inventive and intricately organised, which was what partly made 'Mr Waugh's novels so much superior as entertainment to any other fiction written today'.

The *Daily Telegraph*, piqued at the less than respectful portrait of Sir Percival Phillips, easily recognisable as Sir Jocelyn Hitchcock of the *Daily Brute*, ran a stiff little paragraph in its diary column. '[Mr Waugh] makes Hitchcock return home early in the war ... Actually, as will be well remembered, Phillips's famous message from Addis Ababa to the *Daily Telegraph* revealing the Rickett concession was not only the war's biggest scoop but one of the greatest in modern journalism.'

Scoop was the choice of both the Book Society and the Catholic Book Club but although undoubtedly a success, it could not on its own solve Evelyn's financial problems. Well-paid journalistic work was still hard to come by. The *New Yorker* rejected as too snobbish an article on wine, *Tatler* turned down Peters's suggestion that Waugh should write a regular column, and Elizabeth Penrose of American *Vogue* briskly informed Roughead that, 'Mr Waugh is an expensive luxury that *Vogue* cannot afford except in rather exceptional circumstances.' In May, as a special correspondent for the *Tablet*, Evelyn accompanied by Laura had attended the Eucharistic Conference in Budapest celebrating the ninth centenary of St Stephen, Hungary's patron saint, but although rewarding in other, more spiritual ways the job earned him next to nothing. Then from a wholly unexpected source came an offer which, although unusual and of dubious morality, was in the economic circumstances irresistible.

A few days before leaving for Budapest, Evelyn had told Peters, 'A very rich chap wants me to write a book about Mexico. I gather he is willing to subsidise it. I am seeing him on Wednesday & will turn him on to you for thumb-screwing.' The rich chap was Clive Pearson, second son of the multi-millionaire Viscount Cowdray, head of a vast international business empire. Among Cowdray's most valuable possessions, established at the end of the last century, were oil fields in Mexico so extensive and profitable that they made Cowdray, together with the Standard Oil Company of America, the greatest commercial interest in the country and second only to the president in personal importance. In 1937 the communist Cárdenas government, in an attempt to curtail the power of foreign investors, first ordered the oil companies to increase the wages of their native workers, then the following year passed a law expropriating all foreign-owned assets. For twenty-five years the revenues of the oil companies had been almost limitless; they paid no taxes and there had been no restriction on their export of the country's most valuable natural resource. Needless to say, they did not care for the new régime. Clive Pearson, determined to try to save his golden goose, had the idea of commissioning a well-known name to put his case under the cover of writing a travel book about Mexico. Pearson would pay for the book on the strict understanding that the deal was to be kept secret. On this the contract was clear: 'Mr Waugh shall not disclose to any person or persons whatsoever the existence or contents of this agreement or the fact that he is receiving financial assistance from Mr Pearson unless Mr Pearson shall give his previous consent in writing to such disclosure.'

Although he understood very well that he was being hired to produce a blatant piece of propaganda, Evelyn accepted without hesitation. The money was good (he received a cheque for £989 from Pearson before leaving), the expenses generous, and it was a chance to enjoy a free holiday with Laura in an exotic part of the world. In addition, although his interest in the oil industry was slight, there were aspects of the situation which appealed to his sympathies. From the time of the Spanish conquest, Mexico had been a devoutly Catholic country, but in 1931 under President Calles the churches had been closed, and for five years the government had pursued a policy of brutal and systematic persecution resulting in the murder of hundreds of priests, the desecration of hundreds of places of worship, and crushing penalties imposed on anyone found practising his religion. The republican army epitomised everything Waugh hated: anti-clerical, apparently heavily masonic, opposed to all foreign influence and dedicated to the destruction of the ruling class, in consequence reducing the country to a state of poverty, squalor and spiritual sterility. Under the Cárdenas régime, Waugh wrote, Mexico every year grows 'hungrier, wickeder, and more hopeless'.

Evelyn and Laura sailed for New York on 7 July. From New York they went by ship to Vera Cruz, and from there by train to Mexico City, where they installed themselves at the Ritz.

Evelyn's account of his visit, *Robbery Under Law*, falls uneasily into three divisions: a journalistic account of his experiences as a tourist; a cumbersomely documented essay describing the outrageous treatment of Pearson's company by the Mexican government; and lastly, an impassioned history of the state's persecution of the Church. As a tourist, Waugh complains of the bed-bugs (although not, he hastens to add, at the Ritz), the noise, and the compulsory trip to view 'the infinitely tedious' Aztec and Mayan remains. In his rôle as propagandist, obediently beating Pearson's drum, he berates the Cárdenas government for deliberately destroying the country's one profitable industry. 'To ruin the whole nation in order to reduce the disproportionate prosperity of a part of it, is insane. That has been General Cárdenas's policy.' He goes on to attack the government both for its inefficacy and for its corruption, a corruption which is rendering Mexico ripe for fascism, an inefficacy that would be derisory were its consequences not so destructive.

Waugh's conservative perspective enabled him effectively to ignore the cruelties of the Spanish conquest and largely to overlook the ruthless exploitation of the Mexican peasant; nonetheless, with the country in a state of utter dissolution, he scarcely needed to argue his case. Mexico was desperately poor, hopelessly disorganised and endemically corrupt. In Waugh's eyes, the horror of the situation transcended politics: what he saw was the triumph of chaos over order, the victory of evil over good, of the barbarians over the forces of civilisation. The law of the jungle had taken over, just as the jungle had overtaken Tony

Last's civilised world in *A Handful of Dust*. As an example in microcosm of the country's decay, Waugh describes the experience of a middle-aged Mexican of Spanish descent whom the recent laws had reduced to penury. A model landlord on his small but profitable estate, his property had been confiscated and given to the workers, leaving him destitute.

> We went together to visit his former home. The house was empty and the garden in decay . . . the experimental plantation was no longer in use; the remainder of the estate which had been divided into small holdings was already, in places, reverting to waste. Shade trees and cropping bushes, unpruned, were growing together half buried in weeds . . . We found the old gardener who, on the assumption that he was too close to the patron, had not shared in the spoils. We asked him about the conditions of the people. He said they had no wages now and that many of them had left their holdings and drifted into the town. The others did not bother to grow more than a bare subsistence for themselves; if they did the government claimed it in repayment for the tools and seeds they had been lent; when they were in need of ready cash they set off to the hills and made charcoal.

Interestingly, Graham Greene, who went to Mexico the same year (1938) and politically veered as far to the left as Waugh to the right, came to many of the same conclusions, although very differently expressed. Both men loathed Mexico and the Mexicans, but where Waugh's account is on the whole factual and dogmatic, Greene's is emotional, highly coloured and intensely subjective.[12] Greene's *The Lawless Roads* gives a far more vivid impression of the horror and reality of corruption than does Waugh's *Robbery Under Law*, and yet there is an integrity in Waugh's account that is lacking in Greene's highly wrought version. Where the two writers march closest together is in their condemnation of the state's persecution of the Church, the locking of the churches, the hounding of the clergy, the notorious murder of the young Jesuit, Father Pro; they both cite as evidence of divine partisanship the story of the miraculous visitation of

[12] Evelyn in his book refers to *The Lawless Roads* as 'brilliant'. In a review he says of it, 'Mr Greene's was an heroic journey, mine was definitely homely . . . He makes no disguise of the fact that Mexico disgusted him. In fairness, it must be added that England disgusts him, too.'

Our Lady of Guadaloupe. Where Greene treats his material in a manner both manipulative and melodramatic, Waugh mainly confines himself to a selective but sober statement of fact, rarely giving way to the kind of showy sentimentality which, skilfully employed, was an important part of Greene's stock in trade.

Unlike Greene, who wrote with no external constraints, Waugh was a hired hand; his brief was to expose the appalling injustice inflicted on Pearson's company, his personal concern the appalling injustice inflicted on the Church. Not surprisingly, the result is unsatisfactory, as the author himself recognised; it was the only one of his travel books from which no extract was reprinted in his travel compendium published in 1946, *When the Going Was Good*.[13] There is, however, one long passage in *Robbery Under Law* which is peculiarly revealing, in which, in effect, Waugh states his creed. He must warn the reader, he says near the beginning of the book, that he went to Mexico a conservative, and a conservative he returned, everything he saw there having confirmed him in his opinions.

> I believe that man is, by nature, an exile and will never be self-sufficient or complete on this earth; that his chances of happiness and virtue, here, remain more or less constant through the centuries and, generally speaking, are not much affected by the political and economic conditions in which he lives; that the balance of good and ill tends to revert to a norm; that sudden changes of physical condition are usually ill, and are advocated by the wrong people for the wrong reasons; that the intellectual communists of today have personal, irrelevant grounds for their antagonism to society, which they are trying to exploit. I believe in government; that men cannot live together without rules but that these should be kept at the bare minimum of safety; that there is no form of government ordained from God as being better than any other; that the anarchic elements in society are so strong that it is a whole-time task to keep the peace. I believe that inequalities of wealth and position are inevitable and that it is therefore meaningless to discuss the advantages of their elimination; that men naturally arrange themselves in a system of classes . . . I believe in nationality; not in terms of race or of divine commissions for

[13] Waugh never made further use of the experience, while from Greene's Mexican journey came not only *The Lawless Roads* but a year later the prize-winning *The Power and the Glory*.

world conquest, but simply this: mankind inevitably organises
itself into communities according to its geographical
distribution; these communities by sharing a common history
develop common characteristics and inspire a local loyalty ... I
do not think that British prosperity must necessarily be inimical
to anyone else, but if, on occasions, it is, I want Britain to
prosper and not her rivals. I believe that war and conquest are
inevitable; that is how history has been made and that is how
it will develop ...

When *Robbery Under Law* (originally titled *Pickpocket Government*)
was published in 1939, it was received with little more than polite
interest, typified by a review in the *Guardian* stating that the book
'is admirably written, and few could have set out more ably this
view of Mexico, a view which is open to argument but deserves
to be understood'. Harold Nicolson in the *Daily Telegraph* was one
of the few disparaging voices. 'Mr Evelyn Waugh has written a
short but dull book upon Mexico. He adopts towards that lovely
but misgoverned country the Catholic, the Conservative, the Phal-
angist, point of view ... His account of the oil controversy, as of
the relations between Mexico and the United States, is as jejune
as any blue book.'

In the United States, however, where the book was published
by Little, Brown under the more diplomatic title, *Mexico: an Object
Lesson*,[14] it drew a warmer response, in spite of the author's frank
contempt for America's rôle in the affair. ' ... Mr Waugh's outspoken account of what he saw and heard below the Rio Grande
during the Summer of 1938 is, in its way, a landmark in American
publishing history,' wrote R. L. Martin in the *New York Times*.
'Soberly conceived and wittily executed in the best tradition of
the familiar essay, it is one of those astringent volumes which
appear every now and then as an antidote to complacency,
sweetness and light. The evident sincerity of the author, the
high quality of his literary talent and the calm logic with which
he pursues his theme entitle him to a hearing in this
country.'

On return from Mexico at the end of October 1938, Evelyn's

[14] The United States still maintained diplomatic relations with President
Cárdenas's government, while Britain did not.

most pressing concern was to write the Pearson book so he could start work on a novel, news which came as a relief to Peters, depressed by his client's original intention, suggested to him by Tom Burns of Longmans Green, of undertaking a history of the Jesuits, a proposal that could not from any angle be regarded as commercial. In April Evelyn wrote to Diana Cooper, 'I finished a book today. About Mexico. Like an interminable *Times* leader of 1880. People will say well Waugh is done for; it is marriage and living in the country has done it. But I have a spiffing novel in mind and they must think again.' Before the novel could be got underway, Evelyn had his usual journalistic assignments to complete, mainly book reviews and a short story for *Good House-keeping*, 'An Englishman's Home', notable for the last appearance of that old enemy, C. R. M. F. Cruttwell. His reviews included attacks on a number of writers much in fashion at the time, among them W. H. Auden and Cyril Connolly.

Since Oxford days, Waugh and Connolly had maintained an unbroken if uneasy friendship, Evelyn frequently dining with Connolly and his wife Jean in their house in the King's Road. But although they enjoyed each other's company, their temperaments were in some ways too similar, their politics, particularly since the Spanish Civil War, too different for a tranquil relationship. A friend of both, Christopher Sykes, remarked of this period that when the two of them were together, 'one could feel that each had a pistol in his pocket, and conversation tended to be appropriately over-guarded.' 1938 saw the publication of Connolly's *Enemies of Promise*, a revealing exercise in criticism and autobiography which Waugh dissected with fiendish perception. After giving credit to Connolly for his rare talent as a critic, he goes on to analyse in detail his fatal flaws of both temperament and artistry. The book, he says, is full of 'phrase after phrase of lapidary form, of delicious exercises in parody, of good narrative, of luminous metaphors, and once at any rate – in the passages describing the nightmare of the man of promise – of haunting originality, [but it] is structurally jerry-built . . . Not only in general plan, but in detail, Mr Connolly shirks the extra effort which would have helped him to attain his avowed object of writing a durable book.'

Auden had collaborated with Christopher Isherwood on *Journey to a War*, a collaboration described as '[a] pantomime appearance as hind and front legs of a monster'; Isherwood is allowed a little faint praise, but Auden is condemned as 'awkward and dull', a poet whom vociferous critics have turned into 'a public bore'. When Stephen Spender wrote to protest at this judgment, Waugh, completely unrepentant, took the opportunity to elaborate his argument.

> I am replying to Mr Spender mainly because his letter forms an example of the attitude towards Mr Auden of a certain group of writers. As I said before, it is their fault, not his, that he is a public bore. He writes mediocre verse, as do a multitude of quite decent young men. No particular shame attaches to that. But a group of his friends seem to have conspired to make a booby of him. At a guess, I should say that the literature they have produced about him is, in bulk, about ten times his own work. That is shockingly bad for a man still young, alive and, I fear, productive.

In contrast, Somerset Maugham, a writer whose claims to greatness were largely dismissed by the literary intelligentsia, wins warm praise for his excellent craftsmanship. Reviewing *Christmas Holiday*, Waugh writes that 'one reads it with a feeling of increasing respect for his mastery of his trade. One has the same delight as in watching a first-class cabinet-maker cutting dovetails ... He is, I believe, the only living studio-master under whom one can study with profit.'

Apart from one or two brief visits to London, Evelyn remained at Piers Court, writing, gardening and as far as possible avoiding the neighbours. In July, in order to give their servants a holiday, he and Laura went to Pixton, a visit he enjoyed no more than before. 'Various Amorys and Horners popping in and out, children all over the house, incessant rain, unpunctual uneatable meals, incessant telephoning and changing of plans,' he recorded in the diary. He was nonetheless able to work on his new novel, *Work Suspended*. 'I have rewritten the first chapter of the novel about six times and at last got it into tolerable shape,' he noted with satisfaction at the end of the month.

Returning at the beginning of August to Piers Court, Evelyn was faced with two Herculean labours – his novel, and the restitution of his beloved garden, which he found in a state of decay. 'Weeds had grown prodigious, Prewitt's only effort had been to kill all the grass on the circle with an application of soot, the whole place looked as neglected as it did when we first arrived.' Energetically he began to set it to rights, but then on 24 August, there is this entry in the diary: 'Working in the afternoon in the garden, clearing the alley, I thought: what is the good of this? In a few months I shall be growing swedes and potatoes here and on the tennis court; or perhaps I shall be away and then another two or three years of weeds will feed here until the place looks as it did when we came here two years ago.'

On Sunday, 3 September, the prime minister broadcast to the nation that war with Germany had been declared. Two days later an advertisement appeared on the front page of *The Times*: 'Mr Evelyn Waugh wishes to let Piers Court . . . Low rent to civilised tenant.'

Bloodshed avoided
at the cost of honour

In the weeks leading up to the declaration of war, Evelyn made
a point of seeming to ignore the coming crisis, deliberately avoiding any discussion of the international situation. It was not that
he refused to believe it would happen, more that the enormity
and inevitability of it filled him with dread. He took a morose
pride in the fact that his was one of the few families in England
not to possess a wireless. When Diana Cooper turned up at Piers
Court for a night at the end of June 1939, bursting with insider
information, dying to impart titbits about 'Winston', she was
abruptly snubbed and the subject changed: if she wanted to hear
Halifax's speech on the radio, she was told, she must go outside
and listen to it in the car. Although distancing himself from the
war hysteria afflicting much of the nation, Evelyn was profoundly
depressed by what he saw happening, particularly the signing in
August of the Nazi–Soviet Pact guaranteeing Russian neutrality
in the event of Germany's becoming involved in war. For Evelyn,
Russia and the spread of communism were most to be feared,
conquest by Russia 'a more terrible fate for the allies we are
pledged to defend than conquest by Germany'. More nearly he
dreaded the effects of war on his own affairs, which at last were
relatively settled and relatively happy: there was Laura, again
expecting a child, and Piers Court, and during the summer he
had become absorbed in work on a new novel. All this must now
be abandoned.

Signs of the new order were already in evidence. Stinchcombe
had been alerted to receive parties of evacuees, women and
children mainly from the East End of London, and Miss Metcalfe,

the local schoolmistress, informed Evelyn that Piers Court had been designated as a billet. At the end of that week, full of apprehension, he went down to the village hut as instructed to collect his assignment. 'Most of the notables of the village were there; no children, and complaints that Mrs Barnett had changed all reception arrangements. Meanwhile we listened to wireless in a Mrs Lister's motor-car. It said the evacuation was working like clockwork. Still no children. Then some empty buses. Finally a police officer in a two seater who said the children had come 400 short and there were none for Stinchcombe. Rain came on so we dispersed.'

Over the next few days little groups of white-faced strangers appeared, hanging round the village looking bored and lost. 'Some of the evacuees are under the impression that they are taking refuge from the IRA. Others are extremely discontented at not drawing more pay from the Government and are going home in a huff. Most are settling down. It is now clear that we are going to be immune.' Evelyn relaxed turning his attention to blackout precautions, and to saying goodbye to his butler, Ellwood, who was leaving to join up.

What was easy for Ellwood proved much harder for his employer. At thirty-six Evelyn was at an awkward age, too old for immediate call-up, too young to have earned useful experience in the First World War.[1] Although his priority was regard for his future as a writer, never for one moment did he consider trying to opt out. Determined to involve himself wholly, he had nothing but contempt for those who left their beleaguered country for refuge in the United States or Canada. To Diana Cooper, who was in New York accompanying her husband on a lecture tour of the United States, he sent a letter of heavily ironic commiseration. 'My heart bleeds for you & Duff. I can think of no more painful time to be among Americans & to be obliged by your duties to pay attention to their ghastly opinions.' He was aware, too, of the valuable experience which active service would provide. On 27 August he wrote in his diary,

---

[1] Although at the beginning of the war conscription was extended to include men up to the age of forty-one, the administrative process was so slow that by May 1940 no one over twenty-seven had yet been registered; also, the forces were reluctant to start calling up large numbers before they were equipped to receive them.

My inclinations are all to join the army as a private. Laura is
better placed than most wives, and if I could let the house for
the duration very well placed financially. I have to consider thirty
years of novel-writing ahead of me. Nothing would be more
likely than work in a government office to finish me as a writer;
nothing more likely to stimulate me than a complete change of
habit. There is a symbolic difference between fighting as a
soldier and serving as a civilian, even if the civilian is more
valuable.

As though in direct contradiction of this argument, Evelyn's first
application for a job was to the Ministry of Information, which
together with the BBC was an obvious choice for many writers
and journalists. A. D. Peters was already working there, but was
unable to help. Next Evelyn turned to other, more influential
acquaintance, applying to Robert Bruce-Lockhart, Lord Perth,
General Beith at the War Office, Ian Fleming at the Admiralty,
Basil Dufferin at the Colonial Office. All of them were noncommittal. Eventually a letter arrived from Naval Intelligence asking
him to call when next he was in London. He went up by train
the same day, going straight to the Admiralty, where he saw
Ian Fleming: Fleming politely regretted there was no immediate
prospect of a job. From the Admiralty to the War Office, where
the response was much the same. The following morning Evelyn
called on the Irish Guards, where the interviewing officer was
'genial but unhelpful', and then on the Welsh Guards, where
the Regimental Lieutenant-Colonel, Colonel Leatham, said there
might be something for him in six months' time. Sustained by
this meagre encouragement, he returned to the country, only to
be followed there by a letter from Leatham, 'unaccountably
telling me that their list had been revised and that they had no
room for me'. This sharp disappointment revived all the old
deep-rooted instincts of insecurity and persecution.

My first feeling was that there must be someone at the War
Office occupied in blocking my chances; my second that
Colonel Leatham had become notorious for his generosity in
giving commissions and has been rebuked. Whatever the
reason, I was thrown into despair. I now had no irons in the fire.
That night I tried a new sleeping draught made by the local
doctor. He admitted later that it was what he used to give

mothers in travail. I slept well but woke feeling on the verge
of melancholy mania.

It is just possible that Evelyn's paranoia was for once justified,
that his applications were indeed being blocked. His expressions
of admiration for Mussolini's fascism in *Waugh in Abyssinia* and
for Franco in *Robbery Under Law* may have persuaded official
circles to regard his name with circumspection. Whatever the
reason, the humiliation of his failure to obtain a job was made
keener by the fact that so many of his friends and contemporaries
were already in positions of responsibility; only Harold Acton
could be considered worse off, turned down on all sides and
reduced to giving lectures on Italy for the British Council
and teaching English to Polish airmen in Blackpool. Like Guy
Crouchback, the protagonist of his three-part novel about the
war, the *Sword of Honour*, Evelyn felt bitterly excluded.

> Everywhere little groups of close friends were arranging to spend
> the war together. There was a territorial searchlight battery
> manned entirely by fashionable aesthetes who were called 'the
> monstrous regiment of gentlemen'.[2] Stockbrokers and wine
> salesmen were settling into the offices of London District
> Headquarters. Regular soldiers were kept at twelve hours'
> notice for active service. Yachtsmen were in R.N.V.R.[3] uniform
> growing beards. There seemed no opportunity for Guy in any
> of this.

A further anxiety lay in the difficulties of letting Piers Court;
several people had been to look, but none had made an offer.
'No one wishes to take the house or to employ me,' Evelyn noted
dismally. But then a group of Dominican nuns who were running
a school agreed to take the place for £600 a year. The Waughs
left Piers Court on 29 September but, relieved though he was to
have got the house off his hands, Evelyn now had to face the
prospect of living indefinitely with his mother-in-law. He never
felt at ease at Pixton, and conditions were rendered more objectionable than usual by the addition of over fifty evacuee children
and their helpers. 'We ate (+ helpers) in the hall making a fine

[2] Victor Cazalet's Anti-Aircraft Battery, formed to provide a congenial and
relatively safe environment for artists and writers. It was rumoured to have a
longer waiting list than the Brigade of Guards.
[3] Royal Naval Volunteer Reserve.

target for the children's spittle from the top landing ... Mild flu
and heavy colds are raging.' Demoralised and depressed, Evelyn
endured it for a month, but by the end of October he had had
enough. He longed to return to his novel, and at Pixton 'work
[was] out of the question as the evacuated children are now
admitted to the garden at the back of the house under my
windows. Impetigo, thrush, and various ailments are rampant.'
The birth of Laura's baby was several weeks off; she was surrounded by her family and therefore content, and so he decided
to seek shelter in that cosy, comforting pre-war sanctuary, the
Easton Court Hotel.

At Chagford his spirits immediately improved. 'Wrote all the
morning', he recorded on the first day. 'The second chapter
taking shape and, more important, ideas springing'; and on the
first of November, 'Continuous rain for the last three days and,
in consequence, the novel progressing well and myself not
sleeping ... I take the MS of my novel up to my bedroom for
fear it should be burned in the night. It has in fact got to interest
me so much that for the first time since the war began I have
ceased to fret about not being on active service. Perhaps that
means that I shall shortly get a commission.' No sooner were the
words written than a commission – from the Royal Marines –
arrived. Craved for so long, it now meant little. For four months
Evelyn had been trying his utmost to become a member of the
fighting forces; finally he had accepted defeat and returned to
his writing; the book had taken off, he was deeply immersed, had
completed two chapters which he knew to be good – 'an A1
novel', he told Roughead. None of that mattered now. 'It is clear
to me that I shall not resume my novel for the duration,' he
wrote to Peters. 'Is there a chance of selling the two chapters
under the title 'Work not in Progress' or 'Work Suspended' to a
high-brow paper. Connolly has started one backed by a pansy of
means named Watson. Could they be induced to pay, say £50 for
the serial rights of the fragment?' Evelyn himself had had an idea
of starting a monthly literary magazine, to be called *Duration*,
with Osbert Sitwell and David Cecil as co-editors, but his plans
had been pre-empted by *Horizon*, launched by Peter Watson and
Cyril Connolly in December 1939. And it was in *Horizon* that the
first chapter of *Work Suspended* was published in 1941, the entire

fragment, against Peters's advice,[4] by Chapman & Hall the following year in a small edition of 500 copies.

Evelyn had shown the work to several people, including his
father, who had been favourably impressed. 'Read Ch 1 of
Evelyn's new novel – excellent', Arthur recorded in his journal.
Work Suspended is the only one of Waugh's novels to be written in
the first person, the narrator, John Plant, a successful thriller
writer, who at the beginning of the book is summoned home
from Morocco by the death of his father.

The first section establishes the characters of father and son,
and their distant, formal relationship ('It is about a father with
whom you will be unable to trace any similarities,' Evelyn wrote
to Arthur), the second part telling the story of John Plant's falling
in love with Lucy Simmonds, the wife of an old friend. Plant
senior is an old-fashioned academic painter; profoundly contemptuous of Bloomsbury and the modern movement, he special-
ises in vast religious and historical panoramas, and also in genre
paintings of domestic melodrama very like those which Waugh
himself was to collect later on. He also ran a lucrative sideline in
'restoration' work for a West End gallery. He is an elegant, eccentric, sardonic man, full of scorn for his own times, subject to
persecution mania, and like his creator apt to view much of
contemporary life as 'a huge, grim and solitary jest'. His bachelor
son, bloodless and immature, is just as eccentric, if far less likeable. He, too, despises the modern age and feels little affection
for any of his contemporaries – until he finds himself falling in
love with Lucy. His feelings for her are the first indication of his
coming to life and maturity, a process which would presumably
have provided the main theme of the novel.

There is a great deal of Evelyn Waugh in both Plants, father
and son: John Plant's craftsmanlike attitude to his work, a shared
sense of irony and detachment, their dislike of modernity. After
his father's death, killed by a car while crossing the road, John
Plant comes to understand and respect his father's work and
attitudes, very much as Evelyn came to do with Arthur. The
tone of the book is balanced and benign, as if the death of
John Plant's father and the subsequent destruction of his house,

---

[4] 'I think you would be wise to keep it until it can be the main part of a book
of collected pieces,' Peters wrote to Waugh in July 1942.

demolished by a cheap-jack property developer, was a symbol of Evelyn's happy liberation, through marriage and the purchase of property, from his own unsatisfactory young manhood and his father's influence. Lucy Simmonds, with her pale beauty ('[which] rang through the room like a peal of bells'), her generosity, her unaffected goodness and sincerity, owes a substantial amount to Diana Guinness. Lucy, like Diana when Evelyn knew her best, is expecting a child, and the course of Plant's friendship with her – days in the country, visits to the zoo, long confidential conversations – closely follows Evelyn's friendship with Diana during the course of her pregnancy. Her friendship, says Plant, employing a favourite Waughian simile, 'was an experience for which I was little qualified, to be admitted, as it were, through a door in the wall to wander at will over that rich estate'. Lucy's turning away from him after the birth of her baby, at which point the fragment ends, is as wounding for Plant as Diana's turning away had been for Evelyn.

Years later when Diana accused him of using her as the model for Lucy, Evelyn for a series of complicated reasons denied it.[5] But then he never regarded himself under obligation to reveal the sources of his inspiration, preferring to pay lip-service to what Graham Greene described as 'the time-old gag that an author can never be identified with his characters'.

The great comic character in *Work Suspended* is Atwater, a relentlessly scrounging, touchy yet insensitive oaf; when asked on whom Atwater was based, Evelyn replied insouciantly that every character in the book was without exception modelled on Baby Jungman.

Atwater is the first of those characters, like Trimmer in the *Sword of Honour* trilogy and Hooper in *Brideshead Revisited*, who to Waugh personified the vulgarity and greed of the modern age. But Atwater, like Apthorpe in *Men at Arms*, is primarily a clown; it is he who lightens the otherwise rather sombre tone, although his amorality, comic in its various manifestations, has a savage, sinister undercurrent. An instance of this is the brilliantly funny scene in which the penurious Atwater is compared with an ape

---

[5] In March 1966, Evelyn wrote a version of the truth to Diana: 'I must not leave you with the delusion that *Work Suspended* was a cruel portrait of you. It was perhaps to some extent a portrait of me in love with you, but there is not a single point in common between you and the heroine except pregnancy. Yours was the first pregnancy I observed.'

at the zoo. He and John Plant are watching the behaviour of a gibbon in its cage.

'Feeding animals while men and women starve,' he [Atwater] said bitterly . . .
'The animals are paid for their entertainment value,' I said. 'We don't send out hampers to monkeys in their own forests' – Or did we? there was no knowing what humane ladies in England would not do – 'We bring the monkeys here to amuse us.'
'What's amusing about that black creature there?'
'Well, he's very beautiful.'
'Beautiful?' Atwater stared into the hostile little face beyond the bars. 'Can't see it myself.' Then rather truculently, 'I suppose you'd say he was more beautiful than me.'
'Well, as a matter of fact, since you raise the point . . .'
'You think that thing beautiful and feed it and shelter it, while you leave me to starve.'
This seemed unfair. I had just given Atwater a pound; moreover, it was not I who had fed the ape. I pointed this out.
'I see,' said Atwater. 'You're paying me for my entertainment value. You think I'm a kind of monkey.'
This was uncomfortably near the truth. 'You misunderstand me,' I said.

On the publication in book form of *Work Suspended* in 1942, Peters was proved right: the critics were puzzled at being presented with such a slender fragment of barely 20,000 words. The *Times Literary Supplement* observed, 'Mr Waugh is often amusing, sometimes acute, at times pleasantly decorative and at other times a trifle shrill with prejudice, but what else this fragment is intended to convey there is no means of knowing'; while Rose Macaulay wrote, 'It is carefully composed; it lacks the earlier sparkle; it has a seriousness of tone that might or might not have been fully justified by its theme as it developed: it did not develop, so we cannot know.'

Most perceptive was a piece by Nigel Dennis in *Partisan Review*. Dennis compared Waugh with the poets of the New Left, specifically with Auden, Spender and Day Lewis, and seizing on the theme of the house. The first section of the book was originally entitled 'My Father's House', and John Plant's search for a house of his own, having until then, like Waugh, led a nomadic existence, was by all indications to be an important strand in the narrative.

For fifteen years Waugh has sung the house, and with it the precious furnishings he finds suited to it . . . And in this love of house, of continuous domicile and individual roof, Waugh appears for the defence in one of the most important struggles in English poetry and letters of the last 20 years . . .

The young men who have written English poetry for the last ten years have been mostly the men of Waugh's class . . . Their battle has been for self-emancipation; freedom, not from riches or love of grandeur but from the far more insidious influences of the houses of their birth and education. What appeared in their writings as a new faith in the proletariat and an enthusiasm for the urban under-privileged was, far more, an effort to purge the author's own personality of its upper-class preferences and trained acceptance of the old, rural order . . . The intellectual pledged his new fidelity to the city, to the waste land that must [be] recreated; he entered the woods only by charabanc . . . And in the new direction, there is clearly indicated the sharp line that had emerged to divide the intellectuals of the Left from such as Evelyn Waugh. Like these intellectuals Waugh saw the ghosts in the old houses, the flies lovely in amber; unlike them, he totally rejected the plea to 'advance to rebuild'. The ghosts must be materialized; or, if that were impossible, they must be preserved as the best available wraiths.

Meanwhile there was the war. It was at the end of November that Evelyn finally secured his commission. The previous month he had received an encouraging letter from Brendan Bracken, Winston Churchill's parliamentary private secretary, whom he had met staying with the Brownlows at Belton; according to Bracken, Churchill, then first lord of the Admiralty, had on Bracken's urging strongly supported Waugh's application for the Royal Marines.

Evelyn went up to London on 24 November for his interview, staying overnight with his parents at Highgate. Arthur had taken an unpaid job teaching Victorian poetry to the sixth form at Highgate School, and there was much talk of this, and of course of Alec back in the Army and already with the British Expeditionary Force in France. But neither Arthur nor Kate seemed very interested in their younger son's career.

Evelyn's first encounter with service life took place in a small flat in St James's, where he had been directed for his medical examination.

> Doctors in shabby white coats strode in and out smoking
> cigarettes. I went first to have my eyes tested and did deplorably.
> When asked to read at a distance with one eye I could not
> distinguish lines, let alone letters. I managed to cheat a little
> by peering over the top. Then I went into the next room where
> the doctor said, 'Let's see your birthday suit. Ah, middle-aged
> spread. Do you wear dentures?' He tapped me with a hammer
> in various organs. Then I was free to dress. I was given a sealed
> envelope to take to the Admiralty. In the taxi I unsealed it and
> found a chit to say that I had been examined and found unfit
> for service. It seemed scarcely worthwhile going to the
> interview . . . A colonel jaunty in khaki greeted me in the most
> affable way, apologized for keeping me waiting and gradually it
> dawned on me that I was being accepted. He said, 'The doctors
> do not think much of your eyesight. Can you read that?',
> pointing to a large advertisement across the street. I could.
> 'Anyway most of your work will be in the dark.' Then he gave
> me the choice between Marine Infantry, a force being raised
> for raiding parties, and Artillery, an anti-aircraft unit for work
> in the Shetlands. I chose the former and left in good humour.

Three days later came the official call-up letter from the Admiralty, ordering Evelyn to present himself on 7 December at Chatham, the historic Royal Navy base at the mouth of the Medway in Kent. 'This is a blow as it gives me no time to do the work which would set my affairs in order. My pay is 6s 10d a day out of which I get 2s 5d pocket money when the deductions are made.' Laura and the children were worth an extra allowance of 7s 6d.

Domestic affairs were further complicated by the birth on 17 November of a son. On the morning of that day Bridget Grant had telephoned Evelyn at Chagford to say that Laura had gone into labour. He left at once for Pixton, arriving in the early afternoon, and the baby was born shortly before midnight. 'It is to be called Auberon Alexander. It is quite big and handsome & Laura is very pleased with it,' Evelyn informed Maimie. The child was christened on 27 November, with Katharine Asquith the only one of the four godparents able to attend. Pleased with the baby though she was, Laura was also tired, tearful and depressed, and Evelyn passed the time in her room, eating his meals off a tray, reading aloud, doing the crossword and '[watching] her get slightly but appreciably better'.

On 6 December, liverish and in low spirits at leaving his wife, Evelyn went to London to be fitted for his second lieutenant's uniform, going down to Chatham the following day. In the train were a group of fellow probationers, among them a solicitor, a sports journalist, a banker, an accountant, a schoolmaster and a wine merchant, with Evelyn at thirty-six the oldest by some years. Most of this very mixed lot had volunteered in response to an appeal on the BBC, it having been discovered somewhat late in the day that the Marines, unlike the Army and Navy, did not have a sufficient reserve to form the special brigade it had been decided was necessary for the performance of various as yet undesignated operations. The formation of this particular brigade was in the nature of an experiment, part of which was the training of wholly inexperienced men as officers without sending them along the normal OCTU[6] route beforehand. Arrived at Chatham and welcomed with pink gins by the colonel, Godfrey Lushington, Evelyn found all his romantic notions about service life made fact – the history, the hierarchy, the noble traditions of chivalry and honour. The regular Marines were discovered to be delightful people, the barracks and mess extremely agreeable. Laura was given a roseate description.

> As soon as we arrived we were surrounded by jaggering colonels & majors who stood us drinks continually from 12 noon until 11 pm.
>
> The commandant made us a speech which was one long apology for everything – our beds, our servants, the fact that the mess paintings & silver were stored away underground. He said, 'Once you use the mess all differences of rank cease to exist. All we expect is the deference which youth naturally pays to age.' Since I am considerably older than most of the captains that suits me well enough. As it happens there is absolutely nothing to apologise for. I have a large bed-room to myself with a fire continually blazing in it; the architecture of the barracks is admirable – Georgian brick; there is a fine portrait of William IV with contemporary frame carved with naval trophies; we drink out of splendid silver goblets; the food is absolutely excellent. On the first evening there was a cold supper

[6] Officer Cadet Training Unit.

on account of a play which was being given us in our own
theatre. I was led to the supper table with profuse apologies and
found lobster, fresh salmon, cold birds, hams, brawn exactly
like the cold table at the St James'. Afterwards several rounds of
excellent vintage port. Everything a great deal better than an
Oxford Senior Common Room but rather like it.

Training started in earnest on 11 December.

Breakfast 7.30; parade 8.15; infantry drill, a tour of the
quartermaster's territory learning among other things how to
distinguish cat from rabbit by the number of its ribs; 10.45
military law; 11.45 PT with degrading games that are designed
to keep us gay and which in fact deny the natural dignity of
man. Luncheon. Parade 2.30 and I[infantry] D[rill] till 4, after
which all the squad fall asleep in armchairs.

The emphasis at this early stage was on military and Marine
history and on physical training – press-ups, vaulting over wooden
horses, running on the spot – which Evelyn hated and skimped
whenever he could. Drill, taken by Colour Sergeant Greensmith
('very decent & very very lazy'), was only slightly less objectionable, hours spent on the square marching, wheeling and presenting arms, the length of each man's paces measured with a long
wooden calliper. Evelyn's reluctance to exert himself and his love
of good living soon became something of a joke, one employed
with relish by the colour sergeant. 'Mr Wuff, that's a rifle in your
hands, not a cigar!' But in spite of the cold and the ineluctable
tedium, Evelyn was enjoying himself, amused by the lore and
language of this unfamiliar world, in particular by the idiosyncratic jargon which to the new recruits quickly became second
nature. 'Temporary second lieutenants who, a few weeks earlier,
had been something in the city, might be heard unblushingly
expressing their intention of "going ashore to see the madam",
when they meant to visit their wives in Croydon.'

At Christmas Evelyn had eight days' leave, dutifully spent at
Pixton. Nothing much had changed there: the house was full of
family, dogs, visitors and evacuees, with Mary Herbert as fiercely
energetic as ever. One guest, arriving shortly before Evelyn's visit,
gave a memorable picture of the scene.

'Mrs Herbert is a huge withered woman, like a moulting eagle with a wild eye and dirty tweeds. She says "What? what?" and "Eh" all the time; the daughters [Bridget and Gabriel] are strong shapeless people with thick calves and great goodness. Talk of Belloc and the Spanish Civil War. The food stinks.'

Laura was in bed with pleurisy, and Evelyn, more than happy to have an excuse for avoiding the 'family fun' downstairs, passed most of the time in her bedroom. Shorter leaves were spent in London lavishly lunching and dining with friends – Tom Burns, Baby Jungman, Trim Asquith, the Howards, the Yorkes, and Maimie and her Russian wine-merchant husband, Prince Vsevelode Joannovitch. By the middle of January Laura was well enough to join her husband in London for a couple of days. Evelyn had grown a moustache and was in high good humour. They dined with Phyllis de Janzé, Hubert Duggan and Gerald Berners, went to the cinema, shopped, lunched with Elizabeth and Raimund von Hofmannsthal, and had tea with Pansy Lamb's sister, Mary Pakenham, who noted that '[Evelyn] was one of the few people who was not made more distinguished-looking by wearing uniform.' On the Saturday evening they dined at Boulestin before going to a revue. On Sunday, '[after] another soft night and morning in bed with the papers', they attended Mass at Farm Street and lunched at the St James' with Phyllis, Hubert, Liz and Raimund. 'It was', Evelyn recorded, 'the happiest forty-eight hours of my life.'

But reunions with Laura, anticipated with such eagerness, were not always so harmonious. When Laura and Evelyn spent a weekend with Laura's friend from childhood, Veronica Fraser, and her husband, Alan Phipps, in a rented house in which the walls were thin, Veronica was distressed to hear Laura, lodged with Evelyn in the bedroom next door, sobbing bitterly through the whole of one night.

Soon after his return to Chatham, Evelyn's group moved to a camp farther down the coast at Kingsdown, due south of Deal, where they were joined by a number of temporary officers from other Marine divisions as well as some of the regular captains, majors and colonels who were to form the skeleton of the brigade. ('When the brigade forms', had been a familiar sentence from the time of Evelyn's first joining up.) Conditions were nothing like as comfortable. Kingsdown was a disused holiday camp, with living quarters improvised in a derelict Victorian villa and a number of small asbestos bathing huts. The cold was appalling, with heavy falls of snow and a biting wind; the laurels round the house were stiff with ice, the sky leaden. 'One bath for sixty men, one washbasin, the WCs all frozen up and those inside the house without seats. Carpetless, noisy, cold. A ping-pong table makes one room uninhabitable, a radio the other. We are put five in a bedroom without a coatpeg between us.' But resourceful as ever when it came to looking after his comfort, Evelyn soon made his own arrangements, moving out of the main house and into one of the huts, keeping himself warm with an oil stove and a fur rug sent from Pixton; for a guinea he became a member of the Deal & Walmer Union Club, a snug refuge where in the evenings he could read and have a drink in peace before dining in an Italian restaurant he had discovered on the esplanade.

At the end of January his situation improved further when officers were given permission to live out with their wives; Evelyn took rooms at the Swan Hotel and sent for Laura. These cosy domestic circumstances at the Swan, and later when living temporarily together in rented accommodation, were accurately recalled two years later in *Put Out More Flags*.

> Alastair had a bath and changed into tweeds . . . Then he took a whisky and soda and watched Sonia cooking; they had fried eggs, sausages, bacon and cold plum pudding; after luncheon he lit a large cigar; it was snowing again, piling up round the steel-framed windows, shutting out the view of the golf course; there was a huge fire and at tea-time they toasted crumpets.
> 'There's all this evening, and all to-morrow,' said Sonia. 'Isn't it lovely . . .'
> . . . During one of these week-ends Sonia conceived a child.

Whereas at Chatham the concentration had been on history and physical training, at Kingsdown the emphasis was on strategy, field exercises and firearms practice. ' "At two hundred yards all parts of the body are distinctly seen. At three hundred yards the outline of the face is blurred. At four hundred yards no face. At six hundred yards the head is a dot and the body tapers. Any questions?" ' In contrast to the routine at Chatham, where everyone was kept busy all day, at Kingsdown there were hours of idleness, with the result that the men grew bored and dispirited. 'We have had too little work,' Evelyn complained. 'An hour's drill every morning would have been excellent for physique and morale. Instead, there have been lectures and tewts,[7] the latter usually quite interesting, long stand-easies throughout the morning, frequent free afternoons, no work ever before 9 or after 4. Result: everyone shabby and cross.'

All this changed in mid-February when the newly formed brigade moved to a tented camp at Bisley near Aldershot in Surrey, premises of the National Rifle Association; here they were met by their colonel with the news that they could 'ship a second pip and go away until Monday'. Evelyn went to his parents at Highgate as he was beginning to be seriously worried by debt. A lieutenant's pay was not generous, and during the last few months almost every weekend had been spent in London, staying at comfortable hotels, lunching and dining at the Ritz, drinking at White's Club, of which he had newly become a member, shopping, and generally 'spending a very great deal of money. We are now about £500 overdrawn. I owe £200 in income tax and see no possibility of getting my finances square except by prodigious national inflation.'

As an economy measure, he decided to remain the following weekend in camp, pleased, therefore, to accept an invitation from his brigadier, Albert St Clair Morford, to lunch and dinner on the Saturday. The brigadier had already made an impression during a course of lectures he had given at Kingsdown. '[He] looks like something escaped from Sing-Sing,' Evelyn had noted with pleasure. 'Teeth like a stoat, ears like a faun, eyes alight like a child playing pirates.' The brigadier drove Evelyn to his house, 'a depraved villa of stockbroker's Tudor'. As they approached,

> I said in a jaggering way 'Did you build this house, sir?' and he said 'Build it! It's 400 years old!' The Brigadier's madam is kept very much in her place and ordered about with great shouts. 'Woman, go up to my cabin and get my boots.' More peculiar, she is subject to booby-traps. He told us with great relish how the night before she had had to get up several times

[7] Tactical Exercises Without Troops.

in the night to look after a daughter who was ill and how, each time she returned, he had fixed up some new horror to injure her – a string across the door, a jug of water on top of it etc . . .

When we came back from our walk he showed me a most embarrassing book of rhymes & drawings composed by himself and his madam in imitation of *Just So Stories*, for one of his daughters. I had to read them all with him breathing stertorously down my neck. Then we did a crossword puzzle until a daughter arrived from London where she is secretary to a dentist. She told me she had been a lift girl at the Times Book Club and had lost her job because at Christmas time, she hung mistletoe in the lift. The Brigadier thought this a most unsuitable story to tell me. When he is in a rage he turns slate grey instead of red. He was in an almost continuous rage with this daughter who is by a previous, dead madam.

The brigade remained at Bisley for another month of firearms training, map-reading, route marches and night operations. In steel helmets decorated with bracken, they lay on their stomachs in the heather, blazing away at the Bisley firing ranges, obediently playing dead as instructed when thunder-flashes were lobbed from behind a gorse-bush. 'The day invariably ended with what the CO called "another bloody awful shambles", what with units arriving at the wrong rendezvous or firing blank cartridges at their own side.'

Near the end of the month there was a route march, 'disastrous from first to last', Evelyn recorded, 'and at every stage of the disaster I occupied a conspicuous place. Until then I had been confident of getting second-in-command of a company . . . On the eve of our Easter leave the company lists came out, I with a platoon in B coy. The work will be more interesting but it means sharing a tent, subsisting on lieutenant's pay; also the knowledge of having disappointed expectations.'

By the beginning of May, Evelyn was at last made captain. The only one of the temporary officers to be thus promoted, Evelyn's rise in rank was due partly to the fact that he was older than his colleagues – the younger subalterns called him Uncle Wu, or just Uncle – partly to his superior intelligence. Colonel Lushington in a report written after the first five months' training commended Waugh's qualities of leadership: '[he] possesses any amount of moral courage and has self confidence when on subjects he

knows. A little impatient... With more military experience...
he will make a first class Company Commander.' In fact, Lushington's initial assessment was over-generous, for Evelyn was too
anarchic, too self-centred and intolerant to make good officer
material.

His chief flaw was an inability to get on with other ranks,
veering awkwardly in his manner between contempt and condescension. He was arrogant when giving orders to the soldier-
servants, or MOAs (Marine Officers' Attendants), who were not
slow to resent it, and he never tried to conceal his impatience
with stupidity, frequently resorting to sarcasm when dealing with
troops, a form of humour which they, familiar with the unsubtle
obscenities of the parade ground, found both bewildering and
objectionable. When instructed by the regimental platoon commander to rebuke his men for swearing, Evelyn was heard addressing them in a refined and petulant manner which, as was clear
from the rows of uncomprehending faces, conveyed very little.
'The continued use of obscenities in conversation is tedious and
undignified. These words punctuate your speech like a hiccup.
Instead they should be savoured and reserved for the creative act
itself or for moments of the most extreme frustration.' 'What is
Captain Wuff on about now?' was the usual response to one of
his lectures. Although it would be an exaggeration to hold, with
Christopher Sykes, that during the war '[Evelyn's] greatest enemies were the men he commanded', it is true that he was not
interested in other ranks; they knew it, and disliked him
accordingly.

This is not to say that officers were compensatingly treated
with deference. Evelyn, like his delinquent alter ego, Basil Seal,
possessed a strong streak of subversiveness, which in its wittier
manifestations delighted his more sophisticated colleagues.

There was a much-treasured occasion when he was heard
enquiring of a pompous visiting brass-hat if it were true that in
the Romanian army no one beneath the rank of major was permitted to wear lipstick; and there were one or two accomplished
performances which always had the class in stitches, one in particular when he argued in favour of using sheep in landings,
driving them ashore first to set off the enemy mines. The class
roared; but the CO watching from the back, sensing danger, was

less amused. Indeed throughout Evelyn's military career he was regarded by his commanding officers as a critical, disruptive and frequently disagreeable influence, and for this reason they were usually delighted to see him move on.

Paradoxically, although Evelyn was by temperament totally unsuited to military life, at this stage he loved it, believed in it, and longed to be accepted as a useful component. In his own idiosyncratic way, he was extremely 'keen', a term of high approbation among soldiers, and always anxious to employ his peculiar talents as best he saw fit. The trouble lay in the crucial difference between Evelyn's romantic vision and the actual realities of modern warfare and of service life. His disillusionment, which took place at many levels and over a long period of time, was harsh and embittering, made more so by the fact that during his early months in the Royal Marines circumstances enabled him to maintain that illusion almost intact. From his first encounter with the Marines at Chatham, with their elegant barracks, their lovingly preserved traditions, the handsome mementoes of a long and heroic past, he was able to construct for himself a military ideal, hierarchical, highly civilised and ritualistic, essentially patrician, redolent in atmosphere of gentlemen's clubs and the drawing-rooms of country houses. It bore little relevance to the mid-twentieth century at war. In those early days Evelyn had no doubt that Britain was fighting a just war, her commanders men of courage and honour. He wanted to be part of that noble adventure. For Evelyn as for Guy Crouchback, the enemy 'was plain in view, huge and hateful . . . It was the Modern Age in arms. Whatever the outcome there was a place for him in that battle.' On his last evening at Chatham, Evelyn had invited Patrick Balfour to a guest night, observing, pleased, that '[Patrick] found the evening very surprising, particularly "the strings" [string band] who came downstairs with the port and the elaborate ceremonies with the snuff horn.' The scene is glowingly reproduced in *Men at Arms*.

> The table was lit with huge many-branched candlesticks which commemorated the military history of the last century in silver palm trees and bowed silver savages . . . Presently the hammer sounded again, the chaplain said Grace and the table was cleared. The removal of the cloth was a feat of dexterity which

never failed to delight Guy. The corporal-of-servants stood at
the foot of the table. The mess orderlies lifted the candlesticks.
Then with a single flick of his wrists the corporal drew the
whole length of linen into an avalanche at his feet.

Port and snuff went round.

The painting of such an attractive picture resulted in a constant
struggle on Evelyn's part to pull the rest of the world inside the
frame. Entranced by the grandeur and formality of Chatham, he
was forever trying to impose standards of a similar excellence,
becoming a stickler for etiquette and proper procedure. While
at Kingsdown he had written 'a long & offensive memorandum
on the disorganization of the camp', reporting to Laura that, 'I
am on the mess committee & am trying to suppress the wireless,
ping-pong table & other, rare recreations of my juniors. So far
my only victory is to insist on correct dress at dinner & grace said
by the mess president.' Soon he was able triumphantly to add,
'Did I tell you that I have won a complete victory over the Stilton
cheese question and it is now properly served.' All the time Evelyn
was looking back to the past, and up to a social class higher than
that of the average marine. Instead of the normal marine practice
of referring to companies as '11 Patrol' or '14 Patrol', he adopted
the Household Division's custom of talking in a lordly way of
'Tom's company', or 'Brian's company', and in the evenings
would impress upon the younger men how much better the world
was before the invention of electricity, how much more 'civilized'
were oil-lamps and candles.

Unsurprisingly, such conduct did not win him much affection
from his fellow officers, although most were prepared to treat
him with indulgence. He was a 'writer chappie', different from
them, clever in an odd way, and his quick wit, if sometimes cruel,
often made them laugh. Occasionally, however, he went too far.
While on the mess committee Evelyn had made a display of his
connoisseurship as a wine-buff; he had insisted on the purchase
of higher quality claret and burgundy, having had several cases of
each sent up from Piers Court for his personal use; these were
kept in his room and referred to as 'Waugh's Stores'. At Chatham
there was a small supply of regimental port, some of it dating
back to 1912, and so precious it was drunk, in very small quantities, only on special occasions. Just before going on Christmas

leave, Evelyn bribed the mess sergeant to let him take away several cases, a crime for which, when discovered, he was severely reprimanded.

Meanwhile, during the spring and early summer of 1940, while the brigade was fighting harmless actions across the lush pastures of the local farms and bivouacking among the scrub and birch of Bisley Common, news of the war in Europe grew increasingly grave. Evelyn had been heartened by the spirited attempt of Finland to hold back the Russians at the Mannerheim Line; now the Finns had capitulated, and the communist ogre was a substantial step nearer. 'The Finnish surrender had an acutely depressing effect on me,' he noted in his diary – which he continued to keep intermittently throughout the war in defiance of official regulations. He and Laura were sharing a rented house with the adjutant, R. D. Houghton, and his wife. The four of them got on well, the Houghtons enjoying Evelyn's provocative arguments on religion, a subject firmly discouraged in the mess, and his reading aloud in the evenings from *Eric, or Little By Little*, a novel he had recently discovered and found irresistibly funny.

But then in May, during a spell of perfect summer weather, came the invasion of the Low Countries, closely followed by the fall of France and the surrender of the Channel ports. 'I lectured to the company upon the international situation and depressed myself so much that I could barely continue speaking.' Overnight the atmosphere in camp changed: all ranks were put on alert, weekend leave cancelled, emergency duties imposed. Evelyn was rarely able to leave his post, and consequently saw little of Laura, although as far as he could he kept her informed of his movements, consoling her by emphasising his unsuitability for military action. 'Col. Lushington speaks of extreme athletic fitness as essential for active service, so I think you can rest easy in your mind that I shall be left behind with the luggage when the more sensational adventures are attempted.'

On 9 June, a late-night signal was received for the brigade to prepare to move instantly to South Wales. 'We hope for Tenby and fear Haverfordwest.' Haverfordwest it was, after a frightful journey by rail which reduced everyone to the lowest spirits. 'The battalion shaken out of camp at 4 am and then left standing about until noon. The mess gave up trying for a week and fed us intermittently on bully beef and biscuits while the corporal of servants took to drink and theft. A long journey and late arrival. Marched in the dark to unlit, filthy billets; all settled in with utmost gloom.' But contrary to expectation, the town was delightful. Evelyn was joined almost at once by Laura, with whom he spent several wholly enjoyable days at the Castle Hotel. But at the end of this agreeable week, the brigade was moved to the coast and embarked on a dirty little ship, its decks still stained with blood from the retreat from Dunkirk, on six hours' notice to sail for Ireland. After a few cramped days of squalor and confusion, these orders were countermanded and the entire company sent by train to Cornwall. 'Our task is the defence of Liskeard. None of us can quite make out why anyone should want to attack it.' The Marines spent ten days setting up coastal defences, effectively wrecking the amenities of the prosperous little resort, to the growing resentment of the local population. '[The battalion] lined the sands with barbed wire and demolished the steps leading from esplanade to beach; they dug weapon pits in the corporation's gardens, sandbagged the bow-windows of private houses and with the co-operation of some neighbouring sappers blocked the roads with dragons' teeth and pill boxes; they stopped and searched all cars passing through this area and harassed the inhabitants with demands to examine their identity cards.' Then with characteristic suddenness new orders arrived, tropical kit was issued, and everyone sent on forty-eight hours' embarkation leave.

It was during this leave, spent partly in London, that Evelyn called on Brendan Bracken in Downing Street and learned of plans for a force of volunteer commandos to be formed under Sir Roger Keyes, director of Combined Operations. Disappointed with his uneventful career so far, Evelyn was attracted by this exciting venture, and at once applied to join 8 Commando under Lieutenant-Colonel Robert Laycock. Afterwards he and Laura lunched with Diana Cooper and dined with Phyllis de Janzé and Hubert Duggan. 'The Woodruffs came in to drink champagne with us after the cinema. They were full of tales of the interesting jobs all my friends are getting – Tom [Burns] in Madrid, Chris [Hollis] in Washington. I felt sad to be going back to the confusion of the Marines. Then my leave was over.' But for nearly another three weeks nothing happened.

Then on Sunday, 18 August, reveille was sounded at 2 a. m., and troops loaded with weapons, ammunition and kit-bags were ferried by lorry to Plymouth, where they were to entrain for the long journey to Birkenhead on the Mersey. Following the usual tedious wait on the platform, the train at last pulled in, but was found to be without drinking water. The C.O., placing a guard on the engine, refused to let the train leave until water was put on board. While this was being done, he heard to his astonishment Captain Waugh giving his quartermaster sergeant, whom for some reason he held responsible for the waterless train, a ferocious dressing-down. Such a public reprimand, in full view and hearing of the men, was unforgivable, and Lushington made up his mind then and there that Waugh must be removed from his command. Once arrived at Birkenhead he sent for Evelyn, and as tactfully as he could explained the circumstances of his demotion and the alternatives available. 'It seems clear that if there is an expedition, which becomes increasingly doubtful, I shall be left to take up my transfer to the Commando while an ungenerous attempt is being made to suggest that I am leaving under a cloud,' Evelyn wrote in his diary, avoiding any explicit reference to his disgrace. 'I was offered choice: (a) leaving the ship at Scapa, which is our first destination, and returning to division for transfer to Commando; (b) becoming brigade intelligence officer; (c) battalion intelligence officer; (d) second-in-command of D Company. After some consideration chose (c), since I do not want to leave battalion when it is going into action ... Some difficulty about my rank, but it is decided I can remain captain in excess of what we are authorized to carry, pending casualties.'

At Birkenhead the brigade had found their ship waiting for them, *Ettrick*, a smart, newly converted P&O passenger vessel, which was to take them to Scapa Flow in the Orkneys. Expected to sail at any moment, in the end she remained in port for a week, rife with rumour, her mess-decks dark and overcrowded, stores and ammunition in disorder, civilians and odd, uniformed detachments swarming everywhere. Eventually at 10 p. m. on 24 August *Ettrick* left the Mersey, arriving at Scapa Flow early on the morning of the twenty-sixth.

Evelyn, no longer in a combatant rôle, now took part in the
various exercises – the usual programme of bivouacs, route marches, landings by night – only as umpire. His chief duties as
intelligence officer were to glean from published and unpublished sources all he could about the battalion's next destination
and the enemy forces deployed there, and, more routinely, to
examine incoming reports, file cables, write up the battalion War
Diary and censor letters. 'Soldiers when writing to their wives and
sweethearts put SWALK, which means "Sealed with a loving kiss",
or ITALY, which means "I trust and love you".' Perhaps because
of his changed responsibilities, Evelyn's attitude towards training
grew increasingly more lax. He was reprimanded on one occasion
when his servant, after clambering ashore on an exercise, was
found to be carrying Waugh's weapon-case holding, instead of its
complement of weaponry, two bottles of wine; after another more
serious incident, Evelyn was summonsed to appear before a court
of inquiry, accused of remaining indoors smoking and drinking
instead of taking part in the organised 'battle' raging outside.

On the last day of August *Ettrick* sailed at eleven in the morning
for Freetown in Sierra Leone, a small component of a powerful
concerted attempt to wrest Dakar from the Vichy government and
install General de Gaulle and the Free French in its place. The
voyage out took fifteen days, the time passing slowly in spite of the
unaccustomed luxury for the officers of having the run of the ship's
first-class cabins and saloons. Now a heavily laden troopship on her
way to battle, *Ettrick* maintained the leisurely routine of a pleasure
cruise in the Mediterranean. The Goanese stewards, still in their
red-and-white P&O livery, continued to call their passengers with a
tray of tea, an apple and a slice of thin brown bread and butter;
continued to arrange symmetrically the ashtrays in the lounges,
and to announce the elaborate five-course meals by means of a tiny
musical gong. Other ranks were not so fortunate, as was testified by
the smell of sweat and vomit which sometimes rose in clouds
from the hot and airless lower decks. Much effort, however, was put
into their entertainment, Evelyn dutifully doing his share by lecturing on Abyssinia and helping to organise concert parties and semi-
facetious debates. Left to himself he read detective stories, and with
gin at a penny a tot drank heavily.

On 14 September they reached Freetown, some four hundred
miles south of Dakar. 'We landed as a battalion and marched

about seven miles to a bathing beach, bathed, and back by same route. I enjoy being in Africa again and among niggers.' With one of his fellow Marines, John St John, he sat drinking on the balcony of a shabby hotel situated among the palms and bougainvillaea on the front, the original of the Bedford Hotel in Graham Greene's novel, *The Heart of the Matter*; here they spent a peaceable hour or two watching the barefoot schoolgirls, the vultures perched on the lych-gate of the little cathedral, the Levantine traders haggling outside their shops.

But this pleasant holiday was short-lived. By dawn on 23 September, *Ettrick*, ready to do battle as part of the large naval force commanded by two British admirals and General de Gaulle, came within sight of Madeleine Bay. Around her lay the cruiser *Cumberland*, the battleships *Barham, Resolution* and *Devonshire*, the aircraft-carrier *Ark Royal*, and an extensive flotilla of destroyers and French sloops. It soon became apparent from signs on shore that de Gaulle was not receiving a cordial welcome from his compatriots; all day the ships lay to, while fighting continued on the beaches as the Free French force tried unsuccessfully to land. The next morning was again foggy and naval operations were announced delayed by bad visibility. An ultimatum calling for the surrender of Dakar was delivered and defied. Still no action was taken, and during the night, in spite of a message from Churchill urging the expedition to complete its mission and stop at nothing, the decision was made to turn round: *Cumberland* had been severely damaged and *Resolution* torpedoed; an attempted landing would be vigorously opposed, and Dakar occupied, if at all, only at the cost of heavy casualties. As the fleet steamed once more south towards Freetown, the immediate sensation was one of intense thankfulness at escape from danger. That evening the gins in the officers' saloon were downed more quickly and in greater number than usual, and there was a noisy, face-saving display of frustration and disappointment; privately, most were light-headed with relief. There were some, however, who were aware of a feeling of shame. John St John in his description of the event used the phrase 'running away',[8] and Evelyn in a letter to Laura wrote bitterly that, 'Bloodshed has been avoided at the

[8] A. J. P. Taylor wrote of the Dakar fiasco, 'The attempt [to seize the port] was beaten off with some loss and much discredit.'

cost of honour.' Two days later he wrote again, expressing at greater length his disgust and disillusionment.

> I have written again to London asking for a transfer from the Brigade because it seems clear to me that we are never going to be employed in a way I can be proud of. Also I want to see you.
>
> ... during the time when we expected to be sent into an operation which could only be disastrous, I realised how much you have changed me, because I could no longer look at death with indifference. I wanted to live & I was pleased when we ran away. That is a bad state of affairs for a marine, but I believe most of the marines felt the same. Perhaps that is a bad thing for the country. I dont know. I know that one goes into a war for reasons of honour & soon finds oneself called on to do very dishonourable things. I do not like the R. M. Brigades part in this war and I do not like the war, but I want to be back in Europe fighting Germans.

In the same letter he told Laura, 'Mr St John writes pages to his artistic girl & when asked what about said "love". I am afraid I do not know how to write that kind of letter.' Evelyn was seldom emotionally demonstrative when writing to his wife, and yet his correspondence is peculiarly revealing of the intensity of his involvement with her. He wrote because he loved her, he wrote to inform and entertain her, often to instruct, sometimes to reprove. Most significantly, he wrote to Laura as to an equal, rarely talking down except when cross, assuming then the manner of a stern father with a recalcitrant child; he took for granted that she had an intelligence and a sharpness of perception on a level with his own. Despite the rules of censorship, which often made it impossible to give more than the briefest hint of where he was[9] or what he had been doing ('I have been in a serious battle,' was his sole specific reference to the Crete campaign), Evelyn gives many closely observed, often very funny descriptions of his military life, working hard to amuse her. 'I do not think you take a great deal of interest in my commando yet,' he wrote to her from Scotland, 'but I hope that this will come with time.'

[9] Rules about giving away location were particularly strict, leading to some elaborate circumlocutions. In a letter to Evelyn, Bloggs Baldwin wrote, 'I can't tell you where I am because of the Germans, but I'm not where I was when you last saw me. I'm on a visit for 3 weeks to where you saw me the last time but two ...'

When away from her for long periods he suffered badly from homesickness, often dwelling nostalgically on their brief married life together in the past and on his hopes for their future. 'I am heavy with homesickness . . . miss you unspeakably . . . I have no other interest or aim than to be with you again . . . You are never out of my thoughts for more than a minute . . . What a lot we shall have to say to each other when we meet. I feel that all our future life will be spent in telling how we have spent this year apart. In danger I have only one fear, that it means further separation from you . . . I read a book *Old Curiosity Shop* in which there was a pony called Whisker[10] & it brought me near to tears.'

He was frequently anxious about her, anxious about her safety – 'though I believe Pixton to be as safe as anywhere' – and in particular what she would do in the event of enemy occupation. 'My worst fear is that England gets into German hands & I shall not be able to get to you . . . If the invasion comes, stay put at Pixton at first, then at your leisure make for Quebec.' He worried, too, that the privations of wartime would put a strain on her always fragile health. The most serious crisis came at the end of 1940. In April Laura had discovered she was expecting another child, her dismay at the news so crushing that Evelyn, who privately referred to the pregnancy as 'regretted by all',[11] was moved to write and comfort her.

> It is sad news for you that you are having another baby and I am sad at your sorrow. For myself, surrounded with the spectacle of a world organized to kill, I cannot help feeling some consolation in the knowledge that new life is being given. Your suffering will be to give life, ours, if we have to suffer, to take it. A child that is a danger & distress now may be your greatest happiness in the future. If I do not live through this war, you will have your childrens love & their need of you . . . I know your patience & resignation will be needed to the full in the coming year, and I thank God that you have them.

The child, a girl, was born on the first of December, and died twenty-four hours later, shortly after Evelyn's arrival at Pixton. 'I saw her when she was dead – a blue, slatey colour. Poor little girl,

[10] Evelyn's pet-name for Laura.
[11] Even the family-minded Arthur wrote of it with uncharacteristic distaste. '[Laura] had a son on November 27. She is expecting another in December. The Roman Catholic priests insist upon it.'

she was not wanted.' Baptised 'Mary', she was buried in the nearby churchyard of Brushford. Arthur Waugh commented sadly, 'There seems to me something quite pathetic in this little star of life, which just flickered and went out. She wasn't wanted, and she did not stay. Evelyn announced her coming as "to the regret of all and the consternation of some". Well, she didn't trouble them for long, and she is spared a great deal.'

A chronic anxiety was, as always, money. On his small salary, Evelyn had to provide for Laura and his children, as well as paying for the wine, cigars, good hotels and restaurants which, luxuries to some, he regarded as basic necessities. With paper shortages and other restrictions, the income from his books was limited, and there was little time or opportunity for journalism. Peters was engaged in a constant struggle to extract payment from laggardly publishers, cheques to be sent direct to Laura. The agency was successful in persuading Penguin to pay in advance, instead of on publication, for the use of *Work Suspended* in one of their anthologies: '[Waugh] is in a commando, fighting like a fiend; meanwhile his wife and kids need money badly. Can't something be done?' Penguin reluctantly complied, only to erupt in protest when they discovered an extract from the same piece had gone to *Horizon* for nothing. 'It strikes me as odd that [Waugh] should have agreed to forgo a fee from *Horizon* in view of the emphasis which members of your staff have laid on his shortage of funds . . . What is the explanation?' 'Even the poorest authors are sometimes ready to forgo commercial considerations for the sake of a friend, or in order to help a magazine which seems to them worthy of support,' Peters smoothly replied.

The main worry was that Evelyn would be unable to meet the demands of the Inland Revenue and that Piers Court would have to be sacrificed. Again with Peters's help, he induced the Revenue to agree to a reduction of his monthly payment from £10 to £5. 'I am glad that the Income Tax men have accepted my offer as it removes the fear that has haunted me, that Stinkers will be sold up in my absence,' he wrote to Laura. 'I have told Roughead to pay straight to you the money for *Work Suspended*. This will pay the tax for six months.'

Piers Court was never far from Evelyn's mind, and Laura was on the receiving end of a flow of detailed instructions about its upkeep and administration.

Will you write to the nuns & call for the full rent. Also, in case they have forgotten, impress on them the importance of keeping the water softener supplied with salt. It suddenly occurred to me during night exercises the other evening that it is just the kind of thing they might economise over and all our pipes get furred up ... Will you please write to the nuns & tell them to air my books. That is to say take them all out shelf by shelf, dust them open the leaves & bang them together. Otherwise they will get worm & damp in them ... I hope that you have not abandoned your plan of going to Stinkers to work on the trees & hedges ... Would you like to have the windows in the drawing room and the breakfast parlour made into glass doors? I want to start building again at Stinchcombe ...

Laura's attempts to do as she was told did not always meet with approval. 'I wonder if you put my vintage port back with the white splash uppermost. I am horrified that you broke into the bins. Talking of keys will you please make sure that you have my keys safely. If they were lost I should go out of my mind ... You told me no Stinchcombe gossip. Please do.' The magisterial tone was frequently adopted in regard to the children, with whom Laura sometimes seemed to be classed. 'For the first & for the last time for some years I have made my son Auberon a present,' Evelyn wrote grandly in November 1941. 'It is a handsomely bound set of *The Children's Encyclopaedia*. This is not to be given to the Grant children or dismembered in the nursery but kept until the boy is of a suitable age to enjoy it. Indeed I think we might give it to him volume by volume birthday & Christmas from his eighth to his twelfth year. In the meantime you may study it. I am sure you will find it instructive. It is scholastic & anti-Catholic in tone but this can be corrected by home influence.' A few days later he added in a postscript, 'Read *Children's Encyclopaedia* assiduously.'

Little of Laura's side of the correspondence remains, nothing from this period. Laura had unique access to a side of Evelyn's nature that was both tender and affectionate; there was no doubt that she loved him, yet her attempts to convey this on paper were childishly inept. During the periods of separation at the begin-

ning of the war, when they were able to see each other at least
every few weeks, she obviously found it easier to meet his expectations. 'You have been good about writing. I love your letters,'
he tells her, making appreciative reference to one in particular
that was 'very sad & affectionate'. However, the longer they were
apart, the more difficult Laura found it adequately to keep in
touch. 'You must assume a more impassioned style,' Evelyn wrote
drily, and later, marooned and miserable in Jugoslavia, he noted
on two consecutive days in his diary, 'a dull letter from Laura',
and 'a bitterly disappointing letter from Laura'. To Laura he
wrote, 'Do try to write me better letters . . . Do realize that a letter
need not be a bald chronicle of events; I know you lead a dull
life now, my heart bleeds for it, though I believe you could make
it more interesting if you had the will. But that is no reason to
make your letters as dull as your life. I simply am not interested
in Bridget's children. Do grasp that. A letter should be a form of
conversation; write as though you were talking to me.'

But Laura was never a good correspondent: she hated writing
and found it next to impossible to pick up a pen. And it was not
only her husband who complained. Her parents-in-law, who relied
on her for information of the whereabouts and well-being of
their younger son, suffered very much from her dilatoriness in
sending news, weeks going by without a word from Pixton. 'It is
a worry not to know [about Evelyn],' Arthur told Alec's wife,
Joan. 'I think K is going to write to Laura & find out but I doubt
if Laura answers for days & days. She is the most lethargic girl I
ever knew . . . Letter-writing, at any rate to in-laws, is not Laura's
strong suit!' When she did write, she gave the bare minimum,
dutifully retailing Evelyn's movements but with not a hint of
warmth or personality. 'Laura's letters are like soppy bread dipped
in tepid water,' Arthur complained with unaccustomed acerbity.
But then Laura was never close to her parents-in-law, a fact which
served only to increase her uncommunicativeness. Gentle, modest
Kate she tolerated, although the two women had little in
common, but Arthur's sentimentality and florid Pickwickian
pose[12] she found unsympathetic and embarrassing. For his part,

[12] A polished performance well described by Donald Cowie, a journalist who
visited Arthur in the Highgate flat. Here he found a 'cosy abode of books,
manuscripts, pleasant chintzes and a modern reincarnation of Mr Pickwick. He
had twinkling eyes, rosy cheeks, silky, white hair and a pleasantly rotund figure.'

Arthur was deeply disappointed in her. At first enchanted by
Laura's shyness, prettiness and fragility, he had hoped for a close
filial relationship, emotional and harmlessly romantic, rather as
he had had once with the Fleming girls and now enjoyed with
Alec's warm-hearted and attractive young wife. Joan had returned
to Australia for the duration, taking the children with her; they
were sorely missed at Highgate, but there was no question of
Laura, enigmatic and remote, taking their place. With Laura,
Arthur never signed himself, as he did in letters to Joan, 'Your
loving Poppa', nor cosily referred to Kate as 'Mrs Wugs'.

> I shall never be able to make anything of Laura. We live in other
> worlds, & talk another language . . . I don't know whether she
> has a very strong character, & is able to keep all her feelings to
> herself; or whether she is a case of arrested development,
> soothed by Papal dope. The only things I have ever discussed
> with her are cross-word puzzles, & the question whether
> Ellwood is actually married to Mrs Ellwood! which does not get
> us very far along the beaten path of confidence!

When the bombing of London was its worst, Laura, prompted by
Evelyn, had offered the Waugh parents a cottage on the Pixton
estate, but they preferred to stay where they were. This meant
that apart from brief visits when Evelyn was home on leave, they
saw nothing of their daughter-in-law, who remained in Somerset,
helping on the farm, driving the tractor, serving in an Air Force
canteen, and in her own eccentric way bringing up her children,
her apparent lack of concern for them worrying their grandparents. When Laura's baby girl died, Arthur noted in his journal,
'it is impossible to say how much, or how little, she minded that,'
and of her behaviour with the other two he commented, 'She is
the very changeling of a mother: half of her seems over the
hills & faraway.' To illustrate what he meant, he transcribed one
of Laura's letters for Joan. ' "Teresa has measles but very slightly &
she is already on the mend. She was normal this morning. In its
way it's quite a good plan as I am beginning to make Bron's
acquaintance, which otherwise I never had a chance to do" . . . !!!'
In adult life Auberon himself recalled that as a small boy '[I]
was certainly not aware that motherhood involved any particular
emotional proximity' he felt, he said, more nearly attached to his
kind and lively Aunt Bridget than he did to his mother.

On 5 October *Ettrick* set sail for Gibraltar, a tedious and uneventful voyage, with no mail from home, all the books in the library read, the good wine drunk, the cigars smoked. 'I have never before been for so long in the same, unvaried society, & though I love the marines still I sometimes wish one or two of them understood my kind of joke ... They are all little boys. Some of them naughty little boys like the Brigadier, most of them delicious & just what I want Bron to be at the age of ten, but not one of them a mature man.' But at Gibraltar good news was waiting in a letter from Colonel Laycock, offering Evelyn the Commando post he had applied for while in Cornwall. Enormously relieved to know for certain he would be leaving the Marines, he was able to enjoy his two days ashore, spent mostly in the garrison library, a 'delicious' place, with 'a large collection of nondescript leather-bound books in a series of clubrooms with leather and mahogany furniture and a sub-tropical garden through the windows ... To my great delight I found Father [Thomas] Gilbey, the Dominican, chaplain in *Renown*. Or rather he found me and took me off to his cabin where I read *Tablet* and *Times* up to the end of September.'

On 27 October *Ettrick* berthed at Gourock on the Clyde. The brigade moved from there to Kilmarnock, where they were immediately given seven days' leave. Evelyn spent the time with Laura at Pixton, 'very happy to forget the war for a week'.

He was happy, too, at the prospect of joining the Commandos, whose raffish reputation and unconventional methods attracted him enormously. Evelyn had only once seen them in action, while he was stationed at Liskeard. 'They were unimpressive to look at, but the umpires, on an exercise which we did with them, spoke enthusiastically of their endurance and enterprise. In fact on that occasion, after marching twenty miles, they made boobies of the directing staff by taking all the defended posts by subterfuge', an incident inspiring a similar coup on the part of Ivor Claire in *Officers and Gentlemen*. 'Bob' Laycock, head of 8 Commando, was the personification in Evelyn's eyes of the soldier hero, 'the commander par excellence'. Brave, intelligent, a bit of a maverick, Laycock possessed great qualities of leadership combined with charm, arrogance and an aristocratic self-assurance, that 'whiff of White's', that to Evelyn was always irresistible. Tall, with the heavy, handsome face of a gentleman boxer, Laycock had been born into a military family, educated at Eton and Sandhurst before being commissioned an officer in the Royal Horse Guards, where he succeeded in combining a brilliant career in this most fashionable of cavalry regiments with such dashing adventures as sailing round the world as an ordinary seaman in a Finnish windjammer.

Returned to Kilmarnock after his week's leave, Evelyn's urgent priority was to make contact with his new commander. The word was that Laycock was at the War House in London. Evelyn went by sleeper to London: no one knew anything at the War Office; nor at the Admiralty; eventually an anonymous brigadier revealed that Laycock had been all the time in Scotland. Evelyn tried to telephone, but was unable to get through.

After lunching at Buck's, he went to the Royal Marines office and tried again to telephone, again without success, going off to recover his temper with dinner at the Dorchester. The following day was equally frustrating, and abandoning his efforts he called on Maimie and her husband in their little cottage behind the Brompton Oratory, a brief return to the timeless, nursery world of Madresfield.

> She is living a life of serene detachment among acres of ruin.
> Her minute house full of opulent furniture, a disorder of
> luxury – lap dogs, orchids, dishes of grapes, boxes of chocolates,
> about 50 mechanical toys with which she and Vsevelode play
> in the evenings. She, very stout, and oddly dressed, exactly like
> eccentric royalty. She was giving a cocktail party at 12 in the
> morning 'because people are so dutch about jaggering me at
> night' . . . When the party left we had a great luncheon of
> oysters & gruyère cheese, with two bottles of very old
> champagne. Then Vsevelode and I smoking cigars a yard
> long & Maimie smoking one of a good six inches, we went to a
> matinée. It is not at all London life as Hitler imagines it.

After a couple more days, during which Evelyn stayed with his parents at Highgate, Laycock was eventually tracked down and Evelyn returned to Scotland.

In a private 'Memorandum on LAYFORCE' describing the formation of the Commandos and the various operations in which he was involved, Evelyn clearly reveals both what it was that initially attracted him and the elements of his disenchantment.

The Commandos, raised originally to supply raiding parties for occupied France, were to be led by youthful officers, 'to consist in all ranks of volunteers for hazardous service, and to have an abnormally high proportion of officers and NCOs to men. Administrative staff was to be reduced to a minimum . . . From the first these units developed individual peculiarities; they attracted divergent types and in all stages of their development it was found difficult to get suitable officers for colonel's appointments.' By the time Evelyn arrived, the seeds of destruction were beginning to take root. Already discipline was deteriorating.

After RM Brigade the indolence and ignorance of the officers seemed remarkable, but I have since realized they were slightly above normal army standards. Great freedom was allowed in costume; no one even pretended to work outside working hours . . . The special lodging allowance did little to cover the very high standard of expenditure in No. 8. Two night operations in which I acted as umpire showed great incapacity in the simplest tactical ideas. One troop leader was unable to read a compass. The troops, however, had a smart appearance on inspection parades, arms drill was good, the officers were clearly greatly liked and respected . . . On the whole, however, I saw few symptoms of their later decay. They had a gaiety and independence which I thought would prove valuable in action. The whole thing was a delightful holiday from the Royal Marines.

8 Commando was stationed at Largs, a prosperous seaside resort on the beautiful west coast of Scotland opposite the Isle of Bute. Believing with Peter Pastmaster in *Put Out More Flags* that as war mostly consists of hanging about, he should at least hang about with his friends, Laycock had recruited his company almost entirely from the smarter regiments, the Household Cavalry, the Grenadiers, Coldstream, Scots Greys and Irish and Welsh Guards. As Evelyn noted with satisfaction in his diary, 'Nothing could be less like the Marines than the Special Service Battalion.'

The men with whom Evelyn found himself billeted at the Marine Hotel were exactly the kind of 'Buck's toughs' by whom he was always fascinated; men such as Peter Beatty, Philip Dunne,

Eddie FitzClarence, Robin Campbell, Randolph Churchill, Peter Milton and Harry Stavordale; dandies in dress, intolerably spoilt in behaviour, most of them superb horsemen, they were urbane, amusing, full of bravado and entirely careless of the impression they made on their inferiors. 'All the officers have very long hair & lap dogs & cigars & they wear whatever uniform they like ... The standard of efficiency and devotion to duty, particularly among the officers is very much lower [than in the Marines] ... Officers have no scruples about seeing to their own comfort or getting all the leave they can.'

In an article written for *Life* and published in 1941, Evelyn, constrained by the rules of censorship, gave a rather more elevated impression of his company. 'The names among our officers of Jellicoe, Keyes, Beatty and Churchill showed how the sons of the last war's leaders saw in the commandos the chance of reliving their fathers' achievements. There was something of the spirit which one reads in the letters and poetry of 1914.'

Restored to his captaincy, Evelyn was given the job of liaison officer working with Harry Stavordale, a life, as he described it, 'of untroubled ease', leaving him free to join with the others in the house-party atmosphere of the Marine Hotel.

Although the weather was often appalling and outdoor exercises were tough, over harsh country often in snow or fog, the living conditions were described by one young officer, Major Patrick Ness, as almost Anglo-Indian in luxury. The smart set, as Evelyn called them, 'drink a very great deal, play cards for high figures, dine nightly in Glasgow, and telephone to their trainers endlessly'. Most of them liked Evelyn ('a likeable wee man, charmingly humble' as Patrick Ness surprisingly described him), without ever accepting him as one of themselves: he was an intellectual, not a regular soldier, not of their world. He was, too, rather 'governessy' in his occasional disapproval of their unbridled behaviour, given to lecturing them on the evils of gambling, and on one occasion scolding Harry Stavordale for telling an off-colour story.

Many of the officers had already been joined by their wives – Pamela Churchill, Peggy Dunne, Mary Campbell and Nell Stavordale adding an element of sophisticated femininity in which Laura, once again heavily pregnant, would have been lost. Knowing this, Evelyn did not encourage her to come, and was carefully selective in his descriptions of his high life at Largs, occasionally adding a reassuringly censorious note.

> I think a minor [military] operation might be salutary to check the lotus eating . . . Today there was a grand inspection & I walked behind with the staff detecting, with my trained, marine eye many imperfections which escaped the foot guards . . . I lead a comparatively ascetic life here, but this hotel is very expensive & very avaricious (they charged one officer 6d a day extra for having his breakfast in bed although his own servant carried it up & down) but I have been unable to find any other accomodation in the town . . . You must not please think of me as drinking up all your children's money.

Money was a particular problem, as Evelyn's comrades-in-arms were well-to-do, thinking nothing of spending recklessly on food and wine or of losing hundreds of pounds a night at cards: on one occasion Randolph Churchill found himself £850 down after two nights' play. Evelyn had only his salary, but, he told Laura, '[I] will try and keep up your monthly £15 & cut down on my own expenses.' Unfortunately the Marine Hotel was not cheap, and owing to the rackety behaviour of some of its guests, growing less so by the week. 'On Friday Robin had to go to London and Mary got tipsy and sat up until four with Lord Milton and Captain Milbanke and made such a noise that the hotel put up its prices for all commando members. The prices are really very severe. Randolph's bill for three weeks was £54. He had a great row with them. They charged him £1 a week for his pekinese dog.'

In December, 8 Commando was sent to Arran for a brief period of intensive training preparatory to action, and at the beginning of February 1941 left for the Middle East, sailing for Egypt in a convoy of three ships of the Glen Line, *Glenroy, Glengyle* and *Glenearn. Glenroy,* carrying 8 and 11 Commando, was a fast merchant vessel that had been adapted for combined operations, her portholes blackened, her holds converted into troop decks and extra cabins built on deck. Intended to hold a battalion, she was carrying nearly twice that number and as a consequence the overcrowding was severe. Evelyn shared a tiny cabin with

Randolph Churchill and Harry Stavordale, 'both of whom', he complained to Laura, 'have brought luggage enough for a film stars honeymoon.' They were looked after by their soldier-servant, Ralph Tanner, an intelligent and obliging young man, who in civilian life had worked at the British Museum and was training to be an archaeologist. In spite of the cramped quarters, the way of life for the upper echelons on *Glenroy* was not all that different from that at the Marine Hotel in Largs. 'We have been at sea for a week now and have reached warm weather & calm water & face the long voyage with patience,' Evelyn wrote to Laura.

> As the voyage goes on gambling gets formidably high. Chemin de fer most nights with banks never lower than £50. Randolph lost over £400 last night. I do not play at this table but have a little poker game with the poor from whom I consistently win small sums . . . Randolph has become quartermaster and does his work with great relish. He is growing a moustache. I, on the other hand, am growing a beard. At present it looks peculiarly repulsive – a mass of isolated, coarse hairs of variegated colouring, but it gives me an interest as they say, like a pet or a pot flower.

Relations between the two Commando units were friendly. The men of 11 Commando were 'very young, quiet, overdisciplined, unlike ourselves in every way but quite companionable'; they trained indefatigably throughout the voyage, '[while] we did very little except PT and one or two written exercises for the officers'. Unfortunately the same could not be said for relations between the two services. Apart from three regular naval officers, including the captain, the ship's company was drawn entirely from Royal Naval Reserve and Royal Naval Volunteer Reserve, a fact which for some reason made them an object of contempt to the officers of 8 Commando, who lost no opportunity in displaying towards their naval counterparts an upper-class loutishness evoking the worst elements of schoolboy snobbery. 'The RNVR lieutenants and sub-lieutenants were a pathetic collection of youths straight from insurance offices,' Evelyn gloated.

> 8 Commando was boisterous, xenophobic, extravagant, imaginative, witty, with a proportion of noblemen which the Navy found disconcerting; while the Navy was jejune, dull, poor, self-conscious, sensitive of fancied insults, with the underdog's

aptitude to harbour grievances . . . [The military] aired their grievances loudly, referred to the Captain as 'the old bugger on the roof' . . . There was a meeting of reconciliation between representative officers which embittered relations still more, chiefly by Philip Dunne comparing the Navy to the guard on a train and the Army to a first-class passenger.

The high proportion of blue blood among the officers in Evelyn's clique excited his social ambitiousness. He knew he was not and never would be one of them, knew that their way of life was not for him – he would soon have grown bored with the preoccupation with racing and cards – and yet they possessed qualities he envied. Small and stout, Evelyn longed to be tall and graceful, like Stavordale, or to have the then striking good looks of Randolph Churchill; he longed to have that patrician arrogance, that unquestioning self-confidence, which he believed came with noble birth.

There were times when Evelyn's obvious striving for acceptance made him look ridiculous. He was a standing joke among the WAAFs at Richmond Terrace, headquarters of Combined Operations, where he would sometimes look in for a drink at the bar; the sight of this plump little man 'toadying up', as the girls put it, made them giggle. 'He'd toady up to anyone with a title. I remember one day seeing him trying to hear what Anthony Head, who was enormously tall, was saying to Brian Franks, and Waugh was standing on his fat chubby tiptoes.' Even Private Tanner, who liked Waugh and found him a considerate master, noted that 'he was a bit fond of the Honourables. He insisted on sharing a cabin with Randolph Churchill and Lord Stavordale, for instance.' Interestingly, Ralph Tanner, unlike the men under Evelyn's command at Kingsdown and Cornwall, saw none of the intolerance and condescension of which they complained; but Tanner was from the professional middle classes, which Marine other ranks were not.

Towards the end of February, the ship called at Cape Town. 'The inhabitants of this town excelled all I have ever heard of colonial hospitality, taking the troops for drives in their motor cars, & feeding them on peaches & grapes,' Evelyn told Laura. He and Randolph, between whom there was by now a strong bond formed mainly on a love of drinking and a demonic sense of humour, went on shore together. 'Randolph and I found a

419

sugar-daddy who crammed us with rich foods & let Randolph tell him all about the political situation.'

On 8 March they finally reached Suez, landing at Geneifa, a tented camp by the side of the Canal. Here training for 'Layforce', as they were now designated, continued, interspersed with periods of leave in Cairo. Cairo was headquarters for the Allied forces in the Middle East, but although its pavements were swarming with pink-faced, blond-haired young men in sweat-stained khaki, its streets jammed with jeeps and armoured cars, the city showed little sign of wartime austerity. The large department stores were well stocked with fabrics and cosmetics, the groceries with butter, sugar and eggs, the greengrocers with mounds of oranges and dates. Cafés still served freshly roasted coffee, hotels and restaurants were well provided with French wines. There was a sophisticated social life centring on the two smart hotels, Shepheard's and the Continental, with tea and cocktail parties held regularly on the shady lawns of the British Embassy. Just as in peacetime, people drove out to see the pyramids and the Sphinx, whose four-thousand-year-old chin now rested on a protective wall of sandbags; and just as in peacetime, foreigners were accosted everywhere by begging children, pedlars hawking flywhisks, and young pimps touting their 'sisters' – 'very nice, very clean, all pink inside like Queen Victoria'. For Evelyn, however, the city's charms were less apparent. On 1 April he told Laura,

I am just back from five days leave in Cairo which I did not greatly enjoy. The whole town is like one huge, heterogeneous and very expensive officers mess. I saw a certain number of friends. Christopher Sykes[13] is staying with his father-in-law Russell Pasha and I had a very gloomy evening there talking to Mrs Russell about Cotswold manor houses which she nearly bought at one time or another. I lunched at the Embassy. The Lampsons were charming & their cooking exceptionally good but the party was exclusively military. I saw a good deal of Joan Aly Khan, also of Mrs Otto Kahn who has a palace full of tuberoses & tubular furniture and vintage champagne. I ate bevies of quails with Peter Stirling. It all sounds very gay but it was really flat & stale. Patrick Balfour is here & Robert Byron is coming . . . I was

[13] Sykes was working in the propaganda section of SOE, Cairo. In 1936 he had married Russell Pasha's only daughter, Camilla.

much troubled by looking glasses in Cairo. It was many weeks
since I had seen myself at full length. I found a middle aged,
portly, ill-dressed figure which upset me.

The original intention in sending the Commandos to Egypt was
for them to take part in the capture of Rhodes, but this operation
had been abandoned, leaving several hundred shock troops,
highly trained, honed to battle pitch, with nothing to do. With the
Germans reoccupying Cyrenaica and Rommel on the Egyptian
frontier, the Allied situation was growing increasingly desperate
and military activity correspondingly intense. But time and again
Layforce was left out. A number of minor operations was devised,
but each at the last moment called off, to the intense disappointment of the men, now moved to Alexandria and kicking their
heels in two comfortless camps at Sidi Bishr and Amiriya. There
was always a good reason for these last-minute cancellations –
weather unpropitious, transport unavailable – but that did little
to prevent the growing atmosphere of frustration, Layforce soon
becoming known facetiously as 'Belayforce', with the feelings of
the brigade summed up by a graffito found on *Glengyle*: 'Never
in the history of human endeavour have so few been buggered
about by so many.'

Finally on 19 April they went into action. The planned operation was a night raid on Bardia, a coastal town situated behind
enemy lines in Libya between Salûm and Tobruk, with a garrison,
according to intelligence, of at least 2000 strong. It was for Laycock and his men to give the enemy a fright, discover their exact
numbers and composition, and by staging a surprise attack draw
reinforcements away from the front. A single commando, 'A'
battalion, under Lieutenant-Colonel Felix Colvin, was chosen for
the job. It was a dark night, and there was a heavy swell. The
battalion transferred from *Glengyle*, anchored four miles out from
shore, into motor landing craft, their heads below the armoured
sides of the boats, all packed so tight it was impossible to move
a muscle. 'The man on my left was sick,' Evelyn recorded. 'The
only movement he was capable of was to turn his head slightly
toward me.' From the moment of landing, the operation was, in
military parlance, 'a balls-up'. The first party ashore killed their
own officer by mistake; another, returning down the wrong *wadi*,
was left behind and later captured; one of the boats ran aground

and had to be destroyed. Fortunately for the invaders, it was soon discovered that Bardia, far from being held by a substantial force, was completely deserted, the only sign of the enemy a couple of patrolling motor-cyclists who roared through the empty streets without anyone managing to stop them. In an article for *Life*, Evelyn, obedient to the rules of censorship, gave an inspiriting version of the event, turning a shambles into a small but pertinent victory. Of the failure to shoot down the motor-cycle patrol, he says,

> It was very lucky really that they did escape for it was through
> them that the enemy learned, as we particularly wanted them
> to learn, that a landing was taking place. Had they merely seen
> the blaze and heard the demolition charges from a distance
> they might have taken us for an air-raid. As it was, the impression
> which these men carried away was of a town strongly in enemy
> hands and it was due to their report that our major success was
> achieved. They did exactly what British higher command
> wanted and sent a strong detachment of tanks and armoured
> cars to repel the imagined invasion.[14]

Privately, however, he did not conceal his disgust at the incompetence with which the raid was carried out, writing in his diary, 'After this operation there was a good deal of talk among the more responsible A Battalion officers that Colonel Colvin had behaved badly. I thought no one had behaved well enough for them to be able to afford a post-mortem and did not pass their criticism on to Bob' – a decision which he was shortly very much to regret.

The following month the Commando, increasingly bored, confused and demoralised, again moved camp, divided between Mersa Matruh, a dusty wasteland flanked by a salt lake on one side, the sea on the other, and Tobruk. 'At Mersa the Commando gave up all pretence of military work and spent the day bathing

[14] Evelyn was not alone in presenting the Bardia raid in an exaggeratedly heroic light. Beverley Nichols in the *Sunday Chronicle* wrote a shamelessly adulatory piece on the operation, extolling the Commandos in general and Evelyn in particular. 'Evelyn at this moment is a hard-bitten, sun-scorched Commando, with the dust of the desert in his eyes, and a rifle in his hand ... The ex-dilettante, writing exquisite froth between cocktails, has proved one of the toughest of the lot ... Few of us in the old days could have imagined Evelyn crawling up the escarpment at Bardia in the dead of night ...' etc.

and fishing . . . The officers' mess had no regular meals and lived on sardines and biscuits.' To Laura Evelyn wrote,

> Yesterday I spent in the Union club here looking at the *Country Life* books of country houses in an orgy of homesickness. Phil Dunne & I found a large scale map of England & it marked Stinkers & his village & we nearly died of maudlinness. Everyone is very sad; even Randolph is less exuberant than usual . . . I live with headquarters and only see my beloved 8 Commando when I go into Alexandria to dine which I do rarely on account of economy. Headquarters are very dull . . . Bob [Laycock] is very lonely in his scarlet & rather wistful . . . He is rather touching, reading jokes from Angie's letters & engaging in intellectual conversation . . . The food in Alexandria is delicious – we live on quails & prawns & wood strawberries. But wine is very expensive. I have given up drinking except for a little Chianti. There is a cinema in the camp with a change of film every night. There is superb bathing. All this while you are living in a state of siege.
>
> I see no women. Celibacy is not so irksome as the lack of female company. The pansy clergyman does not really fill their place.

Then suddenly, on 22 May, orders came through at three a.m. for the battalion to leave at once for Alexandria, prior to embarkation for Crete. Crete, for both Britain and Germany, was the key air and naval base for the Eastern Mediterranean.

Since October 1940 the island had been occupied by the British, but now that the Germans had overrun both Greece and Jugoslavia, only Crete lay between them and Egypt. The first attack was launched on 20 May. The strength of the Royal Navy was such that for the Axis to make a seaborne assault on the island would almost certainly have resulted in failure: their plan, therefore, was for massive air bombardment. An Ultra signal warning of such an intention had been received by C-in-C Crete, General Bernard Freyberg,[15] who for a series of complicated

---

[15] Major-General Bernard Freyberg VC, commander of the New Zealand Division, reached Crete on 29 April, having been appointed Commander-in-Chief by Lord Wavell on Churchill's instructions. Freyberg was the seventh commander of British forces on the island since their arrival the previous November, and appointed over Major-General E. C. Weston.

reasons misread the signal and insisted on continuing to prepare for invasion by sea; with consequences that were inevitably cata-strophic. By the twenty-second, the island was as good as lost, a state of affairs that was far from clear in the orders received in Alexandria: Laycock was given to understand that the situation, although serious, was not desperate, with resistance to enemy attack 'well in hand'. The Commandos were to join Creforce with the specific purpose of putting out of action enemy-held ports and aerodromes, and supporting the garrison at the crucial Maleme aerodrome. In fact by the time Layforce arrived, there was no question of providing either support or resistance: the Allied forces were in turmoil, the Commandos finding themselves in the midst of what their brigade major, F. C. C. Graham, accu-rately described as 'a nightmare of unreality and unexpectedness'.

What they found, Laycock and his men, when they reached Suda Bay on the north of the island just before midnight on 26 May, was nothing less than a vision of hell. The harbour was clogged with the masts and funnels of sunken vessels, some of them still smouldering; the quay, heavily cratered by bomb attack, was littered with burned-out vehicles and abandoned stores, among which were slumped small groups of wounded men. While Laycock and his officers were waiting to go ashore, a man wearing only shorts and a greatcoat burst into the captain's cabin, clearly half out of his mind with terror. ' "My God, it's hell," he said. "We're pulling out. Look at me, no gear. O My God, it's hell. Bombs all the time. Left all my gear behind, etc., etc." ' As Major Graham remarked, 'Cheerful to say the least of it & something of a shock to the little party of Commando officers, armed to the teeth & loaded up like Christmas trees, who stared open-mouthed at this bearer of bad news.' Evelyn, openly contemptuous, observed with distaste, 'We took this to be an exceptionally cow-ardly fellow, but in a few hours realized that he was typical of British forces in the island.'

And it was typical of Evelyn to react so intolerantly. After the frustrating weeks of inaction in Egypt and the humiliation of Bardia, Crete presented the first real chance for Layforce to prove itself: what better opportunity than to come to the rescue of a beleaguered Allied army gallantly fighting for its life? Unfortu-nately, by the time the Commandos arrived, that army had given up the fight, indeed was already on the run, and Evelyn's disappointment and disgust at realising that he was to be involved in yet another fiasco coloured his perceptions of the entire campaign. Failing to take into account that while he and his fellow Commandos were arriving fresh and untried, the forces on Crete had been fighting hard under appalling conditions for a week, had endured continuous air bombardment, were ill-equipped, exhausted and near to starvation, Evelyn saw it all in terms of simple and unforgivable cowardice.

Once landed, Evelyn and Laycock, escorted by Tanner, drove off through the silent, narrow streets of Suda in search of the island's second-in-command, General Weston. As they left the town and came out into open country, they saw that the road was swarming with troops, all of whom to their bewilderment seemed to be going the wrong way, an endless unformed rabble of British, Australians, New Zealanders and Greeks, dirty, half-starving and stupid with fatigue, all in a desperate hurry to reach the coast.

The three men located Weston's headquarters, set up in a farmhouse by the side of a track leading south from the Canea end of Suda Bay. The general himself was asleep on the floor, but a Marine officer briefed them, telling them in effect that the situation was hopeless, that all Allied troops were in retreat, and that the Marines with the Commandos were to form a rearguard covering the withdrawal to Sphakia on the south coast, a distance of some thirty miles. Next they drove on through more crowds of fleeing men to report to General Freyberg, before finally at dawn making their way to their own brigade HQ, sited off the road on the side of a hill.

After a few hours' rest, punctually interrupted at 8 a. m. by the first bombardment of the morning, Evelyn was dispatched by Laycock to take orders to Colonel Colvin, who had arrived with an advance party two days earlier. Evelyn was entirely without fear. At one point, with Stukas screaming overhead, he came to a slit-trench. 'May I share your trench?' Evelyn politely asked the astonished occupant, a private with the Australian Imperial Force, before unhurriedly stepping down, unfolding his map, and locating his position. Then, returning the map to its case, he thanked the soldier for his hospitality and calmly continued through the bombardment. It was another half an hour before he found the colonel.

I said, 'I was told Colonel Colvin was here.'

'He is,' they said.

I looked round, saw no one. Then they pointed under the table where I saw their commanding officer sitting hunched up like a disconsolate ape. I saluted and gave him his orders. He did not seem able to take them in at all.

Only when the bombing stopped for a time did Colvin consent to come out. 'He still looked a soldierly figure when he was on his feet: I took him to Bob. He showed no inclination to go back to his battalion but could still talk quite reasonably when there was no aeroplane overhead. Soon they came back and he lay rigid with his face in the gorse for about four hours.' At sunset Colvin left to return to his battalion, but about ten o'clock he suddenly appeared again, 'with a confused account of having been ambushed on a motor cycle. His battalion was fiercely engaged he said (this was balls), and without explaining why he was not with them he gave us the order to withdraw. It all seemed fishy.' Laycock and Graham having gone on ahead, the remainder had little choice but to obey, obliged to spend the night on the march, Colvin constantly urging them on. 'Colvin kept saying, "We must get as far as we can before light" ... Nothing but daylight would stop him. The moment that came he popped into a drain under the road and sat there.' Finally, revolted by the cowardice shown by his superior officer, Evelyn decided to set off on his own – 'It was always exhilarating as soon as one was alone' – eventually reaching the village where Laycock and Graham had set up base. From there the three of them drove back to the wretched Colvin, still in his drain, and here, 'Bob as politely as possible relieved him of command.'

Brigade HQ was now established just outside the village of Babali Hani, and for a few hours Evelyn and his two companions were able to rest in something near tranquillity. The heat was intense, but their refuge a place of great beauty, a little roadside shrine set beside a spring thickly shaded by trees. Although without food, they had a large bottle of wine which they cooled in the spring, a box of cigars and a book of crossword puzzles, Evelyn resting his head on his most treasured item of campaign equipment, a pillow, which accompanied him everywhere. He later wrote to Laura, 'In case I don't see Auberon again tell him when he goes to war that the *most* important thing an officer can carry with him is a pillow. I stuck to mine to the end after I had jettisoned gas-mask & steel helmet & blanket etc & blessed it every hour.'

The brief day's rest at Babali Hani was followed by forty-eight hours of almost surreal adventure. The Allied position on the island being clearly untenable, General Weston had given the order for retreat and capitulation: as many troops as possible had to be got away from Sphakia, the port of embarkation, and it was for Layforce to act as rearguard. With their truck and a commandeered bus which they filled with wounded, brigade HQ drove through the night over the mountains to the village of Imbros, where there was a first-aid post and assembly points. From Imbros, Laycock moved on to a nearby gorge, only a few miles distant from Sphakia. 'The gorge was magnificent, narrowing and deepening until it looked like a seventeenth-century landscape; halfway down it opened into a circle with a well of cold sweet water. At the end it opened a little and was full of caves,' Evelyn wrote. 'We found a green patch, with some large rocks and olive trees near the path up to the village, and established brigade HQ here. That at least would be the military expression, but in fact we simply rested.'

That evening Laycock and Evelyn went to look for Weston, whom they found sitting outside a cave on the hillside, surrounded by a handful of staff officers. 'He gave us half a cupful of sherry and a spoonful of beans for which we were very grateful. He seemed to have lost all interest in the battle ... Bob asked him about order of embarkation and he said, "You were the last to come so you will be the last to go." ' On the afternoon of 31 May, Laycock and Waugh returned once more to Weston for final orders. That night was to be the last on the island, the C-in-C, who had already gone by flying-boat to Egypt, having dictated an order of priority for embarkation, making it clear that Layforce must stay to the end. The Commandos were to surround the beach and cover the evacuation of other troops, remaining in place until a message was received from the embarkation officer on the spot giving them permission to retire.

By 10 p. m. the Commandos were in position. The scene was one of chaos, with the beach and all approaches to the harbour thronged with men desperate to be taken off, the more fortunate already formed into lines waiting for the boats, others hoping to pass themselves off as wounded or trying to rush the armed pickets in an attempt to reach the landing craft beyond. It was painfully evident that there was neither space nor time to take everyone off, and that a substantial number (in the event over 5000) would have to be abandoned, left to be taken prisoner. Realising their predicament, Laycock, Graham and Waugh tried to find the embarkation officer to ask for authorisation to withdraw, but he, it appeared, had already gone. As Evelyn dispassionately tells it, 'Bob then took the responsibility of ordering Layforce to fight their way through the rabble and embark . . . which we did in a small motor boat. We reached the destroyer Nizam about midnight and sailed as soon as we came aboard . . . We did not see any of the ship's officers and arrived at Alexandria at 5 in the afternoon, June 1st, after an uneventful voyage.'

It was in that small but significant action that the bitter kernel of Evelyn's disillusion was embedded, a disillusion made all the more corrosive by the fact that he could never afterwards give it overt expression. When Laycock took the decision to pull out, he was almost certainly disregarding orders, which were to remain until all fighting troops had been evacuated, and until he received permission to withdraw. In going when he did he disobeyed on both counts, leaving entirely on his own initiative and abandoning on the beach not only the Royal Marines and two battalions of Australians, but a large contingent of his own Commandos.[16]

In the 'Intelligence Summary' for the official *War Diary*, Evelyn clearly sets this out in his entry for 31 May. 'Final orders from CREFORCE for evacuation (a) LAYFORCE positions not be held to last man and last round but only as long as was necessary to cover withdrawal of other fighting forces. (b) No withdrawal before order from H.Q. (c) LAYFORCE to embark after other fighting forces but before stragglers.' There was never any question of cowardice.[17] For Laycock, a man of action who was also

[16] Out of a landed force of nearly 800, Laycock took off only 23 officers and 186 other ranks, leaving the remainder to be taken captive.

[17] Evelyn's servant, Private Ralph Tanner, who throughout the operation had behaved with outstanding bravery and devotion to duty, later observed that 'there's no question that Laycock was a very brave man, but there's no doubt about it, he tried to get out before they were supposed to, tried to get as many of Layforce off as he could, but they were very much jumping the queue, in front of the Australians and the Marines.'

ruthlessly ambitious, it was the obvious thing to do: the situation was hopeless, the daredevil Commandos ill-suited to acting as rearguard, and there was no doubt that he himself would be of greater value to the war effort back in Egypt with his battalions than remaining on Crete to be captured.

Nonetheless his arrogant disregard for orders had its shameful side, to Evelyn made more shameful by his own collusion in it: in his diary the entry for 2200 hours on 31 May includes the crucial statement that Laycock gave the order to depart having first ascertained that 'all fighting forces were now in position for embarkation and that there was no enemy contact', two statements which were patently untrue: neither the Australian 2/7th Battalion nor the Marines had yet reached Sphakia, and the beach-head was known to be surrounded by German troops, whose gunfire at dusk Evelyn recorded having heard.

Although he continued unfailingly to support his commanding officer, and never once made open reference to any suspicion that all was not as it should have been, in Evelyn's eyes Laycock's reputation was sullied, and Evelyn tainted by association. Bob Laycock had been his hero, his glorious military ideal, and his disgust and disappointment at the flawed reality, when eventually expressed, were correspondingly complex and profound. Evelyn continued to admire Laycock's courage and qualities of leadership, but after Crete things were never the same between them. Before he wrote his grim fictionalised account of the débâcle in *Officers and Gentlemen*, the nearest he came to revealing his emotions was in two letters to Laura, one referring to the campaign as 'my tale of shame', the other sent immediately after his return to Alexandria describing the event in terms of unmistakable revulsion. 'Darling Laura . . . I have been in a serious battle and have decided I abominate military life. It was tedious & futile & fatiguing. I found I was not at all frightened; only very bored & very weary.' Once back in Egypt, like a child unable to confess his guilt, Evelyn returned again and again to the subject, furiously expressing his contempt without ever being able to reveal its true source. His angry perorations gave a great deal of offence and shocked his fellow officers in Cairo and Alexandria, in particular the officers and men of 8 Commando. On one occasion, sitting on the beach at Alexandria with Randolph

Churchill and Gerald de Winton,[18] Evelyn began yet again insisting that everyone on Crete had behaved in the most cowardly and shameful fashion, refusing to accept any extenuating circumstances. 'I thought he was quite childish about it,' de Winton said later. To Christopher Sykes, then at GHQ in Cairo, Evelyn was even more outspoken.

> He said that he had never seen anything so degrading as the
> cowardice that infected the spirit of the army. He declared that
> Crete had been surrendered without need; that both the officers
> and men were hypnotized into defeatism by the continuous dive-
> bombing which with a little courage one could stand up to; that
> the fighting spirit of the British armed services was so meagre
> that we had not the slightest hope of defeating the Germans;
> that he had taken part in a military disgrace, a fact that he
> would remember with shame for the rest of his life.

As if in sympathy with Evelyn's feelings, a rumour went round that a special evacuation medal would be presented to all survivors of the Crete campaign, to be inscribed simply, EX CRETA.

Evelyn's sense of moral unease seeps like a stain through *Officers and Gentlemen*. His contempt for the shell-shocked Colonel Colvin is clearly the inspiration for the terrified Major Hound, and the cowardly behaviour of Ivor Claire, at first seen as the most dashing of the dandy officers, reflects his own deep sense of betrayal. In reality Evelyn was prepared to falsify the Layforce war record; in the novel Guy Crouchback burns the Hookforce diary, which alone contains the damning evidence of Claire's dishonour. The novel was dedicated 'TO MAJOR-GENERAL SIR ROBERT LAYCOCK K.C.M.G., C.B., D.S.O. That every man in arms should wish to be',[19] and on its publication in 1955, Evelyn received a telegram from his friend, Ann Rothermere, to whom he had sent a copy. 'Presume Ivor Claire based Laycock dedication ironical.' This provoked a startlingly vehement response. 'Your telegram horrifies me. Of course there is no possible connexion between Bob and Claire. If you suggest such a thing anywhere it will be the end of our beautiful friendship... For Christ's sake lay off the idea

---

[18] Gerald de Winton had commanded the signals squadron in the 1st Armoured Brigade in Greece immediately before the Crete campaign.
[19] From Wordsworth's 'Character of the Happy Warrior': 'Who is the happy Warrior? who is he/That every man in arms should wish to be?'

of Bob=Claire ... Just shut up about Laycock, Fuck You, E Waugh.' 'Panic is foreign to your nature and you rarely use rough words,' Ann shrewdly replied. 'Why do you become hysterical if one attempts to identify your Officers and Gentlemen?' Meanwhile Evelyn recorded in his diary on the day he received her telegram, 'I replied that if she breathes a suspicion of this *cruel fact*[20] it will be the end of our friendship.'

On return from Crete, No. 8 Commando was temporarily disbanded, Laycock flying immediately to England. Evelyn, once more with the Royal Marines, was less fortunate; due to the labyrinthine delays of army life he was unable to leave for home until 12 July, when he embarked on the troopship *Duchess of Richmond*. In order to avoid U-boat patrols the ship undertook a 20,000-mile voyage via Cape Town, Trinidad, and Iceland, not arriving in Liverpool until 3 September. After two weeks' leave Evelyn reported for duty at Plymouth, whence he was posted to the 12th Battalion Land Defence Force stationed on Hayling Island, near Portsmouth. He went to join them, he told Laura, 'with the most profound misgivings ... I suppose Mussolini is sadder & possibly Budeny [sic][21] but I am [the] third saddest man in the world. I wish I could recapture some of that adventurous spirit with which I joined at Chatham.'

---

[20] Author's italics, not Waugh's.
[21] General Budenny was in command of the ᴨussian reserve force on the south-west front which had just been destroyed by the Germans.

XIII

My military future is vague

Evelyn's return to England after the harrowing experience of Crete was followed by two years of futility and frustration, a period of limbo both in his writing and in his military career.

Like Charles Ryder, he had fallen out of love with the Army: 'I was aghast to realize that something within me, long sickening, had quietly died, and felt as a husband might feel, who, in the fourth year of his marriage, suddenly knew that he had no longer any desire, or tenderness, or esteem, for a once-beloved wife . . . we had been through it together, the Army and I, from the first importunate courtship until now, when nothing remained to us except the chill bonds of law and duty and custom.' Apart from a few articles, his only published work was a short novel, *Put Out More Flags*, composed during the long voyage home from Alexandria. On 26 September 1941, Evelyn had written to Randolph Churchill, 'I finished the book, dedicated to you, & it is quite funny but paper is so short that it will not appear until it has lost all point.'

In fact, it came out less than six months later, in March 1942, but far from losing all point, *Put Out More Flags* caught the *Zeitgeist* with extraordinary accuracy, reflecting both the change in the mood of the nation and the change that took place during the early part of the war in Evelyn himself; the first half is an ebullient and sophisticated comedy, the second much more sombre in mood, with several of the leading clowns turning serious and filled with foreboding. By the end a spirit of disillusion prevails, the final pages a valedictory to a past that is gone for ever, as the smart, frivolous world of the now aging bright young things disintegrates into disorder and defeat.

The story begins with a description of Malfrey, a prelapsarian Eden, home of Barbara Sothill, Basil Seal's sister. 'There was something female and voluptuous in the beauty of Malfrey . . . it had been built more than two hundred years ago in days of victory and ostentation and lay, spread out, sumptuously at ease, splendid, defenceless and provocative.' But Malfrey has already been targeted: 'across the sea, Barbara felt, a small and envious mind, a meanly ascetic mind, a creature of the conifers, was plotting the destruction of her home.' This theme of a golden age on the verge of annihilation was weighing on Evelyn's mind. In the prefatory letter to *Work Suspended*[1] he had written, 'It is now clear to me that even if I were again to have the leisure and will to finish it, the work would be in vain, for the world in which and for which it was designed, has ceased to exist', and in the dedication to *Put Out More Flags* he refers to his characters as 'a race of ghosts, the survivors of the world we both knew ten years ago . . . where my imagination still fondly lingers'. The book ends ironically, with that pompous old fool, Sir Joseph Mainwaring, smiling 'with sincere happiness'.

' "There's a new spirit abroad," he said. "I see it on every side." '

'And, poor booby, he was bang right.'

It is the time of the Phoney War. The smart set – Peter Pastmaster, Margot Metroland, Basil Seal, Alastair and Sonia Trumpington – are finding it all a tremendous lark, with husbands boyishly dressing up in dashing uniforms and reserving the best jobs for themselves and their friends. 'Sonia was trying to telephone to Margot, to invite themselves all to luncheon . . . " . . . Peter's here and Basil. We're all feeling very gay and warlike. May we come to luncheon?" ' Only Basil Seal has no inclination to fight, seeing the war simply as the best entrepreneurial opportunity that has yet come his way. 'I want to be one of those people one heard about in 1919; the hard-faced men who did well out of the war,' says Basil. But having been accustomed to operating in an orderly, peace-loving society, he is disconcerted to find himself out of his element. 'In the new, busy, secretive, chaotic world which developed during the first days of the war, Basil for the first time in his life felt himself at a disadvantage. It was like being in

---

[1] The letter is addressed to the influential Alexander Woollcott, to whom the book is dedicated.

433

Latin America at a time of upheaval, and instead of being an Englishman, being oneself a Latin American.' Soon readjusting, however, he hits on a scheme which possesses all the necessary components of illegality, amorality and quick, substantial profit.

Shortly before Evelyn left Stinchcombe in 1939, he was told that Piers Court had been designated as a billet for evacuees. 'My heart sank,' he had written in his diary. In fact the threat was never fulfilled, but the hideous possibility gave him the idea for Basil's ploy: posing as a billeting officer and armed with the Connollys, a trio of extravagantly frightful slum children, Basil blackmails carefully selected members of the local gentry into paying him not to leave these monsters of destruction in their charming, lovingly furnished houses. His first target is the Old Mill, home of Mr and Mrs Harkness, an elderly couple of refined manners and artistic pretensions, who have been discreetly advertising for paying guests at six guineas a week.

'In the summer we take our meals under the old mulberry tree. Music. Every week we have chamber music. There are certain *imponderabilia* at the Old Mill which, to be crude, have their market value . . .'

The moment for which Basil had been waiting was come. This was the time for the grenade he had been nursing ever since he opened the little, wrought-iron gate and put his hand to the wrought-iron bell-pull. 'We pay eight shillings and sixpence a week,' he said. That was the safety pin, the lever flew up, the spring struck home; within the serrated metal shell the primer spat and, invisibly, flame crept up the finger's-length of the fuse. Count seven slowly, then throw. One two, three, four . . .

'Eight shillings and sixpence?' said Mr Harkness. 'I'm afraid there's been some misunderstanding.'

Five, six seven. Here it comes. Bang! 'Perhaps I should have told you at once. I am the billeting officer. I've three children for you in the car outside.'

It was magnificent. It was war. Basil was something of a specialist in shocks. He could not recall a better.[2]

[2] A tamer, but equally effective, version of this particular pyrotechnic appears in a scene between Trimmer and Guy Crouchback in *Men at Arms*: ' "Hullo, Uncle, did I hear you getting a rocket?" "You did." "Quite a change for our blue-eyed boy." A spark was struck in Guy's darkened mind; a fuse took fire. "Go to hell," he said. "Tut, tut, Uncle. Aren't we a little crusty this evening?" Bang. "You bloody, half-baked pipsqueak, pipe down," he said. "One more piece of impudence out of you and I'll hit you." '

The execution of Basil's devilish plan is described with a sublime comic artistry as fine as Evelyn ever wrote, and its dénouement is the high point of the novel's first half. After that the gaiety and frivolity begin to fade.

This altered mood is typified by the change that takes place in Alastair Trumpington. First encountered as one of the aristocratic yahoos in *Decline and Fall*, in *Black Mischief* seen leading a life of spoilt futility, Alastair on the outbreak of war abandons his self-indulgent habits and to his friends' bewilderment joins up as a private soldier. Only his wife Sonia understands. ' "You see he'd never done anything for the country and though we were always broke we had lots of money really and lots of fun. I believe he thought that perhaps if we hadn't had so much fun perhaps there wouldn't have been any war . . . He went into the ranks as a kind of penance or whatever it's called that religious people are always supposed to do." ' An even greater transformation is wrought in Cedric Lyne, husband of Basil's long-established mistress, Angela. In the early chapters, he is presented as a slightly ridiculous figure, a dandy-aesthete impotently fiddling about with his water garden and the six grottoes brought back stone by stone from various parts of Europe. But it is Cedric who in battle turns out to be a hero, fearlessly carrying his message through enemy fire, killed by a stray bullet while only quarter of a mile from his goal.

His wife, Angela, at first appears typical of the chic, superficial women comprising the glamorous society surrounding Margot Metroland. 'She wore the livery of the highest fashion . . . All her properties – the luggage heaped above and around her, the set of her hair, her shoes, her finger-nails, the barely perceptible aura of scent that surrounded her . . . – all these things spoke of what (had she been, as she seemed, American) she would have called her "personality". But the face was mute. It might have been carved in jade, it was so smooth and cool and conventionally removed from the human.'

Angela's silent, solitary descent into alcoholism, although a subject of delicious gossip among her set, is shocking. She bears an undeniable resemblance to Evelyn's first love, Olivia Plunket Greene: Olivia, like Angela, was heavily made-up, paid obsessive attention to her dress, and was given to despair and dipsomania. When Basil goes to see Angela after the humiliating incident of her drunken and very public collapse at a cinema,

He found her up and dressed, but indefinably raffish in
appearance; her make-up was haphazard and rather garish,
like a later Utrillo.

'Angela, you look awful.'

'Yes darling, I feel awful . . .'

She began talking intensely and rather wildly about the
French. Presently she said, 'I must leave you for a minute,' and
went into her bedroom. She came back half a minute later with
an abstracted little smile; the inwardly happy smile of a tired
old nun – almost. There was a difference.

The war transforms everything and everyone ('Change and decay
in all around I see,' as Uncle Theodore used to sing to himself in
Scoop), and no one more than Basil's Oxford contemporary,
Ambrose Silk. Ambrose is a member of an almost extinct species:
once one of those exquisite young men who made such a mark
on the Oxford of the 1920s, he is now sadly out of place, ill at
ease in his wartime post at the Ministry of Information. Evelyn
admitted he had modelled the character of Silk on Brian
Howard,[3] even giving him a German lover like Howard's, who
having been in trouble with the Nazis, had managed to get out
of Germany just in time.[4] Like Howard, Ambrose is part Jewish,
homosexual, flamboyant in manner, facetious in speech, full of
swagger and flash, a prey to melancholia. As with Howard, his
extreme elegance in these more austere times provokes embarrassment rather than admiration. 'A pansy. An old queen. A habit
of dress, a tone of voice, an elegant, humorous deportment that
had been admired and imitated, a swift, epicene felicity of wit,
the art of dazzling and confusing those he despised – these had
been his, and now they were the current exchange of comedians.'
Evelyn treats Ambrose with sympathy while firmly designating
him a failure and consigning him to the past, as at the end he
sends him off to Ireland farcically disguised as a priest. It is as
though with his depiction of Ambrose Evelyn were writing off the
influence of Oxford and of his own period of aestheticism and
homosexuality.

[3] 'I put those words into B. Howard's mouth ten years ago in a book about him
called *Put Out More Flags*,' he wrote to Nancy Mitford in 1951.

[4] When he read the book, Brian Howard wrote to his German lover, Toni,
'Evelyn Waugh has made an absolutely vicious attack on me in his new novel
Put Out More Flags. You come into it, too!'

As usual there are a few darts aimed at personal targets. The barbed friendship with Cyril Connolly is teasingly acknowledged in the bestowal of Connolly's surname on the three delinquent children employed with such hideous effect by Basil. And Evelyn's contempt for those who left for America at the beginning of the war, in particular Christopher Isherwood and Wystan Auden, is lethally indicated in his treatment of those two absurdities, the poets Parsnip and Pimpernell.

> 'What I don't see,' she said (and what this girl did not see was usually a very conspicuous embarrassment to Poppet's friends)
> – 'What I don't see is how these two can claim to be *Contemporary* if they run away from the biggest event in contemporary history. They were contemporary enough about Spain when no one threatened to come and bomb *them*.'
> It was an awkward question; one that in military parlance was called 'a swift one'. At any moment, it was felt in the studio, this indecent girl would use the word 'escapism'.

Harold Acton is another poet whose reputation is punctured, not for avoiding the fight, but (in Evelyn's view) for his affected insistence on the glories of Chinese literature. Harold had before the war spent several years in Peking, and was much given to discoursing on his love and knowledge of Chinese poetry. In a scene in *Put Out More Flags*,[5] Mr Bentley, the publisher, has been listening to Ambrose elaborate for rather too long on his favourite subject.

> 'I read a lot of Chinese poetry once,' said Mr Bentley, 'in the translation, of course. I became fascinated by it. I would read of a sage who, as you say, lived frugally and idyllically . . . This sage had no tame dog, but he had a cat and a mother. Every morning he greeted his mother on his knees and every evening, in winter, he put charcoal under her mattress and himself drew the bed-curtains. It sounded the most exquisite existence.'
> 'It was.'
> 'And then,' said Mr Bentley, 'I found a copy of the *Daily Mirror* in a railway carriage and I read an article there by Godfrey

[5] The book's title is taken from an old Chinese saying, quoted before the dedication, ' . . . a drunk military man should order gallons and put out more flags in order to increase his military splendour.'

Winn[6] about his cottage and his flowers and his moods, and for
the life of me, Ambrose, I couldn't see the difference betweeen
that young gentleman and Yuan Ts'e-tung.'
   It was cruel of Mr Bentley to say this ...

Put Out More Flags was published in March 1942 by Chapman &
Hall, a Book Society choice for the same month. It was an immediate success, the hardback edition selling 18,000 copies, despite
the restrictions imposed by wartime paper quotas. The reviews
were on the whole appreciative, most of them coinciding with
the opinion of Arthur Waugh, who judged the novel 'not I think
one of his best, but containing some v. good scenes'. Two of the
most incisive critics were Nigel Dennis, again in *Partisan Review*,
and Alan Pryce-Jones in the *New Statesman*. According to the
latter, '[Waugh is] a vituperative young man, using the unpopular
weapons of economy, proportion, an eager brilliance inventive
but well controlled, possessing a social sense which is dead-accur-
ate but fundamentally without humour ... where he fails it is
from too facile a cynicism in face of the present day; too indulgent
an eye for any idiosyncrasy that evokes an age in which the
ordinary citizen was more likely to be a boor than a cad ... The
English world is neatly, and to some extent justly, divided into
those who get away with it and those who don't, by a judge who
has a weakness for the former ...' In the United States, where it
was published by Little, Brown in May, the book was more moder-
ately admired. 'Randolph tells me that *Put Out More Flags* is
"sweeping America" but I take this only to mean that Mona
Williams[7] has read it,' Evelyn wrote to Laura.

By this time Evelyn had left Hayling Island, where he had been
posted on return from North Africa in September 1941, and
gone to join the brigade in a hutted camp near Hawick in Rox-
burghshire, where conditions were no less dismal. Miserably he
wrote to Laura,

My life is one of squalor, idleness & loneliness ... The weather

[6] A popular journalist who specialised in articles of a cosy and sentimental
nature much admired by the readers of women's magazines.
[7] Wife of the banker, Harrison Williams, Mona Williams was a fashionable beauty
with whom for a time Randolph was infatuated.

here is said to be unusually clement which means that in spite of intense cold there are intermissions of sunlight between hail storms. One marine committed suicide last night . . . I am always wet, cold and bored. In the mess the wireless plays ceaselessly. My hut is too dark & cold to sit in. Hawick is five miles away & full of soldiers. There is no one here with any sense of humour but they never stop laughing . . . Tomorrow a company competition has been ordered on a run-&-walk (200 yards marching, 200 yds doubling) over a five mile cross country course in full equipment. I think this will be the death of me.

In January 1942, the situation improved slightly when Evelyn was sent on a company commander's course in Edinburgh, housed, to his surprise and gratification, in Bonaly Tower, the pretty Scots baronial house built by his great-great-grandfather, Lord Cockburn. 'I discovered this by recognizing the Cockburn coat of arms on the staircase.' The course was much as anticipated – lectures, tewts, sand-table demonstrations – with the exception of an interview with an army psychologist. 'I was interviewed by a neurotic creature dressed as a major, who tried to impute unhappiness and frustration to me at all stages of adolescence.' This perceptive and accurate analysis was naturally dismissed with derision, the session ending with the wretched major being fiercely reproved for having failed to mention religion.

The course over, Evelyn returned to camp for a month of 'acute depression'. In a letter to Diana Cooper, he harked back to the time of her visit to Piers Court in 1939 when he had refused to let her discuss the war.

Do you understand now why I would have no wireless or talk of Central Europe at Stinchcombe? . . . Are there corners where old friends can still talk as though they were free? If there are, they must say in those corners that there is nothing left – not a bottle of wine nor a gallant death nor anything well made that is a pleasure to handle – and never will be again.

The English are a very base people. I did not know this, living as I did. Now I know them through and through and they disgust me.

This was an old pattern: Evelyn depressed and hating the world meant trouble for those around him. The deeper Evelyn sank into melancholy, the more vituperative he became. No attempt was made to disguise his dislike of his fellow officers, and he put himself out to be offensive to his colonel. The lowest point was reached when, after confidently expecting to be given permanent command of a company, Evelyn was told there was nothing for him, that he was suitable to take command only in the most exigent circumstances, in other words, in battle. Mortified, Evelyn wrote at once to Bob Laycock imploring him to come to the rescue and find a post for him in the Special Service Brigade, of which Laycock was now commander. 'Meanwhile I am going on leave for Easter – Brains Trust at BBC, Mells, Pixton, Diana.'

It was a good leave and a lot of damage was done. First, the BBC: Evelyn had been invited to take part in the *Brains Trust*, a popular discussion programme with a permanent panel of three distinguished experts – Julian Huxley, Secretary of the Zoological Society, Commander Campbell, an omniscient retired naval officer, and Dr C. E. M. Joad, head of Philosophy at Birkbeck College. Every week before transmission it was the custom for the panellists and question-master to meet for an informal lunch at the Café Royal to talk through the topics listed for debate. Evelyn fired his first shot by instructing Peters to inform the Corporation that he would accept their proposed fee of twenty guineas only if he were not obliged to attend the luncheon: otherwise he would expect to be paid thirty. Having by this ruse established an atmosphere of mild odium, he proceeded during the course of the broadcast to insult and embarrass every member of the team, individually described in his diary as 'vulgar', 'insincere', 'conceited', 'goatlike', 'libidinous' and 'garrulous'. This satisfactory state of affairs was followed by a lengthy war of attrition with Chapman & Hall over a cheap reprint of *Put Out More Flags*, and while staying at Bognor one violent quarrel with Duff Cooper and three near-rows with Diana.

Laura was so alarmed by her husband's state of mind that she took the unusual step of confiding in her mother-in-law, but there was little either of them could do. Evelyn was sunk in his Stygian gloom, convinced that the world he knew was in ruins; soon nothing of the old civilisation would remain, and what was left would hardly be worth preserving. London in particular filled him with loathing.

The crowds uglier and more aimless, horrible groups of soldiers

in shabby battledress with their necks open, their caps off or
at extravagant angles, hands in pockets, cigarettes in the sides
of their mouths, lounging about with girls in trousers and high
heels and filmstar coiffures. I never saw so many really ugly girls
making themselves conspicuous. Restaurants crowded; one is
jostled by polyglot strangers, starved, poisoned, and cheated by
the management; theatres at an early hour of the afternoon
when it is unnatural and inconvenient to go; even so they are
all crowded.

In a letter to his father after a heavy air-raid over Golders Green,
Evelyn wrote, 'Sad about the destruction of North End but we
have the consolation of many odious buildings that have disappeared. You cannot really make many mistakes with high explo-
sives in London nowadays.'

In May came good news at last. Laycock had arranged that
pending his secondment from the Marines to the Army Evelyn
should join that smartest of smart regiments, the Royal Horse
Guards, a club to which he most fervently wished to belong.
' "The Blues" have accepted me,' he told Laura delightedly, 'so
I can now grow my hair long and wear a watch chain across my
chest, and you can have a suit made of their check tweed . . .
Lucky I didn't buy you a diamond Marine brooch. Shall I get a
diamond Horse Guards one?' He shaved off his moustache, and
'a free & happy man', went up to Ardrossan, near Glasgow, to
join Brigade HQ as intelligence officer.

Ardrossan is a dour little seaside town looking out towards
Arran on the west coast of Scotland, and here as at Hawick there
was little to do. However, Evelyn was back among friends, with
dice, cards and heavy drinking nightly in the officers' mess. 'I
think we are the only mess in Europe which constantly drinks
claret, port and brandy at dinner,' he noted with satisfaction. His
improved spirits were reflected in a letter to Laura describing an
unfortunate incident involving the military and a local laird.

No. 3 Commando were very anxious to be chums with Lord
Glasgow so they offered to blow up an old tree stump for him
and he was very grateful and he said dont spoil the plantation
of young trees near it because that is the apple of my eye and
they said no of course not we can blow a tree down so that it
falls on a sixpence and Lord Glasgow said goodness you are
clever and he asked them all to luncheon for the great explosion.

So Col. Durnford-Slater D.S.O. said to his subaltern, have you put enough explosive in the tree. Yes, sir, 75 lbs. Is that enough? Yes sir I worked it out by mathematics it is exactly right. Well better put a bit more. Very good sir.

And when Col. D. Slater D.S.O. had had his port he sent for the subaltern and said subaltern better put a bit more explosive in that tree. I don't want to disappoint Lord Glasgow. Very good sir.

Then they all went out to see the explosion and Col. D. S. D.S.O. said you will see that tree fall flat at just that angle where it will hurt no young trees and Lord Glasgow said goodness you are clever.

So soon the[y] lit the fuse and waited for the explosion and presently the tree, instead of falling quietly sideways, rose 50 feet into the air taking with it $^1/_2$ acre of soil and the whole of the young plantation.

And the subaltern said Sir I made a mistake, it should have been $7^1/_2$ lbs not 75.

Lord Glasgow was so upset he walked in dead silence back to his castle and when they came to the turn of the drive in sight of his castle what should they find but that every pane of glass in the building was broken.

So Lord Glasgow gave a little cry & ran to hide his emotion in the lavatory and there when he pulled the plug the entire ceiling, loosened by the explosion, fell on his head.

This is quite true.

In the middle of June Evelyn was sent south for a five-week course on air photograph interpretation at Matlock in Derbyshire, where Laura, convalescing at Pixton from the birth of her most recent baby, was able to join him. The child was another daughter, Margaret. If a boy, Evelyn had cheerfully instructed, he was to be called James; 'if a girl it is kinder to drown her.'

At the beginning of October, Laycock moved his HQ south to Sherborne in Dorset, where again Evelyn was able to live in comfortable lodgings and enjoy frequent visits from Laura. Sherborne provided a pleasant interlude in congenial company – the Laycocks, Brian Franks, Phil Dunne, and Basil Bennett, in peacetime manager of the Hyde Park Hotel, who was able to organise a constant supply of cases of liquor from London. It was a beautiful part of the country and there were a number of old friends living in the neighbourhood, among them Daphne

Weymouth at Sturford Mead and Harry and Nell Stavordale at Emshot. One night at Sturford Mead the party became boisterous, ending with Evelyn on his knees being anointed with 200-year-old Green Chartreuse, which Andrew Cavendish had brought from Chatsworth, while the party chanted, 'When comes the promised time when Waugh shall be no more . . .' In a letter to Laura Evelyn wrote, 'So I had a sleepless night on Saturday & went on to luncheon, unshaven, at Nells . . . We ate decoyed ducks – wild ducks caught in infancy & crammed with corn till they are fat as capons. Goodness they are good. I got drunk mainly with Cockburn 1908 port & seeing myself in the looking glass had a serious fright. I looked like a Chinese dragon in red lacquer.' In his diary Evelyn described the incident in even more startling terms, ' . . . drank a great deal of wine. I saw myself in a mirror afterwards, like a red lacquer Chinese dragon, and saw how I shall look when I die.'

At Sherborne military duties were minimal, and Evelyn was at leisure to make frequent visits to London. The previous year, 1941, he had become a member of White's Club, and it was here that he now spent most of his time.

Evelyn, like his father a club man by nature, had joined his first, the Savile, in 1930, finding it useful in those nomadic days as a base, although it lacked the patrician character that properly suited his self-image. Founded in the middle of the last century, the Savile appears as the Greville in *A Handful of Dust*, 'a club of intellectual flavour, composed of dons, a few writers and the officials of museums and learned societies. It had a tradition of garrulity.' Arthur was a member, so was Alec, which no doubt influenced Evelyn's move to the St James', which had distinguished diplomatic affiliations and was situated in an imposing eighteenth-century house in Piccadilly. Neither, however, could begin to compare with White's. White's to the highest degree and in every last detail fulfilled Evelyn's ideas of what such an establishment should be. The oldest and grandest of the gentlemen's clubs, White's had a rakish, lordly glamour, reflected in its prominent position and its distinctive architecture at the top of St James's. With its handsome staircase hung with portraits of distinguished past members, its pillared billiard room and red-walled dining-room (still referred to as the 'coffee-room' in deference to White's seventeenth-century coffee-house origins), the club was rich in history and tradition, a second home where men could drink and dine in grand, dignified surroundings with companions who if usually grand were often far from dignified. Evelyn revelled in 'this glorious place' and delighted in the kind of company he found there, such as Freddie Birkenhead, Randolph Churchill, Ed Stanley, Bob Boothby and Andrew Cavendish, in the main gamblers and heavy-drinking members of the smart set. He disapproved when other professional, middle-class men such as himself sought to join. '[White's]', he wrote to Nancy Mitford, recoiling in distaste from the news that her publisher, Hamish Hamilton, a *businessman*, had become a member, 'should be a club for gamblers, lords and heroes.'

On 28 October 1942, his thirty-ninth birthday, Evelyn wrote in his diary, 'A good year. I have begotten a fine daughter, published a successful book, drunk 300 bottles of wine and smoked 300 or more Havana cigars. I have got back to soldiering among friends ... I have about £900 in hand and no grave debts except to the Government; health excellent except when impaired by wine; a wife I love, agreeable work in surroundings of great beauty. Well that is as much as one can hope for.'

He remained in Dorset over Christmas. 'I am very glad not to be with my children for Christmas,' he told Laura. 'There is an hotel at Shaftesbury with a very splendid sideboard. I think we might take a week end there soon when you are fuckable.'

The year ended in familiar form with a prodigious drinking bout. 'Zoe Franks[8] who is an absolutely crashing bore and Angie [Laycock] whom I am keen on came to stay at the Plume of Feathers. I went to Daphne Weymouth's for one night. Duff, Diana, Conrad, the Cavendish boys[9] – an excellent pair – Debo [Cavendish],[10] Rex Whistler[11] and many nameless foot guards. Great drunkenness ... Then I came back to Sherborne and off we went again, to a great dinner party given by Bill Stirling & Peter Milton. Last night I suffered from the delusion that black rooks were flying round and round my bed room.' But after

[8] Wife of Brian Franks.
[9] The two sons of the Duke of Devonshire, the Marquess of Hartington and Lord Andrew Cavendish.
[10] Deborah Mitford, youngest sister of Nancy and Diana, married Andrew Cavendish in 1941.
[11] The painter and engraver.

Christmas the alcoholic euphoria wore off, and Evelyn was left to the familiar companionship of 'the Giant Boredom'. The diary entries record days of ineffable tedium interspersed with unrestrained carousing: he told Laura that during one visit to London he had been drunk for twenty hours. At night Evelyn's sleep was disturbed 'by a sort of nightmare that is becoming more frequent with me and I am inclined to believe is peculiar to myself. Dreams of unendurable boredom – of reading page after page of dullness, of being told endless, pointless jokes, of sitting through cinema films devoid of interest.'

The truth was that Evelyn had little to do, nobody seemed to want him, the war was going on elsewhere while he remained in a backwater, forgotten. The ordinary soldiers disliked him to such an extent that for a time Laycock felt obliged to set a guard on his sleeping quarters. Even his fellow officers complained about him, saying that the sight of Waugh drilling his men or in any way assuming a position of command was nothing short of embarrassing: he bullied and bewildered them, '[never hesitating] to take advantage of the fact that while he was a highly educated man, most of them were barely literate'. Not surprisingly, the jobs he hoped for in the brigade went to others, and he was further humiliated by Laycock telling him that he was so unpopular as to be virtually unemployable. From time to time he was dispatched to London on loan to Combined Operations HQ at Richmond Terrace, allotted a little intelligence work of a demeaningly clerical nature. 'Most of my work has been unnecessary, but it has prevented me sleeping, since Sherborne accustomed me to undisturbed repose during the day.' Bored and discontented with this Whitehall soldiering, Evelyn soon made his resentment felt, provoking most of the senior staff by his deliberately 'bolshie' attitude. 'Who's that bloody man in your office who never does a bloody thing?' Major-General Tom Churchill, Waugh's immediate superior, was constantly being asked; and Churchill himself regarded Waugh as 'a complete joke'.

Sometimes the joke went too far. One morning Evelyn was smoking a cigar outside the main door when a Colonel Vaughan, commandant of the Commando Training School in Scotland, strode smartly up, and mistaking for a sign of high rank the crimson hatband which all officers of the Household Cavalry wear, saluted smartly, a salute acknowledged by Captain Waugh

445

with a casual raising of his riding crop. Quickly realising his mistake, the colonel angrily rebuked Waugh, who retaliated by spreading damaging stories about Vaughan's private life, claiming that he believed the salute to have been in the nature of a homosexual invitation.

This unsatisfactory state of affairs continued until April 1943, when Bob Laycock put in a request for Evelyn to join his Special Service Brigade as liaison officer, a request almost certainly inspired more by compassion on Laycock's part than a genuine belief that he was picking the best man for the job. More than one of his officers had warned him against the decision, Brian Franks taking the trouble of calling in person to persuade him to change his mind. 'You'll regret it, sir,' he said. '[Evelyn] will only introduce discord and weaken the Brigade as a coherent fighting force . . . And apart from everything else, he'll probably get shot.' 'That's a chance we all have to take.' 'Oh, I don't mean by the enemy.' But Laycock, on the point of leaving to join the Allied forces in North Africa prior to the invasion of Italy, had no time to concern himself with details of personal incompatability. 'It is my intention that Capt Waugh shall join HUSKY Force in North Africa as soon as it can be arranged,' he informed Lord Lovat, his deputy commander.

On 24 June, after the usual quota of false starts and delays, the brigade finally departed, but it went without Evelyn. Arthur Waugh had died the same day, and Laycock, no doubt privately relieved, insisted that Evelyn stay behind on compassionate grounds, giving a written assurance that he and his soldier-servant should follow with the first reinforcements. 'It was an unfortunate coincidence,' Evelyn wrote in a fury of frustration. 'I was angry with Bob for leaving me behind so easily.'

'My father died with disconcerting suddenness,' was the brief diary entry unemotionally recording the fact. Arthur was seventy-six, and in spite of his chronic asthma had enjoyed reasonably good health. In 1940 he had been asked temporarily to resume the chairmanship of Chapman & Hall, an appointment which pleased him at first, although he soon found it too much of a burden. He fretted under the conditions of the amalgamation with Methuen effected two years earlier, and was badly shaken at

the end of December 1940, when the firm's entire stock was
destroyed in an air-raid. To his daughter-in-law, Joan, he sent a
roll-call of almost biblical lamentation. 'I don't suppose you know
how much the publishing trade has suffered . . . Paternoster Row
is dust & ashes, Longmans, Blackwoods, Hutchinsons, Ward
Locks, Eyre & Spottiswoodes, Simpkin Marshalls are all entirely
destroyed, & the beautiful old historic Stationers' Hall is a complete wreck.' Before long he gave up the struggle, remaining at
home reading manuscripts and dealing with his correspondence.

Although the war told on them both, Arthur coped better with
the strain of continual air-raids than did Kate. Now seventy, she
had grown pale and thin, existing in a state of permanent anxiety,
badly missing her grandchildren and worried about the well-
being of her sons. She had been terrified by the blitz, never able
to grow accustomed to the shuddering explosions that shook the
house and lit up the sky night after night. 'The other evening,
when a bomb burst near us during dinner', Arthur told Joan,
'she left the table & I found her sitting on the stairs, saying –
"Don't speak to me. I can't speak. It is shattering." In five minutes
she had picked up again; but a night later, when an explosion
went off, she jumped up in a way that showed her nerves are all
like harp-strings.'

When in England Alec gave as much time as he could to his
parents, spending most weekends at Highgate. Since his return
from France in 1940, Alec had not prospered; he had been living
in a gloomy little flat off Tottenham Court Road, involved in an
unhappy love affair, enjoying small success as a writer and bored
by his work at the Petroleum Warfare Department. In the autumn
of 1941 he was posted to Syria as part of the Spears Mission,
working with MI5.

Evelyn recorded in his diary that his brother's departure 'is sad
for my parents & me as it means I now have them on my conscience'. He made his infrequent visits to Highgate as brief as
possible. Arthur was always nervous before seeing his younger
son, immensely relieved once the ordeal was over. Although in a
limited context he relished Evelyn's humour – 'He really is the
wittiest dog in the world' – he was too conscious of the lack of
sympathy between them ever to be at ease in his company. 'I
make him itch all over. Everything I say puts his teeth on edge,'
he complained to Joan, generously adding that, 'I know that I

447

am not apt to take Evelyn the right way, and perhaps his air of cold detachment is not so heartless as it seems.' 'Seems' was enough, however, to make these occasions uncomfortable, and Arthur's private comments in his journal on Evelyn's behaviour run to a predictable pattern: 'arrogant & dictatorial', 'haughty but amusing', '[Evelyn] not very communicative'. Shortly before departing for the Middle East in 1941, Evelyn had taken Laura to lunch at Highgate. '[Evelyn] has shaved off his moustache, which is an improvement, and put on a good deal of weight, which is not ... He was really very cold, arrogant, & contemptuous. Considering that this was the only time he was going to spare us out of a 15-day leave, I think he might have been a little more patient.'

For years, and long before his time, Arthur had been acting the old man, an affectation which exasperated Evelyn. But now he *was* old. His asthma was worse, he had become increasingly deaf (had taken to using an ear-trumpet) and had grown worryingly obese. Food had always been a pleasure, and many meals, especially during the meagre years of the war, were lovingly detailed in his journal. One evening in July 1940, 'Evelyn & Laura arrived in a taxi, both looking very well. We had a very successful dinner – Joan's whitebait & salad, fowl with peas & new potatoes, plum pudding (nobody had it), raspberries & cream'; on 12 December 1941, 'Evelyn & Laura arrived, both looking well. The lunch was very good, steak & kidney pie, three sweets, cheese & biscuits ...' Six years earlier Arthur had had a fright when his doctor told him his weight had reached dangerous proportions ('I weighed myself. 15st 1. 6!! Alas!!'), and that he must restrict his diet ('Lunched off a fresh herring & some cheese – nearly starved'). By the early summer of 1943 he was very frail, having trouble with his breathing, and walking with difficulty; he had also suffered a mild stroke, affecting one side of his face. On 19 June he and Kate attended a cricket match at Highgate School; two days later Kate noted with characteristic calm, 'Arthur not so well. Turned out cupboards & boxroom looking for moths.' But then suddenly his condition deteriorated; the doctor was summoned and a nurse installed.

On 24 June Arthur made one last entry in his diary. 'Went to sleep & had to be woke up for my dinner & before I had properly begun to eat feeling very dormant but otherwise amiable.' The next day his kidneys failed, and at eight o'clock on the morning of the twenty-sixth he died.

The funeral, well attended, was held three days later at Hampstead Parish Church. With his brother away, Evelyn was left with sole responsibility for sorting out Arthur's affairs, an obligation which from his tone he clearly resented. 'I spent some weary hours going through my father's papers and destroying letters. He kept up a large correspondence with very dull people.'

Since early childhood Evelyn had erected a barrier between himself and his father, which by adolescence was held immovably in place by irritation and contempt. The two men had never been close, and for Evelyn there was little to mourn in his father's death. Sadder in a sense was the deterioration of the loving relationship he had once enjoyed with his mother, now long outgrown. Kate bored and vexed him, and although prepared to do his duty by her, he was impatient for Alec, always the more satisfactory son, to come home and take over.

> You will already have heard the details of our father's death. It is lucky that I have been in England for this month. I go abroad at the beginning of August. If you can get home it would be a good thing as our mother is désoeuvrée and lonely.
>
> My fathers papers have been arranged in his bureau as follows ... I am having a bookplate engraved to mark his books so that eventually they can remain intact as a personal collection in our respective libraries.
>
> My father's estate will probably be about £5000. This is clearly not enough to support our mother if invested in the ordinary way. I do not know if Chapman & Hall will offer a pension. If not I suggest that she purchase an annuity. She should get £500 or more in this way. Joan might care to make a covenanted allowance which would merely come out of her surtax and leave her (Joan) none the worse off.
>
> Our mother shows no inclination to leave Highgate. The best thing would be for you to live with her; the next best that a friend should be found to share the flat.
>
> I hope you will be able to get back to see to things after I have left.

But Evelyn's hopes of going abroad in August never materialised. He fully expected to be able to join Laycock within weeks of his father's funeral, but permission for departure had to be obtained from Lord Lovat, the deputy brigade commander, and Lovat shared none of Laycock's compassionate view, determined that this contumacious officer should have nothing to do with an operation as vital and delicate as HUSKY. He and Evelyn were old enemies. Shimi[12] Lovat, son of the Laura Lovat whom Evelyn had so taken against on his Adriatic cruise ten years before, was a Highland chief and territorial magnate, a devout Catholic and a natural leader of men. A fine soldier, Lovat was possessed of boundless courage and an equally boundless conceit. According to one admirer, he had the 'dashing good looks, cavalier swagger and gestures of bravado [that] put most people in mind of Gay Lochinvar'. As young men he and Evelyn had slightly known and much disliked each other, Evelyn detecting the innate vulgarity beneath Lovat's showy swank and love of applause – a *palais de danse* hero, as he devastatingly described him – while Lovat despised Waugh's social ambitiousness. 'I had known him vaguely at Oxford, and, while I admired his literary genius, had marked him down as a greedy little man – a eunuch in appearance – who seemed desperately anxious to "get in" with the right people.'

Laycock had requested that Evelyn should remain as liaison officer at COHQ until his embarkation orders arrived, when he would proceed to North Africa in the first wave of reinforcements. It would take at least six weeks for the papers to come through, time which Evelyn decided could most profitably be passed in the bar at White's. This gave Lovat his opportunity. Disgusted at what he regarded as Waugh's slovenly deportment, he ordered him to report to the Commando depot at Achnacarry in Scotland for basic training. For an experienced soldier with the rank of captain, this was a gross humiliation, and Evelyn vehemently protested. But Lovat had himself seen Waugh in what he called ' "shit order" – that is to say, without equipment, belt, boots or anklets, for which suede shoes, a cigar or a glass of wine (drunk in a staff car) were substituted', and had no compunction in dismissing his objections. 'You will report to the Depot on 1st August . . . You will not proceed overseas unless passed physically fit by Achnacarry. I hope I have made myself clear.'

Stunned, Evelyn requested an interview with Lovat's superior,

[12] Shimi comes from the Gaelic MacShimidh meaning 'son of Simon', the traditional Gaelic name as chief of his clan.

General Haydon, who, far from sympathising, sacked him on the spot for insubordination. Later that day Evelyn wrote formally to Lovat. 'My Lord, I have the honour to inform you that I have this morning had an interview with the GOCO in which he advised me to leave the Special Service Brigade for the Brigade's good. I therefore have the honour to request that I may be posted to the Royal Horse Guards.' This was followed up with a long, petulant and self-justifying letter to Bob Laycock, describing Lovat's attempt to get him posted to Scotland as 'only explicable on grounds of personal malice'. When Laycock refused to be drawn, Evelyn appealed to Lord Mountbatten, whom he had met socially, but Mountbatten too preferred to remain aloof. Soon the affair blew over. On 10 August Evelyn recorded that 'the indignation I felt a month ago has subsided and I have got bored with the whole thing. My military future is vague . . . I went with Hubert [Duggan] to Windsor and found the barracks full of fine paintings and middle-aged, embittered subalterns. I suppose I shall go there.'

And so to Windsor he went. The surroundings were dismal, his companions dull, and there was little to do. 'White's is shut,' he wrote to Laura, 'so I have no wish to go to London.' But as soon as the club reopened after the summer holiday, Windsor saw less of him, London more. The aimless days continued. 'Too much drinking at midday and at night. White's all the time.' Sometimes Laura came up for a visit, but when she had gone, 'I returned to my futile hanging about White's.' For all his intelligence and powers of perception, Evelyn seemed unable to grasp the direct correlation between his indiscipline and the refusal of his superiors to entrust him with responsibility. With the latest disappointment over Operation HUSKY, all sense of purpose, all ambition to take active part in the war evaporated, in its place a pressing desire to retreat from the world and return to writing.

> I have got so bored with everything military that I can no longer remember the simplest details. I dislike the Army. I want to get to work again. I do not want any more experiences in life. I have quite enough bottled and carefully laid in the cellar, some still ripening, most ready for drinking, a little beginning to lose its body. I wrote to Frank [Pakenham] very early in the war to say that its chief use would be to cure artists of the illusion that they were men of action. It has worked its cure with me . . . I

don't want to be of service to anyone or anything. I simply want
to do my work as an artist.

Certainly the news that Laura was again pregnant and again
miserable at the prospect was insufficient to distract him,
although he took time to send her his customary letter of condolence.

> I do hope that your nursery life is not proving unendurable. I
> think I have not said enough about how deeply I admire your
> patience & resignation in this and in the threat to your future
> happiness in the birth of another child . . . my heart is all
> yours & sorrowing for you. This life of separation & endurance
> is not what I planned for you when I married. There was a
> brief time when I seemed to be having the worse of the war;
> now I live luxuriously & without responsibility & you bear the
> full weight of the times . . .
> If by any chance my children should die, do come to London.
> I miss you every hour.

But although Evelyn was not to see action again, the Army was
not finished with him yet. David Stirling, founder of the Special
Air Service battalion, had been captured in North Africa, and his
brother Bill was engaged in reforming the disbanded unit, hoping
to increase its strength to the dimension of a small brigade. It
was to be under the overall command of Bob Laycock, who, now
returned from Italy, was on the point of taking over from Lord
Mountbatten as Chief of Combined Operations. The friendship
between Laycock and Waugh remained in a state of delicate
balance, their genuine affection for each other tempered by Laycock's embarrassment at Waugh's obstreperousness and demands
for special treatment, and by Waugh's resentment at these reservations. 'I wrote to congratulate him [on his appointment],'
Evelyn recorded, 'comparing him, not quite sincerely, to the
righteous flourishing like a green bay tree. There is no shade for
me under those wide branches. We lunched together on Thursday
but there was a curtain of reproach between us.' However, it was
probably as a result of Laycock's intervention that at the end of
October Bill Stirling agreed to accept Evelyn into the battalion,
with the specific responsibility of presenting in clear and persua-
sive prose the case for an enlarged SAS regiment, a proposal
strongly resisted by more conventional elements. In spite of the

fact that he was a first cousin of the loathsome Lovat, Evelyn admitted Bill Stirling to his personal pantheon, admiring him for a firm moral sense which in his view Laycock lacked. 'He is a great change as a master from Bob – vague, mystical, imaginative, unsmart, aristocratic – in every quality diametrically opposed to Bob and in many ways preferable.'

The plan was for the SAS to embark immediately for North Africa, but on 9 November a cable was received from Allied Force HQ cancelling their journey: victory in the Southern Mediterranean was virtually complete and back-up forces no longer required in that theatre of war. Again Evelyn was left, one on a long list of unwanted persons with nothing to do. At Stirling's instigation and largely to stave off boredom, he and Christopher Sykes, also a member of the regiment, managed to arrange for unoccupied SAS officers to attend an SOE[13] parachute course held at Tatton Park, near Manchester. 'We had a preliminary medical exam, from which I feared the worst. Instead we all passed and went exultantly to White's. We collected several cases of wine and spirits from Justerini and Brooks. Nothing could have spoiled the elation of our journey except what in fact happened. We all developed heavy colds, I influenza.'

In spite of this reverse, the adventure turned out to be rewarding and strangely memorable. The first jump took place in perfect weather on a late autumnal day. 'On Friday we did two jumps. The first was the keenest pleasure I remember. The aeroplane noisy, dark, dirty, crowded; the harness and parachute irksome. From this one stepped into perfect silence and solitude and apparent immobility in bright sunshine above the treetops.' The experience, almost mystical in its other-worldliness, its intensity and sense of peace, vividly remained with Evelyn, to be recreated for Guy Crouchback in *Unconditional Surrender.*

Guy jumped. For a second, as the rush of air hit him, he lost consciousness. Then he came to himself, his senses purged of the noise and smell and throb of the machine. The hazy November sun enveloped him in golden light. His solitude was absolute.

He experienced rapture, something as near as his earthbound soul could reach to a foretaste of paradise, *locum refrigerii, lucis*

---

[13] Special Operations Executive.

et pacis. The aeroplane seemed as far distant as will, at the moment of death, the spinning earth. As though he had cast the constraining bonds of flesh and muscle and nerve, he found himself floating free; the harness that had so irked him in the narrow, dusky, resounding carriage now almost imperceptibly supported him. He was a free spirit in an element as fresh as on the day of its creation.[14]

But as for Crouchback, so for Evelyn: the pleasure was brief. The second time he jumped, he felt a sharp pain in one leg as he hit the ground. That evening the doctor told him he had cracked the fibula which would have to be put in plaster. Out of action again, Evelyn in a few days returned to London, where he spent a pleasant fortnight with Laura entertaining his friends at the Hyde Park Hotel.

Before this anticlimactic episode, in the unhappy period between his enforced resignation from the Special Service Brigade and his joining the SAS, Evelyn became involved in a spiritual matter which affected him deeply.

Over the past year or so, he had spent some time in the company of Hubert Duggan, younger brother of Alfred, both of whom he had known from Oxford days, Alfred much better than his brother. Alfred seemed determined to play the wastrel, but Hubert, infinitely gregarious though he was, took a more responsible approach, joining the Life Guards, then entering Parliament. A handsome and amusing man, Hubert had a melancholy side which gave him a substance he might otherwise have lacked. Evelyn grew fond of him, fond of the high spirits and sympathetic to the intermittent melancholy; when his daughter, Margaret, was born, he asked Hubert to be a godfather. The Duggans had been born in the Argentine, as their immensely rich American mother was married to the honorary attaché to the British legation in Buenos Aires. The family returned to England when the

---

[14] Evelyn's alter ego, Gilbert Pinfold, also remembered his being dropped by parachute 'as the most serene and exalted experience of his life . . . the dispatching officer had signalled; down he had plunged into a moment of night, to come to himself in a silent, sunlit heaven, gently supported by what had seemed irksome bonds, absolutely isolated. There were other parachutes all round him holding other swaying bodies; there was an instructor on the ground bawling advice through a loudspeaker; but Mr Pinfold felt himself free of all human communication, the sole inhabitant of a private, delicious universe.'

boys were small, and although brought up Catholic, they had both had a conventional English education, sent first to Eton, then Oxford, Alfred to Balliol, Hubert to Christ Church. Their father had died in 1915 while they were still at school, and just over a year later their mother married Lord Curzon, chancellor of Oxford University and one time viceroy of India. Neither their mother nor step-father was Catholic, and both boys allowed their faith to lapse, Alfred taking to drink, Hubert to women – he had left Oxford after only a term disgusted by the lack of feminine society. Hubert had had a number of love affairs, both before and after a brief marriage, with among others Maimie Lygon, Bridget Parsons, Diana Fellowes and Daphne Weymouth. For some time he had been living with the beautiful Phyllis de Janzé in a little house in Chapel Street, but she had died in April 1943, and Hubert, whose health had always been fragile, fell ill that same month with tuberculosis.

When Evelyn visited Hubert at the end of September, he found him in a pathetic state, near to death and tormented by the consequences of his lapse in faith. Convinced he had been living for years in a state of mortal sin, he longed to return to the Church, yet felt it would be a betrayal of the mistress he had loved to repent of his life with her. Realising that his friend urgently needed help, Evelyn went to find a priest who would administer the last rites.

I went to see Father Dempsey who is the Catholic chaplain for West London District, to consult him about Hubert. He was a big fat peasant who said, 'I know a priest who is a fine gentleman. Would it not be better to get him? I should put my foot in it.' He telephoned some Irish nuns: 'It's a great work of charity you will be doing Mother . . . [sic]' to have a sister available in case she was needed. He gave me a medal. 'Just hide it somewhere in the room. I have known most wonderful cases of Grace brought about in just that way.' When I got to Chapel Street Lady Curzon told me that it was not expected Hubert would live through the day. As Dempsey had gone out I went to Farm Street and brought back Father Devas [Rector of the Farm Street community]. Marcella [Hubert's sister] did not want him to come in. She and Ellen [the maid] were sitting by him supporting him in a chair saying, 'You are getting well. You have nothing on your conscience.' I brought Father Devas in and he gave Hubert absolution. Hubert said, 'Thank you father,' which was taken as his assent.

... [In the late afternoon] I went back to Chapel Street. Numerous doctors – one particularly unattractive one from Canada – Marcella more than ever hostile. Father Devas very quiet and simple and humble, trying to make sense of all the confusion, knowing just what he wanted – to anoint Hubert – and patiently explaining, 'Look all I shall do is just to put oil on his forehead and say a prayer. Look the oil is in this little box. It is nothing to be frightened of.' And so by knowing what he wanted and sticking to that, when I was all for arguing it out from first principles, he got what he wanted and Hubert crossed himself and later called me up and said, 'When I became a Catholic it was not from fear,' so he knows what happened and accepted it. So we spent the day watching for a spark of gratitude for the love of God and saw the spark.

Evelyn attended Hubert's Requiem Mass at Farm Street on 3 November. His friend's return to his Church through the simple, good offices of the local priest, and in spite of opposition from the family, had made a lasting impression. Later, in the description of the death of Lord Marchmain, it was to provide an important strand in Charles Ryder's road towards Catholic revelation, the primary theme of *Brideshead Revisited.*

This was the novel now taking shape in Waugh's imagination, and on which he was anxious to start. At the end of January 1944, he wrote to his commanding officer at Windsor requesting permission for three months' leave without pay. After listing in a series of numbered paragraphs his lack of qualifications for modern warfare – insufficient technical training, lack of physical agility, little administrative experience, ignorance of foreign languages – he returns to the crux of his argument.

5. In civil life I am a novelist and I have now formed the plan of a new novel which will take approximately three months to write.

6. This novel will have no direct dealing with the war and it is not pretended that it will have any immediate propaganda value. On the other hand it is hoped that it may cause innocent amusement and relaxation to a number of readers and it is understood that entertainment is now regarded as a legitimate contribution to the war effort.

7. It is a peculiarity of the literary profession that, once an

idea becomes fully formed in the author's mind, it cannot be left unexploited without deterioration. If, in fact, the book is not written now it will never be written.

8. On the completion of the writing I shall be able to return to duty with my mind unencumbered either by other preoccupations or by the financial uncertainty caused by the necessity of supporting a large family on the pay of lieutenant. I shall be able to offer myself in the hope that some opportunity will then have arisen in which I can serve my regiment.

The leave was granted. In January 1944 the war was at a crucial stage, British and American forces having landed at Anzio on the twenty-second, and preparations were well advanced for the invasion of Normandy. Able-bodied men were urgently needed, but as Bill Stirling remarked, 'It was difficult if one was doing a general reorganisation of things to have to deal with Evelyn as well, and particularly when he felt he ought to be writing a book.' On the last day of the month Evelyn went down to Chagford, inwardly convinced that he was about to embark on a work of considerable importance. 'I still have a cold and am low in spirits but I feel full of literary power which only this evening gives place to qualms of impotence,' he wrote on the evening of his arrival. To his great satisfaction he found he had been given a sitting-room as well as a bedroom, the better to ensure he would not be disturbed by maids and housework.

Over the next four weeks, Evelyn, wholly absorbed in his novel, recorded his progress daily. On the first morning, 'Up at 8.30, two and a half hours earlier than in London, and at work before 10. I found my mind stiff and my diction stilted but by dinner-time I had finished 1,300 words, all of which were written twice and many three times before I got the time sequence and the transitions satisfactory, but I think it is now all right.'

At Chagford he kept to a strict routine, working all morning, going for a walk after lunch; then more work until the early evening, when he had a bath and cocktail before dinner; after dinner he did *The Times* crossword and went early to bed in the hope of a long and uninterrupted sleep. The trouble with this was that the better he worked, the worse he slept, and if he slept badly, then the next day's work suffered. While a novel was in progress he lived in terror of not sleeping, and thus the frequent recourse to chloral and other soporifics, which were effective in

457

rendering him unconscious, although they made him feel noticeably less alert the next morning.

Evelyn wrote in longhand with a Relief nib on sheets of lined foolscap paper. Each completed manuscript was bound by Maltby of Oxford, its title stamped in gold on a leather spine. He regarded writing as a craft which demanded meticulous skill and attention. To Christopher Sykes he explained, 'Do remember it is much harder to write a book than to make a watch. There are many more good watches in the world than good books. You must give the same intent care to writing that Patek Philippe gives to watchmaking.' To this end he rewrote obsessively, cutting and rephrasing, testing the weight of each significant word and clause.

It was essential to have a thorough understanding of the rules of grammar, and to know not only the current meaning of a word but its derivation and history; for this he relied on the classical grounding he had received at Lancing, and on constant reference to the *Oxford Dictionary* and to Fowler's *Modern English Usage.* Although unmusical, Evelyn had an almost perfect ear for the rhythm and fall of a sentence, and was acutely aware of nuances of style, both his own and of writers whom he admired, such as Ruskin. ('Read a page of Ruskin a day,' was the advice he gave to a conference of young writers in America.) 'I am getting spinsterish about style,' he wrote in the middle of February, and a month later, 'English writers, at forty, either set about prophesying or acquiring a style. Thank God I think I am beginning to acquire a style.' His own sophisticated style was rooted in a profound understanding of the peculiar grace and flexibility of the English language.

'Brevity is not the hall-mark of precision. The familiar is not necessarily the intelligible. Paraphrase, periphrasis, displacement and inversion are often needed to delimit and define and give the correct emphasis to an apparently simple sentence.' He was not against the occasional and deliberate use of cliché, maintaining that 'to be oversensitive about clichés is like being oversensitive about table manners . . . There are many occasions in writing when one needs an unobtrusive background to action, when the landscape must become conventionalized if the foreground is to have the right prominence.' Evelyn considered the English language to be 'the most lavish and delicate which mankind has ever known', and so careful was he to avoid clumsy or extraneous matter that after reading the day's work he sometimes found himself having to stretch, rather than prune his material. 'It is always my temptation in writing to make everything happen in one day, in one hour on one page and so lose its drama and suspense. So all today I have been rewriting and stretching until I am cramped,' he told Laura.

Language and the structure of the plot were what concerned him, he claimed, rather than psychological motivation. 'I regard writing not as investigation of character, but as an exercise in the use of language, and with this I am obsessed. I have no technical psychological interest. It is drama, speech, and events that interest me.' Up to a point this was disingenuous: Evelyn's novels are remarkable for the subtlety and accuracy of his psychological observation; but it amused him to dismiss such topics as pretentious nonsense, choosing instead to play the part of honest craftsman labouring to do his best with the superb tool (the English language) at his disposal.

During those weeks at the Easton Court his imagination was possessed, and once into his stride he was producing up to 3000 words a day, parcelling up completed chapters and taking them to the post office to be sent to Mr McLachlan for typing. For such concentrated effort it was essential that he live away from his family; Laura was allowed to visit him occasionally, but he could not have her with him while he was working – a fact of life he had clearly explained in his letter proposing marriage, an explanation which Laura seems to have forgotten, failed to take seriously, or perhaps not fully to have understood.

When Evelyn told her he wanted to start on a novel, her immediate reaction was to suggest the two of them move into a cottage on the Pixton estate, a project that was brusquely dismissed. Shortly afterwards he wrote to account for his apparently ungracious behaviour.

> I did not explain why your plan to live with me in a cottage at
> Pixton would not do and may have seemed abrupt in turning
> it down. The reason is that I long for your company at all times
> except one. When I am working I must be alone. I should
> never be able to maintain the fervent preoccupation which is
> absolutely necessary to composition, if you were at close

quarters with me . . . While I am working it is brief fairly frequent visits I want, not solid domesticity.

For the whole of February Evelyn remained at Chagford, only distantly disturbed by world affairs. On 13 February he added a few lines to his journal regarding the depressing turn in international events. 'The battle at Nettuno looks unpromising. It is hard to be fighting against Rome. We bombed Castel Gandolfo. The Russians now propose a partition of East Prussia. It is a fact that the Germans now represent Europe against the world. Thank God Japan is not on our side too.'

But at the end of the month came a brutal intrusion in the form of a telephone call from Windsor: the War Office had cancelled his leave and he was under orders to report immediately to take up a new post as ADC to some unknown general. 'So that ends my hopes of another two months' serious work. Back to military frivolities.'

Now began a game of cat-and-mouse between Evelyn, desperate to return to his novel, and the military authorities, frantically preparing for the Second Front and in need of all available forces. The first round went to Evelyn. Having obediently travelled to London to meet his new chief, Major-General Ivor Thomas, he succeeded in making himself so offensive that Thomas refused to have him. 'This is a great relief. The primary lack of sympathy seemed to come from my being slightly drunk in his mess on the first evening. I told him I could not change the habits of a lifetime for a whim of his.' Round two was a draw. Another general, Major-General Miles Graham, was produced, 'like a rabbit from a hat', and he raised no objection to having Evelyn as his ADC. However, the moment the posting was confirmed, Evelyn persuaded Graham at once to grant him six weeks' leave. 'The new general is very much less assuming than Tomas[15] & fully appreciates, or appears to appreciate, the importance of a gentleman leading his own life.'

[15] The deliberate mistaking or misspelling of a name is a sure indication of Evelyn's dislike. 'Thomas' is spelt variously Tomkins, Thompson, Tomlin, Tomas. There was a Brigadier Twohig whom Evelyn took violently against while stationed in Jugoslavia: 'forehead of an orang-outang, a moustache like Osbert Lancaster's, and a voice which blends Aldershot and Irish in a way which made me repeatedly think he was being facetious only to find my smile frozen on my lips by the gleam of his little ape eyes'. His name appears in the diary as Twigg, Twig, Taowig, Twoigg and Twoig.

At the end of the six weeks the War Office, reinvigorated, struck again, this time ordering the recalcitrant novelist to report for duty at Windsor. It was now the beginning of April, and the book was sufficiently advanced for Evelyn to regard the interruption with relative tranquillity: he had come to a natural break in the story and it might, he conceded, be no bad thing to have a couple of weeks away. In the event he passed the entire fortnight drinking in White's, waiting to conduct journalists around the Second Front. No journalists appeared, and by the end of the month Evelyn lost patience and appealed to Bob Laycock for help 'in getting me six clear weeks to finish my work . . . One day, believing it to be the first of a long period of work, is worth a week of odd days on end of which I expect the summons to move.' This time there was nothing Laycock could do, unable to influence the War Office on behalf of an officer who was no longer under his command; but Evelyn, reading Laycock's refusal as a betrayal of friendship, decided to wait no longer. On the first of May he gave dinner to two old friends, John Sutro and Harold Acton: 'a fine dinner – gulls' eggs, consommé, partridge, haddock on toast, Perrier Jouet '28, nearly a bottle a head, liqueur brandy, Partaga cigars . . . I found their company delightful.' Acton had finally been accepted by the RAF, and 'Harold's descriptions of service life as seen by a bugger were a revelation.'

Two days later, and without official permission, Evelyn returned to Chagford. Here for a week he struggled with 'a very difficult chapter of love-making on a liner . . . I feel very much the futility of describing sexual emotions without describing the sexual act; I should like to give as much detail as I have of the meals, to the two coitions – with his wife and Julia. It would be no more or less obscene than to leave them to the reader's imagination.' The shaping of this delicate passage was disrupted by a telegram from Windsor summoning Evelyn to London for an interview at Hobart House in Grosvenor Place; here Evelyn was offered a choice of job, either as welfare officer in a transit camp in India or assistant registrar in a hospital. Reluctantly he chose the latter; then in a panic he turned again to Laycock, who this time was able to pull strings, arranging with Bill Stirling for Evelyn to be taken back into 2 SAS. The following day Evelyn saw Stirling who, infinitely understanding, simultaneously confirmed his appointment and granted six weeks' leave. Evelyn returned to Chagford.

There were to be further alarms and excursions, including the birth of a fifth child. 'Do not let the Herberts harrow me with information about your baby until it is born and you are well & happy,' Evelyn had instructed Laura. The baby, Harriet, was born on 13 May, her father making a brief visit to Pixton to see her a week later.

No sooner had he returned to Chagford than he learned that the amenable Stirling had been dismissed, his place as commander taken by Brian Franks. Fortunately Colonel Franks needed no convincing of Evelyn's undesirability, and told him he could have all the time he needed to finish his book. For Tuesday 6 June, the diary entry reads,

> This morning at breakfast the waiter told me the Second Front had opened. I sat down early to work and wrote a fine passage of Lord Marchmain's death agonies. Carolyn [Cobb] came to tell me the popular front was open. I sent for the priest to give Lord Marchmain the last sacraments. I worked through till 4 o'clock and finished the last chapter – the last dialogue poor – and took it to the post, walked home by the upper road. There only remains now the epilogue which is easy meat. My only fear is lest the invasion upsets my typist at St Leonard's, or the posts to him with my manuscript.

On 8 June the book was finished, Evelyn sending the final section to Mr McLachlan with instructions to change the name of the hero from 'Charles Fenwick' to 'Charles Ryder' and of the child 'Bridget' to 'Cordelia'.

Evelyn spent a few days with Laura, then went on his own to London. To his surprise and disgust, he found himself badly shaken by the bombardment by V-1s, the new pilotless planes. When rumours about these flying bombs first started to spread, as early as November 1943, Evelyn, realising the weapon's potential for enormously increased destruction, had taken certain precautions.

> [I have] given orders for the books I have been keeping at the Hyde Park Hotel to be sent to Piers Court. At the same time I have advocated my son coming to London. It would seem from this that I prefer my books to my son. I can argue that firemen rescue children and destroy books, but the truth is that a child

is easily replaced while a book destroyed is utterly lost; also a
child is eternal; but most that I have a sense of absolute
possession over my library and not over my nursery.

What he did not expect was the effect on his equilibrium of such
an attack. 'At about 1.30 on the night of Monday June 19th–20th
I heard one flying near and low and for the first and I hope the
last time in my life was frightened. Thinking this disagreeable
experience over I think it was due to weakening my nerves with
drink (I was drinking heavily all those days in London) and I
have therefore resolved today never to be drunk again.' Despite
this grim resolution ('It is a cutting of one of the few remaining
strands that held me to human society'), he was able to tell Laura
that he was now completely happy with his life, looking forward
to joining the regiment in Scotland, able to see 'nothing but
innocent pleasure ahead'.

This rare mood of contentment lasted barely twenty-four hours.
The Headquarters of 2 SAS was at Ardchullery, a shooting-lodge
belonging to Bill Stirling in Perthshire. It was immediately made
clear that Evelyn was far from welcome, with Brian Franks, irritated and embarrassed by his presence, candidly informing him
that he was a liability and on no account to be allowed near the
men. As luck would have it, further awkwardness was avoided by a
message coming through almost at once recalling him to London.
Randolph Churchill, currently employed in Brigadier Fitzroy
Maclean's mission in Jugoslavia, was briefly in England, author-
ised by Maclean to find compatible companions to go with him
to Croatia as liaison between the British military and the resistance. Evelyn was Randolph's first choice, unhesitatingly approved
by Maclean not only for his courage and resilience but, more
important, for his ability 'to contain' Randolph. The two men met
at the Dorchester, where Randolph cunningly whetted Evelyn's
appetite by expatiating on the internecine warfare existing in the
area between the Roman Catholic and Orthodox populations: it
would be Waugh's particular brief to play a part in healing this
great schism. 'I accepted eagerly.'

In 1944 the political situation in Jugoslavia was complex and
dangerous. The country had been overrun by the Germans
and Italians in 1941, since when Britain had been vigorously
supporting the resistance, initially the Chetniks under General

Draza Mihailović, a Serbian and a royalist. Soon, however, another formation was making itself felt, the Partisans, led by Marshal Tito. In September, 1943, Maclean had been dropped into the country, instructed by Winston Churchill to discover one simple truth: 'who was killing the most Germans and how they could be helped to kill more.' In spite of the fact that Tito was avowedly communist, his sympathies veering towards Russia rather than Britain and America, it was Maclean's opinion that the Partisans were stronger, their leader more ruthless and in military terms more effective. British support and resources consequently were diverted from Mihailović to the marshal, and Maclean promoted brigadier and appointed head of the British Military Mission (Macmis) to Tito. Randolph was with Macmis as it was thought that the presence of the prime minister's son would act as a visible symbol of Britain's solidarity with Jugoslavia.

Like Evelyn, if on a much bigger scale, Randolph Churchill had long been a problem to the military. Because of his status he was in a sense inviolable; he was also vulnerable as an enemy target, and useful to certain elements, some of them distinctly undesirable, as a direct conduit to his father. Unfortunately, Randolph lacked both the stability and the maturity to keep his balance in such a delicate position. Longing to be accepted for himself, he was at the same time determined that everyone should know who he was. Loud-mouthed and arrogant, he shamelessly exploited all the perquisites and privileges available to him, while complaining that people paid him attention only because his name was Churchill. But though preposterous, there was also something endearing about Randolph, an almost childlike innocence, a capacity for affection, and an impetuous enthusiasm that could be both touching and infectious.

He and Evelyn were two of a kind, each recognising in the other the same rumbustious, malevolent, anarchic strain, a similarity of temperament which allowed this famously fractious friendship to endure through many years of outrage and insult. Attractive as young men (Randolph had been outstandingly handsome), both had turned heavy-jowled and corpulent in middle age. They were self-indulgent, smoked and drank to excess; were lazy and physically unfit. Evelyn was cleverer, both were choleric; but whereas Evelyn's fits of temper were usually expressed with a malice cruel but controlled, Randolph in a rage bellowed like a bull. They both enjoyed making mischief, and were capable of stunning rudeness. Both were heartily disliked by their fellow soldiers, a fact which Randolph accepted with less fortitude than Evelyn; when told by his commander in the 4th Hussars that the officers disliked him and other ranks found him intolerable, Major Churchill burst into tears. On *Glenroy* on the voyage out to North Africa, Randolph was judged 'a brute and a bore, universally disliked, unapproachable, no charm, only interested in the sound of his own voice'. He was also, like Evelyn, exceptionally courageous, and on his return from Jugoslavia was awarded the MBE and recommended for the Military Cross.

Randolph was an energetic womaniser, noisily and clumsily pursuing every attractive woman who crossed his path, regardless of whether or not she was likely to respond. He fell in love fairly frequently, and was fairly frequently rejected. The women who coped most successfully were those who treated him firmly, like a strict nanny with a spoilt child. This was precisely Evelyn's technique.

On the evening of 4 July Evelyn and Randolph flew from Hendon to Gibraltar, then on to Algiers, where they stayed with Duff and Diana Cooper, Duff at that time acting as British representative to General de Gaulle's Committee of National Liberation.

The embassy was a ramshackle Moorish house of great charm, 'with tiled courtyards not unlike Mexico and peacocks and palm & rubber trees', Evelyn told Laura. 'D & D very popular & happy, good food, one lavatory, one bath, everyone in pyjamas all the morning, like Venice before the war.' The other guests were Bloggs Baldwin, Virginia Cowles, Martha Gellhorn and Victor Rothschild, an agreeable house party whose civilised tranquillity was instantly disrupted by the new arrivals. Randolph rampaged about the house talking incessantly, drinking gin and chain-smoking. 'I should think he must go through two bottles of gin a day,' Diana complained. 'His coughing is like some huge dredger that brings up dreadful sea-changed things. He spews them out into his hand or into the vague – as soon as I get up he takes my place in my bed with his dirt-encrusted feet and cigarette ash and butts piling up around.' Evelyn in a contrasting way was just as difficult, sitting through meals in complete silence, apparently immersed in gloom. When Diana asked him what was wrong, he replied that he had never felt so cheerful: 'he had just written a book that he thought a masterpiece, he had no money troubles, a wife he adored, three fine children,[16] splendid health and now an active life calling him to Yugoslavia with his beloved Randolph. His serenity knew no bounds. I said I wished he could reflect his happiness a little more. He said that other people had said the same.'

After three days in Algiers, Waugh and Churchill continued to Bari, rear HQ of Macmis, and from there to the island of Vis off the Dalmatian coast, where there was a British garrison. Here they were immediately embroiled in an elaborate luncheon in honour of Marshal Tito and his staff. Earlier in the war, before Tito had risen to prominence and was operating under conditions of great secrecy, there had been something of a mystery about him, exactly who he was, whether he even existed, whether (facetiously) he was not in fact a young woman. This latter piece of drollery had attracted Evelyn, who had seized on and embroidered it, telling everyone that he could hardly wait to meet 'her'. On arrival Evelyn and Randolph were taken down to the sea where most of the party had been swimming. Evelyn, smartly turned out in his regimental khakis, was greeted by Brigadier Maclean, who then introduced him to a handsome, powerfully-built man wearing nothing but a pair of close-fitting bathing trunks. 'Ask Captain Waugh', said Tito shaking him by the hand, 'why he thinks I am a woman.'[17] That evening the newcomers dined with Maclean, whom Evelyn in his diary described as 'dour, unprincipled, ambitious, probably very wicked; shaved head and devil's ears . . . saturnine and Nazi', an opinion possibly influenced by Maclean having been witness to his embarrassment earlier in the day.

Evelyn and Randolph then returned to Bari for several days,

---

[16] Four children by this date.

[17] Never one to let a good joke drop, Evelyn kept this one going for years. A couple of American military personnel, to whom he propounded the theory, denied it vigorously. 'I know that's not true,' said one. 'I was in charge of the marshal's security when he was in Rome, and I know he went and visited a woman's room on two successive nights.' 'Well,' said Evelyn, unruffled, 'we always knew she was a Lesbian.' And on the occasion of Tito's visit to London in 1953, he wrote to Randolph, 'The politicians must be heartily sorry they imported the wench. I note that her baleful eye brought down another two aircraft yesterday.'

before taking off for Croatia on the evening of 16 July in a large Dakota transport plane. The flight took several hours; late at night as they approached the runway the aircraft suddenly caught fire and crashed into a field. The next Evelyn knew, 'I was walking in a cornfield by the light of the burning aeroplane talking to a strange British officer about the progress of the war in a detached fashion and that he was saying "You'd better sit down for a bit skipper." I had no recollection of the crash nor, at the time, any knowledge of where I was or why.' He and Randolph were taken by ambulance to Topusko, a town forty miles due south of Zagreb, and from there flown back to Bari. They were fortunate in their escape: of the nineteen people on board, ten were killed. Randolph was hurt in both knees, Evelyn badly burned on hands, legs and head. Bandaged up like a mummy, he suffered less from his injuries than from a painful boil on the neck and from the unrestful nature of Randolph's company. Randolph with nothing to occupy him was drinking, talking, making passes at the night nurse, demanding treatment, sampling everyone else's medicine, and loudly dictating letters. Eventually he left for Algiers, and on 2 August Evelyn was well enough to make the journey to Rome, where it was arranged for him to stay in a flat on the Via Gregoriana. Soon the carbuncle on his neck grew so tormenting that he was obliged to go into hospital for ten days, before returning to the flat to convalesce.

At the end of August, Randolph came back, still lame but 'much calmer', and the two left Rome, driving by jeep to Naples, from where they flew to Corsica. Here they were entertained by a hospitable major at the American base at Isle Russe, before taking off for their original destination in Jugoslavia. Their quarters were located on the outskirts of Topusko, a small spa town surrounded by chestnut forests; there was a park, a wood with ornamental walks, two public gardens, and cobbled streets shaded by plane trees. The communal baths were clean, new and still working, unlike the rest of the town which was in a dilapidated condition, with shops gutted and many of the buildings in ruins. The indigenous population having fled, Topusko was used by Tito as his Croatian headquarters, and by the Allies as the final link in the escape route from the Balkans for prisoners of war. Evelyn and Randolph were allocated a house set in the middle of a farmyard, with an orchard to one side. There were four rooms and a verandah, and what was claimed to be the only indoor privy in Topusko. To cook and look after them there was a good-natured old peasant-woman named Zora.

Their duties were light. Evelyn was second-in-command to Randolph, both acting as military ambassadors between the British army and the Partisans. As such, they were responsible for promoting pro-British propaganda among a communist military naturally inclined to look first to Russia for aid; they had also to supervise airdrops of arms and supplies sent over from Italy, and to report on the military situation. In fact this added up to very little, and the chief problem was to find ways to pass the time. Evelyn described the daily routine in his diary. 'Breakfast, I at 8, the others 9. 10.30, go and visit HQ and ask if there is any news; possibly write a signal for enciphering. Large luncheon. Randolph sleeps. I read. We have a large library given by the British Council – dinner at 8. Storm lanterns too feeble to read or write. Wireless news hourly. Randolph drunk and rhetorical. At 10.30 I go to bed and sleep very well.' In a letter to Laura he wrote, 'We do very little & see little company except a partisan liaison officer, the secretary general of the Communist party, the leader of the Peasant party & such people. We also arrange for the evacuation of distressed Jews . . . We have great quantities of eggs to eat and some very tough meat.'

With little to occupy him, and little variation in either company or routine, inevitably Evelyn grew bored and melancholy. 'Time seems to stand still here,' he told Laura. 'I find nothing to do between meals & there is nothing to tell you . . . Today has lasted about a week already and it is only 4.15 pm. We are like Chekhov characters . . . Oh dear I wish I could go to sleep & wake up when the war was over.' Ten days later he wrote, 'The past week has gone like a fortnight – a great improvement. It rained until Wednesday, stopped for three days and began again.' He thought often and longingly of England.

My window is almost covered with vine leaves & I could not understand why, on waking and seeing the light come through the leaves, I spent the first quarter of an hour of every day thinking of Midsomer Norton. I thought it was because the pattern was like my aunt Constance's church needlework, or like the borders of nineteenth-century printed texts. Then I realised that it was quite simple & direct & that this was how the light came into the smoking-room through the vines on the verandah.

His homesickness was aggravated by the fact that it was weeks since any mail had come through, and he suffered from being deprived of his two main staples, cigars and wine. 'This is not a wine growing district,' he told Coote Lygon. 'I came abroad primarily because of the shortage of wine in England. I think I shall apply for a transfer to a grape country.'

But far and away the largest obstacle to contentment was Randolph. Evelyn at least had a bedroom to himself, but he was obliged to spend the entire day cooped up in Randolph's company, which irritated him almost more than he could bear. Never was there a moment's peace. Hour after hour Randolph trampled and trumpeted, talking, shouting, scratching, farting, belching and yawning; he tapped incompetently on the typewriter, bellowed into the telephone, and sat 'clucking over the signals like an old hen'. Every evening he got drunk on *rakia*, a foul-tasting local liquor which, according to Evelyn who was unable to stomach it, gave off a powerful stench, part sewage, part glue. Evelyn did his best to control Randolph by snubbing him at every opportunity and refusing to be moved by his nightly wallowings in crapulent self-pity; he remained ostentatiously unimpressed by Randolph's boasting, deliberately refusing him the attention he craved. But Randolph, ebullient, thick-skinned and eager for affection, was not to be cowed. 'He is simply a flabby bully who rejoices in blustering and shouting down anyone weaker than himself and starts squealing as soon as he meets anyone as strong,' Evelyn wrote in his diary, adding that Churchill's frequent appeals for kinder treatment 'left me unmoved'.

Then suddenly on 13 October, four weeks after their arrival in Topusko, came an unexpected reprieve. 'Randolph and I at dinner – I wondering how long I could bear his company, even he I think faintly conscious of strain – a telephone call from the airfield: Major Clissold and Major Birkenhead had arrived.' This addition to the Croatian contingent had been organised by Fitzroy Maclean. Freddy Birkenhead, newly released from Political Warfare Executive, had the necessary qualities of courage, tolerance and resourcefulness, as well as being a friend of both Churchill (Randolph had been his fag at Eton) and Waugh.

Stephen Clissold, an amiable and quiet-spoken man, was an expert on the Balkans, had lived and worked in Jugoslavia, and most importantly spoke fluent Serbo-Croat.

As they approached the farmhouse they saw Randolph standing at the door, his arms spread wide in welcome. The two newcomers were noisily fussed over, all three talking at once, when according to Birkenhead's account they were joined by 'a demure figure in a brown woollen dressing-gown ... "There he is!" roared the mission commander – "there's the little fellow in his camel-hair dressing-gown! Look at him standing there!" Evelyn directed on him a stare cold and hostile as the Arctic Ocean, and remarked with poisonous restraint: "You've got drunk very quickly tonight." ' Despite his forbidding demeanour, Evelyn was at first as pleased as Randolph to see fresh faces; best of all, Birkenhead had brought with him two letters from Laura and a box of cigars. It was soon apparent, however, that such benefits had their price. 'It is a pleasure to have Freddy here to take Randolph off my hands for a bit but the result of his arrival has been to undo much of the good work I had done in subduing him. He bursts out in such exuberant, spontaneous, full-hearted joy that it should be a pleasure to see him – but it is no great pleasure to me.' It was not long before Churchill and Waugh were back to their old pattern of bellicose behaviour. 'Both were short and sturdy,' Freddy Birkenhead recalled, '[and] I was reminded of a pair of belligerent robins.'

Clissold kept himself to himself, but inevitably Birkenhead soon began to grate on Evelyn's nerves almost as painfully as the irrepressible Randolph.

Freddy is still with us alternately morose and drunkenly jolly ... [He and Randolph] laugh a great deal but never at new jokes or even at their own; they retell endlessly the memorable retorts their respective fathers made at one time or another to various public personages. Even with that vast repertoire they repeat themselves every day or two, sometimes every hour or two. Then they recite memorable patches from Macaulay's essays, John Betjeman's poems and other classics. Of conversation as I love it, with anecdote occurring spontaneously & aptly, jokes growing & taking shape, fantasy – they know nothing. The good time of day for me is the first two hours of daylight before Randolph is awake.

The view from the other side of the fence was equally unattractive. 'We were not a harmonious trio,' Birkenhead admitted. Evelyn appeared sullen and depressed, refusing to join the heavy drinking of *rakia* in the evenings; he watched in silent disapproval while his companions grew drunk and quarrelsome, only emerging waspishly to attack when he heard something he considered particularly objectionable. And in Birkenhead's opinion, Evelyn's own conversation had its limitations. He was such an intensely private man that it was impossible to discuss any intimate feelings or serious beliefs because of the 'iron visor' kept tight shut over his emotions; any attempt at such discussion would be met by relentless frivolity. This reticence detracted from his conversation, 'because however brilliant and witty, one always felt that he was playing some elaborate charade which demanded from him constant wariness and vigilance . . . it was if he was embarrassed by his own emotions and felt that it would not only be grossly improper but also commonplace to give any hint of their nature, and would indeed be a form of indecent exposure.'

To amuse himself and annoy the others, Evelyn resorted to his usual tactic of inventing outrageous stories about his companions. Freddy Birkenhead tolerated the fiction that he was conducting a homosexual affair and had become a morphine addict; his patience gave out, however, over Evelyn's dangerous obsession with Marshal Tito's gender. Evelyn always referred to the Partisan leader as 'Auntie', and when Birkenhead at one point remarked that Tito was being tiresomely intransigent with the Allied leaders, explained that, 'She has come to a rather difficult age for a woman.' 'For God's sake stop this nonsense!' snapped Freddy. 'Everyone knows that Tito's a man and a good looking one at that.' Unfazed, Evelyn replied, 'Her face is pretty, but her legs are *very* thick.'

With Randolph the most serious quarrel erupted over Evelyn's deliberately provocative behaviour during an air-raid. The raid began shortly before dawn, and all except Evelyn took their places in the slit trench at the back of the house. As bombs exploded on all sides and the farmyard was sprayed with machine-gun fire, Evelyn sauntered out wearing a white duffle-coat which might have been designed to attract enemy aim. 'You bloody little swine, take off that coat!' Randolph screamed at him. 'TAKE OFF THAT FUCKING COAT! It's an order! It's a military order!' Without removing his coat, Waugh slowly lowered himself into the trench, quietly remarking to Churchill, 'I'll tell you what I think of your repulsive manners when the bombardment is over.' Later Randolph, unable to bear the frosty atmosphere, apologised for his abusive manner. 'My dear Randolph,' Evelyn replied, 'it wasn't your manners I was complaining of: it was your cowardice.' This outrageous insult effected a complete breach between the two men which continued for several days.

By the beginning of November, relations between Evelyn and Randolph were very strained indeed; but they were stuck with each other. 'As we are obliged to live together I must exercise self-control and give him the privileges of a commanding officer even though he shirks the responsibilities,' Evelyn resolved. 'He is not a good companion for a long period, but the conclusion is always the same – that no one else would have chosen me, nor would anyone else have accepted him. We are both at the end of our tether as far as war work is concerned and must make what we can of it.' By this time Birkenhead, too, had had enough of the unceasing Churchill volubility, and in a final attempt to dam it, joined Evelyn in laying a wager: they bet Randolph £10 he could not read the entire Bible through in a fortnight. 'He has set to work but not as quietly as we hoped,' Evelyn recorded. 'He sits bouncing about on his chair, chortling and saying, "I say, did you know this came in the Bible 'bring down my grey hairs with sorrow to the grave'?" Or simply, "God, isn't God a shit." '

Official duties were still sporadic, mainly consisting of arguments with Partisan delegates about alleged incidents involving British troops, supervising the storing of arms and provisions dropped by parachute, and acting as a reluctant audience at dire 'entertainments' staged in turn by the various national organisations. 'The entertainment consisted of rousing choruses in Russian, Jugoslav, and a language said to be English; a propaganda playlet from the Russian about a boy getting a medal from the state school; a dialogue between Hitler and Reaction, played by a kind of witch; and a play about a cowardly soldier who becomes brave through shooting a German. My Communist neighbour said, "You see in spite of war we have the arts." . . . We got back at 4 am.'

Evelyn loathed the communists, and saw Britain's alliance with Russia as degrading and dishonourable, depriving the war of any crusading element it might once have possessed. Such an attitude severely diminished his usefulness in liaising with the Partisans. In his official report he described the Partisans as 'an organised, revolutionary army whose main characteristics are extreme youth, ignorance, hardiness, pride in the immediate past, confidence in the immediate future, intolerance of dissent, xenophobia, comradeship, sobriety, chastity. The régime which they impose in the rear of the retreating Germans has, to the superficial observer, most of the signs of Nazism.'

Rather than fostering good relations with such godless people, Evelyn was more interested in investigating the subject first broached by Randolph in London, that of the reported persecution of Roman Catholics. Croatia was predominantly a Catholic province. The Catholic population had already suffered at the hands of the Orthodox Church, and a communist régime was unlikely to prove more tolerant: already there were stories of harsh brutality. But in the course of his researches, although plenty of shocking instances were described, Evelyn uncovered little evidence at first hand of sanctions or censorship. In the company of a handful of peasants he was able to attend Mass every Sunday, even if the proceedings at the altar were closely monitored by a soldier with a sub-machine gun. At the house of the parish priest Evelyn interrogated the local monsignor – how many priests were there? did they recognise the authority of their bishops? what was to happen eventually to the teaching orders? At first the man was evasive, but after a time '[he] chucked the patriotic line . . . said it was the priest's duty to stay with his people however hard it was, and that we had the assurance that evil would not prevail over good. I left him with the assurance that he was a sincere priest.'

On 20 November the proofs of *Brideshead Revisited* arrived from England. Before leaving London Evelyn had done as much as he could to prepare the manuscript for publication, delivering one copy to Chapman & Hall, with instructions to print exactly double the number they had planned, and sending one to Father D'Arcy for verification of details of Catholic practice and morality. For the next week Evelyn seized every opportunity when Randolph was out of the room to concentrate on his corrections. It was not easy. 'Proof corrections. Randolph soaking all the afternoon and attempting to compose verse. He sat with a glass of rakija stinking beside him, grunting, counting the syllables on his fingers and in the end produced the line: "Nostalgia for the limbo of the oblivion of your love". Later he became abusive, and later comatose.' But eventually they were done, '[finished] at 6 in the evening while Randolph was at a cinema show at Glina which failed to happen'.

Once the 'magnum opus' had been dispatched, depression returned, intensified by the frightful weather. 'Drizzle began at midday, developing into heavy rain in the afternoon. It rained all· night'; 'A day of continuous rain. We did not leave the house'; 'Mud underfoot, grey skies overhead, intermittent rain, drizzle, mist'; 'Snow and thaw ... Woke once in the night to rain, later to heavy snowfall.' At the beginning of November Evelyn wrote to Laura, 'People talk of things ending here in a few weeks but the war seems to me to have rolled itself in blubber like an eskimo & settled down for the winter. I don't see much hope of getting back before the spring.' By now he was desperate to leave Topusko, and asked Stephen Clissold to suggest to the authorities in Bari that he be moved. Surprisingly this had results, and an order came through recalling him for posting as the Maclean Mission's representative in Dubrovnik.

Belgrade had fallen to the Russians in October, and to help the Partisans harass the Germans and impede their retreat, the British had assembled Floydforce, a unit of brigade strength whose rear headquarters were at Dubrovnik. Evelyn's task was to act as intermediary between Floydforce and the Partisans. On 6 December he arrived in Bari, where he remained for a fortnight collecting stores for the setting up of the new station, and meeting friends, among them Constant Lambert, George Jellicoe, Bill Deakin, and Coote Lygon, who had been posted to Italy with the WAAFs working on photographic interpretation. Coote, looking 'very thin & almost pretty', had hitch-hiked all the way from San Severo specifically to see him, but although Evelyn had looked forward to the visit, it was not a success. '[Coote] arrived, rather inopportunely, at 3.30. I had a rather sticky time with her until 6, failed to get a bath, took two Benzedrine tablets, found I lost all appetite through fatigue and could eat little of the very fine feast we had arranged. For myself I found it a dull evening and wondered whether Coote found it worth her long hitch-hike.'

On 19 December Evelyn disembarked at Dubrovnik, a city of almost Venetian splendour. Dubrovnik was unravaged by war but dilapidated nonetheless, with the beautiful Renaissance façades daubed with communist slogans, the shops empty, and a hungry population desperately trying to barter household goods for food in the markets. Evelyn was driven to the Mission house, a small, comfortless hotel in a narrow alley, where he was to set up his office. With Tito incontestably at this stage the *de facto* heir to Jugoslavia, the Partisans in Dubrovnik, as elsewhere, had begun to treat their British allies in an increasingly peremptory manner. 'The Partisans have succeeded in reducing the British staff to nervous impotence and completely rule the roost,' Evelyn recorded. His situation was a thankless one, mediating in the endless bickering between British and Partisans, wrangling about supplies, and trying to maintain the military status quo, in particular the British right to patrol the town: 'I said we might give up the patrol but not the right to do so.' As in Topusko, part of his official duty was to attend local functions. 'One never knows what one will get in this country,' he told Nancy Mitford after a characteristically eccentric occasion. 'Today we were seated at tables, without a greeting from our hosts, and given (a) Green chartreuse (b) tea and ham sandwiches (c) cakes & cherry brandy & cigarettes (d) two patriotic speeches. Then it seemed reasonable to think the party was over, but no, in came cold mutton & red wine. It is unsettling at my age.'

On 17 January 1945, he wrote with satisfaction, 'Looking back on the last two days I find that everything I have done, which is not much, has been benevolent – giving jobs to the needy, food to the hungry, arranging to get a Canadian moved towards Canada, helping a Dominican priest swap wine for flour.' An additional responsibility was the investigation of the often Byzantine claims of local families to British nationality; many, terrified of a Stalinist régime, were desperate to leave, and their pathetic situation moved him deeply. 'I struggle so far as one bad tempered man and a wireless station can struggle to get the authorities in Italy to do something to relieve the distress here, but so far nothing has been done,' he told his mother. And to Laura he wrote, 'The bloodiness of the Partisans and my uncertain position depress me continually; more than that there are so many unhappy people who look to me for help which I can ill supply. It seems to comfort them to come & tell me how miserable they are; it saddens me.'

For recreation he visited local churches and the magnificent cathedral, and sat to an elderly and engaging sculptor named Paravicini for a portrait bust. 'It will be the next best thing to having myself stuffed.' Most keenly anticipated were letters from England, and the occasional parcel of books sent from Heywood Hill's shop by Nancy Mitford, who was working there as an assistant. On 25 December he wrote to Nancy, 'I have spent a solitary Christmas which next to having Laura's company or the few friends I can count on the toes of one foot, is just as I like it. I dined alone sitting opposite a looking glass & reflecting sadly that the years instead of transforming me into a reasonable man of middle age, have made me into a very ugly youth ... My nerves are not as steady as they were before my harrowing life with R. S. Churchill.'

That Christmas with Laura would have been preferable is a matter for debate. It was at this period that he was complaining so bitterly about the dullness of her letters. Only semi-facetiously he had described for her edification 'an article in an American magazine telling girls how to write to their sweethearts abroad & it said "comment on his letter. Quote bits you liked. Reminisce about happy times in the past. Go to your photographer with your bathing dress and have a pin-up made for him." ' Instead Laura had sent him an account of the seasonal celebrations at Pixton which must have made him grateful for the solitude of Dubrovnik.

> So Christmas is now over – though alas children's jollifications
> are only just beginning as they have parties every day this week
> and most days next week ... Father D'Arcy is here until
> tomorrow ... Last night we had the great yearly get together
> with the nurses from the library which you always dread so
> much ... It really was worse than usual as they have sunk in
> the social scale & instead of being middle class they are lowest
> of all classes & brutally stupid. However as they are all
> methodist preachers they were teetotal & so we had plenty of
> wine for ourselves – the children are all suffering from a mild
> form of pink eye ... I have no other news.

This was far from scintillating, but a more serious disappointment

was Laura's failure to share her husband's passionate interest in
his novel, dedicated to her. For Christmas presents he had had
fifty copies of *Brideshead* specially bound: he was eager to know
the reactions of his friends, and most particularly the reaction of
his wife. On 7 December he wrote to her,

> Darling Laura, sweet whiskers, do try to write me better letters.
> Your last, dated 19 December received today, so eagerly
> expected, was a bitter disappointment . . .
>
> For instance you say my Christmas presents have arrived and
> Eddie [Grant] is pleased. What do you think of the book? Your
> copy is still binding but you must have seen his. You know I
> have not seen one. Tell me what it is like. It is dedicated to
> you. Are you pleased to see it in this form? Are you curious
> to know what changes I have made in the final proofs? There
> are many changes in this copy from what you read before. Can
> you not see how it disappoints me that this book which I regard
> as my first important one, and have dedicated to you, should
> have no comment except that Eddie is pleased with it?

Obediently Laura replied that she had reread the novel, had
enjoyed it, but that her chief concern was Father D'Arcy's objections to one or two passages he considered coarse. 'Have you
rewritten the patches in *Brideshead Revisited* which F. D'Arcy took
exception to . . . On the whole I do agree with Father D'Arcy's
criticism . . . I think it is a pity when you have written such a great
work that it should be able to upset or debar anyone from reading
it . . . I love you & admire you heartily. Laura.'

Clearly no more would be forthcoming on that subject. What,
then, of the response from friends? 'A lot of letters should be
arriving at Pixton thanking for M[agnum]. O[pus]. If you have
not yet forwarded them, do not do so; keep them in a safe place
– not loose in your drawer but in a tin box – and copy out on
an Air Letter the most interesting sentences from each.'

Evelyn's uncertain position was made more uncertain at the
end of January by the Partisans' demand for his withdrawal. Far
the most important of his duties in Evelyn's view was his writing
of a report on the situation of the Roman Church. Having
obtained the permission of Fitzroy Maclean to embark on the
project, he had interviewed a number of clergy, from the bishop
of Kotor to local parish priests, behaviour which the Partisans,
uneasy at any evidence of sympathetic contact with the Catholic

population, condemned as unacceptable. Evelyn appealed to his superiors in Bari, but they, fully occupied with a rapidly moving situation in the Balkans, were disinclined to involve themselves in such a minor dispute. On 7 February instructions were received for Evelyn to go to Trebinje and stay there. He refused. On 12 February came another order, this one impossible to ignore without serious consequences, commanding him to return to Bari at once. On the twenty-first he arrived defiant, determined to apply for the post of consul in Dubrovnik, an *ad hoc* opportunity provided by the Foreign Office making up for wartime staff shortages by offering appointments to suitable non-civil service personnel. Evelyn was attracted by the prospect of '[returning] to the place I was expelled from, with great authority', but his application was unsuccessful.[18]

On 24 February, having obtained the permission of his immediate superior, Major John Clarke, Evelyn flew to Rome to see Pope Pius XII. After several days of wearying interviews with Vatican officials, he was finally granted an audience. 'The sad thing about the Pope is that he loves talking English and has learned several elegant little speeches by heart parrotwise & delivers them with practically no accent, but he does not understand a word of the language.' After listening politely to the pontiff's well-intentioned small-talk, Evelyn requested that they speak in French. 'I left him convinced that he had understood what I came for. That was all I asked.'

The rest of the time in Rome Evelyn devoted to working on his 7500-word report on 'Church and State in Liberated Croatia'. Its substance was that under communist rule the Roman Church was in grave danger, and that freedom of worship was unlikely to be much longer extended. More than that, 'The Croatian clergy believe that a premeditated plan is being put into operation for the gradual extermination of the Church. They base this belief

[18] Another application was equally unproductive. Many years later Osbert Lancaster asked Christopher Sykes if he had known that early in 1945: 'Evelyn had applied to come out to join the Athens Embassy in some not very clearly specified capacity? As the civil war was still raging, H. E. and G. H. Q. barely on speaking terms, the foreign correspondents, both British and American, communists almost to a man, and Randolph insulting everyone in sight, I advised H. E. on being asked my opinion, strongly against accepting this particular addition to the staff, dearly as I would love to have seen him. Despite a loud crowing of cocks I still think I was right.'

on *a priori* grounds that Communism and Christianity are incompatible and also on the evidence of Partisan behaviour in the territory they control.' Largely dismissing evidence that a section of the clergy, in particular members of the Franciscan and Dominican orders, had been active in anti-communist terrorist organisations, Evelyn argued with zeal for the British government's support in protecting his co-religionists.

> Great Britain has given great assistance to the establishment of
> a régime which threatens to destroy the Catholic Faith in a
> region where there are now some 5,000,000 Catholics. There is
> no hope for them from inside their country. Marshal Tito has
> paid lip-service to many liberal principles including that of
> freedom of worship. He may still be amenable to advice from his
> powerful Allies. If he were informed that the position of the
> Church under his rule is causing alarm, that it is not the policy
> of the Allies to destroy one illiberal régime in Europe in order
> to substitute another, that a Government which violates one of
> the principles of the Atlantic Charter cannot be regarded as
> acceptable, he might be induced to modify his policy far
> enough to give the Church a chance of life.

When Evelyn arrived back in London in the middle of March, his urgent intention was to circulate his report to the widest possible audience, in particular to Catholic publications, MPs and other influential members of the Catholic establishment, if possible to the cardinal archbishop himself. The Foreign Office, however, had other ideas. Any real concern on the part of the British government for the Catholics of Jugoslavia was minimal, their overriding anxiety to maintain good relations with Tito. In their view Captain Waugh was a nuisance who must not be allowed to air his provocative opinions. Fortunately he was constrained by the Official Secrets Act: the information to which he had access was acquired while holding office under the Crown as member of a British Military Mission; it was thus classified material. Outraged, Evelyn appealed first to Douglas Howard, head of the Southern Department at the Foreign Office. In a memo, Howard recorded that Captain Waugh was very 'petulant... & said that even if he could not [show the report] ... presumably we could not prevent his talking to his Catholic friends'. The matter was referred to Sir Orme Sargent, permanent under-secretary, who angrily forbad publication, threatening the possibility of serious reprisals if the document were shown outside official circles. Fitzroy Maclean was consulted. Although privately he judged the report both prejudiced and naïve, Maclean knew his man: giving it as his opinion, therefore, that Waugh had presented a reasonably fair picture, he advised the authorities to tread softly. '[It would] be unwise to attempt to coerce Captain Waugh by threats. Captain Waugh is both a clever man and an ardent Roman Catholic and in Brigadier Maclean's opinion would be likely to respond to such treatment by making as much trouble as he could.'

This was not quite the end of the matter. The foreign secretary, Anthony Eden, sent the report to Ralph Skrine Stevenson, newly appointed ambassador in Belgrade, whose response was unequivocal: the issue could be treated with impartiality neither by Catholics nor non-Catholics, and Captain Waugh was no exception; to expect a concordat mutually satisfactory to both the National Liberation Movement and the Catholic Church was beyond the bounds of reason; and most crucially, however accurate or inaccurate the report, the British government had no right whatsoever to interfere in the internal affairs of the Jugoslav state.[19]

This clear-cut argument was far from satisfactory to Evelyn. Debarred from pursuing his crusade in public, he decided to do what he could behind the scenes. On 30 May Captain John McEwen MP asked the foreign secretary in the House what he intended to do to protect Croatian Catholics from Tito's communist régime. Eden replied with an abbreviated version of Stevenson's memorandum,[20] and there finally the matter rested.

[19] According to Stevenson, Waugh chose to ignore much of the evidence pointing to the involvement of a number of clergy with the Catholic Ustase, a terrorist organisation committed to supporting the Italians during the fascist occupation of Jugoslavia. 'The Catholic clergy of Dubrovnik provided the source of a large part of the information contained in Captain Waugh's report. The evidence produced by them was translated for Captain Waugh by Mr Carey, the assistant press secretary at this embassy, who points out that significant passages of their evidence have been omitted. The priests were unable entirely to gloss over the fact of their collaboration, for this was universally known.'
[20] 'I cannot accept the implication that the assistance rendered by us to the National Liberation Movement of Yugoslavia in the struggle against Germany makes His Majesty's Government responsible for the internal administration of the Yugoslav state. This must remain the responsibility of the Yugoslav Government . . . So far as we have influence in any of these lands, it will be to do all we can to allow the people of a country to choose the government and administration they want.'

Evelyn, restricted to denouncing Tito in two letters to *The Times*, was forced to accept that his miserable months in Jugoslavia had been a futile waste of time, his contribution to both the war effort and the Catholic cause negligible.

Age of the common man

At the end of 1940 Evelyn had told Laura, 'I think I shall start writing a book, for my own pleasure, probably not for publication – a kind of modern Arcadia.' Four years later *Brideshead Revisited: the Sacred and Profane Memories of Captain Charles Ryder* was published. In a sense the novel is both panegyric and valediction, inspired by a yearning for a lost arcadia; inspired also by Evelyn's romantic veneration for the aristocracy, for the past, and for English Catholicism, a Catholicism that had survived centuries of persecution, sheltered and nurtured by the great recusant families. On the dustjacket Evelyn described his general intention as

> perhaps intolerably presumptuous; nothing less than an attempt
> to trace the workings of the divine purpose in a pagan world,
> in the lives of an English Catholic family, half paganised
> themselves, in the world of 1923–1939. The story will be
> uncongenial alike to those who look back on that pagan world
> with unalloyed affection, and to those who see it as transitory,
> insignificant and, already, hopefully passed. Whom then can I
> hope to please? Perhaps those who have the leisure to read a
> book word for word for the interest of the writer's use of
> language; perhaps those who look to the future with black
> forebodings and need more solid comfort than rosy memories.
> For those latter I have given my hero, and them, if they will
> allow me, a hope, not, indeed, that anything but disaster lies
> ahead, but that the human spirit, redeemed, can survive all
> disasters.

There are two main themes in *Brideshead Revisited*: the first, that of the working out of a divine plan in the restoration and creation of faith, encompassing the second, the infatuation of Charles Ryder for an entire noble family, the Flytes. *Brideshead* is undoubtedly a great novel; with a fair claim to be Waugh's finest achievement, it is certainly in subjective terms the most significant. In *The Ordeal of Gilbert Pinfold*, confessedly autobiographical, Waugh was to draw an accurate and revealing self-portrait, but it is in *Brideshead* that he engages with the issues that lay nearest his heart.

The course of Ryder's love affair with the Flytes tracks the course of Evelyn's emotional development, as it were a kind of pilgrim's progress. First, in young manhood there is his romantic experience of Oxford and in particular with Alastair Graham, corresponding to Ryder's university career and his friendship with Sebastian Flyte. Then there is the miserable marriage to Evelyn Gardner and the bleak years after it, similar in spirit to the years Ryder spends unhappily married and cut off from contact with the family at Brideshead. Thirdly, there is Ryder's falling in love with Julia which leads him to the final revelation of Catholic faith, reflected in Evelyn's life by his reception into the Church and the strength he derived from his marriage to Laura.

Prologue and Epilogue, too, act as a distillation of the author's philosophy, his nostalgia and his loathing for the modern world. The first and last pages see Ryder with his regiment, under the command of an oafish colonel and surrounded by all the ugliness and squalor of a military encampment, similar in every detail to Pollock camp outside Glasgow, where Evelyn had spent a brief period before his transfer to Ardrossan in 1942. It is here that we meet Hooper, a young subaltern under Ryder's command, who is seen as the brash personification of the Age of the Common Man. Oddly, Hooper in his way is not unengaging, with his amiable, sloppy, take-it-or-leave-it attitude, but he lacks standards. Hierarchy and tradition convey little to Hooper; he has no sense of history, no interest in the past; the values Ryder holds dear, the values of a patrician pre-war world, mean nothing to him.

> [Hooper] came to attention with a kind of shuffling dance-step and spread a wool-gloved palm across his forehead . . .
> ''M I late? Sorry. Had a rush getting my gear together.'
> 'That's what you have a servant for.'

'Well I suppose it is, strictly speaking. But you know how it is. He had his own stuff to do. If you get on the wrong side of these fellows they take it out of you other ways.'

'Well, go and inspect the lines now.'

'Rightyoh.'

'And for Christ's sake don't say "rightyoh".'

'Sorry. I do try to remember. It just slips out.'

The regiment has been moved overnight to a new camp, located by chance in the park of Brideshead Castle. Hooper cheerfully describes the house, a sacred place to Ryder, as

'Great barrack of a place. I've just had a snoop round. Very ornate, I'd call it . . . There's a frightful great fountain, too, in front of the steps, all rocks and sort of carved animals. You never saw such a thing.'

'Yes, Hooper, I did. I've been here before.'

The words seemed to ring back to me enriched from the vaults of my dungeon.

'Oh well, you know all about it. I'll go and get cleaned up.'

I had been there before; I knew all about it.

From this opening the novel goes straight back in time to Charles Ryder at Oxford, a haunting recreation of the place and period, the enclosed and enchanted garden hidden behind the little door in the wall. The description of the university, golden-hued though it is and prettily embowered in meadow-sweet, is extraordinarily evocative: the tourists and church bells, the picnics and luncheon parties, the chimneypieces of fashionable young men cluttered with invitations from London hostesses.

Charles's intense emotional friendship with Sebastian Flyte is firmly grounded in Evelyn's love affair with Alastair Graham – in the manuscript Alastair's name inadvertently appears from time to time instead of Sebastian's. Sebastian has Alastair's whimsical charm, girlish good looks, and addiction to drink; like Alastair, Sebastian, aimless and self-indulgent, is frightened of the adult world, dominated by his mother, and, like Alastair, a committed Catholic. In appearance and temperament Sebastian owes something also to Hugh Lygon, another weak, charming, not overly bright young man to whom Evelyn was much attached. ('Sebastian gives me many pangs,' Hugh's sister, Coote, told Evelyn when she read the book.) Indeed the Lygons provide one of the plot's

structural supports, in that the disgrace and exile of Lord Beauchamp gave Evelyn the idea for Lord Marchmain's story: richer and
grander (a marquess rather than an earl), Marchmain abandons
his wife, vast properties, his position as a leader of the establishment, to live with his mistress in self-imposed exile in Venice.

Oxford is as crucial to the development of Charles Ryder as it
was to Evelyn, and Ryder's university is inhabited by a number
of familiar figures. That Firbankian exquisite, the fascinating,
malevolent Anthony Blanche, although there are elements in him
of Harold Acton, is closely modelled on Brian Howard. In a letter
to Bloggs Baldwin in 1958, the year of Howard's death, Evelyn
wrote, 'There is an aesthetic bugger who sometimes turns up in
my novels under various names – that was $\frac{2}{3}$ Brian $\frac{1}{3}$ Harold
Acton. People think it was all Harold, who is a much sweeter &
saner man.' Harold's was the distinctive gait, '[moving] as though
he had not fully accustomed himself to coat and trousers and
was more at his ease in heavy, embroidered robes'; Harold's the
reciting of 'The Waste Land' through a megaphone. But it is
Brian Howard who gave Blanche his stammer and affected
speech. '[Blanche] took formal and complimentary leave of each
of us in turn. To Sebastian he said: "My dear, I should like to
stick you full of barbed arrows like a p-p-pin-cushion," and to me:
"I think it's perfectly brilliant of Sebastian to have discovered
you. Where do you lurk? I shall come down your burrow and ch-
chivvy you out like an old st-t-toat" '; Howard who gave him
his extreme elegance; Howard's the sophistication and depravity.
'Criss-cross about the world he travelled . . . waxing in wickedness
like a Hogarthian page boy . . . he dined with Proust and Gide
and was on closer terms with Cocteau and Diaghilev . . . he had
aroused three irreconcilable feuds in Capri; he had practised
black art in Cefalu; he had been cured of drug taking in California and of an Oedipus complex in Vienna.'

Another notable Oxford figure prominent in the story is the
sinister and sycophantic Mr Samgrass, admitted by Evelyn to have
been inspired by Maurice Bowra, whose pedantic wit and unctu-
ous mandarin style are reproduced with devastating accuracy.
Charles arrives at Brideshead to find Mr Samgrass already
installed. 'I have been spending a cosy afternoon before the fire
with the incomparable Charlus. Your arrival emboldens me to
ring for some tea. How can I prepare you for the party? Alas, it

breaks up to-morrow . . . I shall miss the pretty creatures about the house – particularly one Celia; she is the sister of our old companion in adversity, Boy Mulcaster, and wonderfully unlike him.'

This reference to Boy Mulcaster's sister, Celia, is the first mention of the woman Ryder is to marry. We see the marriage only in the final stages of its dissolution. Celia, drawn with a cold and subtle cruelty, shares many qualities with Evelyn Gardner. Like She-Evelyn, Celia is snappily dressed, her very English prettiness possessing a 'curiously hygienic quality'; like She-Evelyn, she has a bright, superficial intelligence, a chic taste in interior decoration, is 'good' with servants, and has a schoolgirl air of innocent mischief which many men find adorable. Celia, too, is unfaithful to her husband. But for Charles her adultery is a liberation. 'She had given me my manumission in that brief, sly lapse of hers; my cuckold's horns made me lord of the forest.'

Waugh brilliantly conveys the hostility and distaste in Charles's sexual feeling for his wife; he is less successful, however, in attempting to describe the erotic element in Charles's love for Julia.[1] He made two attempts at describing their first love-making, neither of them impressive.

> So at sunset I took formal possession of her as her lover. It was no time for the sweets of luxury; they would come, in their season, with the swallow and the lime flowers. Now on the rough water, as I was made free of her narrow loins, and, it seemed now, in assuaging that fierce appetite, cast a burden which I had borne all life, toiled under, not knowing its nature – now, while the waves still broke and thundered on the prow, the act of possession was a symbol, a rite of ancient origin and solemn meaning.

In the later revised edition this is changed to,

> It was no time for the sweets of luxury; they would come, in their season, with the swallow and the lime flowers. Now on the rough water there was a formality to be observed, no more.

---

[1] In a revealing passage written in answer to a question of Ann Rothermere's about the nature of Graham Greene's friendship with Catherine Walston, Evelyn wrote, 'My opinion is valueless on their sexual relations. I have no nose for such things and am constantly bowled over to learn who does & who doesn't go to bed with whom.'

It was as though a deed of conveyance of her narrow loins had been drawn and sealed. I was making my first entry as the freeholder of a property I would enjoy and develop at leisure.[2]

Where Celia is entirely real, the character of Julia is cardboard, remaining from first to last, in Christopher Sykes's memorable phrase, 'dead as mutton'. Although the reader is asked to believe that her love for Charles is profound and sexually charged, one believes no such thing. Ryder, completely credible as a man, is as inadequate a lover as Julia a human being, his lethargic wooing and inhibited sexuality making a mockery of the novelist's intention of showing him in the grip of a grand passion. But Ryder shares a number of characteristics with his creator, among them intolerance and irritability, the artist's love of solitude; and, like Waugh, Ryder maintains an air of detachment towards his two children. His daughter is born while he is abroad; not unnaturally, Celia is eager for her husband to see the little girl as soon as possible. ' "Charles, you *must* come. You haven't seen Caroline." "Will she change much in a week or two?" "Darling, she changes every day." "Then what's the point of seeing her now?" '

Although when challenged Evelyn claimed he put this in as a joke, there is good reason for Ryder's lack of paternal feeling: his mother died when he was a child, and his father was a distant and discomfiting parent. Evelyn's brother was not the only one who read into the novel a close relationship between old Mr Ryder and Arthur Waugh. Alec went so far as to argue that their father's demise had released in Evelyn a depth of sentiment he could never have admitted to before. However, although Evelyn's dislike of his father may well have given colour to Ryder's dislike of his, there was little in Arthur's emotional nature to compare with Mr Ryder's witty malevolence. Evelyn had been distanced from his father for too long to feel much of anything when Arthur died.

Predictably, the most hostile reactions were to the novel's overtly Catholic message. Evelyn always insisted that his response to his faith was purely intellectual and pragmatic; in fact, it was also

[2] Evelyn's difficulty in describing sexual relations can perhaps partly be accounted for by his stated belief that 'Our language took form during the centuries when the subject was not plainly handled with the result that we have no vocabulary for the sexual acts which is not quaintly antiquated, scientific or grossly colloquial.'

romantic and emotional, and in *Brideshead* these emotions are given full expression. 'Feeling in London is running high about it,' Christopher Sykes told him. ' "Roman tract" is being hissed in intellectual circles.' But for Evelyn his religion was the centre of his life and focus of his art. The great theme of *Brideshead* is one of Catholic revelation, the bringing of a lost soul to God by means of 'the unseen hook and invisible line . . . the twitch upon the thread'. From the beginning the resolution of this theme is a foregone conclusion, satisfying artistically as well as theologically. It is completely in character for Ryder, the convinced atheist who emphatically repudiates Catholicism, right up until the last furiously condemning it as 'mumbo-jumbo', to make his submission at the end quickly and quietly.

By the time Evelyn came to write *Brideshead,* he had been a member of the Roman Church for almost fifteen years, and had grown familiar with certain strata of Catholic society. As Sebastian tries to explain to Charles, Catholics are not like other people, 'particularly in this country, where they're so few. It's not just that they're a clique . . . but they've got an entirely different outlook on life; everything they think important, is different from other people.' Such esoteric élitism naturally appealed to Evelyn, and he describes it fondly. Like the Herberts, the Flytes are recent converts, and at Brideshead as at Pixton there is constant religious reference in everyday conversation, to Mass, the 'popping in' to the chapel throughout the day, Lady Marchmain's 'little talks', Cordelia's convent chatter. 'My sister Cordelia's last report said that she was not only the worst girl in the school, but the worst there had ever been in the memory of the oldest nun,' Bridey tells Charles at dinner. Cordelia explains: 'That's because I refused to be an Enfant de Marie. Reverend Mother said that if I didn't keep my room tidier I couldn't be one, so I said, well, I won't be one, and I don't believe our Blessed Lady cares two hoots whether I put my gym shoes on the left or the right of my dancing shoes. Reverend Mother was livid.' The ordinariness of the parish priest brought in to administer the last rites to Lord Marchmain bears a strong resemblance to Father Devas, the priest fetched from Farm Street when Hubert Duggan was dying. Sharpest of all, and brilliantly funny, is the report of Julia's lover, Rex Mottram, hurriedly taking instruction with the sole and cynical purpose of qualifying himself for a Catholic marriage.

> Rex was sent to Farm Street to Father Mowbray, a priest renowned for his triumphs with obdurate catechumens. After the third interview he came to tea with Lady Marchmain.
> 'Well, how do you find my future son-in-law?'
> 'He's the most difficult convert I have ever met . . . The first day I wanted to find out what sort of religious life he had had till now, so I asked him what he meant by prayer. He said: "I don't mean anything. *You* tell *me*." I tried to, in a few words, and he said: "Right. So much for prayer. What's the next thing?" I gave him the catechism to take away. Yesterday I asked him whether Our Lord had more than one nature. He said: "Just as many as you say, Father."
> 'Then again I asked him: Supposing the Pope looked up and saw a cloud and said "It's going to rain," would that be bound to happen? "Oh, yes, Father." "But supposing it didn't?" He thought a moment and said, "I suppose it would be sort of raining spiritually, only we were too sinful to see it." '

For some readers, the embarrassment of the novel's Catholic theme was intensified by the high social standing of its dramatis personae. In 1945, a Labour government was elected, a social revolution was under way, and there was much written in the newspapers of the age of the common man. At such a time and for many people the patrician setting of *Brideshead* rankled; in some indefinable way it was considered morally reprehensible to write about the family of an English marquess: the aristocracy was not 'real' in the good, honest way that the lower, and even middle, classes were 'real'. Henry Green writing about servants and factory workers was more in touch, more true to life, than Evelyn Waugh writing about the nobility. But just as Green was inspired by the lives of welders and housemaids, so was Evelyn by the landed aristocracy. As Waugh himself later expressed it, 'The novelist deals with the experiences which excite his imagination.'[3] He does not romanticise the Flytes, who, with the exception of Corde-

---

[3] In an interview given in 1962 Waugh said of the working classes, 'I don't know them, and I'm not interested in them. No writer before the middle of the nineteenth century wrote about the working classes other than as grotesques or as pastoral decorations. Then, when they were given the vote certain writers started to suck up to them.'

lia, are hardly characters to be admired: Sebastian, for all his beauty and waiflike charm, is a drunk and a wastrel; Bridey dull and insensitive; Lady Marchmain pious and cold; her husband an irresponsible rake. In response to the barrage of accusations of snobbery, Waugh wrote, 'Class consciousness, particularly in England, has been so much inflamed nowadays that to mention a nobleman is like mentioning a prostitute 60 years ago. The new prudes say, "No doubt such people do exist but we would sooner not hear about them." I reserve the right to deal with the kind of people I know best.'

The line from *Lamentations* first quoted to Charles by Cordelia in the drawing-room of Marchmain House, 'Quomodo sedet sola civitas . . .', is the novel's leitmotiv. In the present age Evelyn saw nothing but ugliness and poverty of spirit; modernity was purely a force of destruction. The secure, hierarchical pre-war world he believed in was in the process of disintegration, a disintegration metaphorically represented by the disbanding of the Flytes, the demolition of Marchmain House, the departure from Brideshead in all its voluptuous beauty. Fifteen years later when revising the novel for a new edition, Evelyn admitted to a streak of lush romanticism, due he said to the era in which the book was written, an era of Spam and blackouts and Nissen huts,

> a bleak period of present privation and threatening disaster –
> the period of soya beans and Basic English – and in
> consequence the book is infused with a kind of gluttony, for
> food and wine, for the splendours of the recent past, and
> for rhetorical and ornamental language, which now with a full
> stomach I find distasteful. I have modified the grosser passages
> but have not obliterated them because they are an essential part
> of the book.

Six months before publication, fifty copies were specially bound and sent to friends for Christmas. Evelyn, in Dubrovnik, waited eagerly for the first reactions: never had he been so anxious to know how a book of his would be received, and never had he had such a varied response. One of the first, and most enthusiastic, letters was from Nancy Mitford.

Brideshead has come, *beautiful* in orig. boards, a triumph of book production. And a great English classic in my humble opinion. Oh how I should like to chat about it. – There are one or 2 things I long to know. Are you, or not, on Lady Marchmain's side? I couldn't make out . . . One dreadful error. Diamond clips were only invented about 1930 you wore a diamond *arrow* in your cloche. Its the only one, which I call good – the only one I spotted at least. I think Charles might have had a little more glamour – I can't explain why but he seemed to me a tiny bit dim & that is the only criticism I have to make because I am literally dazzled with admiration.

To this Evelyn replied,

Yes I know what you mean; he *is* dim, but then he is telling the story and it is not his story . . . I think the crucial question is: does Julia's love for him seem real or is he so dim that it falls flat; if the latter the book fails plainly. He was a bad painter. Well he was as bad at painting as Osbert [Sitwell] is at writing; for Christ's sake don't repeat the comparison to anyone.

Lady Marchmain, no I am not on her side; but God is, who suffers fools gladly; and the book is about God. Does that answer it?

. . . 50 copies of *Brideshead Revisited* went out, 40 of them to close friends of yours. Do please keep your ear to the ground & report what they say. For the first time since 1928, I am eager about a book.

Nancy loyally complied.

I quite see how the person who tells is dim but then would Julia *&* her brother *&* her sister all be in love with him if he was? Well love is like that & one never can tell . . . Now about what people think

Raymond [Mortimer]: Great English classic.

Cyril: Brilliant where the narrative is straightforward. Doesn't care for the 'purple passages' i.e. deathbed of Lord M. Thinks you go too much to Whites. But found it impossible to put down (no wonder).

Osbert: jealous, doesn't like talking about it. 'I'm devoted to Evelyn – are you?'

Maurice: showing off to Cyril about how you don't always hit the right word or some nonsense but obviously much impressed & thinks the Oxford part perfect.

SW7 (European royal quarter): Heaven, darling.

Diane Abdy: like me & Raymond, no fault to find.

<u>Lady Chetwode</u> [Penelope Betjeman's mother]: Terribly dangerous propaganda. Brilliant.

<u>General View</u>: It is the Lygon family. Too much Catholic stuff.

A more considered, professional view came in a letter from Henry Yorke.

> To my mind you carry out what you set out to do better than any English writer now writing ... you may have overdone the semi colons a bit yet even then the regret with which the whole book is saturated is beautifully carried out in the long structure of your sentences. The whole thing seems to me deeper & wider than any book you have written ...
>
> It is so curious that we should choose subjects, each of us, so distasteful to each other. Quite soon now another one of mine [*Loving*] about the proletariat & about children will be on its way to you c/o your club & which you will find quite unreadable.[4] You can imagine therefore how shocked & hurt I was when the old man crossed himself on his deathbed. But when he sent the priest out the first time I had an idea it was too good to last. In fact through the whole of the end (when I thought Ryder was winning) I kept on saying to myself Evelyn is reconverted to the fold & there will be wailing & gnashing of teeth in Farm St over this. But it was no go ...
>
> I wish I had been in love at Oxford when I was up. I see now what I have missed.

Congratulations came in from, among others, Mary Herbert, Graham Greene, Penelope Betjeman and Cecil Beaton. Harold Acton sent a characteristic paean of praise.

> I slid my paper-knife through ... [the pages] like an itching bridegroom, and was panting, trembling and exhausted by the time I had finished cutting them ... swept alternatively by pleasure and pain: pleasure at your ever-increasing virtuosity and mastery of our fast-evaporating language ... pain, at the acrid memories of so many old friends you have conjured, with accompanying passions which I am surprised to find still smouldering in my bosom after all those years. It is the only successful evocation of the period that I know.

The clergy expressed one or two minor reservations. 'A small

---

[4] 'Henry has written an obscene book named *Loving* about domestic servants,' Evelyn wrote in his diary.

point, raised by Fr Corbishley S. J. who finished the book here at a sitting. On p. 296 the "oily wad" might *seem*, to the inexperienced reader, to be the vehicle by which the sacrament was administered. Actually of course one applies the oil with one's thumb, and only uses the wad to wipe it off again.' But on the whole they loved the book. Ronald Knox, who had given Evelyn details of the procedure for the deconsecration of a chapel, was reported to have been in tears over Lord Marchmain's deathbed.

On the book's publication, most of the adverse comments were naturally expressed behind Evelyn's back, although he received to his face one or two pieces of sharp criticism. John Russell, a reviewer on the *Sunday Times*, told him that in his view, 'the vulgarity of Ryder and the vulgarity of Mottram are the same . . . But what really destroys the spiritual pretensions of the book is . . . the complete uncharity and the complete unhumility of every line of it.' Katharine Asquith was another whose sensibilities were offended: she felt it wrong, she said, that at this most serious crisis in the world's history Evelyn should be writing of such worthless people. 'Katharine who detested the book to the end & beyond . . . [said] that the characters did not exist either in real life or faery,' Evelyn told Ronnie Knox. 'The sad thing is that "Metroland" is my world that I have grown up in & I don't know any other except at second hand or at a great distance.' Another dissident was Roger Fulford, who confided to Matthew Ponsonby, 'I thought the first $1/3$ as good as anything I have ever read . . . But it tails off sadly. Too literary for me. Gush and purple passages.' But this was mild compared to Conrad Russell, who in a series of spiteful letters to Diana Cooper gloated lengthily over 'Wu's' dismal failure. 'I think it so very bad. Such dull uninteresting people, drinking and catamiting and adultery and becoming and unbecoming Catholics. They are a lot of boring puppets and never come to life. Surely it's a great waste of time to write such books, as it is to read them. I suppose it makes money in an easy way and that's a consideration. What an old snob he is with his showing off.'

As Evelyn hoped and expected, *Brideshead* attracted a great deal of attention from the critics, most of it adulatory. But the sticking point was what was perceived as the author's virulent snobbishness. Representative of this attitude was Henry Reed in the *New*

Statesman. ' "How beautiful they are, the lordly ones", might well stand as epigraph to Mr Waugh's oeuvre so far. A burden of respect for the peerage and for Eton, which those who belong to the former, or who have been to the latter, seem able lightly to discard, weighs heavily upon him.' Edmund Wilson, who was never forgiven for it, continued with the same theme in the *New Yorker*. 'Waugh's snobbery, hitherto held in check by his satirical point of view, has here emerged shameless and rampant . . . his cult of the high nobility is allowed to become so rapturous and solemn that it finally gives the impression of being the only real religion in the book.' Conor Cruise O'Brien[5] in the Irish journal, the *Bell*, said

> [the novel] breathes from beginning to end a loving patience
> with mortal sin among the aristocracy and an unchristian
> petulance towards the minor foibles of the middle class . . . Mr
> Waugh's sincerity is beyond all doubt. Indeed his conservatism
> is so intensely emotional that he is a sort of Jacobite by
> anticipation. In his imagination the class he loves is already
> oppressed; the king has taken to the hills . . . *Brideshead Revisited*
> almost seems to imply that the wretched Hooper has no soul
> at all, certainly nothing to compare with the genuine old landed
> article.

Brideshead was published by Chapman & Hall in London on 28 May 1945, and in the United States by Little, Brown the following September. In both countries it was an immediate and overwhelming success, a Book Society choice in England, and a Book of the Month in America, selling over half a million copies.

For Evelyn this was intensely gratifying, bringing him not only fame and fortune but a new-found status as writer and celebrity. With earnings of £20,000 from *Brideshead* and at least £1000 per annum from journalism, he was able to fix his income for the next five years at £5000 a year, which gave him the freedom to choose what and for whom he wrote. He was now in a position to command the highest fees. Where previously he had earned between twenty and thirty guineas for a 2000 to 3000-word piece, *Life* was prepared to pay a dollar a word. In November 1946, he noted with satisfaction, 'This morning I received the offer of £50

[5] Under the pseudonym Donat O'Donnell.

for fifty words from America. It is the price I had for writing the
life of Rossetti twenty years ago.'[6]

The results of the first post-war general election were
announced on 27 July. Assuming in common with most of his
friends that a Conservative victory was a foregone conclusion,
Evelyn prepared to enjoy himself, accepting an invitation from
Lady Rothermere to an election luncheon and from Lady Pamela
Berry, wife of the chairman of the right-wing *Daily Telegraph*, to a
celebratory ball. As he noted in his diary, the day turned out
'a prodigious surprise . . . I went to White's at about 11. Results
were already coming in on the tape, and in an hour and a half
it was plainly an overwhelming defeat. Practically all my friends
are out.' Contemptuous as he was of political life and all politicians, and ready as always to delight in the discomfiture of an
established majority, the spectacle of Tory defeat gave Evelyn
considerable pleasure. In a letter to Laura, who had declined to
come up to London for the occasion, he wrote,

> You should have been to Ann's [Rothermere] party for although
> the champagne was exiguous & the vodka watery the spectacle
> of consternation as details of the massacre spread, was a strong
> intoxicant. In your absence I began the day at Whites and
> already knew of Bob & Randolph & Bracken & Pakenham &
> Belisha before I went to the Dorchester. Ann's party was full
> of chums dressed up to the nines & down in the dumps. I stayed
> there until about 3 then back to White's then to dinner with
> Pam Berry & to a party at Emeralds [Cunard].

But the new régime brought little comfort. It was from this
coming into power of the socialists, the establishing of 'the
Cripps–Attlee terror', that Evelyn dated the start of the new Dark
Ages, the final routing of the old civilisation, the triumph of all
that was meretricious and barbaric. He had felt little exultation
at the ending of a war which had degenerated into 'a sweaty tug-
of-war between teams of indistinguishable louts', and now he
regarded with disgust all evidence of the modern age. Europe
was overrun with poverty and corruption, his own country in the

[6] Before the war such sums would have made Evelyn a rich man, but the
unprecedentedly high levels of taxation introduced by Attlee's government meant
that any individual earnings over approximately £5000 went to the Revenue. For
this reason Evelyn insisted wherever possible on being paid in tax-free expenses
or in kind – wine, books, a new car, church candles for the dining-room table.

hands of a brutish and philistine proletariat. No egalitarian, Evelyn bitterly and personally resented the attacks launched by the Left on the upper classes. He described the socialists as an occupying army overrunning the country like a plague of grey lice. Increasingly he began to feel that England was no place to live, that he was an exile in hostile territory. In a review in the *Spectator*, Waugh stated, 'In place of the old, simple belief of Christianity that differences of wealth and learning cannot affect the reality and ultimate importance of the individual, there has risen the new, complicated and stark crazy theory that only the poor are real and important and that the only live art is the art of the People.' In a Swiftian piece entitled 'What to Do with the Upper Classes: a Modest Proposal', he wrote,

> [The upper classes] are, so far as the outside world is concerned, the sole, finished product of what is thought to be English culture . . . they provided not only the statesmen and admirals and diplomats but also the cranks, aesthetes and revolutionaries; they formed our speech, they directed our artists and architects; they sent adventurous younger sons all over the world; they created and preserved our conceptions of justice and honour and forbearance; all mention of the middle and lower classes might be expunged from our record and leave only trifling gaps . . . our sole, unique, historic creation is the English Gentleman . . . It has been the experience of a middle-aged Englishman to be born into one of the most beautiful countries in the world and watch it change year by year into one of the ugliest. German bombs have made but a negligible addition to the sum of our own destructiveness. It is arguable that the entire process is traceable to the decay of aristocratic domination . . .

Meanwhile the best must be made of it, and preparations begun for the return to Piers Court. Laura at Pixton with the children received detailed instructions from her husband in London about the packing up of his belongings. 'Will you please take great pains to ensure that all my possessions at Pixton, clothes, books, bookplates etc. are included in your luggage. It will be very disagreeable if anything is left behind.'

Finally, on 10 September, after an absence of six years, Evelyn returned home. He arrived at Stinchcombe 'on a grey, fly-infested, heavy evening with a hangover and the excitement of homecoming contending. It began to rain as I walked up to Piers Court to fetch Laura. At first sight the garden was rank, the paths lost, the trees stunted or overgrown irregularly; inside everything damp but superficially tidy. Slept ill.' Next day was spent taking stock, 'Laura saying how perfect everything looked, I detecting losses and damage everywhere . . . By Saturday night the library was in order and the tanks full enough for a hot bath. It was curious to find sumptuous commonplaces of prewar life – writing paper, old magazines.' On the eighteenth, Evelyn was summoned to Windsor to collect his demobilisation papers, on his return writing to Peters,

> It is delightful to be in my own home again. The house has
> suffered less than most private houses during the war.
> Everything that was smart & modern & Beatonesque looks like
> the scenery of a touring company but we had little like that &
> the good mahogany, tho shabbier, looks solid & homely.
>   The planners have diverted the village water supply so most
> of my day is spent carrying buckets of well-water upstairs. The
> garden is a bomb-site wilderness. There are a few dozen bottles
> of wine in the cellar – Dow's '22 in fine condition. Servants
> gradually assembling.

And by the end of November, 'After long correspondence and threats of legal action I have at last had a boiler installed. Ellwood has returned, and silver, boots and furniture shine.' The world was in a deplorable state, but for the moment Evelyn was content, in spite of the unluxurious conditions.

> Laura grapples vaguely but pertinaciously with her household
> tasks; most of her day is spent boiling potatoes for her chickens,
> who now lay three eggs a day, and making little milk cheeses we
> do not eat . . . We have practically no meat – two meals a week –
> and live on eggs and macaroni, cheese (made by Laura),
> bread and wine; very occasionally we get a rather nasty fish.
> But we have some wine left. When that is gone our plight will
> be grave.

On his forty-second birthday he wrote,

> The last three weeks have been happy and uneventful: Laura
> cooking better, wine lasting out, weather splendid. I have
> written more of the school story ['Charles Ryder's Schooldays'],
> a review of Connolly's *Palinurus* which on rereading I find

feeble ... went to London last week for two nights and drank a vast amount of champagne ... I went to a board meeting at Chapman & Hall ... I am preparing a version of my travel books for a single volume.

Evelyn's review in the *Tablet* of Cyril Connolly's *The Unquiet Grave* caused a stir in social and literary circles, and serious disquiet to Connolly. The friendship between them had always been equivocal – Waugh affectionate, amused, slightly contemptuous of 'Smarty-Boots', Connolly admiring, submissive and extremely wary of Waugh: as one friend remarked, when Cyril came to stay at Piers Court, you could smell the fear in the room. As he had with Randolph Churchill, Evelyn recognised in Cyril many similarities of temperament. Although he ridiculed Cyril's bohemian side and left-wing politics, and condemned his lack of religion, he loved him as a sybarite and connoisseur. Like Evelyn, Cyril was touchy, easily bored and a champion hater; he could nurse a grudge for years and was capable of unforgivable rudeness; he was not, however, a bully. Evelyn was, and bullied Cyril mercilessly; as Maurice Bowra observed, 'It is sad that Evelyn has such an urge to torture him. It must be a form of love.'

The Unquiet Grave had been sent to Evelyn by Nancy Mitford while he was in Jugoslavia. With time hanging heavy, he was able to give the work his undivided attention, telling Nancy that he was 'quite fascinated by it', although forced to admit that Cyril's lovingly garnered collection of *pensées* was essentially 'twaddle'. He amused himself by annotating his copy, sending up Connolly's elegant aphorisms with jokes and jeers, like a rude schoolboy twitting a pedantic master. 'Complacent mental laziness is the English disease,' Cyril had written thoughtfully – 'Says Paddy' appears in the margin; 'The secret of happiness lies in the avoidance of Angst' – 'Voodoo, Bog-magic, the wise woman's cabin'; 'Women are different from men, and to break with the past and mangle their mate in the process fulfils a dark need in them' – Ethel M. Dell + Peter Q[uennell]'.

Evelyn's review appeared on 10 November 1945. '[It] seems to have caused a mild sensation,' he recorded with satisfaction. Connolly's adoption of the pseudonym, 'Palinurus', enabled Waugh to pretend he had no idea of the writer's identity, constructing a lethally accurate portrait of the 'anonymous' author which, while not unaffectionate, made few concessions to friendship. Although reported to be mortified by the review, Cyril behaved well, maintaining, anyway in public, a dignified silence, and the friendship continued on its old embattled course.

Over the next year Evelyn, cushioned by the *Brideshead* royalties, published little except for a few articles and a short story about marital hatred, 'Tactical Exercise', which appeared in the *Strand*. In December 1946, Duckworth brought out *When the Going Was Good*, a compilation of his travel writing. In the preface Evelyn explained,

> The following pages comprise all that I wish to preserve of the four travel books I wrote between the years 1929 and 1935 . . . There was a fifth book, *Robbery under Law*, about Mexico, which I am content to leave in oblivion, for it dealt little with travel and much with political questions . . .
>
> My own travelling days are over, and I do not expect to see many travel books in the near future . . . There is no room for tourists in a world of 'displaced persons' . . . I rejoice that I went when the going was good.

But Evelyn's travelling days were far from over and, although he was no longer inclined towards arduous exploration in undeveloped parts of the world, he still retained his curiosity.

His first journey abroad after the war was to Germany as an observer at the Nuremberg trials. He had been invited to attend by one of the prosecuting counsel, Mervyn Griffith-Jones, whom he happened to run into in White's. Evelyn flew over on a troop carrier on 31 March 1946. He had been categorised VIP, to which he made no objection as the category conferred 'certain substantial advantages, such as a private bath and a select dining-room in the courthouse'. The scene was bizarre, the British and Americans living in a large luxury hotel, 'everything else a waste of corpse-scented rubble with a handful of middle-aged, middle-class Germans in Homburg hats picking their way through the ruins.' Although he had high hopes of the trial as spectator sport, possibly even as the subject for a book, he stayed only two days, finding the reality tedious, with long technical disputes about documents and cumulative evidence. The notorious Nazis appeared shabby and ignominious; Ribbentrop looked like 'a seedy schoolmaster', while Goering '[had] much of Tito's matronly appeal'. After the first day's hearing, 'I went to see the room where a French Jew keeps lampshades of human skin, shrunken heads, soap said to be made of corpses and so forth.'

Leaving these obscene relics behind him, Evelyn went on to Paris to stay with the Coopers. Duff had been appointed British ambassador, and Diana, with whom Evelyn was now 'fully reconciled after seven years' estrangement', had made of the embassy, that beautiful, honey-coloured house on the rue du Faubourg St Honoré, a sumptuous pleasure palace. In spite of the unwelcome presence of two old enemies, Auberon Herbert and Peter Quennell, Evelyn enjoyed himself; indeed his geniality was remarked upon by his hostess, who had been braced for trouble. '[Wu] is temporarily happy in his temper – civil to Quennell and generally gentle, and warm-hearted towards me, whom he has so often stoned ... Auberon Herbert can't get over his mellowness.' There was a cocktail party at which he met Mme Pol Roger, M. de Polignac and Philippe de Rothschild, 'so that I was immersed in wine', three dinner parties and a lunch at an excellent restaurant. But after three days' good behaviour the cloven hoof began to show. Diana was angrily rebuked for wearing trousers; Peter Quennell, suffering from a hang-over, was accused of sexual excess[7]; and another guest, Professor Julian Huxley, the distinguished zoologist, was taunted with unamiable tenacity. 'It was very agreeable to see Huxley ... treated on all sides as a zoo-keeper, by myself from malice, by everyone else in genuine goodwill.' In his thank-you letter to Diana, Evelyn wrote that his visit had been a delight, that it had been a great happiness 'to know that you have kept a warm place for me in your heart all through my ice age. I love you.'

The following month Evelyn, at the suggestion of Douglas Woodruff, accepted an invitation to Spain, the occasion a commemorative conference in honour of Francisco de Vittoria, the sixteenth-century Dominican jurist, at which Woodruff as editor of the *Tablet*, was a guest. With memories of pre-war holidays in

[7] After dinner in Paris one evening, Diana drove Evelyn back to Chantilly and, during the drive, she told Conrad Russell, 'He gave me a past and present picture of Quennell, a good and harmless man, fond of pretty girls, and really he painted something so foetid and sinister that it will colour most unfairly my sentiments for Peter Q.'

the sun, of good food and local wine, the two men set off eagerly
enough. Arriving in Madrid on 15 June, they found themselves
launched on two and a half weeks of discomfort and confusion
typical of an incompetently organised international jamboree. In
the dull company of Swiss, Dutch and American jurists and their
wives, they were whirled off on sightseeing tours in decrepit
charabancs, and obliged to endure interminable speeches, ban-
quets and receptions. At the town hall in Valladolid the *vin
d'honneur* was followed by dinner and an exhibition of flamenco
singing; at Burgos there was a mayoral banquet; at Vitoria they
were obliged to witness the laying of a wreath at the 'hideous'
monument to Vittoria, and a display of children folk-dancing. As
a further outrage, the moment the festivities ended the Spanish
government withdrew its hospitality, leaving Waugh and Woodruff
with little cash in hand and no means of getting home, until a
British official in Madrid took pity on them and found them seats
on a government plane. They returned to a London almost as
hot as Madrid, and Laura at Pixton just delivered of a son, to be
christened James.

Evelyn's irritation with the Spanish expedition is vividly
expressed in a long short story, *Scott-King's Modern Europe*, published by Chapman & Hall the following year, 1947. Scott-King,
a 'dim' classics master in a minor public school, is entrenched in
the past, viewing the modern world with contempt and alarm.
For years he has immersed himself in the study of a little-known
seventeenth-century poet, Bellorius, and accepts with alacrity,
therefore, when invited by the government of Neutralia to take
part in the tercentennial commemoration of Bellorius's death.
The republic of Neutralia bears a close resemblance to Tito's
Jugoslavia, 'a typical modern state, governed by a single party,
acclaiming a dominant Marshal, supporting a vast ill-paid
bureaucracy whose work is tempered and humanised by corruption.' Scott-King, anticipating a pleasant few days of hospitality
and donnish interchange, is caught up instead in a nightmare
round of unbearably tedious official functions. 'Above the clatter
and chatter of the dinner-table and the altercations of the waiters,
a mixed choir of young people sang folk-songs, calculated to
depress the most jovial village festival. It was not thus, in his
class-room at Grantchester, that Scott-King had imagined himself
dining.' Towards the end of this hideous ordeal, the government

changes and Scott-King finds he has no way of leaving the country; eventually he is smuggled out at considerable expense disguised as an Ursuline nun and delivered to a Jewish Illicit Immigrants' Camp in Palestine. Back in Grantchester, Scott-King turns his back once and for all on the modern world, telling his headmaster,

> 'I will stay as I am here as long as any boy wants to read the classics. I think it would be very wicked indeed to do anything to fit a boy for the modern world.'
> 'It's a short-sighted view, Scott-King.'
> 'There, headmaster, with all respect, I differ from you profoundly. I think it the most long-sighted view it is possible to take.'

Although written with characteristic elegance, *Scott-King* is not a success, fretful and arid in tone and marred by too much undigested personal experience. Several reviewers praised the comedy while complaining of the author's cantankerousness. According to the critical consensus this was not first-class Waugh. George Orwell identified the book's essential weakness in his perceptive analysis of Waugh's moral and political stance.

> The modern world, we are meant to infer, is so unmistakably crazy, so certain to smash itself to pieces in the near future, that to attempt to understand it or come to terms with it is simply a purposeless self-corruption . . . There is something to be said for this point of view, and yet one must always regard with suspicion the claim that ignorance is, or can be, an advantage. In the Europe of the last fifty years the diehard, know-nothing attitude symbolized by Scott-King, has helped to bring about the very conditions that Mr Waugh is satirizing. Revolutions happen in authoritarian countries, not in liberal ones, and Mr Waugh's failure to see the implications of this fact not only narrows his political vision but also robs his story of part of its point.

The third European journey was a commission from the *Daily Telegraph* to undertake a tour of Scandinavia. Evelyn left in the middle of August 1947, flying first to Sweden, then going on to Norway and Denmark. In his article describing the trip, Waugh refers to Stockholm and Copenhagen as 'two of the most pleasant cities in the world', while Oslo, '[their] noisy, inelegant youngest sister', had little to recommend it, 'all trams and shirt-sleeves and ice-cream cones'. But his overriding concern was with the conspicuous lack in all three countries of any spiritual component. It was much to be regretted that 'for the vast majority of Scandinavians . . . the religious conception of life, of man existing in relation to his Creator, of the world existing in relation to Heaven and hell, is totally and, humanly speaking, irretrievably lost'.

The religious conception of life for Evelyn had become of paramount importance. Since his return from the war this was evident even to his most atheistical acquaintance. The relationship of man to God, of his own personal relationship to his Creator, dominated his consciousness. The Catholic Church provided a strong, hierarchical and supportive structure, and Evelyn held tenaciously to it, evolving a peculiarly fundamentalist theology whose stark black and white he inflexibly imposed on all the shifting shades of grey around him. The uncompromising views he held for instance on politics and modern art (despising all politicians, dismissing all modern art as 'bosh') were reflected in what he described as his 'rule-of-thumb' approach to religion. Although he had received instruction from one of the subtlest and most sophisticated scholars in the English Jesuit Province, Evelyn's faith was elementary and dogmatic; to him Catholic belief was a matter of simple logic, and he literally could not understand why everyone was not a Catholic. 'The church . . . [is] the normal state of man from which men have disastrously exiled themselves.' Dismissive of modern perceptions of the processes of divine retribution, he held to a literal belief in Hell and everlasting punishment. When Christopher Sykes accused him of holding Hell as his favourite dogma, Evelyn replied, 'If we were allowed favourite dogmas, it might be. If you mean I see nothing to doubt in it, and no cause in it for "modernist" squeamish revulsion, you are quite right.'

For Evelyn there were few doubts and ambiguities; the Way, though often hard, was clearly visible. Man was put on Earth to love and to serve God, 'an all-wise God who has a particular task for each individual soul, which the individual is free to accept or decline at will, and whose ultimate destiny is determined by his response to God's vocation'. Evelyn's vocation was to write; and just as chaos was seen as the Devil's domain, so was the imposition of order by the artist part of the divinely imposed task. More specifically, the novelist's art must be dedicated to its primary purpose.

> The failure of modern novelists since and including James Joyce is one of presumption and exorbitance . . . They try to represent the whole human mind and soul and yet omit its determining character – that of being God's creature with a defined purpose.
>
> So in my future books there will be two things to make them unpopular: a preoccupation with style and the attempt to represent man more fully, which, to me, means only one thing, man in his relation to God.

Like many converts, Evelyn had a simple, meticulous approach to his faith which he clung to with an exaggerated orthodoxy; he was intolerant and quick to condemn, impelled by an almost fanatical search for perfection. To the best of his ability he lived his religion. As Mia Woodruff observed, 'At the bottom of everything, of amusing remarks, and going to parties, and all those grand ladies, and spending hours in White's, and getting very drunk, at the bottom and terribly basic was his religion. I think he hung on to it until his last minute.' The rules were strictly kept: morning and evening prayer, following the mnemonic ACTS – Adoration, Contrition, Thanksgiving, Supplication; Mass every Sunday and on days of obligation; Lenten abstinence, the renouncing of wine, cigars and secular reading, as well as going into retreat for three days during Holy Week. For special favours – fine weather for a garden fête or dance, success for his children in the Oxford entrance examination – Evelyn gave money to an order of nuns, the Poor Clares at Looe, to pray on his behalf. He schooled himself to behave with courtesy and sometimes notable restraint towards the Catholic clergy, not all of whom he found congenial, and of many of whom he was in private highly critical. He regarded it as his duty to accept invitations to lecture from Catholic fellowships and institutions, giving his services for nothing and enduring levels of discomfort he would not have tolerated for a moment in secular society. For a penitential period of twelve months in 1949 to 1950, he accepted every such invitation that came his way. 'At first it was easy because I had built up over the years a fine iron curtain by curt refusals. But it leaked out and I have had an autumn & winter of unspeakable boredom culminating in a "Book Lovers Week End" at Grayshott. Next Sunday I speak at Middlesbrough and Leicester...' With his journalism he frequently favoured the Catholic press, writing for little or no money for the *Month* and the *Tablet,* and for *Commonweal* in America. He regarded with a specific, almost proprietary interest the work of Catholic authors, such as Graham Greene, Antonia White, Georges Bernanos, J. F. Powers, Thomas Merton, Ronald Knox and Muriel Spark.

Through Peters and very privately he channelled a substantial portion of his income to Catholic charities and foundations, amounting over the years to tens of thousands of pounds: all revenue from *Scott-King,* for instance, was made over to the Jesuits, Campion Hall in Oxford regularly received large sums, and translation royalties were donated *in toto* to the Catholic primate of the country concerned. The arrangements were not without their complications, as a letter from Peters's office about Waugh's macabre novel, *The Loved One,* illustrates. 'The Archbishop of Milan is apparently very pleased about your gift, and has informed our Agent in Italy that he is going to assign the royalties to an orphanage in the vicinity of Milan. The Archbishop of Prague is also very pleased that he will be getting the royalties on the Czech edition... The Archbishop of Utrecht has, however, informed the Dutch publishers that he will not accept the gift until he has read the book...'[8]

This is not to say that Evelyn's pious intentions were always fulfilled. In particular his explosive temper and a notorious lack of charity towards his fellow men let him down. 'How to reconcile this indifference to human beings with the obligations of Charity', he wrote to Diana Cooper. 'That is my problem.' On one occasion after an irascible few days spent staying with Nancy Mitford in Paris, Nancy asked him how he reconciled 'being so horrible with being a Christian. He replied rather sadly that were he not a Christian he would be even more horrible... & anyway would have committed suicide years ago.'

Many of the more dedicated Romans among Evelyn's acquaintance, men such as Douglas Woodruff, Tom Burns and Christopher Hollis, moved almost exclusively in Catholic circles; but

---

[8] Having read the book, the archbishop declined the donation.

Evelyn had many friends outside the Church, even though there was a clear distinction in his mind between those who were members of the Household of the Faith and those who were not. In the company of his co-religionists, there was a tacit sympathy and understanding, a kind of freemasonry, a sense of private privilege as among members of the same club. When Penelope Betjeman was received, Evelyn wrote to her, 'You are coming into the Church with vastly more knowledge than most converts but what you cannot know until Tuesday is the delight of membership of the Household, of having your chair at the table, a place laid, the bed turned down, of the love & trust, whatever their family bickerings, of all Christendom. It is this family unity which makes the weakest Catholic nearer the angels & saints, than the most earnest outsider.'

Fellow members were carefully watched for any sign of apostasy. A self-appointed grand inquisitor, punitive and puritanical, he rarely hesitated to apply the scourge where he judged it necessary. Kathleen ('Kick') Kennedy[9] after her wedding to the Marquess of Hartington was given a ferocious lecture not only for marrying 'outside', but even worse, for agreeing to have her children brought up as Anglicans. Clarissa Churchill, who was one of the several women for whom Evelyn developed a romantic infatuation (Angela Laycock was another), nearly broke his heart when she defied the Church to marry Anthony Eden, a divorced man. 'Thousands have died and are dying today in torture for the Faith you have idly thrown aside. Did you never think how you were contributing to the loneliness of Calvary by your desertion? . . . Surely you see that the truth of Christ's death cannot be dependent on your own convenience? . . .' Despite its vehemence, this reproof was administered more in sorrow than in anger; others were less fortunate. During a weekend spent with Daphne and Henry Bath, Evelyn behaved with brutal bad manners towards a fellow guest who turned up with an about-to-be-divorced girl-friend, and he made a memorable scene when dining with Alexander Korda on finding he was expected to sit at table in the company of Korda's mistress.

But there were always exceptions to be made: Graham Greene,

9 Kathleen Kennedy was the daughter of the one-time American ambassador to London, Joseph P. Kennedy, and sister of John F. Kennedy.

for one, whom Evelyn regarded with profound respect and whose Catholicism, if very different, was even more idiosyncratic than his own. Greene had a mistress, Catherine Walston, a Catholic convert living with a rich, complaisant, non-Catholic husband by whom she had children. Far from admonishing Greene or refusing to meet Mrs Walston, unforgettably described by Nancy Mitford as 'a Ritz vision in dark mink', Evelyn allowed himself to be wooed by her. At lunch at Greene's flat in St James's Street, 'She sat on the floor and buttered my bread for me and made simple offers of friendship . . . I was asked to go with her to the country. I couldn't that afternoon as I had to dine with the editor of the *Daily Express*. Very well they would pick me up after dinner. I couldn't do that as I was lunching with Father Caraman next day. Very well she would send a car for me at 2.30.'

The visit was a success, and in return Evelyn asked her and Greene to stay at Piers Court. When challenged later about this unusual show of tolerance, Evelyn justified it by telling the story of an early pope, a man so holy that in order to avoid the sin of spiritual pride he would run through the streets of Rome wearing a paper hat. 'Mrs Walston', said Evelyn, 'is Graham's paper hat.'

The pagan soul Evelyn compared to 'a bird fluttering about in the gloom, beating against the windows when all the time the doors are open to the air and sun.' He was always on the lookout for potential converts, frequently displaying a missionary zeal that although undoubtedly inspired by Christian conviction was more suitable to a playground bully than to a bearer of the Word. Catholicism was used as a cudgel with which to bludgeon his victims into submission. In the marginalia to *The Unquiet Grave*, he had written, 'It is a strong buttress of faith in times when one's problems appear insoluble to study the problems of one's friends and to reflect how they would all be happily resolved by acceptance of the truths of the catechism.' Stuart Boyle, the illustrator of *The Loved One*, was targeted as a promising prospect, as was the novelist Robert Henriques; so too, although she probably never knew it, was the powerful Lady Pamela Berry, and even in later years Maimie Lygon, divorced from her Russian prince and in a pathetic state of loneliness and mental frailty. Jack Donaldson, a farming neighbour at Stinchcombe, was treated to a barrage of propaganda; but in his case the many books lent and the exhaustive conversations 'had the result, not entirely acceptable to Evelyn, of returning him to the Protestant faith of his fathers'. Evelyn failed, too, with Diana Cooper, who, although drawn to the idea of the Church as a cure for her pervasive melancholy, remained faint-hearted in her desire for commitment. Nancy Mitford, with whom Evelyn over the years conducted a kind of Catholic correspondence course, was not to be caught either, countering the cudgel blows with a high-spirited facetiousness that would not be downed.

Evelyn's greatest effort and most resounding failure was with John Betjeman. Betjeman's wife, Penelope, preparing to enter the Roman Church, naturally hoped her husband would join her. Evelyn leapt at the opportunity, eager to convince his old friend of what he called 'the bogosity of the Church of England'. For months he deluged the mild-mannered Betjeman with fire-and-brimstone orations, threatening him with hell and eternal damnation if he refused to see the light. 'Awful about your obduracy in schism and heresy. Hell hell hell. Eternal damnation ... Nothing less than complete abandonment is any good. His will is plain as a pikestaff that there shall be one fold & one shepherd and you spend all your time perpetuating a sixteenth century rift & influencing others to perpetuate it. I wouldnt give a thrushs egg for your chances of salvation at the moment.'

Sword unsheathed, Evelyn pursued like an avenging angel, but to Betjeman, dithering and full of doubt, he appeared demonic. So distraught did Betjeman grow under this unrelenting pressure that Penelope was obliged to call Evelyn off. 'The ONLY thing is to leave him alone at present. He has dreadful persecution mania where Catholics are concerned ... LEAVE JOHN ALONE. IT IS THE WISEST POLICY.' Her point was made, and Evelyn with difficulty desisted. 'I am by nature a bully and a scold and John's pertinacity in error brings out all that is worst in me. I am very sorry. I will lay off him in future ... I think there is very clearly a devil at work in him ... But I will keep silence.' Penelope continued ardently on her road to Rome, while her husband remained true to his upbringing and the Anglican Church. On 4 August 1947, Evelyn recorded in his diary, 'To Farnborough to make my peace with the Betjemans. Successful in this.'

For Evelyn the Catholic Church, universal and unchanging, was the one great bulwark against the new Dark Age. He looked with increasing distaste on all manifestations of working-class culture, on the Welfare State, on urban growth, on ribbon development and arterial roads and housing estates, on the spread of ugliness and mediocrity. 'You can have no idea,' he told Nancy Mitford, 'of the awful flat dreariness of England under Welfare.' One symptom of this sense of despair was a disenchantment with his own home, with Piers Court. At the end of the war, 'I found returning to it with many sentimental tremors that my love for it was quite dead, as so many soldiers found about their wives but not me thank God.' During the months of exile in Jugoslavia he had given a great deal of thought as to how he and Laura should shape their lives. One of the most ruthlessly self-protective artists who ever lived, Evelyn's favoured plan involved a scheme to turn his aunts' house at Midsomer Norton into a private working retreat. 'For some time I have been worried about how, after the war, we are going to reconcile your wish to farm and my wish to have the children brought up on a farm and in the country with my own ineradicable love of collecting bric-a-brac and my need for a harmonious place to write in,' he had informed his wife.

> Why should we not dispose of Stinkers and buy you a simple
> farm house and property near Bridget for yourself & the
> children where I will live when not working, and for my work
> and collecting mania and your frequent visits retain my aunts
> house at Midsomer Norton . . . I could then make the house
> into a museum of Victorian art, put Ellwood there as
> permanent housekeeper to look after me while I was there and
> of everything in my absence. I could keep my library there &
> write my novels there. It would be a secret house to which no
> guests would come. I have the photographs of the rooms as
> they were in 1870 & I could gradually restore them to that
> splendid state. It, and the tranquillity of a provincial town,
> would be precisely suited to the mood in which I work.

He gave Laura authority to buy a house if she found one she liked. 'Please bear in mind that it must be very near a Catholic Church. I find it a great joy to be within two minutes walk of daily mass. I don't want our churchgoing to be a long weekly drive in the half dark.'

But Laura had not found the right property, and now there were rumours that Dursley, the local small town, was to be enormously expanded, both it and Stinchcombe within easy commuting distance from Bristol and Gloucester. Clearly England was finished. Inward-looking and backward-looking, Evelyn had a hostility towards contemporary life that led him to believe he should remove himself from it as far as possible. In fact, no one was less suited to an isolated existence. On the day after Christmas 1945, he wrote in his diary, 'Though I make-believe to be detached from the world, I find a day without post or newspapers strangely flat, and look forward to tomorrow's awakening, with Ellwood laying the papers by my pillow.' Nonetheless, his longing to leave was strong; in England there would soon be only two classes, a proletariat and a bureaucracy; in Europe 'wherever I turn [there is] the reek of the Displaced Persons' Camp.' The obvious move was to Ireland, Catholic, impoverished, and still in many respects entrenched in the nineteenth century. Most of his friends were appalled by the idea of this self-imposed exile; Nancy Mitford was one of the few who saw exactly what he was after.

> Never have I seen a country so much made for somebody as *it*
> is for *you*. The terrible silly politeness of lower classes so
> miserable that they long for any sort of menial task at £1 a week,
> the emptiness, the uncompromising Roman Catholicness, the
> pretty houses of the date you like best, the agricultural country
> for Laura, the neighbours all low brow & armigerous, & all 100
> miles away, the cold wetness, the small income tax, really I
> could go on for ever . . . I remember you went to look at a
> Castle, so what happened? Perhaps you saw an elemental & fled
> incontinent? But any priest can fix an elemental, surely.

The castle in question was in Wicklow, but although Evelyn liked the sound of it, Laura did not. 'I am anxious to emigrate, Laura to remain & face the century of the common man. She is younger, braver & less imaginative than I.' At the beginning of December 1946 a second castle came on the market, and this time Evelyn persuaded Laura to go with him to see it. Twenty miles outside Dublin, Gormanston Castle looked promising, 'a fine, solid, grim, square, half-finished block with tower and turrets . . . The ground-floor rooms were large and had traces of fine Regency decoration . . . There were countless bedrooms, many uninhabitable, squalid plumbing, vast attics . . . the grounds were dreary with no features except some fine box alleys. The chapel unlicensed . . .' Evelyn's Dublin solicitor, Terence de Vere White, was instructed to put in a bid, and the next day the Waughs embarked for home. 'On boarding the ship I bought a local evening paper and read that Butlin had acquired a stretch of property at Gormanston and was setting up a holiday camp there. This announcement made us change all our intentions.'

Over the next eight months Evelyn looked at a number of other houses, returning twice more to Dublin, once in April 1947 and again in June, but he found nothing irresistible and by the autumn had made up his mind to abandon the plan.

Reasons (1) Noble. The Church in England needs me. (2)
Ignoble. It would be bad for my reputation as a writer. (3)
Indifferent. There is no reason to suppose life in Ireland will be
more tolerable than here. My children must be English. I
should become an anachronism. The Socialists are piling up
repressive measures now. It would seem I was flying from them.
If I am to be a national figure I must stay at home. The
Americans would lose interest in an emigrant and the Irish
would not be interested.

Four years later he was writing to Nancy, 'Among the countless blessings I thank God for, my failure to find a house in Ireland comes first. Unless one is mad on fox hunting there is nothing to draw one ... Above all [there is] the certainty that once one pulls up roots & lives abroad there is no particular reason for living anywhere. Why not Jamaica? Why not Sicily? Why not California? On the move like a jew all ones life.'

And there were always the occasional sorties abroad temporarily to escape what were described as the 'Balkan austerities' of home. Much the most lavish of these expeditions was to California in the spring of 1947, on the face of it a surprising destination for one who from the beginning of his career had made such a point of despising 'the bloody Yanks'. Evelyn had always referred with patronising contempt to Alec's fondness for America, and especially since the war had come to regard the United States as the apogee of everything that was tasteless, vulgar and barbaric. There was little natural accord between the New World and the Old, between Europeans with their innate dignity and sense of decorum and Americans with their distressing informality, their lack of veneration for history and tradition. 'The great difference between our manners and those of the Americans', Evelyn wrote with a wealth of irony, 'is that theirs are designed to promote cordiality, ours to protect privacy.' In his correspondence with Peters, Evelyn rarely missed an opportunity of making insulting reference to American publishers and agents, and claimed to be appalled by the great transatlantic acclaim bestowed upon *Brideshead*. 'My book has been a great success in the United States which is upsetting because I thought it in good taste before and now I know it can't be,' he complained to Maimie Lygon, and to John Betjeman, 'Americans write to me by every post, O God.'

A favourite target, and also one of Waugh's most lucrative sources of income, was *Life*, whose artless approaches were frequently met with ingenious rebuff. At the beginning of 1946, for example, Elizabeth Reeve from *Life* had written an ill-advisedly chatty letter proposing a photographic feature to coincide with the announcement of *Brideshead* as selection for Book of the Month, 'dramatizing' characters and scenes from Waugh's novels. Mrs Reeve, confidently expressing the hope that Mr Waugh would co-operate in helping carry out this 'monumental job', ended her letter, 'I would be grateful for your comments and suggestions. We must start work immediately, but without consulting you the project will be like blind flying.' Such innocence was irresistible, and Evelyn replied with relish.

Dear Madam: I have read your letter of yesterday with curiosity and reread it with compassion. I am afraid you are unfamiliar with the laws of my country. The situation is not that my co-operation is desirable, but that my permission is necessary, before you publish a series of photographs illustrating my books. I cannot find any phrase in your letter that can be construed as seeking permission.

You say: 'Without consulting you the project will be like blind flying.' I assure you it will be far more hazardous. I shall send a big blue incorruptible policeman to look you up and the only 'monumental' work Mr Scherman is likely to perform is breaking stones at Dartmoor. Yours faithfully, Evelyn Waugh.

It came as a surprise to Peters that Waugh was now seriously considering going to the United States to discuss the sale of film rights: MGM had shown interest in several of the novels, and made a specific offer for the rights to *Brideshead*. Peters did his best to dissuade him. 'You would suffer the most extreme forms of boredom, irritation and frustration. I know nobody who would hate Hollywood as intensely as you.' But by now Evelyn was determined: Hollywood by all accounts would satisfy his keen appetite for the grotesque, Laura needed a holiday, and he was bored at home; there was also the chance of making a considerable amount of money, much of it (in the form of lavish expenses) tax-free. As Peters was made clearly to understand, Evelyn wanted to extract the best possible terms out of the studio. 'The sort of offer I should find most attractive would be a tax-free trip, lecture-free, with a minimum of work of any kind at the other end. Luxury not lionization is the thing. And all trouble spared me of getting permits & booking cabins etc.'

In November 1946, the offer from MGM was accepted: 'a month's trip to Hollywood for Laura and myself, all expenses paid, for me to discuss the film treatment of *Brideshead*. If we cannot agree, they forfeit their money. If we agree, they pay $140,000 less what they have already spent.' Peters, himself in New York at the time, wrote to Evelyn with details of his negotiations. At the end of his letter he added an admonitory note.

> I am sure that if they are reasonable, you will be, too . . . I really
> believe that you will find the Hollywood producer less awful
> and more intelligent than you expect, and that a good film will
> come out of this, provided that you are yourself well-disposed to
> the idea in principle . . . I must tell you that you have the
> reputation here – both at M.G.M. and everywhere else – of
> being a difficult, tetchy, irritating and rude customer. I hope
> you will surprise and confound them all by behaving like an
> 18th century ambassador from the Court of St James's. They are
> children; and they should receive the tolerance and
> understanding that you show to children. You would (I hope,
> will) be surprised by the result.

Tolerance and understanding were rarely conspicuous in Evelyn's attitude towards children, as Peters might have known, and all hope of good behaviour proved to be vain. 'Dear Pete, Many thanks for your letter,' Evelyn replied with a briskness that to a finely attuned ear might have sounded an ominous note.

> I mean to do business with the Californian savages if it is
> possible. I note with interest your own softening of heart towards

EVELYN WAUGH

these creatures. Is it perhaps because in the general
deterioration of Europe the fine contrast is no longer as
apparent? I am sure Matson [Peters's New York associate] and
his fellow countrymen are, as you say, just little boys at heart,
but I believe little boys should be very frequently whipped and
sent to bed supperless.

The Waughs embarked on the SS *America* on 25 January 1947.
Evelyn had recently come out of hospital after an operation for
piles, which had been unexpectedly painful. 'One of the reasons
for my putting myself under the surgeon's knife was the wish to
be absolutely well and free from ointments for Laura's American
treat. All the reasons for the operation appeared ineffective
immediately afterwards. The pain was excruciating and the humili-
ations constant.' When they arrived in New York he was still
unwell, and found little in his surroundings to raise his spirits:
the suite at the Waldorf Astoria was uncomfortable, the food
tasteless, the wine ruined by 'bad cellarage'; on the first evening
they were taken to a play and walked out in disgust because of
its 'socialist propaganda'. New York itself, of course, was hideous;
to Diana Cooper who, Evelyn knew, loved America and New York
in particular, he wrote that in his opinion it was the most damned
awful country, the inhabitants barbarous, their food and habits
filthy; as for the famous skyscrapers, they were nothing but 'great
booby boxes ... absolutely negligible in everything except
bulk ... they bear the same sort of relation to architecture as
distempering a ceiling does to painting.' Hell was defined as
'sitting through all eternity in a traffic block listening to the
conversation of a New York taxi driver'.

Among the Waughs' hosts were Peters's former colleagues, Carl
Brandt and his wife, Carol, who now had an agency of her
own. Brandt was judged 'three-quarters civilized', but Mrs Brandt
was seen at once to be 'a woman of no intellectual interests ...
She did not disguise that her services to us were personally distasteful but she performed every service brilliantly. She introduced Laura to a good dress shop where Laura spent $2,000 in
a very few minutes.' Dollars were provided by Harold Matson. 'I
went over to the Waldorf to see Waugh about 11 in the morning,'
Matson recalled. 'While he ordered a glass of champagne I told
him I had brought the money he wanted. He said, "That's good,"

and put the envelope in his pocket. I asked, "Aren't you going to count it?" He looked at me, twisted his head a little, gave me a squint, and said, "Should I?" '

From New York Evelyn and Laura took the 20th Century to Chicago, where they changed trains, arriving in Pasadena on 6 February. In a letter to his mother Alec passed on a description he had been given of Evelyn's arrival. '[Evelyn's appearance] was fantastic. The sun was shining, tropical flowers were in bloom, all the young people were dressed in shorts and slacks and open shirts and there was Evelyn in a stiff white collar and a bowler hat, carrying a rolled umbrella.' They were driven to the Bel Air Hotel: 'more like Egypt – the suburbs of Cairo or Alexandria – than anything in Europe . . . with a hint of Addis Ababa in the smell of blue gums', Evelyn noted in his diary. In Bel Air they found Harold Acton, in California visiting an uncle. Harold was amused by Evelyn's formality in dress and demeanour, his refusal to adapt to his surroundings, his insistence on the contrary that they be adapted to him: this was part of the game. Evelyn complained about the food, the 'pathological sloth' of hotel servants, the chewing of gum, smoking at meals, the volubility of taxi drivers, and the deplorable habit of installing a shower in the bathroom. When Harold tried to point out to him some of the attractions of the country, Evelyn growled, 'The trouble with you is that you're really a Yank.'

The suite reserved at the Bel Air never materialised, for the good reason that the former occupant had collapsed with a stroke and could not be moved; but Evelyn wanted his suite, and after a vituperative war of attrition with the management, the Waughs moved to the Beverly Hills Hotel. Here they were happier. 'Jovial banter prevails between the hotel servants and the guests, but our insular aloofness is respected. We have trained the waiters in the dining-room not to give us iced water and our chauffeur not to ask us questions.' During the day Laura was entertained to ladies' luncheons and escorted to shops and dress shows while Evelyn at the MGM studios in Culver City attended 'the aimless, genial coffee-house chatter which the film executives call "conferences".' Day after day the filming of *Brideshead* was discussed but, with Evelyn fiercely protective of his property, small progress was made, and before long the project was recognised as hopeless. The Americans failed to understand the theological implications of the book, of paramount significance to its author, and the Hays Office refused to sanction a script which apparently undermined the whole concept of Christian marriage.

The collapse of talks left the Waughs free to enjoy themselves, with MGM's hospitality continuing 'consistently munificent'. 'Social life gay & refined', Evelyn reported to Peters. 'Not as generally described.' Laura in her expensive new clothes 'grew smarter and younger and more popular daily and was serenely happy. I was well content and, as soon as the danger of the film was disposed of, almost serene.' They met Anna May Wong and Merle Oberon, saw Charlie Chaplin's 'brilliant new film *Monsieur Verdoux* and went to a supper party at his house later which comprised mostly central European Jews. We also went over Walt Disney's studios.' They were taken up by the English colony, among whom were a number of friends, the painter Simon Elwes and his wife (whose hostess, Andrea Cowdin, was exceptionally hospitable), Iris Tree and Ivan Moffat, Randolph Churchill, Sir Charles Mendl. It was Mendl who took them to lunch with Aldous Huxley, whose wife, Maria, described the occasion in a letter to Christopher Isherwood. At one end of the table sat Waugh, 'wearing a little black hat on top of his little face and a striped suit over his little body . . . at the other end a very English, still young, woman with an intensely inner-absorbed face. Unlined unwrinkled without any expression but when she looked out of herself the most despairing eyes . . . I must have put my foot in it when I told her she looked melancholy . . . because Waugh in his little black hat put his arm round her shoulder and assured her that she was the gayest person he knew; and they walked off, all three and we were left – uncomfortable.'

For Evelyn the high point was his discovery of Forest Lawn Memorial Park. He had been told of this extraordinary creation, the inspiration of a Dr Hubert Eaton, by Lady Milbanke, an Englishwoman staying in Los Angeles. Sheila Milbanke had been taken to Forest Lawn, and, she told Evelyn, never in her life had she seen a place which surpassed it for beauty, taste and sensitivity, a place where faith and consolation, religion and art had been brought to their highest possible association. Evelyn saw at once exactly what she meant. The saccharine sentimentality, the repellent cuteness, the grotesque euphemisms, the denial of the actuality of death fascinated him. In a letter to Peters he wrote,

> I am entirely obsessed by Forest Lawns & . . . go there two or
> three times a week, am on easy terms with the chief
> embalmer & next week am to lunch with Dr HUBERT EATON
> himself. It is an entirely unique place – the *only* thing in California
> that is not a copy of something else. It is wonderful literary raw
> material. Aldous [Huxley] flirted with it in *After Many A Summer*
> but only with the superficialities. I am at the heart of it. It will
> be a *very* good story . . . Did you know that the cadaver was
> referred to as 'the loved one' at F. L. I have seen dozens of
> loved ones half painted before the bereaved family saw them . . .[10]

Like Dennis Barlow in *The Loved One*, Evelyn returned to Europe with 'the artist's load, a great, shapeless chunk of experience'. He returned, too, with a thoroughly bad reputation, having succeeded in spreading insult from the east coast to the west. In New York, the top management of *Time-Life*, outraged by an offensive commentary given by Evelyn at a banquet in his honour, left early in a body. In Hollywood, the English actor, David Niven, was infuriated when Evelyn referred to Niven's black housekeeper in her presence as 'your native bearer'. Carol Brandt, who accompanied the Waughs to California, took some trouble to analyse the situation in a letter to Peters.

> Carl and I have found Laura and Evelyn delightful, gracious,
> and appreciative in every sense of the word. But I must say we
> seem to be alone in this land of sunshine. I truly think that
> people here have tried to be friendly and gracious, both in
> terms of the usual dinners and in terms of work, but Evelyn has
> been so constantly arrogant and rude apparently as to have
> left a trail of bloody but unbowed heads behind him. Some of
> this, I gather, has been utter mischief on his part and some
> of it has been complete misunderstanding of his particular
> variety of humor and wit.

[10] The bible of Forest Lawn was Roy Slocum's *Embalming Techniques*, and Waugh
had been presented with a signed copy, which he read with close attention,
marking passages of specific interest: 'The nose is sometimes turned to one side.
This may have been caused by wrapping the sheet too tightly about the face . . .'

Exactly this kind of misunderstanding lay behind much of Waugh's notorious reputation for 'rudeness'. Often he *was* rude: intentionally, woundingly and sometimes unforgivably; his instinctive reaction on meeting someone for the first time was hostility; he was capable of being as rude to women as to men, to servants as to generals. When accepting an invitation from Graham Greene he told him he would have to dine with him in his flat or club, not a restaurant, because 'I fall into ungovernable rages with waiters and am sorry afterwards, too late.'

But the kind of rudeness complained of by the Americans was different, the result not so much of a desire to offend as an attempt to cheer things up. Evelyn, a martyr to boredom, lived always in hope of finding a sparring partner worthy of his own wit and ingenuity. In the initial encounter the manner was bullying and bellicose, but to the discerning eye not entirely serious; if, as usually happened, the victim failed to see the pose for what it was and nervously recoiled, Evelyn would have no mercy: scenting fear, he would move in for the kill. But if his opponent stood up to the bullying, or even better returned it in kind, then Evelyn was delighted and would behave charmingly. An example of a typical encounter is given in an article in the *World*, unintentionally revealing, by the American writer and humorist, Leo Rosten.

Under the pen-name Leonard Q. Ross, Rosten was the author of a comic novel, *The Education of Hyman Kaplan*, described by Waugh in a review in the *Spectator* as 'a book of singular enchantment'. Delighted by praise from a writer whom he extravagantly admired, Rosten when he was next in England sent Waugh a friendly note inviting him to 'drop by' for tea or drinks. By return came a postcard: 'Dear L. R. – Alas, impossible. E. W.' Angry at the snub, Rosten replied with a postcard of his own. 'Dear E. W. – Quite. L. R.' Evelyn, his hopes rising at this indication of a kindred spirit, immediately wrote apologising for his hasty reply and suggesting that he and Laura call the following Wednesday when they would be in London.

The day came, the Waughs arrived. Immediately Rosten took the first false step, launching into an adulatory speech about Waugh's work. This was something Evelyn dreaded, having not the faintest interest in the opinions of strangers and considering it the height of bad manners to discuss a man's professional

occupation, his trade, on a social occasion. Repeatedly he tried
to warn Rosten off by ostentatious changing of the subject.

'Why do you wear a double-breasted blazer?'
  'I beg your pardon?'
'Is that what they're wearing in the States?'
  'Y-yes. I bought it in New York . . . Mr Waugh, I've always
wondered – '
'What do you call those shoes?'
  'Uh, they're moccasins . . . Did you write – '
'*Indian* moccasins?'
  'Yes. When I read your *Put Out More Flags* – '
'*Must* they have such heavy soles?'
  'I suppose so. In *Vile Bodies* – '
'Do you find them comfortable?'
  'As for *Handful of Dust*! Were you ever in South America?'
  'Mmh.'
'How did you happen to get there?'
  'Ship.'
'And to Guiana?'
  'Walked.'

All this while Laura sat quietly watching her husband, making no
attempt to intervene. As soon as they decently could, the Waughs
left. Rosten was offended and bewildered. 'I thought the meeting
a disaster,' he wrote.

Evelyn returned from the United States in March 1947. He
wrote a two-part feature on Hollywood for the *Daily Telegraph*, and
'an article on Death for *Life*', but it was not until the end of May
that the Californian experience began to take shape with the
beginning of the short novel inspired by Forest Lawn. By mid-
September *The Loved One* was finished and dispatched to Peters.
Evelyn had already written to his agent, worried that such a
blatant satire of the American way of life might receive a not
altogether favourable response. Peters's reply was unequivocal.

It is not possible to be funny about corpses for 25,000 words . . .
To my mind – I am being painfully frank – it is not a question
of 'what form it should take in its public appearance in U.S.A.
and England', but of whether it should make any public

appearance at all. I found parts of it very amusing, of course;
but parts were to me revolting, and my overriding conviction
when I had finished the story was that it was not worthy of
[you].

Dismissing Peters's objections – he employed his agent as a man
of affairs, not as a literary critic[11] – Evelyn made it clear that he
intended to publish, although given the sensitive nature of the
subject he would be content with 'a minute public'. He suggested
that before appearing in book form the story should be submitted
first to *Horizon* in England and to the *New Yorker* in the United
States. Cyril Connolly accepted it eagerly for *Horizon*, but the *New
Yorker* turned it down. Not, however, for the reasons Evelyn half-
gleefully expected: far from being shocked by his sending up of
Hollywood and of Californian burial customs, they felt this was
stale stuff, had already been done before, by Nathanael West,
Sinclair Lewis, Aldous Huxley, S. J. Perelman among others. 'The
freshest part of Mr Waugh's story is that part which refers to the
English in Hollywood, and we wish, wistfully, that he had concerned himself more exclusively with that theme.' For much the
same reason *Town & Country* rejected it, as did *Good Housekeeping*
and *Atlantic Monthly*.

There was also a very real danger of libel, with Chapman &
Hall's legal adviser particularly worried about the possible reaction of Dr Eaton and Forest Lawn.[12] To circumvent this, Evelyn
conspired with his friend Ed Stanley. Lord Stanley of Alderley,
with all the prestige of a peer of the realm, agreed to add a
codicil to his will stating that he wished to be buried at Forest
Lawn as he understood it resembled the beautiful cemetery so
movingly described by Evelyn Waugh in *The Loved One*.[13]

The Loved One begins with a description of a little group of
exiles in some unspecified but clearly barbarous region. Only

[11] 'I don't think Peters's <u>literary</u> advice valuable. He is a good negotiator but no
better critic than C. Beaton,' Evelyn was to write to Nancy Mitford in 1957.
[12] Eaton was slow to react, but in 1960 he wrote a letter of complaint. 'It is
becoming more and more evident that people in the United States who have
never visited Forest Lawn believe that Evelyn Waugh's book *The Loved One* is a
true depiction of Forest Lawn Memorial-Park, Glendale. Inasmuch as your
locale was placed in Hollywood, and we are the most prominent cemetery, they
insist on taking this view which has become most detrimental to us.'
[13] This clause was revoked after ten years as the danger was past and Lord
Stanley was afraid it would involve his heirs in great expense.

gradually does it become apparent that these very English gentlemen are not in some half-civilised outpost of empire, but in
Bel Air, California, most of them employees of the all-powerful
Megalopolitan Studios. Newly arrived among them is Dennis
Barlow, who, to his older compatriots' disgust, has turned in his
job as a script-writer to work at the Happier Hunting Ground, a
pets' crematorium. The equivalent of this for human beings is
Whispering Glades, a great necropolis of obscenely euphemistic
design, of great fascination to Dennis not only for its mesmerising
tastelessness but as the place of work of the aptly-named Aimée
Thanatogenos, with whom Dennis is in love. It is with the macabre
details of Aimée's work as an embalmer, and that of her superior,
Mr Joyboy, that Evelyn lovingly decorates his black but ebullient
comedy: the 'little poulterer's pinch' which Mr Joyboy gives to a
suicide's thigh, the tricks of the trade with a 'difficult' corpse.
' "Lovely, Miss Thanatogenos," he [Mr Joyboy] said . . . "Did you
have difficulty with the right eyelid?"
    ' "Just a little."
    ' "A tendency to open in the inside corner?"
    ' "Yes, but I worked a little cream under the lid and then
firmed it with No. 6." '
Surrounding this morbid theme are a number of elements
directly derived from Evelyn's own experience of California: the
slangy language, garish costume, the tacky buildings and informal
manners. And underlying it all the aridity of a community with
no understanding of the spiritual life, a people who are prepared
literally to deny death. At the end Dennis, cynical and wiser,
leaves this corrupt civilisation: 'Others, better men than he, had
foundered here and perished. The strand was littered with their
bones. He was leaving it not only unravished but enriched. He
was adding his bit to the wreckage, something that had long irked
him, his young heart, and was carrying back instead the artist's
load, a great shapeless chunk of experience; bearing it home to
his ancient and comfortless shore; to work on it hard and long,
for God knew how long.'
In a letter to Cyril Connolly, Evelyn listed the ideas he had had
in mind while writing the novel.

1st & quite predominantly over excitement with the scene of
Forest Lawn. 2nd the Anglo-American impasse . . . 3rd there is no

such thing as an American. They are all exiles uprooted, transplanted & doomed to sterility . . . 4th the European raiders who come for the spoils & if they are lucky make for home with them. 5th Memento mori, old style, not specifically Californian.

In his introduction to the story in the issue of February 1948, Connolly quotes this letter, adding his own enthusiastic recommendation. 'In its attitude to death, and to death's stand-in, failure, Mr Waugh exposes a materialist society at its weakest spot, as would Swift or Donne were they alive today . . . [*The Loved One*] is, in my opinion, one of the most perfect short novels of the last ten years.'

When it was published in the United States eight months later the critics on the whole agreed with the original judgment of the magazines which had turned the story down. *Time*, which described the piece as 'Evelyn Waugh caught between laughter and vomiting', applauded the portrait of the British expatriates, while describing as disappointing 'the travelogue of the inanities of Whispering Glades'. English reviewers reacted more positively. John Woodburn in the *New Republic* found it as a piece of writing 'nearly faultless', and as satire 'an act of devastation, an angry, important, moral effort', a view endorsed by Desmond MacCarthy in the *Sunday Times*. 'Beneath satire of any depth there always lies, in addition to a sense of humour and an eye for glaring incongruities, a tragic conception of life. It is that which makes *The Loved One* not only a macabre farce but a significant criticism of life.'

Both the English and American editions, with illustrations by Stuart Boyle, were published at the end of 1948 following the story's appearance in *Horizon*. The novel was dedicated to Nancy Mitford. 'I am afraid I have boasted about it so much that it will seem very flat. Do try & laugh a little. It is dedicated to you as the hardest hearted well no toughest is the word girl I know.' Nancy was entranced.

> The *heaven* of *The Loved One* oh you are kind to dedicate it to me, thank you thank you for it. I've been utterly shrieking ever since it arrived, luckily was lunching alone. I must say I couldn't quite do it & the foie de veau together . . . but combined it happily with a banana, & am now in despair at having finished it . . .
> Dined with a young American last night & told him your book

was to be called *The Loved One.* 'What a beautiful name' he said. Poor him.

Ironically it was only since the end of the war, when Nancy left London to live in Paris, that the friendship had become important to Evelyn. He had known her since the 1920s; originally she had been a friend of Evelyn Gardner's, but, shocked by She-Evelyn's infidelity, Nancy had sided firmly with the betrayed husband.

In 1933 she married Peter Rodd ('Prod'), the clever, pompous and handsome adventurer on whom Evelyn drew for his portrait of Basil Seal. The marriage was not a success, and from 1939 Nancy and Peter lived apart, he on service overseas, she working as an assistant in Heywood Hill's bookshop in Curzon Street. Here, at this famous meeting place for the Mayfair intelligentsia, more club than shop, Evelyn used to drop in to buy books, meet friends and glean from Nancy all the latest gossip. For when it came to gossip she was a purveyor of genius. Like Albertine, the accomplished mistress in her novel, *The Blessing,* Nancy knew exactly how to magic her material, however unexceptional in its original form, into glorious entertainment; like Albertine, '[she] always had something to recount. Not plain slices of life served up on a thick white plate, but wonderful confections embellished with the aromatic and exotic fruits of her own sugary imagination . . . she had endless tales to spin around their mutual friends . . .'

An entry in Waugh's diary for February 1946 recounts, 'Got away in time to catch Nancy as her shop was closing and take her to tea at the Ritz. She was full of funny stories about Prod and the Duchess of Kent, Cyril, Dowager Duchess of Devonshire and *Brideshead.*' To Evelyn such fare was irresistible; and when Nancy, in pursuit of the love of her life, Gaston Palewski, the elusive French 'Colonel', moved to Paris, Evelyn missed her sorely: 'No one departure has left such a yawning (literally) hole in London as yours,' he told her. But the friendship, far from fading, became consolidated by letter. Both were at their best on paper; knew the same people, liked the same jokes, read the same books; shared a highly evolved and idiomatic language; both were brilliant performers, hilariously witty, sometimes cruel, frequently childish; they both drew on deep wells of anger and disappointment; they were both prejudiced, provocative, arrogant and essentially kind-hearted. They quarrelled of course, chiefly on account of Nancy's (in Evelyn's eyes) culpable refusal to treat the spiritual side of life seriously. But Nancy had all the qualities he looked for in his worldly women friends: she was smart, sophisticated, funny, and above all brave. Not only was he unable to cow her with his bullying tactics, but it was Nancy with her unerring eye for psychological truth who saw through what she called his Iron Mask to the bonhomous figure beneath; she saw past the ugly image of irascible old buffer, and forgave him willingly his frequently appalling behaviour. There was no question with Nancy of any romantic attachment, as there had been with Diana Cooper. Nancy lacked Diana's famous loveliness; but she lacked, too, Diana's impenetrable carapace of self-regard, the thin, petulant whine of self-pity that so irritated Evelyn. Even when sad or unhappy, Nancy was a firm believer in what she called 'keeping up the shop front'.

For his part Evelyn acted not only as friend and entertainer, but as literary mentor. Nancy always sent him the manuscripts of her novels. 'You are cher maître to me,' she told him. For her he was the supreme practitioner, '[with] your well known knack of one tap on the nail & in it goes, whereas the rest of us hammer & pound for hours'. It was Evelyn who suggested the title for her first big success, *The Pursuit of Love*, and Evelyn who gave her the idea for the brilliant description of Alconleigh, home of the terrifying Uncle Matthew: 'Within, the key-note, the theme, was death . . .' He corrected her girlish grammar, instructed her on narrative technique, ticked her off for using words carelessly ('You do not understand the meaning of the word "eke". It means to make something last longer by adding something else to it. Eg. eke out butter with margarine. When you write: "I might as well eke out the month in London as anywhere else", you commit a gross vulgarism.') And he tried, on the whole without success, to persuade her to revise thoroughly before publication. After reading the first draft of *Love in a Cold Climate*, he told her sternly,

[It needs] six months hard I am afraid without remission for good conduct. The manuscript was a delight to read, full of wit & fun & fantasy . . . The theme is original & promising. There is not a boring sentence (except p. 274). But it isn't a book at all yet. No more 40 hour week. Blood, sweat & tears. That is to

say if you want to produce a work of art. There is a work of
art there, lurking in a hole, occasionally visible by the tip of its
whiskers.

All Evelyn's fondest and most frequent correspondents were
women. '[Evelyn] needs feminine company by the yard,' as Nancy
rightly said. He chose with care, for his requirements were exact-
ing. As well as Nancy and Diana Cooper, he picked Ann Rothermere, married to the owner of the *Daily Mail*, and Lady Pamela
Berry, wife of the Editor-in-Chief of the *Daily Telegraph*. Between
them these four women, gregarious, glamorous and quick-witted,
covered on both sides of the Channel the world of high English
society of the kind most attractive to Evelyn; the world of Margot
Metroland, but also the literary, publishing and newspaper worlds
he had once moved in and written about, but now in middle age
wished to move in and write about very much less. He was still
intensely curious, however; these worlds amused him enormously.
All four shared Evelyn's love of luxury and privilege, and all four
were secure in their position in the scheme of things.

In spite of the frequent quarrels that broke over 'that jagged
stone our relationship', Evelyn probably loved Diana the most,
although Nancy's letters were by far the best, and inspired the best
replies. Evelyn was an exceptional correspondent, understanding
exactly what a letter should be. 'When you write a letter,' he told
one of his daughters, 'try & put yourself in imagination into the
presence of the person you are writing to. That is the secret of
letter-writing, just as it is the secret of prayer.' He applied his
remarkable stylistic agility, adapting himself to each individual
recipient, employing words such as 'blissikins' and 'heavenly' for
gushing Miss Mitford, omitting the personal pronoun and definite article to match Diana's childlike prose: 'Can't understand
Baby's movements . . . Head is in a whirl.'

Worried by his insane self-destructiveness, the four women
often discussed Evelyn among themselves. 'Poor Wu – he does
everything he can to alienate himself from the affection he is
yearning for,' as Diana perceptively remarked. While staying with
her, Evelyn invariably succeeded in quarrelling with Duff, often
– and bitterly – with Diana as well, and alienating most of his
fellow guests. A visit from Evelyn at rue Monsieur in 1949 left
Nancy feeling, she said, like the morning after an air-raid. 'Most

of the time he was sweet, twice he was bloody & all the time funny. About all one can expect. He had a terrible terrible quarrel with Diana at Chantilly this morning & I was ground between the upper & nether millstones of their two strong passionate & violent characters so now I am feeling weak,' she told Pamela Berry. 'The French are beginning to regard Evelyn as one of the greatest living novelists they call him him Wugg & eat up any crumbs of information about him that I deign to let fall. They all long to meet him in spite of earnest warnings from me that it would be better not.' Pamela Berry invited Evelyn to bring Bron for a children's beach holiday at La Baule, an invitation she lived very much to regret. She was confined to bed with a throat infection, which left Evelyn day after day with no adult company except for the Berrys' nanny. It was a long time before he forgave Pam, and a long time before she forgave him for being so unreasonable. Nancy as usual was the mediator. 'Oh please don't quarrel with poor Evelyn,' she implored Pam. 'Do remember it is all medical & do remember how terrible it would be for me to be his only living friend.'

Nancy received intensive tutoring in literary composition, but Evelyn, secure in his own professional estimation, was always generous with writers who asked for advice. He encouraged young writers and took trouble over those who, as his fame grew, appealed to him for help. He saved from suicidal despair the Scottish novelist, Moray McLaren, who was personally unknown to him, sent him a cheque, and read the typescript of his first book which he persuaded Chapman & Hall to accept. He did much the same for his old friend, Alfred Duggan, who had nearly been destroyed by alcoholism, having been invalided out of the Army at the beginning of the war. Duggan had undergone a cure, was living with his mother and training as a dairyman under a government scheme for helping ex-servicemen return to civilian life. Evelyn encouraged him to start writing, and was instrumental in launching him on a successful career as an historical novelist.

Another writer much in Evelyn's debt was the American Thomas Merton. Merton, a Trappist monk at the monastery of Our Lady of Gethsemani, Kentucky, had written an influential, if long-winded, autobiography, *The Seven-Storey Mountain*, which Tom Burns had bought for publication by Hollis & Carter. Burns, with Merton's agreement, had asked Evelyn to edit the book, an 'enthralling task' Evelyn piously described it, apparently undeterred by the author's vanity and the second-rateness of his prose. The book came out in England in 1949, shortened by a third and much more disciplined in style, under the title *Elected Silence.* Merton was grateful, and from these beginnings a friendship grew, with Evelyn advising Merton on his writing (sent him a copy of Fowler's *Modern English Usage*), the monk in return giving spiritual advice to Evelyn. 'Like all people with intellectual gifts, you would like to argue yourself into a quandary that doesn't exist. Don't you see that in all your anxiety to explain how your contrition is imperfect you are expressing an intense sorrow that it is not so – and that is true contrition,' Merton wrote in September 1948. 'Really I think it might do you a lot of good & give you a certain happiness to say the Rosary every day. If you don't like it, so much the better . . .'

Merton in the silence of his Trappist community might well have been an object of envy to Waugh. Having abandoned the plan to set up a separate residence, Evelyn was obliged to live and work in the company of his large family at Piers Court, and combine the solitary discipline of a writer with the more sociable rôle of father of six. But young children bored him, and although his own were strictly brought up never to disturb him, he found their presence tedious and irritating, as his references to them in letters and the diary make very clear.

I abhor their company because I can only regard children as defective adults, hate their physical ineptitude, find their jokes flat and monotonous . . . My children are home for the holidays – merry, affectionate, sadly boring . . . The presence of my children affects me with deep weariness and depression. I do not see them until luncheon, as I have my breakfast alone in the library, and they are in fact well trained to avoid my part of the house; but I am aware of them from the moment I wake. Luncheon is very painful. Teresa has a mincing habit of speech and a pert, humourless style of wit; Bron is clumsy and dishevelled, sly, without intellectual, aesthetic or spiritual interest; Margaret is pretty and below the age of reason. In the nursery whooping cough rages I believe. At tea I meet the three

elder children again and they usurp the drawing-room until it is
time to dress for dinner.

This was not, of course, the whole story, for Evelyn took his
responsibilities seriously, making strenuous efforts to play the part
expected of him. He was a master of farcical invention, and his
exotic fantasies, hilarious jokes and manic clowning could reduce
his audience to tears of laughter. The childish streak in his own
nature gave him unusual insight into the child's world, but it was
this same streak which led him to behave childishly; instead of
making allowances for the children, he behaved like one of them,
suddenly growing bored, or throwing a tantrum because he considered them impertinent or unappreciative, or having his feelings hurt when the children grew tired of a game of his devising.
'I have become involved in a tedious game with the children of
correspondence in a crack in a cedar tree between them and Bad
Basil Bennett, captain of the robbers. That and a fantasy about
"Dr Bedlam's School for Mad and Bad Children" occupy most of
their conversation,' he recorded during one of the school holidays, adding gloomily that by the next this particular invention
had lost its appeal: 'I used to take some pleasure in inventing
legends for them about Basil Bennett, Dr Bedlam and the Sebag-
Montefiores. But now they think it ingenious to squeal: "It isn't
true." '

A much more serious wound was inflicted by Bron, then aged
five, who was treated by his father to a day in London. 'Yesterday
was a day of supreme self-sacrifice,' Evelyn told the child's mother.

> I fetched him [Bron] from Highgate, took him up the dome of
> St Pauls, gave him a packet of triangular stamps, took him to
> luncheon at the Hyde Park Hotel, took him on the roof of the
> hotel, took him to Harrods & let him buy vast quantities of
> toys (down to your account) took him to tea with Maimie who
> gave him a pound and a box of matches, took him back to
> Highgate, in a state (myself not the boy) of extreme exhaustion.
> My mother said 'Have you had a lovely day?' He replied 'A bit
> dull'. So that is the last time for some years I inconvenience
> myself for my children. You might rub that in to him.

No wonder Bron admitted later that he would willingly have
swopped his father for a bosun's whistle.

But the anger never lasted for long, and the cycle continued:

Evelyn delighting his children with eccentric stories one minute, the next retiring into his library in disgust at their incorrigible childishness. He regarded it as his paternal duty to read aloud, mostly Dickens – like his father – but would close the book with a bang the moment he felt the attention of his audience wandering. 'He read well,' Margaret recalled, 'but claimed never to have enjoyed it partly because of the distress caused him by our loutish postures. He would have liked us all to sit round decorously, our heads bent over intricate embroidery. Instead we sat restlessly, scratching our heads and picking our noses.'

Christmas was the time of year most to be dreaded. Elaborate preparations would be made, presents purchased, the Stinchcombe Silver Band entertained after carols, pantomimes booked in Bristol and Bath, but somehow it all ended badly, with Evelyn in sulks because he had not been given what he hoped. 'I made a fair show of geniality throughout the day though the spectacle of a litter of shoddy toys and half-eaten sweets sickened me . . . Luncheon was cold and poorly cooked . . . Laura gave me a pot of caviare which I ate a week ago. My mother gave me a copy of the *Diary of a Nobody*. But for these I have had no presents though I have given many . . . Thank God Christmas is over. I prefer Ash Wednesday.'

It was Laura on whom the burden fell of bringing up the children – 'your children', as their father usually referred to them; it was she who had to buy their clothes, take them to the dentist, drive them to Mass, deliver them to school, and make sure that the nursery staff – nanny and nursemaid, both of impeccably Catholic origins – would maintain the high standards of cleanliness and tidiness her husband demanded. Laura was a conscientious if undemonstrative mother, fond of her children, but she had little time to spare, and was briskly dismissive of childish squabbles and plaints.

In the early years after the war, Laura had to do much of the cooking and housework, as well as labour on her beloved farm. It was here, in her twenty-five acres and small herd of cows, that her real interest lay. 'Poor Laura's life is one of drudgery, cooking, making beds, milking, feeding hens, all done vaguely but pertinaciously – so slowly that it takes all her waking hours.' Evelyn was prepared to tolerate the farm as long as he was not troubled with domestic detail. Except for Ellwood, who looked after him, the servants, the kitchen and the general running of the house were Laura's responsibility. One side of Evelyn would have liked a wife who wore hat and gloves and left cards on the neighbours, but Laura was careless of her appearance, and dressed for preference in shirt and trousers or baggy skirt and old cardigan, her short hair unkempt, a cigarette nearly always in hand. Laura if left to herself would have let many of the more ceremonial traditions comfortably slide. But Evelyn was a perfectionist, a stickler for ceremony, for polished silver and white table-cloths, and he frequently scolded his wife for her lackadaisical approach: 'The aim of my letter was not to make you unhappy, still less to make you despair, but simply to rouse you from the tribal torpor into which you have sunk & make you think. Please go on thinking, however painful it is ... Cheer up & wake up ... Don't be so bloody wet.' Meals were often eaten to the accompaniment of sighing complaints: ' "Laura, shouldn't there be two salt cellars when there are more than four people?" or "sponge cakes with gooseberry fool?" and so on.' Once, when for several days in a row Evelyn had asked Laura to remove from the table a bowl of rotting bananas, a request she had blandly ignored, he picked up the fruit and threw it at her. But Laura allowed little of this to disturb her, preferring to live as it were underground. If angry, she withdrew, and if necessary she could be scathing. 'When Evelyn is in one of his bad moods,' she said with feeling to a surprised Ann Rothermere, 'we send him to a witch in Somerset who spits at him.'

Just as Evelyn refused to have anything to do with her cows and her kale, so she refused any involvement in his London life, his frequent absences providing necessary relief from that demanding and overpowering presence. She was shy by nature, and his smart friends were of no interest to her; privately she despised most of them, infinitely preferring the company of her family. Her mother, brother and sisters she mostly saw at Pixton, as they were rarely allowed at Stinchcombe unless Evelyn were away – 'I stayed in London for no other reason than that Laura was entertaining her mother at Piers Court,' he wrote in November 1946. Meetings with the hated Auberon Herbert sometimes had to be conducted in a local pub, as Evelyn could not be civil to him, and the strain of his hostility was more than Laura could endure. At Pixton in 1950, after the birth of her last child, she wrote to him. 'I have been thinking deeply about whether it would be a good thing for you to come & visit me again & though I long for it I don't think it would be if Auberon is going to be here ... the mixture of all the children and him would be intolerable to you & even though I know you would be polite to him I should be in a fever & miserable, feeling that things were not right.'

When Evelyn's friends came for a night or two, Laura was civil but elusive, remaining in the room no longer than she had to, always with a good reason for disappearing into the kitchen or upstairs. Even when she seemed most attentive, two thirds of her mind would be elsewhere. She did, however, enjoy the jokes, was immensely entertained by Evelyn's often malicious humour; she had a feline wit of her own, as well as a talent for mimicry unsuspected by those who saw in Laura Waugh the archetype of the mouse-wife. According to her eldest son, '[Laura] saw the funny side of everything, mocked everything, and was a natural subversive.'

In January 1945, Evelyn had written to Laura from Dubrovnik, 'We are stinking rich. Do get magnificent furs if it is not a foolish time.' But Laura never showed much interest in furs or any other kind of personal adornment, leaving it to her husband to dispose of the money he earned, which he did with passionate pleasure and sometimes reckless abandon. Home from the war, he immediately began on a spending spree, buying a gold watch for £125, a 100-guinea cashmere coat for Laura, Victorian paintings and furniture, books, carpets and wall-paper. Most of his shopping was done in London, but the local shops were not overlooked. On 30 August 1946, he wrote in his diary,

> To Gloucester with Laura who bought a cow for more than £100. I went to a junk shop and bought a lion of wood, finely carved for £25, also a bookcase £35, a painting of the baptism of a Jewess £15, a charming Chinese painting £10, a Regency easel £7; all good things and at reasonable prices. Then I lost my reason. Among a pile of old paintings was a very pretty watercolour and gouache of Durham Cathedral. I asked the price. '£150', said the aged shopkeeper. I bought it.

Over the next few years the collection was constantly augmented. There were the bizarre curiosities, such as a bark-bronze bust of

Queen Victoria whose head fell back to reveal an inkwell, an elephant's-foot wastepaper-basket, a rhinoceros-foot stud-box, a gothicised barrel organ and an ebony camel half life-size and weighing nearly a ton. He bought books – first editions of favourite novels, antiquarian books on furniture and architecture – from Handasyde Buchanan at Heywood Hill.

In time a considerable number of pictures were acquired, with the emphasis on the Pre-Raphaelites and Victorian narrative painting. Evelyn bought Rossetti's *Spirit of the Rainbow*, which hung in the dining-room at Piers Court, Holman Hunt's *Oriana*, and a version of *The Woodman's Child* by Arthur Hughes. He bought a Mulready from Hugh Walpole's collection, two travel pictures by Thomas Musgrove Joy (commissioning a third by the war artist, Richard Eurich, to complete the trilogy), a fine emigration scene by Henry Nelson O'Neil, and the most important of his genre paintings, *The General Post Office at One Minute to Six* by George Elgar Hicks. He also had a weakness for humorous pictures, especially those with Catholic connotations; a typical example, purchased in 1948, was *An Embarrassing Question* by George Flemwell, showing an uneasy young couple being questioned by a priest.

The garden for a time provided an interest. Evelyn enjoyed buying statues, temples and follies. He had the garden landscaped at great expense and redesigned, he himself working on the construction of what was known as the Edifice, a semi-circular stone wall about ten feet in height, surmounted with battlements and with a paved area beneath it. Another of his ideas was a path made entirely from empty champagne bottles planted upside down. Later he devised and had made two iron gates, outside which was placed the famous notice, gothic lettering on a brass plate, NO ADMITTANCE ON BUSINESS.

The country provided peace in which to write: it did not unfortunately provide very much else. Evelyn was totally uninterested in rural pursuits and local society. 'God I wish I had some neighbours I could bear to speak to. There must be plenty in this populous countryside but they never come our way,' he complained feelingly to Nancy. In an attempt to pass the time he took long dull walks along the main road, and four times a week went to the cinema in Dursley. 'I suppose I have seen more bad films than any living man ... I forget them like dreams the moment I leave the building.'

To alleviate the boredom, friends were frequently invited to stay. The arrival on Friday evening would be looked forward to with keen excitement, hopes would be high, but nearly always by the next afternoon Evelyn would be in a state of intense irritation, barely able to wait for the moment of departure the following day. Fortunately in 1947 there moved into the neighbourhood a couple whom Evelyn did find congenial. John (Jack) Donaldson and his wife, Frances (Frankie), had come to Gloucestershire to farm; they were both socialists, she the daughter of the playwright Frederick Lonsdale. Curious to meet them, Evelyn sent Laura to call, and on her good report, the Donaldsons were invited to dinner. The evening was a success, and the two families became friends. Neither Jack nor Frankie was frightened of Evelyn. They understood exactly his requirements, his love of gossip, his impatience with conversation about politics or books.

Evelyn needed to live in the country for his own preservation, but he also needed to escape from it at frequent intervals, going up to London nearly every week with the excuse of needing a haircut or having to attend a board meeting at Chapman & Hall. In the summer it became a habit for him to spend six weeks at the Hyde Park Hotel for what Ann Rothermere unflatteringly referred to as his 'annual vomit'.

These London visits were eagerly anticipated, and inevitably the cause of much disillusion. At the end of one of his summer seasons, Evelyn wrote to Nancy, 'My last day in London & goodness I am pleased ... It is six weeks now I have been sitting about in hotels & clubs bored bored bored.' Drink as ever was the antidote to boredom, and some of Evelyn's diary entries at this period might almost have been written during his undergraduate days. On 16 July 1946, he recorded, 'Tuesday a drunken day; lunched at Beefsteak ... Drinking in White's most of the afternoon. Then to Beefsteak again where I got drunk with Kenneth Wagg and insulted R. A. Butler. Then to St James's for another bottle of champagne where I insulted Beverly Baxter. Was sick on retiring to bed.'

Alcohol in reasonable quantities made him jolly, but a large intake made him not only melancholy but aggressive, the effects aggravated by an increasing dependence on narcotics. He complained that his expeditions to London were becoming unduly expensive because of the cost of sending flowers to hostesses whose parties he had ruined by his behaviour. At a dinner of Maimie's he reduced almost to tears an American woman who politely complimented him on *Brideshead*; on John Sutro's birthday he wrecked the evening by sitting in a corner drunkenly shouting 'toss-off, toss-off' at anyone who came near; he distinguished himself at a party of Ann Rothermere's 'by being rude to everybody, pretending he didn't know who Rosamond Lehmann was when she rushed up to greet him with open arms ... criticised Alan Ross's beard and, when Cecil Beaton approached him when he was sitting on the sofa ... exclaimed, "Here's someone who can tell us all about buggery!" He then had to be carried into a taxi at three in the morning.'

Evelyn began to notice that on his return home from one of these jaunts he felt ill for up to three or four days afterwards. 'I have been an invalid for a week recuperating from a brief visit to London,' he wrote to Nancy at the end of 1949. 'I get so painfully drunk whenever I go there (Champagne, the shortest road out of Welfaria) and nowadays it is not a matter of a headache and an aspirin but of complete collapse, with some clear indications of incipient lunacy. I think I am jolly near being mad & need very careful treatment if I am to survive another decade without the strait straight? jacket.'

The symptoms of these prolonged hangovers as listed in the diary were insomnia, a disordered stomach, weakness at the knees, and a trembling of the hands.

> They are at their worst on the day after my return home. I tell myself I have drunk too much, smoked too much and kept late hours. But I grow sceptical of this glib excuse. On this last occasion for instance ... I had an easy train journey as far as bodily comfort was concerned. I drank perhaps three cocktails before luncheon, lunched lightly, took things easy in the afternoon, drank perhaps three cocktails before dinner. From then onwards I drank fairly steadily – champagne, with a little brandy at the end of dinner – until 4 o'clock; but I doubt whether in those eight hours I consumed more than a bottle and a half. Next day I began drinking at 11 and drank two glasses of brandy and ginger ale, later two glasses of gin, and

at luncheon practically nothing – half a glass of white Bordeaux and two tiny glasses of port. This is not enough to make a healthy middle-aged man ill for four days . . .

Smoking was one of Evelyn's greatest pleasures, and much of his correspondence with Peters is concerned with the business of having cigars shipped over from America. 'Dear Pete,' runs a characteristically exigent letter.

Where are my cigars? What explanation do the americans give of their beastly conduct. Have cigars been dispatched? When?

I do not mind the americans putting this blurb on my book but they must send cigars.

I do not mind the Poles publishing short stories. My mind is on cigars.

I have no recent photograph of myself. Nor have I cigars.

Both Alfred McIntyre of Little, Brown and Harold Matson were expected to act as suppliers, Matson sending over boxes wrapped like books, with his agency's address label pasted on them, to avoid duty. From time to time Evelyn toyed with the idea of giving up his cigars – 'I am thinking of giving up smoking: (a) mortification, not only the pleasure of smoking but the swagger of it; cigar in hand I become more boastful and ribald; (b) the saving of money which I could give away without affecting the position of Laura or my family; (c) health, particularly in the way that smoking makes for sloth. I put off doing things until I've finished my cigar' – but was never able to do so, except during Lent, when his abstinence made him more than normally bad-tempered. 'I have not been in London for weeks and shall not be until after Easter,' he wrote to Diana Cooper in 1948. 'I have foregone wine and tobacco and am best alone and at home in those conditions.' From time to time, worried by his corpulence, he tried to reduce his weight, sometimes at a health farm, sometimes by following the régime of a Dr Goller in Harley Street, a fashionable quack who prescribed a strict diet in conjunction with appetite-suppressant pills.

In November 1948 Evelyn went again to the United States, the primary purpose of the trip to undertake research for a substantial article for *Life* on the Catholic Church in America, a suggestion that had been greeted with enthusiasm by the magazine's proprietor, Henry Luce. *Life* agreed to fund the visit, the Luces giving a dinner for Evelyn on his arrival in New York. 'It was not a great success,' he told Laura. 'Caviar, dover soles flown that day from England etc but neither aware of what they ate or drank. He handsome, well mannered, well dressed, densely stupid. She exquisitely elegant, clever as a monkey, self-centred.' Clare Booth Luce was important on a number of levels: rich, powerful, beautiful and spoilt, she was a great star in the States, particularly, as a fanatical convert, among the Catholic *prominenten*, to whom she could give Evelyn access.

Evelyn also saw Alec, who, unofficially separated from his wife, was now living mainly in New York. He renewed a friendship with Anne Fremantle, another convert, whom, as Anne Huth-Jackson, he had known at the time of his first marriage. (She was distinguished for being the only woman reputed to have received a proposal of marriage from C. R. M. F. Cruttwell.) Evelyn met, too, the celebrated Dorothy Day, member of the Catholic Labour Movement and co-founder of the *Catholic Worker*: 'an autocratic ascetic saint who wants us all to be poor . . . I gave a great party of them [Mrs Day and her helpers] luncheon in an Italian restaurant in the district & Mrs Day didn't at all approve of their having cocktails or wine but they had them & we talked till four o'clock . . .'

From New York to Boston to see Alfred McIntyre of Little, Brown; from there to Baltimore to collect an honorary doctorate from the Jesuits at Loyola College, then to New Orleans and back to New York. 'I am not really enjoying it very much,' Evelyn told Laura, 'tho I have had some amusing experiences notably staying with Grail maidens (most embarrassing) and Trappist monks. I had a long talk with Thomas Merton.'

Early the following year Evelyn reluctantly returned to America, this time with Laura, to give a series of lectures on 'Three Vital Writers, Chesterton, Knox and Greene'. The tour began as before with New York, Baltimore, New Orleans, then over the border to Ontario, back to Chicago and Milwaukee, to Kentucky to see Merton, to St Paul to meet J. F. Powers. For Evelyn it was a joyless experience, the unbeautiful campuses, the characterless hotels – in New Orleans he smashed open the window of his air-conditioned bedroom with his stick – the tedium of being 'constantly in the company of people you have to "make allowances for".'

Here and there in the reports of those who met him are glimpses of Waugh trying to alleviate the boredom for himself, teasing an audience of bewildered students, making covert fun of a sycophantic host. At Marquette University, Milwaukee, he was cornered by an enthusiastic member of the faculty, a Sister Thérèse Lentfoehr, whose hobby it was to record on film the literary luminaries who visited the university. After the lecture at a reception given at 'the lovely home of the William Browns', the innocent nun asked Evelyn if he would pose for her.

> Mr Waugh was most gracious . . . he led the way into the spacious
> garden, leaving the receiving line waiting before the
> fireplace . . . But the so readily consented to filming of Mr
> Waugh proved more complicated than I had anticipated. As I
> prepared the camera for the shot he stopped me, and insisted
> that I be in the picture with him. Hurriedly I went back to the
> house to call Charles Weishar . . . . whom I knew was familiar with
> the camera. As I stood beside Mr Waugh for the picture, he had
> a sudden suggestion – wouldn't I recite one of my poems for
> him while the camera was rolling? For this I was totally
> unprepared . . . and I quite frankly told him so. But he would
> not take a refusal. He knew of my collection *Give Joan a Sword*,
> with the Maritain preface, and demanded the title poem. There
> was nothing for me to do but haltingly try the first stanzas.
> He was pleased.

Arriving home at the end of March he wrote to Nancy, 'I've seen enough of USA to last me fifty years.' But he was back for a final visit the very next year, sailing on the *Queen Mary* in October 1950. For two and a half weeks he and Laura, still fragile from the birth of her seventh child (another boy, called Septimus) in July, stayed at the Plaza in New York. With no lectures booked and Evelyn's popularity at a peak, particularly in Catholic circles after the publication in *Life* of his article, 'The American Epoch in the Catholic Church', they could give themselves over to being lionised on a grand scale. *Life* had been delighted with the piece, and the Luces made a great fuss of its author, Clare Luce in particular declaring a passionate interest in the subject. When she came to London, Evelyn put himself out to return her hospitality, giving a dinner at Tom Burns's house for her to meet distinguished co-religionists. 'Clare Luce was very much gratified

537

by the hospitality shown her by Evelyn on her visit last week,'
Pam Berry reported to Nancy, adding drily, 'She sees Evelyn in a
quaint Catholic light as a noble gentle person who is capable, oh
yes, from time to time of naughty spitefullness, but who is on the
whole a saintly, good person healed and beatified by the Church.
What do you know about that?'

Evelyn's last visit to America coincided with the appearance of
his novel *Helena*, which his presence in New York did much to
publicise. He always claimed that *Helena* was his favourite, the
best of his novels: 'It's far the best book I have ever written or
ever will write,' he told Christopher Sykes. Many of his admirers
on the contrary regarded it as an embarrassing aberration, a
distasteful mix of slangy girls' school adventure with an emotional
sanctimoniousness; a number of Catholics of more liberal persuasion were made uneasy, too, by the emphasis on the importance of the relic, and its miraculous properties.

With what turned out to be only slight exaggeration, Evelyn
when he began work on the book had informed Ronald Knox
that he was starting on 'an unhistorical life of St Helena which
absolutely no one will be able to bear'. To its author, however,
the project was the fulfilment of a long-held pious intention – the
idea had first come to him in 1935 when visiting Jerusalem on
the way back from Abyssinia – not only to write the life of a saint,
but to bring to the novel-reading public the literal historical truth
of the founding of the Christian Church as manifested in the
discovery of a simple piece of wood, the true cross. *Helena* is a
short novel, but the writing of it was spread over five years, from
May 1945 to the spring of 1950. The third and fourth centuries
AD, the early Christians, the Roman Empire under Constantine,
were unfamiliar territory, and Evelyn was exceptionally anxious to
do his subject justice. He turned to his friend and ex-Commando
colleague, the Jewish writer Robert Henriques. For help with
Jewish history, and for material on St Helena herself and the
stories of the finding of the cross he consulted the Jesuit scholar,
Father Philip Caraman, recently appointed editor of the *Month*.

With so little known about the early life of the empress, Evelyn
was able to shape her story very much as he pleased, choosing
from the wealth of varying legend to make her the daughter of

a British chieftain, King Coel. The portrayal of Helena in girlhood
– brusque, down-to-earth and mad about horses – was closely
based on Penelope Betjeman, to whom the book is dedicated. 'I
am writing about her [Penelope's] life under the disguise of St
Helena's,' he told John Betjeman. 'She is 16, sexy, full of horse
fantasies. I want to get this right. Will you tell her to write to me
fully about adolescent sex reveries connected with riding. I have
no experience of such things, nor has Laura. I make her always
the horse & the consummation when the rider subdues her. Is
this correct?' For Penelope herself he had further questions. Was
it likely, for instance, that Helena would have lost her interest in
horses after her marriage? 'I describe her as hunting in the
morning after her wedding night feeling the saddle as comforting
her wounded maidenhead. Is that OK?' Keenly interested, Penelope responded with enthusiasm. 'Personally I found it very difficult to separate sex & religion after I married & frequently used
to drive a severely-bitted carriage horse in flights of fancy with
an Anglo or Roman priest seated at my side.' But as always, Evelyn
had difficulty writing of the erotic, and the results were far from
satisfactory. Helena, when 'her womanhood broke bud', is
described on the morning after her wedding night as sitting
astride '[while] the saddle-tree solaced her manmade hurt . . .'

The first three chapters of *Helena* were published in the *Tablet*
in December 1945. Unsure at this point whether he should continue with the book, Evelyn consulted Douglas Woodruff. 'Of
course you must go on with St Helena,' Woodruff assured him.
'Ronnie Knox says it is the only book . . . he has ever read which
gave him the feeling of what upper class 3rd century life was
like.'

But although scrupulously researched, *Helena* evokes in almost
every line not the third but the twentieth century. Part of the
trouble is the idiomatic informality of the dialogue. Helena in
the schoolroom is a pert miss who talks to her tutor in language
more suitable to the nursery at Madresfield. ' "What a lark!" said
Princess Helena. "What a sell! Can't you just see Menelaus ramp-
ing and raging about and being smacked on the back by everyone
and Agamemnon pompously declaring him the winner? And
there was Helen tucked up with Paris all the time. Oh, what
sucks!" ' Even in dignified old age, she is given to fits of giggles,
and to using words like 'beastly' and 'bosh'; when announcing

her intention to search for the cross, she sounds for all the world like one of the Famous Five with torch and cocoa setting off to find the smugglers' cave: ' "I bet He's just waiting for one of us to go and find it . . . Just at this moment when everyone is forgetting it and chattering about the hypostatic union, there's a solid chunk of wood waiting for them to have their silly heads knocked against. I'm going off to find it," said Helena.' Her son, the Emperor Constantine, comes straight out of the Hypocrites' Club, referring to Rome as 'a perfectly beastly place', and like a third-century Brian Howard talking of the green wig he wears while giving audience as 'just a little thing I popped on this morning. I have quite a collection. You must ask to see them. Some of them are *very* pretty.'

All this sits awkwardly with the reverential tone adopted for the great Christian theme that lies at the foundations of the story. Helena is a saint because 'she had completely conformed to the will of God. Others a few years back had done their duty gloriously in the arena. Hers was a gentler task, merely to gather wood. That was the particular, humble purpose for which she had been created. And now it was done.' That is the book's message, simply stated. Less simply stated is the progress of the spread of Christianity through the empire, described as 'a great wind of prayer [that] gathered and mounted, lifted the whole squat smoky dome of the Ancient World, swept it off and up like the thatch of a stable, and threw open the calm and brilliant prospect of measureless space.' The description of the evolution of the holy city, from the fall of Imperial Rome to the dawn of the Renaissance, could be the work of the very same 'tosh-horse' that according to Evelyn had galloped with such damaging effect through Cyril Connolly's *The Unquiet Grave*.[14] Constantine's Rome, corrupt and riddled with cranky cults and heretical sects, was, he says, not beautiful: 'Beauty would come later . . . She was on the way, far distant still, saddling under the paling stars for the huge journey of more than a thousand years. Beauty would come in her own time, capricious, adorable wanderer, and briefly make her home on the seven hills.'

Helena appeared in October 1950, under the customary imprint

[14] Connolly's style, said Waugh, sometimes resembles that of a woman novelist, 'a terror, rattling with clichés . . . [and] giving full rein to the tosh-horse whose hooves thunder through the penultimate passages'.

of Chapman & Hall in London and Little, Brown in the United States. *Time* complained that, 'Waugh's sky-blue prose goes purple with emotion,' the *Times Literary Supplement* disliked 'the Angela Brazil accent', while John Raymond in the *New Statesman* gave it as his opinion that 'Waugh has done nothing in this book that he has not done as well or better elsewhere ... While Graham Greene's characters make the frontal approach to Catholicism – undergoing the betrayal on the pier or the Pascalian agony in the shrubbery – Waugh's converts generally get to Heaven the back way through having the right kind of nanny.' In his biography of Waugh, Christopher Sykes writes that 'The indifferent reception given to what Evelyn believed to be by far his best book was the greatest disappointment of his whole literary life.' In a sense and because of the sanctity of its subject, *Helena* appeared to its author closer to the fulfilling of his vocation even than *Brideshead*. No wonder, then, that the opinion of the critics was disappointing.

Undaunted by hostile reviews, the Luces declared themselves impressed, and on the strength of it commissioned Evelyn to write a series of articles on the holy places of the Near East. Evelyn welcomed the commission: it gave him the chance of a temporary escape from 'Welfaria', from Piers Court and the children, and an opportunity to visit the great shrines before it was too late. 'There is so much to see before the next war obliterates it all. I don't want to be caught again as I was in 1939 with so much not visited.'

Burrowing ever deeper
into the rock

During the decade 1951 to 1961 Evelyn, like his alter ego, Gilbert
Pinfold, 'burrowed ever deeper into the rock'. Moving farther
from the centre, he left Gloucestershire for a house in the west
country; he made fewer visits to London. Although only in his
fifties Evelyn, like his father before him, began to accentuate the
attitudes and posture of an old man. In his writing he was capable
still of great achievement, completing the trilogy eventually published in one volume as *The Sword of Honour*, described by Cyril
Connolly as 'unquestionably the finest novels to have come out
of the war'.

Paradoxically, while these works showed him to be at the height
of his powers, his reputation began to decline: newspapers were
less receptive to his suggestions for articles, and his stance of
unrelenting hostility toward the new wave in literature, the 'Angry
Young Men', encouraged younger critics to regard him as a crusty
old has-been.

In the *Pelican Guide to English Literature*, widely used in schools
and universities in the 1950s and '60s, Waugh was categorised as
a curiosity. 'Even though he still writes, [Waugh] offers mainly a
period interest. He is essentially a pre-war novelist, and the post-
war interest in him is a kind of hang-over, a nostalgic reaction,
socially, but not critically, interesting.' Contrary as ever, Evelyn

might well have taken this as a compliment. With his almost Manichean view of the world, he saw little to admire. He was contemptuous of the new 'teddy-boy school' of novelists, such as John Wain, John Braine and Kingsley Amis (or 'Ames', as he affected to believe the name should be pronounced); was outraged by the new informality in dress and manners; appalled when sockets for electric razors appeared in the bedrooms of the Hyde Park Hotel.

He had little interest in politics – 'I have never voted in a parliamentary election . . . I do not aspire to advise my sovereign in her choice of servants' – but continued to inveigh against the prevailing liberal opinion, in particular the Tories' energetically promoted Welfare State and Classless Society. Referring to Butler's Education Act, which according to Evelyn 'provided for the free distribution of university degrees to the deserving poor', he wrote in *Encounter*, 'I could make your flesh creep by telling you about the new wave of philistinism with which we are threatened by these sour young people who are coming off the assembly lines in their hundreds every year and finding employment as critics, even as poets and novelists.'

Only the Church, rock-solid and unchanging, could not fail him. When a new pope, John XXIII, was elected in 1958, Evelyn wrote contentedly, 'A most trustworthy man and good for 25 years placid inactivity.' In this assumption he could not have been more wrong.

It was in order to fulfil a long-held ambition of a book about the early Church that in January 1951 Evelyn, accompanied by Christopher Sykes, left for a tour of the Christian shrines of the Middle East, a project which, like *Helena*, he had had in mind since his first visit to Jerusalem in 1935. Clare and Henry Luce, undaunted by hostile reviews, had been impressed by *Helena*, and commissioned articles for *Life* from both Waugh and Sykes, agreeing to pay all expenses.

Their route took them via Paris and Rome, where Evelyn had long talks at the Vatican about a cherished plan, never to be fulfilled, of consecrating a private chapel in the grounds of Piers Court. From Rome they visited Damascus and Beirut, then Tel Aviv and Jerusalem, 'the most sacred city in the world'. Here they kept an all-night vigil in the Church of the Holy Sepulchre, an intensely moving experience. 'One fully realizes, perhaps for the first time, that Christianity did not strike its first root at Rome or Canterbury or Geneva or Maynooth, but here in the Levant where everything is inextricably mixed and nothing is assimilated.' For Sykes to fulfil his journalistic obligations – an article on Turkey – they continued to Ankara and Istanbul, returning home at the end of February. The result of the expedition was a long essay which appeared in *Life* in the United States, in the *Month* in England, and was then published in a limited edition in book form under the title *The Holy Places*[1] by the Queen Anne Press in London at the end of 1952.

For Christopher Sykes the expedition remained 'a happy memory' – much happier, for example, than the ill-fated trip to Paris two years before, ending in Evelyn's epic quarrel with the Coopers at Chantilly. Then as now, Sykes had acted as 'jagger', the term coined all those years ago at Madresfield to mean a useful friend, someone prepared to render services as well as act as agreeable companion. 'Christopher is being a <u>fairly</u> good jagger,' Evelyn wrote to Laura from Jerusalem.

On the Paris trip it was Evelyn who paid, Sykes who made all the arrangements and acted as courier, as he did again in the Middle East. For although a member of an old Catholic family which was wealthy and distinguished, Christopher was a younger son and never had any money. After Oxford he had gone briefly into the diplomatic service, before becoming a modestly success-ful writer and journalist, for some years working for the BBC. Married to Camilla, beautiful daughter of Russell Pasha, Sykes was intelligent, congenial, and towards those he considered his superiors, of whom Evelyn was undoubtedly one, inclined to be sycophantic. In their letters the two men adopted a kind of schoolboy banter, addressing each other as 'Darling', 'Wildblood', 'Madge', 'My little man'. Before leaving for the holy places, Evelyn had sent Christopher a postcard. 'I know what it is you want to say where you can have women in your rooms you filthy beast well you wont not with me see we are going somewhere respect-able with no goings on except a game of cards with a crook or

---

[1] *The Holy Places*, with engravings by Reynolds Stone, included also an essay on 'St Helena Empress'.

maybe a bit of buggery but no filthiness with women while I am around please make up your mind to that.'

As writers and Catholics, both men were fascinated by their fellow writer and Catholic, Graham Greene, or 'Grisjambon Vert', as they referred to him between themselves. In character and principle, the slippery, sin-haunted Greene was in almost every respect the polar opposite of Waugh. 'Of course I don't often agree with you,' Evelyn once wrote to him. 'I can never hope to do that this side of death.' The two men admired each other's work (Waugh's style, said Greene, was like the Mediterranean before the war: so clear you could see right down to the bottom); they understood each other's sense of humour, and remained friends for life, although Greene's theological 'impropriety' imposed an increasing strain. Evelyn felt little sympathy for Greene's left-wing politics or free-wheeling sexuality, could never share his prurient interest in the louche, the lavatorial, the squalid, the morally sick. Greene's fascination for the underside of life sat uneasily with a wincing fastidiousness that led him into an attitude of lofty detachment, of distaste for a world for which he felt small affection and no hope. Evelyn, on the other hand, in spite of his self-loathing and melancholia, was always energetically engaged, took his place in the arena.

Despite these differences, Evelyn recognised in Greene a number of important traits similar to his own: for both their faith, although vastly different in interpretation, was crucial; they were both as writers ruthlessly self-protective; they were both in different ways consummate performers, Greene's mysterious loner as polished and deliberate an act as Evelyn's belligerent clown; they both liked to drink, and they were both martyrs to boredom. Evelyn told Nancy of an occasion when Graham came to stay at Piers Court and was so bored that, like Bendrix in *The End of the Affair*, he was reduced to 'patrolling the built up areas round Dursley noting the numbers of motor-cars. He takes omens from them.'

Their religious differences were irreconcilable. When Greene published *The Heart of the Matter*, Evelyn wrote a long review provocatively entitled 'Felix Culpa?'

Is Scobie damned? . . . It is the central question of *The Heart of the Matter.* I believe that Mr Greene thinks him a saint . . . He

[Scobie] dies believing himself damned but also in an obscure
way – at least in a way that is obscure to me – believing that
he is offering his damnation as a loving sacrifice for others . . .
To me the idea of willing my own damnation for the love of God
is either a very loose poetical expression or a mad blasphemy,
for the God who accepted that sacrifice could be neither just
nor lovable.

Greene denied that he regarded Scobie as a saint, and Evelyn
wrote a letter to the *Tablet* revising his opinion. 'A careful re-
reading of *The Heart of the Matter* has convinced me that I was
quite wrong in supposing that Mr Greene anywhere imputes
sanctity to his hero . . .' But that was far from the end of a
long-running dialogue, culminating in Evelyn's accusation on the
publication of *A Burnt-Out Case* that Greene had made a recan-
tation of his faith.

By and large, however, the attitude towards each other's work
was more relaxed. Christopher Sykes was present at an occasion
when Greene was outlining the plot of *The Quiet American*. 'It will
be a relief not to write about God for a change!'

'Oh?' Evelyn replied. 'I wouldn't drop God, if I were you. Not
at this stage anyway. It would be like P. G. Wodehouse dropping
Jeeves halfway through the Wooster series.'

At the end of the summer of 1951, Evelyn suggested that
Graham Greene with Catherine Walston should spend a few quiet
days at Piers Court, warning Greene that with Laura in Portofino
and the servants on holiday he must be prepared for all the
discomforts of a 'Swiss Family Robinson life'. He told him, too,
that he himself was hard at work. Having first accepted, then
rejected proposals for lives of St Thomas More and St Ignatius
Loyola, Evelyn had returned to fiction. 'I am writing an interminable novel about army life, obsessed by memories of military
dialogue.'

The novel, *Men at Arms*, was originally intended to be part of
a four or five volume series. Under the working title, *Honour*, it
was begun in June 1951, while Evelyn was staying at Chantilly,
first at an hotel on his own, then at the Château St Firmin with
the Coopers. 'Yesterday I spent reading all my war diaries &
recapturing the atmosphere of those days,' he told Laura. 'Today
I began writing & it came easy.' Soon he was producing up

to 4000 words a day, charting the work's progress in letters to friends. 'Unreadable & endless. Nothing but tippling in officers' messes and drilling on barrack squares. No demon sex. No blood or thunder . . . In poor taste, mostly about WCs and very very dull . . . Book gets longer and more and more facetious. Practical jokes now and chemical closets and clap.'

In January 1952 it was finished and dispatched to Jack Mc-Dougall at Chapman & Hall, who was full of praise. But Evelyn was uneasy about it. 'I have finished that novel – slogging, inelegant, boring,' he told Nancy. 'What little point it has will only be revealed in the fourth volume at least four years hence.' His anxiety may have been due to the fact that *Men at Arms* was a fresh departure, drawing heavily on his own unvarnished experiences, more overtly autobiographical than anything written before. The book, he said, had been composed 'instinctively . . . I did not know why I felt impelled to introduce certain incidents or place them as I did.'

But although both the action of the novel and its setting faithfully reproduce the early stages of Evelyn's war – the initial, euphoric period with the Marines at Chatham, the dismal conditions at Deal and Kingsdown, the abortive attack on Dakar – the protagonist, Guy Crouchback, is not Evelyn; although there are certain similarities, Guy with his arid piety and emotional detachment more nearly resembles Graham Greene, his passivity and helplessness recalling the passivity of Waugh's early heroes, Paul Pennyfeather and Adam Fenwick-Symes. Middle-aged, Catholic, Guy has been lonely and without direction since his divorce eight years previously, and sees in the outbreak of war the chance to prove himself, to belong. With the forming of the Russian–German alliance he is able to feel a whole-hearted commitment to the coming conflict. 'The enemy at last was plain in view . . . Whatever the outcome there was a place for him in that battle.' After a number of rejections, Guy eventually finds a place with the Royal Corps of Halberdiers, and it is here he falls in love with what he perceives as the military ideal, with the tradition, the ceremony, the noble brotherhood. Much of the narrative tension derives from the contrast of Guy's naïvety, his almost schoolboy infatuation with a chivalric image, and the coarse, mundane realities of service life in a modern army controlled by a 'vast uniformed and bemedalled bureaucracy'. Guy's final disenchantment takes place during the Dakar fiasco, when at the last moment the order to attack is cancelled, and the reaction of the men on board ship is predominantly one of shamefaced relief.

Among Guy's colleagues are two of Waugh's most brilliant comic creations, Apthorpe[2] and Brigadier Ritchie-Hook. Apthorpe is a close relation of the appalling Atwater in *Work Suspended*, as Waugh himself admitted in a letter to Cyril Connolly. 'There is a strong affinity between the two characters – tho Atwater was a blackguard, which Apthorpe was not.' Like Atwater, Apthorpe is a ludicrous combination of touchiness and conceit, a conceit which materialises in an eccentric form of boastfulness. 'It would be a travesty to say that Guy suspected Apthorpe of lying. His claims to distinction – porpoise-skin boots, a High Church aunt in Tunbridge Wells, a friend who was on good terms with gorillas – were not what an impostor would invent in order to impress. Yet there was about Apthorpe a sort of fundamental implausibility . . .' Apthorpe is irresistible in his pomposity and pretentiousness, his success as a comic figure no doubt owing much to the fact that his great original had been a fixture in Evelyn's imagination since boyhood: 'Apthorpe giggled slightly at his cleverness like Mr Toad in *The Wind in the Willows*.' Among his strange impedimenta is a 'thunderbox', an antiquated field latrine, of which he is fiercely protective; and it is this pantomime property that brings him into direct conflict with the wily and terrifying brigadier. In appearance, with his black patch over one eye, Ritchie-Hook resembles a piratical version of General Carton de Wiart, but in character he is a line-by-line portrait of Evelyn's brigade commander, Brigadier St Clair Morford. Morford's is the mad courage, ferocious manner ('the Brigadier's eye teeth flashed like a questing tiger's'), the love of 'biffing', the passion for practical jokes. 'For this remarkable warrior the image of war was not hunting or shooting; it was the wet sponge on the door,

---

[2] There was a Reginald Apthorpe in the same form as Evelyn at Lancing; and in 'Charles Ryder's Schooldays', closely based on Waugh's schooldays, Apthorpe is Ryder's house-captain. ' "Get on with your work, Ryder," said Apthorpe. "Apthorpe has greased into being a house-captain this term," Charles wrote [in his diary]. "This is his first evening school. He is being thoroughly officious and on his dignity." '

the hedgehog in the bed; or, rather, he saw war itself as a prodigious booby trap.'[3]

In *Men at Arms,* as in *Brideshead,* the dominant theme, unre-
solved until the final volume of the trilogy, is that of the regener-
ation of faith. Caught up in what he sees as a glorious cause, Guy
is temporarily shaken from the apathy which had descended upon
him after the break-up of his marriage; but still he feels unable
to communicate with God. 'It was as though eight years back he
had suffered a tiny stroke of paralysis; all his spiritual faculties
were just perceptibly impaired ... Into that wasteland where his
soul languished he need not, could not, enter.' In contrast to
Guy's spiritual sterility is the firm faith of his father, old Mr
Crouchback. Head of an ancient and distinguished recusant
family, Crouchback senior is presented as the epitome of lay
saintliness, gentle, dignified and good. Having given up his great
house, Broome, 'almost unique in contemporary England, having
been held in uninterrupted male succession since the reign of
Henry I', he is living in rooms in a seaside hotel, accepting
uncomplainingly the fall in his fortunes brought about by war.
He is described as a man of tolerance, courtesy and humility, a
man (and this, too, is presented as an estimable quality) possessed
of an overweening family pride. 'He was quite without class consciousness because he saw the whole intricate social structure of
his country divided neatly into two unequal and unmistakable
parts.

On one side stood the Crouchbacks and certain inconspicuous,
anciently allied families; on the other side stood the rest of mankind.' Although to some Mr Crouchback appeared a smug, sancti-
monious old snob ('I don't like Crouchback's father,' Tony Powell
told Evelyn, 'and was sorry that he was not turned out of his
room'), to his creator he is entirely admirable, a noble representative 'of the decencies and true purpose of life'.

His father's adamantine faith is a support to Guy. It is Mr

[3] An ex-Commando colleague, General Sir Alan Bourne, wrote to Evelyn after
he had read the novel, 'a Gunner Lieut: Colonel told me that Morford was
the bravest man he had ever met – that he (the Colonel) had commanded a
battery in support of the R[oyal]. M[arines]. in Gallipoli & that he was always
having to open fire because Morford had started some "hate". He said that if
the Marines were not attacking, Morford attached himself to any unit that was
doing so, & if none were attacking he went up to the front line and played "Life
on the Ocean Wave" to irritate the Turks into attacking.'

Crouchback who sounded the warning note over Guy's 'dis-honourable' marriage to the non-Catholic Virginia: 'Poor Guy, picked a wrong 'un.' It is his father's holy medal that Guy wears round his neck, which, it is implied, saves him from danger. One night in his hotel in London Guy runs into his ex-wife; by the laws of his faith Virginia is the one woman in the world he can make love to without sin, she his only chance of perpetuating the name of Crouchback. But his attempts at love-making are constantly interrupted (Apthorpe drunk on the telephone), and Virginia, suddenly seeing what Guy is up to, leaves him in disgust. 'Tears of rage and humiliation were flowing unresisted. "I thought you'd taken a fancy to me again and wanted a bit of fun for the sake of old times. I thought you'd chosen me specially, and by God you had. Because I was the only woman in the whole world your priests would let you go to bed with. That was my attraction. You wet, smug, obscene, pompous, sexless, lunatic pig." '

The intention behind this scene, described with unparalleled artistry, remains ambiguous. Virginia is flighty, promiscuous, amoral and agnostic; and yet it is not *her* behaviour that shocks us, it is Guy's, acceptable though it is in the eyes of the Church. As Nancy Mitford perceptively remarked, 'You see women through a glass darkly don't you?'

For all her many failings, Virginia is treated with compassion, a quality for which up to now Waugh's fiction had not been conspicuous. When the book was published in the autumn of 1952,[4] some critics regretted this new mellowness, feeling that it detracted from the old *saeva indignatio*, an opinion shared by John Raymond in the *New Statesman* – '*Men at Arms* is good-tempered Waugh – and therefore Waugh at his second best' – and Cyril Connolly in the *Sunday Times*: '[*Men at Arms*] describes what [Mr Waugh] has called the "honeymoon period of his love-affair with the Army" . . . Since it is a honeymoon he is unexpectedly gentle and good-tempered . . . For the first time I found myself bored by the central section of a Waugh novel.' Some objected, as they had with *Brideshead*, to the portrayal of an élitist society. 'If one had no other information on the subject . . . [the novel] would convince one that the Second World War occurred solely to rescue Englishmen from boredom and decadence,' wrote

---

[4] By Chapman & Hall in London, and Little, Brown in Boston.

Delmore Schwartz in *Partisan Review*. Others found Guy 'a sad sack', and were irritated by the manner in which Waugh treated his religion as '[a] huge prep school conspiracy of the faithful, that seeming wish to depict Mother Church as one Big Dorm and her mysteries as so much sacred larking'. There were plenty of enthusiasts, however, plenty who agreed with the critic in *Time* that, 'If [Waugh's] trilogy continues as well as it has begun, it will be the best British novel of World War II.'

Friends as usual were complimentary. Christopher Sykes, to whom *Men at Arms* is dedicated, told Evelyn that he admired the book extravagantly, although he qualified this statement elsewhere. Harold Acton too was highly flattering, while Martin D'Arcy was among those who remarked on the new charitable tone. 'Whereas you have been so outstanding as a satirist in former books, now you write as one who sees the good and lovable in what is imperfect.'

Nancy Mitford, who recently had been bewailing her difficulties in thinking up a plot – 'I do think Catholic writers have that advantage, the story is always there to hand, will he won't he will he won't he will he save his soul? Now don't be cross...' – was as ever cheerfully enthusiastic. She did, however, make some pertinent observations. 'I love the way English Roman Catholics are exactly as snobbish as middle European princes' and 'Was it wise to kill off Apthorpe?'

Evelyn cared less for the judgment of professional critics than for the opinions of his friends, fellow-writers whom he considered his peers. Henry Yorke had been such a one. They had read each other's novels with interest and discussed them at length. But now mysteriously Evelyn turned against the Yorkes. He had much disliked Henry's recent fiction, describing *Loving* as 'obscene', *Doting* as 'pitiable', and confessing he thought 'nothing of *Nothing*'. When, in May 1951, the Yorkes spent a weekend at Piers Court it was clear Evelyn disliked the man as much as his work. 'Henry is decrepid, deaf, toothless, dirty (both morally & physically) disloyal to the Royal Family, long haired, ill dressed. I think he is a communist. He smokes as he eats ... I was very sad to see old friends falling so low.' To Bloggs Baldwin, Evelyn wrote, 'I hate the Yorkes now after twenty-five years friendship.'

Towards the end of Evelyn's life there was an attempt at reconciliation: again the Yorkes were invited to stay, but the occasion (described by Heywood Hill to Nancy Mitford) was no happier than before.

> Henry had looked out of the window and seen Evelyn planting an ivy garden all wrong, and Henry had told him so, and Evelyn hadn't slept all night. Then at luncheon the next day Henry said to Laura, would it be all right for him and Dig to smoke in the middle. Laura said it would be all right for them but not for her, which Henry said he ought to have taken as a warning. So they lit up, and then suddenly there was a crash as Evelyn swept all the china from the table, saying he could not endure people who smoked at meals and they must have been mixing with Jews in New York . . . After that he retired to his library and they never saw him again.

Unpredictable in his irrational hostilities, Evelyn was also capable of lasting loyalty. In spite of the fearsome obstacles he often placed in their paths, many of Evelyn's old friendships meant a great deal to him, even when as sometimes happened they no longer held much attraction. He continued to keep closely in touch with Maimie Lygon long after she had become not only impoverished but simple-minded. Olivia Plunket Greene was another pathetic figure to whom he was kind. He had met her again during the war when staying with Daphne Bath; Olivia and her mother were living in a cottage belonging to Henry Bath on the Longleat estate. 'I went to call . . . on your cousin Olivia Greene,' Evelyn had told Laura, '& found her with no trousers on completely drunk and Gwen blacking the grate.' The Greenes were now desperately poor, and Olivia was alcoholic, mentally unbalanced and in the grip of a religious mania which she managed somehow to combine with an eccentric form of communism. Relentlessly she wrote Evelyn long, crazy letters, to which he replied with patience and affection.

Terence Greenidge was another indigent figure from the past to whom Evelyn continued to write and occasionally send money. Greenidge, impoverished and debilitated, was still acting, dependent on walk-on parts in Shakespeare at Stratford-upon-Avon. 'Quite happy, quite uninteresting', Evelyn wrote to Maurice

Bowra. 'The doctors did that operation on him which removes a part of the brain and all idiosyncracy.'

With *Men at Arms* completed, Evelyn returned to a story he had begun two years before about a young man working in 'the euthanasia trade'. *Love Among the Ruins* is a nasty little tale set in a dystopia of the near future, interesting solely as a reflection of the author's prejudices, his hatred of 'progress', of politicians, psychoanalysis, abstract art, functional architecture and all branches of the Welfare State. His protagonist, Miles Plastic, is the epitome of the Modern Man. Educated by the State at an enormous cost, '[a sum] which, fifty years earlier, would have sent whole quiversful of boys to Winchester and New College', Miles works in the Department for Euthanasia, providing a service for which there is an overwhelming demand among a godless and proletarian population. Miles falls in love with Clara, a young ballet dancer, who as an unfortunate side-effect of an operation for sterilisation has grown a luxuriant beard. To have this removed, she undergoes a second operation, during 'Santa-Claus-Tide', after which Miles visits her in hospital.

> 'He's taken off all the skin and put on a wonderful new
> substance, a sort of synthetic rubber that takes grease-paint
> perfectly,' Clara tells him excitedly. 'Look, feel it.'
>   She sat up in bed, joyful and proud.
>   Her eyes and brow were all that was left of the loved face.
> Below it something quite unhuman, a tight, slippery mask,
> salmon pink . . . Miles retched unobtrusively.

Chapman & Hall published *Love Among the Ruins* in 1953, but it never appeared on its own in book form in the United States, and was turned down by *Life, Atlantic Monthly, Collier's, Esquire, Ladies Home Journal, Harper's Bazaar, Saturday Evening Post*, and the *New Yorker*, the latter voicing the consensus by describing it as 'unfunny and disagreeable'. Evelyn was not unduly distressed, admitting to Peters that he knew the work was not of the highest standard, and later telling Graham Greene that the book had been a bit of nonsense, 'hastily finished & injudiciously published. But I don't think it quite as bad as most reviewers do.'

The failure of *Love Among the Ruins* may have left its author relatively unmoved, but it did him little good in the market-place. The enormous success of *Brideshead* had resulted in a long and lucrative period of celebrity. Evelyn had been a star, but now his star was in decline. Out of step with the times, he had, too, antagonised many of his regular employers by his truculence: an in-house memorandum at the BBC noted, 'Waugh is almost impervious to suggestions . . . His sense of his own importance makes production especially difficult . . . N. B. He demands a very high fee.' But high fees were harder to come by, and Evelyn's preoccupation with Catholic affairs was not, outside the sectarian press, shared by a large readership. At the end of 1952, for instance, entirely on his own initiative he undertook a pilgrimage to Goa, that distant outpost of the faith, to see the final exposition of the relics of St Francis Xavier, a sixteenth-century Jesuit priest whose body until the eighteenth century had remained miraculously uncorrupt. On his return he found little interest in his long article on the subject: not only was it rejected by such mainstream publications as the *Sunday Times* and the *New Yorker*, but by small specialist magazines such as *History Today*, and by the Catholic journals, the *Tablet* and the *Universe*.[5] *Life*, under the influence of Mrs Luce usually so receptive to Catholic subjects, turned it down – but then Evelyn had managed to offend even the powerful Luces. '[Harry] did not appreciate your telling Merton you purposely did your poorest work for *Life*, I can tell you!' Clare Luce wrote to him. 'I expect he won't ask you to do any more, which will be, I gather, a relief for both of you.'

Such antagonistic behaviour was badly timed, for Evelyn's return from Goa coincided with a period of serious financial crisis. In the diary for 16 January 1953, he wrote, 'The editor of *Good Housekeeping* tried to dun me for an advance. My Goan article unpublished. My story [*Love Among the Ruins*] unsold in America.'

Good Housekeeping in the United States had been publishing Evelyn's work since before the war. On his visit to New York in 1947, Evelyn had called on the editor, Herbert Mayes, who had offered him a generous $4000 advance for a short story. Evelyn demurred on the grounds that he had no story in mind and

---

[5] 'Goa: the Home of a Saint' was eventually taken by Evelyn's devoted admirer, Father Caraman, editor of the *Month*, who was allowed to run it for nothing in the issue of December 1953.

could not guarantee being able to provide one the magazine would consider suitable. 'Well it won't break us if you don't,' said Mayes. 'We're easy people to do business with. Maybe in two-five years you'll write us something.' The money had been paid over, half in the form of a new car, delivered in Ireland to avoid tax. Now more than five years had passed, no story acceptable to the magazine had been written, and Mayes was acting tough, threatening to sue for the return of his advance. Evelyn was incensed, believing that Mayes was reneging on the terms of the agreement. At first he refused even to consider repayment, but Peters convinced him that his position was vulnerable, and in the end with extreme reluctance he agreed to refund half the sum.

Angry with Mayes, he was even angrier with his New York agent, Harold Matson, who had been present at the original interview and whom he held responsible for the 'blackmail'. 'The time has come to employ another agent in America,' he told Peters. 'Can you, please, arrange this for me or must I make my own arrangements?' Peters tried to pacify his client, explaining that it would be difficult to find another agent of equal calibre, and persuading him to stay with Matson for the time being. To Matson himself Peters reported his efforts with some pride, only to be unexpectedly rebuffed: it was Matson who wanted to be rid of Waugh. Matson was tired of the insults and had been deeply offended by the implications of the *Good Housekeeping* affair; he was tired, too, of being considered as little more than a purveyor of cigars – a box packed up and sent every week from his office to Evelyn in England – and the falling income from Waugh's work no longer made this troublesome author worth the considerable attentions he demanded. The affair ended with Waugh parting company with Matson, to the satisfaction of both sides, and transferring his business to Helen Strauss at the William Morris Agency.

The year which had started badly continued worse. Bored by business, Evelyn left his financial affairs to Peters and to his accountant, Percy Popkin. Laura had a small income of her own, and Peters's office held Evelyn's earnings for him, transferring sums to his account as he required, spreading his income as evenly as possible over the financial year, and where possible keeping within the limits necessary to avoid the highest rates of taxation. It was a simple procedure and Evelyn rarely gave it much thought. But in January 1950, he had had a shock. 'For

555

some time I have been aware that I seemed to be in easier circumstances than most of my friends,' he told Nancy,

> & accounted for it with saws like 'solvency is a matter of temperament' and by thinking of all the nuns who are praying for me, bringing me in pounds when I give them shillings, and so on. Well last week I said to Laura 'are you sure you aren't over-drawn at the bank?' 'No, I don't think so. I'm sure they'd tell me, if I were.' 'Well do ask'. So she did and, my dear, she had an overdraft of £6,420 which had been quietly mounting up for years. There is no possible way to pay it off, as her capital is in trust and for me to earn that much more, I should have to earn about 150,000 and we cannot possibly spend less although for three years we have been spending 2,000 more than our income . . . Well its a sad prospect isn't it. I shall have to go to prison but that is hell nowadays with wireless & lectures & psychiatry. Oh for the Marshalsea.

On this occasion the crisis was averted by Peters, who came up with an ingenious scheme. Having recently negotiated a £1000 deal with Penguin for the republication of ten of the novels, he suggested that this money be paid into a trust theoretically for the benefit of the children. 'You save tax, ensure their future to some extent, and can also draw on the income for the Trust for their education and maintenance if the Deed is skilfully drawn up.' Jocularly referred to as the Save the Children Fund, the trust was drawn up by a solicitor, Wilfrid Ariel Evill of Evill & Coleman, with Peters and Evill as joint trustees. Into the trust were to be paid all revenue from books already published, with Evelyn's personal income provided by his future writings and any money earned in America. In fact Evelyn, with the trustees' permission, could draw on the fund very much as he pleased, using it to buy pictures, books, silver, furniture, anything that could, however loosely, be regarded as 'investment', even selling to the trust his manuscripts when he needed to release tax-free capital. So attractive was the arrangement that Evelyn soon came to look on the fund as bottomless, and money which should have been regarded as insurance against lean times in the future was spent with abandon almost as soon as it was paid in.

But then came cause for further anxiety. The Inland Revenue inspector in Stroud began to show an unwelcome interest in Waugh's affairs. Having conducted a thorough investigation, he was now pressing for unpaid supertax on all film contracts made since 1944, a considerable sum. 'I am in financial depths from which I see no light & need your advice greatly,' Evelyn appealed to Peters in January 1952. 'Could you . . . come for a night (or longer) any time between 13th and 23rd?' After his visit Peters wrote a letter strongly recommending a programme of serious retrenchment: if Evelyn could reduce his annual expenditure to £4000 the situation could be saved. 'The reduction of your standard of living need not be quite so drastic as you think. You should be able to keep a reasonable staff to run the house and still come out square. The hardest thing of all is to pay back income tax out of current earnings. That is practically impossible.' This sensible advice was listened to, and for a time stern economies were imposed. The five servants were dismissed and replaced by two daily cleaning women from the village.

> The trouble is getting servants to go . . . But go they shall, if I
> have to burn the house down [Evelyn told Nancy]. I shall never
> wear a clean collar again or subscribe to Royal Lifeboat Fund
> and I shall steal peoples books & sell them . . . It is no good
> trying to live decently in modern England. I make £10,000 a
> year, which used to be thought quite a lot, I live like a mouse in
> shabby-genteel circumstances, I keep no women or horses or
> yachts, yet I am bankrupt, simply by the politicians buying votes
> with my money.

If prepared temporarily to economise at home, Evelyn saw no need to extend such austerities further afield, continuing to spend extravagantly on his visits to London and to travel where he wished. During the winter months he suffered painfully from arthritis, and whenever he could arranged to spend the early part of the year abroad. He asked Christopher Sykes to accompany him in March 1952 on a tour of Sicily, but that dependable old jagger had grown wary. 'I had noticed a change coming over Evelyn lately,' Sykes recalled in his memoir. 'He was becoming more arrogant, more quarrelsome, and indulged his horrible delight in needling on sensitive spots more freely than usual . . . When we did meet by chance he was invariably unpleasant.' Evelyn's second choice was Harold Acton, with his equable temperament and wide knowledge of Italy an ideal companion. Unfortunately, the weather was cold and wet, Harold was not fully recovered from flu, and Evelyn, very lame with his arthritis, seemed determined to be as offensive as possible to everyone they met. 'I am afraid the expedition was a failure for you,' Evelyn wrote to Harold on his return to England. 'It was pleasure (and edification) enough for me to be with you & watch your super-abundant charity in operation.' Superabundant charity had been all too necessary.

> '[Evelyn] has become so testy and censorious that he is a very difficult companion indeed [Harold confided to John Sutro]. It would take me pages to catalogue the occasions on which he lost his temper with all and sundry, for no particular reason . . . [Italians] can't help being talkative – and they smile with genuine good will. But Evelyn was determined to see them all as scheming, mocking, cheating, derisive (a favourite adjective of his) "Wops". He snubbed them right and left, attacked them like a Spitfire . . . He made himself odious and seemed to revel in it. If I tried to soften a blow or make up for his insulting manners, he accused me of "flirting" and put it down to the pansy streak . . . He says we shall all end in concentration camps, but at this rate I fear he will end in an asylum – and in the very near future too!'

This was a theme becoming common among Evelyn's friends. More and more, his demonic hostility seemed almost insane in its intensity and unreason. 'Poor Evelyn,' wrote Ann Fleming,[6] 'he is deeply unhappy – bored from morning till night and has developed a personality which he hates but cannot escape from.' Much of his bilious humour was, as Nancy once said, 'medical'. Most of the time now he felt unwell, lethargic, liverish, pains in his joints, increasingly dependent on drink to get him through the day and a heavy mixture of drink and narcotics to enable him to sleep at night. 'I am in deep misanthropy,' he told Nancy. 'I can't bear anyone else being alive at all & when a man goes past the window with a barrow or a child shuts a door upstairs I fall into an extremity of rage . . . L'enfer, c'est les autres I think your favourite sage says.' To Nancy he seemed on the verge of nervous breakdown. 'He might go mad,' she told Raymond Mortimer. 'Madder at least.'

She and Evelyn had had a sharp set-to over an error of hers

[6] Ann and Esmond Rothermere were divorced in 1952, and the same year Ann married Ian Fleming.

concerning the Jesuits in an article for the *Sunday Times*. 'My dear Nancy . . . There is no reason why you should know all this, but if you don't know, would it not be best always to avoid any reference to the Church or to your Creator? Your intrusions into this strange world are always fatuous.' Nancy was annoyed. 'Don't start My dear Nancy I don't like it. I can't agree that I must be debarred from ever mentioning anything to do with your creator. Try & remember that he also created me . . . I don't defend my inaccuracies but it's your TONE that nettles me.'

But this scrapping was nothing to the war which now broke out between Evelyn and the Coopers. Hostilities began when Evelyn went to stay at Chantilly in April 1953, arriving tired and drunk. There had been an unpleasant scene at dinner when the irascible Duff had exploded in an 'alarming outburst of rage and hate'. Hardly had this blown over when Diana infuriated her guest by announcing she was leaving for London for several days. When he returned to Piers Court, Evelyn wrote to her, 'If you had accepted my invitation to come here you would have experienced a very much more tender entertainment than I recently received at your hands. I should neither have left you alone in the middle of your visit nor have permitted Laura to insult you at my table. But of course she is incapable of such behaviour.' Worse was to follow. The next month it came to Diana's ears that Evelyn, having accepted an invitation to spend a weekend with Randolph Churchill, had then refused when he heard that Duff had also been invited. 'Yes, it's true that I chucked Churchill because of Duff,' Evelyn unrepentant told Diana. 'I am very sorry to hear that Duff was surprised and grieved to learn that I have detested him for 23 years. I must have nicer manners than people normally credit me with.' These offensive words were followed by a stiff exchange of letters between the two men, resulting in a formal apology from Evelyn which was accepted with dignity by Duff.

Evelyn now swivelled his sights back onto Diana, her 'spirit-writing', as she described her whimsical style of correspondence, frequently provoking bludgeon-blows of argument and rebuke. Evelyn knew precisely how to annoy, upsetting Diana by referring to her as tough and grasping – 'a ruthless go-getter, enormously accomplished, dauntless, devoid of conscience or delicacy' – when he was well aware that she preferred to see herself as frail and vulnerable, 'a creature with a certain irridescent aura'. But her peevish self-pity irritated him, and he was sometimes genuinely shocked by her selfishness. In 1953, he wrote offering to accompany her to the funeral of Hilaire Belloc, whom they had both known. Diana refused. 'You see I don't go to funerals . . . Public ones I grace . . . but not the burials of those I love . . . The idea jars upon me – exhibition of grief – the society duty side does not, in my heart, fit.' This was too much. 'The chief reason, of course, for attending funerals is to pray for the soul of the dead friend. The other reason is courtesy to the surviving relations who like to think that their "loved one" was loved enough for his friends to inconvenience themselves slightly by making a public demonstration of mourning.' Sensitive to criticism, Diana took this badly, retreating into a petulant third person to make her displeasure felt. '[Baby] will not write again – it's too painful to face the leaden answers devoid of understanding or love.' They made up, of course; until the next falling out, which as Diana knew would never be far away. 'Beloved Bo . . . I know you have a great heart but you hate to put it on your sleeve – rightly up to a point – but rather than let it sometimes fly there by its dear volition, you pin a grinning stinking mask on the site.'

By the autumn of 1953 Evelyn's health was rapidly deteriorating. His face was swollen and congested, the backs of his hands frequently mottled with an angry red; he lacked energy, was growing deaf, and suffered from toothache, sciatica and rheumatism. His memory, too, was playing him tricks. 'My memory is not at all hazy,' he told John Betjeman, 'just sharp, detailed & dead wrong.'

Like many writers, Evelyn was tormented by insomnia, particularly when his work was going well. 'There were periods of literary composition when he would find the sentences he had written during the day running in his head . . . so that he would again and again climb out of bed, pad down to the library, make a minute correction, return to his room, lie in the dark dazzled by the pattern of vocables until obliged once more to descend to the manuscript.' Various were the methods Evelyn had tried to induce sleep, even getting up during the night to shave, as a smooth face on the smooth pillow was sometimes soporific. But now nothing was effective except increasingly heavy doses of chloral and bromide. This he procured not in the orthodox manner from his general practitioner but from a chemist in London on an old prescription; instead of diluting the mixture with water, as instructed, he added reckless quantities of crême de menthe. It was a bitterly cold winter, and Evelyn began taking his oblivion-inducing bromide not only at night but as a painkiller during the day, sitting comatose in front of the fire, reading and drinking gin. Time passed slowly. 'Clocks barely moving. Has half an hour past? no five minutes.' On 27 January 1953, he wrote in his diary, 'By the time I have written my letters the papers come and when I have read them it is nearly noon so I do little work before luncheon and then don't get out after luncheon and then have tired eyes by 8 o'clock and don't want to sit up reading and not sleepy so take drugs at 11. A flaw somewhere.'

One of the few interruptions to this torpid and invalidish routine was provided by the BBC, whose Overseas Service had requested a contribution to *Personal Call*, a series which, transmitted to the Far East, was designed 'to combat the many misunderstandings there about people and life in Britain today'. Reluctantly Evelyn agreed, and an interviewer, Stephen Black, with a recording team came down to Piers Court. 'I well remember the visit,' wrote Bron, at home at the time. 'It was the one which eventually drove my Father mad . . . [the interviewer] did not seem to like my father very much.'

The BBC, however, were delighted with the result, and shortly afterwards they approached Evelyn again, asking him to take part in the popular radio series, *Frankly Speaking*. As usual, '[Waugh] requested a ridiculously large fee and a contract was devised including every conceivable right. He accepted. Had he agreed the original offer the total would have been greatly increased by repeat fees.' This time Evelyn was to be interrogated by three men, one of whom was the same Stephen Black who had appeared so hostile on the previous occasion. After the programme was broadcast, the anonymous 'Notebook' columnist in the *Spectator* remarked critically on the condescending manner of the interviewers, their intrusiveness and insinuatingly malicious tone. 'I never heard an interview conducted in public on such ill-natured terms,' he wrote. 'Protected only by a vulnerable breastwork of prejudices and convictions, Mr Waugh stuck to his dandiacal guns; and although they had the initiative, I thought he emerged with far more credit than the three colourless and curiously uniform voices who prosecuted so relentlessly their purpose of proving that Mr Waugh is somehow letting down the Common Man.'

Apart from this unwelcome disruption, life at Piers Court continued as before. For his fiftieth birthday in October Evelyn was given by John Betjeman an ornate Victorian wash-hand stand by the Puginesque designer, William Burges. Evelyn with enormous pleasure inspected it in London, where it was stored in Patrick Kinross's basement before being transported by pantechnicon to Gloucestershire.

When it was unpacked Evelyn saw to his dismay that a part was missing; he remembered it clearly: a small serpentine bronze pipe projecting from the dragon's-mouth tap into the basin. Evelyn sent a postcard to Kinross, and had an angry row with Pickford's, the carrier, but with no result. Finally he wrote to Betjeman, not only describing the pipe but enclosing a detailed drawing. Betjeman's reply came as an unpleasant surprise. 'Oh no, old boy. There was never a pipe from the tap to the basin such as you envisaged.' 'I must see an alienist,' Evelyn told him, badly shaken. 'These delusions are becoming more frequent.'

But instead of a psychiatrist, or alienist (Evelyn, like his father, delighted in using archaic terms), Evelyn decided to put his faith in the curative effects of a sea voyage to the southern hemisphere. Laura, seriously worried by her husband's condition, felt she ought to accompany him; but it was a particularly difficult time for her to leave home, engaged as she was in a complicated dispute with a tenant farmer.

Evelyn sailed from Liverpool at the end of January 1954, on board a cargo ship en route to Rangoon, the *Staffordshire*, which carried a small number of passengers. Evelyn's intention was to disembark at Colombo, and spend a couple of weeks exploring Ceylon. From the first it was noticed that there was something very wrong. He was staggering as he came on board: was he drunk? or ill? In the dining-room, he appeared to be talking to the lamp on his table, and to the toast-rack at breakfast. One of the passengers, Gwendoline Sparkes, who had the cabin on the deck immediately below his, was disturbed night and day by his knocking on her door and asking for a non-existent Miss Margaret Black. Such behaviour began to make Mrs Sparkes nervous; she appealed for help to another passenger, a young nurse who, realising that Evelyn was ill, put herself out to spend time with him and talk to him soothingly. Others, too, tried to involve him, drawing him in to the conversations in the lounge, asking him to help with their crossword puzzles. It was suggested to the captain that he should give a cocktail party to cheer Waugh up, and this seemed to be a success, but a couple of evenings later when there was a small dance on board, he refused to attend, complaining that the music was driving him mad. Later he was seen in his pyjamas at the top of a flight of stairs, crouching over the banister, then suddenly flinging a stool at an invisible target. When the ship reached Port Said the captain decided it was unsafe to take such an obviously deranged man further, and made a plan for him to disembark in company with a fellow passenger who was going by car to Cairo.

Laura, meanwhile, had received letters from her husband which, intended to be reassuring, had done little to set her mind at rest. After only a couple of days at sea he was already feeling much better, Evelyn had written; his rheumatism had gone, and he had given up taking chloral, with the result that although he had difficulty sleeping, his head was much clearer. The ship was comfortable, the passengers pleasant. The only trouble was the noise in his cabin. 'All the pipes and air shafts in the ship seem to run through [it]. To add to my balminess [sic] there are intermittent bits of 3rd Programme talks played in private cabin and two mentioned me very faintly and my p[ersecution] m[ania] took it for other passengers whispering about me.' Five days later in a letter posted from Cairo came more worrying indications. 'I found myself the victim of an experiment in telepathy which made me think I really was going crazy. I will tell you about it when I get home.' Now he was going on by air to Colombo. 'Hand is steady today and the malevolent telepathy broken for the first time – perhaps not permanently. Please don't be alarmed about the references to telepathy. I know it sounds like acute p.m. but it is real & true. A trick the existentialists invented – half mesmerism – which is most alarming when applied without warning or explanation to a sick man . . . I will write from Colombo.'

Arrived in Ceylon Evelyn found his situation no better.

It is rather difficult to write to you because everything I say or think or read is read aloud by the group of psychologists whom I met in the ship. I hoped that they would lose this art after I went ashore but the artful creatures can communicate from many hundreds of miles away . . . It is a huge relief to realize that I am merely the victim of the malice of others, not mad myself as I really feared for a few days. I must stay on at this island for a week or so & then I will come back & no doubt I shall be able to find some rival telepathist who will teach me how to ward these people off. It is really a very rum predicament. Don't worry darling & tell Tanker I now believe in her box.[7]

By now Laura was extremely worried. She decided to fly out herself to Colombo, accompanied by Jack Donaldson, whom she knew Evelyn liked and whose help she thought she might need. But before they had time to make the necessary preparations, Evelyn was home. Laura went up to London to meet him. He was very thin, and his voice sounded curiously high and nasal. Once alone in their bedroom at the Hyde Park Hotel, he gave her a full account of his persecution, perpetrated specifically by one family on board. Their name was 'Black', and the only one to show any kindness to him was the daughter, a girl whom he and Laura had both met; she was engaged to a young man from Wotton-under-Edge whom she had once brought to lunch at Piers Court. Here Laura interrupted: she remembered the girl well, but her name was not Black. Instantly Evelyn saw that she was speaking the truth, and that his experiences had been entirely illusory.

At Laura's instigation, they asked Father Caraman to dine with them at the hotel that same evening. Evelyn told him the full story, adding that he believed he was the victim of diabolic possession, and that the priest should perform an exorcism. Instead Caraman suggested he should consult E. B. Strauss, a distinguished psychoanalyst and physician who was also Catholic. Strauss was telephoned and came round immediately. He talked to Evelyn in the lounge over coffee, and had no trouble diagnos-

[7] 'Tanker' was Diana Oldridge, a neighbour at Stinchcombe, so called because she was heard to say on entering the house, 'It's only me, just tanking in'. She was a believer in the Black Box, a charlatan cure-all contraption much in vogue in the early 1950s. Evelyn was derisive, but Laura had been persuaded to try its effects on an ailing cow, which had instantly recovered.

ing a simple case of bromide poisoning,[8] a diagnosis soon afterwards confirmed by Evelyn's doctor in Gloucestershire.

Paraldehyde was substituted for chloral, and there was no
further trouble – except that the new sedative, or so Evelyn was
convinced, permanently destroyed his taste for claret.

Far from being embarrassed by his breakdown, Evelyn was exhilarated, and talked of it freely, no doubt relieved that the cause was
judged to be purely physical and external. When Christopher Hollis
saw him at Mass at Downside, and asked him how he was, Evelyn
replied loudly, 'I've been mad! Absolutely mad. Off my onion!' As
well, he was delighted at having a new subject for a novel.

The Ordeal of Gilbert Pinfold is by any criteria an extraordinary
work. Not only does the novel narrate with absolute precision the
circumstances of Evelyn's breakdown, but it also gives a clear-
sighted and unflinching *Portrait of the Artist in Middle-Age*. Pinfold
(named after the recusant family who originally owned Piers
Court) is a novelist, a Catholic, living in the country with his wife
and children.

> His strongest tastes were negative. He abhorred plastics, Picasso,
> sunbathing, and jazz – everything in fact that had happened
> in his own lifetime. The tiny kindling of charity which came to
> him through his religion sufficed only to temper his disgust
> and change it to boredom. There was a phrase in the thirties:
> 'It is later than you think', which was designed to cause
> uneasiness. It was never later than Mr Pinfold thought ... He
> looked at the world *sub specie aeternitatis* and he found it flat as
> a map; except when, rather often, personal annoyance intruded.
> Then he would come tumbling from his exalted point of
> observation. Shocked by a bad bottle of wine, an impertinent
> stranger, or a fault in syntax, his mind like a cinema camera

---

[8] One of the symptoms of bromide poisoning, noted by Mary Jane and Daniel
Hurst in 'Bromide Poisoning in The Ordeal of Gilbert Pinfold' is a high, nasal
voice. Other symptoms include 'headache, irritability, emotional lability, lethargy,
delusions, disorientation, hallucinations, loss of memory, vacuous facies (blank
stares), stupor, blurred vision, fabrication ... ataxia (a staggering gait),
confusion, vertigo ... As the patient takes the drug to excess, he grows dull
and sluggish ... The second variety of bromism is delirium. The essential feature
of this state is disorientation. There may or may not be additional symptoms
– restlessness, mood disturbances, delusions, and hallucinations.' During the
1950s bromide prescriptions were popular, and bromide poisoning is as a result
well documented.

trucked furiously forward to confront the offending object close-
up with glaring lens; with the eyes of a drill sergeant inspecting
an awkward squad, bulging with wrath that was half-facetious,
and with half-simulated incredulity; like a drill sergeant he was
absurd to many but to some rather formidable.

Clearly and cogently, Waugh describes the steps leading to Mr
Pinfold's insanity: the insomnia and dependence on narcotics;
the hostility of the radio interviewer ('the questions were civil
enough in form but Mr Pinfold thought he could detect an
underlying malice'); the delusion of the missing pipe from the
fine Victorian wash-hand stand which Mr Pinfold is given as a
birthday present. Once on board ship, renamed *Caliban*, chaos
reigns. Here there are no cosy middle-aged ladies doing crossword puzzles, but a company of fiends. The demonic hallucinations, unsuspected by his fellow passengers, that tormented
Evelyn on the voyage are here given a terrifying reality. Mr Pinfold
is surrounded by evil conspirators led by 'Angel', his antagonist
from the BBC. In his cabin he overhears voices, voices he can
never seem to escape, and which he attributes to a faulty com-
munications system left over from the war. The voices are those
of Angel and his monstrous cronies, and day and night they plot
and threaten to destroy Mr Pinfold, accusing him at random of
everything most abhorrent to him: he is homosexual, impotent,
a coward, a communist, an arriviste, a Jewish immigrant (real
name Peinfeld), a Catholic who 'doesn't really *believe* in his
religion, you know. He just pretends to because he thinks it
aristocratic.' The only character who is kind, like the others heard
but never seen, is a provocative young woman called Margaret, but
even she is used to torment him, sexually provoking him, her
father at one point urging Pinfold with prurient warmth to take
her into his bed.[9] With the warped but lucid logic of insanity,
Pinfold, like Waugh, tries to find a rational explanation for the
nightmare world in which he finds himself, courageously fighting
back every step of the way. At the end, just as in life, Mr Pinfold is

[9] In 1961 Evelyn recorded in his diary, 'Reading the report of the *Lady Chatterley*
trial I found quoted the ludicrous scene between Mellors and Lady C's father. I
must have read it years ago. It had entirely gone from my mind, but I recognized
in it the germ of the hallucination I suffered and described in *Mr Pinfold*. This
father of Lawrence's was the father I had heard urging his daughter to my
cabin.'

cured quickly and simply by the intervention of Mrs Pinfold, and by his doctor changing his prescription – 'a perfectly simple case of poisoning'. The story ends with Mr Pinfold fully restored to health and back home in his library.

> Mr Pinfold sat down to work for the first time since his fiftieth birthday. He took the pile of manuscript, his unfinished novel, from the drawer and glanced through it. The story was still clear in his mind. He knew what had to be done. But there was more urgent business first, a hamper to be unpacked of fresh, rich experience – perishable goods.
>
> He returned the manuscript to the drawer, spread a new quire of foolscap before him, and wrote in his neat, steady hand:
> The Ordeal of Gilbert Pinfold
> A Conversation Piece
> Chapter One
> Portrait of the Artist in Middle-Age

The Ordeal of Gilbert Pinfold was published by Chapman & Hall and Little, Brown in 1957. It provoked an enormous correspondence, with demented readers writing from all over the world eager to retail similar experiences. Many reviewers, on the other hand, were puzzled by the book, not sure how to place it. Some found it embarrassing or freakish; others applauded Waugh's courage in breaking new ground. In the *Observer*, Philip Toynbee, never an admirer, admitted that, 'These are the self revelations of a remarkably honest and brave man who has also allowed us to see that he is a likeable one.' More approving was John Raymond in the *New Statesman*, who made the important point that, '[Mr Waugh] happens to be the only major writer in English whose work reveals any genuine signs of development. It is possible to predict a new novel by Mr Graham Greene, say, a new Compton-Burnett, a Henry Green even, in a way that is impossible in the case of Mr Waugh.'

With *Pinfold*, the Waugh image became fixed in the public mind, stout and splenetic, red-faced and reactionary, a figure from burlesque complete with cigar, bowler and loud check suit. Evelyn's *beau idéal* was the aristocratic dandy, the languid elegance of a Harry Stavordale or an Andrew Devonshire, and, as that for a man small (five foot six) and stout was unattainable, it was as if he had decided defiantly to go to the other extreme. He dressed fastidiously, at home in the country wearing well-tailored dark suits, in the evening a smoking jacket, black tie and silk shirt. But for town he devised a costume almost clownish in character: there was one suit in particular made from a rich brown cloth checked with red, to which 'a weird touch of obscenity was added, as the tailor cut the cloth in such a way that a bright red line from the checks ran down the fly buttons'. But this was all part of the act.

> The part for which he [Mr Pinfold] cast himself was a combination of eccentric don and testy colonel and he acted it strenuously, before his children at Lychpole and his cronies in London, until it came to dominate his whole outward personality. When he ceased to be alone, when he swung into his club or stumped up the nursery stairs, he left half of himself behind, and the other half swelled to fill its place. He offered the world a front of pomposity mitigated by indiscretion, that was as hard, bright, and antiquated as a cuirass.

Pomposity was a key element in the performance, one frequently misunderstood. 'Women don't understand pomposity,' Evelyn once told Diana Cooper. 'It is nearly always an absolutely private joke – one against the world. The last line of defence.'

Newspaper editors knew they could rely on Waugh to outrage the prevailing liberalism, dependably provocative, stylish and eccentric. 'Fact is,' as Nancy Mitford told him, 'the public looks upon you as the Rev. Brontë & is fearfully disappointed if you don't rush at journalists with a poker.' His friends, too, were led to regard him as a kind of Grand Guignol turn. 'Have you seen *Evelyn?*' they would ask each other in meaningful tones, hopeful of a new horror story to be gloated over. The irony was that for all his belligerence, his cruel, unnerving marksmanship, there was a side of Evelyn that craved affection and approval: as his behaviour grew more notorious, the more he resented his notoriety. 'My chief sorrow at the moment is that, as all epigrams get attributed to Ronnie Knox, all rudeness gets attributed to me. Beasts come to me and say: "I heard something so amusing you said the other day" and then recount an act of hideous boorishness without the shadow of reality,' he complained to Diana Cooper. There was justice in the complaint, of course, even if he had chiefly himself to blame: as he wrote of Max Beerbohm, 'The mask, the style, *is* the man.' Evelyn when on form was the funniest man alive; when in good humour immensely lovable and charming. Frances Donaldson, who saw him often, described him as 'the most charming, enchanting, absolutely outstandingly lovely man I ever met'. But even in mellow mood his company could be a strain: there was that dangerously low threshold of boredom, the constant fear that something would be said to trigger a flash of rage, an unforgettably wounding remark.

Christopher Sykes in his biography recorded some of Evelyn's most coloratura performances. Over lunch at Wilton's one day with Sykes and both Waughs present an argument began between man and wife. Laura had a watch in her handbag which she wanted Evelyn to put in his waistcoat pocket.

> He refused. She protested. 'It's such a bore in my bag . . . All your pockets are empty' . . . 'By no means all,' replied Evelyn with a glare. Laura appealed to me . . . 'Why don't you put the watch in your pocket?' I pleaded . . .
>
> 'Because', he said in a voice of thunder, 'if I were to put the watch in my pocket, and if later someone were to pick me up by the heels and shake me, then *two* watches would fall out of my pockets and I would thus be made to look ridiculous.'

The conversation moved on to a new book which Sykes had brought with him, a life of Logan Pearsall Smith, which Evelyn had agreed to review.

> 'Give me the book.'
> 'All right. I'll send it to you tomorrow.'
> 'Why tomorrow, not today?'
> 'Because I want to read the book myself. You'll have it tomorrow.'
> At this Evelyn began to . . . yell in the manner of a two-year-old child, gurgling between ear-splitting ululations 'I-want-the-book-now'. In the confined space of the little restaurant the noise caused much sensation. I hastily gave him the book and his howls of agony instantly stopped.

Recovered from bromide poisoning, Evelyn returned to better health than he had enjoyed for some time. In April 1956 Nancy Mitford reported from Paris, '[Evelyn] is here, in such a sunny mood eating for 6 (éclairs for tea, even). Very nice.' Evelyn himself told Ann Fleming, 'I have turned over a faded leaf and am all honey & flowers,' while Diana Cooper was enchanted to find him full of benevolence during a visit of hers to Piers Court, funny, charming to everyone, throwing himself into a game of charades with the children. 'Thank you so much for my day of sweetness and light,' Diana wrote to him. 'You unpossessed and as you should always be – the dear darling Papa pug, petted ragged and loved.' Even the diary did not contradict her, written on the first day of the holidays, usually a time of acute depression. 'A most successful day. The girls arrived pretty and loving, Bron tall and polite . . . A gay dinner with speeches and charades afterwards, first the children then Diana joined Laura and me acting and dressing up and singing with gusto.'

Although Evelyn still suffered from insomnia – paraldehyde, he said, gave him only four hours' sleep a night – he was feeling fitter and more alert. His main affliction was deafness; he could hear one person, but not if several were talking in the same room. On his own admission, this was at least partly psychosomatic: when bored, he became deafer. But the annoyance of defective hearing was counterbalanced by the pleasure of using an ear-trumpet. Evelyn had advertised in *The Times*, and from the many offers had selected a black, tin Edwardian model nearly two feet long, comically old-fashioned and with great possibilities as an offensive weapon. Anyone asked to repeat himself more than once into an ear-trumpet must feel foolish. 'My ear-trumpets are a great convenience and a great success socially,' Evelyn boasted to Diana. The greatest success was at a Foyle's literary luncheon given in Evelyn's honour on 19 July 1957. Members of the public paid a guinea for a place at the luncheon; among the invited guests at the top table were Father D'Arcy, Alec Guinness, Rose Macaulay, Frank Pakenham, Vivien Leigh, and the Duke and Duchess of Devonshire. Malcolm Muggeridge, a ludicrous figure in Evelyn's opinion, was to give the address. With Muggeridge's first words, the trumpet was removed from Evelyn's ear and not replaced until Muggeridge sat down at the end of his speech. Muggeridge was hurt, but could do nothing, as he complained to Ann Fleming. Ann was made of sterner stuff, and when Evelyn one night at dinner turned his ear-trumpet on her, she hit it sharply with her spoon, giving him a headache for a week. Diana Cooper,

equally robust, emptied a glass of champagne down it, with unre-
ported results.

Ann Fleming, taking him at his word about the turning of the
new leaf, invited Evelyn to stay in Jamaica in January 1955. His
fellow-guest at Goldeneye was to be Peter Quennell, and Evelyn
was warned to be on his best behaviour. As Ann well knew,
Evelyn disliked most of her close friends – Lucien Freud, Alistair
Forbes, Cecil Beaton – her fuddy-duddies, he called them; but
for Quennell he had a special antipathy. 'Have you noticed how
everything beastly begins with Q?' he once wrote to her. 'Like
Quennell and queers and the queen, quibbles, quod, quagmire,
quantum theory, queues, quiffs, most Quintins, questionnaires,
quarrels – well, everything.'

Evelyn enjoyed the voyage out, but the island was a disappointment. As he promised he would, he maintained at least a 'near-
warm civility to Peter', but it was soon clear that boredom had
set in. Ian Fleming spent most of the day indoors working on
James Bond, leaving the others free to explore the spectacular
natural beauty of the island, which Ann loved and in which Evelyn
was completely uninterested. She took the two men rafting. 'I
requested silence for bird-watching. We were passing a flock of
wading egrets. "Owls!" cried Evelyn loudly, frightening them all
away.' To her brother Hugo, Ann reported that although Evelyn
had behaved himself, the holiday had not been a success, his
boredom had been obvious. 'Poor Evelyn – killing time is
his trouble and not a night without sleeping pills for twenty years
– birds, flowers, fishes mean nothing to him.'

The Jamaican expedition was a holiday Evelyn awarded himself
after finishing *Officers and Gentlemen,* his second novel about the
war. Having begun the book in 1953, he had laid it aside until
after his return from Ceylon, but by the end of 1954 it was done.
Initially entitled 'Happy Warriors', it was, he told Nancy, 'short
and funny'. In fact it is dark, subtle and complex, carrying under-
cover all Evelyn's disillusionment with the army, with Laycock in
particular, reaching a climax with his feelings of humiliation over
the débâcle in Crete.

As with *Men at Arms,* the narrative closely follows Evelyn's own
experience, drawing heavily on the diary written at the time. Guy

has joined the Commandos, and we follow him through his period of training in Scotland, on the voyage by troopship via the Cape to Egypt, then through the harrowing last days on Crete. The two interwoven themes of cowardice and betrayal predominate. At one level, in the person of Trimmer, canny, vulgar and self-serving, they are presented as essentially ludicrous. Trimmer's 'raid' on Normandy is farcical, as is his subsequent renaissance as a national hero. A much graver matter is the crack-up of Major 'Fido' Hound, who, as Major Colvin had done, goes to pieces under fire. As with Colvin, Waugh shows no pity for Hound. He is an objectionable little man, typical of the pompous, unimaginative staff officer, stupid, inflexible, armed only with the rules of his rigid training. Hound is dispensable, lacking even Trimmer's meretricious charm. But it is with the defection of Ivor Claire, most dashing of the dandy officers, that the tone of the novel turns sombre. The aristocratic Claire appears to possess all the Commando virtues, the virtues Evelyn most admired, but it is Claire, so apparently courageous, who turns coward on Crete, saving his skin and dishonourably escaping, instead of obeying orders to stay with his men and surrender.

That Claire gets away with it, spending the rest of the war comfortably in India, instead of being court-martialled, is made possible by Mrs Stitch. Mrs Stitch is holding court in Alexandria, surrounded by a coterie of high-ranking officers. She is regarded by the Commando as 'a beneficent, alert deity, their own protectress'. Only Guy remains wary of her, wary of 'the hypodermic needle of her charm', reluctant to accept her all-embracing hospitality. His instincts prove correct when Mrs Stitch, her loyalties true not to her country but to her own aristocratic kind, connives at concealing and distorting the facts of Claire's disgrace.

At the end Guy returns to England, disillusioned and besmirched. Technically there was nothing shameful in the method of his leaving Crete, escaping by sea with the assistance of the sinister Corporal Ludovic. Unlike Ivor Claire's, Guy's action was justified by official sanction. And yet the fact remained that he had left, passing up the chance of staying with his men and sharing their adversity. His moral failure is subtly implied: at dawn on the last day on the island, '[Guy] had no clear apprehension that this was a fatal morning, that he was that day to resign an immeasurable piece of his manhood.' This coded reference is undoubtedly an allusion to Waugh's own uneasiness at what took place. Twenty years after the event he was still referring in letters to 'Laycock's & my ignominious flight'. Interestingly, Tommy Blackhouse, the character inspired by Laycock, is removed from the action just as the ship carrying his Commando steams into Suda Bay: '[Blackhouse] was returning from the bridge when the ship took an unusually heavy plunge; his nailed boots slipped on the steel ladder and he fell to the steel deck with a crash.' At the end, Guy, back in the real world 'after less than two years' pilgrimage in a Holy Land of illusion', destroys his Cretan journal. 'That afternoon he took his pocket-book to the incinerator which stood in the yard outside the window, and thrust it in. It was a symbolic act.'

Published on both sides of the Atlantic in 1955, *Officers and Gentlemen* was not notably successful. Cyril Connolly in the *Sunday Times* again confessed to disappointment: the characters were sketchy, the pace slow, the plot diffuse, and the humour too gentle and anecdotal. 'Mr Waugh used to be a satirist . . . With middle-age his character has changed, mellowing rather than increasing in bitterness; and in this novel a new element of amiability, even of what might be called Christian charity, informs the pages. This I find absolutely delightful but not conducive to satire.'

One of the longest and most analytical reviews was by Kingsley Amis in the *Spectator.* An admirer of the early novels, Amis regretted Waugh's abandonment of farce; he had been repelled by *Brideshead,* disappointed by *Men at Arms,* and now with *Officers and Gentlemen* was posing the question 'whether Mr Waugh's invention is really impaired'. The *New York Times Book Review* returned to the attack on snobbery: 'Mr Waugh seems to believe that with the passing of the old way of life, which he idealizes and white-washes, all principles and values passed from the earth too. Fortunately it is not so, and until Mr Waugh recognizes this his serious work, for all his great talents, will seem . . . without either wholeness or humanity.'

To Maurice Bowra, one of the many friends who wrote to congratulate him, Evelyn replied, 'I am awfully encouraged that you like *Officers & Gentlemen.* The reviewers don't, fuck them.'

In December 1954, a few months before the publication of the novel, Kate Waugh died, aged eighty-four. She was found by her housekeeper lifeless by the fire after tea in the little flat in Highgate. Evelyn had been largely supporting her financially, austerely dutiful in his obligations, but showing little fondness or compassion. Like Mr Pinfold with his mother, 'There remained now only a firm *pietas*. He no longer enjoyed her company nor wished to communicate.' Kate's death was not an occasion of great grief. To Nancy he wrote, 'You say the English always say "Happy release" at a death. It was really so in her case. Not that she was in pain, but bitterly weary and irked at her dependent state. She was found by her maid dead in her arm chair. So for her it was happy, but it fills me with regret for a lifetime of failure in affection & attention.' Both sons were present at the funeral, but none of the grandchildren. 'I am afraid you will always remember her as very old & feeble. I wish you had known her when she was young and active,' Evelyn wrote to Margaret at school. 'She loved all you children very much. You six were her chief interest in her last years.'

This is more than could be said for Evelyn, whose interest in his children revolved mainly around the dates they left home to return to school, always for their father an occasion for celebration, with charades and champagne and an especially delicious dinner. During the holidays, the children were trained to keep out of their father's way, but such was the force of his personality that the effects of his pervasive moods reached even the nursery. Although their father's jokes and jollity entranced his children, they were never unaware of the threatening black cloud of his melancholia, when for days at a time he would eat his meals alone in his library, and his temper could be terrifying. For them it was like living on the lip of a volcano. When Evelyn left Piers Court for London or to go abroad, there was an immediate lightening of the atmosphere, a feeling of liberation, the younger members of the family able to charge about and make as much noise as they liked. When Laura was alone with her husband, she could treat him briskly and ignore his humours, but when the children were there she had constantly to stand between them and him, forever trying to conceal breakages or hush things up, anything to protect them from their father's anger.

The results of such an upbringing were a resilience and a toughening of the hide, the Herbert hardness combining with the Waugh streak of daring and aggression. One friend who knew the children of both clans well, Herberts and Waughs, said 'that dealing with any of them was like touching wire wool'.

The family structure was strictly hierarchical, with the eldest child always allowed the greatest privilege, whether sitting in front in the car, or staying up later than the others before going to bed. As each child in turn became old enough for boarding-school, he or she became a 'dining-room child', moving down from the nursery to have luncheon in the dining-room, where faultless manners were expected and entertaining conversation. Children were present at table even when adult guests were there, an unusual practice ·in those days, and one not always popular with the guests, who frequently found themselves victims of some elaborate joke devised by Evelyn for the children to act out. Even for the children, eating with their parents was a dubious honour. Bron looked back on luncheons 'often marked by the most appal-ling gloom. While Papa chewed his way through the unappetising meals, with his back to the window, my mother... stared past him out of the window at her beloved cows... she loved them extravagantly, as other women love their dogs or, so I have been told, their children.'

His children bored Evelyn; he had no interest in their intense absorption in chemical experiments, pony clubs and autograph collections. And yet he was a conscientious father, much more so than his father had been towards him. It was he who discussed their prospects and arranged their treats; he, not Laura, who wrote regularly to them at school. From the beginning it had been agreed that Evelyn should write to the girls, Laura to the boys; but while he never failed in his duty, she found it next to impossible to apply herself, and every week Evelyn had to stand over her bullying her to write. His letters to 'the little girls' were perfectly designed to catch their interest. 'Darling Meg & Hatty... Oh this will be sad news for Hatty. The cat was run over & killed while we were away. Foul play is not suspected. James's bantams are in good health – I forget whether you met them...' In a curious way, he was very alert to his children, vividly aware of the child's perspective. 'Children come flooding in by every train,' he wrote to Nancy one Christmas. 'It is rather exhilarating to see their simple excitement & curiosity about every Christmas card. "Look, papa, the Hyde Park Hotel has sent a coloured picture of its new cocktail bar".' Nancy was godmother to his youngest daughter, Harriet. 'Did I tell you about Harriet who came the other day in great excitement to say that the kitchen garden was full of "white things with horns". "Cows?" "No, smaller than cows." I thought there must be some visitation of goats & rushed out. It was full of cabbage butterflies. "You must have seen butterflies before Harriet." "Not with horns." '

Inevitably it was the elder children who came in for the most violent confrontations, the two youngest, James and Septimus, for long periods hardly engaging him at all. Teresa gave comparatively little trouble; she was on the whole sensible and well-behaved, but she was never close to her father, who was irritated by her high, affected voice. He was proud, however, when she won her scholarship to Somerville, and did his duty by giving a coming-out dance for her in London, an experience which caused him considerable suffering, enormous expense, and which he resolved never to repeat. He made the best of it nonetheless, giving a dinner party beforehand at the Hyde Park Hotel ('Non Vintage champagne for all but me,' Evelyn instructed Brian Franks), well-behaved at the dance itself. The next day Evelyn sent a lively description of the event to Meg and Hatty at school.

> It was a great success. Teresa wore a dress of emerald green calico trimmed with zebra skin and a straw hat, button boots of patent leather and woollen gloves . . . For supper there was plenty of stout and kippers and bread & margarine and blancmange and plum jam . . . Your mother insisted on bringing all 14 cows . . . A lot of criminals came uninvited and began robbing everyone so the police charged with truncheons and, I am sorry to say, arrested Alec Waugh and Alick Dru by mistake. They are still in prison but we hope to get them out on bail in a day or two. To make things difficult Alick Dru had five watches, six diamond rings and some silver spoons in his pocket when arrested . . . One of the cows escaped from the ball room into the Kensington Square Convent. The nuns have been milking her ever since & feeding her on sun-flower seeds . . .

With Bron, the second eldest, relations were stormier. Evelyn much preferred girls to boys, and while Bron was growing up there was little sympathy between them. 'The most terrifying aspect of Evelyn Waugh as a parent', Bron wrote many years later, 'was that he reserved the right not just to deny affection to his children but to advertise an acute and unqualified dislike.' Evelyn was unrelentingly critical of his eldest son, and in letters and the diary are many disparaging references. In Bron's estimation, the ten years he lived at Piers Court turned him from 'a mildly delinquent six year old into something approaching a professional criminal of sixteen'. In Evelyn's eyes the unforgivable sin was untruthfulness and, unlike the girls, Bron and his brothers were all in self-defence accomplished liars. Bron, too, was considered lazy, sly, obsessed with money and regrettably lacking in motivation. No fault escaped his father's eye. His bedroom was opposite his father's, and every morning Ellwood would put his head round the door and warn 'Master Auberon' to get out of bed and downstairs minutes before Evelyn appeared for breakfast in the dining-room.

The boy was sent to Downside, which he hated. Like his father Bron was rebellious and anarchic, bored by games, loathed the Corps. There had been trouble with the monks from the start, and after one spectacular row Evelyn arranged for him to be moved to another house, writing to the new housemaster, Father Aelred Watkin, with a candour rare in parent-teacher relationships. 'He is not at all a vicious boy or ill mannered, but I think he is listless, lazy, conceited and not completely truthful . . . I think that this is the stage in his life when he must be in contact with someone he does respect & like. I am sure you are the man.' Bron, furious at being moved, protested passionately in an outburst to which his father replied calmly and with considered judgment. 'Don't write in that silly tone. No one has any motive with regard to you except your own welfare . . . If you have a better suggestion to make I shall be pleased to hear it . . . You have made a mess of things. At your age that is not a disaster, but you must help yourself. Your future, temporal and spiritual, is your own making. I can only provide opportunities for your achievements. Your affectionate papa, E. W.'

In July 1955, there was more trouble when Bron, aged fifteen, was arrested for travelling by train without a ticket. Evelyn and Laura had gone to the cinema in Dursley. 'We were greeted by the manager saying that the Stroud police wished to speak to us. They said that a youth had been arrested incapably drunk carrying Bron's suitcase. From their description it was plain that the prisoner was Bron.' Arrest was followed by a court appearance and a fine of ten shillings. Evelyn was very angry indeed, and for the rest of the summer his son's loafing presence around the house irritated him beyond measure. 'Walked to Mass and communion praying for kindness towards Bron.' Soon after he returned to school, Bron was again writing to his father, this time begging to leave. Patiently Evelyn replied.

> I have much sympathy with your restlessness with school life. I felt as you do at your age, asked my father to remove me, was resentful at the time when he refused. Now I am grateful to him. If there was anything you ardently wished to do . . . I would not stand in your way . . . If you leave prematurely everyone will always think you were sacked. To be sacked from school is not absolutely fatal but it is a grave disadvantage for the early years of whatever career you decide on. I am pretty sure it will prevent your getting a commission in any Household regiment and would make entry into Oxford more difficult.

Evelyn was aware of his failure to feel affection for his eldest son, and made genuine efforts to behave well towards him. In the hope of understanding the boy better, he reread his own Lancing diaries. 'I am appalled at what an odious prig I was,' he told Bron. 'One great advantage you have on me is the contact with a place of prayer. Don't neglect that advantage.' In the end Bron stayed the course, proving the value of his father's advice by joining the Royal Horse Guards for his National Service and winning a scholarship to Christ Church. As Bron grew up and Evelyn grew older, his father became 'more of a friend and less of a figure to dodge'.

Dearest of all Evelyn's children was his second daughter, Margaret, known as Meg. From an early age Meg formed a special relationship with her father, the only one of his offspring totally unafraid of him, the only one who loved him unreservedly. Dark, difficult, often wilful and moody, she was his 'ewe lamb – the star of my existence'. In a sense he fell in love with her when she was still a little girl, and remained in love with her for the rest of his life. From the age of ten, she began to feature prominently in his letters, and he took a perverse pleasure in teasing those of his women friends with daughters of the same age – Ann Fleming, Debo Devonshire, Frankie Donaldson – hoping to shock them with what he described as his incestuous passion. He dwelt linger-

ingly on Meg's sexual attractiveness. 'My sexual passion for my
ten year old daughter is obsessive,' he told Ann. 'I can't keep
my hands off her.' Inevitably, the emotional atmosphere between
father and daughter was often highly charged. '[Margaret] in low
spirits perhaps because I had struck her the evening before for
breaking my "acme" chair the second time ... Meg is sulky and
in my bad books. I had to order her from the dining-room in
tears (hers not mine) last night.'

The other children, far from being jealous of Margaret's privileged position, were glad of it. She could act as mediator for
them with their father, and none of them envied her the pressure
which was an inevitable result of his high expectations. Meg
seemed unfazed by the attention. She loved her father, stood up
to him, knew both how to provoke and to soothe him. More than
once she accused him to his face of being drunk, and sometimes
deliberately courted his disapproval. In the car one day coming
back from Mass she lifted the hem of her skirt to show her
petticoat. 'Look at my petticoat!' she said provocatively, watching
his furious face at this inappropiate behaviour. 'Marks & Spencer's
reduced!'

When Margaret, like Teresa and Bron before her, declared she
hated school and implored him to take her away, Evelyn was
deeply concerned at her distress. 'I really am very worried you
should be unhappy, darling little girl.' Mother Bridget, headmistress of St Mary's Convent, Ascot, complained frequently of
Margaret's behaviour and her deleterious influence on the other
girls: increasingly troublesome ... dissatisfied and defiant ... the
minimum of work ... studied attitude of boredom ... self-pity
and persecution mania. But Evelyn was entirely on his daughter's
side. 'Darling Meg – I am sorry you are in hot water. You do not
have to tell me that you have not done anything really wicked. I
know my pig. I am absolutely confident that you will never never
be dishonourable, impure or cruel ... The part of your letter
that I don't like at all is when you say the nuns "hate you". That
is rubbish ... You are loved far beyond your deserts, especially by
your Papa.' Meg was allowed to come home and be taught by her
father, with not entirely satisfactory results; she was the only one
of the children to try for Oxford and fail. Instead she was found
employment at the Jesuit headquarters in Farm Street, assisting

Father Caraman in his work as vice-postulator of the Cause of the English and Welsh Martyrs.

For the two youngest children, James and Septimus, the experience of life at home was very different, happy for one, wretched for the other. Septimus, the last born, was his mother's favourite. Laura adored him, and Septimus was friends with everyone, quickly learning how to manage his father, who by the time his youngest child had reached the age most likely to annoy, lacked the energy to fight him. With the others away at school or university, Septimus for long periods was the only child at home, and so was indulged and given a licence the others never knew. James, on the other hand, also gentle and sweet-natured, suffered miserably. He was on permanently bad terms with Bron, and bullied by Hatty, the next in seniority, who, longing for the friendship of the older Meg, resented being classed with her younger brother. James had a stutter, of which his father made cruel fun. Evelyn decided that James had no sense of humour, and as a remedial exercise insisted he tell a new joke every day. In desperation James bought a book of a thousand and one American jokes, and stammered through each day's instalment at lunchtime, while his father sat stony-faced, refusing to laugh.

When asked his choice of career, James, hoping to please, said he wanted to become a priest. On the basis of this Evelyn managed to get him a place at reduced fees at Stonyhurst, the old-established Jesuit school in Lancashire. Here he was happy, but when, at fourteen, James changed his mind about entering the Church, and told his father he wanted to be a farmer, Evelyn would not hear of it. Nonsense, he said, and gentle James was sent into the Army.

In June 1955, Piers Court suffered an invasion. Nancy Spain, a popular stunt journalist on the *Daily Express*, had telephoned to request an interview, which naturally was refused. Undeterred Miss Spain turned up just before dinner one evening, accompanied by a man friend, Lord Noel-Buxton. Laura answered the door and told them she could not ask them inside. The strangers persisted, until Evelyn, hearing the altercation, came into the hall and ordered them out. Three days later Miss Spain described the experience for her readers.

I rang the bell. Mrs Waugh, a beautiful woman in a twin set and slacks, came immediately, sighed deeply and leaned against the door jamb. I said who we were. She said she was afraid we could not stay, when I heard a voice calling: 'Who is it? . . . Go away, go away! You read the notice, didn't you? No admittance on business!' Lord Noel-Buxton is rather a tall man. He stood his ground, blinking, looking down at Mr Waugh, who is rather a short man. 'I'm not on business,' was the answer. 'I'm a member of the House of Lords.'

Evelyn, 'tremulous with rage' at this intolerable intrusion of his carefully guarded privacy, countered with a funny but damning piece in the *Spectator* entitled 'Awake my Soul! It is a Lord'.[10] Not unnaturally the incident attracted a good deal of publicity; Miss Spain was added to the list of mortal enemies, and the scene of her attempted forced entry became a favourite in family charades.

The very next year came an opportunity for real revenge. Nancy Spain in an ill-researched article unfavourably and inaccurately compared Evelyn's earnings to Alec's, boasting that a notice from her had caused Alec's recent novel, *Island in the Sun*, to sell 60,000 copies, dwarfing 'the total first edition sales' of all Evelyn's work. On 17 March Evelyn wrote to Peters, 'I have waited a long time to catch the *Express* in libel. I think they have done it this time.'

The case came to court in February 1957, with Gerald Gardiner representing the plaintiff, the great Sir Hartley Shawcross acting for the defendant. Alec came over from Tangier, where he was now living, loyally to give evidence on his brother's behalf.

By this time Evelyn was in a state of acute anxiety, having convinced himself that he would lose and the costs would ruin him. But he did not lose. 'The verdict at the trial was a great surprise to me,' he told Hattie and Meg.

At any moment in the last six months I would have settled for £500. At the end of the first day's hearing I would have taken a fiver. During the long wait while the jury deliberated my lawyer apologised for letting me into a mess and hinted that I might

---

[10] This is an accidental conflation of the first lines of two hymns, 'Awake, my soul, and with the sun', and 'Hark, my soul, it is the Lord'. 'It is a sorrow to me that I got the hymn wrong,' Evelyn wrote to Maurice Bowra. 'I have not heard it since Lancing Chapel. I consulted the head housemaid who sings in the protestant parish choir. She gave me the wrong words.'

have to pay costs of £5000. I contemplated our all having to emigrate to Australia. However things turned out all right. Father Collins (to whom I have sent £200) prayed hard and his prayers were answered in a dramatic, Old Testament way. Sir Hartley Shawcross is the most able barrister in the country and he is permanently engaged by Lord Beaverbrook. From the moment he took up the case he was stricken by a series of private disasters culminating at the very moment when he was cross-examining me & making me feel rather an ass, in a well-nigh fatal motor-accident to his mother-in-law which made him chuck the case and leave it to an understrapper. Miss Spain lied repeatedly and obviously in the box. The judge was a buffoon who behaved as though he were acting in Gilbert & Sullivan. Luckily the jury were good solid, prosperous-looking people with a firm prejudice against the *Daily Express* & they did not think the judge at all funny. Their verdict was not so much for me as against Beaverbrook . . . As you can imagine there was much champagne drinking at White's and the Hyde Park Hotel.

But Miss Spain had done her damage. Within days of her pushing into Piers Court, Evelyn put the house on the market. 'I felt it was polluted,' he said. To Knight, Frank & Rutley, the estate agent from whom he had bought the house before the war, he wrote, 'I would like to sell out . . . I believe that £10,000 is the most I could ask. I would not want to sell for less. I am in no hurry to go. I don't want the house advertised. But if you happen to meet a lunatic who wants to live in this ghastly area, please tell him.' Twelve months later an offer was accepted from a Mrs Gadsden for £9500. 'Now as I move about the house and garden nothing irks me as it used to do. It is Mrs Gadsden's house not mine so I don't care if the stone crumbles and the tap drips and the weeds smother the beds. I am soon going. There is a meditation to be made on death on these lines.'

During that summer of 1956 he and Laura devoted themselves to house-hunting. The most attractive property was a medieval bishop's palace near Exeter, but negotiations fell through, and on 11 September Evelyn made an offer of £7500 for a square, handsome eighteenth-century manor house of red sandstone in the tiny village of Combe Florey in Somerset. Standing on a little eminence, approached through a gate-house and up a steep drive, surrounded by forty acres of woods and fields, Combe Florey was more remote, more secluded than Piers Court. 'I have bought a dull, very private house of sandstone, hidden in a valley behind a demesne wall,' Evelyn wrote to Ann Fleming. 'As it stands it will be a suitable place to end my days and there is a lunatic asylum bang next door which is valuable (a) for me if I get another go of barminess (b) in providing indefatigable gardeners at slave wages (c) husband for Harriet.' As at Piers Court, Evelyn hoped to be allowed a private chapel, but his request for the consecration of the gate-house for this purpose was refused by the Bishop of Clifton on the grounds that there were not enough Catholics locally to provide the required 'Mass attendance' of over 200.

Evelyn and Laura spent their last night at Stinchcombe on 31 October. 'Laura has moped a little at seeing her house dismantled,' he recorded in the diary. 'I am exhilarated.' After some untranquil weeks at Pixton, they finally moved into the new house in January, and almost immediately afterwards Evelyn's libel case came to court, the money from which contributed substantially to the beautification of Combe Florey.[11] 'The house, after weeks of chaos, has quite suddenly begun to look rather decent. I have been buying objects like a drunken sailor – candelabra, carpets, fire places. The prodigious sideboard which I bought at Ston Easton has been erected with an infinity of skilled labour and is very splendid.'

To celebrate his victory over the Beaverbrook press, Evelyn had planned to go to Monte Carlo with Laura, who enjoyed luxury hotels and loved a little unadventurous gambling. Instead they went to Torquay, accompanying a dying Ronald Knox for a penitential fortnight in depressing out-of-season hotels. Knox was in the final stages of cancer of the liver, and Evelyn as an old friend had felt it his duty to agree when Knox asked him to act as companion to provide a respite for Katharine Asquith, with whom for the past ten years he had been living as chaplain at Mells. It was a grim experience. 'We are far from happy here,' Evelyn told Ann Fleming. 'Poor Ronnie is very infirm & fretful, can't sleep, eat, drink or read. All that gives him any relief is laborious cross

---

[11] £2000, with a further £3000 from an out-of-court settlement awarded after yet another hostile article by Nancy Spain in the *Daily Express.*

word puzzles . . . Ronnie talks as though he will be on my hands for a month. I love & revere him but oh dear – ' Laura returned home after a week, and Evelyn moved the invalid to Sidmouth. 'This is plainly the hotel which served as a model for *Separate Tables*. My life here is ghastly . . . All he [Ronnie] likes is to smoke a stinking pipe and to make desultory comments on the news in the paper . . . Sometimes I walk up & down the front for half an hour.' On 20 March Evelyn returned to Combe Florey. In June he received a summons to attend Knox at Mells. Evelyn had agreed to act as the priest's literary executor and, it was understood, would write the biography. '[Your duties] can no longer be regarded as very remote,' Knox informed him.

Ronald Knox died on 24 August, his death galvanising Evelyn into action. 'Ronnie's death has transformed my life,' he wrote to Diana Cooper. 'Instead of sitting about bored and idle I am busy all day long, both writing his life and managing his affairs for Trim [Lord Oxford]. Ronnie's close business associates are all scrupulous dotards who write to me by every post. That part is a fiendish nuisance but I am absolutely absorbed in the biography.' Peters was warned that the book, a 'magnum opus', might well take two years to complete.

Recognising that he was ill equipped to deal with Knox's spiritual life, Evelyn consulted Dom Hubert van Zeller at Downside, Knox's confessor and confidant, asking him 'whether I ought to have a chapter by another hand on Ronald's spirituality'. But the idea was soon rejected. As Evelyn wrote to Daphne Acton, '[Ronald] could think of no one more suitable than me to write his biography. So he plainly wanted to be treated as a man of letters rather than of prayer. But of course a lot of people will say that I miss his essential point and of course they will be right.'

Daphne Acton was a key source. She had converted to Catholicism after her marriage to John, 3rd Lord Acton, head of the distinguished old Catholic family. It was Ronald Knox, then private chaplain to the Actons at Aldenham in Shropshire, who had instructed her, and a long and emotional friendship had ensued. After the war the Actons left England to farm in Rhodesia, and in February 1958 Evelyn went out to stay with them. Daphne, pretty, intelligent and full of verve, could not have been more helpful, lending Evelyn her letters and talking with candour about her intense but impeccable relationship with Knox. 'I think the fact that Ronnie was even older, when I first met him than I am now, as well as being full of grace, meant that he could behave with effortless chastity, whereas I found it more of a strain.' During the weeks he spent with them, Evelyn became very fond of the Actons, and of Daphne in particular, although the living conditions at M'Bebi, twenty-five miles from Salisbury, were far from luxurious. 'The house is a long bungalow stretching across the hillside, roofed with iron, walled with concrete, making no claim to architectural character. A short distance away is the "native compound", the village of round huts from which sounds of revelry can often be heard long into the night.' Daphne was the mother of ten.

> Children were everywhere, no semblance of a nursery or a nanny, the spectacle at meals gruesome, a party-line telephone ringing all day, dreadful food, an ever present tremendously boring ex-naval chaplain, broken aluminium cutlery, plastic crockery, ants in the beds, totally untrained black servants (all converted by Daphne to Christianity, taught to serve Mass but not to empty ash trays). In fact everything that normally makes Hell but Daphne's serene sanctity radiating supernatural peace. She is the most remarkable woman I know.

Evelyn returned home from Rhodesia in March 1958, but his work on the biography was interrupted in the second week of June by appalling news. Bron, in Cyprus with his brigade, had been accidentally shot. Out on patrol he had rashly bent over to examine the barrel of a defective machine-gun when the gun had gone off and fired six bullets into him. His life was despaired of and he had already received the last rites when Laura flew out the day after the accident to be with him. 'Bron's resignation and the way he quietly prayed on the way into hospital has been an inspriring thing to witness & his bravery through it all,' she wrote to Evelyn. She stayed at Government House in Nicosia, visiting the hospital twice a day, and gradually, as Bron's condition began to improve, was able to turn her thoughts towards home. 'Will you tell Giovanni[12] to give 1 spoonful of [cattle-]cake daily to Magdalen & Desdemona this week & two spoonfuls daily to

[12] Giovanni and Maria Manfredi were an Italian couple employed for a time at Combe Florey as general factotum and cook.

them from next Monday . . . Bron continues to improve & slept well again . . . I hope Giovanni is singling the mangolds tell him not to bother about the kale. The mangolds are on the side nearest the house – and must be done.'

Evelyn in letters to enquiring friends wrote with gravity and calm. He asked his Catholic friends to pray, and sent money to the Poor Clares at Looe. When eventually Bron was flown back to London, where he was to spend nearly nine months in hospital, his father dutifully went to see him, and did his best to arrange for regular visits by town-dwelling acquaintance. Friends who were Catholic, it was noted, did much better than their Protestant fellows. 'In the last five months Bron has been able to keep a pretty accurate count of those who have troubled to visit him,' Evelyn told Ann Fleming. '*All*, except two brother-officers and one devout Protestant cousin, are Catholics. Dot Head & Pam Berry and other near neighbours write the name of his ward in their engagment books and do nothing . . . People like Mia Woodruff & Frances Phipps who barely know him go two and three times a week. Even Harold Acton went twice during his brief visit.'

At Christmas Evelyn and Meg left the rest of the family in Somerset while they stayed at the Hyde Park Hotel to be nearby. 'At about this time,' Bron wrote in his memoirs, 'I began to be quite fond of my father, never having liked him much in childhood or early youth.'

With Bron back in England and no longer critically ill, Evelyn was able to return to Knox. The biography was attractive not only as a pious duty, which it undoubtedly was, but also because of Evelyn's admiration and sympathy for the subject. It has been said that Knox, with his élitist and anachronistic view of the Church, did Evelyn a great deal of harm; that if instead he had come under the influence of a more vigorous, less self-absorbed personality, such as Hubert van Zeller or C. C. Martindale, he might have survived better the changes imposed by the Second Vatican Council. In a sense, he and Ronald Knox were too alike. The friendship had begun at the time of Oldmeadow's onslaught on *Black Mischief*; in 1950 Knox had dedicated his book, *Enthusiasm*, to Evelyn, who unblushingly described it as 'the greatest work of literary art of the century'. In history and in temperament there were many similarities. Both were writers, both were converts', both came from middle-class families and preferred the company of the nobility. Knox spent his life looking back with nostalgia on that golden generation – Grenfells, Asquiths, Horners – killed in the First World War; for him leaving Eton, he always said, was like going into exile.

Knox had all the intolerance of the convert, was querulous, critical, easily bored. Sensitive and suffering, he largely disdained the modern world; reclusive by nature, he passed most of his adult life in a form of privileged retreat, established as private chaplain in the houses of great Catholic families, with Lady Lovat at Beaufort, with the Actons at Aldenham, with Katharine Asquith at Mells. When the biography was published, one critic pertinently remarked that it was 'perhaps unfortunate for the three generous women friends with whose families he [Knox] made his successive homes that they fall so smoothly into the framework of *Brideshead Revisited*'.

The Life of the Right Reverend Ronald Knox, Fellow of Trinity College, Oxford, and Protonotary Apostolic to His Holiness Pope Pius XII is a work of appropriate stylistic elegance. Although the author's admiration for his subject is clear, this is no hagiography, Waugh maintaining a delicate tension between the priest's piety and scholarship and the difficulties of his character. Knox did suffer, and Evelyn never underestimates his inner tribulations, but there is an occasional hint of reproof. During Knox's thirteen years as Catholic chaplain at Oxford, he used to complain of the burden of having to deal with undergraduates. 'It may occur to the busy parish priest,' Waugh writes, 'that Ronald's limited responsibilities and his long vacations provided quite unprecedented leisure and that his complaints of overwork have a neurotic flavour.' Waugh praises unreservedly Knox's skill as a writer, vigorously attacking the hierarchy's failure to appreciate his monumental undertaking in translating the Bible, even if privately Evelyn held Knox's version in low esteem.

Although a personal friend, Waugh on the surface maintains a scrupulous objectivity. Referring to Knox's last illness, when he and Laura were with him in Torquay, the reader is told only that '[Knox] went to Torquay accompanied by two friends, a husband and wife.'

There are, however, one or two oblique self-referrals: in the account of Knox closing the chapel at Aldenham in 1947 before the Actons' move to Rhodesia, Waugh writes, 'Three years before, it so happened a novelist had asked his help in describing just such a scene . . .' And there are a couple of old scores settled. Oldmeadow, when editor of the *Tablet*, is described, unnamed, as 'a man of meagre attainments and deplorable manners, under whom the paper became petty in its interests and low in tone'. His much disliked patron, Cardinal Bourne, 'was quite devoid of anything which would have passed for scholarship, taste or humour . . . He had no felicity of expression in speech or writing'; while Bishop Myers, whose extreme dilatoriness was responsible for holding up the annulment of Evelyn's first marriage, is dismissed in a meaningful sentence: 'Delegation of any task to Bishop Myers notoriously meant its relegation to oblivion.'

There was a great deal of sectarian interest in publishing the biography, in particular from Tom Burns at Burns, Oates & Washbourne, and from Mark Longman of Longman, Green. But loyalty to the old firm triumphed, and it was Chapman & Hall's offer of £3000 that was accepted. *Ronald Knox* was published in 1959 in both England and America. The book was extravagantly admired by Evelyn's co-religionists, politely admired by non-Catholic friends. At more elevated levels there were indications of displeasure, with certain members of the episcopate distinctly uneasy at the outspoken criticism of their treatment of Knox, their failure sufficiently to recognise his long work of translation and revision. As Monsignor John Barton, the senior censor, crisply pointed out, 'It is, as you are no doubt aware, a sort of unwritten law that the bishops are not criticized or discussed to their disadvantage in any public way.'

The reviewers liked the book, although not all of them found the subject sympathetic. As Graham Greene said in the *Observer*, 'Every Catholic, I suppose, has his favourite type of priest. The Knox of Oxford, the Knox of the rather precious style and of the Latin verses, the chaplain and the translator, had his apostolate in a region which I have always found uninteresting and even at moments repellent.' Maurice Bowra in the *London Magazine*, was also unimpressed by the man, although full of admiration for the author. 'Mr Waugh writes our language with a mastery in which he has few, if any, living equals.' Angus Wilson was one of the few dissenters, describing the book as 'dull, at times even empty', and oddly concluding, 'Perhaps Mr Waugh has not permitted himself enough anger at what he feels to have been the waste of a good deal of Knox's life, and without anger he has sought refuge in this dismal acceptance.'

In the same year in which *Ronald Knox* was published (1959), an attempt was made to give Evelyn public recognition. In May he received a letter from the prime minister's office informing him that he had been recommended for a CBE, and asking if he were prepared to assure the prime minister 'that this mark of Her Majesty's favour would be agreeable to you'. It was not agreeable, and the honour was refused, a display of discourtesy which Evelyn later regretted. At the end of his life he wrote to Graham Greene, 'Some years back I refused the CBE from side (not good enough, I thought) and am now ashamed.' But at the time he regarded such comparatively low-level awards with scorn. When Anthony Powell was awarded the CBE, Evelyn wrote to Nancy, 'No sour grapes but I think it very WRONG that politicians should treat writers as second grade civil servants. Osbert Sitwell opened the breach by accepting this degrading decoration.'

However, when Maurice Bowra was knighted, Evelyn had been openly, exaggeratedly envious: he would go on his knees to the prime minister, he said, he would lick his boots, he would lie in the mud outside Downing Street, if he promised in return to give him a knighthood. His contempt for officialdom extended to the royal family. Invited to luncheon at Buckingham Palace, he refused: 'Said I was too deaf to obey. Real reason snobbery,' he told Daphne Acton. Unaccountably, he expressed a wish to meet the Queen Mother. One of the Queen Mother's ladies-in-waiting was 'Tortor' Gilmour, whose son, Ian Gilmour, as editor of the *Spectator*, had often employed Evelyn. Lady Gilmour arranged a meeting in her little flat in Dorset Square. Two chairs were drawn up in front of the fire; champagne was poured. The Queen Mother raised her glass.

'Oh, Mr Waugh, champagne! *Isn't* this a luxury?'

'A luxury?' Evelyn enquired, unsmiling. '*Really*, ma'am?'

Evelyn had spent nearly two years working on *Ronald Knox*, refusing other commitments to concentrate on his biography. Now he was in low water financially and in need of a change. 'I would like a long luxurious trip among places of beauty & people of charm,' he wrote to Peters. 'I suppose no shipping company would do for me what PanAmerican have done for Alec – send me round the world free?' Peters came up with the perfect proposal, a promotional deal with the Union Castle line: Evelyn would travel to Africa and back on two of their ships, and write a book about his experiences disguised as an independent travel book and published by his usual publisher. This, their managing director hoped, would stimulate interest in Africa while sowing in the mind of the reader that Union Castle was the best means of going there. The company would have final approval of the text, would pay a fee of £500 as well as £1500 expenses, with a free cruise to Madeira for Mr and Mrs Peters thrown in.

Evelyn left London on 28 January 1959, going by train to Genoa, where he spent two days sightseeing with Diana Cooper, the ubiquitous 'Mrs Stitch', before boarding the *Rhodesia Castle* to Mombasa. This was followed by several weeks touring through Central and East Africa, returning home from Cape Town on the new flagship of the line, *Pendennis Castle*.

The result, *A Tourist in Africa*, a book almost as boring to read as evidently it was to write, was finished by the end of the year with many complaints of mental lethargy and suffering. 'I am writing an account of my African journey of ineffable tedium and triviality . . . the African book is very poor stuff . . . [the book] is hard going because I can only be funny when I am complaining about something.' The material was so thin that Evelyn only half facetiously suggested to Chapman & Hall that he insert adverbs before all adjectives in an attempt to lengthen the text. Instead the account of his uneventful journey is padded out with snippets of African history and passages of guide-book prose. 'The chief hotel stands near the railway station. Luggage is carried there through a tunnel under the traffic, which during the day is thick and fast.' Anything complicated is nimbly side-stepped – 'Another pen than mine is needed to do justice to the really remarkable achievements of the Chagga government' – and potentially interesting expeditions shamefully curtailed by a traveller clearly lacking in curiosity. Arrived at a remote Jesuit mission, 'we had lost so much time in getting there that we could barely greet our friend before setting back.' Here and there are glimpses of the price to be paid for accepting free hospitality. At Government Lodge in Salisbury, 'I was able to see and admire the garden that has been the particular contribution of the Governor's wife,' and at Mbeya in Tanganyika, '[Mrs Newman] very kindly put me up for the night in her own cheerful villa. That evening she collected some of her neighbours for cocktails. All were officials; all on easy, intimate terms with one another. One of the D.O.s kept guinea-pigs; a doctor had a very numerous family; the P.C. was Australian.'

Evelyn was too ashamed of his African pot-boiler to send it to friends, but by the terms of his agreement it could not be kept from the critics. On the whole he was treated kindly, most finding the book a pleasant enough read, even though the author was judged lazy and inaccurate. Cyril Connolly in the *Sunday Times* was more severe. '*A Tourist in Africa* is quite the thinnest piece of book-making which Mr Waugh has undertaken ... the particular pose he affects – of an elderly, infirm and irritable old buffer, quite out of touch with the times – is hardly suited to enthusiasm, a prerequisite of travel-writing ... What a drubbing I should get if I had written it.'

A Tourist in Africa provided an agreeable free holiday, but it brought in little money. 'Wind of change is blowing very cold in my bank,' Evelyn wrote to Ann Fleming, and in a newspaper article he complained that 'in order to enjoy the standard of living I had in 1938 I must now earn £20,750. I find it hard work to earn half that amount and my income has, on paper, greatly increased.'

Even Laura was suffering. 'Laura has at last had to give up her herd of cows and mourns them,' he told Diana Cooper, who had herself kept cows during the war. 'They cost as much to keep as a troupe of ballet girls and the horrible politicians made a law that one can no longer charge them against income tax.' Peters again came to the rescue, this time with a lucrative contract from the *Daily Mail*, providing Evelyn with yet another winter holiday abroad, nearly two months in Venice, Monte Carlo and Greece during January and February 1960. For this he was to write five articles for a fee of £2000. 'I was appalled at the way they cut & titled them,' he told his agent, 'but it is no good quarrelling with one's bread and butter at my age.'

With financial anxieties pressing, he even accepted a proposal from his old enemy, the British Broadcasting Corporation, to appear on television in the prestigious interview series, *Face to Face*, whose subjects had included Carl Jung, Bertrand Russell, Edith Sitwell, Henry Moore and Martin Luther King. There was the usual haggling over fees; the BBC eventually agreed to raise their initial offer of 75 guineas to £250 on the understanding that they would pay neither expenses nor foreign rights. As a result, 'Waugh was left happy in the belief that he had scored financially against the Corporation when in fact he received less than any of the other guests on the programme.' The interviewer was John Freeman, an ex-Labour member of Parliament and a clever and experienced broadcaster. Evelyn took trouble to prepare himself for the encounter. 'I have let myself in for cross-examination on Television by a man named Major Freeman who I am told was a colleague of yours in the Working Class Movement,' he wrote to Tom Driberg, also a Labour MP. 'Do you know anything damaging about him that I can introduce into our conversation if he becomes insolent?' Freeman was exquisitely courteous, but he was also perceptive and persistent, and the results were memorable, Waugh's instinctive hostility only just restrained by a carefully assumed pose of world-weary boredom.

In January 1960, Evelyn wrote to Elizabeth Longford, 'It has been a bad year for the old literary hacks – Elizabeth Bowen, John Betjeman, Leslie Hartley down & out of the race; Tony Powell & Nancy Mitford just clinging to their saddles but out of control.' There were, however, some new writers who were welcomed with enthusiasm. Evelyn much enjoyed and admiringly reviewed first novels by Sybille Bedford (*A Legacy*) and Muriel Spark (*The Comforters*). He was impressed by Angus Wilson, and by V. S. Naipaul, whom he described as a writer 'with an exquisite mastery of the English language,' watching his ascending reputation with approval. Ivy Compton-Burnett was still read with pleasure, as was Hemingway. In an article on 'Literary Style in England and America', Evelyn wrote, '[Mr Hemingway] is lucid and individual and euphonious. He has imposed limits on his powers which only a master can survive.' Regretting the lack of stylistic elegance in the present century, Evelyn continued,

Curiously enough it is not in the universities that one finds fine writing; Sir Maurice Bowra is learned and lucid, but dull; Lord

David Cecil has grace but no grammar; Mr Isaiah Berlin is diffuse and voluble; Mr Trevor-Roper vulgar. Among critics in the press the standard is higher. Mr Raymond Mortimer never fails. Mr Cyril Connolly has fitfully achieved some lovely effects. Among novelists Mr Anthony Powell, Mr Graham Greene, Miss Compton-Burnett, Mr Henry Green all have personal and beautiful styles.

But the non-pareil was P. G. Wodehouse, 'the Master'. In fact, Evelyn himself had a far greater claim to such a title, his own style infinitely superior in elegance, flexibility and range to Wodehouse's highly accomplished but essentially limited repertoire of pyrotechnics. But for Waugh Wodehouse had no rivals. Wodehouse still cheerfully inhabited that golden age to which Evelyn looked back with such a sense of loss and longing. 'For Mr Wodehouse there has been no Fall of Man; no "aboriginal calamity". His characters have never tasted the forbidden fruit. They are still in Eden. The gardens of Blandings Castle are that original garden from which we are all exiled.' Evelyn was a vigorous supporter of the movement to repair Wodehouse's reputation damaged by his broadcasting from Germany during the war, for which he had been publicly denigrated at the instigation of 'cad Cooper' and the Ministry of Information – 'Cooper's blackest hour' as Evelyn called it. He defended 'the Master' in a broadcast for the BBC on 15 July 1961, in honour of Wodehouse's eightieth birthday.

Waugh was generous with praise for those he admired, and generous with derision for those he did not. In 1961 Cecil Beaton, the poor little victim of Heath Mount, published a volume of diaries. 'Judging from this book, most of which is twenty years old, he can't write for toffee. Neither in verbal expression nor in literary construction does he show any but the feeblest talent,' a dismaying judgment as Beaton had gone to the expense of having his diaries professionally ghosted. Another favourite punch-bag, Stephen Spender, came in for a drubbing with his autobiography, *World within World.* 'At one stage of his life Mr Spender took to painting and, he naïvely tells us, then learned the great lesson that "it is possible entirely to lack talent in an art where one believes oneself to have creative feeling." It is odd that this never occurred to him while he was writing, for to see him fumbling

593

with our rich and delicate language is to experience all the horror of seeing a Sèvres vase in the hands of a chimpanzee.'

A more recent enemy was the Oxford historian, Hugh Trevor-Roper, 'the demon don' (soon to be Regius Professor of Modern History), regarded as damagingly anti-clerical and on Church matters shamefully ignorant. Evelyn sparred with him on a number of occasions, by no means always coming off best. 'Sir, Trevor-Roper is bored by Popish writers. We are not bored by him,' began a typical letter in the *New Statesman*. 'For on the rather frequent occasions when he tries to make fun of our religion, he sets us the amusing week-end competition of spotting the first howler. We seldom have to read far . . .'

In April 1960, Evelyn began on the final novel in his war trilogy.[13] There had been a number of offers for quick-to-produce non-fiction, for instance, a book on 'Cities of Enchantment', but although they were financially tempting, Evelyn turned them down.

> I decided on reflection that I had only a year or two ahead in which I was capable of original work and I shouldn't waste that time in hack-work. Soon I shall have to jump at every chance of writing the history of insurance companies or prefaces to school text-books. Squire & Belloc warn us of the horrors of longevity. But meanwhile while I have any vestige of imagination left, I must write novels.

Conventional Weapons, as it was originally titled, took exactly twelve months to complete. On 4 April 1961, Evelyn wrote to Peters, 'I have finished the novel – now called, did I tell you? *Unconditional Surrender*[14] – I don't think the last $^1/_3$ as good as the first $^2/_3$. I shall be interested to hear your opinion.'

As before Evelyn used Writers and Speakers Research, run by

[13] *Sword of Honour* was published by Chapman & Hall in 1965 and in paperback by Penguin in 1984.
[14] According to A. J. P. Taylor many incorrect statements have been made about the birth of the phrase 'Unconditional Surrender', which was in fact first used by Roosevelt to his military advisers immediately before leaving for the Casablanca conference of 1943. At the conference, 'Roosevelt produced his terms for ending the war: "Unconditional Surrender". Churchill endorsed the phrase, after trying, unsuccessfully, to exclude Italy . . .'

Joan Saunders, wife of the official historian of the Commandos, who supplied him with information about the Sword of Stalingrad, buzz-bombs, weather and air-raids. Laycock, with whom amiable relations had been sustained, provided details about the Guards. 'The Ceremonial swords carried by the Other Ranks of the Blues . . . are, technically, sabres, but are never referred to as such being knows as "State swords". They are made of steel & are a bloody nuisance to clean, especially after a guard or Escort on a rainy day.' Douglas Woodruff came up with names of old Catholic families to fill the pews at Mr Crouchback's funeral. (Guy on the way to Broome for his father's funeral is surrounded by fellow mourners. 'They greeted him with murmured words of condolence, and seeing it was necessary, reminded him of their names – Tresham, Bigod, Englefield, Arundell, Hornyold, Plessington, Herningham, and Dacre.') Ann Fleming was consulted over the method of obtaining an illicit abortion in wartime.

Unconditional Surrender strongly conveys Waugh's own feelings of sadness and resignation, his consciousness of having failed in the heroic destiny he had originally hoped to find in the war, his disillusionment in the war itself. Evelyn's own prayer, recorded in the diary at a period of profound depression – 'Here I am again. Show me what to do; help me do it' – is echoed in Guy's prayer at his father's funeral. 'He [Guy] reported for duty saying to God: "I don't ask anything from you. I am here if you want me. I don't suppose I can be any use, but if there is anything I can do, let me know." ' Prayer for Guy had long been an empty ritual. 'For many years now the direction in the *Garden of the Soul*, "Put yourself in the presence of God", had for Guy come to mean a mere act of respect, like the signing of the Visitors' Book at an Embassy or Government House.' His original, misguided attitude towards the war is summed up by Mme Kanyi, one of the Jewish refugees under Guy's aegis in Jugoslavia, her words recalling those spoken by Sonia Trumpington about her husband, Alastair, in *Put Out More Flags.*

'It seems to me there was a will to war, a death wish, everywhere. Even good men thought their private honour would be satisfied by war. They could assert their manhood by killing and being killed. They would accept hardships in recompense for having

been selfish and lazy. Danger justified privilege. I knew Italians
– not very many perhaps – who felt this. Were there none in
England?'
'God forgive me,' said Guy. 'I was one of them.'

The novel, beginning with the grotesque display of the Sword of
Stalingrad in Westminster Abbey, again closely follows the course
of Evelyn's war. Guy, refused permission to go abroad with the
Halberdiers, hangs about Bellamy's hoping for a job; joins a
parachute training course where he damages his knee; is posted
to Bari and en route to Jugoslavia is injured in a plane crash;
after recovering he endures harrowing months in Croatia dealing
with hostile partisans and Jewish refugees. In spite of all he has
been through Guy remains emotionally isolated; even the death
of his father, 'the best man, the only entirely good man, he had
ever known', fails to break him out of his apathy. His father's
example, however, does serve to remind him that, 'One day he
would get the chance to do some small service which only
he could perform ... All that mattered was to recognize the
chance when it offered.' (As Father D'Arcy observed, 'The theme
is the same, isn't it? as *Helena* and *Brideshead.*') The chance comes
not in the form of heroic action but in the saving of one soul.
Virginia has been made pregnant by Trimmer and fails to procure
an abortion. Guy agrees to remarry her. She is killed in an air-
raid, but the baby survives, to be adopted and brought up by
Guy, the progeny of the contemptible Trimmer now the heir to
Broome. At the conclusion of the book, Guy, now that Virginia
is dead, can marry again, his second wife Catholic and of good
family by whom he has children.

Most readers accepted this as a happy ending, but they were
deceived. 'I am disconcerted to find I have given the general
impression of a "happy ending". This was far from my intention,'
Evelyn wrote to Anthony Powell. 'The mistake was allowing Guy
legitimate offspring. They shall be deleted in any subsequent
edition. I thought it more ironical that there should be real heirs
of the blessed Gervase Crouchback dispossessed by Trimmer but
I plainly failed to make that clear. So no nippers for Guy &
Domenica in Penguin.'[15]

[15] The deletion was not made. In the Penguin edition, as in the original, Guy
and Domenica have two boys of their own.

Evelyn in
Royal Marines uniform

Lieut.-Colonel Robert Laycock,
'commander *par excellence*'

Evelyn and the 'smart set'
of 8 Commando training on Arran

Randolph Churchill 'had long been
a problem to the military'

Duff and Diana
Cooper

Nancy Mitford: 'she
had endless tales to
spin around their
mutual friends'

Ann Fleming, one of
Waugh's more
worldly women
friends

Pamela Berry, last of
the great political
hostesses

The Waughs in
Hollywood with
Anna May Wong
and Sir Charles
Mendl

Harold Acton,
arbiter,
innovator
and
iconoclast

A. D. Peters 'knew very well
how to handle his clients'

Christopher Sykes,
a 'fairly faithful jagger'

Laura with Evelyn
on one of her rare
visits to London

The family at Piers
Court: from the left,
Bron, Evelyn with
James, Laura
holding Septimus,
Teresa, Meg, Hatty
sitting cross-legged

The family growing up: Evelyn with Septimus in front,
Teresa, Laura, James, Meg, Hatty, Bron

Evelyn at fifty-six   Evelyn at his desk

The family in 1959: Hatty, Teresa, Laura, Meg and James,
Evelyn and Bron behind, Septimus in front

Bron in the
Royal Horse Guards

Evelyn in front of the
gate-house at Combe Florey

Evelyn about to give
Meg away at her
wedding

Maimie Lygon and
Evelyn with the
newly-married
FitzHerberts

Evelyn with his
grand-daughter,
Emily FitzHerbert

London wartime society is vividly recreated, the dinginess, the shortages, the terrible restaurant meals, the drunken parties behind the blackout, the few oases of illicit luxury. '[Ruben's] restaurant was a rare candle in a dark and naughty world. Kerstie Kilbannock, who had made noxious experiments with custard powder and condiments, once asked: "Do tell me, Ruben, how do you make your mayonnaise?" and received the grave reply: "Quite simply, my lady, fresh eggs and olive oil." ' One of the few stable landmarks among this moving population is Everard Spruce, editor of the literary magazine, *Survival.* The portrait of Spruce in his Charvet shirts, pampered by a group of adoring young women, naturally nettled Cyril Connolly. 'I asked a mutual friend . . . to report if it was me and she said, yes, without a doubt – it was then I began to mind a little I think chiefly because *Horizon* had taken so much trouble about you & because I had been so pleased to publish *My Father's House* in 1941 as well as *The Loved One* . . .'

It is Spruce who publishes the *pensées* of the sinister Ludovic, now after the escape from Crete a major. In *Unconditional Surrender* he plays an even more unpleasant and mysterious part than in *Officers and Gentlemen.* Guy is surprised to find Ludovic as commandant of his parachute training school; Ludovic for his part is appalled to see Guy, convinced that Crouchback must remember certain heinous acts of his on Crete, in particular those connected to the disappearance of Major Hound. To avoid Guy, he retreats into mental breakdown, his affections focused on a Pekinese puppy reminiscently called 'Fido'. Later on, Ludovic, restored, completes a novel, a lush melodrama, entirely unlike the sparse and precious *pensées* published in *Survival,* 'a very gorgeous, almost gaudy, tale of romance and high drama set . . . in the diplomatic society of the previous decade'. Ludovic was not alone in such an undertaking, one which has a familiar ring to it. 'Had he known it, half a dozen other English writers, averting themselves sickly from privations of war and apprehensions of the social consequences of the peace, were even then severally and secretly . . . preparing to compose books which would turn from the drab alleys of the thirties into the odorous gardens of a recent past transformed and illuminated by disordered memory and imagination.'

Although the mood is sombre, and with the coming of peace

the outlook for the future bleak, there is a distinctive element of humour. In the rôle of clown, Uncle Peregrine Crouchback is in a minor league when compared with Apthorpe or Ritchie-Hook, but he is memorable nonetheless. A pious and dried-up old bachelor, he is, if unintentionally, a more engaging figure than his elder brother. The scene between Uncle Peregrine and Virginia over dinner in a restaurant is a small masterpiece of comic balance and timing.

'Didn't you ever want to marry?'

'Not really.'

Uncle Peregrine was not at all put out by these direct personal questions. He was essentially imperturbable. No one, so far as he could remember, had ever shown so much interest in him. He found the experience enjoyable, even when Virginia pressed further.

'Lots of affairs?'

'Good heavens, no.'

'I'm sure you aren't a pansy.'

'Pansy?'

'You're not homosexual?'

'Good gracious, no. Besides the "o" is short. It comes from the Greek not the Latin.'

'Peregrine, have you never been to bed with a woman?'

'Yes,' said Uncle Peregrine smugly, 'twice. It is not a thing I normally talk about.'

'Do tell.'

'Once when I was twenty and once when I was forty-five. I didn't particularly enjoy it.'

'Tell me about them.'

'It was the same woman.'

Virginia's spontaneous laughter had seldom been heard in recent years . . . She sat back in her chair and gave full, free tongue . . . Uncle Peregrine smirked. He had never before struck success.

Unconditional Surrender, dedicated 'To my daughter Margaret, Child of the Locust Years', was published in 1961, in America under the title *The End of the Battle*. As with *Brideshead*, the reviewers were divided between admiration for an impressive artistic achievement and distaste for the author's snobbishness and reactionary views. Kingsley Amis in a witty and perceptive analysis praised all three novels for mobility, economy and breadth, but stuck at being asked to accept as exemplary the moral standards of the Crouchbacks. Guy's passivity would be sympathetic 'if he seemed to be really trying, but he never looks back from that stage, early in *Men at Arms*, when he appears in England in the first weeks of the war "looking for a job" by button-holing powerful friends at Bellamy's and writing to Cabinet Ministers' wives. What about all those jobs in the ranks of, say, Signals or the RASC? Unthinkable, naturally.' Joseph Heller in *Nation* was even more condemnatory; he found Crouchback pitiful and boring, and thought it was 'doubtful that a more unflattering portrait of Roman Catholics will soon appear in literature than the one Waugh draws of his favorite people in these novels... For someone who has never read Evelyn Waugh, this would be a poor place to begin. For many who always read him, this may, unfortunately, seem a good place to stop.'

Fortunately there were others whose critical faculties were able to rise above an instinctive antipathy to the subject. Bernard Bergonzi in the *Guardian*, made the priorities plain. 'To anyone brought up as a Catholic Mr Waugh's image of Catholicism is, to say the least, peculiar; and the same thing may well be true of his picture of the gentry. But that is beside the point; it is enough that Mr Waugh has found the myth creatively valuable... The quality of the writing is, throughout, superb, and confirms my belief that Mr Waugh is the best living writer of English prose.' In the *New York Times Book Review* Gore Vidal, with a dash of irony worthy of Waugh himself, hailed him as 'Our time's first satirist... [writing] in a prose so chaste that at times one longs for a violation of syntax to suggest that its creator is fallible, or at least part American.'

The completion of his trilogy gave Evelyn little sense of elation. He was worried about money, and haunted by the fear that his creative imagination would dry up, that inspiration would fail him. In an article for the *Sunday Times* about Rudyard Kipling, he wrote, 'Kipling was conscious of a "demon"... who entered him from outside and directed his work. Most story-tellers are aware of this influence. They do not know where they are tending; worse, they fear the ending of this guidance from some undiscovered place in their minds.' It was this demon, he felt, that was now deserting him. In March 1961, he wrote gloomily to Peters, 'I should like to come & discuss my dark future with you.'

There is no refuge

Evelyn's forecast was grimly accurate: it was a dark future that lay ahead.

During the early 1960s – while the nation was caught up in a cultural and economic renaissance, a social revolution, an explosion of new trends and ideas, with the young, as in the 1920s, coming into fashionable prominence – Evelyn sank deeper into premature old age. Physically he was in poor condition, arthritic, lethargic, smoking heavily, drinking too much, taking almost no exercise, every night imbibing quantities of paraldehyde to induce a few hours' unconsciousness. His hair was silver, he walked with a stick, and like his father he had grown extremely stout, his face so bloated that his already small features seemed to have shrunk into miniature. More than this, he began to yield to a form of spiritual torpor, losing all appetite for life, his vigorous intellectual energy ebbing away. In January 1962, he contributed an article on Sloth to a series in the *Sunday Times* on the Seven Deadly Sins, interpreting the word in its strict theological sense. 'It is in that last undesired decade [of life], when passion is cold, appetites feeble, curiosity dulled and experience has begotten cynicism, that accidie lies in wait as the final temptation to destruction. That is the time which is given a man to "make his soul".'

At first Evelyn's withdrawal and decline were gradual, seeming no more than a slight intensification of his habitual melancholy and general hostility towards the world. After finishing *Unconditional Surrender*, he informed Peters, 'I don't think I shall write another novel for five or six years.' But there was no immediate cause for alarm in that, and as it happened events within the family now made any sustained attempt at work difficult. Within a few months of each other, the two eldest children, Teresa and Bron, had announced that they wished to marry. Teresa while at Oxford had fallen in love with a young American, John D'Arms, and Bron had become engaged to Lady Teresa Onslow, daughter of the Earl and Countess of Onslow.

Apart from an instinctive antipathy towards any man wishing to take possession of one of his daughters, Evelyn took little interest in John D'Arms, accepting the situation calmly, if without enthusiasm. As an American, D'Arms was at a natural disadvantage, but otherwise unobjectionable. 'He is not superficially very American,' Evelyn reported, 'dresses sombrely, parts his hair and speaks in low tones. But he has the basic earnestness of his compatriots which I should find unendurable. However, that is Teresa's business, not mine.'

Bron in his father's view had done rather better. Relations between father and son had continued to improve, Bron writing in retrospect that in the final ten years of Evelyn's life, his father's comportment towards him 'was never so benign or so gentle'. Bron was already earning a good living as a journalist, his mission, as he explained to his father, 'to try and bring the lower classes to their senses'.

In November 1965, thanking for a birthday present of wine, Bron sent a letter that might have been written by the young Evelyn. 'I have found a new *métier* in journalism. A newspaper called *Sun* prints a weekly sermon, rather on the lines of my old *Catholic Herald* pieces, but pays 25 guineas a time. So far they have had the moral beauty of suffering inflicted by fireworks, the wickedness of allowing State-supported undergraduates to demonstrate, the idiocy of allowing Old Age Pensioners free medicine and the injustice of free public school education for children of the working class. Money for jam.' When in 1960 Bron had brought out his first novel, *The Foxglove Saga*, published by Chapman & Hall, Evelyn had been encouraging – 'Very funny, I thought' he told Ann Fleming. His son's bachelor existence was described with approval, very much the kind of dashing social life that Evelyn had aspired to at the same age. 'My son, Bron, has had an undeserved but gratifying success with a novel and is a dandy with rooms in Clarges Street and a thousand cards of invitation & is enjoying himself top hole.'

Evelyn took to Bron's fiancée, Teresa Onslow, pretty, clever and frightened of no one. To Jack Donaldson, he wrote good-humouredly, 'It is very distressing that my son should think of marriage at an age when he should give himself to the education of a femme du monde de quarante ans, but, as you remark, in this age of miscegenation it is agreeable that he should have chosen a consort of his own class.' Of his own class perhaps, but not of the same faith. Neither Teresa Onslow nor John D'Arms was Catholic, but while D'Arms had agreed to take instruction, Teresa had not, thus destroying Evelyn's hopes of a double ce-remony on the same day. But with Teresa Onslow an Anglican, 'she & Bron would not be admitted to the sanctuary but would have to stand outside the rails. This would cause offence to Lady Onslow. Both weddings fill me with gloom.'

Teresa Waugh was married on the third of June in Taunton, Bron on the first of July in London. To Diana Cooper Evelyn wrote, 'The boredom and expense of two weddings in a month is breaking my great spirit.' For his daughter, Evelyn had given a dance three days before at Quaglino's, having first consulted Brian Franks about hiring a military band for the occasion. 'I went last week to the Academy banquet and was much struck by the efficacy of military music in suspending conversation... Is there an agency for such things or does one have to write round to every regiment?... All I ask is noise.'

In spite of this precaution, the celebrations were 'extremely painful', and no less painful at Bron's wedding the following month at the Church of the Assumption, Warwick Street, with a reception afterwards at the House of Lords. Next day there was a photograph of the father of the groom, grossly corpulent in top hat and morning coat, which shocked Evelyn profoundly. 'The photograph of me in the paper has changed my life. I have drunk no wine or spirits since,' he wrote to Alec, reporting a month later, 'I have not yet touched wine or spirits since I saw the photograph of myself at Bron's wedding. Twice a day I drink a small glass of cider. I have halved my consumption of cigars. I have become totally silent.'

After these purgatorial experiences, a plan was formed which was temporarily reviving, a trip to British Guiana for the *Daily Mail*. Guiana was on the eve of independence, and the idea was for Evelyn to retrace his journey of nearly thirty years before, describing the changes that had taken place. The attraction of the project was not Guiana, of small interest to him in 1933 and of smaller interest now, but the fact that he would be escaping the English winter and able to take with him his nineteen-year-old second daughter as 'secretary'. 'Margaret is my darling still,' he told Diana Cooper. 'Much prettier again after a time of looking like a toad.' They had travelled together before: Evelyn had taken Meg to Paris when she was only thirteen and she had gone with him to Greece in 1960.

She was now living in London during the week, working for Father Caraman at Farm Street, returning home to Combe Florey nearly every weekend. The relationship was as highly charged as ever, Evelyn at one moment writing to his daughter as a stern and reproving father, at another with words as tender as a lover's. He missed her constant companionship, and was heavily censorious of her behaviour when away from him. He thought she drank too much, smoked too much – 'I beg you to consider the effect of smoking on your mother who has not stopped coughing day or night for fifteen years' – went out too often, stayed up too late. When she came to Combe Florey she should rest. 'By "rest" I don't mean hogging it in bed, but composing your disordered life, mending your clothes, writing your letters. Not painting your fingers with red ink and complaining of the lack of lively company.' He was emotionally demanding, easily wounded by signs on her part of slight or indifference, and inevitably there were frequent tiffs.

> It is kind of you to enquire after my melancholy. It is provoked
> by many causes not least by yourself. It was churlish of you,
> after your promise, to leave me a fortnight without word from
> you – and then a very meagre note dashed off in the hope of
> appeasing me before coming here. I gave you good warning that
> I should lose interest in you if you neglected me. I don't, of

course, expect a formal collins every time I give you a treat
because a treat for you is a treat for me. But one of the marks of
love is the wish to communicate.

'Please don't be cross with me because I can't bear it,' wrote Meg
from Farm Street. 'It would be the last straw for this old camel.
I am very sorry – it was more incompetent than discourteous
though.' And after another jealous outburst, 'You know I love
you more than anyone else in the world. Please don't stop loving
me I couldn't bear it. You didn't mean that letter seriously,
did you? . . . it's made me dreadfully unhappy . . . Papa I'll
give up living in London and come home for good if you like. I
don't love any of my friends here one quarter as much as I
love you.'

They left for Guiana at the end of November 1961, aboard the
Stella Polaris, the ship on which thirty years before Evelyn
had taken the ill-fated voyage with his first wife. On arrival
in Georgetown father and daughter were deluged with invitations.
'We flit about in private aeroplanes & launches and live
in luxurious guesthouses but I am awfully bored at seeing welfare
activities,' Evelyn wrote to Laura. 'It is like being
Princess Margaret.' They visited the old Jesuit with whom
Evelyn had stayed at the St Ignatius Mission. Father Mather,
still very much the craftsman, made Meg a handbag out of
monkey skin.

Despite her charm, Meg had a wintry side, with a full share of
the Herbert toughness and intolerance; with her father, however,
she was an engaging companion, cheerful, a good sailor, and
prepared to drink almost as much as he did. But Evelyn's pleasure
in his daughter could not disguise the fact that the places they
visited and their inhabitants bored him. 'We have had ten days
in Georgetown – too long . . . People have asked us out a lot but
they are not really very interesting people. Today we go off for a
brief excusion into the N.W. district. Then back to Georgetown
simply to tranship to Trinidad. Then another change of ship and
(I hope) a comfortable voyage home.' On the way back, the ship
called at Lisbon, where they were invited to lunch by Daphne
and Xan Fielding, now living in Portugal. Daphne was struck by
her old friend's melancholy. 'For a moment his spirits were
restored by the prospect of a dish of lampreys cooked with cream

and brandy and port, a local speciality. "I'm sure I shall die of a surfeit," he said, beaming with greed.' But then he caught sight of one of the passengers from the ship, whom he disliked, and his mood turned surly and captious.[1]

Evelyn's lack of interest in the expedition clearly conveyed itself in his written account. The *Mail*, which had contracted for five articles for a fee of £2,000, including expenses, expressed severe disappointment. Instead of five, they were now prepared to take only one article on Guiana, the other four to be written on subjects as yet unspecified. Having spent the money, Evelyn was obliged to agree, but when he received galley proofs of the piece in its diminished form he was horrified. 'They have cut it down to insignificance, removing almost every personal note. It was not a very good article before. Now it is contemptible & calculated to injure my reputation,' he wrote in distress to Peters. 'Do you think it is still possible to get back from the *Mail* all I have written about Guiana, and to get a respectable paper e.g. *Telegraph, Sunday Times* to take a long article 'Portrait of a Distressed Dependency'? *Mail*, for a consideration to surrender all rights on my voyage?' Fortunately John Montgomery managed to extract his client's work from the *Mail*, selling it instead to the *Sunday Times*, where it appeared under the heading 'Eldorado Revisited'.

The cool reception of Evelyn's account of his trip was lowering enough, but not as lowering as his effect on some of the people he met during it. In Trinidad he and Meg had stayed with Lord Hailes, governor general of the West Indies. It was now kindly passed on to him by Ann Fleming, who never could resist making mischief, that she had heard from Clarissa Avon that the Haileses had found him a bore. To Evelyn, with his horror of bores, this came as a bad shock, one compounded by an incident which happened shortly afterwards in White's. He gave a searing account of it to Nancy. 'I was sitting in the hall at 7 pm being no trouble to anyone, when a man I know by sight but not by name – older than I, the same build, better dressed, commoner – came up & said: "Why are you alone?" "Because no one wants to speak to me." "I can tell you exactly why. Because you sit there on your

---

[1] The passenger may have been Harold Nicolson, who in his diary of the voyage recorded, 'I talk to Margaret Waugh – a charming girl, intelligent and lovely . . . [I] talk to Waugh as a penance.'

arse looking like a stuck pig." ' Nancy tried to calm him down, but in spite of her disclaimer – 'Do try & get it into your head that whatever else you may be you are not a bore,' – he was still registering shock a month later.

> My writing again. How you will groan . . . But I must explain about boring the Haileses because it has been what young people call 'traumatic' . . . The crucial point is that I was confident they both enjoyed my visit . . . I talked loud & long & they laughed like anything. Now I find I bored them. Well of course everyone is a bore to someone. One recognizes that. But it is a ghastly thing if one loses the consciousness of being a bore. You do see it means I can never go out again.

For consolation he turned to the one sure source, writing to Margaret, 'I am in low spirits and in low water.' But Meg, far from comforting him, was now the cause of extreme anguish. Like her older brother and sister, Meg too wanted to marry. Having ended an unhappy romance shortly before leaving for Guiana, Meg on her return from South America had fallen seriously in love. For a time she was careful to say nothing, keeping her young man, Giles FitzHerbert, well away from Combe Florey, waiting till the summer to break the news. But even Meg could not have suspected the force of her father's reaction, the violent feelings of grief and jealousy which with almost super-human control he battened down out of sight. It was not that he had never contemplated the possibility of his favourite wishing to leave him for another man, but there was a painful difference between hypothesis and reality.

Three years earlier, when Teresa was being courted by John D'Arms, he had written cheerfully to Meg, 'Please marry someone very rich very soon, let him die, then you can set up house for me on a luxurious scale. I would not mind your having one daughter if she were like you. No sons please.' From time to time he had been introduced to some of her men friends, among whom there was one he regarded as suitable, Alexander Dunluce, son of Ran and Angela Antrim, a viscount, Catholic, educated at Downside and Christ Church, nephew of Christopher Sykes. 'If Dunluce proposes marriage, accept, unless he is positively repellant to you,' he had instructed Meg in March 1961. But it was Giles FitzHerbert she wanted, not Lord Dunluce.

Meg's defection broke her father's heart. She knew her marrying would hurt him, but not the extent of the hurt. 'I haven't really thanked you properly for being so kind about my engagement,' she wrote to him in August. 'You are the best father anyone can ever have had in the history of the world ... And there need be no divorce between us – I will come just as often for week ends – Giles won't mind ... Darling Papa I love you very much please don't stop loving me.' As friends wrote to congratulate him, Evelyn put on a brave face: FitzHerbert was not exactly the husband he would have chosen, he told Ann Fleming, 'an Irish stock-broker's clerk ... penniless, rather raffish in looks, small, a Catholic (thank God)', but there it was. To Nancy he came nearer the truth. '[Margaret] has fallen head over heels in love and I can't find it in my heart to forbid consummation ... She wants children & that is a thing I can't decently provide for her. I expect that in ten years time she will be back on my doorstep with a brood.' However, it was only to Diana Cooper that he was completely candid, her compassionate and sensitive response provoking an admission of profound misery.

> Your letter full of understanding. It is, to me, a bitter pill and ungilded. I would forbid the marriage if I had any other cause than jealousy and snobbery. As it is, I pretend to be complaisant. Little Meg is ripe for the kind of love I can't give her. So I am surrendering with the honours of war ... You see I feel that with Meg I have exhausted my capacity for finding objects of love. How does one exist without them? I haven't got the Gaiety euphoria that makes old men chase tarts.

Evelyn would not prevent the marriage, but he could in imagination do the next best thing. 'Do you remember books I wrote about a character called "Basil Seal"?' he continued in his letter to Diana. 'I suddenly yesterday began a story about Basil Seal at 60. Jolly good so far.'

Basil Seal Rides Again, or the Rake's Regress, is Evelyn's last work of fiction, thin on plot and technically undistinguished, but as a reflection of the author's state of mind significant. Basil Seal, prematurely aging, corpulent and lame, is married to the very rich Angela Lyne, by whom he has one daughter, Barbara ('Babs'), whom he adores. Returning to the house one night, he finds Babs at home with a handsome but dishevelled young man who is wearing one of Basil's shirts and insolently helping himself to Basil's drink. This is Charles Albright, whom, Babs informs her father, she intends to marry. Bewildered and appalled, Basil stumps off to consult Sonia Trumpington (widow of Alastair), to whom it is given to point out the obvious. 'Perhaps you can tell me what Barbara sees in him,' Basil says to her.

' "Why, *you*, of course," said Sonia. "Haven't you noticed? He's the dead spit – looks, character, manner, everything." ' It is then that something stirs in Basil's memory, recollections of a brief wartime affair with Charles's mother. A way out. He takes Babs into the park where he can talk to her quietly. There is something he has to tell her: Charles is her brother. 'Soundlessly Barbara rose from the seat and sped through the twilight, stumbled on her stiletto heels across the sand of the Row . . .' Basil, well content, drops in for a drink at Bellamy's before returning home. 'Angie, if it suits you, I think we might all three of us go to Bermuda tomorrow,' he says to his wife. 'I daresay Babs needs a change of scene.'

The relationship between Babs and her father carries an undeniably erotic undertone, his paternal possessiveness both tender and passionate. When at the beginning of the story Basil arrives back at the house, he is lovingly embraced by his daughter. 'It was not thus that Basil had often been greeted in limber youth. Two arms embraced his neck and drew him down, an agile figure inclined over the protuberance of his starched shirt, a cheek was pressed to his and teeth tenderly nibbled the lobe of his ear.' After Babs's shocking announcement that she intends to marry Charles, Basil with difficulty controls an explosion of rage, then brusquely interrogates her. ' "Have you been to bed with this man?"

"Not to *bed*."

"Have you slept with him?"

"Oh, no *sleep*."

"You know what I mean. Have you had sexual intercourse with him?" '

After a little more of this, 'There followed one of those scuffles that persisted between father and daughter even in her eighteenth year which ended in her propulsion, yelping.' As Evelyn did with Meg, Basil makes Babs cry – 'She pressed her face on his thigh and wept'; he addresses her as 'chattel' – "You stay where you're put, chattel", he tells her, fondly stern. In a letter to Meg shortly before her marriage Evelyn wrote, 'as long as you are my chattel you must pay attention to me.' As Nancy remarked when she read it, '[the story] gives rise to certain reflections . . . Was he [Basil] meant to be jealous? If so we are in deep waters indeed . . .'

There is a half-hearted attempt to trick out the theme with some familiar old friends – Ambrose Silk, Parsnip and Pimpernell, Margot Metroland now living in rooms in the Ritz and transfixed by television – but they barely materialise. The shape and balance of the story are oddly unsatisfactory; as John Montgomery complained, 'Why, when it has such pace and humour, should it finish at the end of the preliminary skirmish?' But for once Evelyn sacrificed artistry to wish-fulfilment.

In the past Basil Seal had shared several traits of character with his creator, and now in old age they were more alike than ever, not only in their incestuous passion, but in appearance, decrepitude, and attitude towards the young. ' "You complain of speechlessness, a sense of heat and strangulation, dizziness and subsequent trembling?" asks the doctor.

' "I feel I'm going to burst," said Basil.

' "Exactly. And these symptoms only occur when you meet young men?"

' "Hairy young men especially." '

And Evelyn at the Ritz had exactly the same experience as Basil after luncheon there one day. In the diary for December 1960 is this entry. 'I must have given my hat many hundreds of times to the old porter at the Ritz (London). The other day when I came to leave after luncheon he was not on duty, so I went behind his counter and collected my belongings. In my hat he had put a label with the one word "Florid".' The same for Basil: 'A day came when he sat longer than usual over luncheon and found the man off duty. Lifting the counter he had penetrated to the rows of pegs and retrieved his bowler and umbrella. In the ribbon of the hat he found a label, put there for identification. It bore the single pencilled word "Florid".'

For the generous fee of £3000, *Basil Seal* first appeared in Britain in the *Sunday Telegraph*, and in *Esquire* in America. The book, dedicated to Ann Fleming, was published by Chapman & Hall in 1963 in a signed, limited edition of 750, with a frontispiece by Kathleen Hale, creator of *Orlando the Marmalade Cat*. A thousand extra copies were printed for sale in the United States by Little, Brown. With such a small print-run it attracted only cursory attention. Among the few who noticed it, Jocelyn Brooke in the *Listener* regretted its brevity and praised its impeccable prose, while V. S. Pritchett, paying homage to Waugh as 'the most accomplished comic of his period', lamented the decision to portray the buccaneering Basil as old, fat and respectable. 'Sequels rob fictions of their immortality . . . the real Basil Seal can never be in his fifties.'

Margaret was married on 20 October 1962, she and Giles leaving immediately afterwards for Italy on their honeymoon. 'The young couple are now, it is hoped, enjoying congress in Porto Fino,' was how Evelyn in a dismaying choice of phrase described it to Ann Fleming. From the Villa Carnarvon, Meg wrote to her father, 'You were quite wrong about honeymoons – I'm enjoying mine awfully & not cried once or even considered it . . . Thank you very much . . . for behaving so beautifully at the wedding.'

With Meg gone, all pleasure in life evaporated, and Evelyn fell into deep melancholy. Not yet sixty, he felt eighty; he was enfeebled by senile infirmities and talked openly of his wish to die. Most of the day was spent indoors reading and writing letters, every evening doing *The Times* crossword with Laura.

It was a gloomy period for her, her husband's unhappiness weighing heavy on the household. If an old friend proposed a visit, Laura now had to calculate whether to tell Evelyn in advance, knowing that he would suffer days of agonising, convinced the visit would be a failure and he himself an intolerable bore, or to spring it on him at the last moment and risk his rage.

More and more Laura took refuge in her work out of doors, growing more silent and withdrawn when with her husband. Having given up her cows, she started market gardening, in which she was helped by Walter Coggan, a villager whose dubious expertise she unreservedly admired and depended upon. Soon it seemed that she preferred his company to that of anyone else, Evelyn sarcastically referring to the unprepossessing Coggan as 'my rival' or 'Laura's lover'. Evelyn now ate little, but he and

Laura both smoked heavily and drank too much, she sherry, Evelyn gin. Refusing an invitation to stay with the Walstons, he explained, 'The sad truth is that I am not sortable these days – too deaf & crotchety,' and to Nancy, 'I very seldom mind people's deaths. I long for my own.'

The winter of 1962–3 was exceptionally hard. 'The frost here has been very severe. Drive impassable. Very few taps or lavatories working. Deluges impending when there is a thaw.' To escape the worst of it, Evelyn decided to take Laura to Menton for a holiday. They would spend a week together before Laura joined Teresa and John D'Arms in Naples, leaving her husband for ten days alone in his favourite working environment, a comfortable, out-of-season hotel. But Evelyn was too depressed to work. 'On Sunday I felt so low that I nearly telegraphed for your return,' he told her. 'I am bored & idle . . . Evenings are the worst time. Very lonely then.' To Diana Cooper he described his sojourn in terms more appropriate to a sentence of solitary confinement. 'Sometimes the *Times* arrived in the evening. Sometimes next morning. I used to be glad when it was late because it gave me something to look forward to.'

Once home, Evelyn realised that something must be done. 'I am very lame. Rheumatic limbs can't carry the weight. Can't reduce weight by healthy exercise on account of lameness. Vicious circle.' Almost worse, as he told Nancy, 'I found in the last year that I could no longer get tight (a condition I enjoy) however much I drank.' On Ann Fleming's advice he booked himself in for a fortnight at Forest Mere, a health hydro in Hampshire, where on a diet of fruit and vegetable juice he succeeded in losing over a stone.

The work on which Evelyn had intended to start while staying in Menton was the first volume of an autobiography. In 1961 he had told Peters he was planning a three-volume work to be written over a period of ten years, a suggestion to which Peters responded with enthusiasm, soon returning with a handsome offer from the *Sunday Times* for £15,000 for the serial rights to all three volumes; Jack McDougall at Chapman & Hall would pay not less than £3000 for each volume, he told his client, and Little, Brown at least $5000. 'It is therefore safe to assume that the three volumes will bring in over £29,000 – say £5,000 a year for six years.' In July Evelyn began sorting through his papers, 'preparing to start on my autobiography (with some misgivings about what Alec is going to say in his)'.

Alec had begun writing the serial story of his life at a young age, publishing his first volume of reminiscences, *Myself When Young*, as early as 1923. Four more were to follow, the idea for the second, on which he was now at work, having evolved when he was stationed in Baghdad during the war. 'I am thinking of writing an autobiography of the years 1919–1931,' he had told his parents. 'I shall write it in the third person though, and omit my brother. It would be impossible to hit the right note...' Obviously with the two brothers covering much of the same ground, there was danger of overlap, and Evelyn suggested that they meet to decide on a division of territory, just as so many years before they had agreed to divide the world between them. Alec welcomed the proposal. With his parents dead, divorced from his wife, his children grown up, Alec came less frequently to England; his home base was now Tangier, although he still travelled extensively and spent at least a couple of months every year in the United States. He had felt out of touch. 'Now that our mother is not here,' he had written plaintively to Evelyn, 'no family news comes to me except from A. D. Peters.'

Scrupulously, Evelyn wrote to those who had been his closest friends at Lancing and Oxford asking for permission to refer to their youthful delinquencies. 'I think it may have caused a seasonable chill in some reformed breasts,' he told Nancy. 'There is a pompous ass called Hot-lunch Molson whom I don't suppose you ever met. I have a full diary of his iniquities in 1921–2. Perhaps he will fly the country.' Hugh Molson was appalled by the prospect, one of only two of those approached who begged Evelyn not to mention him, the other being Matthew Ponsonby, a magistrate and anxious about the effect on his reputation of the drunken arrest. Another who was expected to refuse was Dick Young, the licentious one-legged schoolmaster at Arnold House, but he on the contrary was delighted. 'Publish and be damned so far as I am concerned,' he wrote cheerfully from retirement in an almshouse in Winchester. 'I always flatter myself that I was the original Capt. Grimes.'

Amusing although some of this correspondence was, however,

the project failed to ignite. 'I distil a few daily drops of exquisite boredom about my early life,' Evelyn told Ann Fleming. 'The difficulty is that I am really not much interested in myself & too many of my associates are still alive.'

This lack of engagement comes through in the book, written from beginning to end with an elegant and stylised detachment. Starting with the statement, 'Only when one has lost all curiosity about the future has one reached the age to write an autobiography,' the narrative moves gracefully forward through an account of the Waugh and Raban forebears, to a description of Evelyn's parents and his own early life. To his mother he devotes barely more than a paragraph, but of his father he draws a full and affectionate portrait. 'There were times when I was inclined to regard his achievement as somewhat humdrum. Now I know that the gratitude I owe him for the warm stability he created, which I only dimly apprehended, can best be measured by those less fortunate than myself.'

The description of the three aunts at Midsomer Norton is intensely evocative, as are the childhood games with the Flemings (here named the 'Rolands'), the Pistol Troop, Heath Mount. Lancing is looked back on without affection – 'I do not seek to harrow with these mild austerities the reader who has vicariously supped full with the horrors of the concentration camp. I merely assert that *I* was harrowed' – although Evelyn's debt to both Crease and Roxburgh is handsomely acknowledged in vivid character studies of both. The section on Oxford is fairly brief and understandably reticent, with Alastair Graham, under the pseudonym 'Hamish Lennox', only glancingly mentioned as 'the friend of my heart'.

A final chapter on schoolmastering, 'In which Our Hero's Fortunes Fall Very Low', deals with Arnold House, and ends with the abortive suicide attempt. 'I turned about, swam back through the track of the moon to the sands . . . Then I climbed the sharp hill that led to all the years ahead.'

A Little Learning was published by Chapman & Hall and Little, Brown in September 1964. Among the critics there was an expression of mild disappointment: something more exceptional had been anticipated than this accomplished if unrevealing piece, a work of consummate artistry, but one in a minor key. 'Mr Waugh is a thoughtful rather than intimate autobiographer,'

wrote V. S. Pritchett in the *New Statesman.* 'He keeps the lid on.'
Much was made of the author's stylistic mastery, although William
Plomer in the *Listener* criticised the use of affectedly archaic
language. 'Mr Waugh's vocabulary and syntax do now and then
have an old-world air, like a well-dressed sexagenarian wearing
spats.' Anthony Burgess in *Encounter* also referred to Waugh's
'carefully outmoded elegance . . . The perfect mastery of the exact
conceptual locution, often implying . . . a moral judgment that is
not really there, is the source of all of Mr Waugh's humour and
irony.' Alec wrote a rambling and nervously noncommittal review
for *Cosmopolitan,* beginning, 'It is a curious experience to read
the autobiography of a brother – so much is familiar, yet so
much is strange,' and generously if lamely concluding, 'It is an
important book because it presents and interprets the seed-time
of one of the most important writers of our day. What would we
not give for a similar book from Balzac, Turgenev, or Thomas
Hardy? I do not see how it could have been better done.'

To Evelyn personally his brother wrote, 'Many many
congratulations . . . What different lives we led under the same
roof. Your life ended when his [Arthur's] key turned in the lock
and mine began.' Reactions from friends were almost wholly
favourable, with one or two exceptions. Katharine Asquith as
usual was 'shocked' by the book, in particular by the episodes
concerning the pederastic Dick Young. To her familiar litany of
pious indignation Evelyn patiently replied, 'There is no one
whose opinion I value more than yours. I assure you that I do
not introduce obscene passages in my work with the motive of
offending you. I rightly feared that there was an anecdote
in my memoirs which would offend you & therefore was in two
minds about sending you a copy. But affection overcame discre-
tion.' But by far the most hostile reaction came from Dudley
Carew, Evelyn's old schoolfriend, who in the section on Lancing
had been enraged to find that he had been almost ignored,
the friendship referred to harmlessly, anonymously and only in
passing.

Why on earth you should deliberately spit in the eye of one who
has always wished you well passes my comprehension. I have
long letters of yours over a period of years which give a very
different picture of an old friendship from the contemptuous

615

squiggle of a caricature you have of our relationship . . . Many
people whose opinion of me I value will have little difficulty,
thanks to your gratuitous clues, in identifying me with the
grotesque figure of the 'boy in another house'. As for my
private feelings, you have hurt them most damnably.[2]

Evelyn wrote him a pacifying letter, but ten years later, with his
old mentor safely dead, Carew took his revenge in a spiteful
memoir,[3] in which *A Little Learning* is described as 'the worst book
Evelyn ever wrote.'

But such annoyances were nothing compared to the storm that
was now about to break. It had long been clear that some changes
in the Church were inevitable. As early as 1949, Evelyn had
written, 'It may well be that Catholics of today, in their own
lifetime, may have to make enormous adjustments in their conception of the temporal nature of the Church.' But at that stage
he had no conception of how enormous those adjustments would
be. When on the election of John XXIII he had asserted that the
new pope was 'good for 25 years placid inactivity', he was voicing
the majority opinion of traditional Catholics of his generation.
The reign of John's predecessor, Pius XII, had lasted for nearly
twenty years, during which an extreme ultramontanism had prevailed throughout the Holy See, with the pope in old age becoming increasingly isolated and reactionary, largely ignoring the
growing unrest widespread in the Church, particularly in France
and Germany, where the work of some of the most outstanding
liberal theologians was officially condemned by Rome. The movement for change was based chiefly on a desire for liturgical
reform, for a lay apostolate, and for an approach towards some
degree of ecumenism. Pius had made a gesture in this direction
with his reform of the Holy Week liturgy, much resented by
Evelyn. At Downside for the Easter retreat of 1956 he had written
in his diary, '[the triduum was] rather boring since the new

---

[2] The offending passage begins, 'In the role of iconoclast which I assumed, I
fascinated and dominated a boy of my own age in another House . . . I set out to
ridicule his loyalties, particularly his devotion to myself, which secretly I rather
relished. He was warmly confidential; I patronising and sardonic.'
[3] *A Fragment of Friendship: a Memory of Evelyn Waugh When Young* (Everest Books,
1974).

liturgy introduced for the first time this year leaves many hours unemployed'. And in a later article for the *Spectator* he complained bitterly of the new Holy Week services.

> For centuries these had been enriched by devotions which were dear to the laity – the anticipation of the morning office of Tenebrae, the vigil at the Altar of Repose, the Mass of the Presanctified . . . Now nothing happens before Thursday evening. All Friday morning is empty. There is an hour or so in church on Friday afternoon. All Saturday is quite blank until late at night. The Easter Mass is sung at midnight to a weary congregation who are constrained to 'renew their baptismal vows' in the vernacular and later repair to bed. The significance of Easter as a feast of dawn is quite lost.

It was confidently assumed that the new pope, seventy-six when he took office, would do nothing to disturb the status quo while the search went on for a suitable younger man. However, in January 1959, only three months after his election, John announced his intention of summoning a general council. Amid intense excitement around the world, the Second Vatican Council was opened by the pope in St Peter's on 11 October 1962, the last of its four annual sessions convened on 8 December 1965, by which time John XXIII was dead.

Pope John, said Evelyn, 'had no idea of the Pandora's box he was opening'.

At first there seemed no great cause for anxiety. Evelyn wrote to Nancy in October 1962, 'The Council is of the highest importance. As in 1869–70 the French & Germans are full of mischief but, as then, the truth of God will prevail.' Before long, however, a horrified realisation of what was intended began to dawn. For over five hundred years the Latin Mass had remained almost unchanged. Now suddenly it was to be radically reformed, with the emphasis on popular participation and the demystification of the priest's rôle. Latin would be largely replaced by the vernacular, the priest was to face the congregation, and communal responses were to be encouraged. For Evelyn as for many British Catholics these changes were deeply disturbing, as though the bulwarks they had manned for generations had suddenly been swept away.

At the end of the Council's first month, Evelyn expressed his apprehensions.

> As the months pass and the Council becomes engrossed in its essential work, it is likely that the secular press will give less attention to it than it has done to its spectacular assembly. The questions for discussion are a matter of speculation to all outside the inner circle but there is a persistent rumour that changes may be made in the liturgy . . .
>
> As the service proceeded in its familiar way I wondered how many of us wanted to see any change. The church is rather dark. The priest stood rather far away. His voice was not clear and the language he spoke was not that of everyday use. This was the Mass for whose restoration the Elizabethan martyrs had gone to the scaffold. St Augustine, St Thomas à Becket, St Thomas More, Challoner and Newman would have been perfectly at their ease among us . . .
>
> . . . I think it highly doubtful whether the average churchgoer either needs or desires to have complete intellectual, verbal comprehension of all that is said . . . In most of the historic Churches the act of consecration takes place behind curtains or doors. The idea of crowding round the priest and watching all he does is quite alien there . . . Awe is the natural predisposition to prayer. When young theologians talk, as they do, of Holy Communion as 'a social meal' they find little response in the hearts or minds of their less sophisticated brothers.

As the Council moved relentlessly on, destroying the hallowed traditions of centuries, Evelyn's feelings of despair deepened. At first, before he conceded the hopelessness of any rearguard action, he did his best to organise resistance. He wrote to the *Tablet*, 'Will you promote an appeal to the Holy See for the establishment of a Uniate Latin Church which shall observe all the rites as they existed in the reign of Pius IX?'[4] To Daphne Acton,

---

[4] Evelyn much admired the reactionary Pius IX (1846–78), the first pope to identify wholeheartedly with ultramontanism, who in 1864 published an encyclical denouncing the principal errors of the age, including the view that the Pope can or should reconcile himself to progress, liberalism, and modern civilization. It was during his pontificate that the hierarchy was re-established in England and the First Vatican Council summoned. Among much else, that Council declared the infallibility of the Pope in faith and morals, and published a constitution deploring contemporary pantheism, materialism and atheism, thus clearly declaring its enmity to the neutral modern state.

who had sent him a pamphlet on liturgical reform, he explained his vehement objections, predominantly to communal response and the use of the vernacular.

> I am returning the tract you kindly lent me with some very cross marginalia. I didn't like it at all ... Some people, like Penelope Betjeman, like making a row in church and I don't see why they shouldn't ... Every parish might have one rowdy Mass a Sunday for those who like it. But there should be silent ones for those who like quiet ... The word 'vernacular' is almost meaningless. If they intend to have versions of the liturgy in the everyday speech of everyone, they will have to have some hundreds of thousands of versions ... They also say that we must have the same version as the Americans, heaven help us.

The tract, *Liturgy and Doctrine: the Doctrinal Basis of the Liturgical Movement*[5] by Charles Davis,[6] was returned to Daphne heavily annotated: 'Patronising pig! ... I suspect the author of being American ... Rot, ha ha ... old stuff ... Rot ... HERESY ... Ass ...' On the title page he had returned to the main theme of his grievance. ' "Active participation" doesn't necessarily mean making a noise. Only God knows who are participating. People can pray loudly like the Pharisee & not be heard while the silent publican is ... Multa obstant Nole imprimare.'

Increasingly, anger gave way to desolation. 'The Vatican Council weighs heavy on my spirits,' he wrote to Diana Cooper. 'I do not believe that there is much immediate prospect of reversing the disagreeable trend in the Church. In her inspired wisdom she will come right but not in our time.' For Easter 1964 he went to Rome 'to avoid the horrors of the English liturgy,' and in September met Archbishop (later Cardinal) Heenan to discuss what, if anything, could be done. 'I had been summoned to London to dine tête-à-tête with Archbishop Heenan to discuss the attitude of the laity to the liturgical innovations. He showed himself as deeply conservative and sympathetic to those of us who are scared of the new movement,' he reported to Katharine Asquith. But the archbishop, traditionalist by reputation, had progressive tendencies, and was not as reactionary as many of the

---

[5] Sheed & Ward, 1960.
[6] Father Charles Davis, editor of *Clergy Review,* was a well-known liberal theologian.

older Catholics among his flock hoped and believed. The following year Evelyn wrote in his diary, 'Cardinal Heenan has been double-faced in the matter,' and to Christopher Sykes, 'The hierarchy are like Gadarene swine.'

As if distress over the Church was not enough, Evelyn now found himself again in serious trouble financially. His solicitor, Wilfrid Evill, had died, leaving behind an unconscionable mess. The Save the Children Fund, it was now discovered, had been incompetently drafted, with the trust owing the Inland Revenue some fifteen years of back tax. Evelyn was appalled. He wrote to Meg, '[Evill] has been exposed as a charlatan and it seems possible that huge sums of back taxes will have to be paid. In fact we may have to auction our carpets and pictures and silver.' But it was not as bad as that. Peters managed the crisis deftly and was soon able to reassure Evelyn that in all probability he would not have to pay more than six years' tax, and for this amount, about £5000, there was enough money in hand. Knowing his client's extravagant habits, however, he was careful to add that, 'it would be dangerous for you to use any of the funds until we knew the worst.'

The next priority was to generate income. Film rights to *Decline and Fall* and *A Handful of Dust* had recently been sold, and the English director, Tony Richardson, had taken over Buñuel's option on *The Loved One* (for which, for one fleeting moment, Richard Burton and Elizabeth Taylor were considered for the rôles of Dennis and Aimée). In 1965 the war trilogy, with minor textual emendations, was published by Chapman & Hall in one volume under the title *Sword of Honour.* But Evelyn lacked both energy and inspiration; he had no plot in mind for a novel and was reluctant to start the next volume of autobiography: '[it] will be much harder to write as I have used almost all adult experiences already in one form or another.' Fortunately offers were coming in, from Doubleday for a history of the papacy, from George Rainbird, a publisher specialising in high-quality, lavishly illustrated books, for a history of the crusades. 'It certainly would be easy enough & agreeable to write 70,000 words in paraphrase of Runciman & Duggan,' Evelyn told Peters. 'All that worries me is the time limit.' He had been idle the previous year, 'not diseased, but enfeebled', and now there were three books to be written, with Rainbird pressing for an early delivery date. Evelyn had no wish to be hurried. 'I think those three books may be my last & with rising taxation there is no point in making more than a bare living. I don't want any money until I have work to show for it. We have both seen too many elderly writers fussed with advances they have accepted & can't satisfy. I would be happier to have no fixed day for delivery. If they *must* have a date ·can you satisfy them with the end of 1967?'

With small appetite for work, Evelyn had little desire either for amusement. A short holiday in Spain with Laura in the autumn of 1964 had been a failure. 'Can't speak the lingo,' he wrote to Bloggs Baldwin from Madrid, '& don't like the grub.' The truth was that he had lost all curiosity for foreign places and all capacity for enjoyment. He felt ill most of the time, but had no real wish to get better, was certainly not prepared to deny himself the debilitating quantities of drink and drugs to which he was addicted. He had, however, agreed to consult his doctor, he told Ann Fleming. 'I said "I have practically given up drinking – only about 7 bottles of wine & 3 of spirits a week." "A week? Surely you mean a month?" "No, and· I smoke 30 cigars a week & take 40 grains of sodium amytal." He looked graver & graver.' He even checked himself into hospital for a couple of days' examination, but checked out again when he discovered Randolph in the next room. 'I have been a fellow patient with him before.' Randolph was about to undergo an operation for the removal of a tumour on the lung, which fortunately turned out to be not malignant. Soon after hearing the news, Evelyn ran into Ed Stanley in White's. 'I remarked that it was a typical triumph of modern science to find the only part of Randolph that was not malignant and remove it. Ed repeated this to Randolph whom I met on my return from Rome, again in White's. He looked so pale and feeble and was so breathless that we there and then made up our estrangement of some twelve years.'

Although he drank heavily, Evelyn had lost interest in food and ate very little,. part of the trouble being that his teeth were bad and he found it difficult to chew. 'Most of my lack of appetite comes from the boredom of chewing with my few, loose teeth. Not eating drives me to the bottle – both spirits and drugs. One can't sleep hungry.' He took the drastic decision to have all his teeth removed, eccentrically disdaining an anaesthetic, a horrifying experience which left him weak and shaken; the false teeth which he had fitted were uncomfortable, and the ordeal fatally diminished him. 'My snappers are a failure,' he told Ann; and to Jack McDougall he wrote, 'I am toothless, deaf, melancholic, shaky on my pins, unable to eat, full of dope, quite idle – a wreck.' When Brian Franks invited him to the annual luncheon of old cronies at the Hyde Park Hotel in December 1964, Evelyn refused on the grounds that his presence could be only a burden and a bore. Franks wrote again, urging him to change his mind, and Evelyn, touched, agreed to come. 'I accept with gratitude & the repeated warning that I can only be regarded as a ghost. People get a macabre pleasure in observing the decay of their contemporaries. That is the only pleasure I can hope to give the assembled company.' Christopher Sykes, also at the luncheon, was placed opposite Evelyn and described the occasion. 'He had felt too ill to come down from his room before luncheon. He ate nothing. He drank nothing. He sat silent. I caught a glance from him which plainly said, "You see my state." After quarter of an hour he left, leaning on the arm of a waiter.'

In his life of Ronald Knox, Evelyn had written, 'Mystical writers agree that it is a common, if not universal, sign of advance in the spiritual life when "consolations" are withdrawn, and the soul is left without any sensible delights often for very long periods.' Certainly he himself seemed without consolation. His grief over the Church weighed crushingly on him, the vast brocade disintegrating before his eyes as the measures prescribed by the Council in Rome began to make themselves felt. To Diana Evelyn complained, 'They are destroying all that was superficially attractive about my Church. It is a great sorrow to me.' In his preface to *Sword of Honour* Evelyn stated, 'On reading the book I realized that I had done something quite outside my original intention. I had written an obituary of the Roman Catholic Church in England as it had existed for many centuries . . . Despite the faith of many of the characters, *Sword of Honour* was not specifically a religious book. Recent developments have made it, in fact, a document of Catholic usage of my youth.'

Instead of solace and inspiration, the Church daily became more remote. Evelyn was so distressed by the new liturgy and the communal celebration that he sought official advice on the minimal obligation for attending Mass, writing to the *Clergy Review* for guidance. 'I do not ask what is best for me; merely what is the least I am obliged to do without grave sin. I find the new liturgy a temptation against Faith, Hope and Charity but I shall never, pray God, apostatise.' Always stronger on faith than either hope or charity, he found himself under severe strain. To Diana Guinness (now Diana Mosley), with whom he had recently renewed a friendship begun and almost ended so many years before, he wrote, 'The Vatican Council has knocked the guts out of me ... I have not yet soaked myself in petrol and gone up in flames, but I now cling to the Faith doggedly without joy. Church going is a pure duty parade.'

Deep in 'the bowered world' of Combe Florey, as John Betjeman described it, Evelyn was drowning in melancholy, ill, aimless and miserable. He did no work, spending the day, he said, breathing on the library window, playing noughts and crosses, and drinking gin. To Nancy he wrote, 'Laura finds consolation in horticulture. I am a dreary companion for her these days.' His friends now began seriously to worry about his state. 'My darling Bo,' wrote Diana Cooper. 'I *am* exercised about your condition ... Find a way to feel better than you do – and I am almost sure that a disagreeable restraint ... more reading, less calmatives would slowly restore your appetite ... Don't resent this appeal, it is written in love.' Father D'Arcy, too, was anxious. 'I had not realised the depth of your depression, & wish to heaven that I could be of some help to you'. He compared Evelyn's disillusion with the Church to that of Robert Peckham, member of a distinguished recusant family, who fled England on the accession of Elizabeth I and sought refuge in Rome. Evelyn thanked D'Arcy for his letter, but rejected the parallel. 'Peckham had an easy choice of exile. Today there is no refuge.'

Behind the scenes there was much anxious debate as to what could be done. Patrick Kinross and Moray McLaren were in favour of trying to persuade Evelyn to see a psychiatrist, or failing that at least to change his medication, but predictably nothing came of it. Meg in London, having received a depressed letter from her father – 'You must not worry about my condition. I am growing old ... The awful prospect is that I may have more than 20 years ahead. Pray that I "make my soul" in this period' – wrote in alarm to Philip Caraman. 'I am *very* worried by Papa. I think he is seriously ill. He eats quite literally nothing & is physically weaker than I have ever seen him. I wrote him a long letter begging him to see a doctor but he hasn't answered . . . I don't think he really cares.' Father Caraman passed this on to Graham Greene, who replied that in his opinion Waugh was not suffering from despair in the theological sense, but from severe depression for which there was probably a clinical cure.

It was true: Evelyn no longer cared. He wanted to die. In January 1966, he told Ann Fleming, 'No work. Feeble health. Those who love me tell me I am dying but professional opinion does not confirm them.' Frail and dispirited, he asked Peters to cancel his contracts with Rainbird and Doubleday. 'Tell them I have temporarily lost my reason as the result of the Vatican Council. Tell them anything. Get them to release me from my foolhardy promise.' Meanwhile he undertook to start work on the second volume of autobiography, to be entitled, *A Little Hope*.[7] But his efforts were at best desultory. When Christopher Sykes encountered him in White's, Evelyn told him, 'My life is roughly speaking over. I sleep badly except occasionally in the morning. I get up late. I try to read my letters. I try to read the paper. I have some gin. I try to read the paper again. I have some more gin. I try to think about my autobiography. Then I have some more gin and it's lunch time. That's my life. It's ghastly.'

For Easter that year, Evelyn had asked his old friend at Downside, Dom Hubert van Zeller, to celebrate a Latin Mass at Combe Florey, but the request had been rejected. 'When the Abbot refused permission for this – the idea being that I should be with the community at that time,' van Zeller wrote later, '[Evelyn] felt that every man's hand was now against him, and that even Downside had let him down – judging him to be an unsuitable influence on one of its monks. He was quite wrong about this of course but I knew it would be useless to explain.' Evelyn then turned to Philip Caraman, who had become a confidant, staying frequently at Combe Florey and giving Evelyn what spiritual support he could. 'A gentle, uncomplaining visitor', Evelyn described him to Ann Fleming. Caraman would be at Pixton over Easter,

---

[7] From the poem by Alfred de Musset:
  'La vie est brève:
  Un peu d'espoir,
  Un peu de rêve
  Et puis – bonsoir'.

and was willing to say Mass, as a Jesuit needing no permission from a higher authority to do so.

On Easter Sunday, 10 April, at ten o'clock in the morning Father Caraman celebrated a Latin Mass at the Catholic chapel in Wiveliscombe, a village five miles from Combe Florey. In the congregation were Bridget Grant from Nutcombe, Auberon and Mary Herbert from Pixton, Evelyn and Laura, Meg and Giles FitzHerbert with their two children, Hatty, James and Septimus. As they came out of church, several people noticed how cheerful Evelyn seemed. Mary Herbert was surprised that he greeted even Auberon warmly, and Philip Caraman remarked how calm and contented he appeared, his depression evaporated, almost as though he had finally come through some dark night of the soul. 'He was benign and at peace, with a kind of tranquillity and serenity that as a priest one often meets in people who are dying.' The Waughs, Meg and Giles, Father Caraman and Mary Herbert drove to Combe Florey, where everyone gathered in the morning-room except Laura who went to the kitchen to make coffee. Evelyn was in high good humour, happy to have Meg staying in the house, full of talk about a new book by Martin D'Arcy which he was to review for the *Sunday Times*. Sitting in the bay window Philip Caraman and Hatty started a game of Scrabble.

Shortly before lunch Evelyn left the room. When after an interval he had not returned, James knocked on the door of the downstairs lavatory, which was locked. Climbing on Septimus's shoulders, James looked in through an outside window and saw his father collapsed on the floor.

The FitzHerberts' nanny tried to give him the kiss of life, but there was no response. Father Caraman administered Conditional Absolution, the Last Rites given on the supposition that life may not yet be extinct: 'Si vivis, ego te absolvo . . .' Then he telephoned Father Formosa, the priest from Wiveliscombe, to come with his oils to anoint the dead man. The police were asked to make contact with Bron, then living near Hungerford; he and Teresa had gone out to lunch and it was important to find them before the news broke. Bron arrived that evening, by which time his father's body had been removed from the house.

On 15 April, by special arrangement, Evelyn was buried just outside the boundaries of the Anglican churchyard at Combe

Florey, after a funeral conducted by Father Caraman at the Church of St Teresa of Lisieux in Taunton.

On 21 April 1966, a full Requiem Mass was held at Westminster Cathedral, permission having been obtained from the cathedral authorities for the Mass to be said in Latin. Father Caraman gave the address, with Cardinal Heenan on the Sanctuary throne. Present in the congregation were Laura and all the children, as well as Alec and Joan, and Alec's elder son, Andrew, who as a little boy had been a page at Evelyn's wedding. Among many old friends were Christopher Sykes, Patrick Kinross, Tom Driberg, Pansy Lamb, the Woodruffs, Antrims, Donaldsons, Sutros and Birkenheads. Brian Franks was there, also Tony Powell, Roger Fulford, and John Betjeman. Ann Fleming came, and so, perhaps mindful of the lecture she had once received, did Diana Cooper. There was a representative from Chapman & Hall, from the Royal Horse Guards, from the Abbot of Downside, and from the Latin Mass Society.

At the other end of Victoria Street, outside the Palace of Westminster, could faintly be heard the guns firing in salute to the queen as she arrived for the opening of Parliament. At the end of the service the 'Last Post' was sounded by trumpeters of the Blues.

Evelyn's last years were bleak and wretched, but his death was an unparalleled blessing, dying shriven on Easter Sunday, the most joyful day in the Church's year. As Meg wrote afterwards to Diana Cooper, 'You know how he longed to die and dying as he did on Easter Sunday, when all the liturgy is about death and resurrection, after a Latin Mass and holy communion, would be exactly what he wanted. I am sure he had prayed for death at Mass.'

Evelyn had made no secret of the fact that he longed to die; death held no fears for him. He had had a prevision of it once, years before. 'Guy jumped. For a second, as the rush of air hit him, he lost consciousness. Then he came to himself, his senses purged of the noise and smell and throb of the machine. The hazy November sun enveloped him in golden light. His solitude was absolute. He experienced rapture, something as near as his earthbound soul could reach to a foretaste of paradise, *locum refrigerii, lucis et pacis . . .*'

After Evelyn's death, Laura remained at Combe Florey. Wrongly convinced that she had been left in near poverty, she agreed to the sale of her husband's papers to the University of Texas. Among them were the bound manuscript volumes of his diary which, largely unread by Laura, caused waves of shock and horror when parts of them were published in a Sunday newspaper, later all of them in book form, fixing unmovably in the public mind the image of Evelyn Waugh as monster. In 1971 Bron and his family moved in to Combe Florey, Laura retiring to an apartment at the back of the house, where she lived with her spaniel, Credit, drinking copious quantities of Cyprus sherry and passing the time with crosswords and jigsaw puzzles. She died of pneumonia on 17 June 1973, and was buried on her fifty-seventh birthday, 'more deeply mourned than her modest nature could ever have understood'.

Meanwhile Evelyn's reputation continued to grow, and the sales of his best-known novels in the English-speaking world steadily increased. In the year of his death, *Vile Bodies* sold 9,108 copies, and in 1993, 11,729. *Brideshead Revisited* sold 7,644 in 1966, and 12,234 in 1993, its popularity reaching an apogee with the novel's dramatisation for television which brought the work to the attention of millions of new admirers, particularly among the vilified inhabitants of the United States of America.

Alec married again in 1969, his third wife, Virginia Sorensen, an American Mormon and writer of children's books, with whom he lived quietly in Tangier. At the very end of his life he and Virginia moved to Tampa, Florida, where Alec died on 3 September 1981.

All Evelyn's children married. Bron, although the author of five novels, never rivalled his father as a writer of fiction. He easily surpassed him, however, as a journalist, early establishing himself as the most original, provocative and successful columnist of his generation. Hatty, too, wrote novels, as well as regular reviews of films and fiction.

Margaret published a life of her grandfather, Aubrey Herbert, and there was talk of her producing a memoir of her father. But in January 1986, while crossing Chalk Farm Road in London, she was hit by a car and killed.

Source Notes

Of the many published sources consulted in the preparation of this book, I would like in particular gratefully to acknowledge the following: *The Letters of Evelyn Waugh*, ed. Mark Amory (Weidenfeld & Nicolson 1980); *The Diaries of Evelyn Waugh*, ed. Michael Davie (Weidenfeld & Nicolson 1976); *The Essays, Articles and Reviews of Evelyn Waugh*, ed. Donat Gallagher (Methuen 1983); *Evelyn Waugh: the Critical Heritage*, ed. Martin Stannard (Routledge & Kegan Paul 1984); *A Catalogue of the Evelyn Waugh Collection at the Humanities Research Center at the University of Texas at Austin*, Robert Murray Davis (Whitston 1981); *A Bibliography of Evelyn Waugh*, Robert Murray Davis, Paul A. Doyle, Donat Gallagher, Charles E. Linck, Winnifred M. Bogaards (Whitston 1986); *Mr Wu and Mrs Stitch: the Letters of Evelyn Waugh and Diana Cooper*, ed. Artemis Cooper (Hodder & Stoughton 1991); *The Letters of Ann Fleming*, ed. Mark Amory (Collins Harvill 1985); *The Letters of Nancy Mitford: Love from Nancy*, ed. Charlotte Mosley (Hodder & Stoughton 1993).

The sources of Evelyn Waugh's correspondence are various: letters written to Waugh and originally owned by the Waugh Estate are held by the British Library; the largest collection of letters written by Waugh is in the Humanities Research Center at the University of Texas at Austin. Most of Alec Waugh's papers, including the diaries of Arthur Waugh, are at the Twentieth Century Archives at Boston University. Much of Christopher Sykes's correspondence is at Georgetown University, Washington, DC; Patrick Balfour's at the Huntington Library, California and the National Library of Scotland. Many letters quoted here were in private collections when I saw them: some remain so, others have since been sold. Dates are marked in the list below only when the letter itself is dated by the writer or by postmark.

Abbreviations

Editions of the writings of Evelyn Waugh quoted in this book:

ALL   *A Little Learning: the First Volume of an Autobiography* (Chapman & Hall 1964).

BM   *Black Mischief* (Penguin 1965).

BR   *Brideshead Revisited: the Secret and Profane Memoirs of Captain Charles Ryder* (Penguin 1962).

DF   *Decline and Fall* (Penguin 1937).

EAR   *The Essays, Articles and Reviews of Evelyn Waugh*, ed. Donat Gallagher (Methuen 1983).

EC   *Edmund Campion* (Penguin 1953).

EWD   *The Diaries of Evelyn Waugh*, ed. Michael Davie (Weidenfeld & Nicolson 1976).

EWL   *The Letters of Evelyn Waugh*, ed. Mark Amory (Weidenfeld & Nicolson 1980).

HD   *A Handful of Dust* (Penguin 1951).

LO   *The Loved One* (Penguin 1951).

MA   *Men at Arms* (Penguin 1964).

MLLO   *Mr Loveday's Little Outing and other Sad Stories* (Chapman & Hall 1936).

NTD   *Ninety-Two Days* (Penguin 1985).

OG   *Officers and Gentlemen* (Penguin 1964).

OGP   *The Ordeal of Gilbert Pinfold* (Penguin 1962).

POMF   *Put Out More Flags* (Penguin 1943).

RP   *Remote People* (Penguin 1985).

RUL   *Robbery Under Law: the Mexican Object Lesson* (Chapman & Hall 1939).

S-K   *Scott-King's Modern Europe* (Chapman & Hall 1947).

US   *Unconditional Surrender* (Penguin 1964).

VB   *Vile Bodies* (Penguin 1938).

WIA   *Waugh in Abyssinia* (Methuen 1984).

WS   *Work Suspended and Other Stories including Charles Ryder's Schooldays* (Penguin 1982).

Other:

BL: British Library; BU: Mugar Memorial Library at Boston University; CWD: Catherine Waugh's Diary; DE: *Daily Express*; DM: *Daily Mail*; DT: *Daily Telegraph*; EW: *Evelyn Waugh, a Biography*, Christopher Sykes (Penguin

1977); *EWCH: Evelyn Waugh: the Critical Heritage*, ed. Martin Stannard (Routledge & Kegan Paul 1984); *EWW: Evelyn Waugh and His World*, ed. David Pryce-Jones (Weidenfeld & Nicolson 1973); Georgetown: Georgetown University, Washington, DC; HRC: Harry Ransom Humanities Research Center, University of Texas at Austin; Huntington: Huntington Library, California; *MBE: My Brother Evelyn and Other Profiles*, Alec Waugh (Cassell 1967); *MWMS: Mr Wu and Mrs Stitch: the Letters of Evelyn Waugh and Diana Cooper*, ed. Artemis Cooper (Hodder & Stoughton 1991); *MWY: Myself When Young: Confessions*, Alec Waugh (Grant Richards 1923); *NS: New Statesman; OMR: One Man's Road, Being a Picture of Life in a Passing Generation*, Arthur Waugh (Chapman & Hall 1931); *ST: Sunday Times; STel: Sunday Telegraph; TLS: Times Literary Supplement.*

Chapter I

1 **the nastiest tempered man**... *Ancestral Voices*, James Lees-Milne (Chatto & Windus 1977), 169.

1 **a saint** Malcolm Muggeridge to Christopher Sykes, 7 December 1973. Private collection.

1 **Why does everyone**... *OGP*, 30.

5 **the temptations of the greasepaint** *OMR*, 158.

5 **the inky virus** *OMR*, 163.

7 **All these books**... Peter Waugh, interview with author.

7 **With the dawn of May**... *Fortnightly Review*, May 1931.

8 **I had a lovely dress**... *CWD*. Private collection.

9 **by nature and education**... *OMR*, 270.

11 **We must remember**... ibid., 172.

11 **His manner is now**... Arthur Waugh to Kenneth McMaster, February 1904. HRC.

12 **An appalling outburst**... *ALL*, 22.

13 **Shopped in morning**... *CWD*.

15 **like a linseed meal poultice** Arthur Waugh to Kenneth McMaster, 6 June 1905. HRC.

15 **a dark-eyed, curly-haired**... ibid., 6 January 1927. HRC.

16 **Arthur sang & nursed**... *CWD*.

16 **I am much too fat**... Arthur Waugh to Kenneth McMaster, 26 April 1906. HRC.

17 **Knights of the Pen**... *A Hundred Years of Publishing*, Arthur Waugh (Chapman & Hall 1930), 1.

17 **Lucy & the boys**... *CWD*.

Chapter II

19 **Once more the borders**... Arthur Waugh to Kenneth McMaster, 26 May 1905. HRC.

20 **stout timbers** *ALL*, 44.

20 **a kindly, grateful** *OMR*, 269.

21 **quite raw, absolutely uneatable**... Arthur Waugh to Alec Waugh, 18 January 1917. BU.

22 **Lucy has no business**.., Stella Rhys to Christopher Sykes, 19 April 1974. Private collection.

23 **a world of privacy**... *ALL*, 86.

23 **the terrible autocracy**... *OMR*, 373.

23 **young with the young**... ibid., 374.

24 **Charming, entirely charming**... *ALL*, 69.

24 **Blast it! Darn it!**... ibid., 37.

24 **Nobody loves me**... ibid., 71.

24 **When this feeble voice**... 'My Father', *STel*, 2 December 1962.

25 **creating a little aura**... *ALL*, 54.

25 **Mrs Fleming cordially told me**... Arthur Waugh to Alec Waugh, 4 May 1914. HRC.

25 **Welcome home**... *MBE*, 164.

25*n* **The three great things**... Arthur Waugh to Andrew Waugh, 1933. Private collection.

26 **I know that I worry**... Arthur Waugh to Kenneth McMaster, 13 December 1913. HRC.

26 **I think your terms**... Arthur Waugh to Alec Waugh, 5 April 1916. Private collection.

26 **Dear Boy, I am sure**... Arthur Waugh to Alec Waugh, 29 August 1915. BU.

26 **The result of self-abuse**... ibid., 20 May 1914. BU.

27 **I might almost be said**... *OMR*, 332.

27 **the blue-and-gold**... Arthur Waugh to Alec Waugh, 25 May 1915. BU.

27 **My life centred**... **For my first**... 'My Childhood', Alec Waugh (unpub. ms.). HRC.

27*n* **Sunshine is wasted**... *MWY*, 41.

27*n* **in the possibility**... Arthur Waugh to Kenneth McMaster 28 August 1902. HRC.

28 **Daddy loves Alec**... *MBE*, 164.

28 Have you been hiding... Alec Waugh to Evelyn Waugh, 22 May 1909. HRC.

28n You are so like me ... Catherine Waugh to Alec Waugh, 31 January 1917. BU.

29 I had a nice book... Diary 1914 (unpub. ms.). HRC.

29 We all disliked him ... Marjorie Watts, interview with author.

29 Oh no, he has a brother... *MBE*, 164.

30 Are you blackmailed?... Diary 1915–1916 (unpub. ms.). HRC.

30 It's very nice... My Diary Voll 2 (unpub. ms.). HRC.

30 a whopping success... Arthur Waugh to Kenneth McMaster, 21 January 1914. HRC.

31 Eve! Fancy you... Arthur Waugh to Alec Waugh, 4 May 1914. HRC.

32 Shut your jaw... 'The Sheriff's Daughter' (unpub. ms.). HRC.

32 Fine is the clan ... 'Come to the Coach House Door Boys' (unpub. ms.). HRC.

32 I'm sorry, dear... ibid.

32 The applause was tremendous... Arthur Waugh to Kenneth McMaster, 1 January 1915. HRC.

33 Never be polite to Germans... *The Pistol Troop Magazine*, 1912. HRC.

33 a dark bushy mistarsh... 'The Curse of the Horse Race' published in *Seeds in the Wind: 20th Century Juvenilia from W. B. Yeats to Ted Hughes*, ed. Neville Braybrooke (Hutchinson 1989).

34 a great collector... 'Multa Pecunia'.

34 Sudenly the door opened... 'Fidon's Confetion' (unpub. ms.). HRC.

34 We allways have sausages... *EWD*, 5.

34 My name is Evelyn... 'My History & Diary' 1912 (unpub. ms.). HRC.

35 developed a vindictive... Arthur Waugh to Alec Waugh. Private collection.

35 We set out... Diary 1915–1916 (unpub. ms.). HRC.

36 Mother and Aunt Elsie ... Diary 1914 (unpub. ms.). HRC.

36n an obscure seat... *Harper's Bazaar*, May 1935.

36n My father belonged... *ALL*, 55.

37 Mother read me... *EWD*, 5.

38 With a thorough knowledge... *ALL*, 48.

38 no longer any good ibid., 68.

39 Despite all Mr Bourchier's... ibid., 92.

39 intensely curious... ibid., 93.

39 serving at the altar... Arthur Waugh to 'Diana', 30 August 1918. Private collection.

39 We are all struck... ibid.

39 **promised to make me** . . . *EWD*, 9.

39*n* **incuriously, without expectation** . . . *Charles Ryder's Schooldays* in *Work Suspended and Other Stories* (Penguin 1982), 306.

40 **Here the Devil** . . . 'The World to Come', Arthur Waugh to Kenneth McMaster, 24 August 1916. HRC.

40 **Not bad for twelve** . . . ibid.

40 **You know, mother** . . . *MBE*, 167.

40 **In the evening** . . . *EWD*, 8.

41 **I am very pleased** . . . Granville Grenfell to Catherine Waugh, 31 October 1910. BL.

42 **Geoghegan minor** . . . *ALL*, 82.

42 *Molior,* **to contrive** . . . ibid., 86.

42 **Fletcher got liked** . . . Diary 1914. HRC.

43 **Cynical without being cheaply so** . . . *The Cynic*. HRC.

43 **By George when the term** . . . Diary 1916. HRC.

43 **Rostail entered** . . . *EWD*, 9.

44 **It was a game** . . . 'The Balance' in *Georgian Stories* (Chapman & Hall 1926), 316.

44 **Awful score to a chap** . . . Stella Rhys to Christopher Sykes, 19 April 1974. Private collection.

44 **Evelyn is very sinister** . . . Cecil Beaton to Greta Garbo, 18 April 1948, quoted by permission of the executors of the Estate of the late Sir Cecil Beaton.

45 **I lost half my income** . . . Arthur Waugh to Kenneth McMaster, 25 August 1914. HRC.

45 **hypnotised by the war** ibid., 3 March 1915. HRC.

45 **My wife continues** . . . ibid.

46 **I feel rather sorry** . . . *EWD*, 8.

46 **Some of our soles** . . . ibid., 90.

46 **Kate is plunged in nursing** . . . Arthur Waugh to Kenneth McMaster, 24 August 1915. HRC.

46 **really nearly broken** . . . Arthur Waugh to Alec Waugh, 29 August 1915. BU.

47 **sacredly to yourself** Arthur Waugh to Alec Waugh, 5 June 1915. BU.

47*n* **Thus began a friendship** . . . *The Loom of Youth*, Alec Waugh (Richards Press 1917), 244.

Chapter III

49 a flint-girt fortress *EWD*, 21.

50 a bleak, untouchable epoch *WS*, 294.

51 my wife's gone . . . *EWD*, 27.

52 Ascension Day never passes . . . ibid., 678.

53 Not a word about Barbara . . . Alec Waugh to Hugh Mackintosh, 31 July 1916. Private collection.

54 Barbara & Evelyn have been busy . . . Arthur Waugh to Jean Fleming, 14 April 1914. Private collection.

55 The dance in the evening . . . *EWD*, 49.

55 Their loud laughter . . . Arthur Waugh to Jean Fleming, 14 April 1918. Private collection.

56 Evelyn has become quite amorous . . . Alec Waugh to Hugh Mackintosh, 31 January 1919. Private collection.

56 I think I shall have to snub her . . . *EWD*, 95.

56 I have shut down . . . ibid., 109.

57 bound in a sort of greasy . . . Undated ms. fragment (1918?). HRC.

57 Evelyn is a misfit . . . Alec Waugh to Hugh Mackintosh, 13 October 1917. Private collection.

57 Poor Evelyn has been getting into trouble . . . Catherine Waugh to Alec Waugh, 19 May 1918. BU.

58 Could you send me a few pennies . . . EW to Arthur and Catherine Waugh, 29 February 1920. BU.

58 They began with crumpets . . . *ALL*, 125.

59 Roxborough's French is really a joy . . . *EWD*, 20.

60 The Bowlby family were having a smart wedding . . . ibid., 87.

60 the most joyous of my life *ALL*, 124.

60 [Peter] was seventeen and a half . . . Ms. fragment. HRC.

61 Much has been written . . . ibid.

62 I did not admire . . . *ALL*, 109.

63 courageous and witty and clever . . . *Mallowan's Memoirs*, Max Mallowan (Collins 1977), 19.

63 In Head's House . . . *ALL*, 130.

63 We want it to be perfectly democratic . . . *EWD*, 35.

64 This is really most encouraging . . . ibid., 24.

64 If ever I paint anything . . . ibid., 41.

64 It is printed very well . . . ibid., 24.

64 I have spent a lot of today . . . ibid., 23.

65 **received me with exquisite charm** . . . *ALL*, 146.

65 **Letters are things** . . . *Eric Gill*, Fiona MacCarthy (Faber 1989), 44.

65 **Once the barest respect** . . . *Thirty-Four Decorative Designs*, Francis Crease (privately printed 1927), vii.

66 **He worked happily** . . . *WS*, 308.

66 **saying that I had real instinct** . . . *EWD*, 53.

67 **Threw up his eyes** . . . *ALL*, 148.

67 **as far as the turn** . . . introduction to *Thirty-Four Decorative Designs*.

67 **What is the matter is impatience** . . . Francis Crease to EW, 25 March 1920. Private collection.

68 **I asked Carew about Dick's objection** . . . *EWD*, 65.

68 **I am feeling very depressed** . . . ibid., 78.

68 **I see the only way** . . . ibid., 56.

68 **I owe anything at Lancing** . . . ibid., 74.

69 **The spell is broken** . . . ibid., 132.

69 **He seemed diminished** . . . *ALL*, 162.

69 **We lunched modestly** . . . *EWD*, 88.

69 **I do wish I could get a little taller** ibid., 77.

69 **the contagion of disillusionment** J. F. Roxburgh to EW, 12 March 1922. BL.

70 **a detached, critical Hyde** . . . *WS*, 311.

70 **could smell the cleaning stuff** . . . Ms. fragment (1918?). HRC.

70 **bulged with incorrect folding** . . . ibid.

70 **either hid from action** . . . *ALL*, 132.

71 **the House was in a fever** . . . ibid., 134.

71 **I lead as pure a life** . . . *EWD*, 147.

72 **All that day I wrestled** . . . ibid., 138.

72 **filth experience . . . with Roberts** . . . J. A. Hill to EW, December 1921. BL.

72 **Yet I knew** . . . *EWD*, 128.

72 **I mentioned the 'just you two' of the poem** . . . Dudley Carew, unpublished diary. Private collection.

72*n* **Apparently he wants to see him** . . . *EWD*, 61.

74 **a short, broad, strong-looking boy** . . . *et seq.*, *The Next Corner*, Dudley Carew (Lane 1924), 17, 125, 142, 187.

74 **I must write prose** . . . *EWD*, 123.

74 **The Tragedy of Youth in three burlesques** . . . ibid., 127.

74 **The chief result of the increased insight** . . . ibid., 92.

75 **Alec has an extraordinary chilling** . . . Carew diary, unpublished.

75 **Basil, to enliven the time** . . . *EWD*, 96.

75 **I am astoundingly elated** . . . ibid., 100.

76 **I have been put in the Upper Sixth** . . . ibid., 102.

76 **We had an excellent lunch** . . . ibid., 107.

76 **he went about in a depressed manner** ... Catherine Waugh to Alec Waugh, April 1921. BU.

76 **in great danger** ... *EWD*, 125.

77 **I am bitterly unhappy** ... ibid., 119.

77 **I am burdened with failure** ... ibid., 132.

77 **Your mother and I** ... *ALL*, 136.

77 **Father has been ineffably silly** ... *EWD*, 125.

77 **I am rather glad** ... ibid., 127.

78 **No mean theologian, Waugh** ibid., 755.

78 **This learned and devout man** ... 'Come Inside', Evelyn Waugh, from *The Road to Damascus*, ed. John O'Brien (1949), *EAR*, 367.

78 **Evelyn has come to the realisation** ... Carew diary, unpublished.

79 **If it's good enough for me** ... *Tom Driberg: His Life and Indiscretions*, Francis Wheen (Chatto & Windus 1990), 30.

79 **In the last few weeks** ... *EWD*, 127.

79 **for people who are bored stiff** ibid., 147.

79 **I am hating this term** ... ibid., 141.

79 **that it is better to go up to Oxford** ... ibid., 142.

79 **blushing scarlet with British Imperialism** Basil Handford, interview with author.

80 **Most of your work** ... C. R. M. F. Cruttwell to EW, 14 December 1921. BL.

80 **I am sure I have left** ... *EWD*, 154.

Chapter IV

82 **My chief memory of the staircase** ... *ALL*, 166.

82 **an hungering OL** *EWL*, 6.

82 **say of me now** ... ibid., 50.

82 **If I came down to Lancing** ... EW to Tom Driberg, June 1922. Christ Church, Oxford.

82 **I imagine I am pretty well disliked** ... EW to Dudley Carew, March 1922, *EWL*, 8.

83 **the sound of the English county families** ... *DF*, 10.

83 **there was the difficulty** ... *Pack My Bag*, Henry Green (Oxford University Press 1989), 219.

83 **entirely happy in a subdued fashion** *ALL*, 166.

83*n* **There appeared at my window** ... *BR*, 31.

84 **On my first afternoon** ... ibid., 29.

84 **not over well** ... *EWL*, 6.

84 **[there] is a pleasant old world violence**... EW to Tom Driberg, 13 February 1922, *EWL*, 6.

84 **which opened on an enclosed and enchanted garden**... *BR*, 32.

84 **I can say little**... EW to Dudley Carew, March 1922, *EWL*, 8.

85 **When asked by my tutor**... *ALL*, 172.

85 **for the biting criticism**... *Disjointed Recollections: Hertford College*, W. L. Ferrar (unpub. ms.). Hertford College, Oxford.

85 **He was tall, almost loutish**... *ALL*, 173.

86 **a silly little suburban sod**... *Seven Hundred Years of an Oxford College (Hertford College 1284–1984)* ed. Andrew Goudie (Hertford College, Oxford).

87 **Cruttwell dog, Cruttwell dog**... *Oxford in the Twenties*, Christopher Hollis, (Heinemann 1976), 86.

87 **Do you hear that?**... 'Evelyn Waugh's Lost Rabbit', Claud Cockburn, *Atlantic*, 1973.

87 **It is the memorial biography**... *Author-Biography*, Cecil Hunt (Hutchinson 1935).

87n **Crouching in his stall**... *Labels: a Mediterranean Journal*, Evelyn Waugh (Penguin 1985), 156.

88 **We are all of us young**... *Isis*, 2 May 1923.

89 **it seemed as though I was being given**... *BR*, 45.

90 **At Oxford I was reborn**... *ALL*, 171.

90 **with (as one of them said later)**... *Ruling Passions*, Tom Driberg (Cape 1977).

91 **very pink in the cheeks**... *EW*, 84.

91 **'Why do you make so much noise?'**... *Cyril Connolly: Journal and Memoir*, David Pryce-Jones (Collins 1983).

91 **We are of the stout South Country stuff**... *The First Drinking Song*, Hilaire Belloc.

91 **the hot spring of anarchy**... *BR*, 45.

91 **There was a drinking set**... *ALL*, 191.

91 **Do let me most seriously advise you**... EW to Tom Driberg, 1922, *EWL*, 10.

92 **that noisy alcohol-soaked rat-warren**... *In Time of Trouble*, Claud Cockburn (Hart-Davis 1956), 64.

92 **I did not greatly like**... *ALL*, 204.

92 **to barge about in the corridors**... *Brian Howard: Portrait of a Failure*, ed. Marie-Jacqueline Lancaster (Blond 1968).

93 **Oh my de-ar**... *A Cornishman at Oxford*, A. L. Rowse (Mott 1983), 24.

94 **I think much of it excellent** EW to Dudley Carew, 1923. HRC.

95 **that nice old maid** Harold Acton to EW, 21 September 1923. BL.

95 **Please forgive me**... Harold Acton to EW. BL.

96 Life here is very beautiful... EW to Tom Driberg, 1922, *EWL*, 10.

96 By the way a friend of mine... ibid., June 1922. HRC.

96 I have been inwardly faithful... Richard Pares to EW. BL.

96 My dear, *he lends his body*... A. L. Rowse to the author, 4 June 1991.

96 In vain that you ate the bread... Richard Pares to EW. BL.

97 his gift for absurdity... *Isis*, 3 December 1924.

97 When I felt most intimate... *ALL*, 192.

97 I have been rather gone on him... Cyril Connolly, 23 March 1923, *Cyril Connolly*, 63.

98 I have been having one of my periodic fits... EW to Dudley Carew, 1923. HRC.

98 A thoroughly sincere artist... *Cherwell*, 10 November 1923, *EAR*, 13.

100 that this was purely a question... *Isis*, 28 February 1923.

100 expressed his surprise... ibid., 14 November 1923.

100 supported the motion... ibid., 29 November 1922.

100 at best a technical question... *RP*, 120.

100 I proclaimed myself a Tory... *ALL*, 182.

101 a badger-like figure... *Isis*, 5 March 1924.

101 a strange shambling man... *Cherwell*, 5 September 1923.

101 Edward hated him... ibid., 1 August 1923.

102 and so the Lady Elizabeth... *Oxford Broom*, vol. 1, no. 3, June 1923.

102 I am depressed... EW to Dudley Carew. HRC.

102 Believe me my dear Carey... ibid.

102 There is no harm... *Isis*, 28 May 1923.

102n Evelyn was particularly dear to me... Harold Acton to Christopher Sykes, 16 October 1972. Private collection.

103 Dear Uncle Julius... *Cherwell*, 24 May 1924.

104 premature decrepitude... *Quarterly Review*, October 1916.

104 I hardly know how I shall live... EW to Tom Driberg. Christ Church, Oxford.

105 He was then in his late fifties... *BR*, 61.

105 Because I can choose my friends... Lord Molson to Nicholas Shakespeare (*The Waugh Trilogy*, BBC 1987).

106 There is far too much religion... EW to Dudley Carew, *EWL*, 4.

106 [I] never go to Chapel... EW to Tom Driberg, 13 February 1922, *EWL*, 7.

106 the friend of my heart... *ALL*, 192.

107 I could not have fallen under an influence... ibid., 193.

108 had no repugnance to the bottle... ibid., 192.

108 I have found the ideal way... Alastair Graham to EW. BL.

108 I've got a motor-car... *BR*, 25.

109 All the beautiful things... Alastair Graham to EW. BL.

110   **I was doing no good** ... *ALL*, 175.

110   **My life here has been extremely precarious** ... EW to Dudley Carew, *EWL*, 12.

111   **God made them in his own image** ... EW to Tom Driberg, 28 February 1922. Christ Church, Oxford.

112   **I cannot say that your 3rd** ... C. R. M. F. Cruttwell to EW. BL.

112   **heart-breaking dreariness** ... *Isis*, 12 March 1924, *EAR*, 20.

Chapter V

113   **strangely enough Joyce Fagan** ... *EWD*, 171.

114   **I cannot write or think** ... ibid., 177.

114   **Quite soon I am going to write a little book** ... EW to Dudley Carew. HRC.

114   **a suspicion settles on me** ... *EWD*, 177.

115   **Everything was inexpressibly sordid** ibid., 178.

115   **feeling more than a little disconsolate** ibid., 179.

115   **by illustrating *Punch*** ... ibid., 180.

115   **[The model] disclosed** ... 'The Balance' in *Georgian Stories*, 288.

116   **Every evening I return** ... *EWD*, 180.

116   **obsession with solid form** ... *ALL*, 211.

116   **I learned that it is not possible** ... *EWD*, 183.

116   **there is no stronger deterrent** ... *MWY*, 7.

117   **To me he was someone** ... Ms. fragment. HRC.

117   **sends him to Jermyn Street** ... *EWD*, 253.

118   **Looking back on it** ... ibid., 170.

118   **one wants a Bohemia of one's own** ... EW to Dudley Carew. HRC.

119   **pansies, prostitutes and journalists** ... *EWD*, 169.

119   **There's a drunken beast** ... Philippa Fleming to the author, 27 March 1991.

120   **Now with Alastair a thousand miles away** ... *EWD*, 194.

120   **like some baffled archangel** ... ibid., 185.

120   **After about this stage of the evening** ... ibid., 187.

121   **one man was sick** ... ibid., 188.

122   **no one in our class** ... EW to Dudley Carew. HRC.

122   **writing out letters of praise** ... *EWD*, 191.

123   **I met Mrs Greene** ... ibid., 196.

124   **Evelyn was here yesterday afternoon** ... Olivia Plunket Greene to Matthew Ponsonby. Private collection.

125   **A book, a play, a film** ... *ALL*, 217.

126 snapped like a lizard ... ibid., 225.
126 I wonder whether I am falling in love ... *EWD*, 193.
126 When he was washed ... ibid., 195.
126 I had promised to go to tea ... ibid., 197.
126 a ghost with a glass of gin in her hand 'He-Evelyn and She-Evelyn', Dudley Carew, *EWW*, 40.
127 almost wholly spoiled ... *EWD*, 198.
127 a tall old man ... ibid., 195.
128 'Oh, sir, will you take my bag?' ... *ALL*, 221.
128 tall and grand and elderly *EWD*, 200.
128 healthy, happy, well-fed ... *ALL*, 220.
128 There are no timetables ... *EWD*, 200.
129 He was a distinct success ... *DF*, 41.
129 Mr Banks frequently expresses himself ... *EWD*, 203.
129n Everyone was wearing ... ibid.
129n [I] look exactly ten years old ibid., 197.
130 A short time ago ... ibid., 201.
130 I got up late for chapel ... ibid., 204.
130 the result was that I was sick ibid., 202.
130 an aged eunuch ... ibid., 204.
131 On Wednesday Gordon and I ... ibid., 203.
131 There was no happiness ... *ALL*, 225.
131 We all do nothing ... *EWD*, 204.
131 All the term I have been allowing her ... ibid.
131 It makes me sad for them ... ibid., 202.
131 I should dearly like ... ibid., 203.
131 about Silenus – very English ... *EWL*, 23.
131 Gordon and Dean and I ... *EWD*, 204.
132 considered gravely how very little ... ibid., 205.
132 rather ill-naturedly, I thought ibid., 206.
132 After all I was rather more ... EW to Matthew Ponsonby, 27 April 1925. Private collection.
133 in spite of the insistent sorrows ... *EWD*, 207.
134 it seems unkind ... ibid., 210.
134 I am making the first chapter ... ibid., 212.
134 a fidgety, learned, humorous bachelor ... 'A Little Hope', ms. fragment. HRC.
135 has left four schools ... *EWD*, 213.
135 'What did you find to enjoy?' ... *ALL*, 227.
135 Too English for my exotic taste ... ibid., 228.
135 I debate the paradoxes ... *EWD*, 211.
135n It was an airy Firbankian trifle ... Harold Acton to Christopher Sykes, 25 September 1972. Private collection.

137 **I was tired and ill at ease** ... *EWD*, 217.

137 **My dearest Evelyn, I feel very lonely now** ... Alastair Graham to EW. BL.

137 **Thank you for your letter** ... ibid.

138 **dull, but tolerable** ... Richard Plunket Greene to EW. BL.

138 **I took languid, lengthy** ... *EWD*, 224.

138 **taught the poor mad boys** ... ibid., 226.

138 **they act contemptibly** ibid., 237.

139 **dined at the George** ... ibid., 245.

139 **I was behaving very oddly** ... ibid., 232.

139 **I want to write a book** ... ibid., 233.

140 **Very tired and sad** ibid., 229.

140 **I am writing in the middle of the night** ... ibid., 216.

140 **remote from me** ... ibid., 233.

140 **that disgusting dance of hers** ibid., 238.

141 **Olivia as usual** ... ibid., 234.

141 **Olivia could talk of nothing** ... ibid., 281.

141*n* **⅓ drunk** ... ibid., 698.

142 **Alastair and I both got very drunk indeed** ibid., 265.

142 **went at the bottle** ... *EWW*, 46.

143 **I arranged a tableau** ... *EWD*, 240.

143 **so ignorant about Paris** ... ibid., 263.

143 **My account there** ... *EWD*, 246.

143 **it rained all the time** ibid., 256.

143*n* **At first the boys despised me** ... *Nash's Pall Mall Magazine*, March 1937, *EAR*, 191.

144 **was rather a bore** ... *EWD*, 250.

144 **rather odd in shape** ... EW to Chatto & Windus, 3 September 1925. Reading University.

144*n* **Adam is lying on his face** ... 'The Balance' in *Georgian Stories*, 312.

145 **Poor Adam, I never thought** ... ibid., 280.

145 **Imogen, you never really cared** ... ibid., 295.

145 **a very silly review** ... *EWD*, 268.

145 **made savage inroads** ... ibid., 254.

146 **and got very drunk** ... *EWD*, 256.

146 **now nearly sixteen** ... *Rossetti: His Life and Works*, Evelyn Waugh (Duckworth 1975), 11.

146 **the noblest painting** ... ibid., 39.

146 **a life of sobriety** ... *EWD*, 265.

146*n* **Poor Mr Toad** ... *Rossetti*, 22.

147 **increasingly given to sordid malefactions** ibid., 270.

147 **very modern indeed** ... ibid., 274.

148 **It seemed to me then** ... *Labels*, 128.

148 I am afraid I have inherited overmuch . . . *EWD*, 276.

148 rather a blow . . . ibid., 280.

149 Dear Evelyn, I cannot tell you how sorry . . . 'Edmund' to EW, 21 February 1927. BL.

149 the time has arrived . . . *EWD*, 281.

149*n* The early hours, the close association . . . *Passing Show*, 16 February 1929, *EAR*, 51.

150 esurient narcotics Harold Acton to EW, 1 January 1928. BL.

150 simply unintelligent to confine . . . Robert Speaight to Christopher Sykes, 3 April 1974. Private collection.

150 a face like a fungus Georgiana Blakiston, interview with author.

150 found her packing bottles . . . *EWD*, 249.

151 the Cross *and* the Crown *Letters from Baron Friedrich von Hügel to a Niece*, Gwendolen Greene (Dent 1928), xix.

151 rather a charming flat in John Street . . . *EWD*, 281.

151*n* Holy suffering is the very crown . . . *Letters from Baron Friedrich von Hügel*, 156.

152 I have met such a nice girl . . . ibid., 284.

Chapter VI

153 was a girl it was impossible to dislike . . . *A Fragment of Friendship*, Dudley Carew (Everest 1974), 79.

153 Utterly delightful . . . Anthony Powell, interview with Nicholas Shakespeare (BBC 1987).

154 like a china doll . . . Diana Mosley, interview with author.

155 More like a bare fairy! 'Evelyn Gardner', Mary Clive (unpub. ms.) (1987).

155 some of us suffered *Evening Standard*, 9 January 1930.

156 *I* think it's time . . . Pansy Lamb, interview with Nicholas Shakespeare (BBC 1987).

157 the correct procedure . . . *Passing Show*, 26 January 1929, *EAR*, 48.

158 which I spent in a week *EWD*, 284.

158 Balston will never see that book . . . *MBE*, 180.

158 beginning decorously at Basso's . . . *EWD*, 285.

158 Could you have seen my enjoyment . . . Francis Crease to EW, 4 October 1927. BL.

158 that unquiet lady *EWD*, 290.

159 He received me in bed . . . ibid., 289.

159 Turner was seventy-one years old . . . *Rossetti*, 20.

159 **in later life [Rossetti] was inclined** ... ibid., 119.
160 **the baffled and very tragic figure** ... ibid., 13.
160 **the *moral* stability of the great artist** ... ibid., 98.
160 **All his brooding about magic** ... ibid., 226.
160 **There is no reason why** ... ibid., 152.
160 **yet in some measure coherent** ... Brian Howard to Robert Byron, *Brian Howard: Portrait of a Failure*, 253.
160 **I deal with God as best I can** ... EW to Robert Byron, 13 February 1928. Private collection.
161 **How I detest this house** ... *EWD*, 289.
161 **Oh, Tolstoy, and that sort of thing** Anthony Powell, interview with Nicholas Shakespeare (BBC 1987).
161 **all except the carving in the evenings** *EWD*, 293.
161 **Those were delightful days** ... *Nash's Pall Mall Magazine*, March 1937, *EAR*, 191.
161*n* **Furniture is so useful** ... *MBE*, 193.
162 **An awful old woman** ... Evelyn Gardner to John Maxse, 21 November 1927. University of Columbia.
162 **Evelyn got a little tight too** ... ibid.
162 **immense charm & a very generous nature** ... *EW*, 119.
163 **Lately we have become** ... Evelyn Gardner to John Maxse, 21 November 1927.
163 **at that moment had some of the air** ... *Messengers of Day*, Anthony Powell (Heinemann 1978), 67.
163 **rang up Pansy** ... *EWD*, 294.
163 **Went to Southampton Row** ... ibid.
163 **'I'm going to be married'** *Messengers of Day*, 64.
164 **She is an impossible person** ... Evelyn Gardner to John Maxse, November 1927. Columbia.
165 **a Mr Crutwell (palpitating with perverse vices)** ... ibid., May 1928. Columbia.
165 **The late Lord Burghclere** ... Pansy Pakenham to John Maxse, 8 May 1928. Columbia.
165 **Victory for the Evelyns!** Evelyn Gardner to John Maxse, 2 May 1928. Columbia.
165 **but then my opinion** ... Pansy Pakenham to John Maxse, 29 December 1927. Columbia.
166 **Old Mr Waugh is a complete Pinkle-Wonk** ... ibid., 21 November 1927. Columbia.
166 **a tight-lipped, snobby little thing** Philippa Fleming, interview with author.
166 **Somehow I thought that you wouldn't be pleased** ... Evelyn Gardner to Catherine Waugh, 28 December 1927. HRC.

167 **[It] does not get on** . . . EW to Harold Acton, 1928, *EWL*, 25.

167 **I do not see much hope** . . . Evelyn Gardner to John Maxse, February 1928. Columbia.

167 **the first fine careless rapture** . . . Pansy Pakenham to John Maxse, 1 February 1928. Columbia.

167 **. . . Unfortunately, [she] is really afraid of poverty** . . . ibid., 8 May 1928. Columbia.

168 **As soon as I see any hope** . . . EW to Patrick Balfour, 20 February 1928, *EWL*, 26.

168 **[Waugh's] engagement still prospers** . . . Pansy Pakenham to John Maxse, 12 June 1928. Columbia.

168 **Mama has gone off to Egypt** . . . Evelyn Gardner to John Maxse, 2 February 1928. Columbia.

168 **book on Rossetti is a success** . . . Pansy Pakenham to John Maxse, 19 March 1928. Columbia.

168 **Peter Quennell . . . said it might have been made** . . . Harold Acton to EW, 1 May 1928, *EWCH*, 69.

168 **I am not proud of the book** . . . EW to Harold Acton, 27 April 1928, *EWL*, 27.

169 **He is fully alive** . . . *Nation & Athenaeum*, 19 May 1928, *EWCH*, 71.

169 **Miss Waugh approaches** . . . *TLS*, 10 May 1929.

169 **Your reviewer refers to me** . . . EW to *TLS*, 17 May 1928, *EWL*, 28.

169 **Dear Mr Waugh, May I tell you** . . . Rebecca West to EW, *EWCH*, 79.

169 **Do you like 'Untoward Incidents'?** . . . EW to Anthony Powell, 7 April 1928, *EWL*, 26.

169 **The phrase, you remember** . . . ibid.

169n **Certainly I didn't mean** . . . Peter Quennell to EW. HRC.

170 **I have finished the novel** . . . EW to Harold Acton, 27 April 1928, *EWL*, 27.

170 **[Evelyn] roared with laughter** . . . *EWW*, 43.

170 **it is really screamingly funny** . . . Evelyn Gardner to John Maxse, 18 July 1928. Columbia.

170 **my sincere great admiration** . . . Harold Acton to EW. BL.

172 **[Firbank's] later novels** . . . *Life & Letters*, March 1929, *EAR*, 58.

172 **a creditable career** . . . *DF*, 11.

172 **A novelist's trade . . . is the only one** . . . *Graphic*, 31 May 1930.

173 **Went to a quarry with four dogs** . . . *EWD*, 290.

173 **a stout elderly woman** . . . *DF*, 67.

173 **emerged with little shrieks** . . . ibid., 128.

174 **two eloquent photographs** . . . ibid., 150.

174 **'If there's another word . . .'** ibid., 38.

174 **Peter Pastmaster came into the room** . . . ibid., 213.

175   [Evelyn Gardner's] marriage still seems remote ... Pansy Pakenham to John Maxse, 12 June 1928. Columbia.

175   as their own rooms are so disgusting ... Robert Byron to Margaret Byron, 7 June 1928, *Robert Byron: Letters Home*, ed. Lucy Butler (John Murray 1991), 103.

175   Evelyn and I began to go to Dulwich ... *EWD*, 294.

176   this elusive, timid creature ... Pansy Pakenham to John Maxse, 26 July 1928. Columbia.

176   forked out handsomely ... EW to Laura Herbert. BL.

176   to avoid scandal & misconstruction ... Evelyn Gardner to John Maxse, 18 July 1928. Columbia.

177   Half a house in a slum ... EW to Henry Yorke. HRC.

177   find him squatted on the floor ... *Memoirs of an Aesthete*, Harold Acton (Methuen 1948), 204.

178   a pair of squirrels ... Daphne Fielding to Christopher Sykes, 21 October 1973. Private collection.

178   a fauness with a little snub nose ... *Memoirs of an Aesthete*, 202.

178   How *could* she leave all that delicious *food?* ... Mary Clive (unpub. ms.).

178   [which] will be rather amusing ... Evelyn Gardner to John Maxse, 28 March 1928. Columbia.

178   The happy pair will not be poorer ... Pansy Pakenham to John Maxse, 26 July 1928. Columbia.

179   full of scandal about the Sitwells ... *EWD*, 296.

179   more or less kindly comments ... ibid., 298.

180   *Decline and Fall* is an uncompromising ... *Evening Standard*, 11 October 1928, *EWCH*, 82.

180   [Mr Waugh] is an important addition ... *Observer*, 23 September 1928, *EWCH*, 81.

180   there is a love of life ... *NS*, 3 November 1928, *EWCH*, 85.

180   I remember that lunch ... *Good Talk: an Anthology from BBC Radio*, ed. Derwent May (Gollancz 1968), 16.

181   As a satire ... *NS*, 3 November 1928.

181   [Waugh's] book is dedicated 'In Homage' ... *Evening News*, 2 November 1928, *EWCH*, 84.

181   I don't know what to say ... *Oxford in the Twenties*, 105.

181   *Decline & Fall* seems to be going well ... EW to Tom Balston, 1 October 1928. Private collection.

181   Our finances have vastly improved ... Evelyn Gardner to John Maxse, 2 January 1929. Columbia.

182   Please fix up anything ... EW to A. D. Peters, *EWL*, 30.

182   The misunderstanding is unfortunate ... ibid. HRC.

182   a humorous serial called *Young Man* ... ibid., *EWL*, 30.

183 **Could you get the** *Express* ... EW to W. N. Roughead, November 1928. HRC.

183 **The** *Daily Express* **say** ... A. D. Peters to EW, 27 November 1928. HRC.

183 **I find humorous articles an awful strain** ... EW to W. N. Roughead, November 1928, *EWL*, 30.

183 **[choosing] as a subject** ... *Passing Show*, 2 February 1929, *EAR*, 49.

183 **It seems to me that it would be nice** ... EW to W. N. Roughead, *EWL*, 30.

183 **In business, in the professions** ... *Evening Standard*, 22 January 1929, *EAR*, 46.

184 **Would anyone like travel articles** ... EW to A. D. Peters, January 1929. HRC.

184 **[Mr and Mrs Waugh] were about to spend the proceeds** ... *Daily Sketch*, 30 January 1929.

184 **from the icy contact of a cocktail glass** ... *Labels*, 8.

185 **I did not really enjoy** ... ibid., 55.

185 **distressingly like a corpse** ... ibid., 57.

185 **In spite of all reports** ... EW to Harold Acton, *EWL*, 31.

186 **There are three good bookshops** ... EW to Arthur Waugh, 1929, *EWL*, 31.

186 **Today she is sitting up** ... EW to Tom Balston. Private collection.

186 **We have had to give up** ... EW to Arthur Waugh, *EWL*, 31.

186 **I hope now things are easier** ... EW to Harold Acton, *EWL* 31.

186 **I am struggling to write** ... EW to Tom Balston, 12 March 1929. Private collection.

186 **a pathetic S.O.S. from the Evelyns** ... Alastair Graham to Mark Amory, 7 December 1978. Private collection.

186 **struggle along for another week or two** ... EW to Arthur Waugh, *EWL*, 31.

186 **enormous and hideously expensive** ... EW to Harold Acton, 1 April 1929, *EWL*, 32.

187 **The travel book is going to be** *very* **good** ... EW to Tom Balston. Private collection.

187 **I am growing a moustache** ... EW to A. D. Peters. HRC.

187 **We are getting a little fed up** ... Evelyn Gardner to John Maxse, 26 May 1929. Columbia.

187 **combining a gay enthusiasm** ... *Labels*, 120.

187 **little Evelyns Waugh** ... *Sacheverell Sitwell: Splendours and Miseries*, Sarah Bradford (Sinclair-Stevenson 1993), 202.

187 **Their new hobby is to talk Greek** ... EW to Henry Yorke, 4 May 1929, *EWL*, 33.

188 **I will send you about twenty articles** ... EW to A. D. Peters. HRC.

188   that obsession by panic ... *Labels*, 45.

188   They were quite naked ... ibid., 47.

188   They seem to have been unable ... ibid., 116.

188   Gaudì bears to these anonymous contractors ... ibid., 144.

189   The young man was small ... ibid., 24.

189   The hills were covered with asphodel ... ibid., 54.

189   looking distressingly like a corpse ... ibid., 57.

189   Geoffrey was not to be consoled so easily ... ibid., 58.

189   I woke up several times ... ibid., 167.

190   It would be difficult to imagine ... *Observer*, 12 October 1930, *EWCH*, 114.

190   a minute house ... EW to Harold Acton. Private collection.

190   We found bills of over £200 ... EW to Henry Yorke, *EWL*, 35.

190   To be left entirely alone ... Evelyn Gardner to John Maxse, 28 March 1928. Columbia.

190*n*   I don't think it is complete ... Carl Brandt to A. D. Peters, 14 April 1930. HRC.

191   We hardly ever saw the light of day ... Nancy Mitford, *Arts et Loisirs*, 1966.

191   I danced blissfully with Evelyn ... Harold Acton to EW, 26 June 1929. BL.

191   the Hon. Nancy Mitford ... *Bystander*, 3 July 1929.

193   a welter of sex and snobbery ... EW to Harold Acton, *EWL*, 37.

193   In the evenings I sit with the farmers ... EW to Henry Yorke, *EWL*, 36.

193   [Evelyn] was dressed in a rough shirt ... *Twenty-One Years*, Randolph S. Churchill (Weidenfeld 1965), 97.

193   I have written 25,000 words ... EW to Henry Yorke, *EWL*, 36.

194   butter not melting in her mouth ... Margaret Wyndham to John Maxse, 30 July 1929. Columbia.

194   It's terrible ... *MBE*, 190.

195   I am afraid my book is not written ... EW to Tom Balston. Private collection.

195   Evelyn so obviously was determined ... Pansy Pakenham to John Maxse, 26 September 1929. Columbia.

195*n*   has to work hard for him ... ibid., 19 March 1928. Columbia.

196   constriction from He-Evelyn's brain ... John Heygate to Alec Waugh, 6 December 1967. BU.

196   I explained to her a lot ... *EWD*, 315.

197   my smutty lawsuit ... EW to Tom Balston. Private collection.

197   It's going to be a great blow ... *MBE*, 192.

197   I asked Alec to tell you ... EW to Catherine and Arthur Waugh, *EWL*, 38.

197 **Are you so very male** ... Harold Acton to EW, 5 August 1929. BL.

198 **Certainly the fact that she should have chosen** ... EW to Harold Acton, *EWL*, 38.

198 **It is extraordinary how homosexual people** ... EW to Henry Yorke, *EWL*, 39.

198 **my mock marriage** EW to Laura Herbert. BL.

198 **I fear [She-]Evelyn's affairs** ... Pansy Pakenham to John Maxse, 26 September 1929. Columbia.

198 **He was miserable** ... Margaret Wyndham to John Maxse, 10 September 1929. Columbia.

198 **Well, you can't call life dull!** ... Mary Clive (unpub. ms.).

Chapter VII

200 **the all-encompassing chaos** ... *HD*, 137.

200 **I wish I was handing Evelyn over** ... EW to Tom Balston. Private collection.

201 **My horror and detestation** ... EW to Henry Yorke, *EWL*, 39.

201 **wires arrive in green envelopes** ... EW to Tom Balston. Private collection.

201 **everyone is talking so much nonsense** ... EW to Harold Acton, *EWL*, 38.

201 **I confess to being shy** ... EW to Tom Balston. Private collection.

201 **Can you suggest anything** ... EW to Henry Yorke, *EWL*, 39.

201 **Have you tried quickly sleeping** ... Claud Cockburn to EW. BL.

201 **strange mixture of dash and melancholy** ... V. S. Pritchett's memorial address.

202 **I do hope that you are in a towering rage** ... Henry Yorke to EW, 15 September 1929. BL.

202 **I am escaping to Ireland** ... EW to Harold Acton, *EWL*, 38.

202 **The real value of marriage** ... *DM*, 8 October 1929.

202 **they will be printing my austere views** ... EW to A. D. Peters. HRC.

202 **Do you & Dig share my admiration** ... EW to Henry Yorke, *EWL*, 39.

203 **He was the best company** ... *Loved Ones: Pen Portraits*, Diana Mosley (Sidgwick & Jackson 1985), 57.

203 **One couldn't have had him constantly in the house** ... Diana Mosley to Christopher Sykes, 30 September 1975. Private collection.

204 **The chief instrument in the band** ... *Cyril Connolly: Journal and Memoir*, David Pryce-Jones (Collins 1983), 221.

204   **I am going to stop hiding away** . . . EW to Henry Yorke, *EWL*, 41.

205   **It has been infinitely difficult** . . . ibid., *EWL*, 390.

205   **one of the meanest and most fraudulent** . . . Richard Aldington, *Sunday Referee*, 9 February 1930, *EWCH*, 103.

205   **cocktail parties given in basement flats** . . . *VB*, 111.

205   **'I don't know if it sounds absurd** . . .' ibid., 123.

205   **'My dear, I never hated anything** . . .' ibid., 83.

206   **to admit that perhaps love was a thing** . . . ibid., 91.

206   **The truth is that like so many people** . . . *VB* (Chapman & Hall 1930), 95.

206   **'After all, damn it** . . .' *VB*, 196.

206   **a horizon of straggling red suburb** . . . ibid., 200.

206   **a splintered tree stump** . . . ibid., 223.

206   **'Oh, Nina, what a lot of parties'** . . . ibid., 123.

206   **'Well,' they said, 'Well** . . .' ibid., 28.

206   **those two poles of savagery** . . . ibid., 115.

207   **the Presence of Royalty** . . . ibid., 126.

207   **'What I always wonder, Kitty, dear** . . .' ibid., 130.

207   **There was a famous actor** . . . ibid., 53.

207   **The new drink is green beer** . . . *DE*, 18 October 1930.

207   **One can go to Shepheard's** . . . *VB*, 36.

208   **true to the sound old snobbery** . . . ibid., 38.

208   **'What about a little drink?** . . .' ibid., 40.

208   **Rosa was having some trouble** . . . EW to Daphne Fielding, 30 July 1962, *EWL*, 589.

208   **There are two bastards** . . . *EW*, 147.

208   **Not long ago I published a novel** . . . *DM*, 31 May 1930, *EAR*, 73.

209   **by ambiguous telephone calls** . . . *VB*, 110.

209   **a perfectly sheepish house in Hertford Street** . . . ibid., 29.

209   **I think there would be something wrong** . . . *Paris Review*, April 1962.

209   **[Adam] went up the steps** . . . *VB*, 68.

210   **rescued from Red Indians** . . . ibid., 211.

210   **six important new books** . . . ibid., 9.

210   **Father Rothschild pulled on a pair** . . . ibid., 133.

210   **I know very few young people** . . . ibid., 132.

211   **a most frightfully depressing book** . . . Henry Yorke to EW, 21 December 1929. BL.

211   **the chief in my view** . . . *Evening Standard*, 29 January 1930, *EWCH*, 99.

211   **an extremity of desperation** . . . *Fortnightly Review*, February 1930. *EWCH*, 107.

211   **Those *Vile Bodies* seem to be selling** . . . EW to A. D. Peters, 29 January 1930. HRC.

211 **you know how deep our interest** . . . Carl Brandt to Arthur Waugh, 3 April 1930. HRC.

212 **crash through with a swell offer** . . . Carol Hill to A. D. Peters, 16 April 1930. HRC.

212 **Did I tell you I saw a man** . . . EW to A. D. Peters. HRC.

212 **He is so tremendously amusing** . . . Joyce Reynolds to A. D. Peters, 15 February 1930. HRC.

212 **£15.15 a thousand** . . . EW to A. D. Peters. HRC.

212 **temporarily up to £2500 a year** . . . *EWD*, 309.

212 **The book that interests me most** . . . *Graphic*, 4 October 1930, *EWCH*, 113.

212 **Thinking things over I feel very strongly** . . . EW to Tom Balston, 30 August 1930. Private collection.

213 **to avoid the manners of the new rich** . . . *EW*, 149.

213 **No-one has a keener appreciation** . . . *DM*, 12 July 1930.

213 **climbed the slopes of London society together** . . . Frank Longford, interview with author.

214 **Lady C. very restless** . . . *EWD*, 324.

214 **Stale buns and no chairs** . . . ibid., 310.

214 **They talked of spiritualism** . . . ibid., 322.

214 **He has a simple, friendly nature** . . . ibid., 320.

214 **There were two ambassadors** . . . ibid., 318.

215 **Sachie likes talking about sex** . . . ibid., 328.

215 **I have seen at Pakenham** . . . *Observer*, 2 December 1961.

216 **like a couple of twins** . . . Elizabeth Longford, interview with author.

216 **Go after Frank** . . . ibid.

216 **Frank and Harman slept together** . . . *EWD*, 328.

216 **lean, dark and singular** . . . *ALL*, 213.

217 **the manual dexterity of the workers** . . . *EWD*, 317.

217 **[Your review] was quite excellent** . . . Henry Yorke to EW, 24 September 1929. BL.

217 **I am longing to read it** . . . ibid., 22 June 1929. BL.

217 **Most unsatisfactory and I am afraid** . . . *EWD*, 311.

217 **Vain, jealous and too rich** . . . Robert Byron to EW. BL.

217 **I have just read *Brothers & Sisters*** . . . EW to Harold Acton, 23 January 1930, *EWL*, 49.

218 **an umbrella from Brigg** . . . *EWD*, 315.

218 **Diana and I quarrelled** . . . ibid., 320.

218 **trying to explain that it was my fault** . . . ibid., 322.

219 **I must have seemed unfriendly** . . . EW to Diana Guinness, 17 July 1930, *Loved Ones*, 64.

219 **You ask why our friendship petered out** . . . EW to Diana Mosley, 9 March 1966, *EWL*, 638.

219*n* **When Evelyn got fed up with me** ... Diana Mosley to Nancy Mitford. Private collection.

220 **He was able for the first time** ... *MBE*, 196.

221 **fate accorded me the delights of dalliance** ... *A Year to Remember: a Reminiscence of 1931*, Alec Waugh (W. H. Allen 1975), 40.

221 **that absorption in and ultimate identification** ... *MBE*, 196.

221 **You cannot appraise** ... ibid., 198.

221 **Audrey felt ill all the week** ... *EWD*, 314.

221 **Audrey says she thinks** ... ibid., 316.

221 **Went back and slept with Varda** ... ibid., 314.

222 **such passades** ... *MBE*, 197.

222 **anxious to be friendly** ... *EWD*, 311.

223 **she couldn't stick him** ... Diana Mosley, interview with author.

223 **[Baby] left early** ... *EWD*, 313.

223 **[I] saw Baby in the distance** ... ibid., 322.

223 **chucked ... on Friday** ... ibid., 314.

223 **The trouble comes entirely from young women** ... *DM*, 14 June 1930.

223 **I must tell you** ... Gwen Plunket Greene to Dolly Ponsonby, 2 March 1930. Private collection.

223*n* **Wrote my *Mail* and *Graphic* articles** ... *EWD*, 314.

224 **the great, tremendous and dazzling lure** ... *Letters of Conrad Russell 1897–1947*, ed. Georgiana Blakiston (John Murray 1987), 110.

224 **[She] is marvellously happy** ... Gwen Plunket Greene to Dolly Ponsonby. Private collection.

224 **the call came unadorned** ... *Letters from Baron Friedrich von Hügel*, xli.

224 **about the habits of some strange tribe** ... Mia Woodruff, interview with author.

224 **grim reality** ... ibid.

224 **noli me tangere atmosphere** ... Edward Yarnold SJ, obituary notice.

225 **Went to Father D'Arcy** ... *EWD*, 320.

225 **They are very settled in their minds** ... ibid., 325.

225 **I wonder whether it will be possible** ... *Evelyn Waugh's Officers, Gentlemen and Rogues*, Gene D. Philips (Chicago 1975), 53.

225 **With me, [D'Arcy] saw it was no good** ... EW to Penelope Betjeman, 18 February 1948, *EWL*, 269.

226 **watching critically from the balcony** ... *DE*, 30 September 1930.

226 **a first interest in the Catholic Church** ... *The Road to Damascus*, ed. John O'Brien (1949), *EAR*, 366.

226*n* **What I fear is that the popular papers** ... EW to Philip Caraman, 19 July 1955, *EWL*, 448.

227 **a proposition [which] seemed so plain** ... *The Road to Damascus*.

227 I have never myself met a convert ... *EW,* 156.

227n I reverence the Catholic Church ... *Paris Review,* April 1962.

228 unintelligible and unendurable without God ... *The Road to Damascus.*

228 he needed to cling to something ... Graham Greene, interview with Nicholas Shakespeare (BBC 1987).

228 the essential issue is no longer ... *DE,* 20 October 1930, *EAR,* 103.

229 God give our wavering clergy back ... from *The Secret History of the Oxford Movement,* a Protestant propaganda poem by Walter Walsh.

229 Superficially he was an aesthete ... introd. to *Richard Raynal, Solitary,* Robert Hugh Benson (Regnery, Chicago, 1956).

229 stumped up to the altar ... *EWD,* 792.

230 a Catholic Cathedral is a sort of world ... *A Packet of Letters: a Selection from the Correspondence of John Henry Newman,* ed. Joyce Sugg (Oxford 1983).

230 it took me years to begin to glimpse ... EW to Penelope Betjeman, 10 February 1948, *EWL,* 267.

Chapter VIII

231 hidden in the mountains ... *RP,* 11.

231 I want very much to go to Abyssinia ... EW to A. D. Peters, 12 September 1930, *EWL,* 49.

232 inconceivably ill-disciplined children ... *EWD,* 329.

232 preposterous Alice in Wonderland fortnight ... *RP,* 22.

232 peculiar flavour of galvanized and translated reality ... ibid., 23.

233 but for the bare feet ... ibid., 21.

233 the tin and tarmac squalor ... *WIA,* 89.

234 Evelyn Waugh after various interviews ... Irene Ravensdale's diaries. Private collection.

234 It was highly interesting to me ... *RP,* 39.

234 Coronation cable hopelessly late ... *EWD,* 333.

234 After all, Evelyn ... ibid., 332.

234 I have rarely seen anything so hysterical ... EW to Henry Yorke, *EWL,* 51.

235 expert of high transatlantic reputation ... *RP,* 44.

235 who, we learned later ... ibid., 59.

235 of which the world stood in awe ... ibid., 61.

235 It would take many weeks ... ibid., 71.

236   **He struck me as flaccid** ... *The Life of My Choice*, Wilfred Thesiger (Collins 1987), 92.

236   **I'd have been tempted to knock him off** ... Wilfred Thesiger, interview with author.

236   **[Rimbaud] used to live with a native woman** ... *RP*, 79.

237   **spoke a queer kind of French** ... ibid., 76.

237   **all very much like Rat's preparation** ... ibid., 80.

237   **He knew it all by heart** ... ibid., 102.

238   **After the torpid atmosphere of Aden** ... ibid., 106.

238   **Besse gave a lithe skip** ... *EWD*, 342.

238   **my shoes were completely worn through** ... *RP*, 109.

239   **Raymond de T. is something of a handful** ... EW to Dorothy Lygon, *EWL*, 64.

239   **[Raymond] told me what horses to back** ... *RP*, 135.

239*n*   **[Besse] never wore crêpe de chine shirts** ... *Antonin Besse of Aden: the Founder of St Antony's College, Oxford*, David Footman (Macmillan 1986).

240   **[Raymond] got very drunk** ... *EWD*, 347.

240   **Mr Waugh has failed to observe** ... *DT*, 4 December 1931, *EWCH*, 121.

240   **Never have I been so desperately** ... *RP*, 89.

240   **to everyone in England** ... ibid., 92.

241   **I fought boredom** ... ibid., 174.

241   **island sanity in raving town** ... *EWD*, 332.

241   **At the convent they manage a small farm** ... *RP*, 159.

242   **For anyone accustomed to the Western rite** ... ibid., 67.

243   **The district is full of chums** ... EW to Henry Yorke, *EWL*, 55.

244   **all the biggest bores on the Riviera** ... EW to Jean Connolly, *Cyril Connolly*, 242.

244   **How I hate the south of France** ... EW to Martin D'Arcy, 20 June 1931. Private collection.

244   **I am living in a pension** ... EW to Patrick Balfour, 22 June 1931. Huntington.

244   **I regret slight delay** ... Alex McLachlan to A. D. Peters, 6 July 1931. HRC.

244   **Henry amazingly cheerful** ... EW to Patrick Balfour. Huntington.

245   **That girl has made a fool of me** ... ibid.

245   **I said some hard things** ... ibid.

246   **If there was only the cat in the room** ... *The Seven Ages*, Christopher Hollis (Heinemann 1974), 129.

246   **The difficulty is that it simply isn't amusing** ... Carl Brandt to A. D. Peters, 27 August 1931. HRC.

246   **Africa eludes him** ... *TLS*, 5 November 1931, *EWCH*, 120.

246 **well beneath his proper form**... *DT*, 4 December 1931, *EWCH*, 121.

246 **[Waugh] is not ashamed**... *Spectator*, 23 January 1932, *EWCH*, 125.

246 **writing what I take**... EW to Henry Yorke. Private collection.

247 **Authors, especially young authors**... A. D. Peters to Bernice Baumgarten, 9 October 1931. HRC.

247 **a real dyed in the wool**... EW to W. N. Roughead. HRC.

247 **Cape agreed fulfill contractual commitments**... Carl Brandt to A. D. Peters, 24 November 1931. HRC.

247 **One very important literateur**... John Farrar to Bernice Baumgarten, 20 January 1932. HRC.

247 **We just sit about**... EW to Patrick Balfour. Huntington.

247 **rightful place of composition**... *Enemies of Promise*, Cyril Connolly (Penguin 1961), 126.

248 **very odd. Kept by a deserter**... EW to Mary Lygon, *EWL*, 60.

250 **Angels in printed cotton smocks**... *BR*, 40.

250 **my brothers were rather reticent**... *Good Talk*, 16.

250*n* **'Is it good art?'**... *BR*, 89.

252 **When we meet again**... EW to Mary and Dorothy Lygon, *EWL*, 65.

252 **Very very sorry for lacocking tea**... EW to Mary Lygon, *EWL*, 64.

252 **What a difficult book it will be**... ibid., *EWL*, 89.

252 **So sorry I was mad Carew**... ibid., *EWL*, 78.

252 **I went to Stonyhurst**... ibid. Private collection.

252 **I am going to spend a very studious autumn**... ibid., *EWL*, 89.

253 **We hindered more than we helped**... Dorothy Lygon, *EWW*, 50.

253 **The trouble about poor Bo**... EW to Dorothy Lygon. HRC.

253 **What fools we were**... *EWW*, 51.

254 **It was like having Puck**... ibid., 50.

254 **Darling Maimie, Thank you 100 times**... EW to Mary Lygon. Private collection.

254 **Look after that dear Dutch girl**... ibid.

254 **I may say that the Captain is dead nuts**... EW to Mary and Dorothy Lygon, *EWL*, 56.

255 **As for poor Boaz**... ibid., *EWL*, 57.

255 **Well this is the last time**... EW to Sibell, Mary and Dorothy Lygon, *EWL*, 58.

256 **It is always difficult**... A. D. Peters to Carl Brandt, 11 May 1934. HRC.

256 **Well, I am living like a swell**... EW to Arthur Windham Baldwin, 14 January 1932, *EWL*, 60.

256 **I wish we could see Gothic**... ibid.

257 **The new version of *V.B.* is stinking**... EW to A. D. Peters, 23 March 1932. HRC.

257 **So Boaz is momentarily a social lion** . . . EW to Arthur Windham Baldwin, *EWL*, 63.

257*n* **Although I loved him very much** . . . Teresa Jungman, letter to author.

258 **I was so sad to see you again** . . . Teresa Jungman to EW. BL.

258 **Darling Evelyn – don't be cross** . . . ibid.

258 **I wish I were dead** . . . EW to Mary Lygon. Private collection.

259 *Accession* **as such** . . . John Farrar to A. D. Peters, 20 April 1932.

259 **'Seth, what's the Imperial Bank of Azania?'** . . . *BM*, 154.

260 **Each had a separate telephone** . . . ibid., 78.

261 **'No, the truth about Basil . . .'** ibid., 71.

261 **'Was the party a success?'** . . . ibid., 84.

261 **hard, bare feet rhythmically kicking** . . . ibid., 35.

262 **'I think you're effeminate . . .'** ibid., 45.

262 **the brook Kedron conveyed there** . . . ibid., 172.

262 **an all-round growth of strength** . . . *Spectator*, 19 October 1932, *EWCH*, 129.

262 **amazingly well-written** . . . *Spectator*, 1 October 1932.

262 **[Mr Waugh] grows a trifle weary** . . . *DT*, 4 October 1932.

262 **With all respect to Mr Evelyn Waugh** . . . *Bookman*, November 1932, *EWCH*, 131.

263 **Of course you know how I deplore travel** . . . Henry Yorke to EW, 8 October 1932, *Evelyn Waugh & Others: from the Library of Michael M. Thomas* (Glen Horowitz, G. Heywood Hill Ltd 1989), 50.

263 **one cannot neglect the study** . . . *DM*, 16 January 1933, *EAR*, 133.

264 **I went to a disgusting thing** . . . EW to Dorothy Lygon, 16 April 1932, *EWL*, 61.

264 **My passion for shows** . . . EW to Christine Longford. Private collection.

265 **A house of staggering beauty** . . . ibid.

265 **a strained hour in Diana's dressing-room** . . . *EWD*, 355.

265 **his dribbling, dwarfish, little amorous singeries** . . . *Diana Cooper*, Philip Ziegler (Hamish Hamilton 1981), 160.

265 **Wish I could persuade you** . . . EW to Diana Cooper, *MWMS*, 18.

265 **My word I am glad** . . . EW to Dorothy Lygon, *EWL*, 63.

266 **We cooked them on a charcoal brazier** . . . *Harper's Bazaar* (London), October 1932, *EAR*, 132.

266 **among the wildest possible forest people** . . . EW to A. D. Peters. HRC.

266 **far flung stuff** . . . ibid., *EWL*, 65.

267 **we don't deal with scenery** . . . Alison Settle to A. D. Peters, 7 December 1932. HRC.

267 **She sat quiet** . . . *EWD*, 355.

267 Usual Ritz usual Dutch girl ... EW to Diana Cooper, *MWMS*, 16.
267 [I] had a very pious few days ... ibid., 18.
268 [The Dutch girl] gave me a St Christopher ... ibid., 20.
268 Deadly lonely, cold, and slightly sick ... *EWD*, 355.

Chapter IX

269 What a snare this travelling business ... P. G. Wodehouse to Leonora Cazalet, *P. G. Wodehouse*, Frances Donaldson (Weidenfeld & Nicolson 1982), 155.
269 distant and barbarous places ... *NTD*, 11.
269 unattractive, squat and dingy ... ibid., 122.
270 the greatest physical and mental well-being ... ibid., 114.
270 was as depressing a time ... ibid., 12.
270 The sailors will not clear up ... EW to Mary Lygon, December 1932. Private collection.
270 Very little sleep at nights ... *MWMS*, 21.
270 I feel less tied to London ... *EWD*, 357.
271 General impression of Trinidad ... ibid., 359.
271 Like me, poor fish ... *NTD*, 15.
271 I have never seen a less attractive harbour ... ibid., 19.
271 not at all a nice town ... *MWMS*, 22.
271 I don't mind how soon I leave it ... *EWD*, 360.
271 Saw countless ants ... ibid., 361.
272 an opinionated and rather disagreeable old man ... ibid.
272 too lethargic even to switch away ... *NTD*, 37.
272 A hammock is one of the most agreeable things ... ibid., 36.
273 Many of his stories ... ibid., 32.
273 There was one insect ... ibid., 43.
273 a large middle-aged black ... ibid., 36.
273 I was sorry that this stage ... ibid., 43.
274 All through the blazing afternoon ... ibid., 83.
274 a minute red creature ... ibid., 69.
274 It is quite accurate to say ... ibid.
274 One-eyed horse played up ... *EWD*, 366.
274 the fantastic figure of Mr Christie ... *NTD*, 168.
275 Lately he had been privileged ... ibid., 65.
275 'I always know the character ...' ibid., 63.
275 a dish of fried eggs ... ibid., 69.
275 a curious library ... ibid., 72.

275 **in a third of the time** ... ibid., 73.

275 **firm, finely jointed and fitted** ... ibid., 74.

276 **He had once been desperately ill** ... ibid., 76.

276 **a squalid camp of ramshackle cut-throats** ... ibid., 92.

276 **they are naturally homicidal** ... ibid., 90.

276 **I do not think he ever liked me** ... ibid., 97.

277 **I will not say I was bored** ... ibid., 98.

277 **Goodness the boredom of Boa Vista** ... *MWMS*, 26.

277 **It was in a despondent and rather desperate mood** ... *NTD*, 99.

278 **a grade A short story** ... EW to A. D. Peters, 15 February 1933. HRC.

278 **thought of plot for short story** ... *EWD*, 371.

278 **They were of German manufacture** ... *HD*, 189.

278 **Whenever he went to Georgetown** ... *NTD*, 145.

279 **It is made from sweet cassava roots** ... ibid., 122.

279 **'I have all Dickens's books here ...'** *HD*, 209.

279 **except the desire to visit the manager** ... *NTD*, 108.

280 **It was one of the low spots** ... ibid., 110.

280 **I had just returned to the carpenter's shop** ... extract from Father Mather's diary, 22 February 1933, transcribed by him in a letter to Frederick J. Stopp, 5 July 1954. Cambridge University Library.

281 **While I was riding** ... *NTD*, 140.

281 **Father Keary went off at 9** ... *EWD*, 381.

281 **The delight of these simple people** ... EW to Mary and Dorothy Lygon, *EWL*, 70.

281 **after a journey of the greatest misery** ... EW to Henry Yorke, *EWL*, 71.

281 **cheery, red-cheeked** ... Arthur Waugh's diary. BU.

282 **mostly Christmas cards** ... EW to Henry Yorke, *EWL*, 71.

282 **I think people may enjoy it** ... *MWMS*, 15.

282 **Whether Mr Waugh still considers himself** ... *Tablet*, 21 January 1933, *EWCH*, 132.

282 **We think these sentences** ... ibid.

283 **had fallen from heaven quite unexpectedly** ... *BM*, 173.

283 **the twelve signatories of the above protest** ... *Tablet*, 18 February 1933, *EWCH*, 134.

283 **Had the Editor of *The Tablet*** ... 'An Open Letter to His Eminence the Cardinal Archbishop of Westminster', May 1933, *EWL*, 72.

284 **Influential priests induced him** ... *DE*, 10 September 1934.

285 **So I am in the sea of Marmora** ... EW to Mary and Dorothy Lygon, *EWL*, 79.

285 **There was the usual rather unusual conversation** ... Katharine

Asquith's 'Diary of the Hellenic Cruise August-September 1933'. Private collection.

286 **big on good sense** ... *MWMS*, 34.

286 **The lovely Magdalen Fraser** ... EW to Mary and Dorothy Lygon, *EWL*, 79.

286 **gets into such odd postures** ... *MWMS*, 31.

286 **to bring about a greater mutual appreciation** ... Katharine Asquith's Diary.

287 **white mouse named Laura** ... EW to Katharine Asquith and Julian Oxford, *EWL*, 80.

287 **a very dangerous house** ... *MWMS*, 34.

287 **It is most enjoyable here** ... EW to Katharine Asquith and Julian Oxford, *EWL*, 80.

288 **A weekly literary page** ... A. D. Peters to EW, 5 May 1933. HRC.

288 **I am very sorry about this piece** ... Richard T. Sharman to Carl Brandt, 6 September 1933. HRC.

288 **one of the most uninteresting** ... Mark Goulden to A. D. Peters, 9 January 1935. HRC.

288 **Evelyn has not been doing his best** ... A. D. Peters to Carl Brandt, 19 October 1933. HRC.

288*n* **Here is the boring article on Boredom** EW to A. D. Peters. HRC.

289 **I wasn't greatly surprised** ... A. D. Peters to EW, 24 August 1933. HRC.

289 **You can't tell me a thing** ... EW to A. D. Peters. HRC.

289 **Hard words, hard words** ... ibid.

289 **The heading of the article** ... Mark Goulden to A. D. Peters, 9 January 1935. HRC.

289 **Mr Goulden must be off his rocker** ... EW to A. D. Peters. HRC.

289 **Please transfer my American business** ... ibid.

289 **The book has begun** ... *MWMS*, 39.

290 **I am much under compliment** ... ibid., 38.

290 **It is a very sad life** ... EW to Dorothy Lygon. HRC.

290 **Trouble is I think of dutch girl** ... *MWMS*, 38.

290 **The pope G.B.H. won't let me use her** ... EW to Mary Lygon. HRC.

290 **Can't help loving that girl** ... ibid., *EWL*, 81.

290 **I was thirty on Saturday** ... ibid. HRC.

290 **Oh dear oh dear I wish I was dead** ... ibid.

291 **I shall be in London on Wed** ... EW to Dorothy Lygon. HRC.

292 **but that when financial considerations** ... 'Evelyn Waugh and Vatican Divorce', Donat Gallagher, from *Evelyn Waugh: New Directions*, ed. Alan Blayac (Macmillan 1992).

293 *Post hoc* **and possibly** *propter hoc* ... Private collection.

293 **no matter how 'discreditable'** ... *Evelyn Waugh's Gentlemen, Officers and Rogues,* 41.

293*n* **So I am in the eternal city** ... EW to Mary Lygon. Private collection.

294 **Just heard yesterday** ... ibid., *EWL,* 81.

294 **I enjoy that situation too much** ... Teresa Jungman to EW. BL.

295 **Did you like him?** ... Julian Oxford, interview with author.

295 *Remoters* **and** *Blackers* ... EW to Katharine Asquith, *EWL,* 78.

296 **Just to see if Mrs Heygate is dead** ... Christopher Hollis to Christopher Sykes, 1 December 1972. Private collection.

296 **a city of astonishing beauty** ... EW to Katharine Asquith, *EWL,* 83.

297 **I have formed an attachment** ... *MWMS,* 42.

297 **I used to work on the verandah** ... *WS,* 108.

298 **WOT¿ KARSA BLANKER** ... EW to Mary Lygon, *EWL,* 86.

298 **What I have done is** *excellent* ... *MWMS,* 43.

298 **It may be much the same ending** ... EW to A. D. Peters. HRC.

298*n* **I am aware that John Farrar** ... A. D. Peters to Carol Hill, 4 June 1934. HRC.

299 **God how I hate Americans** ... EW to A. D. Peters. HRC.

299 **Evelyn is more interested in money** ... A. D. Peters to Carol Hill, 11 May 1934. HRC.

299 **No one here, on the strength of past work** ... Blanche Knopf to Carol Hill, 7 August 1934.

299 **[Waugh's] sales record** ... Carol Hill to A. D. Peters, 16 August 1934. HRC.

299 **rather more than Evelyn Waugh** ... A. D. Peters to Carol Hill, 9 October 1934. HRC.

300 **[They] are not interested in continuing** ... Carol Hill to A. D. Peters, 6 September 1934. HRC.

300 **Whether you think it is advisable** ... ibid., 24 September 1934. HRC.

300 **Farrar and Rinehart are keeping the publication** ... ibid., 17 October 1934. HRC.

300 **Though the book is far from being dull** ... *Spectator,* 23 March 1934.

301 **I have finished the G[ood] T[aste] book** ... EW to Mary Lygon. Private collection.

301 **tender Miss Herberts** ... ibid.

301 **While I was in my bath** ... *EWD,* 386.

302 **disgracefully gibberingly drunk** ... *Edith Olivier: From Her Journals 1924–48,* ed. Penelope Middelboe (Weidenfeld & Nicolson 1989), 150.

302 **To Farm Street to confess Winnie** ... *EWD,* 387.

304 **We made two journeys** ... 'Fiasco in the Arctic', Evelyn Waugh from *The First Time I . . .*, ed. Theodora Benson (Chapman & Hall 1935), 155.
305 **The flow was terrific** ... ibid., 159.
306 **the first time I despaired of my life** ... ibid., 162.
306 **This is typical of your folly** ... Sir Alexander Glen, interview with author.
306 **hell – a fiasco** ... EW to Tom Driberg, *EWL*, 88.

Chapter X

307 **I peg away at the novel** ... EW to Katharine Asquith, *EWL*, 83.
307 **I wanted to discover** ... *Life*, 8 April 1946, *EAR*, 303.
308 **Not a worry in the world** ... *HD*, 12.
308 **the habit of loving** ... ibid., 129.
308 **I often think Tony Last's** ... ibid., 12.
308 **Fortune is the least capricious** ... *Labels*, 167.
309 **After all the last thing one wants** ... *HD*, 115.
309 **all-encompassing chaos** ... ibid., 137.
309 **half-lit by day** ... ibid., 14.
309 **He hung up the receiver** ... ibid., 151.
309 **Me? I *detest* it** ... ibid., 36.
309 **My poor Brenda** ... ibid., 79.
310 **a transfigured Hetton** ... ibid., 160.
310 **I will tell you what I have learned** ... ibid., 207.
310 **'You know,' said Tony** ... *MLLO*, 36.
311 **rehearsing over and over** ... *HD*, 132.
311 **very fair, under-water look** ... ibid., 9.
311 **She leant forward to him** ... ibid., 16.
311 **[Tony] had always rather enjoyed** ... ibid., 210.
312 **'What is it Jock? ...'** ... ibid., 118.
312 **'Where's mummy gone?'** ... ibid., 44.
313 **Tony is so incapable** ... *TLS*, 6 September 1934, *EWCH*, 149.
313 **There is no waste** ... *Spectator*, 14 September 1934, *EWCH*, 153.
313 **All the people in the book** ... J. B. Priestley to EW, 7 September 1934. BL.
313 **O Evelyn the book!** ... Katharine Asquith to EW. BL.
314 **The book was entirely spoilt for me** ... Henry Yorke to EW, 2 September 1934. BL.
314 **Very many thanks for your letter** ... EW to Henry Yorke, *EWL*, 88.
314 **and wherever I go** ... EW to Mary Lygon, *EWL*, 89.

315 **I am doing a little book** . . . EW to W. N. Roughead. HRC.

315 **a funny short story** . . . EW to Dorothy Lygon, *EWL*, 90.

315 **It is not very good** . . . EW to A. D. Peters. HRC.

315 **I personally like it** . . . Joyce Reynolds to W. N. Roughead, 30 October 1934. HRC.

315 **If it was anyone else** . . . EW to W. N. Roughead. HRC.

315 **BBC LSD NBG** . . . ibid., *EWL*, 92.

316 **well read without being literary** . . . *Cyril Connolly*, 252.

316 **the way he made drunk people talk** . . . *Paris Review*, April 1962.

316 **One has to regard a man** . . . *Evelyn Waugh: Portrait of a Country Neighbour*, Frances Donaldson (Weidenfeld & Nicolson 1968), 73.

316 **I simply don't understand** . . . EW to T. W. Gadd, 11 April 1955, *EWL*, 439.

316 **I had not for ten years** . . . *NTD*, 166.

317 **the worst book in the world** . . . EW to Laura Waugh, 23 January 1945, *EWL*, 197.

317 **I'm afraid not quite a gentleman** . . . *Oxford in the Twenties*, 83.

317 **always always Mr Wu** . . . *Letters of Conrad Russell*, 129.

317 **[it] doesn't amuse me much** . . . ibid., 124.

319 **I have taken a *great* fancy** . . . EW to Mary Lygon, *EWL*, 92.

320 **[Laura had] a very definite personality** . . . Chloe MacCarthy, interview with author.

320 **pretty unforthcoming** . . . John Jolliffe, interview with author.

320 **Mummy had a very strong character** . . . Harriet Waugh, interview with author.

320 **Behind the veil of good manners** . . . *Laura Waugh 1916–1973*, Auberon Waugh (*Antigonish Review*).

320 **a quality of self-containedness** . . . *EW*, 210.

322 **I am not sure yet about all the girls** . . . Laura Herbert to Chloe Buxton. Private collection.

323 **Holds herself badly** . . . Private collection.

323 **Darling Laura, it's discouraging that we never meet** . . . EW to Laura Herbert, *EWL*, 94.

323 **I thought we had heard the last of that young man** . . . *EWD*, 407n.

323 **I am sad and bored** . . . EW to Laura Herbert, *EWL*, 91.

324 **something historically and continuously English** . . . *EC*, 47.

324n **I daresay I am at fault.** EW to Canon F. E. Hutchinson. Private collection.

325 **which lies at the root** . . . *EC*, 100.

325 **[a] pure light shining in darkness, uncomprehended** . . . ibid., 8.

325 **dry, witty, well-modulated** . . . *NS*, 28 September 1935, *EWCH*, 163.

325 **You can't know how happy** . . . Laura Herbert to EW. BL.

326 **It is in the nature of civilization** . . . *Evening Standard*, 13 February 1935, *EAR*, 163.

327 **So it is all OK about Abyssinia** . . . *MWMS*, 49.

327 **so I have to wait wait wait** . . . EW to Mary Lygon, *EWL*, 93.

328 **It is odd I don't say more** . . . EW to Laura Herbert, *EWL*, 99.

329 **a natty young man** . . . Dominic Gill, interview with author.

330 **It is too difficult not to write to you now** . . . Joyce Gill to EW. BL.

331 **Was it absolutely necessary** . . . Claire Mackenzie to EW. BL.

332 **like a malignant demon** . . . *A Look at My Life*, Eileen Agar (Methuen 1988), 104.

332 **I remember being very shocked** . . . Penelope Betjeman, interview with Martin Stannard from *Evelyn Waugh: the Early Years 1903–1939* (Dent 1986), 282.

332 **[it] was rather like that of a child** . . . Mary Clive, letter to author, 20 July 1992.

333 **The *Daily Mail* have given me** . . . EW to Laura Herbert, *EWL*, 95.

333 **'He says the prospects for cubbin' are excellent'** . . . *WIA*, 57.

333 **I want particularly to know** . . . EW to Penelope Betjeman, *EWL*, 96.

334 **Badly left oil concession** . . . *WIA*, 109.

334 **Evelyn comes next week** . . . Patrick Balfour to Caroline Kinross, 16 August 1935. National Library of Scotland.

334 **I am universally regarded** . . . EW to Laura Herbert, 24 August 1935, *EWL*, 97.

336 **men with strong cockney tastes** . . . William Deedes, *Sunday Telegraph Magazine*, 15 February 1987.

336 **Colour is just a lot of bull's-eyes about nothing** . . . *Scoop: a Novel About Journalists*, Evelyn Waugh (Penguin 1943), 66.

337 **I do my work very badly** . . . *MWMS*, 54.

337 **Evelyn gets hell from the *Daily Mail*** . . . Patrick Balfour to Caroline Kinross, 2 September 1935. National Library of Scotland.

337 **There is no news** . . . EW to Laura Herbert, 24 August 1935, *EWL*, 97.

338 **[Evelyn] is getting pretty depressed** . . . Patrick Balfour to Caroline Kinross, 24 August 1935. National Library of Scotland.

338 **I am a very bad journalist** . . . EW to Penelope Betjeman, *EWL*, 102.

338 **The journalists are lousy competitive** . . . EW to Katharine Asquith, 5 September 1935, *EWL*, 98.

338 **If you were conscientious** . . . 'Fiasco in Addis Ababa', Patrick Balfour in *Abyssinia Stop Press*, ed. Ladislas Farago (Hale 1936).

339 **a certain disenchantment** . . . William Deedes, interview with author.

339 **armed to teeth** . . . *MWMS*, 54.

339 **but he seemed incapable of affection** . . . EW to Laura Herbert, *EWL*, 99.

340 **It is a chaste life** ... *MWMS*, 54.

340 **well I have chucked the *Mail*** ... ibid., 52.

340 **On account of my great honour** ... ibid., 53.

340 **They began their war last week** ... EW to Laura Herbert, *EWL*, 99.

340 **the Abyssinians lacked everything but courage** ... *The Life of My Choice* (Collins 1987), 223.

340 **I think I shall be home soon** ... EW to Laura Herbert, 25 October 1935. Georgetown.

341 **I didn't realise how much I hated this job** ... *MWMS*, 58.

341 **Off to Africa full of the gloomiest forebodings** ... EW to Katharine Asquith, 4 August 1936, *EWL*, 109.

341 **Evelyn is back in Abyssinia** ... Arthur Waugh to Kenneth McMaster, 26 August 1936. HRC.

342 **Truth appears to be Wops in jam** ... *EWD*, 398.

342 **like many others before him** ... *WIA*, 246.

342 **attended by the spread of order** ... ibid., 250.

343 **tarmac, concrete parapets** ... *EWD*, 403.

343 **[Soon] new roads will be radiating** ... *WIA*, 253.

343 **[I] had intended to bathe** ... *EWD*, 405.

344 **It is the saddest news I ever heard** ... EW to Mary Lygon, *EWL*, 110.

344 **If the book bores its readers** ... EW to Daphne Acton, 27 April 1936.

345 **his venality, treachery** ... *London Mercury and Bookman*, June 1937, *EAR*, 193.

345 **[Mr Waugh] should perhaps temper** ... *TLS*, 7 November 1936, *EWCH*, 190.

345 **the American swine** ... EW to W. N. Roughead, 21 September 1936. HRC.

Chapter XI

346 **Tell you what you might do** ... EW to Laura Herbert, *EWL*, 103.

348 **Lovely child, you have been sweet** ... ibid., 107.

348 **It has been a very happy summer** ... *MWMS*, 60.

348 **La jeune fille paresseuse** ... EW to Mary Lygon, *EWL*, 105.

349 **the most important literary award** ... A. D. Peters to Carol Hill, 16 June 1936. HRC.

349 **that a prize of that kind** ... EW to Henry Yorke. Private collection.

349 the confident touch of an accomplished master . . . *Spectator*, 10 July 1936, *EWCH*, 182.

349 no wish whatever . . . Carol Hill to A. D. Peters, 4 May 1936. HRC.

349 It was delightful of you and Alec . . . EW to Joan Waugh. BU.

350 shop-soiled and second-hand . . . *EWD*, 132.

350 In evening wrote free stuff for Belloc . . . ibid., 412.

351 Yes, the pay is rather disappointing . . . EW to Graham Greene. Georgetown.

351 I had no conception . . . ibid.

351 I received your telegram . . . EW to Graham Greene, *The Life of Graham Greene Volume One: 1904–1939*, Norman Sherry (Cape 1989), 263.

352 vulgar film about cabaret girls . . . *EWD*, 413.

352 itching & full of ideas . . . EW to Laura Herbert. BL.

352 The grimmest pilgrimage in Christendom . . . *MWMS*, 118.

352 [It] very rarely fails and is *horrible* . . . EW to Penelope Betjeman, 4 February 1950.

352 Bathed, shaved . . . *EWD*, 391.

352 They had both been caught in a storm . . . Nancy Mitford (broadcast).

353 You will be greatly surprised . . . EW to Mary Lygon, *EWL*, 108.

354 My darling, it is a night of inconceivable beauty . . . EW to Laura Herbert. BL.

354 My darling, I'm afraid I've got one hard blow . . . Laura Herbert to EW. BL.

354 Decided nothing . . . *EWD*, 406.

355 My dear Father, I hope that you do not think . . . EW to Arthur Waugh. Private collection.

355 Afternoon with Diana . . . *EWD*, 408.

356 I don't imagine the story . . . EW to Tom Driberg, *EWL*, 112.

356 When i get home i shall buy a cottage . . . EW to Laura Herbert, *EWL*, 99.

357 professed a specialized enthusiasm . . . *WS*, 143.

357 the solid, spacious houses of the bourgeoisie . . . *Country Life*, 26 February 1938, *EAR*, 215.

357 Very small, next to the castle . . . *EWD*, 406.

357 Laura and I have found a house . . . *MWMS*, 62.

359 Low spirited, sleeping badly . . . *EWD*, 413.

359 Went to drink sherry with Grants . . . ibid., 409.

359 Family fun. No sleep . . . ibid., 417.

359 Xmas was great hell . . . EW to Mary Lygon. Private collection.

360 The main objection to the house . . . *MWMS*, 62.

360 Re. Hancock. What he must do . . . EW to Laura Herbert. BL.

360 [I] bought a chimney-piece . . . *EWD*, 420.

361 **Lord Cockburn was ennobled** ... *EW,* 20.

361 **It is the kind of house** ... Ms. fragment. HRC.

361 **marrying procreating & purchasing property** ... EW to Alec Waugh, *EWL,* 114.

362 **You should write to her** ... EW to Laura Herbert. BL.

362 **Joan Waugh is mean as hell** ... ibid.

362 **My mama is giving us** ... ibid.

362 **Presents have come in** ... *EWD,* 420.

362 **we were able to put together** ... *MWMS,* 64.

363 **Capt. Hance G.B.H. has said yes** ... EW to Mary Lygon. Private collection.

363 **Cocktail party that afternoon** ... *EWD,* 421.

364 **Lovely day, lovely house** ... ibid., 422.

364 **So it is very decent** ... EW to Dorothy Lygon, *EWL,* 113.

364 **Honeymoon is being all that honeymoon should be** ... EW to A. D. Peters. HRC.

365 **The Misses Leigh and the parish priest** ... *EWD,* 427.

365 **Dined with Lady Featherstone Godley** ... ibid., 431.

365 **As the men were away** ... ibid., 425.

366 **yesterday we took our driving tests** ... *MWMS,* 63.

366 **Lovely house: quite big** ... Patrick Balfour to Caroline Kinross, 15 December 1937. National Library of Scotland.

366 **Laura's baby was born yesterday** ... EW to A. D. Peters, 10 March 1938, *EWL,* 116.

366 **I foresee that she will be a problem** ... EW to Tom Balston. Private collection.

367 **Work on *Scoop* going slowly** ... *EWD,* 429.

368 **massive double doors** ... *Scoop,* 41.

368n **This is a light satire** ... *Evelyn Waugh: the Early Years,* 472.

368n **[Beaverbrook] used his papers** ... *Beaverbrook,* Anne Chisholm and Michael Davie (Hutchinson 1992), 231.

369 **[Lord Copper's] massive head, empty of thought** ... *Scoop,* 179.

369 **ignominiously sandwiched** ... ibid., 16.

369 **His mail had been prodigious** ... *Scoop,* 20.

369n **Waugh was furious at its inadequacies** ... Richard Acton, *Spectator,* 19 September 1992.

370 **'And you'd go on paying me my wages?'** ... *Scoop,* 32.

370 **Shumble, Whelper, and Pigge knew Corker** ... ibid., 84.

370 **NEWS EXYOU UNRECEIVED** ... ibid., 121.

371 **'Tell me ...'** ... ibid., 29.

371 **Ten servants waited upon the household** ... ibid., 119.

371 **'But you see I don't like restaurants ...'** ibid., 33.

371 **[William's] mother, Priscilla, and his three uncles** ... ibid., 195.

372 **Made a very good start** ... *EWD*, 409.

372 **[Mrs Stitch's] normally mobile face** ... *Scoop*, 6.

372 **I like Mr Waugh best** ... *NS*, 7 May 1938, *EWCH*, 194.

372*n* **Message to call on Diana** ... *EWD*, 391.

373 **The shop paid him six hundred a year** ... *Scoop*, 44.

373 **Various courageous Europeans** ... ibid., 74.

374 **had both, in another age** ... ibid., 218.

374 **ingenious, satirical, extremely funny** *TLS*, 7 May 1938, *EWCH*, 197.

374 **as good as some of Mr Waugh's other books** ... *Spectator*, 13 May 1938, *EWCH*, 199.

374 **[Mr Waugh] makes Hitchcock return home** ... *DT*, 2 June 1938.

374 **Mr Waugh is an expensive luxury** ... Elizabeth Penrose to W. N. Roughead, 16 May 1938. HRC.

375 **A very rich chap** ... EW to A. D. Peters. HRC.

375 **Mr Waugh shall not disclose** ... 23 June 1938. HRC.

376 **hungrier, wickeder, and more hopeless** *RUL*, 205.

376 **To ruin the whole nation** ... ibid., 178.

377 **We went together to visit his former home** ... ibid., 483.

377*n* **Mr Greene's was an heroic journey** ... *Spectator*, 10 March 1939, *EAR*, 249.

378 **I believe that man is, by nature** ... *RUL*, 16.

379 **is admirably written** ... *Guardian*, 28 July 1939, *EWCH*, 204.

379 **Mr Evelyn Waugh has written a short but dull book** ... *DT*, 30 June 1939, *EWCH*, 203.

379 **Mr Waugh's outspoken account** ... *New York Times*, 19 November 1939, *EWCH*, 205.

380 **I finished a book today** ... *MWMS*, 66.

380 **one could feel that each had a pistol** ... *EW*, 262.

380 **phrase after phrase of lapidary form** ... *Tablet*, 3 December 1938, *EAR*, 238.

380 **[a] pantomime appearance** ... *Spectator*, 24 March 1939, *EAR*, 251.

381 **I am replying to Mr Spender** ... ibid., 21 April 1939.

381 **one reads it with a feeling** ... ibid., 17 February 1939, *EAR*, 247.

381 **Various Amorys and Horners** ... *EWD*, 433.

381 **Weeds had grown prodigious** ... ibid., 435.

382 **Working in the afternoon** ... ibid., 437.

382 **Mr Evelyn Waugh wishes to let Piers Court** ... *Times*, 5 September 1939.

Chapter XII

383   **a more terrible fate** ... *EWD*, 443.

384   **Most of the notables of the village** ... ibid., 439.

384   **My heart bleeds for you & Duff** ... EW to Diana Cooper, *EWL*, 131.

385   **My inclinations are all to join** ... *EWD*, 438.

385   **unaccountably telling me** ... ibid., 447.

386   **Everywhere little groups of close friends** ... *MA*, 19.

386   **No one wishes to take the house** ... *EWD*, 441.

386   **We ate (+ helpers)** ... ibid., 444.

387   **work [was] out of the question** ... ibid., 447.

387   **It is clear to me** ... EW to A. D. Peters, *EWL*, 137.

388   **It is about a father** ... EW to Arthur Waugh, *EWL*, 158.

388   **a huge, grim and solitary jest** *WS*, 116.

388n   **I think you would be wise to keep it** ... A. D. Peters to EW. HRC.

389   **[which] rang through the room** ... *WS*, 171.

389   **was an experience for which I was little qualified** ... ibid., 167.

389   **the time-old gag** ... *A Burnt-out Case*, Graham Greene (Heinemann & Bodley Head 1974), introd. xii.

389n   **I must not leave you with the delusion** ... EW to Diana Mosley, 30 March 1966, *EWL*, 639.

390   **'Feeding animals while men and women starve ...'** *WS*, 184.

390   **Mr Waugh is often amusing** ... *TLS*, 23 January 1943, *EWCH*, 227.

390   **It is carefully composed** ... *Horizon*, 7 December 1946, *EWCH*, 232.

391   **For fifteen years Waugh has sung the house** ... *Partisan Review*, 28 July 1943, *EWCH*, 228.

392   **Doctors in shabby white coats** ... *EWD*, 451.

392   **It is to be called Auberon Alexander** ... EW to Mary Lygon. Private collection.

393   **[watching] her get slightly but appreciably better** *EWD*, 452.

393   **As soon as we arrived** ... EW to Laura Waugh, *EWL*, 128.

394   **Breakfast at 7.30** ... *EWD*, 459.

394   **very decent & very very lazy** EW to Laura Waugh. HRC.

394   **Temporary second lieutenants** ... *The Globe and Laurel*, April 1940, *EAR*, 262.

394   **Mrs Herbert is a huge withered woman** ... *A Lonely Business: a Self-Portrait of James Pope-Hennessy*, ed. Peter Quennell (Weidenfeld & Nicolson 1981).

395 [Evelyn] was one of the few people . . . 'Wuff: my personal memories of him', Mary Clive (unpub. ms., 1987).

395 [after] another soft night . . . *EWD*, 461.

396 Alastair had a bath . . . *POMF,* 109.

396 'At two hundred yards . . .' *MA*, 75.

397 We have had too little work . . . *EWD*, 462.

397 spending a very great deal of money . . . ibid., 465.

397 [He] looks like something escaped . . . ibid., 461.

397 I said in a jaggering way . . . EW to Laura Waugh, *EWL*, 137.

398 The day invariably ended . . . *To the War with Waugh*, John St John (Whittington 1973), 25.

398 disastrous from first to last . . . *EWD*, 465.

398 [he] possesses any amount of moral courage . . . Unpub. report, 18 May 1940, ref. S. 260B, section III, Old Admiralty Building, Whitehall. *Evelyn Waugh: No Abiding City, 1939–1966*, Martin Stannard (Dent 1992), 12.

399 'The continued use of obscenities . . .' *To the War with Waugh*, 24.

399 [Evelyn's] greatest enemies . . . *EW*, 265.

400 was plain in view . . . *MA*, 11.

400 [Patrick] found the evening very surprising . . . *EWD*, 461.

400 The table was lit . . . *MA*, 43.

401 a long & offensive memorandum . . . EW to Laura Waugh, 22 January 1940, *EWL*, 135.

401 I am on the mess committee . . . ibid., *EWL*, 136.

401 Did I tell you that I have won . . . ibid., 15 January 1940. BL.

402 The Finnish surrender . . . *EWD*, 466.

402 I lectured to the company . . . ibid., 469.

402 Col. Lushington speaks of extreme athletic fitness . . . EW to Laura Waugh, 15 January 1940. BL.

402 We hope for Tenby . . . *EWD*, 471.

403 [The battalion] lined the sands . . . *POMF,* 216.

403 The Woodruffs came in to drink champagne . . . *EWD*, 473.

404 It seems clear that if there is an expedition . . . ibid., 476.

405 Soldiers when writing to their wives . . . ibid., 479.

405 We landed as a battalion . . . ibid., 480.

406 Bloodshed has been avoided . . . EW to Laura Waugh, 26 September 1940.

406n The attempt [to seize the port] . . . *English History, 1914–1945*, A. J. P. Taylor (Oxford 1965).

407 I have written again to London . . . EW to Laura Waugh, 28 September 1940, *EWL*, 141.

407 I have been in a serious battle ibid., 2 June 1941, *EWL*, 152.

407 I do not think you take a great deal of interest . . . ibid., *EWL*, 147.

407n **I can't tell you where I am** ... Arthur Windham Baldwin to EW. BL.

408 **I am heavy with homesickness** EW to Laura Waugh, 1 April 1941. BL.

408 **miss you unspeakably** ibid., *EWL*, 155.

408 **I have no other interests** ... ibid., 3 August 1941. BL.

408 **You are never out of my thoughts** ... ibid., 6 March 1941. BL.

408 **What a lot we shall have to say** ... ibid., 2 June 1941, *EWL*, 152.

408 **though I believe Pixton** ... ibid., 25 April 1941. BL.

408 **My worst fear is that England** ... ibid., 13 September 1940, *EWL*, 139.

408 **It is sad news for you** ... EW to Laura Waugh, *EWL*, 139.

408 **I saw her when she was dead** ... *EWD*, 489.

408n **[Laura] had a son** ... Arthur Waugh to Kenneth McMaster, 25 August 1940. HRC.

409 **There seems to me something quite pathetic** ... Arthur Waugh to Joan Waugh, 6 December 1940. Private collection.

409 **[Waugh] is in a commando** ... W. N. Roughead to D. Kilham Roberts, 25 March 1941. HRC.

409 **It strikes me as odd** ... D. Kilham Roberts to A. D. Peters, 6 October 1941. HRC.

409 **Even the poorest authors** ... A. D. Peters to D. Kilham Roberts, 7 October 1941. HRC.

409 **I am glad that the Income Tax** ... EW to Laura Waugh, 8 February 1941. BL.

410 **Will you write to the nuns** ... ibid., 3 January 1941. BL.

410 **Will you please write to the nuns** ... ibid., *EWL*, 145.

410 **I hope that you have not abandoned** ... ibid., 23 February 1941, *EWL*, 150.

410 **Would you like to have the windows** ... ibid., 3 August 1941. BL.

410 **I wonder if you put my vintage port** ... ibid.

410 **For the first & for the last time** ... ibid., 2 November 1941. BL.

410 **Read** *Children's Encyclopaedia* **assiduously** ibid.

411 **You have been good about writing** ... ibid., 22 January 1940, *EWL*, 135.

411 **You must assume a more impassioned style** ibid., 7 December 1940. BL.

411 **a dull letter from Laura** *EWD*, 607.

411 **Do try to write me better letters** ... EW to Laura Waugh, 7 January 1945, *EWL*, 195.

411 **It is a worry not to know** ... Arthur Waugh to Joan Waugh, 15 August 1940. Private collection.

411   Letter-writing, at any rate to in-laws . . . ibid., 19 May 1941. Private collection.

411   Laura's letters are like soppy bread . . . ibid., 10 September 1940. Private collection.

411*n*   cosy abode of books . . . *Publishers' Circular & Booksellers' Record*, 15 July 1939.

412   I shall never be able to make anything of Laura . . . Arthur Waugh to Joan Waugh, 1 September 1940. Private collection.

412   I don't know whether she has a very strong character . . . ibid., 2 November 1940. Private collection.

412   'Teresa has measles . . .' ibid., 1 September 1940. Private collection.

412   [I] was certainly not aware . . . *Will This Do?*, Auberon Waugh (Century 1991).

413   I have never before been for so long . . . EW to Laura Waugh, 13 October 1940, *EWL*, 142.

413   a large collection of nondescript . . . *EWD*, 484.

413   They were unimpressive to look at . . . ibid., 490.

414   She is living a life of serene detachment . . . EW to Laura Waugh, *EWL*, 142.

414   to consist in all ranks . . . *EWD*, 489.

415   Nothing could be less like the Marines . . . ibid., 487.

416   All the officers have very long hair . . . EW to Laura Waugh, *EWL*, 145.

416   The standard of efficiency . . . *EWD*, 487.

416   The names among our officers . . . *Life*, 17 November 1941, *EAR*, 264.

416   drink a very great deal . . . *EWD*, 488.

417   I think a minor operation . . . EW to Laura Waugh. BL.

417   [I] will try and keep up . . . ibid., *EWL*, 143.

417   On Friday Robin had to go to London . . . ibid., *EWL*, 147.

418   both of whom have brought luggage . . . ibid., 8 February 1941. BL.

418   very young, quiet, overdisciplined . . . *EWD*, 493.

418   The RNVR lieutenants . . . ibid., 492.

419   He'd toady up to anyone . . . Mary Dups, interview with author.

419   he was a bit fond of the Honourables . . . Ralph Tanner, *Punch*, 19 November 1975.

419   The inhabitants of this town . . . EW to Laura Waugh, 23 February 1941, *EWL*, 150.

420   'very nice, very clean . . .' *Cairo in the War 1939–1945*, Artemis Cooper (Hamish Hamilton 1989), 114.

420   I am just back from five days leave . . . EW to Laura Waugh, 1 April 1941. BL.

421   **Never in the history of human endeavour** . . . *EWD*, 495.
421   **The man on my left was sick** . . . *Life*, 17 November 1941, *EAR*, 266.
422   **It was very lucky really** . . . ibid.
422   **After this operation** . . . *EWD*, 496.
422*n*   **Evelyn at this moment** . . . *Sunday Chronicle*, 23 November 1941.
423   **Yesterday I spent in the Union Club** . . . EW to Laura Waugh, 7 May 1941, *EWL*, 151.
424   **a nightmare of unreality** . . . 'Cretan Crazy Week', F. C. C. Graham (unpub. ms.).
424   **'My God, it's hell'** . . . ibid.
424   **We took this to be an exceptionally cowardly fellow** . . . *EWD*, 499.
426   **In case I don't see Auberon again** . . . EW to Laura Waugh, 2 June 1941, *EWL*, 152.
427   **The gorge was magnificent** . . . *EWD*, 506.
428   **Bob then took the responsibility** . . . ibid., 509.
428   **Final orders from CREFORCE** . . . *War Diary* ref no. WO 218/166.
428*n*   **there's no question that Laycock** . . . Ralph Tanner, interview with author.
429   **all fighting forces** . . . *Crete: the Battle and the Resistance*, Antony Beevor (John Murray 1991), 220.
429   **my tale of shame** EW to Laura Waugh. BL.
429   **Darling Laura** . . . **I have been in a serious battle** . . . EW to Laura Waugh, 2 June 1941, *EWL*, 152.
430   **'I thought he was quite childish about it'** *Crete*, 230.
430   **He said that he had never seen** . . . *EW*, 295.
430   **Presume Ivor Claire** . . . Ann Rothermere to EW, *The Letters of Ann Fleming*, ed. Mark Amory (Collins 1985), 155.
430   **Your telegram horrifies me** . . . EW to Ann Rothermere, ibid.
431   **Why do you become hysterical** . . . Ann Rothermere to EW, ibid., 156.
431   **I replied that if she breathes** . . . *EWD*, 728.
431   **with the most profound misgivings** . . . EW to Laura Waugh, *EWL*, 156.

Chapter XIII

432   **I was aghast to realize** . . . *BR*, 9.
432   **I finished the book** . . . EW to Randolph Churchill, 26 September 1941, *EWL*, 154.
433   **There was something female and voluptuous** . . . *POMF*, 9.

433 across the sea, Barbara felt . . . ibid.

433 smiling 'with sincere happiness . . .' ibid., 222.

433 Sonia was trying to telephone . . .' ibid., 42.

433 'I want to be one of those people . . .' ibid., 46.

433 In the new, busy, secretive . . . ibid., 49.

434 'In the summer we take our meals . . .' ibid., 95.

434n 'Hullo, Uncle, did I hear you getting a rocket?' . . . MA, 82.

435 'You see he'd never done anything . . .' POMF, 106.

435 She wore the livery of the highest fashion . . . ibid., 25.

436 He found her up and dressed . . . ibid., 159.

436 A pansy. An old queen . . . ibid., 41.

436n I put those words . . . EW to Nancy Mitford, EWL, 356.

436n Evelyn Waugh has made an absolutely vicious attack . . . Brian Howard, 428.

437 'What I don't see,' she said . . . POMF, 39.

437 'I read a lot of Chinese poetry once,' . . . ibid., 177.

438 [Waugh is] a vituperative young man . . . NS, 11 April 1942, EWCH, 214.

438 Randolph tells me . . . EW to Laura Waugh, EWL, 159.

438 My life is one of squalor . . . ibid., 2 November 1941. BL.

439 I am always wet, cold and bored . . . ibid., 16 November 1941, EWL, 157.

439 I discovered this by recognizing . . . EWD, 517.

439 I was interviewed by a neurotic creature . . . ibid., 518.

439 Do you understand now . . . MWMS, 77.

440 Meanwhile I am going on leave . . . EWD, 519.

440 The crowds uglier and more aimless . . . ibid., 536.

441 Sad about the destruction of North End . . . EW to Arthur Waugh, 5 November 1940, quoted in a letter from Arthur Waugh to Joan Waugh, 8 November 1940. Private collection.

441 'The Blues' have accepted me . . . EW to Laura Waugh. BL.

441 I think we are the only mess in Europe . . . EWD, 528.

441 No. 3 Commando were very anxious to be chums . . . EW to Laura Waugh, 31 May 1942, EWL, 160.

442 if a girl it is kinder to drown her ibid. HRC.

443 So I had a sleepless night . . . ibid.

443 drank a great deal of wine . . . EWD, 529.

443 a club of intellectual flavour . . . HD, 157.

444 this glorious place EWD, 163.

444 [White's] should be a club for gamblers . . . EW to Nancy Mitford, 10 October 1949, EWL, 310.

444 A good year . . . EWD, 530.

444 **I am very glad not to be with my children** ... EW to Laura Waugh. BL.

444 **Zoe Franks, who is an absolutely crashing bore** ... ibid., *EWL*, 164.

445 **by a sort of nightmare** ... *EWD*, 531.

445 **[never hesitating] to take advantage** ... *EW*, 311.

445 **Most of my work has been unnecessary** ... *EWD*, 535.

445 **'Who's that bloody man** ...' *Evelyn Waugh: No Abiding City*, 81.

446 **'You'll regret it, sir'** ... *EW*, 312.

446 **'It is my intention** ...' *EWD*, 539.

447 **I don't suppose you know** ... Arthur Waugh to Joan Waugh, 7 January 1941. Private collection.

447 **The other evening** ... ibid., 25 October 1940. Private collection.

447 **is sad for my parents** ... EW to Laura Waugh, *EWL*, 156.

447 **He really is the wittiest dog in the world'** Arthur Waugh to Joan Waugh, 15 August 1940. Private collection.

447 **I make him itch all over** ... ibid., 22 January 1941. Private collection.

447 **I know that I am not apt to take Evelyn** ... ibid., 8 November 1940. Private collection.

448 **[Evelyn] has shaved off his moustache** ... ibid., 22 January 1941. Private collection.

449 **I spent some weary hours** ... *EWD*, 539.

449 **You will already have heard** ... EW to Alec Waugh. HRC.

450 **dashing good looks, cavalier swagger** ... *Mercury Presides*, Daphne Fielding (Eyre & Spottiswoode 1954), 202.

450 **I had known him vaguely at Oxford** ... *March Past*, Lord Lovat (Weidenfeld & Nicolson 1978), 233.

450 **'You will report to the Depot** ...' *EWD*, 542.

451 **My Lord, I have the honour to inform you** ... ibid., 543.

451 **Only explicable on grounds of personal malice** ... EW to Robert Laycock, *EWD*, 543.

451 **The indignation I felt** ... *EWD*, 545.

451 **White's is shut** ... EW to Laura Waugh, 24 August 1943, *EWL*, 168.

451 **Too much drinking at midday** ... *EWD*, 552.

451 **I have got so bored** ... ibid., 547.

452 **I do hope that your nursery life** ... EW to Laura Waugh, 19 September 1943, *EWL*, 169.

452 **I wrote to congratulate him** ... *EWD*, 553.

453 **He is a great change as a master** ... EW to Laura Waugh, *EWL*, 171.

453 **We had a preliminary medical exam** ... *EWD*, 555.

453 **Guy jumped. For a second** ... *US*, 102.

454n **as the most serene and exalted experience of his life** ... *OGP*, 142.

455   I went to see Father Dempsey . . . *EWD*, 552.

456   5. In civil life I am a novelist . . . ibid., 557.

457   It was difficult if one was doing a general reorganisation . . . *Good Talk*, 23.

457   I still have a cold . . . *EWD*, 558.

458   Do remember it is much harder . . . EW to Christopher Sykes, 25 November 1946. Georgetown.

458   I am getting spinsterish about style *EWD*, 558.

458   English writers, at forty . . . ibid., 560.

458   Brevity is not the hall-mark of precision . . . EW to the *Universe*, 27 February 1949. HRC.

458   to be oversensitive about clichés . . . *Life*, 8 April 1946, *EAR*, 300.

459   It is always my temptation . . . *EWD*, 561.

459   I regard writing not as investigation of character . . . *Paris Review*, April 1962.

459   I did not explain why . . . EW to Laura Waugh, 25 January 1944, *EWL*, 176.

459   When I am working . . . ibid. BL.

460   The battle at Nettuno . . . *EWD*, 558.

460   The new general is very much less assuming . . . EW to Laura Waugh, *EWL*, 179.

460n   forehead of an orang-outang . . . *EWD*, 600.

461   in getting me six clear weeks . . . ibid., 562.

461   a very difficult chapter . . . ibid., 564.

462   Do not let the Herberts harrow me . . . EW to Laura Waugh, 12 May 1944, *EWL* 183.

462   [I have] given orders for the books . . . *EWD*, 555.

463   At about 1.30 on the night of Monday . . . ibid., 568.

463   It is a cutting of one of the few remaining strands . . . EW to Laura Waugh, 25 June 1944. BL.

463   nothing but innocent pleasure ahead ibid., 17 June 1944. BL.

463   I accepted eagerly *EWD*, 569.

464   who was killing the most Germans . . . Fitzroy Maclean to Michael Davie, January 1976. *EWD*, 651.

465   a brute and a bore . . . Patrick Ness, interview with author.

465   with tiled courtyards not unlike Mexico . . . EW to Laura Waugh, 6 July 1944, *EWL*, 185.

465   I should think he must go through . . . *Diana Cooper*, 221.

466   he had just written a book . . . *Trumpets from the Steep*, Diana Cooper (Hart-Davis 1960), 201.

466   Ask Captain Waugh . . . Fitzroy Maclean, *EWW*, 135.

466   dour, unprincipled, ambitious . . . *EWD*, 571.

466n   'I know that's not true' . . . *Good Talk*, 24.

466*n* The politicians must be heartily sorry ... EW to Randolph Churchill, 29 March 1953.

467 I was walking in a cornfield ... *EWD*, 573.

468 Breakfast, I at 8 ... ibid., 579.

468 We do very little ... EW to Laura Waugh, 16 September 1944, *EWL*, 187.

468 Time seems to stand still here ... ibid., 27 September 1944, *EWL*, 188.

468 The past week has gone like a fortnight ... *EWD*, 582.

468 My window is almost covered with vine leaves ... EW to Laura Waugh, 27 September 1944, *EWL*, 188.

469 This is not a wine growing district ... EW to Dorothy Lygon, 14 October 1944. HRC.

469 clucking over the signals ... *EWD*, 585.

469 He is simply a flabby bully ... ibid., 587.

469 Randolph and I at dinner ... ibid., 582.

470 a demure figure in a brown woollen dressing-gown ... *EWW*, 143.

470 It is a pleasure to have Freddy here ... EW to Laura Waugh, 14 October 1944, *EWL*, 189.

470 Both were short and sturdy ... *EWW*, 143.

470 Freddy is still with us ... EW to Laura Waugh, 24 October 1944, *EWL*, 191.

471 We were not a harmonious trio *Good Talk*, 26.

471 because however brilliant and witty ... *EWW*, 139.

472 As we are obliged to live together ... *EWD*, 587.

472 He has set to work ... ibid., 591.

472 The entertainment consisted of rousing choruses ... ibid., 581.

473 an organised, revolutionary army ... *Salisbury Review*, 'Church and State in Liberated Croatia', PRO 371/48910.

473 [he] chucked the patriotic line ... *EWD*, 586.

473 Proof corrections. Randolph soaking all the afternoon ... ibid., 593.

474 Drizzle began at midday ... ibid., 587.

474 People talk of things ending here ... EW to Laura Waugh, 5 November 1944, *EWL*, 192.

474 [Coote] arrived, rather inopportunely ... *EWD*, 596.

475 The Partisans have succeeded ... ibid., 600.

475 One never knows what one will get ... EW to Nancy Mitford, 7 January 1945, *EWL*, 196.

475 Looking back on the last two days ... *EWD*, 609.

475 I struggle so far as one bad tempered man ... EW to Catherine Waugh, 5 February 1945, *EWL*, 199.

475 **The bloodiness of the Partisans** . . . EW to Laura Waugh, 19 February 1945, *EWL*, 200.

476 **It will be the next best thing** . . . *EWD*, 608.

476 **I have spent a solitary Christmas** . . . EW to Nancy Mitford, 25 December 1944, *EWL*, 194.

476 **an article in an American magazine** . . . EW to Laura Waugh, 13 December 1944. BL.

476 **So Christmas is now over** . . . Laura Waugh to EW, 26 December 1944. BL.

477 **Darling Laura, sweet whiskers** . . . EW to Laura Waugh, 7 December 1944, *EWL*, 195.

477 **Have you rewritten the patches** . . . Laura Waugh to EW, 26 December 1944. BL.

477 **A lot of letters should be arriving** . . . EW to Laura Waugh, 9 January 1945, *EWL*, 196.

478 **[returning] to the place I was expelled from** . . . *EWD*, 616.

478 **The sad thing about the Pope** . . . EW to Laura Waugh, 8 March 1945, *EWL*, 201.

478 **I left him convinced** . . . *EWD*, 618.

478*n* **Evelyn had applied to come out** . . . Osbert Lancaster to Christopher Sykes, 19 October 1975. Private collection.

479 **petulant** . . . **& said that even if he could** . . . 30 March 1945, FO R 5927/1059/92; *Evelyn Waugh: No Abiding City*, 139.

480 **[It would] be unwise to attempt** . . . ibid., *No Abiding City*, 140.

480 **The Catholic clergy of Dubrovnik** . . . FO R 8555/1059/92 (no. 66), *No Abiding City*, 142.

Chapter XIV

482 **I think I shall start writing a book** . . . EW to Laura Waugh, *EWL*, 145.

483 **[Hooper] came to attention** . . . *BR*, 13.

484 **'Great barrack of a place . . .'** ibid., 19.

484 **Sebastian gives me many pangs** Dorothy Lygon to EW, 25 February 1945. BL.

485 **There is an aesthetic bugger** . . . EW to Arthur Windham Baldwin, 14 March 1958, *EWL*, 506.

485 **[moving] as though he had not fully accustomed himself** . . . *BR*, 30.

485 **[Blanche] took formal and complimentary leave** . . . ibid., 31.

485 **Criss-cross about the world** ... ibid., 42.

485 **'I have been spending a cosy afternoon ...'** ibid., 111.

486 **a curiously hygienic quality** ibid., 201.

486 **She had given me my manumission** ... ibid., 235.

486 **So at sunset I took formal possession of her** ... ibid., 228.

486 **It was no time for the sweets of luxury** ... *BR* (1960), 248.

486*n* **My opinion is valueless** ... EW to Ann Rothermere, 7 April 1953. Private collection.

487 **'Charles, you *must* come ...'** *BR*, 231.

487*n* **Our language took form** ... *Month*, 6 September 1951.

488 **Feeling in London is running high** ... Christopher Sykes to EW, 27 December 1944. BL.

488 **the unseen hook and invisible line** ... *BR*, 195.

488 **particularly in this country** ... ibid., 80.

488 **'My sister Cordelia's last report ...'** ibid., 81.

489 **Rex was sent to Farm Street** ... ibid., 170.

489 **The novelist deals with the experiences** ... *Helena* (Penguin 1963), 9.

489*n* **I don't know them** ... *Paris Review*, April 1962.

490 **Class consciousness, particularly in England** ... *Life*, 8 April 1946, *EAR*, 300.

490 **a bleak period of present privation** ... Preface to *BR* (1960).

490 ***Brideshead* has come** ... Nancy Mitford to EW, 22 December 1944. BL.

491 **Yes I know what you mean** ... EW to Nancy Mitford, 7 January 1945, *EWL*, 196.

491 **I quite see how the person who tells** ... Nancy Mitford to EW, 17 January 1945. BL.

492 **To my mind you carry out** ... Henry Yorke to EW, 25 December 1944. BL.

492 **I slid my paper-knife** ... Harold Acton to EW, 30 May 1945. BL.

492 **A small point, raised by Fr Corbishley** ... Ronald Knox to EW. BL.

492*n* **Henry has written an obscene book** ... *EWD*, 624.

493 **the vulgarity of Ryder** ... John Russell to EW, 19 January 1948. BL.

493 **Katharine who detested the book** ... EW to Ronald Knox, 14 May 1945, *EWL*, 206.

493 **I thought the first $1/3$ as good** ... Roger Fulford to Matthew Ponsonby, 8 July 1945. Private collection.

493 **I think it so very bad** ... *Letters of Conrad Russell*, 236.

493 **How beautiful they are** ... NS, 23 June 1945, *EWCH*, 239.

494 **Waugh's snobbery, hitherto held in cheek** ... *New Yorker*, 5 January 1946, *EWCH*, 245.

494 [the novel] breathes from beginning to end . . . *Bell*, December 1946, *EWCH*, 255.

494 This morning I received the offer . . . *EWD*, 664.

495 a prodigious surprise . . . ibid., 629.

495 You should have been to Ann's party . . . EW to Laura Waugh, 28 July 1945. BL.

495 a sweaty tug-of-war . . . *S-K*, 5.

496 In place of the old, simple belief . . . *Spectator*, 6 November 1942, *EAR*, 272.

496 [The upper classes] are, so far as the outside world is concerned . . . *Town and Country*, September 1946, *EAR*, 312.

496 Will you please take great pains . . . EW to Laura Waugh. BL.

497 on a grey, fly-infested heavy evening . . . *EWD*, 634.

497 It is delightful to be in my own home . . . EW to A. D. Peters, 25 September 1945. HRC.

497 After long correspondence and threats . . . *EWD*, 638.

497 Laura grapples vaguely . . . ibid., 637.

498 It is sad that Evelyn . . .' Maurice Bowra to Ann Fleming, *The Letters of Ann Fleming*, 295.

498 quite fascinated by it EW to Nancy Mitford, 17 January 1945. Private collection.

498 [It] seems to have caused . . . *EWD*, 638.

498 certain substantial advantages . . . ibid., 645.

500 [had] much of Tito's matronly appeal EW to Randolph Churchill, *EWL*, 226.

500 fully reconciled . . . *EWD*, 641.

500 [Wu] is temporarily happy . . . Diana Cooper to Conrad Russell, 5 April 1946. Private collection.

500 so that I was immersed in wine *EWD*, 647.

500 It was very agreeable to see Huxley . . . ibid., 648.

500 to know that you have kept a warm place . . . *MWMS*, 85.

501 a typical modern state . . . *S-K*, 4.

501 Above the clatter and chatter . . . ibid., 41.

502 'I will stay as I am here . . .' ibid., 88.

502 The modern world, we are meant to infer . . . *New York Times Book Review*, 20 September 1949, *EWCH*, 294.

502 two of the most pleasant cities . . . *DT*, 11 November 1947, *EAR*, 339.

503 for the vast majority . . . *DT*, 13 November 1947, *EAR*, 343.

503 The church . . . [is] the normal state of man . . . EW to Edward Sackville West, 2 July 1948. Private collection.

503 If we were allowed favourite dogmas . . . *EW*, 440.

503 an all-wise God . . . *Tablet*, 27 July 1946, *EAR*, 309.

504   **The failure of modern novelists**... *Life*, 8 April 1946, *EAR*, 300.

504   **At the bottom of everything**... Mia Woodruff, interview with author.

504   **At first it was easy**... EW to Penelope Betjeman, 7 January 1950, *EWL*, 317.

505   **The Archbishop of Milan is apparently very pleased**... Peter Janson-Smith to EW, 19 November 1948. HRC.

505   **How to reconcile this indifference**... *MWMS*, 88.

505   **being so horrible with being a Christian**... Nancy Mitford to Pamela Berry, 17 May 1950. Private collection.

506   **You are coming into the Church**... EW to Penelope Betjeman, 7 March 1948, *EWL*, 271.

506   **Thousands have died**... EW to Clarissa Eden, 2 September 1952, *EWL*, 381.

507   **a Ritz vision in dark mink** Nancy Mitford to EW, 28 January 1950. BL.

507   **She sat on the floor**... *EWD*, 701.

507   **Mrs Walston is Graham's paper hat** Peter Quennell, *STel*, 28 July 1991.

507   **a bird fluttering about in the gloom**... *EWD*, 783.

507   **had the result, not entirely acceptable to Evelyn**... *Portrait of a Country Neighbour*, 34.

508   **the bogosity of the Church of England** EW to Penelope Betjeman, 10 February 1948, *EWL*, 267.

508   **Awful about your obduracy**... EW to John Betjeman, *EWL*, 248.

508   **Nothing less than complete abandonment**... ibid., *EWL*, 249.

508   **The ONLY thing is to leave him alone**... Penelope Betjeman to EW. BL.

508   **I am by nature a bully**... EW to Penelope Betjeman, 4 June 1947, *EWL*, 252.

509   **You can have no idea**... EW to Nancy Mitford, 27 September 1950, *EWL*, 336.

509   **I found returning to it**... *MWMS*, 93.

509   **For some time I have been worried**... EW to Laura Waugh, 17 October 1944. BL.

509   **Please bear in mind**... ibid., 29 January 1945, *EWL*, 198.

510   **wherever I turn [there is]**... *EWD*, 661.

510   **Never have I seen a country**... Nancy Mitford to EW, 26 April 1952. BL.

510   **I am anxious to emigrate**... EW to Nancy Mitford, 16 October 1946, *EWL*, 235.

510   **a fine, solid, grim**... *EWD*, 664.

511   **Reasons: (1) Noble**... ibid., 689.

511　**Among the countless blessings** . . . EW to Nancy Mitford, 1 May 1952, *EWL*, 373.

511　**The great difference between our manners** . . . *ST*, 12 August 1962, *EAR*, 590.

512　**My book has been a great success** . . . EW to Mary Lygon, 4 February 1946, *EWL*, 223.

512　**Americans write to me by every post** . . . EW to John Betjeman, 11 June 1946, *EWL*, 230.

512　**I would be grateful for your comments** . . . Elizabeth Reeve to EW, 30 January 1946. HRC.

512　**Dear Madam: I have read your letter of yesterday** . . . EW to Elizabeth Reeve, 31 January 1946, *EWL*, 221.

513　**You would suffer the most extreme forms** . . . A. D. Peters to EW, 16 October 1946. HRC.

513　**The sort of offer** . . . EW to A. D. Peters, 3 October 1946, *EWL*, 235.

513　**a month's trip to Hollywood** . . . *EWD*, 662.

513　**I am sure that if they are reasonable** . . . A. D. Peters to EW, 15 November 1946. HRC.

513　**Dear Pete, Many thanks for your letter** . . . EW to A. D. Peters, 21 November 1946. HRC.

514　**One of the reasons for my putting myself** . . . *EWD*, 668.

514　**great booby boxes** . . . *MWMS*, 94.

514　**sitting through all eternity** . . . Ms. fragment. HRC.

514　**a woman of no intellectual interests** . . . *EWD*, 670.

514　**I went over to the Waldorf** . . . Harold Matson, interview with Edwin McDowell, *New York Times*, 1 May 1986.

515　**[Evelyn's appearance] was fantastic** . . . Alec Waugh to Catherine Waugh, 22 February 1948. BU.

515　**more like Egypt** . . . *EWD*, 672.

515　**'The trouble with you . . .'** Harold Acton, *More Memoirs of an Aesthete* (Methuen 1970), 226.

515　**Jovial banter prevails** . . . *EWD*, 673.

515　**the aimless, genial coffee-house chatter** . . . *Life*, 29 September 1947, *EAR*, 331.

516　**Social life gay & refined** . . . EW to A. D. Peters, 6 March 1947, *EWL*, 247.

516　**grew smarter and younger** . . . *EWD*, 675.

516　**wearing a little black hat** . . . Maria Huxley to Christopher Isherwood, 6 March 1947. Private collection.

517　**I am entirely obsessed by Forest Lawns** . . . EW to A. D. Peters, 6 March 1947, *EWL*, 247.

517　**the artist's load** . . . *LO*, 127.

517 **Carl and I have found Laura and Evelyn** ... Carol Brandt to A. D. Peters, 18 March 1947. HRC.

518 **I fall into ungovernable rages** ... EW to Graham Greene, 26 September 1948. Georgetown.

518 **a book of singular enchantment** *Spectator,* 16 October 1959.

519 **'Why do you wear a double-breasted blazer?'** ... Leo Rosten, *The World,* 21 September 1974

519 **It is not possible to be funny** ... A. D. Peters to EW, 13 September 1947. HRC.

520 **The freshest part of Mr Waugh's story** ... quoted in a letter from A. D. Peters to EW, 10 November 1947. HRC.

520n **I don't think Peters's literary advice valuable** ... EW to Nancy Mitford, 23 August 1957. Private collection.

520n **It is becoming more and more evident** ... Hubert Eaton to EW, 8 January 1960. HRC.

521 **'Lovely, Miss Thanatogenos,'** ... *LO,* 57.

521 **Others, better men than he** ... ibid., 127.

521 **1st & quite predominantly** ... EW to Cyril Connolly, 2 January 1948, *EWL,* 265.

522 **Evelyn Waugh caught between laughter and vomiting** ... *Time,* 12 July 1948, *EWCH,* 301.

522 **an act of devastation** ... *New Republic,* 26 July 1948, *EWCH,* 304.

522 **Beneath satire of any depth** ... *ST,* 21 November 1948, *EWCH,* 308.

522 **I am afraid I have boasted** ... EW to Nancy Mitford. Private collection.

522 **The *heaven* of *The Loved One*** ... Nancy Mitford to EW, 9 February 1948. BL.

523 **[she] always had something to recount** ... Nancy Mitford, *The Blessing* (Hamish Hamilton 1951), 76.

523 **Got away in time** ... *EWD,* 643.

523 **No one departure** ... EW to Nancy Mitford, 16 October 1946, *EWL,* 235.

524 **You are cher maître to me** Nancy Mitford to EW, 30 July 1949. BL.

524 **[with] your well known knack** ... ibid., 27 May 1950. BL.

524 **Within, the key-note, the theme, was death** Nancy Mitford, *The Pursuit of Love* (Hamish Hamilton 1945), 39.

524 **You do not understand the meaning** ... EW to Nancy Mitford, 8 July 1953, *EWL,* 405.

524 **[It needs] six months hard I am afraid** ... ibid., 24 October 1948, *EWL,* 285.

525 **[Evelyn] needs feminine company by the yard** Nancy Mitford to Pamela Berry, 1 May 1952. Private collection.

525 **that jagged stone our relationship** ... *MWMS,* 109.

525 **When you write a letter** . . . EW to Margaret Waugh, 9 May 1956. Private collection.

525 **Can't understand Baby's movements** . . . *MWMS*, 271.

525 **Poor Wu – he does everything he can** . . . Diana Cooper to Conrad Russell, 7 April 1946. Private collection.

526 **Most of the time he was sweet** . . . Nancy Mitford to Pamela Berry, 20 May 1949. Private collection.

526 **The French are beginning to regard Evelyn** . . . ibid., 14 November 1949. Private collection.

526 **Oh please don't quarrel with poor Evelyn** ibid., 4 October 1949. Private collection.

527 **Like all people with intellectual gifts** . . . Thomas Merton to EW, 22 September 1948. BL.

527 **I abhor their company** . . . *MWMS*, 82.

527 **My children are home for the holidays** . . . *MWMS*, 87.

527 **The presence of my children** . . . *EWD*, 667.

528 **I have become involved** . . . ibid., 649.

528 **I used to take some pleasure** . . . ibid., 667.

528 **Yesterday was a day of supreme self-sacrifice** . . . EW to Laura Waugh, 25 August 1945. BL.

529 **He read well** . . . *EW*, 597.

529 **I made a fair show of geniality** . . . *EWD*, 668.

529 **Thank God Christmas is over** . . . EW to Philip Caraman. Boston College.

529 **Poor Laura's life is one of drudgery** . . . *MWMS*, 82.

530 **The aim of my letter** . . . EW to Laura Waugh. BL.

530 **Don't be so bloody wet** ibid., *EWL*, 261.

530 **'Laura, shouldn't there be two salt cellars . . .'** *Portrait of a Country Neighbour*, 43.

530 **When Evelyn is in one of his bad moods** . . . Ann Fleming, *EWW*, 237.

530 **I stayed in London for no other reason.** . . . *EWD*, 661.

530 **I have been thinking deeply** . . . Laura Waugh to EW. BL.

531 **[Laura] saw the funny side of everything** . . . Auberon Waugh in *Singular Encounters*, Naim Atallah (Quartet 1990), 547.

531 **We are stinking rich** . . . EW to Laura Waugh, 9 January 1945, *EWL*, 196.

532 **God I wish I had some neighbours** . . . EW to Nancy Mitford, 16 October 1946, *EWL*, 235.

532 **I suppose I have seen** . . . ibid., 24 October 1946, *EWL*, 237.

533 **My last day in London** . . . ibid., 7 August 1946, *EWL*, 232.

534 **by being rude to everybody** . . . Barbara Skelton, *Tears Before Bedtime* (Hamish Hamilton 1987), 135.

534   **I have been an invalid** . . . EW to Nancy Mitford, 5 December 1949, *EWL*, 315.

534   **They are at their worst** . . . *EWD*, 682.

535   **Where are my cigars?** . . . EW to A. D. Peters, *EWL*, 488.

535   **I am thinking of giving up smoking** . . . *EWD*, 676.

535   **I have not been in London for weeks** . . . *MWMS*, 99.

536   **It was not a great success** . . . EW to Laura Waugh, 9 November 1948, *EWL*, 287.

536   **an autocratic ascetic saint** . . . ibid., 14 November 1948, *EWL*, 289.

536   **I am not really enjoying it very much** . . . ibid., 1 December 1948. BL.

536   **constantly in the company** . . . EW to Nancy Mitford, 2 April 1949. Private collection.

537   **Mr Waugh was most gracious** . . . Thérèse Lentfoehr, *Evelyn Waugh Newsletter*, vol. 11 no. 1.

537   **I've seen enough of USA** . . . EW to Nancy Mitford, 2 April 1949. Private collection.

538   **Clare Luce was very much gratified** . . . Pamela Berry to Nancy Mitford, 27 November 1949. Private collection.

538   **It's far the best book** . . . EW to Christopher Sykes, *EWL*, 318.

538   **an unhistorical life of St Helena** . . . EW to Ronald Knox, 14 May 1945, *EWL*, 206.

539   **I am writing about her life** . . . EW to John Betjeman, *EWL*, 207.

539   **I describe her as hunting** . . . EW to Penelope Betjeman, 15 January 1946, *EWL*, 218.

539   **Personally I found it very difficult** . . . Penelope Betjeman to EW, 23 January 1946. BL.

539   **her womanhood broke bud** *Helena*, 24.

539   **[while] the saddle-tree solaced her man-made hurt** ibid., 33.

539   **Of course you must go on** . . . Douglas Woodruff to EW. BL.

539   **'What a lark!' said Princess Helena** . . . *Helena*, 20.

540   **'I bet He's just waiting . . .'** ibid., 128.

540   **'just a little thing I popped on . . .'** ibid., 104.

540   **she had completely conformed to the will of God** . . . ibid., 156.

540   **a great wind of prayer** . . . ibid., 89.

540   **Beauty would come later** . . . ibid., 92.

540*n* **a terror, rattling with clichés** . . . *Tablet*, 10 November 1945, *EAR*, 281.

541   **Waugh's sky-blue prose** . . . *Time*, 23 October 1950, *EWCH*, 323.

541   **the Angela Brazil accent** *TLS*, 13 October 1950.

541   **Waugh has done nothing in this book** . . . *NS*, 20 October 1950, *EWCH*, 320.

541   **The indifferent reception given** . . . *EW*, 451.

541 **There is so much to see** ... EW to Diana Cooper, 24 November 1950.

Chapter XV

542 **burrowed ever deeper into the rock** *OGP,* 13.

542 **unquestionably the finest novels** *ST,* 29 October 1961.

542 **Even though he still writes** ... Graham Martin in *The Modern Age,* vol. 7 of the *Pelican Guide to English Literature,* ed. Boris Ford (1961), 394.

543 **I have never voted in a parliamentary election** ... *Spectator,* 2 October 1959, *EAR,* 537.

543 **provided for the free distribution** ... *Encounter,* December 1955, *EAR,* 494.

543 **A most trustworthy man** ... EW to Daphne Acton, 2 November 1958, *EWL,* 515.

543 **the most sacred city in the world** *The Holy Places* (Queen Anne Press 1952), 15.

544 **One fully realizes, perhaps for the first time** ... ibid., 37.

544 **Christopher is being a** *fairly* **good jagger** EW to Laura Waugh, *EWL,* 345.

544 **I know what it is you want** ... EW to Christopher Sykes, *EWL,* 344.

545 **Of course I don't often agree with you** ... EW to Graham Greene, 17 March 1951, *EWL,* 346.

545 **patrolling the built up areas** ... EW to Nancy Mitford, *EWL,* 356.

545 **Is Scobie damned?** ... *Commonweal,* 16 July 1948, *EAR,* 360.

546 **A careful re-reading of** *The Heart of the Matter* ... EW to *Tablet,* 17 July 1948.

546 **'It will be a relief not to write about** *God* ...' Christopher Sykes, *ST,* 17 April 1966.

546 **I am writing an interminable novel** ... EW to Graham Greene, 18 August 1951, *EWL,* 352.

546 **Yesterday I spent reading** ... EW to Laura Waugh, *EWL,* 351.

547 **Unreadable & endless** ... EW to Nancy Mitford, 24 August 1951, *EWL,* 354.

547 **In poor taste, mostly about WCs** ... EW to Mary Lygon, 23 January 1952, *EWL,* 366.

547 **Book gets longer** ... *MWMS,* 122.

547 **I have finished that novel** ... EW to Nancy Mitford, 8 January 1952. Private collection.

547 **instinctively ... I did not know why ...** EW to F. J. Stopp, 19 January 1954. Cambridge University Library.

547 **The enemy at last was plain in view ...** *MA*, 11.

547 **a vast uniformed and bemedalled bureaucracy** ibid., 107.

548 **There is a strong affinity ...** EW to Cyril Connolly, 8 September 1952, *EWL*, 382.

548 **It would be a travesty to say ...** *MA*, 85.

548 **Apthorpe giggled slightly at his cleverness ...** ibid., 186.

548 **the Brigadier's eye teeth flashed ...** ibid., 110.

548 **For this remarkable warrior ...** ibid., 57.

548*n* **'Get on with your work, Ryder,' ...** *Charles Ryder's Schooldays*, 287.

549 **It was as though eight years back ...** *MA*, 13.

549 **almost unique in contemporary England ...** ibid., 16.

549 **He was quite without class consciousness ...** ibid., 28.

549 **I don't like Crouchback's father ...** Anthony Powell to EW, 1 July 1955. BL.

549 **of the decencies and true purpose of life** Frederick J. Stopp, *Evelyn Waugh: Portrait of an Artist* (Chapman & Hall 1958), 168.

549*n* **a Gunner Lieut. Colonel told me ...** Alan Bourne to EW, 15 August 1955. BL.

550 **'Poor Guy, picked a wrong 'un'** *MA*, 67.

550 **Tears of rage and humiliation ...** ibid., 104.

550 **You see women through a glass ...** Nancy Mitford to EW, 27 September 1952. BL.

550 **Men at Arms is good-tempered** Waugh *NS*, 20 September 1952, *EWCH*, 339.

550 **[Men at Arms] describes ...** *ST*, 7 September 1952, *EWCH*, 337.

550 **If one had no other information ...** *Partisan Review*, 3 November 1952, *EWCH*, 344.

551 **a sad sack** *New Republic*, 10 November 1952, *EWCH*, 345.

551 **[a] huge prep school conspiracy ...** *NS*, 20 September 1952, *EWCH*, 339.

551 **If [Waugh's] trilogy continues ...** *Time*, 27 October 1952, *EWCH*, 341.

551 **Whereas you have been so outstanding ...** Martin D'Arcy to EW, 14 September 1952. BL.

551 **I do think Catholic writers ...** Nancy Mitford to EW, 16 June 1952. BL.

551 **I love the way English Roman Catholics ...** ibid., 27 September 1952. BL.

551 **Henry is decrepid, deaf, toothless ...** EW to Mary Lygon. Private collection.

552 **I hate the Yorkes now...** EW to Arthur Windham Baldwin, 30 October 1951.

552 **Henry had looked out of the window...** Heywood Hill to Nancy Mitford, 6 March 1962. Private collection.

552 **I went to call ... on your cousin...** EW to Laura Waugh, *EWL*, 164.

552 **Quite happy, quite uninteresting...** EW to Maurice Bowra, 29 September 1964.

553 **[a sum] which fifty years earlier...** *Love Among the Ruins: a Romance of the Near Future* (Chapman & Hall 1953), 6.

553 **'He's taken off all the skin...'...** ibid., 39.

553 **hastily finished & injudiciously published...** EW to Graham Greene, 5 June 1953, *EWL*, 403.

554 **Waugh is almost impervious...** 17 May 1951. HRC.

554 **[Harry] did not appreciate...** Clare Luce to EW, 1 February 1953. BL.

554 **The editor of *Good Housekeeping* tried to dun me...** *EWD*, 713.

555 **Well it won't break us...** ibid., 671.

555 **The time has come to employ another agent...** EW to A. D. Peters, 3 March 1953. HRC.

555 **For some time I have been aware...** EW to Nancy Mitford, 11 January 1950, *EWL*, 318.

556 **You save tax, ensure their future...** A. D. Peters to EW, 8 December 1949. HRC.

557 **I am in financial depths...** EW to A. D. Peters. HRC.

557 **The reduction of your standard of living...** A. D. Peters to EW. HRC.

557 **The trouble is getting servants to go...** EW to Nancy Mitford, 14 January 1952, *EWL*, 365.

557 **I had noticed a change...** *EW*, 472.

558 **I am afraid the expedition was a failure...** EW to Harold Acton, 26 March 1952.

558 **[Evelyn] has become so testy...** Harold Acton to John Sutro. Private collection.

558 **'Poor Evelyn, he is deeply unhappy...'** Ann Fleming to Hugo Charteris, 14 February 1955, *Letters of Ann Fleming*, 150.

558 **I am in deep misanthropy...** EW to Nancy Mitford, 12 April 1949, *EWL*, 296.

558 **He might go mad...** Nancy Mitford to Raymond Mortimer, 12 December 1953. Princeton.

559 **My dear Nancy... There is no reason...** EW to Nancy Mitford. Private collection.

559 **Don't start My dear Nancy** ... Nancy Mitford to EW, 6 September 1951. BL.

559 **alarming outburst of rage and hate** *EWD*, 719.

559 **If you had accepted my invitation** ... *MWMS*, 175.

559 **Yes, it's true that I chucked Churchill** ... ibid., 178.

559 **I am very sorry to hear that Duff was surprised** ... ibid., 180.

559 **a ruthless go-getter** ... ibid., 268.

560 **a creature with a certain irridescent aura** ibid., 193.

560 **You see I don't go to funerals** ... ibid., 175.

560 **[Baby] will not write again** ... ibid., 176.

560 **Beloved Bo** ... **I know you have a great heart** ... ibid., 202.

560 **My memory is not at all hazy** ... EW to John Betjeman, 17 September 1953, *EWL*, 410.

560 **There were periods of literary composition** ... *OGP*, 17.

561 **Clocks barely moving** ... *EWD*, 722.

561 **I well remember the visit** ... Auberon Waugh to Martin Stannard, 9 February 1989, *No Abiding City*, 334.

561 **[Waugh] requested a ridiculously large fee** ... Hugh Burnett, *Oldie*, 29 October 1993.

561 **I never heard an interview** ... *Spectator*, 20 November 1953.

562 **Oh no, old boy** ... John Betjeman to EW, 31 December 1953. BL.

562 **I must see an alienist** ... EW to John Betjeman.

563 **All the pipes and air shafts** ... EW to Laura Waugh, 3 February 1954, *EWL*, 418.

563 **I found myself the victim** ... ibid., 8 February 1954, *EWL*, 418.

564 **It is rather difficult to write to you** ... ibid., 12 February 1954, *EWL*, 419.

565 **'I've been mad ...'** *Oxford in the Twenties*, 82.

565 **His strongest tastes were negative** ... *OGP*, 14.

565*n* **headache, irritability, emotional lability** ... *Bromide Psychoses: Four Varieties*, Max Levin 1948, *Evelyn Waugh Newsletter*, Autumn 1982.

566 **the questions were civil enough** ... *OGP*, 19.

566 **'who doesn't really believe in his religion ...'** ibid., 101.

566*n* **Reading the report of the Lady Chatterley trial** ... *EWD*, 781.

567 **a perfectly simple case of poisoning** *OGP*, 156.

567 **Mr Pinfold sat down to work** ... ibid., 157.

567 **These are the self revelations** ... *Observer*, 21 July 1957, *EWCH*, 386.

567 **[Mr Waugh] happens to be** ... *NS*, 20 July 1957, *EWCH*, 384.

568 **a weird touch of obscenity** ... *EW*, 397.

568 **The part for which he cast himself** ... *OGP*, 15.

568 **Women don't understand pomposity** ... EW to Diana Cooper, 21 December 1949, *MWMS*, 104.

568 **Fact is the public looks upon you** ... Nancy Mitford to EW, 26 April 1956. BL.

568 **My chief sorrow at the moment** ... *MWMS*, 150.

569 **The mask, the style, *is* the man** *National Review,* 22 April 1961, *EAR,* 558.

569 **the most charming, enchanting** ... Frances Donaldson, interview with author.

569 **He refused. She protested** ... *EW*, 425.

570 **[Evelyn] is here, in such a sunny mood** ... Nancy Mitford to Heywood Hill, 14 April 1956. Private collection.

570 **I have turned over a faded leaf** ... EW to Ann Fleming. Private collection.

570 **Thank you so much for my day of sweetness** ... *MWMS*, 208.

570 **A most successful day** ... *EWD*, 731.

570 **My ear-trumpets are a great convenience** ... *MWMS*, 233.

571 **Have you noticed how everything beastly** ... EW to Ann Fleming. Private collection.

571 **near-warm civility to Peter** Ann Fleming to Hugh Charteris, 14 February 1955, *Letters of Ann Fleming*, 150.

571 **I requested silence for bird-watching** ... Ann Fleming, *EWW*, 238.

571 **Poor Evelyn – killing time is his trouble** ... Ann Fleming to Joan Rayner and Patrick Leigh Fermor, 27 March 1955, *EWW*, 153.

572 **a beneficent, alert deity** ... *OG*, 316.

572 **the hypodermic needle of her charm** ibid., 382.

572 **[Guy] had no clear apprehension** ... ibid., 368.

573 **Laycock's & my ignominious flight** EW to Dorothy Lygon, 27 November 1962. Private collection.

573 **[Blackhouse] was returning from the bridge** ... *OG*, 322.

573 **after less than two years' pilgrimage** ... ibid., 383.

573 **Mr Waugh used to be a satirist** ... *ST*, 3 July 1955, *EWCH*, 369.

573 **whether Mr Waugh's invention is really impaired** *Spectator,* 8 July 1955.

573 **Mr Waugh seems to believe** ... *New York Times Book Review,* 10 July 1955, *EWCH*, 375.

573 **I am awfully encouraged** ... EW to Maurice Bowra, 14 July 1955, *EWL*, 443.

574 **There remained now only a firm pietas** ... *OGP*, 30.

574 **You say the English always say** ... EW to Nancy Mitford, *EWL*, 434.

574 **I am afraid you will always remember her** ... EW to Margaret Waugh, 11 December 1954, *EWL*, 434.

575 **that dealing with any of them** ... Geoffrey Wheatcroft, *Absent Friends* (Hamish Hamilton 1989), 130.

575 **often marked by the most appalling gloom** ... *Will This Do?*, 46.

575 **Darling Meg & Hatty... Oh this will be sad news...** EW to Margaret and Harriet Waugh, 8 February 1956.

575 **Children come flooding in by every train...** EW to Nancy Mitford, 18 December 1954, *EWL*, 434.

576 **Did I tell you about Harriet...** ibid., 18 August 1949, *EWL*, 305.

576 **Non Vintage champagne for all but me** EW to Brian Franks, *EWL*, 473.

576 **It was a great success...** EW to Margaret and Harriet Waugh, 8 July 1956, *EWL*, 474.

576 **The most terrifying aspect of Evelyn Waugh...** *Will This Do?*, 46.

577 **He is not at all a vicious boy...** EW to Aelred Watkin, 18 May 1955. Downside.

577 **Don't write in that silly tone...** EW to Auberon Waugh, 23 May 1955, *EWL*, 441.

577 **We were greeted by the manager...** *EWD*, 732.

578 **Walked to Mass and communion...** ibid., 737.

578 **I have much sympathy with your restlessness...** EW to Auberon Waugh, 20 February 1956, *EWL*, 466.

578 **I am appalled at what an odious prig I was...** ibid.

579 **My sexual passion for my ten year old daughter...** EW to Ann Fleming, 1 September 1952, *EWL*, 379.

579 **[Margaret] in low spirits...** *EWD*, 767.

579 **Meg is sulky and in my bad books...** EW to Ann Fleming, 5 August 1957. Private collection.

579 **I really am very worried...** EW to Margaret Waugh, 24 May 1953, *EWL*, 402.

579 **Darling Meg – I am sorry you are in hot water...** ibid., 3 June 1957, *EWL*, 489.

581 **I rang the bell...** *DE*, 23 June 1955.

581 **the total first edition sales** ibid., 17 March 1956.

581 **I have waited a long time...** EW to A. D. Peters, 17 March 1956, *EWL*, 468.

581 **The verdict at the trial was a great surprise...** EW to Margaret and Harriet Waugh, 17 February 1957. Private collection.

581*n* **It is a sorrow to me...** EW to Maurice Bowra, 14 July 1955, *EWL*, 443.

582 **I felt it was polluted** EW to Nancy Mitford, 28 February 1966, *EWL*, 636.

582 **I would like to sell out...** EW to Knight, Frank & Rutley, 4 July 1955, *EWL*, 443.

582 **Now as I move about the house...** *EWD*, 764.

583 **I have bought a dull, very private house...** EW to Ann Fleming, 13 September 1956, *Letters of Ann Fleming*, 186.

583 **Laura has moped a little** . . . *EWD*, 770.

583 **The house, after weeks of chaos** . . . EW to Ann Fleming, 28 January 1957, *EWL*, 484.

583 **We are far from happy here** . . . ibid. Private collection.

584 **This is plainly the hotel** . . . ibid., 19 March 1957, *EWL*, 487.

584 **[Your duties] can no longer be regarded as very remote** Ronald Knox to EW, 17 June 1957. BL.

584 **Ronnie's death has transformed my life** . . . *MWMS*, 244.

584 **whether I ought to have a chapter** . . . EW to Hubert van Zeller, 30 December 1957, *EWL*, 500.

584 **[Ronald] could think of no one more suitable** . . . EW to Daphne Acton. Private collection.

585 **I think the fact that Ronnie was even older** . . . Daphne Acton to EW, 25 August 1958. BL.

585 **The house is a long bungalow** . . . *A Tourist in Africa* (Chapman & Hall 1960), 121.

585 **Children were everywhere** . . . EW to Ann Fleming, 10 March 1958, *EWL*, 504.

585 **Bron's resignation and the way he quietly prayed** . . . Laura Waugh to EW, 11 June 1958. BL.

585 **Will you tell Giovanni** . . . ibid., 17 June 1958. BL.

586 **Bron continues to improve** . . . ibid., 19 June 1958. BL.

586 **In the last five months** . . . EW to Ann Fleming, 3 December 1958, *Letters of Ann Fleming*, 225.

586 **At about this time** . . . *Will This Do?*, 112.

586 **the greatest work of literary art of the century** *Books on Trial*, October 1955, *EAR*, 477.

587 **perhaps unfortunate for the three generous women friends** . . . *TLS*, 9 October 1959, *EWCH*, 397.

587 **It may occur to the busy parish priest** . . . *The Life of the Right Reverend Ronald Knox* (Chapman & Hall 1959), 237.

587 **[Knox] went to Torquay** . . . ibid., 327.

588 **Three years before, it so happened** . . . ibid., 306.

588 **a man of meagre attainments** . . . ibid., 243.

588 **was quite devoid of anything** . . . ibid., 166.

588 **Delegation of any task** . . . ibid., 291.

588 **It is, as you are no doubt aware** . . . John Barton to EW, 1 October 1959. BL.

588 **Every Catholic, I suppose** . . . *Observer*, 11 October 1959, *EWCH*, 400.

588 **Mr Waugh writes our language** . . . *London Magazine*, December 1959, *EWCH*, 402.

589 **Perhaps Mr Waugh has not permitted himself** . . . *Encounter,* January 1960, *EWCH*, 405.

589 **that this mark of Her Majesty's favour** . . . T. J. Bligh to EW, 7 May 1959, BL.

589 **Some years back I refused the CBE** . . . EW to Graham Greene, 7 May 1964, *EWL*, 619.

589 **No sour grapes** . . . EW to Nancy Mitford, 7 June 1956, *EWL*, 472.

589 **Said I was too deaf to obey** . . . EW to Daphne Acton, 30 June 1958. Private collection.

589 **'Oh, Mr Waugh, champagne! . . .'** Frances Donaldson, interview with author.

589 **I would like a long luxurious trip** . . . EW to A. D. Peters. HRC.

590 **I am writing an account of my African journey** . . . EW to Auberon Waugh, 28 July 1959. Private collection.

590 **[the book] is hard going** . . . EW to Daphne Acton, 20 October 1959, *EWL*, 529.

590 **The chief hotel stands near** . . . *Tourist in Africa*, 23.

590 **Another pen than mine** . . . ibid., 102.

590 **we had lost so much time** . . . ibid., 146.

591 **I was able to see and admire** . . . ibid., 159.

591 **[Mrs Newman] very kindly put me up** . . . ibid., 113.

591 *A Tourist in Africa* **is quite the thinnest piece** . . . *ST,* 25 September 1960, *EWCH*, 414.

591 **Wind of change is blowing very cold** . . . EW to Ann Fleming, 10 November 1960, *EWL,* 552.

591 **in order to enjoy the standard of living** . . . *DM,* 28 December 1959, *EAR,* 539.

591 **Laura has at last had to give up** . . . EW to Diana Cooper, 24 December 1960, *EWL,* 555.

592 **I was appalled at the way** . . . EW to A. D. Peters, 5 April 1960. HRC.

592 **Waugh was left happy** . . . *Evelyn Waugh: New Directions,* 107.

592 **I have let myself in** . . . EW to Tom Driberg, 11 June 1969. Christ Church.

592 **It has been a bad year** . . . EW to Elizabeth Longford, 4 January 1960, Elizabeth Longford, *The Pebbled Shore* (Weidenfeld & Nicholson 1986), 303.

592 **with an exquisite mastery of the English language** *Month,* November 1962, *EAR,* 601.

592 **[Mr Hemingway] is lucid and individual** . . . *Books on Trial,* October 1955, *EAR,* 477.

593 **For Mr Wodehouse there has been no Fall of Man** . . . *ST,* 16 July 1961, *EAR,* 561.

593 Judging from this book . . . *Spectator*, 21 July 1961, *EAR*, 568.

593 At one stage of his life . . . *Tablet*, 5 May 1951, *EAR*, 394.

594 Sir, Trevor-Roper is bored . . . *NS*, 1 September 1956.

594 I decided on reflection . . . EW to John MacDougall, *EWL*, 564.

594 I have finished the novel . . . EW to A. D. Peters, 4 April 1961, *EWL*, 564.

594n Roosevelt produced his terms . . . A. J. P. Taylor, *English History, 1914–1945*.

595 The Ceremonial swords . . . Robert Laycock to EW, 10 May 1960. HRC.

595 They greeted him with murmured words . . . *US*, 60.

595 Here I am again . . . *EWD*, 722.

595 He [Guy] reported for duty . . . *US*, 66.

595 'It seems to me . . .' *POMF*, 232.

596 the best man, the only entirely good man . . . *US*, 65.

596 The theme is the same . . . Martin D'Arcy to EW, 21 October 1961. BL.

596 I am disconcerted to find . . . EW to Anthony Powell, 31 October 1961, *EWL*, 579.

597 [Ruben's] restaurant was a rare candle . . . *US*, 23.

597 I asked a mutual friend . . . Cyril Connolly to EW, 25 October 1961. BL.

597 a very gorgeous, almost gaudy, tale . . . *US*, 187.

598 'didn't you ever want to marry?' ibid., 35.

599 if he seemed to be really trying . . . *Spectator*, 27 October 1961, *EWCH*, 419.

599 doubtful that a more unflattering portrait . . . *Nation*, 20 January 1962, *EWCH*, 443.

599 To anyone brought up as a Catholic . . . *Guardian*, 27 October 1961, *EWCH*, 423.

599 Our time's first satirist . . . *New York Times Book Review*, 7 January 1962, *EWCH*, 438.

600 I should like to come & discuss . . . EW to A. D. Peters, 8 March 1961. HRC.

Chapter XVI

601 It is in that last undesired decade . . . *ST*, 7 January 1962, *EAR*, 572.

602 I don't think I shall write another novel . . . EW to A. D. Peters, 4 April 1961, *EWL*, 564.

602   **He is not superficially very American** ... EW to Auberon Waugh, 28 July 1959. Private collection.

602   **was never so benign or so gentle** *Spectator*, 6 May 1966.

602   **to try and bring the lower classes** ... Auberon Waugh to EW, 29 January 1964. BL.

602   **I have found a new** *métier* ... ibid., 19 November 1965. BL.

602   **Very funny, I thought** EW to Ann Fleming, 26 May 1960, *EWL*, 541.

603   **My son, Bron, has had an undeserved** ... EW to Diana Cooper, 24 December 1960, *EWL*, 555.

603   **It is very distressing** ... EW to John Donaldson, 24 April 1961. Private collection.

603   **she & Bron would not be admitted** ... EW to Ann Fleming, 27 March 1961, *EWL*, 562.

603   **The boredom and expense** ... *MWMS*, 285.

603   **I went last week to the Academy banquet** ... EW to Brian Franks, 1 May 1961. Private collection.

603   **The photograph of me in the paper** ... EW to Alec Waugh, 12 July 1961. BU.

603   **I have not yet touched wine** ... EW to Ann Fleming, 8 August 1961. Private collection.

604   **Margaret is my darling still** ... EW to Diana Cooper, 24 December 1960, *EWL*, 555.

604   **I beg you to consider** ... EW to Margaret Waugh, 12 April 1962. Private collection.

604   **It is kind of you to enquire** ... ibid., 24 May 1961.

605   **Please don't be cross with me** ... Margaret Waugh to EW, 4 September 1961. BL.

605   **You know I love you** ... ibid., 6 April 1961.

605   **We flit about in private aeroplanes** ... EW to Laura Waugh, 12 January 1962, *EWL*, 580.

605   **We have had ten days in Georgetown** ... ibid., 22 January 1962. BL.

605   **For a moment his spirits were restored** ... Daphne Fielding, *The Nearest Way Home* (Eyre & Spottiswoode 1970), 166.

606   **They have cut it down to insignificance** ... EW to A. D. Peters, 4 April 1962, *EWL*, 584.

606   **I was sitting in the hall at 7 pm** ... EW to Nancy Mitford, 27 March 1962, *EWL*, 582.

606   **Do try & get it into your head** ... Nancy Mitford to EW, 10 April 1962. BL.

606*n*   **I talk to Margaret Waugh** ... Harold Nicolson, *Diaries and Letters vol III* (Collins 1968), 407 (and typescript Balliol College Library).

607 **My writing again. How you will groan** . . . EW to Nancy Mitford, *EWL*, 584.

607 **I am low spirits and in low water** EW to Margaret Waug , 12 April 1962. Private collection.

607 **Please marry someone very rich** . . . ibid., 9 March 1959. Private collection.

607 **If Dunluce proposes marriage** . . . ibid., 22 March 1961. Private collection.

608 **I haven't really thanked you properly** . . . Margaret Waugh to EW, 7 August 1962. BL.

608 **Darling Papa I love you very much** ibid., 30 August 1962. BL.

608 **an Irish stock-broker's clerk** . . . EW to Ann Fleming, 22 August 1962. Private collection.

608 **[Margaret] has fallen head over heels in love** . . . EW to Nancy Mitford, *EWL*, 591.

608 **Your letter full of understanding** . . . *MWMS*, 293.

609 **'Perhaps you can tell me what Barbara sees in him,'** 'Basil Seal Rides Again or The Rake's Regress' in *Work Suspended and Other Stories* (Penguin 1982), 277.

609 **Soundlessly Barbara rose from the seat** . . . ibid., 281.

609 **It was not thus that Basil** . . . ibid., 259.

609 **'Have you been to bed with this man?'** ibid., 273.

609 **'You stay where you're put, chattel,'** ibid., 264.

609 **as long as you are my chattel** . . . EW to Margaret Waugh. HRC.

610 **[the story] gives rise to certain reflections** . . . Nancy Mitford to EW, 26 October 1963. BL.

610 **Why, when it has such pace** . . . John Montgomery to EW, 20 September 1962. BL.

610 **'You complain of speechlessness . . .'** 'Basil Seal', 263.

610 **I must have given my hat** . . . *EWD*, 777.

610 **A day came when he sat longer than usual** . . . 'Basil Seal', 257.

611 **the most accomplished comic of his period** . . . *NS*, 15 November 1963, *EWCH*, 452.

611 **The young couple are now** . . . EW to Ann Fleming, 22 October 1962. Private collection.

611 **You were quite wrong about honeymoons** . . . Margaret Waugh to EW, 26 October 1962. BL.

612 **The sad truth is I am not sortable** . . . EW to Harry Walston, 15 November 1962. Private collection.

612 **I very seldom mind people's deaths** . . . EW to Nancy Mitford, 15 January 1963. Private collection.

612 **The frost here has been very severe** . . . ibid.

612 **On Sunday I felt so low** . . . EW to Laura Waugh. BL.

612   **Sometimes the *Times* arrived in the evening** . . . *MWMS*, 297.

612   **I am very lame** . . . ibid.

612   **I found in the last year** . . . EW to Nancy Mitford, 4 October 1963. Private collection.

612   **It is therefore safe to assume** . . . A. D. Peters to EW, 27 April 1961. HRC.

612   **preparing to start on my autobiography** . . . *EWD*, 782.

613   **I am thinking of writing an autobiography** . . . Alec Waugh to Arthur and Catherine Waugh, 23 June 1943. HRC.

613   **Now that our mother is not here** . . . Alec Waugh to EW, 13 May 1962. HRC.

613   **I think it may have caused** . . . EW to Nancy Mitford, 28 December 1962. Private collection.

613   **Publish and be damned** . . . W. R. B. Young, 21 November 1963. BL.

613   **I distil a few daily drops** . . . EW to Ann Fleming, 7 August 1963, *EWL*, 611.

614   **The difficulty is that I am really** . . . EW to Auberon Waugh, 11 June 1963. Private collection.

614   **Only when one has lost all curiosity** . . . *ALL*, 1.

614   **There were times when I was inclined** . . . ibid., 79.

614   **I do not seek to harrow** . . . ibid., 115.

614   **the friend of my heart** ibid., 192.

614   **I turned about, swam back** . . . ibid., 230.

615   **Mr Waugh is a thoughtful** . . . *NS*, 25 September 1964, *EWCH*, 459.

615   **My Waugh's vocabulary and syntax** . . . *Listener*, 10 September 1964, *EWCH*, 454.

615   **carefully outmoded elegance** . . . *Encounter*, December 1964, *EWCH*, 470.

615   **It is a curious experience** . . . *Cosmopolitan*, November 1964. *EWCH*, 467.

615   **Many many congratulations** . . . Alec Waugh to EW, 10 December 1962. BL.

615   **There is no one whose opinion** . . . EW to Katharine Asquith, 14 September 1964, *EWL*, 623.

615   **Why on earth you should deliberately** . . . Dudley Carew to EW, 4 September 1964. BL.

616   **It may well be that Catholics of today** . . . *Life*, 19 September 1949, *EAR*, 377.

616   **good for 25 years placid inactivity** EW to Daphne Acton, 2 November 1958, *EWL*, 515.

616   **[the triduum was] rather boring** . . . *EWD*, 758.

616*n*   **In the role of iconoclast** . . . *ALL*, 129.

617 **For centuries these had been enriched** ... *Spectator,* 23 November 1962, *EAR,* 602.

617 **had no idea of the Pandora's box** ... EW to Ann Fleming. Private collection.

617 **The Council is of the highest importance** ... EW to Nancy Mitford, 27 October 1962, *EWL,* 595.

618 **As the months pass** ... *Spectator,* 23 November 1962, *EAR,* 602.

618 **Will you promote an appeal** ... EW to *Tablet,* 12 March 1963.

619 **I am returning the tract** ... EW to Daphne Acton, 15 March 1963, *EWL,* 602.

619 **The Vatican Council weighs heavy on my spirits** *MWMS,* 311.

619 **I do not believe that there is much immediate prospect** ... EW to Ruth McQuillan, 19 February 1964. National Library of Scotland.

619 **to avoid the horrors of the English liturgy** EW to Ann Fleming, 3 March 1964, *EWL,* 618.

619 **I had been summoned to London** ... EW to Katharine Asquith, 14 September 1964, *EWL,* 623.

620 **Cardinal Heenan has been double-faced in the matter** *EWD,* 793.

620 **The hierarchy are like Gadarene swine** EW to Christopher Sykes, 24 August 1965. Georgetown.

620 **[Evill] has been exposed** ... EW to Margaret Waugh, 18 January 1965. Private collection.

620 **it would be dangerous for you** ... A. D. Peters to EW, 19 January 1965. HRC.

620 **[it] will be much harder to write** ... EW to Handasyde Buchanan, 13 April 1964. Georgetown.

620 **It certainly would be easy enough** ... EW to A. D. Peters, 12 February 1965. Private collection.

621 **I think those three books** ... ibid.

621 **Cant speak the lingo** ... EW to Arthur Windham Baldwin, 20 October 1964.

621 **I said 'I have practically ...'** EW to Ann Fleming, 3 March 1964, *EWL,* 618.

621 **I remarked that it was a typical** ... *EWD,* 792.

621 **Most of my lack of appetite** ... *MWMS,* 315.

622 **My snappers are a failure** EW to Ann Fleming, 11 May 1965. Private collection.

622 **I am toothless, deaf** ... EW to John MacDougall, 7 June 1965. Reading University.

622 **I accept with gratitude** ... EW to Brian Franks, 20 November 1964, *EWL,* 627.

622 **He had felt too ill** ... *EW,* 590.

622 **Mystical writers agree** ... *Knox,* 169.

622   **They are destroying all . . .** *MWMS*, 316.

622   **I do not ask what is best for me . . .** EW to Monsignor McReavy, 15 April 1965, *EWL*, 630.

623   **The Vatican Council has knocked the guts out of me** EW to Diana Mosley, 9 March 1966, *EWL*, 638.

623   **I have not yet soaked myself . . .** ibid., 30 March 1966, *EWL*, 638.

623   **Laura finds consolation in horticulture . . .** EW to Nancy Mitford, 5 September 1965, *EWL*, 632.

623   **My darling Bo, I am exercised about your condition . . .** *MWMS*, 315.

623   **I had not realised the depth of your depression . . .** Martin D'Arcy to EW, 14 September 1965. BL.

623   **Peckham had an easy choice . . .** EW to Martin D'Arcy, 9 September 1965. Private collection.

623   **You must not worry about my condition . . .** EW to Margaret Waugh, 6 December 1965, *EWL*, 635.

623   **I am *very* worried by Papa . . .** Margaret Waugh to Philip Caraman, 5 January 1966. Boston College.

624   **No work. Feeble health . . .** EW to Ann Fleming, *EWL*, 635.

624   **Tell them I have temporarily lost my reason . . .** EW to A. D. Peters, 29 January 1966. Private collection.

624   **My life is roughly speaking over . . .** *EW*, 589.

624   **When the Abbot refused permission . . .** Hubert van Zeller to Christopher Sykes, 27 April 1973. Private collection.

625   **He was benign and at peace . . .** Philip Caraman, interview with Nicholas Shakespeare (BBC 1987).

626   **You know how he longed to die . . .** Margaret Waugh to Diana Cooper, *MWMS*, 326.

627   **more deeply moved . . .** *Will This Do?*, 210.

Index

NOTES: Works by EW appear directly under title; works by others appear under the name of the author. Titles and ranks are generally the highest mentioned in the text.

G.K.'s Weekly, 350
Glasgow, Patrick James Boyle, 8th Earl of, 442
Glen, Sir Alexander ('Sandy'), 301, 303–6
Glengyle (ship), 417, 421
Glenroy (ship), 417–18, 465
Gloucester, Prince Henry, Duke of, 232
Goa: EW visits, 554
'Goa: the Home of a Saint' (EW; article), 554n
Goering, Hermann, 500
Golden Hind (magazine), 103
Golders Green, London, 20, 104
Goldring, Douglas, 119–20, 329
Goller, Dr, 535
Good Housekeeping (magazine), 380, 554–5
Goossens, Eugene, 94
Gordon (Arnold House teacher), 131
Gordon, E.B., 65–6
Gore, Arthur ('Boofy'; *later* 8th Earl of Arran), 222
Gormanston Castle, Ireland, 510–11
Gosse, Edmund: helps Arthur, 6; literary salon, 11; EW offends at Oxford, 89–90; EW despises, 116; *Father and Son*, 3
Gosse, Philip, 13
Gosse, Sylvia, 13, 121
Gosse, Thomas, 3
Goulden, Mark, 288–9
Graham, Alastair: friendship and relations with EW, 106–10, 112–13, 134, 137, 142, 145–6, 158, 196, 360; holiday in Ireland with EW, 113–14; leaves for Kenya, 113, 115, 120; received into Roman Catholic Church, 114, 228; returns from Kenya, 126; visits EW at Arnold House, 128; diplomatic post in Athens, 136, 147, 187; visits EW at Aston Clinton, 138; visits Paris with EW, 143; depicted in *Decline and Fall*, 174; visits EW in Port Said, 186; and EW's divorce, 201; introduces EW to Cavendish Hotel, 208; portrayed in *Vile Bodies*, 209; accompanies EW to Pakenham Hall, 215; qualities, 222; and coronation of Haile Selassie, 231–2; letters to EW, 257–8; depicted in *Brideshead Revisited*, 484

Graham, Major F.C.C., 424, 426, 428
Graham, Jessie (*née* Low; Alastair's mother): EW visits at Barford, 106–7, 120, 126, 145, 158–9; concern for Alastair, 109–10, 113–14; on Alastair in Kenya, 115n; visits EW at Arnold House, 128; absence from Barford, 134; takes EW to Kelmscott, 159; depicted in *Decline and Fall*, 173
Graham, Major-General Miles, 460
Graham, Sibyl (Alastair's sister), 106, 109, 113, 115n
Grant, Bridget (*née* Herbert; Laura's sister), 287, 301, 321–2, 346n, 359n, 395, 412, 625
Grant, Edward, 346n, 359n, 477
Graphic (journal): EW writes for, 212, 223n; and EW's trip to Haile Selassie's coronation, 232
Graziani, Marshal Rodolfo, 342
Green, Henry *see* Yorke, Henry
Green, Romney, 163
Greene, Graham: Catholicism, 105, 228, 505, 507, 541, 545; EW admires writing, 316, 545, 593; reviews *Edmund Campion*, 325; edits *Night & Day*, 351; on identification of author with characters, 389; and Catherine Walston, 486n, 507; praises *Brideshead Revisited*, 492; EW's relations with, 507, 545–6; invites EW to meal, 518; and EW's *Love Among the Ruins*, 553; on Knox, 588; and EW's refusal of CBE, 589; *A Burnt-Out Case*, 546; *British Dramatists*, 496n; *The End of the Affair*, 545; *The Heart of the Matter*, 406, 545–6; *The Lawless Roads*, 377; *The Power and the Glory*, 378n; *The Quiet American*, 546
Greenidge, John, 118, 138
Greenidge, Terence: friendship with EW at Oxford, 87–8, 90, 120; literary style, 103; lends money to EW, 111; visits EW at Aston Clinton, 138; dines at EW's parents with Evelyn Gardner, 166; EW maintains relations with, 552
Greensmith, Colour Sergeant, 394
Gregory the Great, Pope, 300–1
Griffith-Jones, Mervyn, 499
Guiana, 271–2, 274, 279–81, 604–6
Guinness, Bryan (*later* 2nd Baron Moyne): at Oxford, 139; pays for